Mazda Pick-ups Automotive Repair Manual

by Mike Stubblefield
and John H Haynes

Member of the Guild of Motoring Writers

Models covered:
All Mazda pick-ups
1972 through 1993
Does not include diesel or rotary engine information

(1W8 - 267)

ABCD

Haynes Publishing Group
Sparkford Nr Yeovil
Somerset BA22 7JJ England

Haynes North America, Inc.
861 Lawrence Drive
Newbury Park
California 91320 USA

Acknowledgements

We are grateful for the help and cooperation of the Mazda Motor Company for their assistance with technical information, certain illustrations and vehicle photos. The Champion Spark Plug Company supplied the illustrations of various spark plug conditions. Technical writers who contributed to this project include Larry Warren, Bob Henderson and Ken Freund.

© **Haynes North America, Inc.   1989, 1990, 1992, 1993**

. With permission from J.H. Haynes & Co. Ltd.

A book in the **Haynes Automotive Repair Manual Series**

Printed in the U.S.A.

ISBN 1 56392 084 0

Library of Congress Catalog Card Number 93-79165

Contents

1988 Mazda Cab Plus pick-up

About this manual

Its purpose

The purpose of this manual is to help you get the best value from your vehicle. It can do so in several ways. It can help you decide what work must be done, even if you choose to have it done by a dealer service department or a repair shop; it provides information and procedures for routine maintenance and servicing; and it offers diagnostic and repair procedures to follow when trouble occurs.

It is hoped that you will use the manual to tackle the work yourself. For many simpler jobs, doing it yourself may be quicker than arranging an appointment to get the vehicle into a shop and making the trips to leave it and pick it up. More importantly, a lot of money can be saved by avoiding the expense the shop must pass on to you to cover its labor and overhead costs. An added benefit is the sense of satisfaction and accomplishment that you feel after having done the job yourself.

Using the manual

The manual is divided into Chapters. Each Chapter is divided into numbered Sections, which are headed in bold type between horizontal lines. Each Section consists of consecutively numbered paragraphs.

At the beginning of each numbered section you will be referred to any illustrations which apply to the procedures in that section. The reference numbers used in illustration captions pinpoint the pertinent Section and the Step within that section. That is, illustration 3.2 means the illustration refers to Section 3 and Step (or paragraph) 2 within that Section.

Procedures, once described in the text, are not normally repeated. When it is necessary to refer to another Chapter, the reference will be given as Chapter and Section number i.e. Chapter 1/16). Cross references given without use of the word ''Chapter'' apply to Sections and/or paragraphs in the same Chapter. For example, ''see Section 8'' means in the same Chapter.

Reference to the left or right side of the vehicle is based on the assumption that one is sitting in the driver's seat, facing forward.

Even though extreme care has been taken during the preparation of this manual, neither the publisher nor the author can accept responsibility for any errors in, or omissions from, the information given.

NOTE

A **Note** provides information necessary to properly complete a procedure or information which will make the steps to be followed easier to understand.

CAUTION

A **Caution** indicates a special procedure or special steps which must be taken in the course of completing the procedure in which the **Caution** is found which are necessary to avoid damage to the assembly being worked on.

WARNING

A **Warning** indicates a special procedure or special steps which must be taken in the course of completing the procedure in which the **Warning** is found which are necessary to avoid injury to the person performing the procedure.

Introduction to the Mazda pick-ups

The Mazda pick-up truck is a conventional front engine-rear wheel drive design with four-wheel drive (4WD) available on later models.

The inline four-cylinder engines used in these models are equipped with a carburetor. The engine drives the rear wheels through either a four or five-speed manual or an automatic transmission via a driveshaft and solid rear axle. On 4WD models, a transfer case is used to drive the front wheels via a driveshaft and independent driveaxles.

Front suspension is independent, featuring coil springs on earlier models and torsion bars on later models, with power assisted steering available on later models. Leaf springs are used in the rear suspension.

Earlier models used drum brakes on all four wheels while later models feature disc brakes at the front and drums at the rear.

Vehicle identification numbers

Modifications are a continuing and unpublicized process in vehicle manufacturing. Since spare parts manuals and lists are compiled on a numerical basis, the individual vehicle numbers are essential to correctly identify the component required.

Vehicle Identification Number (VIN)

This very important identification number is stamped on a plate attached to the left side cowling just inside the windshield on the driver's side of the vehicle **(see illustration)**. The VIN also appears on the Vehicle Certificate of Title and Registration. It contains information such as where and when the vehicle was manufactured, the model year and the body style.

Chassis number

The vehicle chassis number is stamped on the frame itself and is visible by looking to the rear of the right front wheel **(see illustration)**.

Vehicle Certification Regulation Plate

The Vehicle Certification Regulation Plate (VC label) is affixed to the left (driver's) door pillar **(see illustration)**. The plate contains the name of the manufacturer, the month and year of manufacture, the Gross Vehicle Weight Rating (GVWR), the Gross Axle Weight Rating (GAWR) and the certification statement.

The VC label also contains a 17-character Vehicle Identification Number which is used for warranty identification of the vehicle and indicates such things as manufacturer, type of restraint system, line, series, body type, engine, model year and consecutive unit number.

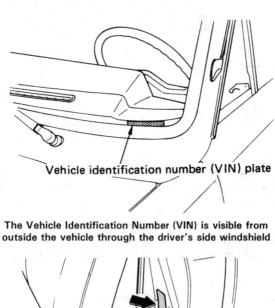

The Vehicle Identification Number (VIN) is visible from outside the vehicle through the driver's side windshield

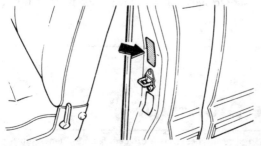

The Certification Regulation Plate is located on the driver's side door pillar

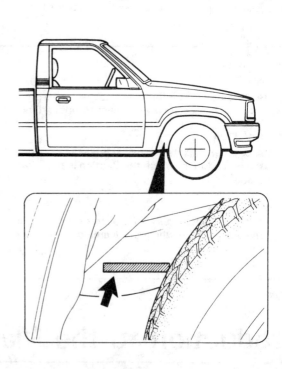

The chassis number is located on the frame rail and can be viewed by looking behind the front wheel

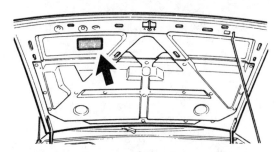

The Vehicle Emission Control Information (VECI) label is located on the under side of the hood

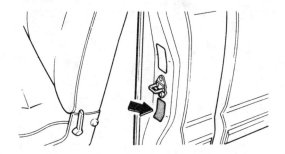

The tire pressure label can be found on the driver's side door pillar

The engine number is stamped at the front of the block

Vehicle Emission Control Information label

The Vehicle Emission Control Information (VECI) label is located on the under side of the hood **(see illustration)**. It contains information on the emission controls with which your vehicle is equipped.

Tire pressure label

The tire pressure label is found on the driver's side door pillar and contains the recommended tire pressures **(see illustration)**.

Engine number

The engine number for most models is stamped on a pad on the right front side of the block, near the distributor **(see illustration)**.

Buying parts

Replacement parts are available from many sources, which generally fall into one of two categories – authorized dealer parts departments and independent retail auto parts stores. Our advice concerning these parts is as follows:

Retail auto parts stores: Good auto parts stores will stock frequently needed components which wear out relatively fast, such as clutch components, exhaust systems, brake parts, tune-up parts, etc. These stores often supply new or reconditioned parts on an exchange basis, which can save a considerable amount of money. Discount auto parts stores are often very good places to buy materials and parts needed for general vehicle maintenance such as oil, grease, filters, spark plugs, belts, touch-up paint, bulbs, etc. They also usually sell tools and general accessories, have convenient hours, charge lower prices and can often be found not far from home.

Authorized dealer parts department: This is the best source for parts which are unique to the vehicle and not generally available elsewhere (such as major engine parts, transmission parts, trim pieces, etc.).

Warranty information: If the vehicle is still covered under warranty, be sure that any replacement parts purchased – regardless of the source – do not invalidate the warranty!

To be sure of obtaining the correct parts, have engine and chassis numbers available and, if possible, take the old parts along for positive identification.

Maintenance techniques, tools and working facilities

Maintenance techniques

There are a number of techniques involved in maintenance and repair that will be referred to throughout this manual. Application of these techniques will enable the home mechanic to be more efficient, better organized and capable of performing the various tasks properly, which will ensure that the repair job is thorough and complete.

Fasteners

Fasteners are nuts, bolts, studs and screws used to hold two or more parts together. There are a few things to keep in mind when working with fasteners. Almost all of them use a locking device of some type, either a lockwasher, locknut, locking tab or thread adhesive. All threaded fasteners should be clean and straight, with undamaged threads and undamaged corners on the hex head where the wrench fits. Develop the habit of replacing all damaged nuts and bolts with new ones. Special locknuts with nylon or fiber inserts can only be used once. If they are removed, they lose their locking ability and must be replaced with new ones.

Rusted nuts and bolts should be treated with a penetrating fluid to ease removal and prevent breakage. Some mechanics use turpentine in a spout-type oil can, which works quite well. After applying the rust penetrant, let it work for a few minutes before trying to loosen the nut or bolt. Badly rusted fasteners may have to be chiseled or sawed off or removed with a special nut breaker, available at tool stores.

If a bolt or stud breaks off in an assembly, it can be drilled and removed with a special tool commonly available for this purpose. Most automotive machine shops can perform this task, as well as other repair procedures, such as the repair of threaded holes that have been stripped out.

Flat washers and lockwashers, when removed from an assembly, should always be replaced exactly as removed. Replace any damaged washers with new ones. Never use a lockwasher on any soft metal surface (such as aluminum), thin sheet metal or plastic.

Fastener sizes

For a number of reasons, automobile manufacturers are making wider and wider use of metric fasteners. Therefore, it is important to be able to tell the difference between standard (sometimes called U.S. or SAE) and metric hardware, since they cannot be interchanged.

All bolts, whether standard or metric, are sized according to diameter, thread pitch and length. For example, a standard 1/2 — 13 x 1 bolt is 1/2 inch in diameter, has 13 threads per inch and is 1 inch long. An M12 — 1.75 x 25 metric bolt is 12 mm in diameter, has a thread pitch of 1.75 mm (the distance between threads) and is 25 mm long. The two bolts are nearly identical, and easily confused, but they are not interchangeable.

In addition to the differences in diameter, thread pitch and length, metric and standard bolts can also be distinguished by examining the bolt heads. To begin with, the distance across the flats on a standard bolt head is measured in inches, while the same dimension on a metric bolt is sized in millimeters (the same is true for nuts). As a result, a standard wrench should not be used on a metric bolt and a metric wrench should not be used on a standard bolt. Also, most standard bolts have slashes radiating out from the center of the head to denote the grade or strength of the bolt, which is an indication of the amount of torque that can be applied to it. The greater the number of slashes, the greater the strength of the bolt. Grades 0 through 5 are commonly used on automobiles. Metric bolts have a property class (grade) number, rather than a slash, molded into their heads to indicate bolt strength. In this case, the higher the number, the stronger the bolt. Property class numbers 8.8, 9.8 and 10.9 are commonly used on automobiles.

Strength markings can also be used to distinguish standard hex nuts from metric hex nuts. Many standard nuts have dots stamped into one side, while metric nuts are marked with a number. The greater the number of dots, or the higher the number, the greater the strength of the nut.

Metric studs are also marked on their ends according to property class (grade). Larger studs are numbered (the same as metric bolts),

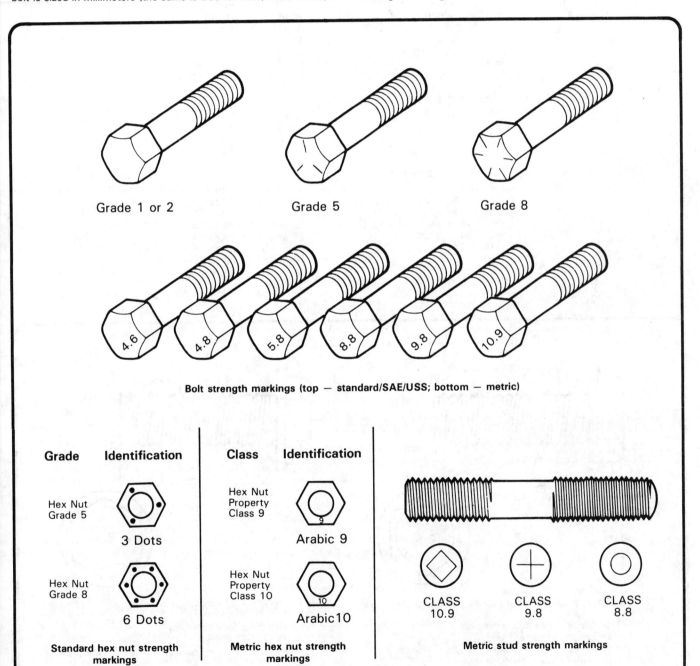

Grade 1 or 2　　　　Grade 5　　　　Grade 8

Bolt strength markings (top — standard/SAE/USS; bottom — metric)

Grade	Identification
Hex Nut Grade 5	3 Dots
Hex Nut Grade 8	6 Dots

Standard hex nut strength markings

Class	Identification
Hex Nut Property Class 9	Arabic 9
Hex Nut Property Class 10	Arabic 10

Metric hex nut strength markings

CLASS 10.9　　CLASS 9.8　　CLASS 8.8

Metric stud strength markings

while smaller studs carry a geometric code to denote grade.

It should be noted that many fasteners, especially Grades 0 through 2, have no distinguishing marks on them. When such is the case, the only way to determine whether it is standard or metric is to measure the thread pitch or compare it to a known fastener of the same size.

Standard fasteners are often referred to as SAE, as opposed to metric. However, it should be noted that SAE technically refers to a non-metric *fine thread* fastener only. Coarse thread non-metric fasteners are referred to as USS sizes.

Since fasteners of the same size (both standard and metric) may have different strength ratings, be sure to reinstall any bolts, studs or nuts removed from your vehicle in their original locations. Also, when replacing a fastener with a new one, make sure that the new one has a strength rating equal to or greater than the original.

Tightening sequences and procedures

Most threaded fasteners should be tightened to a specific torque value (torque is the twisting force applied to a threaded component such as a nut or bolt). Overtightening the fastener can weaken it and cause it to break, while undertightening can cause it to eventually come loose. Bolts, screws and studs, depending on the material they are made of and their thread diameters, have specific torque values, many of which are noted in the Specifications at the beginning of each Chapter. Be sure to follow the torque recommendations closely. For fasteners not assigned a specific torque, a general torque value chart is presented here as a guide. These torque values are for dry (unlubricated) fasteners threaded into steel or cast iron (not aluminum). As was previously mentioned, the size and grade of a fastener determine the amount of torque that can safely be applied to it. The figures listed here are approximate

Metric thread sizes	Ft-lb	Nm/m
M-6	6 to 9	9 to 12
M-8	14 to 21	19 to 28
M-10	28 to 40	38 to 54
M-12	50 to 71	68 to 96
M-14	80 to 140	109 to 154

Pipe thread sizes		
1/8	5 to 8	7 to 10
1/4	12 to 18	17 to 24
3/8	22 to 33	30 to 44
1/2	25 to 35	34 to 47

U.S. thread sizes		
1/4 — 20	6 to 9	9 to 12
5/16 — 18	12 to 18	17 to 24
5/16 — 24	14 to 20	19 to 27
3/8 — 16	22 to 32	30 to 43
3/8 — 24	27 to 38	37 to 51
7/16 — 14	40 to 55	55 to 74
7/16 — 20	40 to 60	55 to 81
1/2 — 13	55 to 80	75 to 108

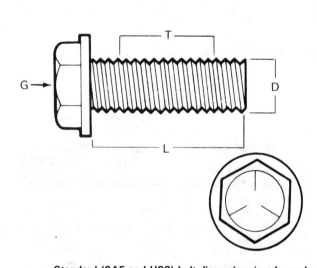

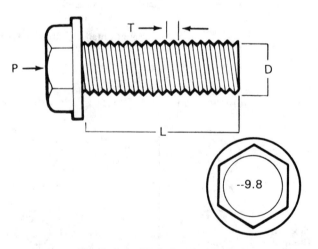

Standard (SAE and USS) bolt dimensions/grade marks

    G Grade marks (bolt strength)
    L Length (in inches)
    T Thread pitch (number of threads per inch)
    D Nominal diameter (in inches)

Metric bolt dimensions/grade marks

    P Property class (bolt strength)
    L Length (in millimeters)
    T Thread pitch (distance between threads in millimeters)
    D Diameter

for Grade 2 and Grade 3 fasteners. Higher grades can tolerate higher torque values.

Fasteners laid out in a pattern, such as cylinder head bolts, oil pan bolts, differential cover bolts, etc., must be loosened or tightened in sequence to avoid warping the component. This sequence will normally be shown in the appropriate Chapter. If a specific pattern is not given, the following procedures can be used to prevent warping.

Initially, the bolts or nuts should be assembled finger-tight only. Next, they should be tightened one full turn each, in a criss-cross or diagonal pattern. After each one has been tightened one full turn, return to the first one and tighten them all one-half turn, following the same pattern. Finally, tighten each of them one-quarter turn at a time until each fastener has been tightened to the proper torque. To loosen and remove the fasteners, the procedure would be reversed.

Component disassembly

Component disassembly should be done with care and purpose to help ensure that the parts go back together properly. Always keep track of the sequence in which parts are removed. Make note of special characteristics or marks on parts that can be installed more than one way, such as a grooved thrust washer on a shaft. It is a good idea to lay the disassembled parts out on a clean surface in the order that they were removed. It may also be helpful to make sketches or take instant photos of components before removal.

When removing fasteners from a component, keep track of their locations. Sometimes threading a bolt back in a part, or putting the washers and nut back on a stud, can prevent mix-ups later. If nuts and bolts cannot be returned to their original locations, they should be kept in a compartmented box or a series of small boxes. A cupcake or muffin tin is ideal for this purpose, since each cavity can hold the bolts and nuts from a particular area (i.e. oil pan bolts, valve cover bolts, engine mount bolts, etc.). A pan of this type is especially helpful when working on assemblies with very small parts, such as the carburetor, alternator, valve train or interior dash and trim pieces. The cavities can be marked with paint or tape to identify the contents.

Whenever wiring looms, harnesses or connectors are separated, it is a good idea to identify the two halves with numbered pieces of masking tape so they can be easily reconnected.

Gasket sealing surfaces

Throughout any vehicle, gaskets are used to seal the mating surfaces between two parts and keep lubricants, fluids, vacuum or pressure contained in an assembly.

Many times these gaskets are coated with a liquid or paste-type gasket sealing compound before assembly. Age, heat and pressure can sometimes cause the two parts to stick together so tightly that they are very difficult to separate. Often, the assembly can be loosened by striking it with a soft-face hammer near the mating surfaces. A regular hammer can be used if a block of wood is placed between the hammer and the part. Do not hammer on cast parts or parts that could be easily damaged. With any particularly stubborn part, always recheck to make sure that every fastener has been removed.

Avoid using a screwdriver or bar to pry apart an assembly, as they can easily mar the gasket sealing surfaces of the parts, which must remain smooth. If prying is absolutely necessary, use an old broom handle, but keep in mind that extra clean up will be necessary if the wood splinters.

After the parts are separated, the old gasket must be carefully scraped off and the gasket surfaces cleaned. Stubborn gasket material can be soaked with rust penetrant or treated with a special chemical to soften it so it can be easily scraped off. A scraper can be fashioned from a piece of copper tubing by flattening and sharpening one end. Copper is recommended because it is usually softer than the surfaces to be scraped, which reduces the chance of gouging the part. Some gaskets can be removed with a wire brush, but regardless of the method used, the mating surfaces must be left clean and smooth. If for some reason the gasket surface is gouged, then a gasket sealer thick enough to fill scratches will have to be used during reassembly of the components. For most applications, a non-drying (or semi-drying) gasket sealer should be used.

Hose removal tips

Warning: *If the vehicle is equipped with air conditioning, do not disconnect any of the A/C hoses without first having the system depressurized by a dealer service department or an air conditioning specialist.*

Hose removal precautions closely parallel gasket removal precautions. Avoid scratching or gouging the surface that the hose mates against or the connection may leak. This is especially true for radiator hoses. Because of various chemical reactions, the rubber in hoses can bond itself to the metal spigot that the hose fits over. To remove a hose, first loosen the hose clamps that secure it to the spigot. Then, with slip-joint pliers, grab the hose at the clamp and rotate it around the spigot. Work it back and forth until it is completely free, then pull it off. Silicone or other lubricants will ease removal if they can be applied between the hose and the outside of the spigot. Apply the same lubricant to the inside of the hose and the outside of the spigot to simplify installation.

As a last resort (and if the hose is to be replaced with a new one anyway), the rubber can be slit with a knife and the hose peeled from the spigot. If this must be done, be careful that the metal connection is not damaged.

If a hose clamp is broken or damaged, do not reuse it. Wire-type clamps usually weaken with age, so it is a good idea to replace them with screw-type clamps whenever a hose is removed.

Tools

A selection of good tools is a basic requirement for anyone who plans to maintain and repair his or her own vehicle. For the owner who has few tools, the initial investment might seem high, but when compared to the spiraling costs of professional auto maintenance and repair, it is a wise one.

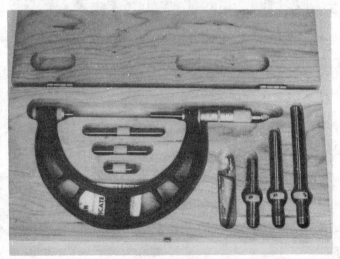

Micrometer set

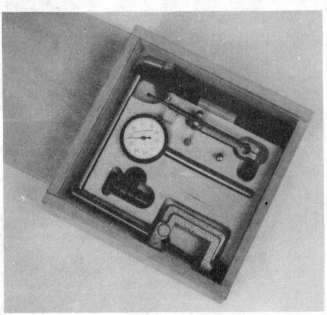

Dial indicator set

Dial caliper

Hand-operated vacuum pump

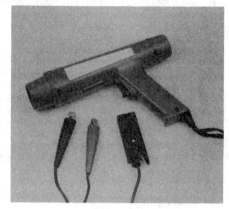

Timing light

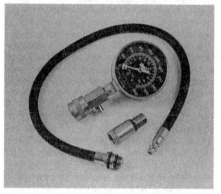

Compression gauge with spark plug
hole adapter

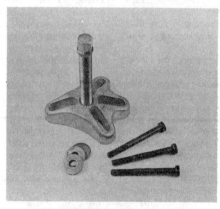

Damper/steering wheel puller

General purpose puller

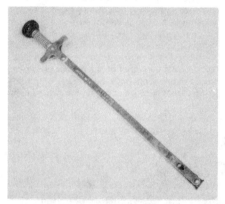

Hydraulic lifter removal tool

Valve spring compressor

Valve spring compressor

Ridge reamer

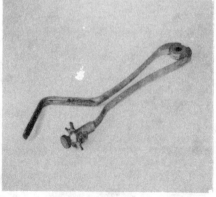

Piston ring groove cleaning tool

Ring removal/installation tool

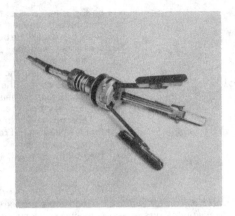
Ring compressor

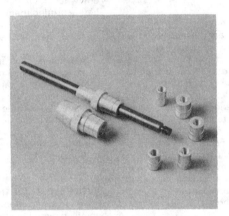
Cylinder hone

Brake hold-down spring tool

Brake cylinder hone

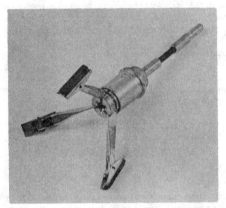
Clutch plate alignment tool

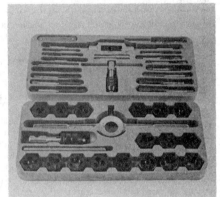
Tap and die set

To help the owner decide which tools are needed to perform the tasks detailed in this manual, the following tool lists are offered: *Maintenance and minor repair, Repair/overhaul* and *Special.*

The newcomer to practical mechanics should start off with the maintenance and minor repair tool kit, which is adequate for the simpler jobs performed on a vehicle. Then, as confidence and experience grow, the owner can tackle more difficult tasks, buying additional tools as they are needed. Eventually the basic kit will be expanded into the repair and overhaul tool set. Over a period of time, the experienced do-it-yourselfer will assemble a tool set complete enough for most repair and overhaul procedures and will add tools from the special category when it is felt that the expense is justified by the frequency of use.

Maintenance and minor repair tool kit

The tools in this list should be considered the minimum required for performance of routine maintenance, servicing and minor repair work. We recommend the purchase of combination wrenches (box-end and open-end combined in one wrench). While more expensive than open end wrenches, they offer the advantages of both types of wrench.

Combination wrench set (1/4-inch to 1 inch or 6 mm to 19 mm)
Adjustable wrench, 8 inch
Spark plug wrench with rubber insert
Spark plug gap adjusting tool
Feeler gauge set
Brake bleeder wrench
Standard screwdriver (5/16-inch x 6 inch)
Phillips screwdriver (No. 2 x 6 inch)
Combination pliers — 6 inch
Hacksaw and assortment of blades
Tire pressure gauge
Grease gun
Oil can
Fine emery cloth
Wire brush

Battery post and cable cleaning tool
Oil filter wrench
Funnel (medium size)
Safety goggles
Jackstands (2)
Drain pan

Note: *If basic tune-ups are going to be part of routine maintenance, it will be necessary to purchase a good quality stroboscopic timing light and combination tachometer/dwell meter. Although they are included in the list of special tools, it is mentioned here because they are absolutely necessary for tuning most vehicles properly.*

Repair and overhaul tool set

These tools are essential for anyone who plans to perform major repairs and are in addition to those in the maintenance and minor repair tool kit. Included is a comprehensive set of sockets which, though expensive, are invaluable because of their versatility, especially when various extensions and drives are available. We recommend the 1/2-inch drive over the 3/8-inch drive. Although the larger drive is bulky and more expensive, it has the capacity of accepting a very wide range of large sockets. Ideally, however, the mechanic should have a 3/8-inch drive set and a 1/2-inch drive set.

Socket set(s)
Reversible ratchet
Extension — 10 inch
Universal joint
Torque wrench (same size drive as sockets)
Ball peen hammer — 8 ounce
Soft-face hammer (plastic/rubber)
Standard screwdriver (1/4-inch x 6 inch)
Standard screwdriver (stubby — 5/16-inch)
Phillips screwdriver (No. 3 x 8 inch)
Phillips screwdriver (stubby — No. 2)

Pliers — vise grip
Pliers — lineman's
Pliers — needle nose
Pliers — snap-ring (internal and external)
Cold chisel — 1/2-inch
Scribe
Scraper (made from flattened copper tubing)
Centerpunch
Pin punches (1/16, 1/8, 3/16-inch)
Steel rule/straightedge — 12 inch
Allen wrench set (1/8 to 3/8-inch or 4 mm to 10 mm)
A selection of files
Wire brush (large)
Jackstands (second set)
Jack (scissor or hydraulic type)

Note: *Another tool which is often useful is an electric drill motor with a chuck capacity of 3/8-inch and a set of good quality drill bits.*

Special tools

The tools in this list include those which are not used regularly, are expensive to buy, or which need to be used in accordance with their manufacturer's instructions. Unless these tools will be used frequently, it is not very economical to purchase many of them. A consideration would be to split the cost and use between yourself and a friend or friends. In addition, most of these tools can be obtained from a tool rental shop on a temporary basis.

This list primarily contains only those tools and instruments widely available to the public, and not those special tools produced by the vehicle manufacturer for distribution to dealer service departments. Occasionally, references to the manufacturer's special tools are inluded in the text of this manual. Generally, an alternative method of doing the job without the special tool is offered. However, sometimes there is no alternative to their use. Where this is the case, and the tool cannot be purchased or borrowed, the work should be turned over to the dealer service department or an automotive repair shop.

Valve spring compressor
Piston ring groove cleaning tool
Piston ring compressor
Piston ring installation tool
Cylinder compression gauge
Cylinder ridge reamer
Cylinder surfacing hone
Cylinder bore gauge
Micrometers and/or dial calipers
Hydraulic lifter removal tool
Balljoint separator
Universal-type puller
Impact screwdriver
Dial indicator set
Stroboscopic timing light (inductive pick-up)
Hand operated vacuum/pressure pump
Tachometer/dwell meter
Universal electrical multimeter
Cable hoist
Brake spring removal and installation tools
Floor jack

Buying tools

For the do-it-yourselfer who is just starting to get involved in vehicle maintenance and repair, there are a number of options available when purchasing tools. If maintenance and minor repair is the extent of the work to be done, the purchase of individual tools is satisfactory. If,

on the other hand, extensive work is planned, it would be a good idea to purchase a modest tool set from one of the large retail chain stores. A set can usually be bought at a substantial savings over the individual tool prices, and they often come with a tool box. As additional tools are needed, add-on sets, individual tools and a larger tool box can be purchased to expand the tool selection. Building a tool set gradually allows the cost of the tools to be spread over a longer period of time and gives the mechanic the freedom to choose only those tools that will actually be used.

Tool stores will often be the only source of some of the special tools that are needed, but regardless of where tools are bought, try to avoid cheap ones, especially when buying screwdrivers and sockets, because they won't last very long. The expense involved in replacing cheap tools will eventually be greater than the initial cost of quality tools.

Care and maintenance of tools

Good tools are expensive, so it makes sense to treat them with respect. Keep them clean and in usable condition and store them properly when not in use. Always wipe off any dirt, grease or metal chips before putting them away. Never leave tools lying around in the work area. Upon completion of a job, always check closely under the hood for tools that may have been left there so they won't get lost during a test drive.

Some tools, such as screwdrivers, pliers, wrenches and sockets, can be hung on a panel mounted on the garage or workshop wall, while others should be kept in a tool box or tray. Measuring instruments, gauges, meters, etc. must be carefully stored where they cannot be damaged by weather or impact from other tools.

When tools are used with care and stored properly, they will last a very long time. Even with the best of care, though, tools will wear out if used frequently. When a tool is damaged or worn out, replace it. Subsequent jobs will be safer and more enjoyable if you do.

Working facilities

Not to be overlooked when discussing tools is the workshop. If anything more than routine maintenance is to be carried out, some sort of suitable work area is essential.

It is understood, and appreciated, that many home mechanics do not have a good workshop or garage available, and end up removing an engine or doing major repairs outside. It is recommended, however, that the overhaul or repair be completed under the cover of a roof.

A clean, flat workbench or table of comfortable working height is an absolute necessity. The workbench should be equipped with a vise that has a jaw opening of at least four inches.

As mentioned previously, some clean, dry storage space is also required for tools, as well as the lubricants, fluids, cleaning solvents, etc. which will soon become necessary.

Sometimes waste oil and fluids, drained from the engine or cooling system during normal maintenance or repairs, present a disposal problem. To avoid pouring them on the ground or into a sewage system, pour the used fluids into large containers, seal them with caps and take them to an authorized disposal site or recycling center. Plastic jugs, such as old antifreeze containers, are ideal for this purpose.

Always keep a supply of old newspapers and clean rags available. Old towels are excellent for mopping up spills. Many mechanics use rolls of paper towels for most work because they are readily available and disposable. To help keep the area under the vehicle clean, a large cardboard box can be cut open and flattened to protect the garage or shop floor.

Whenever working over a painted surface, such as when leaning over a fender to service something under the hood, always cover it with an old blanket or bedspread to protect the finish. Vinyl covered pads, made especially for this purpose, are available at auto parts stores.

Booster battery (jump) starting

Certain precautions must be observed when using a booster battery to start a vehicle.

a) Before connecting the booster battery, make sure the ignition switch is in the Off position.
b) Turn off the lights, heater and other electrical loads.
c) Your eyes should be shielded. Safety goggles are a good idea.
d) Make sure the booster battery is the same voltage as the dead one in the vehicle.
e) The two vehicles MUST NOT TOUCH each other!
f) Make sure the transmission is in Neutral (manual) or Park (automatic).
g) If the booster battery is not a maintenance-free type, remove the vent caps and lay a cloth over the vent holes.

Connect the red jumper cable to the *positive* (+) terminals of each battery.

Connect one end of the black jumper cable to the *negative* (–) terminal of the booster battery. The other end of this cable should be connected to a good ground on the vehicle to be started, such as a bolt or bracket on the engine block **(see illustration)**. Use caution to ensure that the cable will not come into contact with the fan, drivebelts or other moving parts of the engine.

Start the engine using the booster battery, then, with the engine running at idle speed, disconnect the jumper cables in the reverse order of connection.

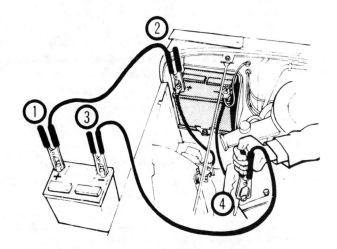

Make the booster battery cable connections in the numerical order shown (note that the negative cable of the booster battery is NOT attached to the negative terminal of the dead battery)

Jacking and towing

Jacking

The jack supplied with the vehicle should only be used for raising the vehicle when changing a tire or placing jackstands under the frame. **Warning:** *Never work under the vehicle or start the engine while this jack is being used as the only means of support.*

The vehicle should be on level ground with the wheels blocked and the transmission in Park (automatic) or Reverse (manual). On 4WD models, the transfer case must be in the 2H, 4H or 4L position (never in Neutral). If a wheel is being changed, loosen the lug nuts one-half turn and leave them in place until the wheel is raised off the ground.

Place the jack under the vehicle suspension in the indicated position **(see illustrations)**. Turn the jack handle clockwise until the wheel is raised off the ground. Remove the lug nuts, pull off the wheel, install

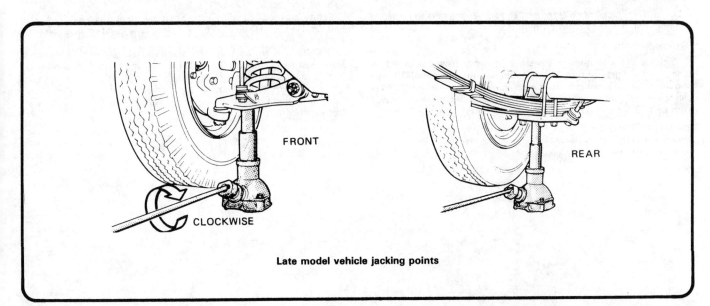

Late model vehicle jacking points

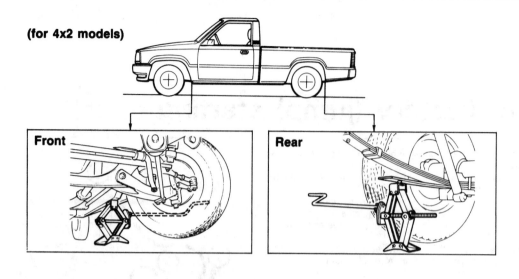

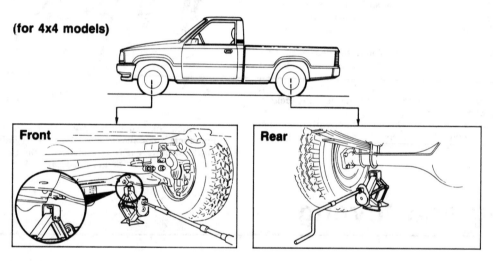

Early model vehicle jacking points

the spare and thread the lug nuts back on with the bevelled sides facing in. Tighten them snugly, but wait until the vehicle is on the ground to finish tightening them.

Lower the vehicle, remove the jack and tighten the nuts (if loosened or removed) in a criss-cross pattern.

Towing

Vehicles with an automatic transmission can be towed with all four wheels on the ground, provided that speeds do not exceed 30 mph and the distance is not over 10 miles, otherwise transmission damage can result. Vehicles equipped with a manual transmission may be towed with all four wheels on the ground at moderate speeds.

Towing equipment specifically designed for this purpose should be used and should be attached to the main structural members of the vehicle, not the bumper or brackets.

Safety is a major consideration when towing and all applicable state and local laws must be obeyed. A safety chain system must be used for all towing.

While towing, the parking brake should be released and the transmission must be in Neutral. On 4WD models, the control lever must be in Neutral and the free running hubs should be in the Free position. The steering must be unlocked (ignition switch in the Off position). Remember that power steering and power brakes will not work with the engine off.

Automotive chemicals and lubricants

A number of automotive chemicals and lubricants are available for use during vehicle maintenance and repair. They include a wide variety of products ranging from cleaning solvents and degreasers to lubricants and protective sprays for rubber, plastic and vinyl.

Cleaners

Carburetor cleaner and choke cleaner is a strong solvent for gum, varnish and carbon. Most carburetor cleaners leave a dry-type lubricant film which will not harden or gum up. Because of this film it is not recommended for use on electrical components.

Brake system cleaner is used to remove grease and brake fluid from the brake system where clean surfaces are absolutely necessary. It leaves no residue and often eliminates brake squeal caused by contaminants.

Electrical cleaner removes oxidation, corrosion and carbon deposits from electrical contacts, restoring full current flow. It can also be used to clean spark plugs, carburetor jets, voltage regulators and other parts where an oil-free surface is desired.

Demoisturants remove water and moisture from electrical components such as alternators, voltage regulators, electrical connectors and fuse blocks. It is non-conductive, non-corrosive and non-flammable.

Degreasers are heavy-duty solvents used to remove grease from the outside of the engine and from chassis components. They can be sprayed or brushed on, and, depending on the type, are rinsed off either with water or solvent.

Lubricants

Motor oil is the lubricant formulated for use in engines. It normally contains a wide variety of additives to prevent corrosion and reduce foaming and wear. Motor oil comes in various weights (viscosity ratings) from 5 to 80. The recommended weight of the oil depends on the season, temperature and the demands on the engine. Light oil is used in cold climates and under light load conditions. Heavy oil is used in hot climates and where high loads are encountered. Multi-viscosity oils are designed to have characteristics of both light and heavy oils and are available in a number of weights from 5W-20 to 20W-50.

Gear oil is designed to be used in differentials, manual transaxles and other areas where high-temperature lubrication is required.

Chassis and wheel bearing grease is a heavy grease used where increased loads and friction are encountered, such as for wheel bearings, balljoints, tie rod ends and universal joints.

High temperature wheel bearing grease is designed to withstand the extreme temperatures encountered by wheel bearings in disc brake equipped vehicles. It usually contains molbdenun disulfide (moly), which is a dry-type lubricant.

White grease is a heavy grease for metal to metal applications where water is a problem. White grease stays soft under both low and high temperatures (usually from –100°F to +190°F), and will not wash off or dilute in the presence of water.

Assembly lube is a special extreme pressure lubricant, usually containing moly, used to lubricate high-load parts such as main and rod bearings and cam lobes for initial start-up of a new engine. The assembly lube lubricates the parts without being squeezed out or washed away until the engine oiling system begins to function.

Silicone lubricants are used to protect rubber, plastic, vinyl and nylon parts.

Graphite lubricants are used where oils cannot be used due to contamination problems, such as in locks. The dry graphite will lubricate metal parts while remaining uncontaminated by dirt, water, oil or acids. It is electrically conductive and will not foul electrical contacts in locks such as the ignition switch.

Moly penetrants loosen and lubricate frozen, rusted and corroded fasteners and prevent future rusting or freezing.

Heat-sink grease is a special electrically non-conductive grease that is used for mounting HEI ignition modules where it is essential that heat be transferred away from the module.

Sealants

RTV sealant is one of the most widely used gasket compounds. Made from silicone, RTV is air curing, it seals, bonds, waterproofs, fills surface irregularities, remains flexible, doesn't shrink, is relatively easy to remove, and is used as a supplementary sealer with almost all low and medium temperature gaskets.

Anaerobic sealant is much like RTV in that it can be used either to seal gaskets or to form gaskets by itself. It remains flexible, is solvent resistant and fills surface imperfections. The difference between an anaerobic sealant and an RTV-type sealant is in the curing. RTV cures when exposed to air, while an anaerobic sealant cures only in the absence of air. This means that an anaerobic sealant cures only after the assembly of parts, sealing them together.

Thread and pipe sealant is used for sealing hydraulic and pneumatic fittings and vacuum lines. It is usually made from a teflon compound, and comes in a spray, a paint-on liquid and as a wrap-around tape.

Chemicals

Anti-seize compound prevents seizing, galling, cold welding, rust and corrosion in fasteners. High temperature anti-seize, usually made with copper and graphite lubricants, is used for exhaust system and manifold bolts.

Anaerobic locking compounds are used to keep fasteners from vibrating or working loose, and cure only after installation, in the absence of air. Medium strength locking compound is used for small nuts, bolts and screws that you expect to be removing later. High strength locking compound is for large nuts, bolts and studs which you don't intend to be removing on a regular basis.

Oil additives range from viscosity index improvers to chemical treatments that claim to reduce internal engine friction. It should be noted that most oil manufacturers caution against using additives with their oils.

Gas additives perform several functions, depending on their chemical makeup. They usually contain solvents that help dissolve gum and varnish that build up on carburetor and intake parts. They also serve to break down carbon deposits that form on the inside surfaces of the combustion chambers. Some additives contain upper cylinder lubricants for valves and piston rings, and others chemicals to remove condensation from the gas tank.

Miscellaneous

Brake fluid is specially formulated hydraulic fluid that can withstand the heat and pressure encountered in brake systems. Care must be taken that this fluid does not come in contact with painted surfaces or plastics. An opened container should always be resealed to prevent contamination by water or dirt.

Weatherstrip adhesive is used to bond weatherstripping around doors, windows and trunk lids. It is sometimes used to attach trim pieces.

Undercoating is a petroleum-based tar-like substance that is designed to protect metal surfaces on the underside of the vehicle from corrosion. It also acts as a sound-deadening agent by insulating the bottom of the vehicle.

Waxes and polishes are used to help protect painted and plated surfaces from the weather. Different types of paint may require the use of different types of wax and polish. Some polishes utilize a chemical or abrasive cleaner to help remove the top layer of oxidized (dull) paint on older vehicles. In recent years many non-wax polishes that contain a wide variety of chemicals such as polymers and silicones have been introduced. These non-wax polishes are usually easier to apply and last longer than conventional waxes and polishes.

Safety first!

Regardless of how enthusiastic you may be about getting on with the job at hand, take the time to ensure that your safety is not jeopardized. A moment's lack of attention can result in an accident, as can failure to observe certain simple safety precautions. The possibility of an accident will always exist, and the following points should not be considered a comprehensive list of all dangers. Rather, they are intended to make you aware of the risks and to encourage a safety conscious approach to all work you carry out on your vehicle.

Essential DOs and DON'Ts

DON'T rely on a jack when working under the vehicle. Always use approved jackstands to support the weight of the vehicle and place them under the recommended lift or support points.

DON'T attempt to loosen extremely tight fasteners (i.e. wheel lug nuts) while the vehicle is on a jack — it may fall.

DON'T start the engine without first making sure that the transmission is in Neutral (or Park where applicable) and the parking brake is set.

DON'T remove the radiator cap from a hot cooling system — let it cool or cover it with a cloth and release the pressure gradually.

DON'T attempt to drain the engine oil until you are sure it has cooled to the point that it will not burn you.

DON'T touch any part of the engine or exhaust system until it has cooled sufficiently to avoid burns.

DON'T siphon toxic liquids such as gasoline, antifreeze and brake fluid by mouth, or allow them to remain on your skin.

DON'T inhale brake lining dust — it is potentially hazardous (see *Asbestos* below)

DON'T allow spilled oil or grease to remain on the floor — wipe it up before someone slips on it.

DON'T use loose fitting wrenches or other tools which may slip and cause injury.

DON'T push on wrenches when loosening or tightening nuts or bolts. Always try to pull the wrench toward you. If the situation calls for pushing the wrench away, push with an open hand to avoid scraped knuckles if the wrench should slip.

DON'T attempt to lift a heavy component alone — get someone to help you.

DON'T rush or take unsafe shortcuts to finish a job.

DON'T allow children or animals in or around the vehicle while you are working on it.

DO wear eye protection when using power tools such as a drill, sander, bench grinder, etc. and when working under a vehicle.

DO keep loose clothing and long hair well out of the way of moving parts.

DO make sure that any hoist used has a safe working load rating adequate for the job.

DO get someone to check on you periodically when working alone on a vehicle.

DO carry out work in a logical sequence and make sure that everything is correctly assembled and tightened.

DO keep chemicals and fluids tightly capped and out of the reach of children and pets.

DO remember that your vehicle's safety affects that of yourself and others. If in doubt on any point, get professional advice.

Asbestos

Certain friction, insulating, sealing, and other products — such as brake linings, brake bands, clutch linings, torque converters, gaskets, etc. — contain asbestos. *Extreme care must be taken to avoid inhalation of dust from such products since it is hazardous to health.* If in doubt, assume that they *do* contain asbestos.

Fire

Remember at all times that gasoline is highly flammable. Never smoke or have any kind of open flame around when working on a vehicle. But the risk does not end there. A spark caused by an electrical short circuit, by two metal surfaces contacting each other, or even by static electricity built up in your body under certain conditions, can ignite gasoline vapors, which in a confined space are highly explosive. Do not, under any circumstances, use gasoline for cleaning parts. Use an approved safety solvent.

Always disconnect the battery ground (–) cable *at the battery* before working on any part of the fuel system or electrical system. Never risk spilling fuel on a hot engine or exhaust component.

It is strongly recommended that a fire extinguisher suitable for use on fuel and electrical fires be kept handy in the garage or workshop at all times. Never try to extinguish a fuel or electrical fire with water.

Fumes

Certain fumes are highly toxic and can quickly cause unconsciousness and even death if inhaled to any extent. Gasoline vapor falls into this category, as do the vapors from some cleaning solvents. Any draining or pouring of such volatile fluids should be done in a well ventilated area.

When using cleaning fluids and solvents, read the instructions on the container carefully. Never use materials from unmarked containers.

Never run the engine in an enclosed space, such as a garage. Exhaust fumes contain carbon monoxide, which is extremely poisonous. If you need to run the engine, always do so in the open air, or at least have the rear of the vehicle outside the work area.

If you are fortunate enough to have the use of an inspection pit, never drain or pour gasoline and never run the engine while the vehicle is over the pit. The fumes, being heavier than air, will concentrate in the pit with possibly lethal results.

The battery

Never create a spark or allow a bare light bulb near the battery. The battery normally gives off a certain amount of hydrogen gas, which is highly explosive.

Always disconnect the battery ground (–) cable *at the battery* before working on the fuel or electrical systems.

If possible, loosen the filler caps or cover when charging the battery from an external source. Do not charge at an excessive rate or the battery may burst.

Take care when adding water and when carrying a battery. The electrolyte, even when diluted, is very corrosive and should not be allowed to contact clothing or skin.

Always wear eye protection when cleaning the battery to prevent the caustic deposits from entering your eyes.

Household current

When using an electric power tool, inspection light, etc., which operates on household current, always make sure that the tool is correctly connected to its plug and that, where necessary, it is properly grounded. Do not use such items in damp conditions and, again, do not create a spark or apply excessive heat in the vicinity of fuel or fuel vapor.

Secondary ignition system voltage

A severe electric shock can result from touching certain parts of the ignition system (such as the spark plug wires) when the engine is running or being cranked, particularly if components are damp or the insulation is defective. In the case of an electronic ignition system, the secondary system voltage is much higher and could prove fatal.

Conversion factors

Length (distance)

Inches (in)	X 25.4	= Millimetres (mm)	X 0.0394	= Inches (in)
Feet (ft)	X 0.305	= Metres (m)	X 3.281	= Feet (ft)
Miles	X 1.609	= Kilometres (km)	X 0.621	= Miles

Volume (capacity)

Cubic inches (cu in; in³)	X 16.387	= Cubic centimetres (cc; cm³)	X 0.061	= Cubic inches (cu in; in³)
Imperial pints (Imp pt)	X 0.568	= Litres (l)	X 1.76	= Imperial pints (Imp pt)
Imperial quarts (Imp qt)	X 1.137	= Litres (l)	X 0.88	= Imperial quarts (Imp qt)
Imperial quarts (Imp qt)	X 1.201	= US quarts (US qt)	X 0.833	= Imperial quarts (Imp qt)
US quarts (US qt)	X 0.946	= Litres (l)	X 1.057	= US quarts (US qt)
Imperial gallons (Imp gal)	X 4.546	= Litres (l)	X 0.22	= Imperial gallons (Imp gal)
Imperial gallons (Imp gal)	X 1.201	= US gallons (US gal)	X 0.833	= Imperial gallons (Imp gal)
US gallons (US gal)	X 3.785	= Litres (l)	X 0.264	= US gallons (US gal)

Mass (weight)

Ounces (oz)	X 28.35	= Grams (g)	X 0.035	= Ounces (oz)
Pounds (lb)	X 0.454	= Kilograms (kg)	X 2.205	= Pounds (lb)

Force

Ounces-force (ozf; oz)	X 0.278	= Newtons (N)	X 3.6	= Ounces-force (ozf; oz)
Pounds-force (lbf; lb)	X 4.448	= Newtons (N)	X 0.225	= Pounds-force (lbf; lb)
Newtons (N)	X 0.1	= Kilograms-force (kgf; kg)	X 9.81	= Newtons (N)

Pressure

Pounds-force per square inch (psi; lbf/in²; lb/in²)	X 0.070	= Kilograms-force per square centimetre (kgf/cm²; kg/cm²)	X 14.223	= Pounds-force per square inch (psi; lbf/in²; lb/in²)
Pounds-force per square inch (psi; lbf/in²; lb/in²)	X 0.068	= Atmospheres (atm)	X 14.696	= Pounds-force per square inch (psi; lbf/in²; lb/in²)
Pounds-force per square inch (psi; lbf/in²; lb/in²)	X 0.069	= Bars	X 14.5	= Pounds-force per square inch (psi; lbf/in²; lb/in²)
Pounds-force per square inch (psi; lbf/in²; lb/in²)	X 6.895	= Kilopascals (kPa)	X 0.145	= Pounds-force per square inch (psi; lbf/in²; lb/in²)
Kilopascals (kPa)	X 0.01	= Kilograms-force per square centimetre (kgf/cm²; kg/cm²)	X 98.1	= Kilopascals (kPa)

Torque (moment of force)

Pounds-force inches (lbf in; lb in)	X 1.152	= Kilograms-force centimetre (kgf cm; kg cm)	X 0.868	= Pounds-force inches (lbf in; lb in)
Pounds-force inches (lbf in; lb in)	X 0.113	= Newton metres (Nm)	X 8.85	= Pounds-force inches (lbf in; lb in)
Pounds-force inches (lbf in; lb in)	X 0.083	= Pounds-force feet (lbf ft; lb ft)	X 12	= Pounds-force inches (lbf in; lb in)
Pounds-force feet (lbf ft; lb ft)	X 0.138	= Kilograms-force metres (kgf m; kg m)	X 7.233	= Pounds-force feet (lbf ft; lb ft)
Pounds-force feet (lbf ft; lb ft)	X 1.356	= Newton metres (Nm)	X 0.738	= Pounds-force feet (lbf ft; lb ft)
Newton metres (Nm)	X 0.102	= Kilograms-force metres (kgf m; kg m)	X 9.804	= Newton metres (Nm)

Power

Horsepower (hp)	X 745.7	= Watts (W)	X 0.0013	= Horsepower (hp)

Velocity (speed)

Miles per hour (miles/hr; mph)	X 1.609	= Kilometres per hour (km/hr; kph)	X 0.621	= Miles per hour (miles/hr; mph)

Fuel consumption*

Miles per gallon, Imperial (mpg)	X 0.354	= Kilometres per litre (km/l)	X 2.825	= Miles per gallon, Imperial (mpg)
Miles per gallon, US (mpg)	X 0.425	= Kilometres per litre (km/l)	X 2.352	= Miles per gallon, US (mpg)

Temperature

Degrees Fahrenheit = (°C x 1.8) + 32   Degrees Celsius (Degrees Centigrade; °C) = (°F - 32) x 0.56

*It is common practice to convert from miles per gallon (mpg) to litres/100 kilometres (l/100km),
where mpg (Imperial) x l/100 km = 282 and mpg (US) x l/100 km = 235

Troubleshooting

Contents

This Section provides an easy reference guide to the more common problems that may occur during the operation of your vehicle. Various symptoms and their probable causes are grouped under headings denoting components or systems, such as Engine, Cooling system, etc. They also refer to the Chapter and/or Section that deals with the problem.

Remember that successful troubleshooting isn't a mysterious 'black art' practiced only by professional mechanics, it's simply the result of knowledge combined with an intelligent, systematic approach to a problem. Always use a process of elimination starting with the simplest solution and working through to the most complex — and never overlook the obvious. Anyone can run the gas tank dry or leave the lights on overnight, so don't assume that you're exempt from such oversights.

Finally, always establish a clear idea why a problem has occurred and take steps to ensure that it doesn't happen again. If the electrical system fails because of a poor connection, check all other connections in the system to make sure they don't fail as well. If a particular fuse continues to blow, find out why — don't just go on replacing fuses. Remember, failure of a small component can often be indicative of potential failure or incorrect functioning of a more important component or system.

Engine and performance

1 Engine will not rotate when attempting to start

1   Battery terminal connections loose or corroded. Check the cable terminals at the battery; tighten cable clamp and/or clean off corrosion as necessary (see Chapter 1).
2   Battery discharged or faulty. If the cable ends are clean and tight on the battery posts, turn the key to the On position and switch on the headlights or windshield wipers. If they won't run, the battery is discharged.
3   Automatic transmission not engaged in park (P) or Neutral (N).
4   Broken, loose or disconnected wires in the starting circuit. Inspect all wires and connectors at the battery, starter solenoid and ignition switch (on steering column).
5   Starter motor pinion jammed in flywheel ring gear. If manual transmission, place transmission in gear and rock the vehicle to manually turn the engine. Remove starter (Chapter 5) and inspect pinion and flywheel (Chapter 2) at earliest convenience.
6   Starter solenoid faulty (Chapter 5).
7   Starter motor faulty (Chapter 5).
8   Ignition switch faulty (Chapter 13).
9   Engine seized. Try to turn the crankshaft with a large socket and breaker bar on the pulley bolt.

2 Engine rotates but will not start

1   Fuel tank empty.
2   Battery discharged (engine rotates slowly). Check the operation of electrical components as described in previous Section.
3   Battery terminal connections loose or corroded. See previous Section.
4   Fuel not reaching carburetor or fuel injection system. Check for clogged fuel filter or lines and defective fuel pump. Also make sure the tank vent lines aren't clogged (Chapter 4).
5   Choke not operating properly (Chapter 1).
6   Faulty distributor components. Check the cap and rotor (Chapter 1).
7   Low cylinder compression. Check as described in Chapter 2.
8   Valve clearances not properly adjusted (Chapter 1).
9   Water in fuel. Drain tank and fill with new fuel.
10   Dirty or clogged carburetor jets. Carburetor out of adjustment. Check the float level (Chapters 1 and 4).
11   Wet or damaged ignition components (Chapters 1 and 5).
12   Worn, faulty or incorrectly gapped spark plugs (Chapter 1).
13   Broken, loose or disconnected wires in the starting circuit (see previous Section).

14   Loose distributor (changing ignition timing). Turn the distributor body as necessary to start the engine, then adjust the ignition timing as soon as possible (Chapter 1).
15   Broken, loose or disconnected wires at the ignition coil or faulty coil (Chapter 5).
16   Timing belt or chain failure or wear affecting valve timing (Chapter 2).

3 Starter motor operates without turning engine

1   Starter pinion sticking. Remove the starter (Chapter 5) and inspect.
2   Starter pinion or flywheel/driveplate teeth worn or broken. Remove the inspection cover on the left side of the engine and inspect.

4 Engine hard to start when cold

1   Battery discharged or low. Check as described in Chapter 1.
2   Fuel not reaching the carburetor or fuel injection system. Check the fuel filter, lines and fuel pump (Chapters 1 and 4).
3   Choke inoperative (Chapters 1 and 4).
4   Defective spark plugs (Chapter 1).

5 Engine hard to start when hot

1   Air filter dirty (Chapter 1).
2   Fuel not reaching carburetor or fuel injection system (see Section 4). Check for a vapor lock situation, brought about by clogged fuel tank vent lines.
3   Bad engine ground connection.
4   Choke sticking (Chapter 1).
5   Defective pick-up coil in distributor (Chapter 5).
6   Float level too high (Chapters 1 and 4).

6 Starter motor noisy or engages roughly

1   Pinion or flywheel/driveplate teeth worn or broken. Remove the inspection cover on the left side of the engine and inspect.
2   Starter motor mounting bolts loose or missing.

7 Engine starts but stops immediately

1   Loose or damaged wire harness connections at distributor, coil or alternator.
2   Intake manifold vacuum leaks. Make sure all mounting bolts/nuts are tight and all vacuum hoses connected to the manifold are attached properly and in good condition.
3   Insufficient fuel flow (see Chapter 4 for the fuel pump testing procedure).

8 Engine 'lopes' while idling or idles erratically

1   Vacuum leaks. Check mounting bolts at the intake manifold for tightness. Make sure that all vacuum hoses are connected and in good condition. Use a stethoscope or a length of fuel hose held against your ear to listen for vacuum leaks while the engine is running. A hissing sound will be heard. A soapy water solution will also detect leaks. Check the intake manifold gasket surfaces.
2   Leaking EGR valve or plugged PCV valve (see Chapters 1 and 6).
3   Air filter clogged (Chapter 1).
4   Fuel pump not delivering sufficient fuel (Chapter 4).
5   Leaking head gasket. Perform a cylinder compression check (Chapter 2).
6   Timing chain or belt worn or (Chapter 2).
7   Camshaft lobes worn (Chapter 2).
8   Valve clearance out of adjustment (Chapter 1). Valves burned or otherwise leaking (Chapter 2).
9   Ignition timing out of adjustment (Chapter 1).
10   Ignition system not operating properly (Chapters 1 and 5).

11 Thermostatic air cleaner not operating properly (Chapter 1).
12 Choke not operating properly (Chapters 1 and 4).
13 Carburetor dirty, clogged or out of adjustment. Check the float level (Chapters 1 and 4).
14 Idle speed out of adjustment (Chapter 1).
15 Clogged fuel injectors or other problems in the fuel injection system (Chapter 4).

9 Engine misses at idle speed

1 Spark plugs faulty or not gapped properly (Chapter 1).
2 Faulty spark plug wires (Chapter 1).
3 Wet or damaged distributor components (Chapter 1).
4 Short circuits in ignition, coil or spark plug wires.
5 Sticking or faulty emissions systems (see Chapter 6).
6 Clogged fuel filter and/or foreign matter in fuel. Remove the fuel filter (Chapter 1) and inspect.
7 Vacuum leaks at intake manifold or hose connections. Check as described in Section 8.
8 Incorrect idle speed (Chapter 1) or idle mixture (Chapter 4).
9 Incorrect ignition timing (Chapter 1).
10 Low or uneven cylinder compression. Check as described in Chapter 2.
11 Choke not operating properly (Chapter 1).

10 Excessively high idle speed

1 Sticking throttle linkage (Chapter 4).
2 Choke opened excessively at idle (Chapter 4).
3 Idle speed incorrectly adjusted (Chapter 1).
4 Valve clearances incorrectly adjusted (Chapter 1).

11 Battery will not hold a charge

1 Alternator drivebelt defective or not adjusted properly (Chapter 1).
2 Battery cables loose or corroded (Chapter 1).
3 Alternator not charging properly (Chapter 5).
4 Loose, broken or faulty wires in the charging circuit (Chapter 5).
5 Short circuit causing a continuous drain on the battery (Chapter 13).
6 Battery defective internally.
7 Faulty regulator (Chapter 5).

12 Alternator light stays on

1 Fault in alternator or charging circuit (Chapter 5).
2 Alternator drivebelt defective or not properly adjusted (Chapter 1).

13 Alternator light fails to come on when key is turned on

1 Faulty bulb (Chapter 12).
2 Defective alternator (Chapter 5).
3 Fault in the printed circuit, dash wiring or bulb holder (Chapter 12).

14 Engine misses throughout driving speed range

1 Fuel filter clogged and/or impurities in the fuel system. Check fuel filter (Chapter 1) or clean system (Chapter 4).
2 Faulty or incorrectly gapped spark plugs (Chapter 1).
3 Incorrect ignition timing (Chapter 1).
4 Cracked distributor cap, disconnected distributor wires or damaged distributor components (Chapter 1).
5 Defective spark plug wires (Chapter 1).
6 Emissions system components faulty (Chapter 6).

7 Low or uneven cylinder compression pressures. Check as described in Chapter 2.
8 Weak or faulty ignition coil (Chapter 5).
9 Weak or faulty ignition system (Chapter 5).
10 Vacuum leaks at intake manifold or vacuum hoses (see Section 8).
11 Dirty or clogged carburetor or fuel injectors (Chapter 4).
12 Leaky EGR valve (Chapter 6).
13 Carburetor out of adjustment (Chapter 4).
14 Idle speed out of adjustment (Chapter 1).

15 Hesitation or stumble during acceleration

1 Ignition timing incorrect (Chapter 1).
2 Ignition system not operating properly (Chapter 5).
3 Dirty or clogged carburetor or fuel injectors (Chapter 4).
4 Low fuel pressure. Check for proper operation of the fuel pump and for restrictions in the fuel filter and lines (Chapter 4).
5 Carburetor out of adjustment (Chapter 4).

16 Engine stalls

1 Idle speed incorrect (Chapter 1).
2 Fuel filter clogged and/or water and impurities in the fuel system (Chapter 1).
3 Choke not operating properly (Chapter 1).
4 Damaged or wet distributor cap and wires.
5 Emissions system components faulty (Chapter 6).
6 Faulty or incorrectly gapped spark plugs (Chapter 1). Also check the spark plug wires (Chapter 1).
7 Vacuum leak at the carburetor, intake manifold or vacuum hoses. Check as described in Section 8.
8 Valve clearances incorrect (Chapter 1).

17 Engine lacks power

1 Incorrect ignition timing (Chapter 1).
2 Excessive play in distributor shaft. At the same time check for faulty distributor cap, wires, etc. (Chapter 1).
3 Faulty or incorrectly gapped spark plugs (Chapter 1).
4 Air filter dirty (Chapter 1).
5 Spark timing control system not operating properly (Chapter 6).
6 Faulty ignition coil (Chapter 5).
7 Brakes binding (Chapters 1 and 10).
8 Automatic transmission fluid level incorrect, causing slippage (Chapter 1).
9 Clutch slipping (Chapter 8).
10 Fuel filter clogged and/or impurities in the fuel system (Chapters 1 and 4).
11 EGR system not functioning properly (Chapter 6).
12 Use of sub-standard fuel. Fill tank with proper octane fuel.
13 Low or uneven cylinder compression pressures. Check as described in Chapter 2.
14 Air leak at carburetor or throttle body or intake manifold (check as described in Section 8).
15 Dirty or clogged carburetor jets or malfunctioning choke (Chapters 1 and 4).

18 Engine backfires

1 EGR system not functioning properly (Chapter 6).
2 Ignition timing incorrect (Chapter 1).
3 Thermostatic air cleaner system not operating properly (Chapter 6).
4 Vacuum leak (refer to Section 8).
5 Valve clearances incorrect (Chapter 1).
6 Damaged valve springs or sticking valves (Chapter 2).
7 Intake air leak (see Section 8).
8 Carburetor float level out of adjustment (Chapter 4).
9 Problem in the fuel injection system (Chapter 4).

19 Engine surges while holding accelerator steady

1 Intake air leak (see Section 8).
2 Fuel pump not working properly (Chapter 4).

20 Pinging or knocking engine sounds when engine is under load

1 Incorrect grade of fuel. Fill tank with fuel of the proper octane rating.
2 Ignition timing incorrect (Chapter 1).
3 Carbon build-up in combustion chambers. Remove cylinder head(s) and clean combustion chambers (Chapter 2).
4 Incorrect spark plugs (Chapter 1).

21 Engine diesels (continues to run) after being turned off

1 Idle speed too high (Chapter 1).
2 Ignition timing incorrect (Chapter 1).
3 Incorrect spark plug heat range (Chapter 1).
4 Intake air leak (see Section 8).
5 Carbon build-up in combustion chambers. Remove the cylinder head and clean the combustion chambers (Chapter 2).
6 Valves sticking (Chapter 2).
7 Valve clearance incorrect (Chapter 1).
8 EGR system not operating properly (Chapter 6).
9 Fuel shut-off system not operating properly (Chapter 6).
10 Check for causes of overheating (Section 27).

22 Low oil pressure

1 Improper grade of oil.
2 Oil pump regulator valve not operating properly (Chapter 2).
3 Oil pump worn or damaged (Chapter 2).
4 Engine overheating (refer to Section 27).
5 Clogged oil filter (Chapter 1).
6 Clogged oil strainer (Chapter 2).
7 Oil pressure gauge not working properly (Chapter 2).

23 Excessive oil consumption

1 Loose oil drain plug.
2 Loose bolts or damaged oil pan gasket (Chapter 2).
3 Loose bolts or damaged front cover gasket (Chapter 2).
4 Front or rear crankshaft oil seal leaking (Chapter 2).
5 Loose bolts or damaged rocker arm cover gasket (Chapter 2).
6 Loose oil filter (Chapter 1).
7 Loose or damaged oil pressure switch (Chapter 2).
8 Pistons and cylinders excessively worn (Chapter 2).
9 Piston rings not installed correctly on pistons (Chapter 2).
10 Worn or damaged piston rings (Chapter 2).
11 Intake and/or exhaust valve oil seals worn or damaged (Chapter 2).
12 Worn valve stems.
13 Worn or damaged valves/guides (Chapter 2).

24 Excessive fuel consumption

1 Dirty or clogged air filter element (Chapter 1).
2 Incorrect ignition timing (Chapter 1).
3 Incorrect idle speed (Chapter 1).
4 Low tire pressure or incorrect tire size (Chapter 10).
5 Fuel leakage. Check all connections, lines and components in the fuel system (Chapter 4).

6 Choke not operating properly (Chapter 1).
7 Dirty or clogged carburetor jets (Chapter 4).

25 Fuel odor

1 Fuel leakage. Check all connections, lines and components in the fuel system (Chapter 4).
2 Fuel tank overfilled. Fill only to automatic shut-off.
3 Charcoal canister filter in Evaporative Emissions Control system clogged (Chapter 1).
4 Vapor leaks from Evaporative Emissions Control system lines (Chapter 6).

26 Miscellaneous engine noises

1 A strong dull noise that becomes more rapid as the engine accelerates indicates worn or damaged crankshaft bearings or an unevenly worn crankshaft. To pinpoint the trouble spot, remove the spark plug wire from one plug at a time and crank the engine over. If the noise stops, the cylinder with the removed plug wire indicates the problem area. Replace the bearing and/or service or replace the crankshaft (Chapter 2).
2 A similar (yet slightly higher pitched) noise to the crankshaft knocking described in the previous paragraph, that becomes more rapid as the engine accelerates, indicates worn or damaged connecting rod bearings (Chapter 2). The procedure for locating the problem cylinder is the same as described in Paragraph 1.
3 An overlapping metallic noise that increases in intensity as the engine speed increases, yet diminishes as the engine warms up indicates abnormal piston and cylinder wear (Chapter 2). To locate the problem cylinder, use the procedure described in Paragraph 1.
4 A rapid clicking noise that becomes faster as the engine accelerates indicates a worn piston pin or piston pin hole. This sound will happen each time the piston hits the highest and lowest points in the stroke (Chapter 2). The procedure for locating the problem piston is described in Paragraph 1.
5 A metallic clicking noise coming from the water pump indicates worn or damaged water pump bearings or pump. Replace the water pump with a new one (Chapter 3).
6 A rapid tapping sound or clicking sound that becomes faster as the engine speed increases indicates "valve tapping" or improperly adjusted valve clearances. This can be identified by holding one end of a section of hose to your ear and placing the other end at different spots along the rocker arm cover. The point where the sound is loudest indicates the problem valve. Adjust the valve clearance (Chapter 1).
7 A steady metallic rattling or rapping sound coming from the area of the timing chain cover indicates a worn, damaged or out-of-adjustment timing chain. Service or replace the chain and related components (Chapter 2).

Cooling system

27 Overheating

1 Insufficient coolant in system (Chapter 1).
2 Drivebelt defective or not adjusted properly (Chapter 1).
3 Radiator core blocked or radiator grille dirty and restricted (Chapter 3).
4 Thermostat faulty (Chapter 3).
5 Fan not functioning properly (Chapter 3).
6 Radiator cap not maintaining proper pressure. Have cap pressure tested by gas station or repair shop.
7 Ignition timing incorrect (Chapter 1).
8 Defective water pump (Chapter 3).
9 Improper grade of engine oil.
10 Inaccurate temperature gauge.

28   Overcooling

1   Thermostat faulty (Chapter 3).
2   Inaccurate temperature gauge.

29   External coolant leakage

1   Deteriorated or damaged hoses. Loose clamps at hose connections (Chapter 1).
2   Water pump seals defective. If this is the case, water will drip from the weep hole in the water pump body (Chapter 3).
3   Leakage from radiator core or header tank. This will require the radiator to be professionally repaired (see Chapter 3 for removal procedures).
4   Engine drain plugs or water jacket freeze plugs leaking (see Chapters 1 and 2).
5   Leak from coolant temperature switch (Chapter 3).
6   Leak from damaged gaskets or small cracks (Chapter 2).
7   Damaged head gasket. This can be verifed by checking the condition of the engine oil as noted in Section 30.

30   Internal coolant leakage

Note: *Internal coolant leaks can usually be detected by examining the oil. Check the dipstick and inside the rocker arm cover for water deposits and an oil consistency like that of a milkshake.*

1   Leaking cylinder head gasket. Have the system pressure tested or remove the cylinder head (Chapter 2) and inspect.
2   Cracked cylinder bore or cylinder head. Dismantle engine and inspect (Chapter 2).
3   Loose cylinder head bolts (tighten as described in Chapter 2).
4   Damaged oil cooler (Chapter 2A).

31   Abnormal coolant loss

1   Overfilling system (Chapter 1).
2   Coolant boiling away due to overheating (see causes in Section 27).
3   Internal or external leakage (see Sections 29 and 30).
4   Faulty radiator cap. Have the cap pressure tested.
5   Cooling system being pressurized by engine compression. This could be due to a cracked head or block or leaking head gasket(s).

32   Poor coolant circulation

1   Inoperative water pump. A quick test is to pinch the top radiator hose closed with your hand while the engine is idling, then release it. You should feel a surge of coolant if the pump Is working properly (Chapter 3).
2   Restriction in cooling system. Drain, flush and refill the system (Chapter 1). If necessary, remove the radiator (Chapter 3) and have it reverse flushed or professionally cleaned.
3   Loose water pump drivebelt (Chapter 1).
4   Thermostat sticking (Chapter 3).
5   Insufficient coolant (Chapter 1).

33   Corrosion

1   Excessive impurities in the water. Soft, clean water is recommended. Distilled or rainwater is satisfactory.
2   Insuffiecient antifreeze solution (refer to Chapter 1 for the proper ratio of water to antifreeze).
3   Infrequent flushing and draining of system. Regular flushing of the cooling system should be carried out at the specified intervals as described in (Chapter 1).

Clutch

Note: *All clutch related service information is located in Chapter 8, unless otherwise noted.*

34   Fails to release (pedal pressed to the floor — shift lever does not move freely in and out of Reverse)

1   Clutch contaminated with oil. Remove clutch plate and inspect.
2   Clutch plate warped, distorted or otherwise damaged.
3   Diaphragm spring fatigued. Remove clutch cover/pressure plate assembly and inspect.
4   Leakage of fluid from clutch hydraulic system. Inspect master cylinder, operating cylinder and connecting lines.
5   Air in clutch hydraulic system. Bleed the system.
6   Insufficient pedal stroke. Check and adjust as necessary.
7   Piston seal in operating cylinder deformed or damaged.
8   Lack of grease on pilot bushing.

35   Clutch slips (engine speed increases with no increase in vehicle speed)

1   Worn or oil soaked clutch plate.
2   Clutch plate not broken in. It may take 30 or 40 normal starts for a new clutch to seat.
3   Diaphragm spring weak or damaged. Remove clutch cover/pressure plate assembly and inspect.
4   Flywheel warped (Chapter 2).
5   Debris in master cylinder preventing the piston from returning to its normal position.
6   Clutch hydraulic line damaged.

36   Grabbing (chattering) as clutch is engaged

1   Oil on clutch plate. Remove and inspect. Repair any leaks.
2   Worn or loose engine or transmission mounts. They may move slightly when clutch is released. Inspect mounts and bolts.
3   Worn splines on transmission input shaft. Remove clutch components and inspect.
4   Warped pressure plate or flywheel. Remove clutch components and inspect.
5   Diaphragm spring fatigued. Remove clutch cover/pressure plate assembly and inspect.
6   Clutch linings hardened or warped.
7   Clutch lining rivets loose.

37   Squeal or rumble with clutch engagad (pedal released)

1   Improper pedal adjustment. Adjust pedal free play.
2   Release bearing binding on transmission shaft. Remove clutch components and check bearing. Remove any burrs or nicks, clean and relubricate before reinstallation.
3   Pilot bushing worn or damaged.
4   Clutch rivets loose.
5   Clutch plate cracked.
6   Fatigued clutch plate torsion springs. Replace clutch plate.

38   Squeal or rumble with clutch disengaged (pedal depressed)

1   Worn or damaged release bearing.
2   Worn or broken pressure plate diaphragm fingers.

39   Clutch pedal stays on floor when disengaged

1   Binding linkage or release bearing. Inspect linkage or remove clutch components as necessary.

2   Linkage springs being over extended. Adjust linkage for proper free play. Make sure proper pedal stop (bumper) is installed.

Manual transmission

Note: *All manual transmission service information is located in Chapter 7, unless otherwise noted.*

40   Noisy in Neutral with engine running

1   Input shaft bearing worn.
2   Damaged main drive gear bearing.
3   Insufficient transmission oil (Chapter 1).
4   Transmission oil in poor condition. Drain and fill with proper grade oil. Check old oil for water and debris (Chapter 1).
5   Noise can be caused by variations in engine torque. Change the idle speed and see if noise disappears.

41   Noisy in all gears

1   Any of the above causes, and/or:
2   Worn or damaged output gear bearings or shaft.

42   Noisy in one particular gear

1   Worn, damaged or chipped gear teeth.
2   Worn or damaged synchronizer.

43   Slips out of gear

1   Transmission loose on clutch housing.
2   Stiff shift lever seal.
3   Shift linkage binding.
4   Broken or loose input gear bearing retainer.
5   Dirt between clutch lever and engine housing.
6   Worn linkage.
7   Damaged or worn check balls, fork rod ball grooves or check springs.
8   Worn mainshaft or countershaft bearings.
9   Loose engine mounts (Chapter 2).
10   Excessive gear end play.
11   Worn synchronizers.

44   Oil leaks

1   Excessive amount of lubricant in transmission (see Chapter 1 for correct checking procedures). Drain lubricant as required.
2   Side cover loose or gasket damaged.
3   Rear oil seal or speedometer oil seal damaged.
4   To pinpoint a leak, first remove all built-up dirt and grime from the transmission. Degreasing agents and/or steam cleaning will achieve this. With the underside clean, drive the vehicle at low speeds so the air flow will not blow the leak far from its source. Raise the vehicle and determine where the leak is located.

45   Difficulty engaging gears

1   Clutch not releasing completely.
2   Loose or damaged shift linkage. Make a thorough inspection, replacing parts as necessary.
3   Insufficient transmission oil (Chapter 1).

4   Transmission oil in poor condition. Drain and fill with proper grade oil. Check oil for water and debris (Chapter 1).
5   Worn or damaged striking rod.
6   Sticking or jamming gears.

46   Noise occurs while shifting gears

1   Check for proper operation of the clutch (Chapter 8).
2   Faulty synchronizer assemblies. Measure baulk ring-to-gear clearance. Also, check for wear or damage to baulk rings or any parts of the synchromesh assemblies.

Automatic transmission

Note: *Due to the complexity of the automatic transmission, it's difficult for the home mechanic to properly diagnose and service. For problems other than the following, the vehicle should be taken to a reputable mechanic.*

47   Fluid leakage

1   Automatic transmission fluid is a deep red color, and fluid leaks should not be confused with engine oil which can easily be blown by air flow to the transmission.
2   To pinpoint a leak, first remove all built-up dirt and grime from the transmission. Degreasing agents and/or steam cleaning will achieve this. With the underside clean, drive the vehicle at low speeds so the air flow will not blow the leak far from its source. Raise the vehicle and determine where the leak is located. Common areas of leakage are:
   a)   Fluid pan: tighten mounting bolts and/or replace pan gasket as necessary (Chapter 1).
   b)   Rear extension: tighten bolts and/or replace oil seal as necessary.
   c)   Filler pipe: replace the rubber oil seal where pipe enters transmission case.
   d)   Transmission oil lines: tighten fittings where lines enter transmission case and/or replace lines.
   e)   Vent pipe: transmission overfilled and/or water in fluid (see checking procedures, Chapter 1).
   f)   Speedometer connector: replace the O-ring where speedometer cable enters transmission case.

48   General shift mechanism problems

Chapter 7 deals with checking and adjusting the shift linkage on automatic transmissions. Common problems which may be caused by out of adjustment linkage are:
   a)   Engine starting in gears other than P (park) or N (Neutral).
   b)   Indicator pointing to a gear other than the one actually engaged.
   c)   Vehicle moves with transmission in P (Park) position.

49   Transmission will not downshift with the accelerator pedal pressed to the floor

Chapter 7 deals with adjusting the kickdown switch to enable the transmission to downshift properly.

50   Engine will start in gears other than Park or Neutral

Chapter 7 deals with adjusting the Neutral start switch installed on automatic transmissions.

51 Transmission slips, shifts rough, is noisy or has no drive in forward or Reverse gears

1   There are many probable causes for the above problems, but the home mechanic should concern himself only with one possibility; fluid level.
2   Before taking the vehicle to a shop, check the fluid level and condition as described in Chapter 1. Add fluid, if necessary, or change the fluid and filter if needed. If problems persist, have a professional diagnose the transmission.

Driveshaft

Note: *Refer to Chapter 8, unless otherwise specified, for service information.*

52 Leaks at front of driveshaft

Defective transmission rear seal. See Chapter 7 for replacment procedure. As this is done, check the splined yoke for burrs or roughness that could damage the new seal. Remove burrs with a fine file or whetstone.

53 Knock or clunk when transmission is under initial load (just after transmission is put into gear)

1   Loose or disconnected rear suspension components. Check all mounting bolts and bushings (Chapters 1 and 11).
2   Loose driveshaft bolts. Inspect all bolts and nuts and tighten them securely.
3   Worn or damaged universal joint bearings. Replace driveshaft (Chapter 8).
4   Worn sleeve yoke and mainshaft spline.
5   Defective center bearing or insulator.

54 Metallic grating sound consistent with vehicle speed

Pronounced wear in the universal joint bearings. Replace U-joints or driveshafts, as necessary.

55 Vibration

Note: *Before blaming the driveshaft, make sure the tires are perfectly balanced and perform the following test.*

1   Install a tachometer inside the vehicle to monitor engine speed as the vehicle is driven. Drive the vehicle and note the engine speed at which the vibration (roughness) is most pronounced. Now shift the transmission to a different gear and bring the engine speed to the same point.
2   If the vibration occurs at the same engine speed (rpm) regardless of which gear the transmission is in, the driveshaft is NOT at fault since the driveshaft speed varies.
3   If the vibration decreases or is eliminated when the transmission is in a different gear at the same engine speed, refer to the following probable causes.
4   Bent or dented driveshaft. Inspect and replace as necessary.
5   Undercoating or built-up dirt, etc. on the driveshaft. Clean the shaft thoroughly.
6   Worn universal joint bearings. Replace the U-joints or driveshaft as necessary.
7   Driveshaft and/or companion flange out of balance. Check for missing weights on the shaft. Remove driveshaft and reinstall 180° from original position, then recheck. Have the driveshaft balanced if problem persists.
8   Loose driveshaft mounting bolts/nuts.
9   Defective center bearing, if so equipped.
10   Worn transmission rear bushing (Chapter 7).

56 Scraping noise

Make sure the dust cover (if equipped) on the sleeve yoke isn't rubbing on the transmission extension housing.

57 Whining or whistling noise

Defective center bearing, if so equipped.

Rear axle and differential

Note: *For differential servicing information, refer to Chapter 8.*

58 Noise — same when in drive as when vehicle is coasting

1   Road noise. No corrective action available.
2   Tire noise. Inspect tires and check tire pressures (Chapter 1).
3   Front wheel bearings loose, worn or damaged (Chapter 1).
4   Insufficient differential oil (Chapter 1).
5   Defective differential.

59 Knocking sound when starting or shifting gears

Defective or incorrectly adjusted differential.

60 Noise when turning

Defective differential.

61 Vibration

See probable causes under Driveshaft. Proceed under the guidelines listed for the driveshaft. If the problem persists, check the rear wheel bearings by raising the rear of the vehicle and spinning the wheels by hand. Listen for evidence of rough (noisy) bearings. Remove and inspect (Chapter 8).

62 Oil leaks

1   Pinion oil seal damaged (Chapter 8).
2   Axleshaft oil seals damaged (Chapter 8).
3   Differential cover leaking. Tighten mounting bolts or replace the gasket as required.
4   Loose filler or drain plug on differential (Chapter 1).
5   Clogged or damaged breather on differential.

Transfer case (4WD models)

63 Gear jumping out of mesh

1   Incorrect control lever free play.
2   Interference between the control lever and the console.
3   Play or fatigue in the transfer case mounts.
4   Internal wear or incorrect adjustments.

64 Difficult shifting

1   Lack of oil.
2   Internal wear, damage or incorrect adjustment.

65 Noise

1 Lack of oil in transfer case.
2 Noise in 4H and 4L, but not in 2H indicates cause is in the front differential or front axle.
3 Noise in 2H, 4H and 4L indicates cause is in rear differential or rear axle.
4 Noise in 2H and 4H but not in 4L, or in 4L only, indicates internal wear or damage in transfer case.

Brakes

Note: *Before assuming a brake problem exists, make sure the tires are in good condition and inflated properly, the front end alignment is correct and the vehicle is not loaded with weight in an unequal manner. All service procedures for the brakes are included in Chapter 9, unless otherwise noted.*

66 Vehicle pulls to one side during braking

1 Defective, damaged or oil contaminated brake pad on one side. Inspect as described in Chapter 1. Refer to Chapter 9 if replacement is required.
2 Excessive wear of brake pad material or disc on one side. Inspect and repair as necessary.
3 Loose or disconnected front suspension components. Inspect and tighten all bolts securely (Chapters 1 and 10).
4 Defective caliper assembly. Remove caliper and inspect for stuck piston or damage.
5 Brake pad to rotor adjustment needed. Inspect automatic adjusting mechanism for proper operation.
6 Scored or out of round rotor.
7 Loose caliper mounting bolts.
8 Incorrect wheel bearing adjustment.

67 Noise (high-pitched squeal)

1 Front brake pads worn out. Replace pads with new ones immediately!
2 Glazed or contaminated pads.
3 Dirty or scored rotor.
4 Bent support plate.

68 Excessive brake pedal travel

1 Partial brake system failure. Inspect entire system (Chapter 1) and correct as required.
2 Insufficient fluid in master cylinder. Check (Chapter 1) and add fluid — bleed system if necessary.
3 Air in system. Bleed system.
4 Excessive lateral rotor play.
5 Brakes out of adjustment. Check the operation of the automatic adjusters.
6 Defective check valve. Replace valve and bleed system.

69 Brake pedal feels spongy when depressed

1 Air in brake lines. Bleed the brake system.
2 Deteriorated rubber brake hoses. Inspect all system hoses and lines. Replace parts as necessary.
3 Master cylinder mounting nuts loose. Inspect master cylinder bolts (nuts) and tighten them securely.
4 Master cylinder faulty.
5 Incorrect shoe or pad clearance.

6 Defective check valve. Replace valve and bleed system.
7 Clogged reservoir cap vent hole.
8 Deformed rubber brake lines.
9 Soft or swollen caliper seals.
10 Poor quality brake fluid. Bleed entire system and fill with new approved fluid.

70 Excessive effort required to stop vehicle

1 Power brake booster not operating properly.
2 Excessively worn linings or pads. Check and replace if necessary.
3 One or more caliper pistons seized or sticking. Inspect and rebuild as required.
4 Brake pads or linings contaminated with oil or grease. Inspect and replace as required.
5 New pads or linings installed and not yet seated. It'll take a while for the new material to seat against the rotor or drum.
6 Worn or damaged master cylinder or caliper assemblies. Check particularly for frozen pistons.
7 Also see causes listed under Section 69.

71 Pedal travels to the floor with little resistance

Little or no fluid in the master cylinder reservoir caused by leaking caliper piston(s) or loose, damaged or disconnected brake lines. Inspect entire system and repair as necessary.

72 Brake pedal pulsates during brake application

1 Wheel bearings damaged, worn or out of adjustment (Chapter 1).
2 Caliper not sliding properly due to improper installation or obstructions. Remove and inspect.
3 Rotor not within specifications. Remove the rotor and check for excessive lateral runout and parallelism. Have the rotors resurfaced or replace them with new ones. Also make sure that all rotors are the same thickness.
4 Out of round rear brake drums. Remove the drums and have them turned or replace them with new ones.

73 Brakes drag (indicated by sluggish engine performance or wheels being very hot after driving)

1 Output rod adjustment incorrect at the brake pedal.
2 Obstructed master cylinder compensator. Disassemble master cylinder and clean.
3 Master cylinder piston seized in bore. Overhaul master cylinder.
4 Caliper assembly in need of overhaul.
5 Brake pads or shoes worn out.
6 Piston cups in master cylinder or caliper assembly deformed. Overhaul master cylinder.
7 Rotor not within specifications (Section 72).
8 Parking brake assembly will not release.
9 Clogged brake lines.
10 Wheel bearings out of adjustment (Chapter 1).
11 Brake pedal height improperly adjusted.
12 Wheel cylinder needs overhaul.
13 Improper shoe to drum clearance. Adjust as necessary.

74 Rear brakes lock up under light brake application

1 Tire pressures too high.
2 Tires excessively worn (Chapter 1).
3 Defective proportioning valve.

75 Rear brakes lock up under heavy brake application

1 Tire pressures too high.
2 Tires excessively worn (Chapter 1).
3 Front brake pads contaminated with oil, mud or water. Clean or replace the pads.
4 Front brake pads excessively worn.
5 Defective master cylinder or caliper assembly.

Suspension and steering

Note: *All service procedures for the suspension and steering systems are included in Chapter 11, unless otherwise noted.*

76 Vehicle pulls to one side

1 Tire pressures uneven (Chapter 1).
2 Defective tire (Chapter 1).
3 Excessive wear in suspension or steering components (Chapter 1).
4 Front end alignment incorrect.
5 Front brakes dragging. Inspect as described in Section 73.
6 Wheel bearings improperly adjusted (Chapter 1).
7 Wheel lug nuts loose.
8 Worn upper or lower link or tension rod bushings.

77 Shimmy, shake or vibration

1 Tire or wheel out of balance or out of round. Have them balanced on the vehicle.
2 Loose, worn or out of adjustment wheel bearings (Chapter 1).
3 Shock absorbers and/or suspension components worn or damaged. Check for worn bushings in the upper and lower links.
4 Wheel lug nuts loose.
5 Incorrect tire pressures.
6 Excessively worn or damaged tire.
7 Loosely mounted steering gear housing.
8 Steering gear improperly adjusted.
9 Loose, worn or damaged steering components.
10 Damaged idler arm.
11 Worn balljoint.

78 Excessive pitching and/or rolling around corners or during braking

1 Defective shock absorbers. Replace as a set.
2 Broken or weak leaf springs and/or suspension components.
3 Worn or damaged stabilizer bar or bushings.
4 Worn or damaged upper or lower links or bushings.

79 Wandering or general instability

1 Improper tire pressures.
2 Worn or damaged upper and lower link or tension rod bushings.
3 Incorrect front end alignment.
4 Worn or damaged steering linkage or upper or lower link.
5 Improperly adjusted steering gear.
6 Out of balance wheels.
7 Loose wheel lug nuts.
8 Worn rear shock absorbers.
9 Fatigued or damaged rear leaf springs.

80 Excessively stiff steering

1 Lack of lubricant in power steering fluid reservoir, where appropriate (Chapter 1).
2 Incorrect tire pressures (Chapter 1).
3 Lack of lubrication at balljoints (Chapter 1).
4 Front end out of alignment.
5 Steering gear out of adjustment or lacking lubrication.
6 Improperly adjusted wheel bearings.
7 Worn or damaged steering gear.
8 Interference of steering column with turn signal switch.
9 Low tire pressures.
10 Worn or damaged balljoints.
11 Worn or damaged steering linkage.
12 See also Section 79.

81 Excessive play in steering

1 Loose wheel bearings (Chapter 1).
2 Excessive wear in upper or lower link or tension rod bushings (Chapter 1).
3 Steering gear improperly adjusted.
4 Incorrect front end alignment.
5 Steering gear mounting bolts loose.
6 Worn steering linkage.

82 Lack of power assistance

1 Steering pump drivebelt faulty or not adjusted properly (Chapter 1).
2 Fluid level low (Chapter 1).
3 Hoses or pipes restricting the flow. Inspect and replace parts as necessary.
4 Air in power steering system. Bleed system.
5 Defective power steering pump.

83 Steering wheel fails to return to straight-ahead position

1 Incorrect front end alignment.
2 Tire pressures low.
3 Steering gears improperly engaged.
4 Steering column out of alignment.
5 Worn or damaged balljoint.
6 Worn or damaged steering linkage.
7 Improperly lubricated idler arm.
8 Insufficient oil in steering gear.
9 Lack of fluid in power steering pump.

84 Steering effort not the same in both directions (power system)

1 Leaks in steering gear.
2 Clogged fluid passage in steering gear.

85 Noisy power steering pump

1 Insufficient oil in pump.
2 Clogged hoses or oil filter in pump.
3 Loose pulley.
4 Improperly adjusted drivebelt (Chapter 1).
5 Defective pump.

86   Miscellaneous noises

1   Improper tire pressures.
2   Insufficiently lubricated balljoint or steering linkage.
3   Loose or worn steering gear, steering linkage or suspension components.
4   Defective shock absorber.
5   Defective wheel bearing.
6   Worn or damaged upper or lower link or tension rod bushing.
7   Damaged leaf spring.
8   Loose wheel lug nuts.
9   Worn or damaged rear axleshaft spline.
10   Worn or damaged rear shock absorber mounting bushing.
11   Incorrect rear axle end play.
12   See also causes of noises at the rear axle and driveshaft.
13   Worn or damaged driveaxle joints (4WD models).

87   Excessive tire wear (not specific to one area)

1   Incorrect tire pressures.
2   Tires out of balance. Have them balanced on the vehicle.
3   Wheels damaged. Inspect and replace as necessary.
4   Suspension or steering components worn (Chapter 1).

88   Excessive tire wear on outside edge

1   Incorrect tire pressure.
2   Excessive speed in turns.
3   Front end alignment incorrect (excessive toe-in).

89   Excessive tire wear on inside edge

1   Incorrect tire pressure.
2   Front end alignment incorrect (toe-out).
3   Loose or damaged steering components (Chapter 1).

90   Tire tread worn in one place

1   Tires out of balance. Have them balanced on the vehicle.
2   Damaged or buckled wheel. Inspect and replace if necessary.
3   Defective tire.

Chapter 1 Tune-up and routine maintenance

Contents

Specifications

Recommended lubricants and fluids

Engine oil type . . . . SF, SF/CC or SF/CD
Engine oil viscosity . . . . See accompanying chart

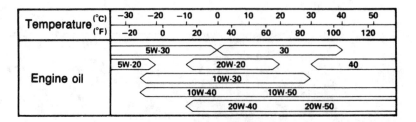

ENGINE OIL VISCOSITY

Automatic transmission fluid type*
  1972 thru 1986 . . . .   ATF type F automatic transmission fluid
  1987 on . . . .   Dexron II automatic transmission fluid
*Correct fluid type is printed on the dipstick
Manual transmission lubricant type . . . .   API GL-4 SAE 75W90W or 80W90W gear oil
Differential lubricant type . . . .   API GL-5 SAE 80W90W hypoid gear oil
Brake fluid type . . . .   DOT 3 brake fluid
Clutch fluid type . . . .   DOT 3 brake fluid
Power steering system fluid . . . .   ATF type F automatic transmission fluid
Steering gear box oil . . . .   API GL-4 SAE 90W
Transfer case lubricant type . . . .   API GL-4 or GL-5 SAE 80W or 90W gear oil
Suspension and steering balljoint grease . . . .   NLGI No. 1 or 2 molybdenum-disulfide lithium base grease
Driveshaft
  Slip yokes . . . .   Molybdenum-disulfide base, NLGI No. 2
  Universal joints . . . .   Lithium base multi-purpose, No.1
Steering gear box oil . . . .   API GL-4 SAE 90W
Wheel bearing grease . . . .   NLG1 No. 2 lithium base multi-purpose grease

Ignition system

Spark plug type and gap . . . .   Refer to the *Emission Control Information* label
Ignition timing . . . .   Refer to the *Emission Control Information* label
Engine firing order   1-3-4-2
Ignition contact point gap . . . .   0.020-in (0.5 mm)
Dwell angle . . . .   49 to 55°

Carburetor

Idle speed . . . .   Refer to the *Emission Control Information* label
Idle speed switch voltage
  At idle 12V
  Above 1000 to 1200 rpm . . . .   Below 1.5V

Cooling system

Drivebelt (fan belt) deflection
Air pump
  New . . . .   0.39 to 0.59 in (10 to 15 mm)
  Used . . . .   0.59 to 0.70 in (15 to 18 mm)
Alternator
  New . . . .   0.28 to 0.32 in (7 to 8 mm)
  Used . . . .   0.32 to 0.36 in (8 to 9 mm)
Air conditioning compressor
  New . . . .   0.39 to 0.47 in (10 to 12 mm)
  Used . . . .   0.47 to 0.55 in (12 to 14 mm)
Power steering pump
  New . . . .   0.32 to 0.39 in (8 to 10 mm)
  Used . . . .   0.43 to 0.51 in (11 to 13 mm)

Clutch

Clutch pedal free play . . . .   0.02 to 0.12 in (0.5 to 3.0 mm)
Clutch pedal height
  1600/1800/2000/2200 engine . . . .   8.43 to 8.62 in (214 to 219 mm)
  2600 engine . . . .   8.82 to 9.02 in (224 to 229 mm)

Brakes

Disc brake pad lining thickness (minimum) . . . .   0.040 in (1 mm)
Drum brake shoe lining thickness (minimum) . . . .   0.040 in (1 mm)
Brake pedal
  Height . . . .   8.1 in (205 mm)
  Free travel
    1972 through 1979 . . . .   0.02 to 0.12 in (0.5 to 3.0 mm)
    1980 on . . . .   0.28 to 0.35 in (7 to 9 mm)

Valve clearances

1600/1800/2000/2200 engine
1972 through 1984
  Valve side
    Intake valve . . . .   0.012 in (0.3 mm)
    Exhaust valve . . . .   0.012 in (0.3 mm)
  Cam side
    Intake valve . . . .   0.009 in (0.2 mm)
    Exhaust valve . . . .   0.009 in (0.2 mm)

1985 through 1987
  Valve side
    Intake valve . . . .   0.012 in (0.3 mm)
    Exhaust valve . . . .   0.012 in (0.3 mm)
  Cam side
    Intake valve . . . .   0.012 in (0.3 mm)
    Exhaust valve . . . .   0.012 in (0.3 mm)
  1988 and later 2200 engine . . . .   Self-adjusting hydraulic lifters

2600 engine
Intake and exhaust valves . . . .   Self-adjusting hydraulic lifters
Jet valve (1988 and earlier models) . . . .   0.10 in (0.2 mm)

Torque specifications   Ft-lbs
Automatic transmission pan bolts . . . .   4 to 7
EGR valve bolt . . . .   5 to 9
Front wheel bearing nut preload (2WD) . . . .   14 to 22

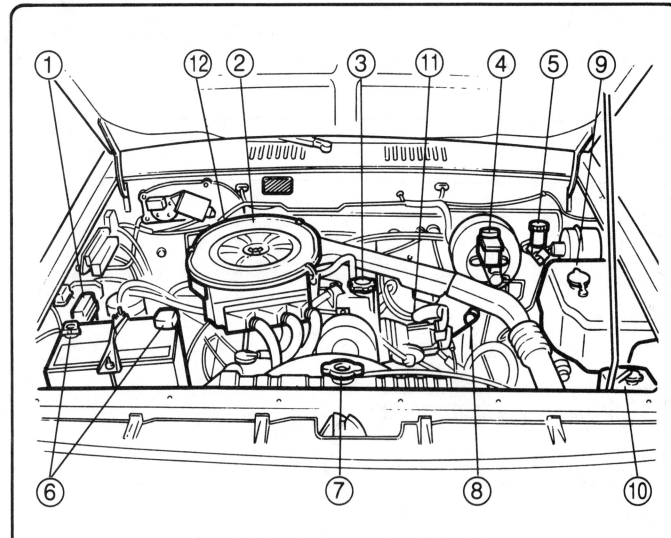

1.1a   Typical underhood component layout (2200 engine)

1 Main fuse block	*8 Engine oil dipstick*
2 Air cleaner	*9 Windshield washer*
3 Oil filler cap	* fluid reservoir*
4 Brake fluid reservoir	*10 Engine coolant reservoir*
5 Clutch fluid reservoir	*11 Power steering fluid reservoir*
6 Battery terminals	*12 Automatic transmission*
7 Radiator cap	* fluid dipstick*

1   Introduction

This Chapter is designed to help the home mechanic maintain the Mazda pick-up with the goals of maximum performance, economy, safety and reliability in mind.

Included is a master maintenance schedule, followed by procedures dealing specifically with each item on the schedule. Visual checks, adjustments, component replacement and other helpful items are included. Refer to the accompanying illustrations of the engine compartment and the underside of the vehicle for the locations of various components.

Servicing your vehicle in accordance with the planned mileage/time maintenance schedule and the step-by-step procedures should result in maximum reliability and extend the life of your vehicle. Keep in mind that it's a comprehensive plan — maintaining some items but not others at the specified intervals will not produce the same results.

As you perform routine maintenance procedures, you'll find that many can, and should, be grouped together because of the nature of the procedures or because of the proximity of two otherwise unrelated components or systems.

For example, if the vehicle is raised for chassis lubrication, you should inspect the exhaust, suspension, steering and fuel systems while you're under the vehicle. When you're rotating the tires, it makes good sense to check the brakes since the wheels are already removed. Finally, let's suppose you have to borrow or rent a torque wrench. Even if you only need it to tighten the spark plugs, you might as well check the torque of as many critical fasteners as time allows.

The first step in this maintenance program is to prepare yourself before the actual work begins. Read through all the procedures you're planning to do, then gather up all the parts and tools needed. If it looks like you might run into problems during a particular job, seek advice from a mechanic or experienced do-it-yourselfer.

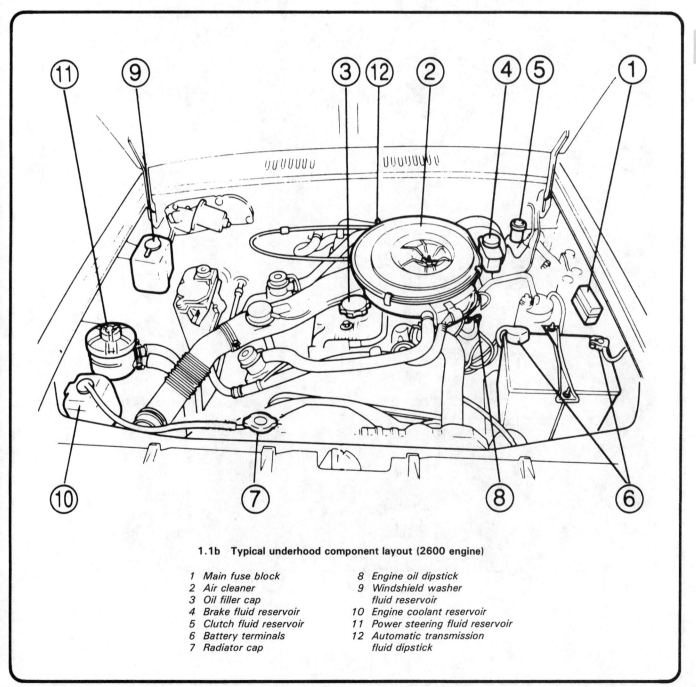

1.1b   Typical underhood component layout (2600 engine)

1   Main fuse block
2   Air cleaner
3   Oil filler cap
4   Brake fluid reservoir
5   Clutch fluid reservoir
6   Battery terminals
7   Radiator cap
8   Engine oil dipstick
9   Windshield washer
    fluid reservoir
10 Engine coolant reservoir
11 Power steering fluid reservoir
12 Automatic transmission
    fluid dipstick

1.1c Typical engine underside components

1 Front engine undercover
2 Tension rod
3 Stabilizer bar
4 Lower control arm
5 Engine oil pan
6 Front exhaust pipe
7 Torsion bar
8 Transmission
9 Clutch operating cylinder
10 Engine mount

2 Mazda pick-up Routine maintenance schedule

The following maintenance intervals are based on the assumption that the vehicle owner will be doing the maintenance or service work, as opposed to having a dealer service department do the work. Although the time/mileage intervals are based on factory recommendations, most have been shortened to ensure, for example, that such items as lubricants and fluids are checked/changed at intervals that promote maximum engine/driveline service life. Also, subject to the preference of the individual owner interested in keeping his or her vehicle in peak condition at all times and with the vehicle's ultimate resale in mind, many of the maintenance procedures may be performed more often than recommended in the following schedule. We encourage such owner initiative.

When the vehicle is new it should be serviced initially by a factory authorized dealer service department to protect the factory warranty. In many cases the initial maintenance check is done at no cost to the owner – check with your dealer service department for more infomation.

Every 250 miles or weekly, whichever comes first

Check the engine coolant level (Section 4)
Check the windshield washer fluid level (Section 4)
Check the brake fluid and clutch fluid levels (Section 4)
*Check the automatic transmission fluid level (Section 5)
*Check the power steering fluid level (Section 6)
Check the tires and tire pressures (Section 7)
Check the engine oil level (Section 4)

Every 7500 miles or 12 months, whichever comes first

All items listed above plus:
Check and service the battery (Section 8)
Check the cooling system (Section 9)
Inspect and replace if necessary the windshield wiper blades (Section 10)
Inspect and replace if necessary all underhood hoses (Section 11)
*Change the engine oil and oil filter (Section 12)

Every 15,000 miles or 12 months, whichever comes first

All items listed above plus:
Check the choke operation and clean the linkage (Section 13)
Replace the ignition points (Section 14)
Check and adjust the valve clearances (Section 15)
Lubricate the chassis components (Section 16)
*Inspect the suspension and steering components (Section 17)
*Inspect the exhaust system (Section 18)
Check the clutch pedal height and freeplay (Section 19)
*Check the manual transmission oil level (Section 20)
*Check the transfer case oil level (Section 21)
*Check the differential oil level (Section 22)
Rotate the tires (Section 23)
*Check the brakes (Section 24)
Inspect the fuel system (Section 25)
Check the thermostatically-controlled air cleaner (Section 26)

Check and adjust if necessary, the engine drivebelts (Section 27)
Check the seat belts (Section 28)

Every 30,000 miles or 24 months, whichever comes first

All items listed above plus:
Replace the air and PCV filter (Section 29)
Replace the fuel filter (Section 30)
Check the evaporative emissions system (Section 31)
Check the carburetor mounting torque (Section 32)
Check and adjust if necessary the engine idle speed (Section 33)
Check and adjust if necessary, the engine idle switch (1985 and later carbureted models) (Section 34)
Check and adjust if necessary, the carburetor float level (1600/1800/2000/2200 engine) (Section 35)
Change the transfer case oil (Section 36)
Change the manual transmission oil (Section 37)
Change the differential oil (Section 38)
**Change the automatic transmission fluid and filter (Section 39)
Check and repack the front wheel bearings (2WD models) (Section 40 or 41)
Service the cooling system (drain, flush and refill) (Section 42)
Inspect and replace if necessary the PCV valve (Section 43)
Replace the spark plugs (Section 44)
Inspect the spark plug wires (Section 45)
Inspect the distributor cap and rotor (Section 46)
Check and adjust if necessary the ignition timing (Section 47)

Every 60,000 miles or 24 months, whichever comes first

Replace the oxygen sensor (1985 through 1987 models with 2000/2200 engine) (Section 48)
Replace the EGR valve (1985 and later models with 2000/2200 engine) (Section 49)

Every 80,000 miles or 36 months, whichever comes first

Replace the oxygen sensor (1988 and later models with 2200 engine) (Section 48)

*This item is affected by "severe" operating conditions as described below. If your vehicle is operated under "severe" conditions, perform all maintenance indicated with a * at 3000 mile/3 month intervals.*
Severe conditions are indicated if you mainly operate your vehicle under one or more of the following conditions:
Operating in dusty areas
Towing a trailer
Idling for extended periods and/or low speed operation
Operating when outside temperatures remain below freezing and when most trips are less than 4 miles

** If operated under one or more of the following conditions, change the automatic transmission fluid every 15,000 miles:
In heavy city traffic where the outside temperature regularly reaches 90-degrees F (32-degrees C) or higher
In hilly trailer pulling
Frequent trailer pulling

3   Tune-up general information

The term *tune-up* is used in this manual to represent a combination of individual operations rather than one specific procedure.

If, from the time the vehicle is new, the routine maintenance schedule is followed closely and frequent checks are made of fluid levels and high wear items, as suggested throughout this manual, the engine will be kept in relatively good running condition and the need for additional work will be minimized.

More likely than not, however, there will be times when the engine is running poorly due to lack of regular maintenance. This is even more likely if a used vehicle, which has not received regular and frequent maintenance checks, is purchased. In such cases, an engine tune-up will be needed outside of the regular routine maintenance intervals.

The first step in any tune-up or diagnostic procedure to help correct a poor running engine is a cylinder compression check. A compression check (see Chapter 2 Part B) will help determine the condition of internal engine components and should be used as a guide for tune-up and repair procedures. If, for instance, a compression check indicates serious internal engine wear, a conventional tune-up will not improve the performance of the engine and would be a waste of time and money. Because of its importance, the compression check should be done by someone with the right equipment and the knowledge to use it properly.

The following procedures are those most often needed to bring a generally poor running engine back into a proper state of tune.

Minor tune-up

   Check all engine related fluids
   Clean and check the battery (Section 8)
   Check and adjust the drivebelts (Section 27)
   Replace the spark plugs (Section 44)
   Check the cylinder compression (Chapter 2)
   Inspect the distributor cap and rotor (Section 46)
   Inspect the spark plug and coil wires (Section 45)
   Replace the air and PCV filters (Section 29)
   Check and adjust the idle speed (Section 33)
   Check the carburetor float level (Section 35)
   Check the idle speed switch (1985 through 1988 2000/2200 engine (Section 34)
   Check and adjust the ignition timing (Section 47)
   Replace the fuel filter (Section 30)
   Check the PCV valve (Section 43)
   Adjust the valve clearances (Section 15)
   Check and service the cooling system (Section 42)

Major tune-up

All items listed under Minor tune-up plus . . .
   Check the EGR system (Chapter 6)
   Check the charging system (Chapter 5)
   Check the ignition system (Chapter 5)

   Replace the ignition points (if equipped) (Section 14)
   Check the fuel system (Section 25 and Chapter 4)
   Replace the spark plug wires, distributor cap and
     rotor (Sections 45 and 46)

4   Fluid level checks

Note: *The following are fluid level checks to be done on a 250 mile or weekly basis. Additional fluid level checks can be found in specific maintenance procedures which follow. Regardless of how often the fluid levels are checked, watch for puddles under the vehicle — if leaks are noted, make repairs immediately.*

1   Fluids are an essential part of the lubrication, cooling, brake, clutch and windshield washer systems. Because the fluids gradually become depleted and/or contaminated during normal operation of the vehicle, they must be periodically replenished. See *Recommended lubricants and fluids* at the beginning of this Chapter before adding fluid to any of the following components. **Note:** *The vehicle must be on level ground when fluid levels are checked.*

Engine oil

Refer to illustrations 4.4a, 4.4b and 4.6

2   The engine oil level is checked with a dipstick that extends through a tube and into the oil pan at the bottom of the engine.

3   The oil level should be checked before the vehicle has been driven, or about 15 minutes after the engine has been shut off. If the oil is checked immediately after driving the vehicle, some of the oil will remain in the upper engine components, resulting in an inaccurate reading on the dipstick.

4   Pull the dipstick from the tube **(see illustration)** and wipe all the oil from the end with a clean rag or paper towel. Insert the clean dipstick all the way back into the tube, then pull it out again. Note the oil at the end of the dipstick. Add oil as necessary to keep the level between the L (low) mark and the F (full) mark on the dipstick **(see illustration)**.

5   Don't overfill the engine by adding too much oil since this may result in oil fouled spark plugs, oil leaks or oil seal failures.

6   Oil is added to the engine after removing a threaded cap from the rocker arm cover **(see illustration)**. An oil can spout or funnel may help to reduce spills.

7   Checking the oil level is an important preventive maintenance step. A consistently low oil level indicates oil leakage through damaged seals, defective gaskets or past worn rings or valve guides. If the oil looks milky in color or has water droplets in it, the cylinder head gasket(s) may be blown or the head(s) or block may be cracked. The engine should be checked immediately. The condition of the oil should also be checked. Whenever you check the oil level, slide your thumb and index finger up the dipstick before wiping off the oil. If you see small dirt or metal particles clinging to the dipstick, the oil should be changed (Section 12).

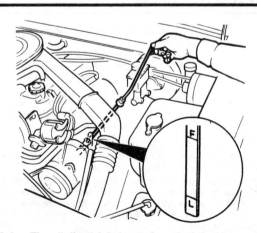

4.4a   The oil dipstick is located on the left side of the engine

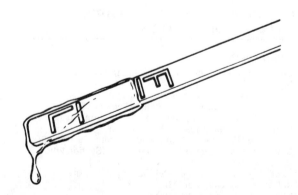

4.4b   The oil level must be kept between the F and L lines on the dipstick

4.6   After unscrewing the filler cap from the rocker arm cover, oil can be added to the engine

9   The coolant level in the reservoir should be checked regularly. **Warning:** *Do not remove the radiator cap to check the coolant level when the engine is warm.* The level in the reservoir varies with the temperature of the engine. When the engine is cold, the coolant level should be at or slightly above the lower mark on the reservoir. Once the engine has warmed up, the level should be at or near the upper mark. If it isn't, allow the engine to cool, then remove the cap from the reservoir and add a 50/50 mixture of ethylene glycol-based anti-freeze and water.

10   Drive the vehicle and recheck the coolant level. If only a small amount of coolant is required to bring the system up to the proper level, water can be used. However, repeated additions of water will dilute the antifreeze and water solution. In order to maintain the proper ratio of antifreeze and water, always top up the coolant level with the correct mixture. An empty plastic milk jug or bleach bottle makes an excellent container for mixing coolant. Do not use rust inhibitors or additives.

11   If the coolant level drops consistently, there may be a leak in the system. Inspect the radiator, hoses, filler cap, drain plugs and water pump (see Section 9). If no leaks are noted, have the radiator cap pressure tested by a service station.

12   If you have to remove the radiator cap, wait until the engine has cooled, then wrap a thick cloth around the cap and turn it to the first stop. If coolant or steam escapes, let the engine cool down longer, then remove the cap.

13   Check the condition of the coolant as well. It should be relatively clear. If it's brown or rust colored, the system should be drained, flushed and refilled. Even if the coolant appears to be normal, the corrosion inhibitors wear out, so it must be replaced at the specified intervals.

Engine coolant

Refer to illustration 4.8

Warning: *Don't allow antifreeze to come in contact with your skin or painted surfaces of the vehicle. Flush contaminated areas immediately with plenty of water. Don't store new coolant or leave old coolant lying around where it's accessible to children or pets — they're attracted by its sweet taste. Ingestion of even a small amount of coolant can be fatal! Wipe up garage floor and drip pan coolant spills immediately. Keep antifreeze containers covered and repair leaks in your cooling system immediately.*

8   All later vehicles covered by this manual are equipped with a pressurized coolant recovery system. A white plastic coolant reservoir located in the engine compartment is connected by a hose to the radiator filler neck **(see illustration)**. If the engine overheats, coolant escapes through a valve in the radiator cap and travels through the hose into the reservoir. As the engine cools, the coolant is automatically drawn back into the cooling system to maintain the correct level.

Windshield washer fluid

Refer to illustration 4.14

14   Fluid for the windshield washer system is stored in a plastic reservoir located on the driver's side of the engine compartment **(see illustration)**. If necessary, refer to the underhood component illustration(s) at the beginning of this Chapter to locate the reservoir.

15   In milder climates, plain water can be used in the reservoir, but it should be kept no more than 2/3 full to allow for expansion if the water freezes. In colder climates, use windshield washer system anti-freeze, available at any auto parts store, to lower the freezing point of the fluid. Mix the antifreeze with water in accordance with the manufacturer's directions on the container. **Caution:** *Don't use cooling system antifreeze — it will damage the vehicle's paint.*

16   To help prevent icing in cold weather, warm the windshield with the defroster before using the washer.

4.8   The coolant level must be kept between the two marks on the side of the reservoir — coolant is added after removing the cap

4.14   The windshield washer level must be near the top of the reservoir, shown here to the left of the coolant reservoir. Fluid is added after snapping the cap up, making sure to close it securely when you're done

Battery electrolyte

17   To check the electrolyte level in the battery, remove all of the cell caps. If the level is low, add *distilled* water until it's above the plates. Original equipment batteries are translucent so the electrolyte level can be checked by looking at the side of the case **(see illustration)**. Most aftermarket replacement batteries have a split-ring indicator in each cell to help you judge when enough water has been added — don't overfill the cells!

Brake and clutch fluid

Refer to illustrations 4.19a and 4.19b

18   The brake master cylinder is mounted on the front of the power booster unit in the engine compartment. The clutch cylinder used on manual transmissions is mounted adjacent to it on the firewall.
19   The fluid inside is readily visible. The level should be between the MIN and MAX marks on the reservoirs **(see illustrations)**. If a low level is indicated, be sure to wipe the top of the reservoir cover with a clean rag to prevent contamination of the brake and/or clutch system before removing the cover.

20   When adding fluid, pour it carefully into the reservoir to avoid spilling it onto surrounding painted surfaces. Be sure the specified fluid is used, since mixing different types of brake fluid can cause damage to the system. See *Recommended lubricants and fluids* at the front of this Chapter or your owner's manual. **Warning:** *Brake fluid can harm your eyes and damage painted surfaces, so be very careful when handling or pouring it. Don't use brake fluid that's been standing open or is more than one year old. Brake fluid absorbs moisture from the air. Excess moisture can cause a dangerous loss of brake efficiency.*
21   At this time the fluid and master cylinder can be inspected for contamination. The system should be drained and refilled if deposits, dirt particles or water droplets are seen in the fluid.
22   After filling the reservoir to the proper level, make sure the cover is on tight to prevent fluid leakage.
23   The brake fluid level in the master cylinder will drop slightly as the pads and the brake shoes at each wheel wear down during normal operation. If the master cylinder requires repeated additions to keep it at the proper level, it's an indication of leakage in the brake system, which should be corrected immediately. Check all brake lines and connections (see Section 24 for more information).
24   If, upon checking the master cylinder fluid level, you discover one or both reservoirs empty or nearly empty, the brake system should be bled (Chapter 9).

4.19a   The brake master cylinder fluid level should be kept between the Min and Max marks on the reservoir

5   Automatic transmission fluid level check

Refer to illustration 5.3

1   The automatic transmission fluid level should be carefully maintained. Low fluid level can lead to slipping or loss of drive, while overfilling can cause foaming and loss of fluid.
2   With the parking brake set, start the engine, then move the shift lever through all the gear ranges, ending in Park. The fluid level must be checked with the vehicle level and the engine running at idle. **Note:** *Incorrect fluid level readings will result if the vehicle has just been driven at high speeds for an extended period, in hot weather in city traffic, or if it has been pulling a trailer. If any of these conditions apply, wait until the fluid has cooled (about 30 minutes).*
3   With the transmission at normal operating temperature, remove the dipstick from the filler tube. The dipstick is located at the rear of the engine compartment on the passenger's side **(see illustration)**.
4   Carefully touch the fluid at the end of the dipstick to determine if it's cool (86 to 122 °F) or hot (123 to 176 °F). Wipe the fluid from the dipstick with a clean rag and push it back into the filler tube until the cap seats.
5   Pull the dipstick out again and note the fluid level.

4.19b   The clutch fluid level should be kept between the Max and Min marks on the reservoir

5.3   The automatic transmission dipstick is located at the right rear of the engine compartment

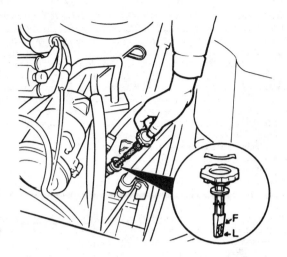

6.5 On 2000/2200 engines, check the power steering
fluid level on the dipstick after twisting off the cap

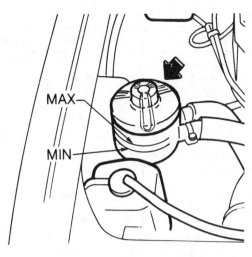

6.7 On 2600 engines, the power steering reservoir is
located on the inner fender panel and the fluid level can be
checked visually without removing the cap

6   The fluid level should be between the F mark and 1/4-inch below
the mark with the transmission fluid at normal operating temperature
(hot) (see illustration 5.3).
7   If additional fluid is required, add it directly into the tube using a
funnel. It takes about one pint to raise the level from the L mark to
the H mark with a hot transmission, so add the fluid a little at a time
and keep checking the level until it's correct.
8   The condition of the fluid should also be checked along with the
level. If the fluid at the end of the dipstick is a dark reddish-brown color,
or if it smells burned, it should be changed. If you are in doubt about
the condition of the fluid, purchase some new fluid and compare the
two for color and smell.

6   Power steering fluid level check

Refer to illustrations 6.5 and 6.7

1   Unlike manual steering, the power steering system relies on fluid
which may, over a period of time, require replenishing.
2   The fluid reservoir for the power steering pump is located on the
pump body at the front of the engine. On vehicles with a 2600 V6
engine, the reservoir is separate from the pump and is mounted
remotely.
3   For the check, the front wheels should be pointed straight ahead
and the engine should be off. The engine and power steering fluid
should be cold.
4   Use a clean rag to wipe off the reservoir cap and the area around
it. This will help prevent any foreign matter from entering the reservoir during the check.

2000/2200 engine

5   Twist off the cap — it has a dipstick attached to it (see illustration).
6   Wipe off the fluid with a clean rag, reinsert the dipstick, then
withdraw it and note the fluid level. The level should be within the range
marked on the dipstick. Never allow the fluid level to drop below the
lower range mark.

2600 engine

7   On these models, the fluid reservoir is mounted on the inner fender
panel. The reservoir is translucent plastic and the level can be checked visually (see illustration).
8   The level must be maintained between the MAX and MIN marks
and fluid can be added after twisting off the cap.
9   If additional fluid is required, pour the specified type directly into
the reservoir, using a funnel to prevent spills.

10 If the reservoir requires frequent fluid additions, all power steering
hoses, hose connections and the power steering pump should be carefully checked for leaks.

7   Tire and tire pressure checks

Refer to illustrations 7.2, 7.3, 7.4a, 7.4b and 7.8

1   Periodic inspection of the tires may spare you the inconvenience
of being stranded with a flat tire. It can also provide you with vital information regarding possible problems in the steering and suspension
systems before major damage occurs.
2   The original tires on this vehicle are equipped with wear indicator
bars that will appear when tread depth reaches a predetermined limit,
usually 1/16-inch, but they don't appear until the tires are worn out.
Tread wear can be monitored with a simple, inexpensive device known
as a tread depth indicator (see illustration).

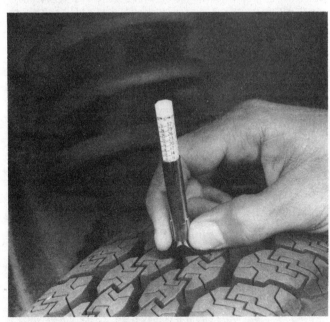

7.2 A tire wear tread depth indicator should be used to
monitor tire wear — they are available at auto parts stores
and service stations and cost very little

Condition	Probable cause	Corrective action	Condition	Probable cause	Corrective action
Shoulder wear	• Underinflation (both sides wear) • Incorrect wheel camber (one side wear) • Hard cornering • Lack of rotation	• Measure and adjust pressure. • Repair or replace axle and suspension parts. • Reduce speed. • Rotate tires.	Feathered edge Toe wear	• Incorrect toe	• Adjust toe-in.
Center wear	• Overinflation • Lack of rotation	• Measure and adjust pressure. • Rotate tires.	Uneven wear	• Incorrect camber or caster • Malfunctioning suspension • Unbalanced wheel • Out-of-round brake drum • Lack of rotation	• Repair or replace axle and suspension parts. • Repair or replace suspension parts. • Balance or replace. • Turn or replace. • Rotate tires.

7.3   This chart will help you determine the condition of your tires, the probable cause(s) of abnormal wear and the corrective action necessary

3   Note any abnormal tread wear **(see illustration)**. Tread pattern irregularities such as cupping, flat spots and more wear on one side than the other are indications of front end alignment and/or balance problems. If any of these conditions are noted, take the vehicle to a tire shop or service station to correct the problem.

4   Look closely for cuts, punctures and embedded nails or tacks. Sometimes a tire will hold air pressure for a short time or leak down very slowly after a nail has embedded itself in the tread. If a slow leak persists, check the valve stem core to make sure it's tight **(see illustra-** tion). Examine the tread for an object that may have embedded itself in the tire or for a ''plug'' that may have begun to leak (radial tire punctures are repaired with a plug that's installed in a puncture). If a puncture is suspected, it can be easily verified by spraying a solution of soapy water onto the puncture area **(see illustration)**. The soapy solution will bubble if there's a leak. Unless the puncture is unusually large, a tire shop or service station can usually repair the tire.

5   Carefully inspect the inner sidewall of each tire for evidence of brake fluid leakage. If you see any, inspect the brakes immediately.

7.4a   If a tire loses air on a steady basis, check the valve core first to make sure it's snug (special inexpensive wrenches are commonly available at auto parts stores)

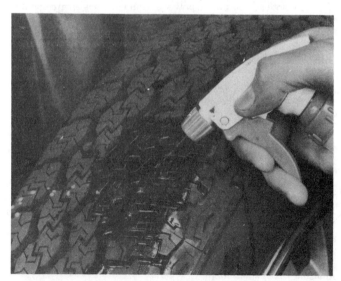

7.4b   if the valve core is tight, raise the corner of the vehicle with the low tire and spray a soapy water solution onto the tread as the tire is turned slowly — slow leaks will cause small bubbles to appear

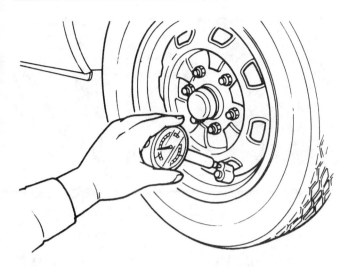

7.8   To extend the life of your tires, check the air pressure at least once a week with an accurate gauge (don't forget the spare!)

6   Correct air pressure adds miles to the lifespan of the tires, improves mileage and enhances overall ride quality. Tire pressure cannot be accurately estimated by looking at a tire, especially if it's a radial. A tire pressure gauge is essential. Keep an accurate gauge in the vehicle. The pressure gauges attached to the nozzles of air hoses at gas stations are often inaccurate.
7   Always check tire pressure when the tires are cold. Cold, in this case, means the vehicle has not been driven over a mile in the three hours preceding a tire pressure check. A pressure rise of four to eight pounds is not uncommon once the tires are warm.
8   Unscrew the valve cap protruding from the wheel or hubcap and push the gauge firmly onto the valve stem **(see illustration)**. Note the reading on the gauge and compare the figure to the recommended tire pressure shown on the placard on the glove compartment door. Be sure to reinstall the valve cap to keep dirt and moisture out of the valve stem mechanism. Check all four tires and, if necessary, add enough air to bring them up to the recommended pressure.
9   Don't forget to keep the spare tire inflated to the specified pressure (refer to your owner's manual or the tire sidewall).

8   Battery check and maintenance

Refer to illustrations 8.1, 8.7a, 8.7b, 8.7c and 8.7d
Warning: *Several precautions must be followed when checking and servicing the battery. Hydrogen gas, which is highly flammable, is always present in the battery cells, so keep lighted tobacco and all other open flames and sparks away from the battery. The electrolyte in the cells is actually dilute sulfuric acid, which will cause injury if splashed on your skin or in your eyes. It'll also ruin clothes and painted surfaces. When removing the battery cables, always detach the negative cable first and hook it up last!*

Check

1   Battery maintenance is an important procedure which will help ensure that you aren't stranded because of a dead battery. Several tools are required for this procedure **(see illustration)**.
2   On vehicles equipped with a conventional battery, the electrolyte level should be checked every week (see Section 4).
3   If the vehicle is equipped with a battery electrolyte level warning light, the electrolyte should still be visually checked on a regular basis to make sure all cells are full.
4   On some models a sealed maintenance-free battery is used. Unlike a conventional battery, it has no removable cell caps and is completely sealed except for a small vent hole. Because of its sealed design, water cannot be added to the cells.

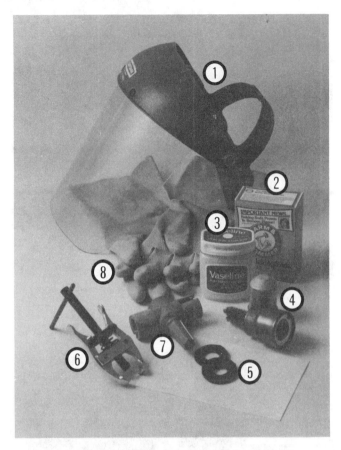

8.1   Tools and materials required for battery maintenance

1   **Face shield/safety goggles** — *When removing corrosion with a brush, the acidic particles can easily fly up into your eyes*
2   **Baking soda** — *A solution of baking soda and water can be used to neutralize corrosion*
3   **Petroleum jelly** — *A layer of this on the battery posts will help prevent corrosion*
4   **Battery post/cable cleaner** — *This wire brush cleaning tool will remove all traces of corrosion from the battery posts and cable clamps*
5   **Treated felt washers** — *Placing one of these on each post, directly under the cable clamps, will help prevent corrosion*
6   **Puller** — *Sometimes the cable clamps are very difficult to pull off the posts, even after the nut/bolt has been completely loosened. This tool pulls the clamp straight up and off the post without damage*
7   **Battery post/cable cleaner** — *Here is another cleaning tool which is a slightly different version of number 4 above, but it does the same thing*
8   **Rubber gloves** — *Another safety item to consider when servicing the battery; remember that's acid inside the battery!*

Maintenance

5   Periodically clean the top and sides of the battery. Remove all dirt and moisture. This will help prevent corrosion and ensure that the battery doesn't become partially discharged by leakage through moisture and dirt. Check the case for cracks and distortion.
6   Check the tightness of the battery cable bolts to ensure good electrical connections. Inspect the entire length of each cable, looking for cracked or abraded insulation and frayed conductors.
7   If corrosion, which usually appears as white, fluffy deposits, is evident, remove tha cables from the terminals, clean them with a battery brush and reinstall them **(see illustrations)**. Corrosion can be kept

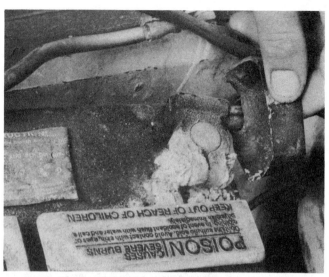

8.7a   Battery terminal corrosion usually appears as light
fluffy powder

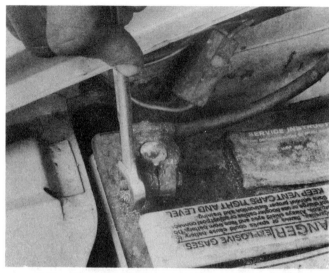

8.7b   Removing a cable from the battery post with a
wrench — sometimes a special battery pliers is required for
this procedure if corrosion has caused deterioration of the
nut hex (always remove the ground cable
first and hook it up last!)

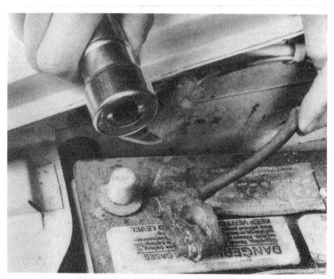

8.7c   Regardless of the type of tool used to clean the
battery posts, a clean, shiny surface should be the result

8.7d   When cleaning the cable clamps, all corrosion must
be removed (the inside of the clamp is tapered to match
the taper on the post, so don't remove too much material)

to a minimum by applying a layer of petroleum jelly to the terminals after the cables are in place.

8   Make sure the battery carrier is in good condition and the hold-down clamp is tight. If the battery is removed, make sure that nothing is in the bottom of the carrier when it's reinstalled and don't overtighten the clamp nuts.

9   A temperature-compensated hydrometer is built into the top of maintenance-free batteries. It gives an indication of the electrolyte level and the battery's state of charge. If a blue dot is seen in the indicator window on top of the battery, the battery is properly charged. If the indicator is transparent, the battery should be recharged from an external source and the charging system should be checked (Chapter 5).

10   The freezing point of electrolyte depends on its specific gravity. Since freezing can ruin a battery, it should be kept in a fully charged state to protect against freezing.

11   If you frequently have to add water to a conventional battery and the case has been inspected for cracks that could cause leakage, but none are found, the battery is being overcharged; the charging system should be checked as described in Chapter 5.

12   If any doubt exists about the battery state of charge, a hydrometer

should be used to test it by withdrawing a little electrolyte from each cell, one at a time.

13   The specific gravity of the electrolyte at 80 °F will be approximately 1.270 for a fully charged battery. For every 10 °F that the electrolyte temperature is above 80 °F, add 0.04 to the specific gravity. Subtract 0.04 if the temperature is below 80 °F.

14   A specific gravity reading of 1.240 with an electrolyte temperature of 80 °F indicates a half-charged battery.

15   Some of the common causes of battery failure are:

a) Accessories, especially headlights, left on overnight or for several hours.

b) Slow average driving speeds for short intervals.

c) The electrical load of the vehicle being more than the alternator output. This is very common when several high draw accessories are being used simultaneously (such as radio/stereo, air conditioning, window defoggers, lights, etc.).

d) Charging system problems such as short circuits, slipping drivebelt, defective alternator or faulty voltage regulator.

e) Battery neglect, such as loose or corroded terminals or loose battery hold-down clamp.

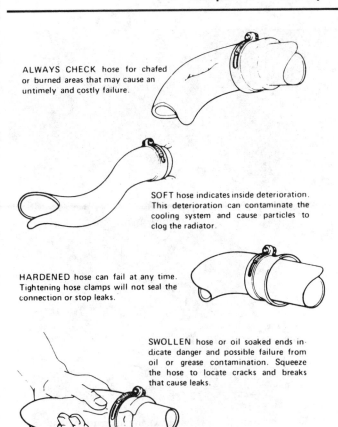

ALWAYS CHECK hose for chafed or burned areas that may cause an untimely and costly failure.

SOFT hose indicates inside deterioration. This deterioration can contaminate the cooling system and cause particles to clog the radiator.

HARDENED hose can fail at any time. Tightening hose clamps will not seal the connection or stop leaks.

SWOLLEN hose or oil soaked ends indicate danger and possible failure from oil or grease contamination. Squeeze the hose to locate cracks and breaks that cause leaks.

9.4 Hoses, like drivebelts, have a habit of failing at the worst possible time — to prevent the inconvenience of a blown radiator or heater hose, inspect them carefully as shown here

Battery charging

16 In winter when heavy demand is placed upon the battery, it's a good idea to occasionally have it charged from an external source.

17 When charging the battery, the negative cable should be disconnected. The charger leads should be connected to the battery *before* the charger is plugged in or turned on. If the leads are connected to the battery terminals after the charger is on, a spark could occur and the hydrogen gas given off by the battery could explode!

18 The battery should be charged at a low rate of about 4 to 6 amps, and should be left on for at least three or four hours. A trickle charger charging at the rate of 1.5 amps can be safely used overnight.

19 Special rapid boost charges which are claimed to restore the power of the battery in a short time can cause serious damage to the battery plates and should only be used in an emergency situation.

20 The battery should be left on the charger only until the specific gravity is brought up to a normal level. On maintenance-free batteries, continue to charge only until the blue dot is seen in the indicator window. Don't overcharge the battery! **Note:** *Some battery chargers will automatically shut off after the battery is fully charged, making it unnecessary to keep a close watch on the state of charge.*

21 When disconnecting the charger, unplug it before disconnecting the charger leads from the battery.

9   Cooling system check

Refer to illustration 9.4

1 Many major engine failures can be attributed to a faulty cooling system. If the vehicle is equipped with an automatic transmission, the cooling system also cools the transmission fluid, prolonging transmission life.

2 The cooling system should be checked with the engine cold. Do

this before the vehicle is driven for the day or after it has been shut off for at least three hours.

3 Remove the radiator cap by turning it counterclockwise until it reaches a stop. If you hear a hissing sound (indicating there's still pressure in the system), wait until it stops. Now press down on the cap with the palm of your hand and continue turning until it can be removed. Thoroughly clean the cap, inside and out, with clean water. Also clean the filler neck on the radiator. All traces of corrosion should be removed. The coolant inside the radiator should be relatively transparent. If it's rust colored, the system should be drained and refilled (Section 42). If the coolant level is not up to the top, add additional antifreeze/coolant mixture (see Section 4).

4 Carefully check the large upper and lower radiator hoses along with the smaller diameter heater hoses which run from the engine to the firewall. Inspect each hose along its entire length, replacing any hose that's cracked, swollen or deteriorated. Cracks may become more apparent if the hose is squeezed **(see illustration)**. Regardless of condition, it's a good idea to replace hoses with new ones every two years.

5 Make sure that all hose connections are tight. A leak in the cooling system will usually show up as white or rust colored deposits on the areas adjoining the leak. If wire-type clamps are used at the ends of the hoses, it may be a good idea to replace them with more secure screw-type clamps.

6 Use compressed air or a soft brush to remove bugs, leaves, etc. from the front of the radiator or air conditioning condenser. Be careful not to damage the delicate cooling fins or cut yourself on them.

7 Every other inspection, or at the first indication of cooling system problems, have the cap and system pressure tested. If you don't have a pressure tester, most gas stations and repair shops will do this for a minimal charge.

10   Wiper blade inspection and replacement

1 The windshield wiper and blade assembly should be inspected periodically for damage, loose components and cracked or worn blade elements.

2 Road film can build up on the wiper blades and affect their efficiency, so they should be washed regularly with a mild detergent solution.

3 The action of the wiping mechanism can loosen the bolts, nuts and fasteners, so they should be checked and tightened, as necessary, at the same time the wiper blades are checked.

4 If the wiper blade elements (sometimes called inserts) are cracked, worn or warped, they should be replaced with new ones.

5 Pull the wiper blade/arm assembly away from the glass.

6 Squeeze the latch lock release at the end of the blade and then pull the blade element out of the lever jaws.

7 Compare the new element with the old for length, design, etc.

8 Slide the new element through the lever jaws into place. It will automatically lock at the correct location.

9 Reinstall the blade assembly on the arm, wet the windshield and check for proper operation.

11   Underhood hose check and replacement

General

1 **Caution:** *Replacement of air conditioning hoses must be left to a dealer service department or air conditioning shop that has the equipment to depressurize the system safely. Never remove air conditioning components or hoses until the system has been depressurized.*

2 High temperatures in the engine compartment can cause the deterioration of the rubber and plastic hoses used for engine, accessory and emission systems operation. Periodic inspection should be made for cracks, loose clamps, material hardening and leaks. Information specific to the cooling system hoses can be found in Section 9.

3 Some, but not all, hoses are secured to the fittings with clamps. Where clamps are used, check to be sure they haven't lost their tension, allowing the hose to leak. If clamps aren't used, make sure the hose has not expanded and/or hardened where it slips over the fitting, allowing it to leak.

Vacuum hoses

4   It's quite common for vacuum hoses, especially those in the emissions system, to be color coded or identified by colored stripes molded into them. Various systems require hoses with different wall thicknesses, collapse resistance and temperature resistance. When replacing hoses, be sure the new ones are made of the same material.

5   Often the only effective way to check a hose is to remove it completely from the vehicle. If more than one hose is removed, be sure to label the hoses and fittings to ensure correct installation.

6   When checking vacuum hoses, be sure to include any plastic T-fittings in the check. Inspect the fittings for cracks and the hose where it fits over the fitting for distortion, which could cause leakage.

7   A small piece of vacuum hose (1/4-inch inside diameter) can be used as a stethoscope to detect vacuum leaks. Hold one end of the hose to your ear and probe around vacuum hoses and fittings, listening for the "hissing" sound characteristic of a vacuum leak. **Warning:** *When probing with the vacuum hose stethoscope, be very careful not to come into contact with moving engine components such as the drivebelts, cooling fan, etc.*

Fuel hose

Warning: *There are certain precautions which must be taken when inspecting or servicing fuel system components. Work in a well ventilated area and don't allow open flames (cigarettes, appliance pilot lights, etc.) or bare light bulbs near the work area. Mop up any spills immediately and don't store fuel soaked rags where they could ignite.*

8   Check all rubber fuel lines for deterioration and chafing. Check carefully for cracks in areas where the hose bends and where it's attached to fittings.

9   High quality fuel line, usually identified by the word *Fluroelastomer* printed on the hose, should be used for fuel line replacement. **Warning:** *Never, under any circumstances, use unreinforced vacuum line, clear plastic tubing or water hose for fuel lines!*

10   Spring-type clamps are commonly used on fuel lines. They often lose their tension over a period of time, and can be "sprung" during removal. Replace all spring-type clamps with screw clamps whenever a hose is replaced.

Metal lines

11   Sections of metal line are often used for fuel line between the fuel pump and carburetor or fuel injection unit. Check carefully to be sure the line has not been bent or crimped and look for cracks.

12   If a section of metal fuel line must be replaced, only seamless steel tubing should be used, since copper and aluminum tubing don't have the strength necessary to withstand normal engine vibration.

13   Check the metal brake lines where they enter the master cylinder and brake proportioning unit (if used) for cracks in the lines and loose fittings. Any sign of brake fluid leakage means an immediate thorough inspection of the brake system should be done.

---

12   Engine oil and filter change

Refer to illustrations 12.3, 12.9a, 12.9b and 12.18

1   Frequent oil changes are the most important preventive maintenance procedures that can be done by the home mechanic. As engine oil ages, it becomes diluted and contaminated, which leads to premature engine wear.

2   Although some sources recommend oil filter changes every other oil change, the minimal cost of an oil filter and the fact that it's easy to install dictate that a new filter be used every time the oil is changed.

3   Gather all necessary tools and materials before beginning this procedure **(see illustration)**.

4   You should have plenty of clean rags and newspapers handy to mop up any spills. Access to the underside of the vehicle is greatly improved if the vehicle can be lifted on a hoist, driven onto ramps or supported by jackstands. **Warning:** *Do not work under a vehicle which is supported only by a bumper, hydraulic or scissors-type jack!*

5   If this is your first oil change, get under the vehicle and familiarize yourself with the locations of the oil drain plug and the oil filter. The engine and exhaust components will be warm during the actual work, so note how they're situated to avoid touching them when working under the vehicle.

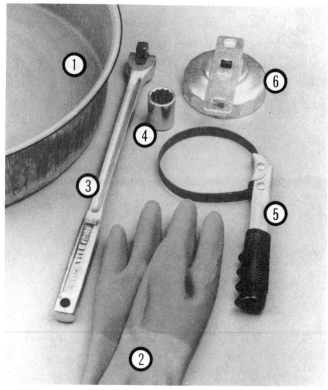

12.3   These tools are required when changing the engine oil and filter

1   **Drain pan** — *It should be fairly shallow in depth, but wide in order to prevent spills*
2   **Rubber gloves** — *When removing the drain plug and filter it is inevitable that you will get oil on your hands (the gloves will prevent burns)*
3   **Breaker bar** — *Sometimes the oil drain plug is pretty tight and a long breaker bar is needed to loosen it*
4   **Socket** — *To be used with the breaker bar or a ratchet (must be the correct size to fit the drain plug)*
5   **Filter wrench** — *This is a metal band-type wrench, which requires clearance around the filter to be effective*
6   **Filter wrench** — *This type fits on the bottom of the filter and can be turned with a ratchet or breaker bar (different size wrenches are available for different types of filters)*

6   Warm the engine to normal operating temperature. If the new oil or any tools are needed, use the warm-up time to obtain everything necessary for the job. The correct oil for your application can be found in *Recommended lubricants and fluids* at the beginning of this Chapter.

7   With the engine oil warm (warm engine oil will drain better and more built-up sludge will be removed with it), raise and support the vehicle. Make sure it's safely supported!

8   Move all necessary tools, rags and newspapers under the vehicle. Set the drain pan under the drain plug. Keep in mind that the oil will initially flow from the pan with some force; position the pan accordingly.

9   Being careful not to touch any of the hot exhaust components, use a wrench to remove the drain plug near the bottom of the oil pan **(see illustrations)**. Depending on how hot the oil is, you may want to wear gloves while unscrewing the plug the final few turns.

10   Allow the old oil to drain into the pan. It may be necessary to move the pan as the oil flow slows to a trickle.

11   After all the oil has drained, wipe off the drain plug with a clean rag. Small metal particles may cling to the plug and would immediately contaminate the new oil.

12   Clean the area around the drain plug opening and reinstall the plug. Tighten the plug securely with the wrench. If a torque wrench is available, use it to tighten the plug.

13   Move the drain pan into position under the oil filter.

14   Use the filter wrench to loosen the oil filter. Chain or metal band

12.9a   Removing the oil pan drain plug

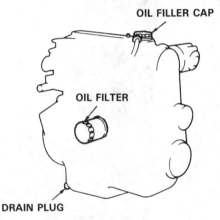

12.9b   Engine oil drain plug location

filter wrenches may distort the filter canister, but it doesn't matter since the filter will be discarded anyway.
15 Completely unscrew the old filter. Be careful; it's full of oil. Empty the oil inside the filter into the drain pan.
16 Compare the old filter with the new one to make sure they're the same type.
17 Use a clean rag to remove all oil, dirt and sludge from the area where the oil filter mounts to the engine. Check the old filter to make sure the rubber gasket isn't stuck to the engine. If the gasket is stuck to the engine, remove it.
18 Apply a light coat of clean oil to the rubber gasket on the new oil filter (see illustration).
19 Attach the new filter to the engine, following the tightening directions printed on the filter canister or packing box. Most filter manufacturers recommend against using a filter wrench due to the possibility of overtightening and damage to the seal.
20 Remove all tools, rags, etc. from under the vehicle, being careful not to spill the oil in the drain pan, then lower the vehicle.
21 Move to the engine compartment and locate the oil filler cap.
22 If an oil can spout is used, push the spout into the top of the oil can and pour the fresh oil through the filler opening. A funnel may also be used.
23 Pour three or four quarts of fresh oil into the engine. Wait a few minutes to allow the oil to drain into the pan, then check the level on the oil dipstick (see Section 4 if necessary). If the oil level is above the L mark, start the engine and allow the new oil to circulate.
24 Run the engine for only about a minute and then shut it off. Immediately look under the vehicle and check for leaks at the oil pan drain plug and around the oil filter. If either one is leaking, tighten it a little more.

12.18   Lubricate the oil filter gasket with clean engine oil before installing the filter on the engine

25 With the new oil circulated and the filter now completely full, recheck the level on the dipstick and add more oil as necessary.
26 During the first few trips after an oil change, make it a point to check frequently for leaks and correct oil level.
27 The old oil drained from the engine cannot be reused in its present state and should be disposed of. Oil reclamation centers, auto repair shops and gas stations will normally accept the oil, which can be refined and used again. After the oil has cooled it can be poured into a container (capped plastic jugs or bottles, milk cartons, etc.) for transport to a disposal site.

13   Carburetor choke check

Refer to illustrations 13.3 and 13.9

1   The choke operates only when the engine is cold, so this check should be performed before the engine has been started for the day.
2   Open the hood and remove the top plate of the air cleaner assembly. If any vacuum hoses must be disconnected, tag them to ensure reinstallation in their original positions.
3   Look at the center of the air cleaner housing. You'll notice a flat plate at the carburetor opening (see illustration).

13.3   The carburetor choke plate

4　Have an assistant press the throttle pedal to the floor. The plate should close completely. Start the engine while you watch the plate at the carburetor. Don't position your face near the carburetor, as the engine could backfire, causing serious burns! When the engine starts, the choke plate should open slightly.

5　Allow the engine to continue running at an idle speed. As the engine warms up to operating temperature, the plate should slowly open, allowing more air to enter through the top of the carburetor.

6　After a few minutes, the choke plate should be completely open to the vertical position. Blip the throttle to make sure the fast idle cam disengages.

7　You'll notice that engine speed corresponds to the plate opening. With the plate closed, the engine should run at a fast idle speed. As the plate opens and the throttle is moved to disengage the fast idle cam, the engine speed will decrease.

8　With the engine off and the throttle held half-way open, open and close the choke several times. Check the linkage to see if it's hooked up correctly and make sure it doesn't bind.

9　If the choke or linkage binds, sticks or works sluggishly, clean it with choke cleaner (an aerosol spray available at auto parts stores) **(see illustration)**. If the condition persists after cleaning, replace the troublesome parts.

10　Visually inspect all vacuum hoses to be sure they're securely connected and look for cracks and deterioration. Replace as necessary.

11　If the choke fails to operate normally, but no mechanical causes can be found, check the choke electrical circuits.

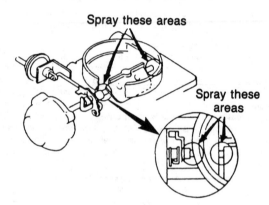

13.9　Use aerosol carburetor spray to clean the choke linkage contact areas

14　Ignition point replacement

Refer to illustration 14.1

1　The ignition points must be replaced at regular intervals on vehicles not equipped with electronic ignition. Occasionally the rubbing block will wear enough to require adjustment of the points. It's also possible to clean and dress them with a fine file, but replacement is recommended since they are relatively inaccessible and very inexpensive. Several special tools are required for this procedure **(see illustration)**.

2　After removing the distributor cap and rotor (Section 46), the ignition points are plainly visible. They can be examined by gently prying them open to reveal the condition of the contact surfaces. If they're rough, pitted, covered with oil or burned, they should be replaced, along with the condenser. **Caution:** *This procedure requires the removal of small screws which can easily fall down into the distributor. To retrieve them, the distributor would have to be removed and disassembled. Use a magnetic or spring-loaded screwdriver and be extra careful.*

3　Note how they are routed, then disconnect the primary circuit and condenser wires from the ignition point assembly quick disconnect terminal.

4　Remove the point assembly mounting screw and detach the points from the breaker plate.

5　Remove the screw and detach the condenser from the distributor body.

6　Before installing the new points and condenser, clean the breaker plate and the cam on the distributor shaft to remove all dirt, dust and oil.

7　Apply a small amount of distributor cam lube (usually supplied with

the new points, but also available separately) to the cam lobes. If the cam lubricator is in good shape, several drops of oil can be applied to it instead of using distributor cam lube.

8　Position the new condenser and tighten the mounting screw securely.

9　Install the new points, but don't tighten the mounting screw completely. Make sure the peg on the point assembly fits into the hole in the breaker plate before installing the screw.

10　Reconnect the primary circuit and condenser wires.

11　*If a dwell meter is available*, hook it up by following the manufacturer's instructions.

12　Make sure the point assembly mounting screw is snug, but not tight, then insert a screwdriver into the adjustment slot.

13　Have an assistant crank the engine over with the starter while you note the dwell reading on the meter. If the dwell is incorrect, turn the screwdriver as required to bring it into the specified range, then tighten the point assembly mounting screw and recheck the dwell. Dwell angle specifications can be found at the beginning of this Chapter and on the tune-up decal in the engine compartment. If there's a discrepancy between the two, assume the tune-up decal is correct. **Note:** *When*

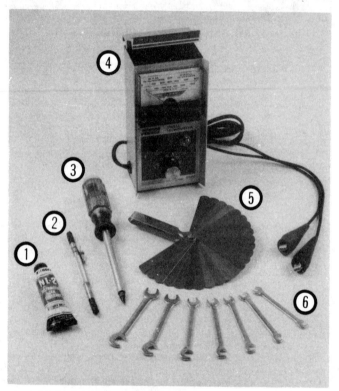

14.1　Tools needed for point replacement and dwell angle adjustment

1　**Distributor cam lube** — *Sometimes this special lubricant comes with the new points; however, its a good idea to buy a tube and have it on hand*

2　**Screw starter** — *This tool has special claws which hold the screw securely as it is started, which helps prevent accidental dropping of the screw*

3　**Magnetic screwdriver** — *Serves the same purpose as 2 above. If you do not have one of these special screwdrivers, you risk dropping the point mounting screws down into the distributor body*

4　**Dwell meter** — *A dwell meter is the only accurate way to determine the point setting (gap). Connect the meter according to the instructions supplied with it*

5　**Blade-type feeler gauges** — *These are required to set the initial point gap (space between the points when they are open)*

6　**Ignition wrenches** — *These special wrenches are made to work within the tight confines of the distributor. Specifically, they are needed to loosen the nut/bolt which secures the leads to the points*

adjusting the dwell, aim for the lower end of the dwell specification range. Then, as the points wear, the dwell will remain within the specified range over a longer period of time.

14   If a dwell meter isn't available, the dwell can be set close enough to allow the engine to run by adjusting the point gap. Make sure that the point rubbing block is resting on one of the high points of the cam. If it isn't, turn the ignition switch to Start in short bursts to reposition the cam. You can also turn the crankshaft with a breaker bar and socket attached to the large bolt that holds the vibration damper in place.

15   With the rubbing block on a cam high point (points open), insert the specified feeler gauge between the contact surfaces and turn the screwdriver in the adjustment slot (see Step 13) to open or close the points slightly as needed to change the gap. The gap is correct when a slight amount of drag is felt as the feeler gauge is withdrawn. Tighten the point mounting screw, then recheck the gap.

16   Check the distributor cap and rotor as described in Section 46, then install them, along with the shield (if equipped).

17   Start the engine and allow it to reach normal operating temperature, then check the dwell again. **Note:** *If you don't have a dwell meter, have the dwell checked/adjusted with a meter as soon as possible to ensure optimum performance.*

18   If the dwell isn't as specified, remove the distributor cap, readjust the dwell, reinstall the cap and check it again.

15   Valve clearance check and adjustment

1   Although the valves can be adjusted with the engine cold, it's better to adjust them with the engine hot. If they're adjusted cold they should be rechecked once the engine has warmed up and readjusted if necessary to conform to the hot engine specifications.

1600/1800/2000/2200 engine (1972 thru 1988 only)
Note: *The valves on 1988 and later 2200 engines are not adjustable.*
Refer to illustrations 15.3, 15.4 and 15.7
2   Run the engine until normal operating temperature is reached.

Remove the rocker arm cover from the engine as described in Chapter 2.
3   Position the number one piston at top dead center (TDC) on the compression stroke (see Chapter 2). The valve clearances for valves 1 and 2 intake and 1 and 3 exhaust can now be checked **(see illustration)**.
4   Insert the specified feeler gauge between the valve stem and the adjusting screw. If the feeler gauge fits between the stem and screw with a slight amount of drag, the clearance is correct **(see illustration)**.
5   If adjustment is required, loosen the adjusting screw locknut and carefully loosen or tighten the adjusting screw until you feel a slight drag on the feeler gauge as it's withdrawn from between the valve stem and screw.
6   Hold the adjusting screw and tighten the locknut securely. Recheck the clearance to make sure it didn't change.
7   Turn the crankshaft one complete revolution (360-degrees) clockwise so the number four piston is at TDC on the compression stroke. Verify this by checking where the distributor rotor is pointing. Adjust the number 3 and 4 intake and 2 and 4 exhaust valves **(see illustration)**.
8   Install the rocker arm cover.

1988 and earlier (carbureted) 2600 engine (jet valve only)
Refer to illustration 15.13
Note: *1989 and later (2600i) engines do not require periodic valve adjustment).*

9   Only the small jet valves require adjustment on this engine because the intake and exhaust valves are actuated by self adjusting hydraulic lifters.
10   With the engine at normal operating temperature and the rocker arm cover removed, position the number 1 cylinder at top dead center (TDC) on the compression stroke.
11   On the number 1 cylinder, loosen the jet valve locknut and back off the adjusting screw.
12   Turn the jet valve adjusting screw counterclockwise and insert the appropriate size feeler gauge between the jet valve stem and the adjusting screw.
13   Carefully tighten the adjusting screw until you feel a slight drag on the feeler gauge as you withdraw it from between the stem and the adjusting screw **(see illustration)**. Since the jet valve spring is

1

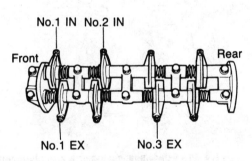

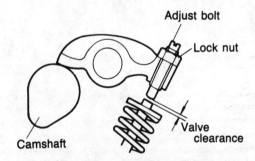

15.3   With the number 1 piston at Top Dead Center (TDC), these valves can be adjusted (1986 and later models shown)

15.4   Insert a feeler gauge between the valve stem and the rocker arm and adjust the valve clearance by turning the adjusting bolt with a screwdriver after loosening the locknut

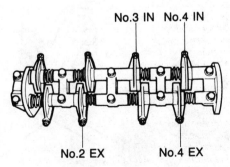

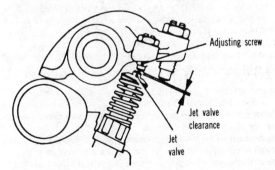

15.7   When the number 4 piston is at TDC, adjust these valves (1986 and later models shown)

15.13   Jet valve adjustment details (2600 engine)

relatively weak, use special care not to force the valve open.

14 Hold the adjusting screw with a screwdriver and tighten the locknut. Recheck the clearance to make sure it hasn't changed.

15 Repeat the procedure for the remaining jet valves, following the firing order of 1-3-4-2.

16 Chassis lubrication

Refer to illustrations 16.1, 16.3a and 16.3b

1   A grease gun and cartridge filled with the recommended grease are the only items required for chassis lubrication other than some clean rags and equipment needed to raise and support the vehicle safely **(see illustration)**.

2   There are several points on the vehicle's suspension, steering and drivetrain components that must be periodically lubricated with lithium or moly based multi-purpose grease. Included are the upper suspension idler arm, the arm shafts on the steering linkage and, on some 4WD models, the front and rear driveshafts.

3   The grease points for each upper suspension arm shaft **(see illustration)** are accessible by removing the front wheel and tire. The steering linkage idler arm is designed to be lubricated **(see illustration)** and the driveshaft sleeve yoke(s) and some universal joints require lubrica-

tion as well.

4   For easier access under the vehicle, raise it with a jack and place jackstands under the frame. Make sure the vehicle is safely supported on the stands!

5   If grease fittings aren't already installed, the plugs will have to be removed and fittings screwed into place.

6   Force a little of the grease out of the gun nozzle to remove any dirt, then wipe it clean with a rag.

7   Wipe the grease fitting and push the nozzle firmly over it. Squeeze the trigger on the grease gun to force grease into the component. Both the balljoints and swivel joints should be lubricated until the rubber reservoir is firm to the touch. Don't pump too much grease into the fittings or it could rupture the reservoir. If the grease seeps out around the grease gun nozzle, the fitting is clogged or the nozzle isn't seated all the way. Resecure the gun nozzle to the fitting and try again. If necessary, replace the fitting.

8   Wipe excess grease from the components and the grease fittings.

9   While you're under the vehicle, clean and lubricate the parking brake cable along with the cable guides and levers. This can be done by smearing some of the chassis grease onto the cable and its related parts with your fingers.

10 Lower the vehicle to the ground for the remaining body lubrication process.

11 Open the hood and rear gate and smear a little chassis grease on the latch mechanisms. Have an assistant pull the release knob from inside the vehicle as you lubricate the cable at the latch.

12 Lubricate all the hinges (door, hood, hatch) with a few drops of light engine oil to keep them in proper working order.

13 The key lock cylinders can be lubricated with spray-on graphite, which is available at auto parts stores.

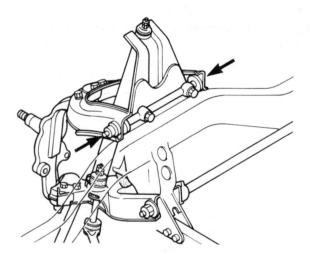

16.3a   Upper suspension arm shaft lubrication points (arrows)

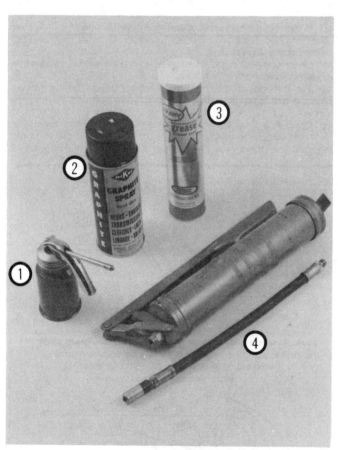

16.1   Materials required for chassis and body lubrication

1 **Engine oil** — *Light engine oil in a can like this can be used for door and hood hinges*
2 **Graphite spray** — *Used to lubricate lock cylinders*
3 **Grease** — *Grease, in a variety of types and weights, is available for use in a grease gun. Check the Specifications for your requirements*
4 **Grease gun** — *A common grease gun, shown here with a detachable hose and nozzle, is needed for chassis lubrication. After use, clean it thoroughly!*

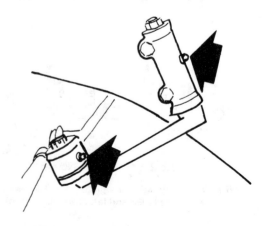

16.3b   Idler arm lubrication fittings (arrows)

17   Suspension and steering check

1   Indications of a fault in these systems are excessive play in the steering wheel before the front wheels react, excessive sway around corners, body movement over rough roads or binding at some point as the steering wheel is turned.

2   Raise the front of the vehicle periodically and visually check the suspension and steering components for wear. Because of the work to be done, make sure the vehicle cannot fall from the stands.

3   Check the wheel bearings. Do this by spinning the front wheels. Listen for any abnormal noises and watch to make sure the wheel spins true (doesn't wobble). Grab the top and bottom of the tire and pull in-and-out on it. Notice any movement which would indicate a loose wheel bearing assembly. If the bearings are suspect, refer to Sections 40 and 41 and Chapter 10 for more information.

4   From under the vehicle check for loose bolts, broken or disconnected parts and deteriorated rubber bushings on all suspension and steering components. Look for grease or fluid leaking from the steering assembly. Check the power steering hoses and connections for leaks.

5   On 4WD models, check the fornt wheel driveaxle CV joint boots for damage, leaks and tight clamps.

6   Have an assistant turn the steering wheel from side-to-side and check the steering components for free movement, chafing and binding. If the steering doesn't react with the movement of the steering wheel, try to determine where the slack is located.

18   Exhaust system check

1   With the engine cold (at least three hours after the vehicle has been driven), check the complete exhaust system from the manifold to the end of the tailpipe. Be careful around the catalytic converter, which may be hot even after three hours. The inspection should be done with the vehicle on a hoist to permit unrestricted access. If a hoist isn't available, raise the vehicle and support it securely on jackstands.

2   Check the exhaust pipes and connections for signs of leakage and/or corrosion indicating a potential failure. Make sure that all brackets and hangers are in good condition and tight.

3   Inspect the underside of the body for holes, corrosion, open seams, etc. which may allow exhaust gases to enter the passenger compartment. Seal all body openings with silicone sealant or body putty.

4   Rattles and other noises can often be traced to the exhaust system, especially the hangers, mounts and heat shields. Try to move the pipes, mufflers and catalytic converter. If the components can come in contact with the body or suspension parts, secure the exhaust system with new brackets and hangers.

19   Clutch pedal height and free play check and adjustment

Refer to illustration 19.2

1   On vehicles equipped with a manual transmission, the clutch pedal height and free play must be correctly adjusted.

2   The height of the clutch pedal is the distance the pedal pad sits off the dash bracket (see illustration). The distance should be as specified. If the pedal height is not within the specified range, loosen the locknut (A) on the pedal stopper located to the rear of the clutch pedal and turn the stopper in or out until the pedal height is correct. Retighten the locknut.

3   The free play is the pedal slack, or the distance the pedal can be depressed before it begins to have any effect on the clutch (pedal play in illustration 19.2). The distance should be as specified. If it isn't, loosen the locknut (C) on the clutch master cylinder pushrod, turn the pushrod (D) until the free play is correct, then retighten the locknut.

20   Manual transmission oil level check

Refer to illustration 20.1

1   Manual transmissions don't have a dipstick. The oil level is checked by removing a plug from the side of the transmission case (see illustration). Locate the plug and use a rag to clean the plug and the area around it. If the vehicle is raised to gain access to the plug, be sure to support it safely on jackstands — DO NOT crawl under the vehicle when it's supported only by a jack!

2   With the engine and transmission cold, remove the plug. If lubricant immediately starts leaking out, thread the plug back into the transmission — the level is correct. If it doesn't, completely remove the plug and reach inside the hole with your little finger. The level should be

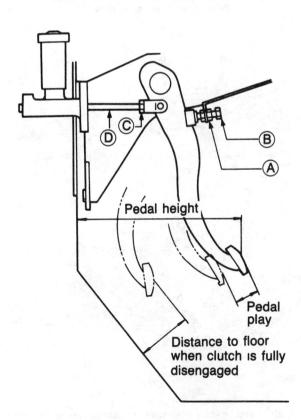

19.2   Clutch pedal adjusting details

20.1   The manual transmission fill plug is accessible from under the vehicle

even with the bottom of the plug hole.

3   If the transmission needs more lubricant, use a syringe or small pump to add it through the plug hole.

4   Thread the plug back into the transmission and tighten it securely. Drive the vehicle, then check for leaks around the plug.

21   Transfer case oil level check

Refer to illustration 21.1

1   The transfer case oil level is checked by removing a plug from the rear of the case **(see illustration)**. Remove the rock guard (if equipped), then locate the plug and use a rag to clean the plug and the area around it. If the vehicle is raised to gain access to the plug, be sure to support it safely on jackstands — DO NOT crawl under the vehicle when it's supported only by a jack!

2   With the engine and transfer case cold, remove the plug. If lubricant immediately starts leaking out, thread the plug back into the case — the level is correct. If it doesn't, completely remove the plug and reach inside the hole with your little finger. The level should be even with the bottom of the plug hole.

3   If more oil is needed, use a syringe or small pump to add it through the opening.

4   Thread the plug back into the case and tighten it securely. Drive the vehicle, then check for leaks around the plug. Install the rock guard.

22   Differential oil level check

Refer to illustrations 22.2a and 22.2b

1   The differential has a check/fill plug which must be removed to check the oil level. If the vehicle is raised to gain access to the plug, be sure to support it safely on jackstands — DO NOT crawl under the vehicle when it's supported only by a jack.

2   Remove the oil check/fill plug from the differential **(see illustrations)**.

3   The oil level should be at the bottom of the plug opening. If not, use a syringe to add the recommended lubricant until it just starts to run out of the opening.

4   Install the plug and tighten it securely.

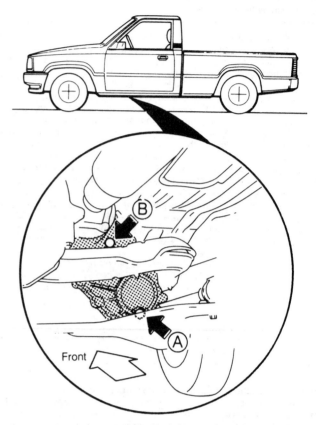

21.1   It may be necessary to remove the transfer case rock guard for access to the oil check/fill plug (B) — DO NOT remove the drain plug (A)

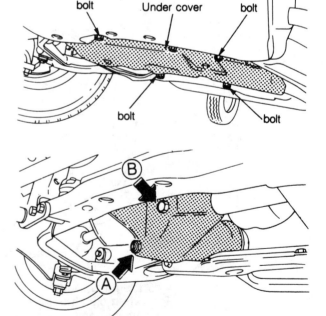

22.2b   Remove the under cover to gain access to the front differential oil check/fill plug (B) — DO NOT remove the drain plug (A)

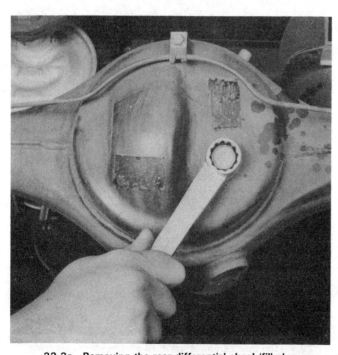

22.2a   Removing the rear differential check/fill plug

23 Tire rotation

Refer to illustration 23.2

1   The tires should be rotated at the specified intervals and whenever uneven wear is noticed.
2   Refer to the accompanying illustration for the preferred tire rotation pattern.
3   Refer to the information in *Jacking and towing* at the front of this manual for the proper procedures to follow when raising the vehicle and changing a tire. If the brakes are to be checked, don't apply the parking brake as stated. Make sure the tires are blocked to prevent the vehicle from rolling as it's raised.
4   Preferably, the entire vehicle should be raised at the same time. This can be done on a hoist or by jacking up each corner and then lowering the vehicle onto jackstands placed under the frame rails. Always use four jackstands and make sure the vehicle is safely supported.
5   After rotation, check and adjust the tire pressures as necessary and be sure to check the lug nut tightness.
6   For additional information on the wheels and tires, refer to Chapter 10.

BIAS AND BIAS BELTED TIRES

4 wheel rotation

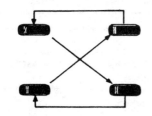

5 wheel rotation

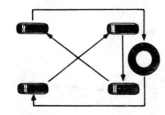

RADIAL TIRES

4 wheel rotation

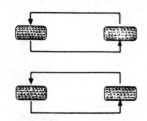

5 wheel rotation

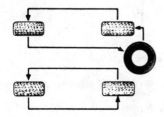

23.2 Tire rotation diagram

24 Brake check

Refer to illustrations 24.5, 24.11, 24.13 and 24.22
Note: *For detailed photographs of the brake system, refer to Chapter 9.*

1   In addition to the specified intervals, the brakes should be inspected every time the wheels are removed or whenever a defect is suspected.
2   To check the brakes, raise the vehicle and place it securely on jackstands. Remove the wheels (see *Jacking and towing* at the front of the manual, if necessary).

Disc brakes

3   Disc brakes are used on the front wheels of later models. Extensive rotor damage can occur if the pads are not replaced when needed.
4   The disc brake calipers, which contain the pads, are visible with the wheels removed. There is an outer pad and an inner pad in each caliper. All pads should be inspected.
5   The caliper has a ''window'' to inspect the pads. Check the thickness of the lining by looking into the caliper at each end and down through the inspection window at the top of the housing **(see illustration)**. If the wear sensor is very close to the rotor or the pad material has worn to about 1/8-inch or less, the pads require replacement.
6   If you are unsure about the exact thickness of the remaining lining material, remove the pads for further inspection or replacement (refer to Chapter 9).
7   Before installing the wheels, check for leakage and/or damage (cracking, splitting, etc.) around the brake hose connections. Replace the hose or fittings as necessary, referring to Chapter 9.
8   Check the condition of the rotor. Look for scoring, gouging and burned spots. If these conditions exist, the hub/rotor assembly should be removed for servicing (Chapter 9).

Drum brakes

9   On front drum brakes, remove the hub/drum (see Section 39).
10   On rear brakes, remove retaining screws (early models) and remove the drum by pulling it off the axle and brake assembly. If this proves difficult, make sure the parking brake is released, then squirt penetrating oil around the center hub areas. Allow the oil to soak in and try again to pull the drum off. If the drum still cannot be pulled off, the brake shoes will have to be adjusted. This is done by first removing the plugs from the backing plate.

24.5   The disc brake pads are visible through the opening slot in the caliper

11   Push the lever off the star wheel and then use a small screwdriver to turn the star wheel, which will move the linings away from the drum **(see illustration)**.

12   With the drum removed, do not touch any brake dust. **Warning:** *Brake system dust contains asbestos, which is harmful to your health. Never blow it out with compressed air and do not inhale any of it.*

13   Note the thickness of the lining material on both the front and rear brake shoes. If the material has worn away to within 1/32-inch of the recessed rivets or metal backing, the shoes should be replaced **(see illustration)**. The shoes should also be replaced if they are cracked, glazed (shiny surface) or wet with brake fluid.

14   Check that all the brake assembly springs are connected and in good condition.

15   Check the brake components for any signs of fluid leakage. With your finger, carefully pry back the rubber cups on the wheel cylinders located at the top of the brake shoes. Any leakage is an indication that the wheel cylinders should be overhauled immediately (Chapter 9). Also check brake hoses and connections for signs of leakage.

16   Wipe the inside of the drum with a clean rag and brake cleaner or denatured alcohol. Again, be careful not to breath the dangerous asbestos dust.

17   Check the inside of the drum for cracks, score marks, deep scratches and hard spots, which will appear as small discolorations. If these imperfections cannot be removed with fine emery cloth, the drum must be taken to a machine shop equipped to turn the drums.

18   If after the inspection process all parts are in good working condition, reinstall the brake drum (using a metal or rubber plug if the knock-out was removed).

19   Install the wheels and lower the vehicle.

Parking brake

20   The parking brake operates from a hand lever and locks the rear brake system. The easiest, and perhaps most obvious method of periodically checking the operation of the parking brake assembly is to park the vehicle on a steep hill with the parking brake set and the transmission in Neutral. If the parking brake cannot prevent the vehicle from rolling, it is in need of adjustment (see Chapter 9).

Brake pedal height

21   The brakes should be periodically checked for pedal height, which is the distance the brake pedal moves toward the floor from a fully released position. The brakes must be cold while performing this test.

22   Using a ruler, measure the distance from the floor to the brake pedal **(see illustration)**.

23   Pump the brakes at least three times. On power brake models do this without starting the engine. Press firmly on the brake pedal and measure the distance between the floor and the pedal.

24   The distance the pedal travels should not exceed specifications.

25   To adjust the pedal height, unplug the stop light switch, loosen the locknut and turn the switch until the specified height is achieved. Tighten the locknut.

Brake pedal free travel

26   The distance the brake pedal moves before resistance is felt is free travel **(see illustration 24.22)**.

27   To adjust the free travel, loosen the brake pushrod locknut and turn the pushrod until the specified free travel is reached. Tighten the locknut.

---

25   Fuel system check

Warning: *There are certain precautions to take when inspecting or servicing the fuel system components. Work in a well ventilated area and don't allow open flames (cigarettes, appliance pilot lights, etc.) in the work area. Mop up spills immediately and don't store fuel soaked rags where they could ignite.*

1   On most models the main fuel tank is located at the rear of the vehicle.

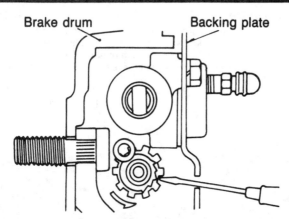

24.11   Back off the brake drum adjuster with a screwdriver (the adjuster locking lever must be held away from the starwheel with a punch or rod)

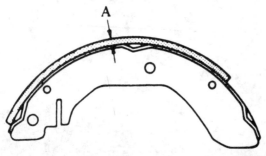

24.13   The rear brake shoe lining thickness (A) is measured from the outer surface of the lining to the metal shoe

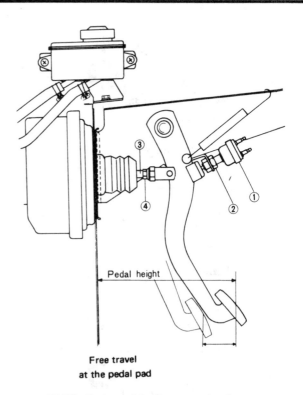

Pedal height

Free travel
at the pedal pad

24.22   Brake pedal adjustment details

1 Stoplight switch (turn to adjust height)	3 Pushrod (turn to adjust free travel)
2 Stoplight switch locknut	4 Locknut

2   The fuel system should be checked with the vehicle raised on a hoist so the components underneath the vehicle are readily visible and accessible.

3   If the smell of gasoline is noticed while driving or after the vehicle has been in the sun, the system should be thoroughly inspected immediately.

4   Remove the gas tank cap and check for damage, corrosion and an unbroken sealing imprint on the gasket. Replace the cap with a new one if necessary.

5   With the vehicle raised, check the gas tank and filler neck for punctures, cracks and other damage. The connection between the filler neck and the tank is especially critical. Sometimes a rubber filler neck will leak due to loose clamps or deteriorated rubber, problems a home mechanic can usually rectify. **Warning:** *Do not, under any circumstances, try to repair a fuel tank yourself (except rubber components). A welding torch or any open flame can easily cause the fuel vapors to explode if the proper precautions are not taken!*

6   Carefully check all rubber hoses and metal lines leading away from the fuel tank. Look for loose connections, deteriorated hoses, crimped lines and other damage. Follow the lines to the front of the vehicle, carefully inspecting them all the way. Repair or replace damaged sections as necessary.

7   If a fuel odor is still evident after the inspection, refer to Chapter 6 and check the EEC system.

---

26   Thermostatic air cleaner check

Refer to illustrations 26.4 and 26.5

1   All models are equipped with a thermostatically controlled air cleaner, which draws air to the carburetor from different locations depending on engine temperature.

2   This is a simple visual check. However, if access is tight, a small mirror may have to be used.

3   Open the hood and find the air control valve on the air cleaner assembly. It's located inside the long snorkel portion of the metal air cleaner housing.

4   If there's a flexible air duct attached to the end of the snorkel, disconnect it so you can look through the end of the snorkel and see the air control valve inside **(see illustration)**. A mirror may be needed

if you can't safely look directly into the end of the snorkel.

5   The check should be done when the engine and outside air are cold. Start the engine and watch the air control valve, which should move up and close off the snorkel air passage. With the valve closed, air can't enter through the end of the snorkel, but instead enters the air cleaner through the hot air duct attached to the exhaust manifold **(see illustration)**.

6   As the engine warms up to operating temperature, the valve should open to allow air through the snorkel end. Depending on outside air temperature, this may take 10 to 15 minutes. To speed up the check you can reconnect the snorkel air duct, drive the vehicle and then check the position of the valve.

7   If the thermostatic air cleaner isn't operating properly, see Chapter 6 for more information.

26.4   Remove the flexible air inlet duct from the air cleaner to check the thermostatic system

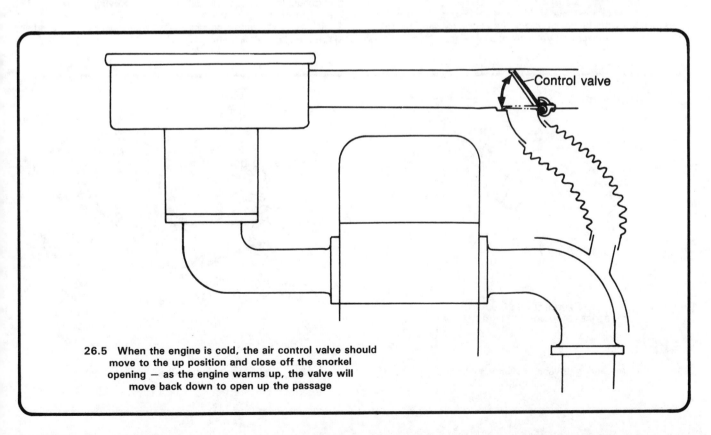

26.5   When the engine is cold, the air control valve should move to the up position and close off the snorkel opening — as the engine warms up, the valve will move back down to open up the passage

27   Drivebelt check, adjustment and replacement

Refer to illustrations 27.3, 27.4 and 27.6

1   The drivebelts, or V-belts as they are often called, are located at the front of the engine and play an important role in the overall operation of the engine and accessories. Due to their function and material make-up, the belts are prone to failure after a period of time and should be inspected and adjusted periodically to prevent major engine damage.

2   The number of belts used on a particular vehicle depends on the accessories installed. Drivebelts are used to turn the alternator, power steering pump (some models), water pump and air conditioning compressor. Depending on the pulley arrangement, more than one of the components may be driven by a single belt.

3   With the engine off, locate the drivebelts at the front of the engine. Using your fingers (and a flashlight, if necessary), move along the belts checking for cracks and separation of the belt plies. Also check for fraying and glazing, which gives the belt a shiny appearance **(see illustration)**. Both sides of each belt should be inspected, which means you'll have to twist each belt to check the underside. Check the pulleys for nicks, cracks, distortion and corrosion.

4   The tension of each belt is checked by pushing on it at a distance halfway between the pulleys. Push firmly with your thumb and see how much the belt moves (deflects) **(see illustration)**. A rule of thumb is that if the distance from pulley center-to-pulley center is between 7 and 11 inches, the belt should deflect 1/4-inch. If the belt travels between pulleys spaced 12-to-16 inches apart, the belt should deflect 1/2-inch.

5   If adjustment is needed, either to make the belt tighter or looser, it's done by moving the belt-driven accessory on the bracket.

6   Each component usually has an adjusting bolt and a pivot bolt. Both bolts must be loosened slightly to enable you to move the component. Some components have an adjusting bolt that can be turned to change the belt tension after the mounting bolt is loosened **(see illustration)**.

7   After the two bolts have been loosened, move the component away from the engine to tighten the belt or toward the engine to loosen the belt. Hold the accessory in position and check the belt tension. If it's correct, tighten the two bolts until just snug, then recheck the tension. If the tension is correct, tighten the bolts.

8   You may have to use some sort of pry bar to move the accessory while the belt is adjusted. If this must be done to gain the proper leverage, be very careful not to damage the component being moved or the part being pried against.

9   To replace a belt, follow the above procedures for drivebelt adjustment but slip the belt off the pulleys and remove it. Since belts tend to wear out more or less at the same time, it's a good idea to replace all of them at the same time. Mark each belt and the corresponding pulley grooves so the replacement belts can be installed properly.

10   Take the old belts with you when purchasing new ones in order to make a direct comparison for length, width and design.

11   Adjust the belts as described earlier in this Section.

28   Seatbelt check

1   Check the seatbelts, buckles, retractors and anchors for any obvious damage or signs of wear.

2   Make sure the seatbelt reminder light comes on when the key is turned on.

3   The seatbelts are designed to lock up during a sudden stop or impact, yet allow free movement during normal driving. The retractors should hold the belt against your chest while driving and rewind the belt when the buckle is unlatched.

4   If any of the above checks reveal problems with the seatbelt system, replace parts as necessary.

SMALL CRACKS   GREASE

GLAZED   ALWAYS CHECK the underside of the belt.

27.3   Here are some of the more common problems associated with drivebelts (check the belts very carefully to prevent an untimely breakdown)

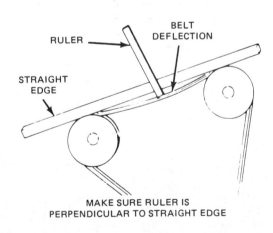

27.4   Measuring drivebelt deflection with a straightedge and ruler

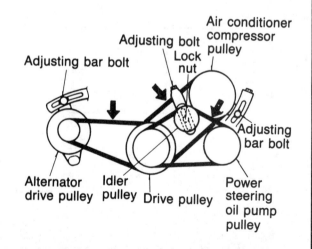

27.6   Typical later model drivebelt adjustment points

29 Air filter and PCV filter replacement

Refer to illustrations 29.4 and 29.6

1   At the specified intervals, the air filter should be replaced with a new one. A thorough program of preventative maintenance would also call for the filter to be inspected periodically between changes, especially if the vehicle is often driven in dusty conditions.

2   The air filter is located inside the air cleaner which is mounted on top of the carburetor or, on fuel injection-equipped models, in a housing on the driver's side of the engine compartment.

3   Remove the wingnut or bolts that hold the top plate or cover to the air cleaner body, release any clips and lift it off.

4   Lift the air filter out of the housing (**see illustration**). If it's covered with dirt, replace it with a new one.

5   Wipe out the inside of the air cleaner housing with a rag.

6   Pull out the old PCV filter (if equipped) and press a new one into the housing (**see illustration**).

7   Place the new filter into the air cleaner housing.

8   Reinstall the top plate on the air cleaner housing and install the nut/bolts and clips.

30 Fuel filter replacement

Refer to illustration 30.4

Warning: *Gasoline is extremely flammable, so extra precautions must be taken when working on any part of the fuel system. DO NOT smoke or allow open flames or bare light bulbs near the work area.*

Also, don't work in a garage if a natural gas appliance (such as a water heater or clothes dryer) is present.

1   This job should be done with the engine cold (after sitting for three hours). Place a metal container, rags or newspapers under the filter to catch spilled fuel.

2   Disconnect the cable from the negative battery terminal.

3   Locate the fuel filter, which is located under the vehicle, near the gas tank on early models, or on later models, is mounted on the inner fender panel (carburetor) or on the firewall near the windshield wiper motor (fuel injection).

4   On fuel injected models, depressurize the fuel system (Chapter 4, Section 10). Loosen the clamps and slide the hoses off (**see illustrations**). Allow the fuel to drain out of the filter.

5   Pull the filter out of the clip (carbureted) or remove the bolts and detach the filter from the bracket (fuel injected), (note the directions of any arrows on the housing). Install the new filter, then hook up the hoses and tighten the clamps securely.

31 Evaporative emissions control system check

Refer to illustration 31.2

1   The function of the evaporative emissions control system is to draw fuel vapors from the gas tank and fuel system, store them in a charcoal canister and route them to the intake manifold during normal engine operation.

2   The most common symptom of a fault in the evaporative emissions system is a strong fuel odor in the engine compartment. If a fuel odor is detected, inspect the canister, located in the engine compartment (**see illustration**). Check the canister and all hoses for damage

29.4   After the top plate has been removed from the air cleaner housing, lift the air filter out of position — be careful not to drop any dirt, tools, etc. down the center of the carburetor

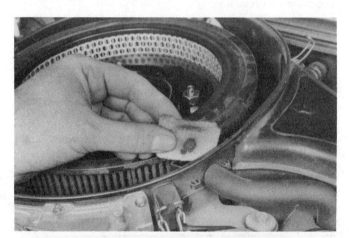

29.6   On models so equipped, grasp the PCV filter and pull it out of the housing inside the air cleaner

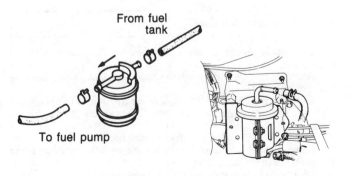

30.4   Fuel filter details (carbureted models – left, fuel injected model – right)

31.2   The evaporative emissions canister is located in the engine compartment — inspect the various hoses attached to it and check the canister itself for damage

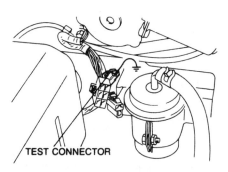

33.2 On fuel injected models, ground the test connector before checking the idle speed or ignition timing

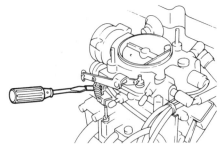

33.8a Use a screwdriver to the turn the idle speed adjustment screw on the carburetor

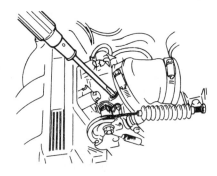

33.8b Adjust the idle speed on fuel injected models by turning the adjusting screw on the top of the throttle body

and deterioration.

3   The evaporative emissions control system is explained in more detail in Chapter 6.

32   Carburetor mounting nut torque check

1   The carburetor is attached to the top of the intake manifold by several bolts or nuts. The fasteners can sometimes work loose from vibration and temperature changes during normal engine operation and cause a vacuum leak.

2   If you suspect that a vacuum leak exists at the bottom of the carburetor or throttle body, obtain a two-foot length of fuel line hose. Start the engine and place one end of the hose next to your ear as you probe around the base with the other end. You'll hear a hissing sound if a leak exists (be careful of hot or moving engine components).

3   Remove the air cleaner assembly, tagging each hose that's disconnected with a piece of numbered tape to make reassembly easier.

4   Locate the mounting nuts or bolts at the base of the carburetor. Decide what special tools or adapters will be necessary, if any, to tighten the fasteners.

5   Tighten the nuts or bolts securely. Don't overtighten them, as the threads could strip.

6   If, after the nuts or bolts are properly tightened, a vacuum leak still exists, the carburetor must be removed and a new gasket installed. See Chapter 4 for more information.

7   After tightening the fasteners, reinstall the air cleaner and return all hoses to their original positions.

33   Idle speed check and adjustment

Refer to illustrations 33.2, 33.8a and 33.8b

1   Engine idle speed is the speed at which the engine operates when no throttle pressure is applied. The idle speed is critical to the performance of the engine, as well as many engine sub-systems.

2   A hand-held tachometer must be used when adjusting the idle speed to get an accurate reading. The exact hook-up for these meters varies with the manufacturer, so follow the particular directions included. On fuel injected models, use a jumper wire to ground the green test connector to the body **(see illustration)**. Fuel injected models also have a tachometer check connector so make this easier.

3   Set the parking brake and block the wheels. Be sure the transmission is in Neutral (manual trans) or Park (automatic trans).

4   Turn off the air conditioner (if equipped), the headlights and any other accessories during this procedure.

5   Start the engine and allow it to reach operating temperature.

6   On automatic transmission equipped models, have an assistant shift to Drive while keeping the brake pedal firmly depressed. Place manual transmission equipped vehicles in Neutral.

7   Check the engine idle speed with the tachometer and compare it to the VECI label.

8   If the idle speed is not correct, turn the idle speed adjusting screw until the idle speed is correct **(see illustrations)**.

9   After adjustment, shift the automatic transmission into Park and turn the engine off. On fuel injected models, remove the jumper wire and plug in the test connector.

34   Idle speed switch (1985 through 1988 2000/2200 engine) – check and adjustment

Refer to illustration 34.2

1   With the engine idling at normal operating temperature, connect a tachometer to the engine.

2   Connect a voltmeter to the terminals (LgB on 1985 through 1987 models, LgR for 1988 models) **(see illustration)**.

3   Increase the speed of the engine above 2000 rpm and then allow it to gradually decelerate.

4   Check the voltmeter reading with the engine at idle and then above 1000 to 1200 rpm to make sure they are as specified. If they are not, turn the adjusting screw **(see illustration 34.2)**.

35   Carburetor float level (1600/1800/2000/2200 engine) – check and adjustment

Refer to illustration 35.1

1   With the engine idling at normal operating temperature, check the sight glass on the side of the carburetor to make sure the fuel level is even with the mark on the glass, indicating that the float level is properly adjusted **(see illustration)**.

2   If necessary, turn the float adjusting screw until the fuel level is correct.

36   Transfer case oil change

1   Drive the vehicle for at least 15 minutes in 4WD to warm up the oil in the case.

2   Raise the vehicle and support it securely on jackstands. Remove the rock guard.

3   Move a drain pan, rags, newspapers and a breaker bar or ratchet (to fit the square drive hole in the transfer case plugs) under the vehicle.

4   Remove the check/fill plug **(see illustration 21.1)**.

5   Remove the drain plug from the lower part of the case and allow the old oil to drain completely.

6   Carefully clean and install the drain plug after the case is completely drained. Tighten the plug to the specified torque.

7   Fill the case with the specified lubricant until it's level with the lower edge of the filler hole.

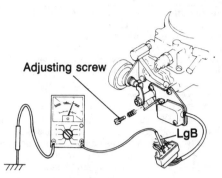

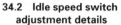

34.2   Idle speed switch
adjustment details

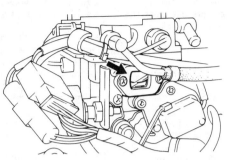

35.1   Check the carburetor float level by
looking through the sight glass

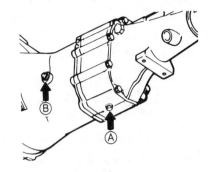

37.3   The manual transmission fill (B)
and drain (A) plugs

8   Install the check/fill plug and tighten it securely.
9   Install the rock guard, then lower the vehicle.
10   Check carefully for leaks around the drain plug after the first few
miles of driving.

37   Manual transmission oil change

Refer to illustration 37.3

1   Drive the vehicle for a few miles to thoroughly warm up the transmission oil.
2   Raise the vehicle and support it securely on jackstands.
3   Move a drain pan, rags, newspapers and a 1/2-inch drive breaker
bar or ratchet with an extension under the vehicle. With the drain pan
and newspapers in position under the transmission, use the ratchet
and extension to loosen the drain plug located in the bottom of the
transmission case **(see illustration)**. Some later models have two drain
and two fill plugs. Make sure to remove all four when changing the oil.
4   Once loosened, carefully unscrew it with your fingers until you
can remove it from the transmission. Allow all of the oil to drain into
the pan. If the plug is too hot to touch, use the wrench to remove it.
5   If the transmission is equipped with a magnetic drain plug, see if
there are bits of metal clinging to it. If there are, it's a sign of excessive
internal wear, indicating that the transmission should be carefully inspected in the near future. If the transmission isn't equipped with a
magnetic drain plug, allow the oil in the pan to cool, then feel with
your hands along the bottom of the drain pan for debris.
6   Clean the drain plug, then reinstall it in the transmission and tighten
it to the specified torque.
7   Remove the transmission oil check/fill plug (see Section 20). Using
a hand pump or syringe, fill the transmission with the correct amount
and grade of oil (see the Specifications), until the level is just at the
bottom of the plug hole.
8   Reinstall the check/fill plug and tighten it securely.

38   Differential oil change

Refer to illustration 38.3

Note: *The following procedure can be used for the rear differential as
well as the front differential used on 4WD vehicles.*

1   Drive the vehicle for several miles to warm up the differential oil,
then raise the vehicle and support it securely on jackstands.
2   Move a drain pan, rags, newspapers and a 1/2-inch drive breaker
bar or ratchet with an extension and socket under the vehicle. If equipped, remove the under cover.
3   With the drain pan under the differential, use the breaker bar or
ratchet and socket to loosen the drain plug. It's the lower of the two
plugs **(see illustrations)**.
4   Once loosened, carefully unscrew it with your fingers until you
can remove it from the case.
5   Allow all of the oil to drain into the pan, then replace the drain plug
and tighten it to the specified torque.

38.3   The drain plug is located at the bottom of the
differential housing

6   Feel with your hands along the bottom of the drain pan for any
metal bits that may have come out with the oil. If there are any, it's
a sign of excessive wear, indicating that the internal components should
be carefully inspected in the near future.
7   Remove the differential check/fill plug located above the drain plug.
Using a hand pump, syringe or funnel, fill the differential with the correct
amount and grade of oil (see the Specifications) until the level is just
at the bottom of the plug hole.
8   Reinstall the plug and tighten it securely.
9   Lower the vehicle. Check for leaks at the drain plug after the first
few miles of driving.

39   Automatic transmission fluid and filter change

Refer to illustration 39.10

1   At the specified time intervals, the transmission fluid should be
drained and replaced. Since the fluid should be hot when it's drained,
drive the vehicle for 15 or 20 minutes before proceeding.
2   Before beginning work, purchase the specified transmission fluid
(see *Recommended lubricants and fluids* at the front of this Chapter).
Note: *Most vehicle manufacturers also have specific fluid requirements
on the dipstick.*
3   Other tools necessary for this job include jackstands to support
the vehicle in a raised position, a drain pan capable of holding at least
eight pints, newspapers and clean rags.
4   Raise the vehicle and support it securely on jackstands.
5   With a drain pan in place, remove the rear and side transmission
fluid pan mounting bolts. Be careful not to burn yourself on anything —
it may be wise to wear gloves.
6   Loosen the front pan bolts approximately four turns, but don't
remove them.
7   Carefully pry the transmission pan loose with a screwdriver, allowing the fluid to drain. Be very careful not to damage the pan or transmission gasket surfaces! Save the fluid so you can estimate how much

new fluid to add to the transmission.

8   Remove the remaining bolts, pan and gasket. Carefully clean the gasket surface of the transmission to remove all traces of the old gasket and sealant.

9   Drain the fluid from the transmission pan, clean it with solvent and dry it with compressed air.

10 Remove the bolts and detach the filter from the mount inside the transmission **(see illustration)**.

11 Install a new filter and install the bolts. Tighten the bolts securely.

12 Apply a thin layer of sealant to the transmission case side of the new gasket.

13 Make sure the gasket surface on the transmission pan is clean, then apply a thin layer of sealant to it and position the new gasket on the pan. Put the pan in place against the transmission, install the bolts and, working around the pan, tighten each bolt a little at a time until the final torque figure is reached.

14 Lower the vehicle and add new automatic transmission fluid through the filler tube (Section 5). The amount should be equal to the amount of fluid that was drained (you don't want to overfill it).

15 With the transmission in Park and the parking brake set, run the engine at a fast idle, but don't race it.

16 Move the gear selector through each range and back to Park, then check the fluid level (Section 5). Add more fluid as required.

17 Check under the vehicle for leaks during the first few miles of driving.

---

40   Front wheel bearing check, repack and adjustment (2WD models)

Refer to illustrations 40.1, 40.24, and 40.25

1   In most cases the front wheel bearings will not need servicing until the brake pads are changed. However, the bearings should be checked whenever the front of the vehicle is raised for any reason. Several items, including a torque wrench and special grease, are required for this procedure **(see illustration)**.

2   With the vehicle securely supported on jackstands, spin each wheel and check for noise, rolling resistance and free play.

3   Grasp the top of each tire with one hand and the bottom with the other. Move the wheel in-and-out on the spindle. If there's any noticable movement, the bearings should be checked and then repacked with grease or replaced if necessary.

4   Remove the wheel(s).

5   Fabricate a wood block to slide between the brake pads to keep them separated. Remove the brake caliper (Chapter 9) and hang it out of the way on a piece of wire.

6   Pry the dust cap out of the hub using a screwdriver or hammer and chisel.

7   Straighten the bent ends of the cotter pin, then pull the cotter pin out of the adjusting nut cap. Discard the cotter pin and use a new one during reassembly.

8   Remove the adjusting nut and washer from the end of the spindle.

9   Pull the hub out slightly, then push it back into its original position. This should force the outer wheel bearing off the spindle enough so it can be removed.

10 Pull the hub off the spindle.

11 Use a screwdriver to pry the grease seal out of the rear of the hub. As this is done, note how the seal is installed.

12 Remove the inner wheel bearing from the hub.

13 Use solvent to remove all traces of the old grease from the bearings, hub and spindle. A small brush may prove helpful; however make sure no bristles from the brush embed themselves inside the bearing rollers. Allow the parts to air dry.

14 Carefully inspect the bearings for cracks, heat discoloration, worn rollers, etc. Check the bearing races inside the hub for wear and damage. If the bearing races are defective, the hubs should be taken to a machine shop with the facilities to remove the old races and press new ones in. Note that the bearings and races come as matched sets and old bearings should never be installed on new races.

15 Use high-temperature front wheel bearing grease to pack the bearings. Work the grease completely into the bearings, forcing it between the rollers, cone and cage from the back side.

16 Apply a thin coat of grease to the spindle at the outer bearing seat, inner bearing seat, shoulder and seal seat.

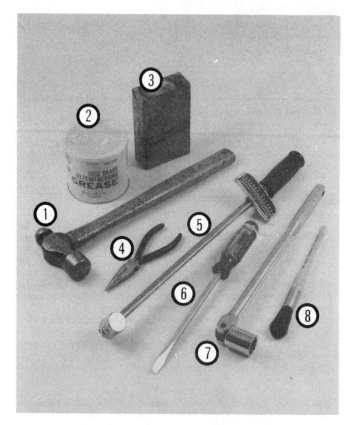

40.1   Tools and materials needed for front wheel bearing maintenance

1   **Hammer** — *A common hammer will do just fine*
2   **Grease** — *High-temperature grease which is formulated specially for front wheel bearings should be used*
3   **Wood block** — *If you have a scrap piece of 2x4, it can be used to drive the new seal into the hub*
4   **Needle-nose pliers** — *Used to straighten and remove the cotter pin in the spindle*
5   **Torque wrench** — *This is very important in this procedure; if the bearing is too tight, the wheel won't turn freely — if it is too loose, the wheel will 'wobble' on the spindle. Either way, it could mean extensive damage*
6   **Screwdriver** — *Used to remove the seal from the hub (a long screwdriver would be preferred)*
7   **Socket/breaker bar** — *Needed to loosen the nut on the spindle if it is extremely tight*
8   **Brush** — *Together with some clean solvent, this will be used to remove old grease from the hub and spindle*

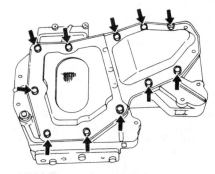

39.10   Automatic transmission fluid filter bolt locations (arrows)

CARBON DEPOSITS

Symptoms: Dry sooty deposits indicate a rich mixture or weak ignition. Causes misfiring, hard starting and hesitation.

Recommendation: Check for a clogged air cleaner, high float level, sticky choke and worn ignition points. Use a spark plug with a longer core nose for greater anti-fouling protection.

OIL DEPOSITS

Symptoms: Oily coating caused by poor oil control. Oil is leaking past worn valve guides or piston rings into the combustion chamber. Causes hard starting, misfiring and hesition.

Recommendation: Correct the mechanical condition with necessary repairs and install new plugs.

TOO HOT

Symptoms: Blistered, white insulator, eroded electrode and absence of deposits. Results in shortened plug life.

Recommendation: Check for the correct plug heat range, over-advanced ignition timing, lean fuel mixture, intake manifold vacuum leaks and sticking valves. Check the coolant level and make sure the radiator is not clogged.

PREIGNITION

Symptoms: Melted electrodes. Insulators are white, but may be dirty due to misfiring or flying debris in the combustion chamber. Can lead to engine damage.

Recommendation: Check for the correct plug heat range, over-advanced ignition timing, lean fuel mixture, clogged cooling system and lack of lubrication.

HIGH SPEED GLAZING

Symptoms: Insulator has yellowish, glazed appearance. Indicates that combustion chamber temperatures have risen suddenly during hard acceleration. Normal deposits melt to form a conductive coating. Causes misfiring at high speeds.

Recommendation: Install new plugs. Consider using a colder plug if driving habits warrant.

GAP BRIDGING

Symptoms: Combustion deposits lodge between the electrodes. Heavy deposits accumulate and bridge the electrode gap. The plug ceases to fire, resulting in a dead cylinder.

Recommendation: Locate the faulty plug and remove the deposits from between the electrodes.

NORMAL

Symptoms: Brown to grayish-tan color and slight electrode wear. Correct heat range for engine and operating conditions.

Recommendation: When new spark plugs are installed, replace with plugs of the same heat range.

1

ASH DEPOSITS

Symptoms: Light brown deposits encrusted on the side or center electrodes or both. Derived from oil and/or fuel additives. Excessive amounts may mask the spark, causing misfiring and hesitation during acceleration.

Recommendation: If excessive deposits accumulate over a short time or low mileage, install new valve guide seals to prevent seepage of oil into the combustion chambers. Also try changing gasoline brands.

WORN

Symptoms: Rounded electrodes with a small amount of deposits on the firing end. Normal color. Causes hard starting in damp or cold weather and poor fuel economy.

Recommendation: Replace with new plugs of the same heat range.

DETONATION

Symptoms: Insulators may be cracked or chipped. Improper gap setting techniques can also result in a fractured insulator tip. Can lead to piston damage.

Recommendation: Make sure the fuel anti-knock values meet engine requirements. Use care when setting the gaps on new plugs. Avoid lugging the engine.

SPLASHED DEPOSITS

Symptoms: After long periods of misfiring, deposits can loosen when normal combustion temperature is restored by an overdue tune-up. At high speeds, deposits flake off the piston and are thrown against the hot insulator, causing misfiring.

Recommendation: Replace the plugs with new ones or clean and reinstall the originals.

MECHANICAL DAMAGE

Symptoms: May be caused by a foreign object in the combustion chamber or the piston striking an incorrect reach (too long) plug. Causes a dead cylinder and could result in piston damage.

Recommendation: Remove the foreign object from the engine and/or install the correct reach plug.

17 Put a small quantity of grease behind each bearing race inside the hub. Using your finger, form a dam at these points to provide for extra grease and to keep thinned grease from flowing out of the bearing.

18 Place the grease-packed inner bearing into the rear of the hub and put a little more grease outside of the bearing.

19 Place a new seal over the inner bearing and tap the seal evenly into place with a hammer and block of wood until it's flush with the hub.

20 Carefully place the hub assembly onto the spindle and push the grease-packed outer bearing into position.

21 Install the washer and adjusting nut. Tighten the nut to the specified torque.

22 Turn the hub to seat the bearings and remove any grease or burrs which could cause excessive bearing play later.

23 Loosen the nut enough that it can be turned by hand.

24 Pull on one of the wheel studs with a spring tension gauge and measure the initial torque necessary to turn the hub **(see illustration)**. This measurement is the frictional force.

25 Adjust the nut using a wrench until the torque required to turn the hub (initial turning torque) measured by the spring scale equals the frictional force measured in step 24 plus 1.3 to 2.4 ft-lb (6 to 11 Nm) **(see illustration)**.

26 Install the adjusting nut cap and see if the hole in the spindle is aligned with the slot in the cap. Install a new cotter pin.

27 Bend the ends of the cotter pin until they're flat against the nut. Cut off any extra length which could interfere with the dust cap.

28 Install the dust cap, tapping it into place with a hammer.

29 Place the brake caliper near the rotor and carefully remove the wood spacer. Install the caliper (Chapter 9).

30 Install the tire/wheel assembly on the hub and tighten the lug nuts.

31 Grasp the top and bottom of the tire and check the bearings in the manner described earlier in this Section.

32 Lower the vehicle.

41 Front wheel bearing check, repack and adjustment (4WD models)

Refer to illustrations 41.7, 41.8, 41.9 and 41.23

1   In most cases, the front wheel bearings will not need servicing until the brake pads are changed. However, these bearings should be checked whenever the front wheels are raised for any reason. Several items, including grease and a torque wrench are required for this procedure **(see illustration 40.1)**

2   With the vehicle securely supported on jackstands, spin the wheel and check for noise, rolling resistance or free play. Now grab the top of the tire with one hand and the bottom of the tire with the other. Move the tire in and out on the spindle. If it moves more than 0.005 in, the bearings should be checked, then repacked with grease or replaced if necessary.

3   To remove the bearings for replacing or repacking, begin by removing the wheel.

4   Remove the caliper mounting bolts (Chapter 9).

5   Fabricate a wood block which will be slid between the brake pads to keep them separated. Carefully slide the caliper off the disc and insert the wood block between the pads. Use wire to hang the caliper assembly out of the way. Be careful not to kink or damage the brake hose.

6   Remove the free wheel hub assembly (Chapter 8).

7   Using snap-ring pliers, remove the hub bearing snap-ring and spacer **(see illustration)**.

8   Use a screwdriver to remove the set bolts and remove the bearing set plate **(see illustration)**.

9   Remove the bearing locknut and adjusting nut. A special large wheel bearing nut wrench (Mazda special tool number 49 S231 635) is required for this job **(see illustration)**.

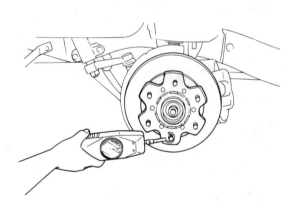

40.24 Pull on one of the wheel studs with a spring scale to measure the initial force required to turn the wheel

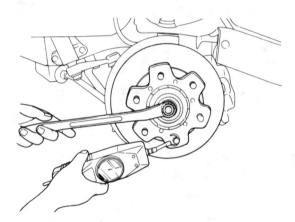

40.25 Adjust the nut while measuring the initial turning torque with the spring scale

41.7 Remove the hub bearing snap ring and spacer with snap ring pliers

41.8 Unscrew the two bearing set plate bolts with a screwdriver

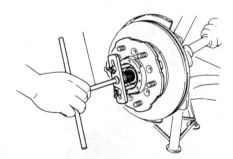

41.9 A special wrench is required for removing and installing the bearing nuts

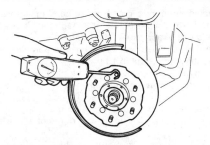

41.23 Measure the frictional force required to initially turn the hub by pulling on one of the wheel studs with a spring scale

10 Pull the hub assembly out slightly and then push it back into its original position. This should force the outer bearing off the spindle enough so that it can be removed with your fingers. Remove the outer bearing, noting how it is installed on the end of the spindle.
11 Now the hub assembly can be pulled off the spindle.
12 The inner bearing can now be removed from the hub, again noting how it is installed.
13 Use clean solvent to remove all traces of the old grease from the bearings, hub and spindle. A small brush may prove useful; however, make sure no bristles from the brush embed themselves inside the bearing rollers. Allow the parts to air dry.
14 Carefully inspect the bearings for cracks, heat discoloration, bent rollers, etc. Check the bearing races inside the hub for cracks, scoring or uneven surfaces. If the bearing races are in need of replacement, the job should be left to a repair shop which can press the new races into position.
15 Use an approved high temperature wheel bearing grease (see the Recommended lubricants Section) to pack the bearings. Work the grease fully into the bearings, forcing the grease between the rollers, cone and cage.
16 Apply a thin coat of grease to the spindle at the outer bearing seat, inner bearing seat, shoulder and seal seat.
17 Put a small quantity of grease inboard of each bearing race inside the hub. Using your finger, form a dam at these points to provide extra grease availability and to keep thinned grease from flowing out of the bearing.
18 Place the grease-packed inner bearing into the rear of the hub and put a little more grease outboard of the bearing.
19 Place a new seal over the inner bearing and tap the seal with a block of wood and a hammer until it is flush with the hub.
20 Carefully place the hub assembly onto the spindle and push the grease-packed outer bearing into position.
21 Install the locknut and adjusting nut. Tighten the nuts and turn the hub two or three times to seat the bearings.
22 Loosen the locknut and adjusting nut until they can be turned by hand.
23 Pull on one of the wheel studs with a spring tension gauge and measure and record the initial turning torque required to turn the hub (**see illustration**). This measurement is the frictional force.
24 Tighten the locknut with the special wrench until the preload is reached. The preload is the frictional force plus 1.3 to 2.6 Ft-lb (6 to 12 Nm).
25 Install the bearing set plate and bolts.
26 Coat the spacer with multi purpose grease and secure it in place with the snap-ring.
27 Remove the wood blocks, slide the caliper over the rotor and install the bolts. Tighten the caliper mounting bolts to the specified torque (Chapter 9).
28 Install the free wheel hub assembly (Chapter 8).
29 Install the wheel on the hub and tighten the mounting nuts.
30 Grab the top and bottom of the tire and check the bearings in the same manner as described at the beginning of this Section.
31 Lower the vehicle to the ground and tighten the wheel nuts.

42 Cooling system servicing (draining, flushing and refilling)

Warning: *Antifreeze is a corrosive and poisonous solution, so be careful not to spill any of the coolant mixture on the vehicle's paint or your skin. If you do, rinse it off immediately with plenty of clean water. Consult local authorities regarding proper disposal of antifreeze before draining the cooling system. In many areas, reclamation centers have*

been established to collect used oil and coolant mixtures.

1 Periodically, the cooling system should be drained, flushed and refilled to replenish the antifreeze mixture and prevent formation of rust and corrosion, which can impair the performance of the cooling system and cause engine damage. When the cooling system is serviced, all hoses and the radiator cap should be checked and replaced if necessary.
2 Apply the parking brake and block the wheels. If the vehicle has just been driven, wait several hours to allow the engine to cool down before beginning this procedure.
3 Once the engine is completely cool, remove the radiator cap. Place the heater temperature control in the maximum heat position.
4 Move a large container under the radiator drain to catch the coolant, then unscrew the drain plug (a pair of pliers may be required to turn it).
5 After the coolant stops flowing out of the radiator, move the container under the engine block drain plug, located near the rear of the block. Remove the plug and allow the coolant in the block to drain.
6 While the coolant is draining, check the condition of the radiator hoses, heater hoses and clamps (refer to Section 9 if necessary).
7 Replace any damaged clamps or hoses.
8 Once the system is completely drained, flush the radiator with fresh water from a garden hose until it runs clear at the drain. The flushing action of the water will remove sediments from the radiator but will not remove rust and scale from the engine and cooling tube surfaces.
9 These deposits can be removed with a chemical cleaner. Follow the procedure outlined in the manufacturer's instructions. If the radiator is severely corroded, damaged or leaking, it should be removed (Chapter 3) and taken to a radiator repair shop.
10 Remove the overflow hose from the coolant recovery reservoir. Drain the reservoir and flush it with clean water, then reconnect the hose.
11 Reinstall and tighten the radiator drain plug. Install and tighten the block drain plug.
12 Slowly add new coolant (a 50/50 mixture of water and antifreeze) to the radiator until it's full. Add coolant to the reservoir up to the lower mark.
13 Leave the radiator cap off and run the engine in a well-ventilated area until the thermostat opens (coolant will begin flowing through the radiator and the upper radiator hose will become hot).
14 Turn the engine off and let it cool. Add more coolant mixture to bring the level back up to the lip on the radiator filler neck.
15 Squeeze the upper radiator hose to expel air, then add more coolant mixture if necessary. Replace the radiator cap.
16 Start the engine, allow it to reach normal operating temperature and check for leaks.

43 Positive Crankcase Ventilation (PCV) valve check and replacement

Refer to illustration 43.2
1 The PCV valve is usually located in the rocker arm cover.
2 With the engine idling at normal operating temperature, pull the valve (with hose attached) from the rubber grommet in the cover (**see illustration**).

43.2 The PCV valve (arrow) is located in the rocker cover on these models (1988 and later model shown)

3   Place your finger over the valve opening. If there's no vacuum at the valve, check for a plugged hose, manifold port, or the valve itself. Replace any plugged or deteriorated hoses.

4   Turn off the engine and shake the PCV valve, listening for a rattle. If the valve doesn't rattle, replace it with a new one.

5   To replace the valve, pull it from the end of the hose, noting its installed position and direction.

6   When purchasing a replacement PCV valve, make sure it's for your particular vehicle and engine size. Compare the old valve with the new one to make sure they're the same.

7   Push the valve into the end of the hose until it's seated.

8   Inspect the rubber grommet for damage and replace it with a new one if necessary.

9   Push the PCV valve and hose securely into position.

44   Spark plug replacement

Refer to illustrations 44.2, 44.5a, 44.5b, 44.6 and 44.10

1   Replace the spark plugs with new ones at the intervals recommended in the *Routine maintenance schedule.*

2   In most cases, the tools necessary for spark plug replacement include a spark plug socket which fits onto a ratchet (spark plug sockets are padded inside to prevent damage to the porcelain insulators on the new plugs), various extensions and a gap gauge to check and adjust the gaps on the new plugs **(see illustration)**. A special plug wire removal tool is available for separating the wire boots from the spark plugs, but it isn't absolutely necessary. A torque wrench should be used to tighten the new plugs.

3   The best approach when replacing the spark plugs is to purchase the new ones in advance, adjust them to the proper gap and replace them one at a time. When buying the new spark plugs, be sure to obtain the correct plug type for your particular engine. This information can be found on the *Emission Control Information label* located under the hood and in the factory owner's manual. If differences exist between the plug specified on the emissions label and in the owner's manual, assume the emissions label is correct.

4   Allow the engine to cool completely before attempting to remove any of the plugs. While you're waiting for the engine to cool, check the new plugs for defects and adjust the gaps.

5   The gap is checked by inserting the proper thickness gauge between the electrodes at the tip of the plug **(see illustration)**. The gap between the electrodes should be the same as the one specified on the *Emissions Control Information label.* The wire should just slide between the electrodes with a slight amount of drag. If the gap is incor-

rect, use the adjuster on the gauge body to bend the curved side electrode slightly until the proper gap is obtained **(see illustration)**. If the side electrode is not exactly over the center electrode, bend it with the adjuster until it is. Check for cracks in the porcelain insulator (if any are found, the plug shouldn't be used).

6   With the engine cool, remove the spark plug wire from one spark plug. Pull only on the boot at the end of the wire — don't pull on the wire. A plug wire removal tool should be used if available **(see illustration)**.

7   If compressed air is available, use it to blow any dirt or foreign material away from the spark plug hole. A common bicycle pump will

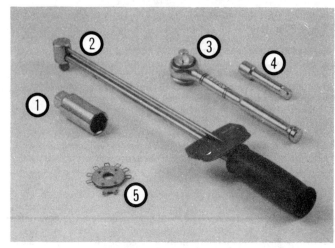

44.2   Tools required for changing spark plugs

1   *Spark plug socket* — This will have special padding inside to protect the spark plug porcelain insulator

2   *Torque wrench* — Although not mandatory, use of this tool is the best way to ensure that the plugs are tightened properly

3   *Ratchet* — Standard hand tool to fit the plug socket

4   *Extension* — Depending on model and accessories, you may need special extensions and universal joints to reach one or more of the plugs

5   *Spark plug gap gauge* — This gauge for checking the gap comes in a variety of styles. Make sure the gap for your engine is included

44.5a   Spark plug manufacturers recommend using a wire-type gauge when checking the gap — if the wire does not slide between the electrodes with a slight drag, adjustment is required

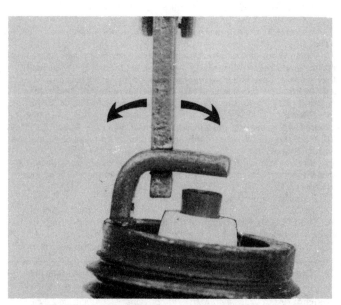

44.5b   To change the gap, bend the side electrode only, as indicated by the arrows, and be very careful not to crack or chip the porcelain insulator surrounding the center electrode

also work. The idea here is to eliminate the possibility of debris falling into the cylinder as the spark plug is removed.

8   Place the spark plug socket over the plug and remove it from the engine by turning it in a counterclockwise direction.

9   Compare the spark plug to those shown in the accompanying photos to get an indication of the general running condition of the engine.

10   Thread one of the new plugs into the hole until you can no longer turn it with your fingers, then tighten it with a torque wrench (if available) or the ratchet. It might be a good idea to slip a short length of rubber hose over the end of the plug to use as a tool to thread it into place **(see illustration)**. The hose will grip the plug well enough to turn it, but will start to slip if the plug begins to cross-thread in the hole – this will prevent damaged threads and the accompanying repair costs.

11   Before pushing the spark plug wire onto the end of the plug, inspect it following the procedures outlined in Section 45.

12   Attach the plug wire to the new spark plug, again using a twisting motion on the boot until it's seated on the spark plug.

13   Repeat the procedure for the remaining spark plugs, replacing them one at a time to prevent mixing up the spark plug wires.

45   Spark plug wire check and replacement

1   The spark plug wires should be checked at the recommended intervals and whenever new spark plugs are installed in the engine.

2   The wires should be inspected one at a time to prevent mixing up the order, which is essential for proper engine operation.

3   Disconnect the plug wire from one spark plug. To do this, grab the rubber boot, twist slightly and pull the wire free. Do not pull on the wire itself, only on the rubber boot **(see illustration 44.6)**.

4   Check inside the boot for corrosion, which will look like a white

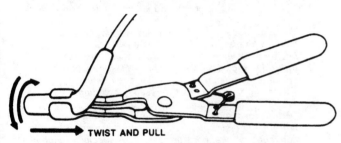

44.6   When removing the spark plug wires, pull only on the boot and use a twisting/pulling motion — a tool such as the one shown can make the job easier

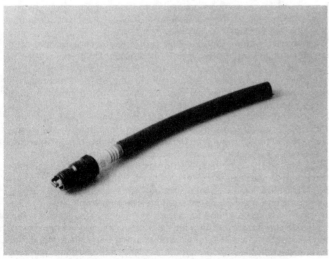

44.10   A length of 3/16-inch rubber hose will save time and prevent damaged threads when installing the spark plugs

crusty powder. Push the wire and boot back onto the end of the spark plug. It should be a tight fit on the plug. If it isn't, remove the wire and use a pair of pliers to carefully crimp the metal connector inside the boot until it fits securely on the end of the spark plug.

5   Using a clean rag, wipe the entire length of the wire to remove any built-up dirt and grease. Once the wire is clean, check for holes, burned areas, cracks and other damage. Don't bend the wire excessively or the conductor inside might break.

6   Disconnect the wire from the distributor cap. Again, pull only on the rubber boot. Check for corrosion and a tight fit in the same manner as the spark plug end. Reattach the wire to the distributor cap.

7   Check the remaining spark plug wires one at a time, making sure they are securely fastened at the distributor and the spark plug when the check is complete.

8   If new spark plug wires are required, purchase a new set for your specific engine model. Wire sets are available pre-cut, with the rubber boots already installed. Remove and replace the wires one at a time to avoid mix-ups in the firing order. The wire routing is extremely important, so be sure to note exactly how each wire is situated before removing it.

46   Distributor cap and rotor check and replacement

Refer to illustrations 46.4 and 46.7

Note: *It's common practice to install a new distributor cap and rotor whenever new spark plug wires are installed.*

1   Although the breakerless distributor used on later vehicles requires much less maintenance than a conventional distributor, periodic inspections should be performed at the intervals specified in the routine maintenance schedule and whenever any work is performed on the distributor.

2   Disconnect the ignition coil wire(s) from the coil(s), then unsnap the spring clips or loosen the screws that hold the cap to the distributor body. Detach the distributor cap and wires.

3   Place the cap, with the spark plug and coil wires still attached, out of the way. Use a length of wire or rope to secure it, if necessary.

4   The rotor is now visible on the end of the distributor shaft. Check it carefully for cracks and carbon tracks. Make sure the center terminal spring tension is adequate (not all models) and look for corrosion and wear on the rotor tip **(see illustration)**. If in doubt about its condition, replace it with a new one.

5   If replacement is required, detach the rotor from the shaft and install a new one. On some models, the rotor can simply be pulled off the shaft. On some later models, the rotor is retained on the shaft by two screws.

6   While the distributor cap is off, check the air gap on 2600 engine equipped models as described in Chapter 5.

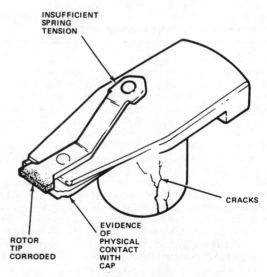

46.4   The ignition rotor should be checked for wear and corrosion as indicated here (if in doubt about its condition, buy a new one)

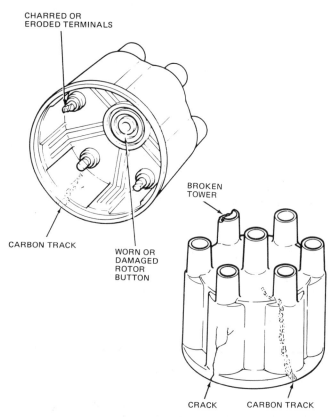

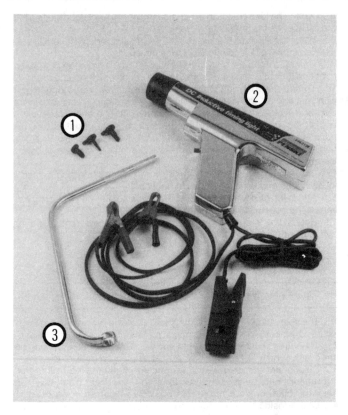

46.7   Shown here are some of the common defects to look for when inspecting a distributor cap (if in doubt about its condition, install a new one)

7   Check the distributor cap for carbon tracks, cracks and other damage. Closely examine the terminals on the inside of the cap for excessive corrosion and damage (**see illustration**). Slight deposits are normal. Again, if in doubt about the condition of the cap, replace it with a new one.
9   Reattach the cap to the distributor, then tighten the screws or re-position the spring clips to hold it in place.
8   When replacing the cap, simply transfer the spark plug and coil wires, one at a time, from the old cap to the new cap. Be very careful not to mix up the wires!

---

47   Ignition timing check and adjustment

Refer to illustrations 47.1, 47.4 and 47.11

1   The proper ignition timing setting for your vehicle is printed on the VECI label located on the underside of the hood. Some special tools will be required for this procedure (**see illustration**).
2   On 2600 engines, locate the timing plate on the front of the engine, near the crankshaft pulley. The T mark is Top Dead Center (TDC). To locate which mark the notch in the pulley must line up with for the timing to be correct, count back from the 0 mark the number of degrees BTDC (Before Top Dead Center) noted on the VECI label. Normally each mark on the timing plate equals 5 degrees, so if your vehicle Specifications call for 6-degrees BTDC, you should make a mark with white paint or chalk at the 5 mark on the timing plate.
3   Locate the timing notch in the pulley and mark it with a dab of paint or chalk so it will be visible under the strobe light. To locate the notch it may be necessary to have an assistant temporarily turn the ignition off and on in short bursts to turn the crankshaft. **Warning:** *Stay clear of all moving engine components if the engine is turned in this manner!*
4   On the 1600/1800/2000/2200 engine, the timing mark scale is on the vibration damper and timing indicator (pointer) is stationary, attached to the engine (**see illustration**). Highlight the pointer and the

47.1   Tools needed to check and adjust the ignition timing

1   *Vacuum plugs — Vacuum hoses will, in most cases, have to be disconnected and plugged. Molded plugs in various shapes and sizes are available for this*
2   *Inductive pick-up timing light — Flashes a bright concentrated beam of light when the number one spark plug fires. Connect the leads according to the instructions supplied with the light*
3   *Distributor wrench — On some models, the hold-down bolt for the distributor is difficult to reach and turn with conventional wrenches or sockets. A special wrench like this must be used*

appropriate mark on the vibration damper with chalk or white paint (refer to the Emissions Control Information label).
5   Connect a tachometer according to the manufacturer's instructions and make sure the idle speed is correct. Adjust if necessary as described in Section 33.
6   Allow the engine to warm up to normal operating temperature. Be sure the air conditioner, if equipped, is off. On some models as noted on the VECI label, you must disconnect the distributor vacuum hose and plug it. On fuel injected models, unplug the green test connector and connect a jumper wire between the connecter terminal and a good ground (**see illustration 33.2a**).
7   With the ignition switch off, connect the pick-up of the timing light to the number one (front, closest to the radiator) spark plug wire. Use either a jumper lead between the wire and plug or an inductive-type pick-up. Don't piece the wire or attempt to insert a wire between the boot and plug wire. Connect the timing light power leads according to the manufacturer's instructions.
8   Make sure the wiring for the timing light is clear of all moving engine components, then start the engine. Race the engine two or three times, then allow it to idle for a minute.
9   Point the flashing timing light at the timing marks, again being careful not to come in contact with moving parts. The marks you highlighted should appear stationary. If the marks are in alignment, the timing is correct. If the marks aren't lined up, turn off the engine.
10   Loosen the distributor mounting bolt until the distributor can be rotated.

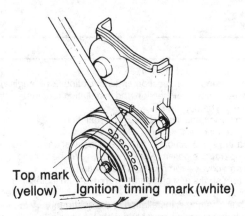

47.4   The timing marks are located on the pulley and the pointer is attached to the engine on 1600/1800/2000/2200 engines

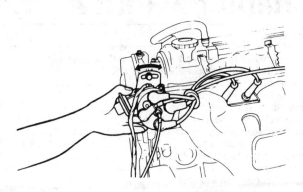

47.11   Ignition timing is adjusted by swiveling the distributor slightly either clockwise or counterclockwise

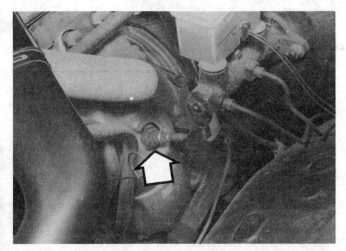

48.2   The oxygen sensor (arrow) threads into the exhaust manifold and is accessible in the engine compartment

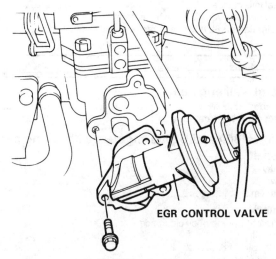

EGR CONTROL VALVE

49.2   EGR valve details

11   Start the engine and slowly rotate the distributor either left or right until the timing marks are aligned **(see illustration)**.
12   Shut off the engine and tighten the distributor mounting/adjusting bolts, being careful not to move the distributor.
13   Restart the engine and recheck the timing to make sure the marks are still in alignment.

48   Oxygen sensor replacement

Refer to illustration 48.2

1   The oxygen (exhaust gas) sensor, used on later models, should be replaced at the specified intervals.
2   The sensor is threaded into the exhaust manifold and can be identified by the wires attached to it **(see illustration)**. Replacement consists of disconnecting the wire harness and unthreading the sen-

sor from the manifold. Tighten the new sensor securely, then reconnect the wire harness.

49   EGR valve replacement (1985 and later 2000/2200 engine)

Refer to illustration 49.2

1   With the engine cold, disconnect the vacuum tube from the EGR valve.
2   Remove the retaining bolts and lift the EGR valve from the exhaust manifold **(see illustration)**.
3   To install, place the new EGR valve in position and install the retaining bolts. Tighten the bolts securely.
4   Connect the vacuum hose.
5   Start the engine, run it at idle and check for exhaust leaks.

Chapter 2 Part A   Engines

Contents

Specifications

General – all engines

Firing order	1-3-4-2
Cylinder numbers (front-to-rear)	1-2-3-4

B1600, B1800 and B2000 engines (with timing chain)

Camshaft
End play
New	0.001 to 0.007 in (0.02 to 0.18 mm)
Wear limit	0.008 in (0.20 mm)

Oil pump
Outer rotor-to-pump body clearance
New	0.006 to 0.010 in (0.14 to 0.25 mm)
Wear limit	0.012 in (0.30 mm)

Rotor end play
New	0.002 to 0.004 in (0.04 to 0.10 mm)
Wear limit	0.006 in (0.15 mm)

Clearance between rotor lobes
New	0.002 to 0.006 in (0.04 to 0.15 mm)
Wear limit	0.010 in (0.25 mm)

Clearance between pump shaft and body
New	0.0002 to 0.0020 in (0.006 to 0.051 mm)
Wear limit	0.004 in (0.10 mm)
Oil pump chain slack	0.157 in (4.0 mm) maximum

Torque specifications

	Ft-lbs
Rocker arm cover nuts	1.1 to 1.4
Intake manifold nuts/bolts	14 to 19
Exhaust manifold nuts/bolts	
B1600 and B1800	12 to 17
B2000	16 to 21
Camshaft sprocket nut	51 to 58
Cylinder head bolts	
B1600 and B1800	
Cold engine (initial)	56 to 60
Warm engine (final)	69 to 72
B2000	
Cold engine (initial)	65 to 69
Warm engine (final)	69 to 72
Crankshaft pulley-to-crankshaft bolt	101 to 108
Distributor drive gear nut	51 to 58
Oil pump sprocket nut	22 to 25
Oil pan bolts	5 to 7
Flywheel bolts	112 to 118
Miscellaneous	
6 mm bolt	5.8
8 mm bolt	13.7
10 mm bolt	27.5

Cylinder locations and firing order

12 mm bolt	47
14 mm bolt	66

B2000 and B2200 engines (with timing belt)
Camshaft
End play

New	0.003 to 0.006 in (0.08 to 0.16 mm)
Wear limit	0.008 in (0.20 mm)

Timing belt deflection . . . . 0.43 to 0.51 in (11 to 13 mm)

Oil pump (gear type)
Inner gear-to-crescent clearance

New	0.0010 to 0.0015 in (0.26 to 0.38 mm)
Wear limit	0.016 in (0.40 mm)

Outer gear-to-crescent clearance

New	0.0078 to 0.0126 in (0.02 to 0.32 mm)
Wear limit	0.016 in (0.40 mm)

Gear-to-cover clearance

New	0.0012 to 0.0025 in (0.03 to 0.063 mm)
Wear limit	0.040 in (0.10 mm)

Oil pump (rotor type)

Inner rotor-to-outer rotor clearance limit	0.007 in (0.018 mm)
Rotor-to-pump cover clearance limit	0.004 in (0.10 mm)
Outer rotor-to-pump body clearance limit	0.008 in (0.20 mm)

Torque specifications　　　　　　　　　　　　　　　　　　**Ft-lbs**

Rocker arm cover nuts	2 to 3
Intake manifold nuts/bolts	14 to 19
Exhaust manifold nuts/bolts	16 to 21
Camshaft sprocket bolt	35 to 48
Cylinder head bolts	59 to 64
Crankshaft pulley bolt	9 to 12.3
Oil cooler/filter adapter bolts	10.8 to 14.5

Oil pump **(see illustration 15.14)**

Bolt A*	14 to 19
Bolt B**	27 to 38
Oil strainer bolts	5.8 to 8.7
Oil pan bolts	5 to 9.0
Flywheel/driveplate bolts	71 to 76
Block end plate bolts	14 to 22
Timing belt cover nuts/bolts	5 to 7.2
Rear oil seal housing bolts	5.8 to 8.7
Rocker arm shaft assembly bolts	13 to 20
Front housing-to-cylinder head bolts	14 to 19
Timing belt tensioner lock bolt	27 to 38
Idler pulley bolt	27 to 38

Miscellaneous

6 mm bolt	5.8
8 mm bolt	13.7
10 mm bolt	27.5
12 mm bolt	47
14 mm bolt	66

*All bolts on 1986 and 1987 models　　**1988 and later models only*

B2600 (2.6L) engine (through 1988)
Timing chain tensioner spring free length . . . . 2.587 in (65.7 mm)

Balance shaft

Left bearing journal diameter	0.906 in (23 mm)
Left bearing oil clearance	0.0008 to 0.0024 in (0.02 to 0.06 mm)
Right bearing journal diameter	1.693 in (43 mm)
Right bearing oil clearance	0.0020 to 0.0035 in (0.05 to 0.09 mm)
Chain-to-guide clearance (slack)	0.008 to 0.031 in (0.2 to 0.8 mm)

Oil pump

Relief spring free length	1.850 in (47 mm)
Gear-to-housing clearance	0.0043 to 0.0059 in (0.11 to 0.15 mm)
Gear-to-pump body clearance	0.0008 to 0.0020 in (0.02 to 0.05 mm)
Gear-to-pump cover bearing clearance	0.0016 to 0.0028 in (0.04 to 0.07 mm)

Gear end play

Drive	0.0020 to 0.0043 in (0.05 to 0.11 mm)
Driven	0.0016 to 0.0039 in (0.04 to 0.10 mm)

Camshaft
End play

Standard	0.0008 to 0.007 in (0.02 to 0.18 mm)
Wear limit	0.008 (0.20 mm)

2A

Torque specifications   Ft-lbs

Intake manifold nuts	11 to 14
Exhaust manifold nuts	11 to 14
Cylinder head-to-block bolts (HOT)	72 to 79
Cylinder head-to-block bolts (COLD)	65 to 72
Cylinder head-to-timing chain case bolts	11 to 16
Crankshaft sprocket/pulley bolt	80 to 94
Camshaft bearing cap bolts	
All except bolt number 5	14 to 15
Bolt number 5	15 to 20
Flywheel/driveplate-to-crankshaft bolts	
1972 through 1988	94 to 101
1989 and later	67 to 72
Rocker arm cover bolts	3.6 to 5.1
Jet valves	13 to 15
Engine mount bracket	36 to 43
Distributor drive gear/camshaft sprocket bolt	
Timing chain cover bolts	8.7 to 10.2
Oil pan bolts	4.3 to 5.1
Timing chain guide bolts	7.2 to 8.7
Balance shaft drive gear/oil pump sprocket bolt	22 to 29
Balance shaft sprocket bolt	43 to 50
Balance shaft thrust plate bolts	7.3 to 7.9
Balance shaft chain guide bolts	
Left guide (A) and upper guide (B)	3.6 to 5.8
Lower guide (C)	
Upper bolt	5.8 to 6.5
Lower bolt	11 to 15
Oil pump sprocket bolt	22 to 29
Oil pump mounting bolt	5.7 to 6.5
Oil strainer bolts	11 to 16

B2600I (2.6L) engine (1989 and later)

General

Displacement	158.97 cubic inches (2.6 liters)
Intake/exhaust manifold warpage limit	0.006 inch
Balance shaft chain slack	1/8-inch

Camshaft

Endplay	0.0008 to 0.0059 inch
Runout	0.0012 inch
Camshaft journal diameters	
Journals 1 and 5	1.1788 to 1.1797 inches
Journals 2, 3 and 4	1.1776 to 1.1785 inches
Journal oil clearances	
Standard	
Journals 1 and 5	0.0014 to 0.0033 inch
Journals 2, 3 and 4	0.0026 to 0.0045 inch
Service limit	0.006 inch
Lobe height	
Intake	1.6423 inches
Exhaust	1.6531 inches
Balance shaft oil clearance	
Front	0.0020 to 0.0045 in
Center and rear	0.0031 to 0.0057 in
Oil pump	
Side clearance	0.0039 maximum
Tooth tip clearance	0.0071 maximum
Outer rotor-to-pump body clearance	0.0078 maximum
Pressure relief valve spring – free length	1.827 inches

Torque specifications   Ft-lbs (unless otherwise indicated)

Camshaft bearing cap bolts	14 to 19
Valve cover bolts	52 to 78 in-lbs
Balance shaft chain guide bolts	156 in-lbs
Timing chain guide bolts	70 to 95 in-lbs
Camshaft sprocket bolt	37 to 40
Crankshaft pulley bolt	131 to 144
Cylinder head bolts (except bolts "A" in illustration 19.27d)	
First step	21
Second step	42
Third step	59 to 64
Cylinder head-to-timing chain cover bolts (bolt A)	12 to 16
Flywheel/driveplate-to-crankshaft bolts	68 to 72
Intake manifold bolts	14 to 18
Exhaust manifold bolts	16 to 20

Balance shaft sprocket bolt	27 to 39
Oil pan-to-engine bolts	70 to 95 in-lbs
Oil pump pick-up tube bolts	70 to 95 in-lbs
Oil pump body bolts	14 to 18
Oil pump pressure relief valve	28 to 44
Rear main oil seal housing bolts	70 to 95 in-lbs
Timing chain/balance shaft chain access cover	
Bolts	70 to 95 in-lbs
Nuts	61 to 86 in-lbs
Timing chain cover bolts	14 to 18
Water pump bolts	See Chapter 3

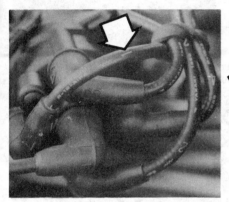

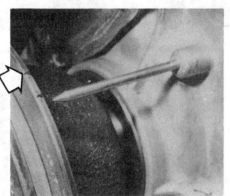

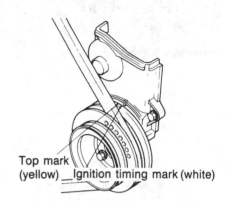

Top mark (yellow) __ Ignition timing mark (white)

2A

3.5 Mark the distributor directly under the number one plug wire terminal in the cap – the wires may be marked (arrow)

3.8a Align the second notch in the drivebelt pulley (arrow) with the pointer on the front of the engine (early models)

3.8b Align the yellow (TDC) mark with the pointer on the timing cover (2.2L engine shown, others similar)

1 General information

This Part of Chapter 2 is devoted to in-vehicle repair procedures for the engine. All information concerning engine removal and installation and engine block and cylinder head overhaul can be found in Part B of this Chapter.

The following repair procedures are based on the assumption that the engine is installed in the vehicle. If the engine has been removed from the vehicle and mounted on a stand, many of the steps outlined in this Part of Chapter 2 will not apply.

The Specifications included in this Part of Chapter 2 apply only to the procedures contained in this Part. Part B of Chapter 2 contains the Specifications necessary for cylinder head and engine block rebuilding.

2 Repair operations possible with the engine in the vehicle

Many major repair operations can be accomplished without removing the engine from the vehicle.

Clean the engine compartment and the exterior of the engine with some type of degreaser before any work is done. It will make the job easier and help keep dirt out of the internal areas of the engine.

Depending on the components involved, it may be helpful to remove the hood to improve access to the engine as repairs are performed (refer to Chapter 11 if necessary). Cover the fenders to prevent damage to the paint. Special pads are available, but an old bedspread or blanket will also work.

If vacuum, exhaust, oil or coolant leaks develop, indicating a need for gasket or seal replacement, the repairs can generally be made with the engine in the vehicle. The intake and exhaust manifold gaskets, timing chain cover gasket, oil pan gasket, crankshaft oil seals and cylinder head gasket are all accessible with the engine in place.

Exterior engine components, such as the intake and exhaust manifolds, the oil pan (and the oil pump), the water pump, the starter motor, the alternator, the distributor and the fuel system components can be removed for repair with the engine in place.

Since the cylinder head can be removed without pulling the engine, valve component and camshaft servicing can also be accomplished with the engine in the vehicle. Replacement of the timing chain or belt and sprockets is also possible with the engine in the vehicle.

In extreme cases caused by a lack of necessary equipment, repair or replacement of piston rings, pistons, connecting rods and rod bearings is possible with the engine in the vehicle. However, this practice is not rec-

ommended because of the cleaning and preparation work that must be done to the components involved.

3 Top Dead Center (TDC) for number one piston – locating

Refer to illustrations 3.5, 3.8a and 3.8b

Note: *The following procedure is based on the assumption that the distributor is correctly installed. If you are trying to locate TDC to install the distributor correctly, piston position must be determined by feeling for compression at the number one spark plug hole, then aligning the ignition timing marks as described in Step 8.*

1   Top Dead Center (TDC) is the highest point in the cylinder that each piston reaches as it travels up-and-down when the crankshaft turns. Each piston reaches TDC on the compression stroke and again on the exhaust stroke, but TDC generally refers to piston position on the compression stroke.

2   Positioning the piston(s) at TDC is an essential part of many procedures such as rocker arm removal, camshaft and timing chain/belt/sprocket removal and distributor removal.

3   Before beginning this procedure, be sure to place the transmission in Neutral and apply the parking brake or block the rear wheels. Also, disable the ignition system by detaching the coil wire from the center terminal of the distributor cap and grounding it on the block with a jumper wire. Remove the spark plugs (see Chapter 1).

4   In order to bring any piston to TDC, the crankshaft must be turned using one of the methods outlined below. When looking at the front of the engine, normal crankshaft rotation is *clockwise.*

   a) The preferred method is to turn the crankshaft with a socket and ratchet attached to the bolt threaded into the front of the crankshaft.

   b) A remote starter switch, which may save some time, can also be used. Follow the instructions included with the switch. Once the piston is close to TDC, use a socket and ratchet as described in the previous paragraph.

   c) If an assistant is available to turn the ignition switch to the Start position in short bursts, you can get the piston close to TDC without a remote starter switch. Make sure your assistant is out of the vehicle, away from the ignition switch, then use a socket and ratchet as described in Paragraph a) to complete the procedure.

5   Note the position of the terminal for the number one spark plug wire on the distributor cap **(see illustration)**. If the wire/terminal isn't marked, follow the plug wire from the number one cylinder spark plug to the cap.

4.10   Engines with a timing chain have a semi-circular plug at the front (arrow) that must be in place

6   Use a felt-tip pen or chalk to make a mark on the distributor body directly under the terminal.
7   Detach the cap from the distributor and set it aside (see Chapter 1 if necessary).
8   Turn the crankshaft (see Paragraph 3 above) until the notch in the crankshaft pulley is aligned with the 0, T or pointer on the timing plate (located at the front of the engine) **(see illustrations)**.
9   Look at the distributor rotor – it should be pointing directly at the mark you made on the distributor body.
10   If the rotor is 180 degrees off, the number one piston is at TDC on the exhaust stroke.
11   To get the piston to TDC on the compression stroke, turn the crankshaft one complete turn (360-degrees) clockwise. The rotor should now be pointing at the mark on the distributor. When the rotor is pointing at the number one spark plug wire terminal in the distributor cap and the ignition timing marks are aligned, the number one piston is at TDC on the compression stroke.
12   After the number one piston has been positioned at TDC on the compression stroke, TDC for any of the remaining pistons can be located by turning the crankshaft and following the firing order. Mark the remaining spark plug wire terminal locations on the distributor body just like you did for the number one terminal, then number the marks to correspond with the cylinder numbers. As you turn the crankshaft, the rotor will also turn. When it's pointing directly at one of the marks on the distributor, the piston for that particular cylinder is at TDC on the compression stroke.

---

4   Rocker arm cover – removal and installation

Refer to illustration 4.10

1   Disconnect the negative cable from the battery.
2   Remove the air cleaner assembly (see Chapter 4).
3   Disconnect the hoses and wires from the rocker arm cover.
4   Detach the wire holders from the rocker arm cover.
5   Clearly label and then disconnect any emission hoses which cross over the rocker arm cover.
6   Disconnect the throttle cable from the rocker arm cover and carburetor (see Chapter 4).
7   If so equipped, detach the cruise control and automatic transmission cables from the rocker arm cover.
8   Unbolt the rocker arm cover and lift it off. If the cover sticks to the cylinder head, gently pry all around it. Take your time to avoid damaging the cover.
9   Thoroughly clean the rocker arm cover and remove all traces of old gasket material.
10   Install the cover with a new gasket and, on timing chain equipped models, the end seal **(see illustration)**. Tighten the fasteners to the specified torque.
11   The remaining steps are the reverse of removal.

---

5   Intake manifold – removal and installation

Refer to illustration 5.8
Warning: *Gasoline is extremely flammable, so extra precautions must be*

5.8   Slip the intake manifold off the cylinder head studs and lift it out of the engine compartment

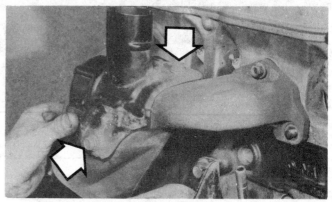

6.6   The exhaust manifold heat shield may have to be removed to gain access to the manifold nuts/bolts

taken when working on any part of the fuel system. Make sure the engine is cool. Don't smoke or allow open flames or bare light bulbs near the work area. Also, do not work in a garage if a natural gas-type appliance with a pilot light is present. Have a fire extinguisher handy.
1   Disconnect the negative cable from the battery.
2   Drain the cooling system (see Chapter 1).
3   Remove the air cleaner (carbureted models) or disconnect the intake duct from the throttle body (fuel injected models) (see Chapter 4).
4   Clearly label and then disconnect all hoses, brackets and emission lines which run to the carburetor or throttle body/intake manifold assembly.
5   Disconnect the fuel lines from the carburetor or fuel rail (relieve the fuel pressure first) and cap the fittings to prevent leakage (see Chapter 4).
6   Disconnect the throttle cable from the carburetor or throttle body (see Chapter 4).
7   Detach the cable which runs from the carburetor or throttle body to the transmission (automatic transmission only) and the cruise control cable, on vehicles so equipped.
8   Unbolt the intake manifold and remove it from the engine **(see illustration)**. If it sticks, tap the manifold with a soft-face hammer. **Caution:** *Do not pry between the gasket sealing surfaces.*
9   Thoroughly clean the manifold and cylinder head mating surfaces, removing all traces of gasket material.
10   Install the manifold, using a new gasket and tighten the nuts in several stages, working from the center out, until the specified torque is reached.
11   The remaining steps are the reverse of removal.
12   Add coolant, run the engine and check for leaks and proper operation.

---

6   Exhaust manifold – removal and installation

Refer to illustrations 6.6 and 6.11
Warning: *Allow the engine to cool completely before beginning this procedure.*

1   Disconnect the negative cable from the battery.
2   Raise the vehicle and support it securely on jackstands.

6.11 Be sure to position new gaskets over the studs before installing the exhaust manifold – do not use sealant!

7.4 When using a chain wrench to keep the crankshaft from turning, protect the pulley with a rag – if the pulley is nicked or otherwise damaged, it will destroy the drivebelt

3   Disconnect the exhaust pipe from the bottom of the exhaust manifold (see Chapter 4).
4   On carbureted models, remove the air cleaner assembly (see Chapter 4).
5   Unplug the oxygen sensor wire, on models so equipped.
6   Remove the heat shield **(see illustration)** from the exhaust manifold (except models with permanent "spot welded in place" shields).
7   Remove the brackets and emission components from the exhaust manifold (see Chapter 6).
8   Unbolt the manifold and remove it from the engine compartment.
9   Clean and inspect all the threaded fasteners and repair as necessary.
10   Remove any traces of gasket material from the mating surfaces and inspect them for wear and cracks.
11   Using new gasket(s) **(see illustration)**, install the manifold and tighten the nuts in several steps, working from the center out, to the specified torque.
12   The remaining steps are the reverse of removal.
13   Run the engine and check for exhaust leaks.

3   Remove the timing belt and crankshaft sprocket, if equipped (see Section 11).
4   On timing chain equipped models, remove the crankshaft bolt. To keep the crankshaft from turning, set the parking brake, block the wheels and put the transmission in high gear (manual transmission only) or wrap a chain wrench around the pulley **(see illustration)**. **Caution:** *Don't overtighten the chain wrench, as it may damage the pulley, which could result in rapid belt failure.*
5   Unbolt and remove the lower crankshaft pulley **(see illustration)**.
6   Using a screwdriver or a seal puller, pry the seal out of the housing. Be careful not to damage the crankshaft or seal bore.
7   Thoroughly clean and inspect the seal bore and sealing surface.
8   Lubricate the outer edge of the new seal with engine oil and drive it into place with a large socket or piece of pipe and a hammer.
9   Reinstall the timing belt, (if removed) and crankshaft pulley and bolt. Be sure to align the pulley keyway with the key **(see illustration)**. Tighten the bolt to the specified torque.
10   Reinstall the drivebelts, radiator and shroud. Run the engine and check for leaks.
11   Reinstall the belly pan.

---

7   Crankshaft front oil seal – replacement

Refer to illustrations 7.4, 7.5 and 7.9

1   Remove the drivebelts (see Chapter 1) and unbolt the belly pan.
2   Remove the radiator and shroud (see Chapter 3). On B2600i models (1989 and later), remove the cooling fan and water pump pulley.

---

8   Timing chain tensioner – adjustment, removal and installation

---

Note: *This procedure applies to pre-1985 models only. For 2.6L engine timing chain tensioner information, see Section 10.*

7.5 The crankshaft pulley may slip off by hand, but it may require a puller if it's stuck

7.9 After the seal is installed flush with the housing, align the key (arrow) with the slot in the pulley

8.4   Wedge a screwdriver in the tensioner while compressing the snubber spring

1   Timing chain adjustment is normally taken care of automatically. However, after removal and installation of the timing chain, it is recommended that the adjustment procedure in this Section be followed (Steps 2 through 9, or 15 through 22, as appropriate).

Hydraulic type

Adjustment

Refer to illustration 8.4

2   Remove the water pump (refer to Chapter 3 if necessary).
3   Remove the cover from the timing chain tensioner (three nuts and washers). Be careful not to damage the sealing surfaces if the cover is stuck to the engine.
4   Rotate the crankshaft slightly in the direction of normal rotation (clockwise), then lift the release on the tensioner and compress the snubber spring as far as possible. Wedge a screwdriver in the tensioner to prevent it from releasing **(see illustration)**.
5   Remove the two plugs and aluminum washers from the holes in the timing chain cover. Loosen the chain guide screws through the holes in the cover.
6   Push on the top of the guide through the adjusting hole in the cylinder head, then tighten the guide screws.
7   Remove the screwdriver from the tensioner to allow the snubber to take up the spring slack.
8   Install the chain tensioner cover and gasket, using a new gasket and RTV sealant.
9   Install the water pump (refer to Chapter 3 if necessary).

Removal and installation

Refer to illustration 8.11

10 To remove the tensioner, initially proceed as described in Steps 2 and 3.
11 Remove the bolts from the tensioner, then withdraw it through the hole in the timing chain cover. Hold the body and shoe together as there is a spring inside **(see illustration)**.
12 When installing the tensioner, wedge a screwdriver in the tensioner release mechanism while compressing the snubber spring **(see illustration 8.4)**.
13 Without removing the screwdriver, insert the tensioner through the hole in the cover, then install and tighten the bolts.
14 Adjust the tensioner as described above.

Spring type

Adjustment

Refer to illustration 8.17

15 Remove the water pump (see Chapter 3) and the rocker arm cover (see Section 4).
16 Remove the cover from the timing chain tensioner (three nuts and

8.11   Hydraulic chain tensioner components — exploded view

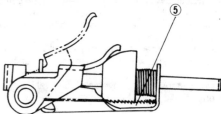

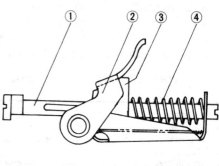

8.17   Spring type chain tensioner components

    1 Slide pin   4 Spring
    2 Arm   5 Wedge plate
    3 Wedge

washers). Be careful not to damage the sealing surfaces if the cover is stuck to the engine.
17 Rotate the crankshaft slightly in the direction of normal rotation, then pass a screwdriver down the opening at the side of the camshaft sprocket. Depress the slide pin as far as possible and turn it clockwise 90 degrees **(see illustration)**.
18 Remove the two plugs and aluminum washers from the holes in the timing chain cover. Loosen the chain guide through the holes.
19 Push on the top of the guide through the adjusting hole in the cylinder head, then tighten the guide screws.
20 Release the tensioner slide pin by turning it counterclockwise.
21 Install the chain tensioner cover and gasket using a new gasket and RTV sealant.
22 Install the water pump (refer to Chapter 3 if necessary).

Removal and installation

23 To remove the tensioner, initially proceed as described in Steps 15 and 16.
24 Remove the bolt and withdraw the tensioner through the hole in the timing chain cover.
25 When installing the tensioner, depress the slide pin all the way and turn it clockwise 90 degrees to lock the wedge.
26 Insert the tensioner through the hole in the timing chain cover, then install and tighten the bolt.
27 Adjust the tensioner as described above.

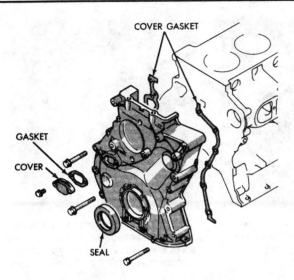

9.9a 2.6L engine timing chain cover and related components –
exploded view (models through 1988 shown, later models similar)

9 Timing chain cover – removal and installation

Refer to illustrations 9.9a and 9.9b

1 Remove the radiator and water pump (see Chapter 3).
2 Remove the oil pan (see Section 20).
3 Remove the cylinder head (see Section 19). **Note:** *Although it is possible to remove the timing chain cover without removing the cylinder head, it is not recommended. The head gasket seals the gap between the timing chain cover and head. During disassembly the gasket will probably tear, leading to oil leaks later.*
4 Remove the crankshaft pulley (see Section 7). On 1989 and later B2600i models, remove the power steering pump and bracket (see Chapter 10).
5 Remove the air pump (if equipped) and brackets (see Chapter 6). On 1989 and later B2600i models, remove coolant bypass pipe.
6 On A/C equipped models, unbolt the compressor and set it aside without disconnecting the refrigerant hoses. **Warning:** *Do not disconnect any refrigerant lines unless the system pressure has been discharged by an A/C technician.*
7 On 1989 and later B2600i models, remove the alternator and bracket. On all other models, remove the bolt holding the alternator adjusting bracket to the timing chain cover, then move the bracket toward the alternator.
8 Remove all wires, lines and brackets from the timing chain cover.
9 Remove the timing chain cover bolts, noting the locations of the various size bolts **(see illustrations)**. Tap on the cover with a soft-face hammer to separate it from the engine block. If the cover doesn't come loose easily, recheck for any remaining bolts.
10 Thoroughly clean away all traces of gasket material. Take extra care when scraping aluminum parts since they gouge easily.
11 Affix a new gasket with RTV sealer on both sides and position the cover on the engine.
12 Install the bolts and tighten them to the specified torque in three or four steps.
13 Perform the remaining steps in the reverse order of removal.
14 Be sure to add oil and coolant. Run the engine and check for leaks.

10 Timing chain/sprockets – removal, inspection and installation

2.6L engine

Refer to illustrations 10.5, 10.6, 10.7, 10.8, 10.9a, 10.9b, 10.9c and 10.10

1 The balance shaft chain and sprockets must be removed to gain access to the timing chain assembly (Section 12) and the number one piston

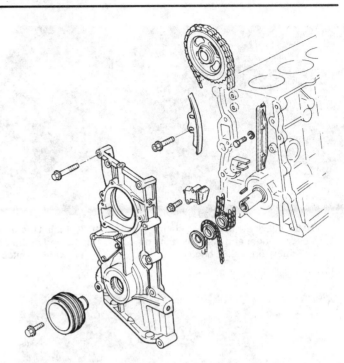

9.9b Mazda engine timing chain cover and related components –
exploded view

must be at TDC (see Section 3).
2 Depress the timing chain tensioner plunger on the oil pump (models through 1988) or unbolt and remove the tensioner (1989 and later models) and slide the camshaft sprocket, the crankshaft sprocket and the timing chain off the engine as an assembly. Do not lose the key that indexes the crankshaft sprocket in the proper place. On 1988 and earlier models, remove the timing chain tensioner plunger and spring from the oil pump.
3 Remove the camshaft sprocket holder (if equipped) and the right and left timing chain guides from the front of the engine block.
4 Inspect the sprocket teeth for wear and damage. Check the chain for cracked plates and pitted or worn rollers. Check the chain tensioner rubber shoe (if equipped) for wear and the tensioner spring for cracks and deterioration. Measure the tensioner spring free length and compare it to the Specifications (if the spring is a separate part). Check the chain guides for wear and damage. Replace any defective parts with new ones.
5 Install the sprocket holder **(see illustration)** and the right and left timing chain guides on the engine block. Tighten the bolts securely. The upper bolt in the left timing chain guide should be installed fingertight only. Then coat the entire length of the chain contact surfaces of the guides with clean, high-quality moly-base grease.

10.5 Installing the camshaft sprocket holder on the
engine block (2.6L engine)

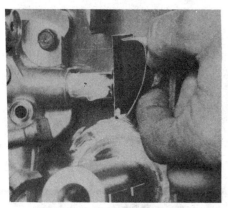

10.6   Lubricate the timing chain tensioner plunger and install it in the oil pump bore (2.6L engine)

10.7   Install the timing chain sprocket on the end of the crankshaft with the wide shoulder facing out

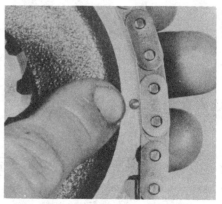

10.8   Mesh the camshaft sprocket and the timing chain with the mark on the sprocket directly opposite the plated link on the chain (1988 and earlier models shown)

10.9a   Installing the timing chain on the crankshaft sprocket (note that the sprocket mark and the plated link are opposite each other) (1988 and earlier models)

8   Mesh the camshaft sprocket with the chain, lining up the plated link on the chain with the marked tooth on the sprocket (**see illustration**). On 1988 and later models, the mark on the sprocket is a line.

9   Slip the chain over the crankshaft sprocket, lining up the plated links on the chain with the marked tooth on the sprocket (**see illustration**). Slide the crankshaft sprocket all the way onto the crankshaft while, on 1988 and earlier models, depressing the chain tensioner so the chain fits into place between the guides. Rest the camshaft sprocket on the sprocket holder (**see illustration**) and make sure the plated links and mating marks are aligned properly. **Caution:** *Do not rotate the crankshaft for any reason until the cylinder head and camshaft have been properly installed.*

10   On 1989 and later push the timing chain tensioner plunger into the tensioner, lift the lever on the tensioner to lock it in place, then insert a fabricated pin through the hole in the lever to hold the lever in place (**see illustration**). **Note:** *Leave the pin in this position until the cylinder head is installed and the camshaft sprocket is bolted to the camshaft.*

11   On 1989 and later models, after installation of the timing chain cover and the cylinder head (and the camshaft sprocket has been bolted to the camshaft), remove the tensioner access cover from the timing chain cover and remove the retaining pin from the chain tensioner. Reinstall the service cover with a new gasket and tighten the bolts to the torque listed in this Chapter's Specifications.

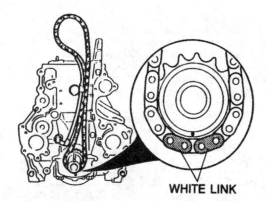

WHITE LINK

10.9b   On 1989 and later models, install the timing chain on the crankshaft sprocket with the plated chain links flanking the mark on the crank gear

6   Turn the crankshaft bolt with a large wrench until the number one piston is at top dead center. The piston is at TDC when it's flush with the top of the engine block. On 1988 and earlier models, apply a layer of clean moly-base grease or engine assembly lube to the timing chain tensioner plunger and install the tensioner spring and plunger loosely into the oil pump body (**see illustration**).

7   Position the timing chain sprocket on the end of the crankshaft with the wide shoulder facing out (**see illustration**). Line up the keyway in the sprocket with the key on the crankshaft.

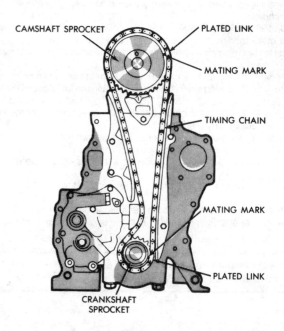

CAMSHAFT SPROCKET — PLATED LINK

— MATING MARK

— TIMING CHAIN

— MATING MARK

— PLATED LINK

CRANKSHAFT SPROCKET

10.9c   Correct timing chain and sprocket relationship – 2.6L engines through 1988

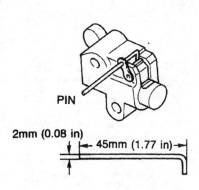

PIN

2mm (0.08 in)
45mm (1.77 in)

10.10   On 1989 and later models, insert a pin fabricated from a piece of coat hanger or welding rod through the tensioner lock lever to keep the tensioner plunger in the retracted position

10.13   The oil slinger (arrow) fits over the crankshaft outside of the oil pump drive chain (Mazda engine)

10.15   A spacer (arrow) fits between the oil pump sprocket and timing chain sprocket (Mazda engine)

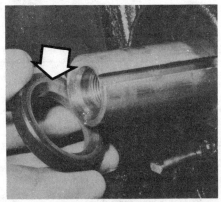

10.17   Be sure the inner spacer is in place – the chamfered side (arrow) must face in (Mazda engine)

17   Mesh the crankshaft sprocket in the timing chain with the mark on the sprocket between the two bright chain links, then position them both on the crankshaft. Where applicable, install the spacer and key first **(see illustration)**.
18   Slide the spacer on first, then position the oil pump drive chain and sprocket on the crankshaft.
19   Make sure the sprockets are seated, then install the oil slinger.
20   Install the oil pump as described in Section 16.
21   If they were removed, install the camshaft, sprocket and chain. Align the nickel plated links on the chain with the marks on the camshaft and crankshaft sprockets as they are reinstalled **(see illustrations)**.

2A

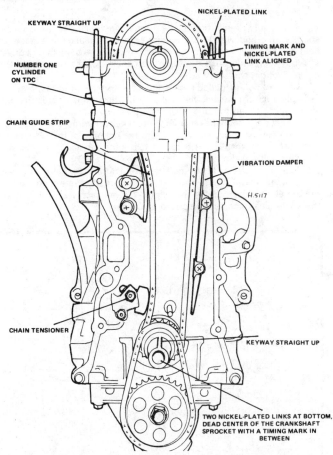

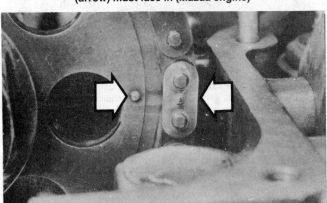

10.21a   The single bright link must align with the dot on the camshaft sprocket (arrows) – Mazda engine with timing chain

Pre-1985 models

Refer to illustrations 10.13, 10.15, 10.17, 10.21a and 10.21b

12   Position the number one piston at TDC (see Section 3) and remove the timing chain cover (see Section 9) and loosen the screws which retain the timing chain guide.
13   Remove the oil slinger from the crankshaft **(see illustration)**.
14   Remove the oil pump as described in Section 16, then take off the oil pump drive chain.
15   Remove the oil pump sprocket from the crankshaft. Where applicable, remove the spacer from the crankshaft **(see illustration)**.
16   Pull the chain and sprocket off the crankshaft. If the chain and sprocket must be removed from the camshaft, the camshaft will have to be removed first (see Section 18).

10.21b   Make sure the timing chain and sprockets are installed with the marks aligned as shown here – Mazda engine with timing chain

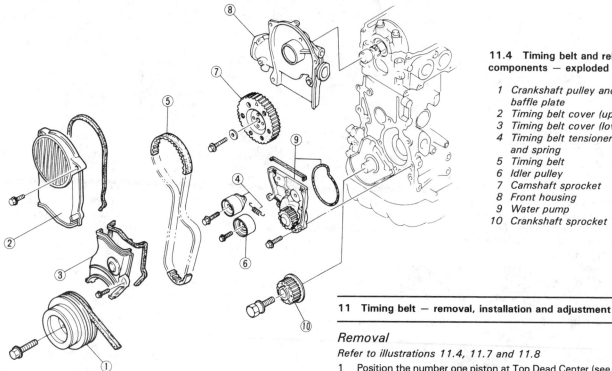

11.4   Timing belt and related components — exploded view

1   Crankshaft pulley and baffle plate
2   Timing belt cover (upper)
3   Timing belt cover (lower)
4   Timing belt tensioner and spring
5   Timing belt
6   Idler pulley
7   Camshaft sprocket
8   Front housing
9   Water pump
10 Crankshaft sprocket

11   Timing belt — removal, installation and adjustment

Removal

Refer to illustrations 11.4, 11.7 and 11.8

1   Position the number one piston at Top Dead Center (see Section 3).
2   Disconnect the negative cable from the battery.
3   Remove the drivebelts and spark plugs (see Chapter 1).
4   Remove the crankshaft pulley **(see illustration)**. Refer to Section 7 if necessary.
5   If so equipped, remove the three air injection tubes which run in front of the timing belt cover (see Chapter 6).
6   Unbolt and remove the upper and lower timing belt covers **(see illustration 11.4)**. Don't lose the rubber seals.
7   Be sure the camshaft mark (A) lines up with the mark on the front housing and the crankshaft sprocket notch lines up with the pointer on the oil pump housing **(see illustration)**.
8   If you plan on reinstalling the timing belt, paint an arrow on it to indicate the direction of rotation **(see illustration)**.
9   Loosen the timing belt tensioner lock bolt, move the tensioner toward the intake side of the engine and retighten the lock bolt.
10 Slip the belt off the sprockets and remove it from the engine.
11 Inspect the belt for damage, peeling, wear, cracks, hardening, crimping and signs of oil or other fluid contamination. The belt should be replaced if any of these conditions exist or if the specified mileage has elapsed (see Chapter 1).

22 Where a hydraulic timing chain tensioner is used, compress the snubber ring and wedge a screwdriver in the release mechanism to hold it in place. Install the tensioner and tighten the bolts (screwdriver still in place), then push the top of the chain guide strip toward the chain. Tighten the screws.
23 Where a spring loaded timing chain tensioner is used, depress the slide pin and turn it clockwise 90° to lock the wedge. Install the tensioner and tighten the bolt.
24 Remove the screwdriver from the tensioner (hydraulic type) or turn the slide pin using a screwdriver from the opening at the side of the camshaft sprocket (spring type), to allow the tensioner to release.
25 Reinstall the timing chain cover (see Section 9).
26 The remainder of the installation procedure is the reverse of the removal procedure. When finished, fill the cooling system and adjust the drivebelt tension (refer to Chapter 1 if necessary). Finally adjust the valve clearances as described in Chapter 1.

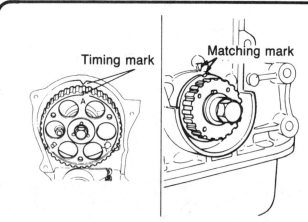

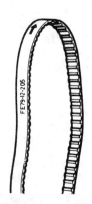

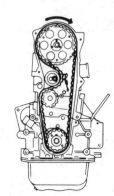

11.7   Be sure the marks are aligned as shown here before and after timing belt installation

11.8   If you plan to reuse the belt, paint an arrow on it to indicate the direction of rotation

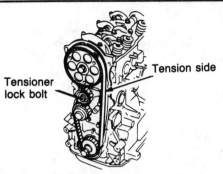

**11.14   Slip the belt over the sprockets so that moderate
tension is maintained**

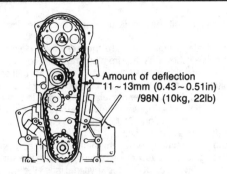

**11.17   Check the belt deflection midway between the crankshaft
and camshaft sprockets**

2A

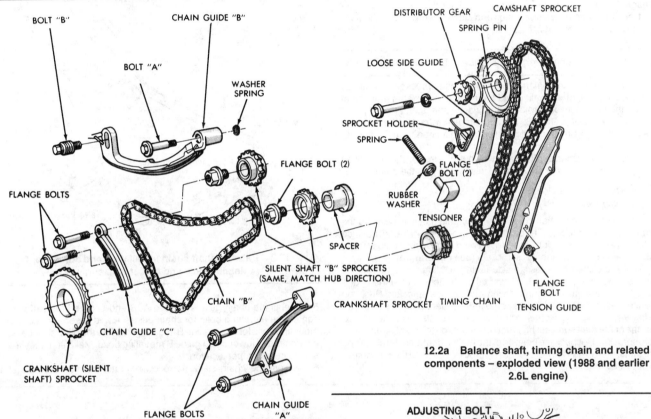

**12.2a   Balance shaft, timing chain and related
components – exploded view (1988 and earlier
2.6L engine)**

Installation

Refer to illustration 11.14

12   Make sure the crankshaft and camshaft sprocket timing marks are still aligned.

13   If the old belt is being reinstalled, make sure the arrow is pointed in the proper direction.

14   Slip the belt onto the camshaft and crankshaft sprockets from the tension (right) side so the tension is maintained **(see illustration)**.

Adjustment

Refer to illustration 11.17

15   Loosen the tensioner lock bolt so only the spring is applying pressure.

16   Install the crankshaft pulley bolt and use it to turn the crankshaft in the normal direction of rotation (clockwise) through two complete revolutions (720-degrees) so equal tension is applied to both sides of the timing belt. Tighten the lock bolt to the specified torque.

17   Recheck the timing mark alignment and check the deflection of the belt midway between the crankshaft and camshaft sprockets on the tension side **(see illustration)**. Compare it to the Specifications. If the deflection is incorrect, repeat the adjustment operation.

18   Reinstall the remaining parts in the reverse order of removal.

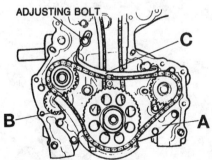

**12.2b   Locations of balance shaft chain guide A, B and C (1989
and later models)**

**12   Balance shaft chain/sprockets – removal and inspection
(2.6L engine only)**

Refer to illustrations 12.2a and 12.2b

1   Remove the timing chain cover (Section 9).

2   Remove the chain guides labeled A, B and C **(see illustrations)**. Each guide is held in place by two bolts. Draw a simple diagram showing

the location of each bolt so it can be returned to the same hole from which it was removed.

3   Reinstall the large bolt in the end of the crankshaft. Hold it in place with a wrench to prevent the crankshaft from turning while loosening the bolt on the end of the right balance shaft, the bolt attaching the right balance shaft drive sprocket to the oil pump shaft and the bolt in the end of the left balance shaft. On 1988 and earlier models, if the bolt in the end of the right balance shaft is difficult to loosen, remove the oil pump and balance shaft as an assembly (see Section 17), then remove the bolt with the balance shaft securely clamped in a vise.

4   Slide the crankshaft sprocket, the balance shaft sprockets and the chain off the engine as an assembly. Leave the bolt in the end of the right balance shaft in place. Do not lose the keys that index the sprockets to the shafts.

5   Check the sprocket teeth for wear and damage. Check the sprocket cushion rings and ring guides (balance shaft sprockets only) for wear and damage. Rotate the cushion rings and check for smooth operation. Inspect the chain for cracked side plates and pitted or worn rollers. Replace any defective or worn parts.

---

13   Balance shaft chain/sprockets – installation (2.6L engine only)

1   Before installing the balance shaft chain and sprockets, the timing chain must be properly installed and the number one piston must be at TDC on the compression stroke. Both balance shafts and the oil pump should also be in place. On 1989 and later models, retract the timing chain tensioner and hold it in this position, following the procedure in Section 10, Step 10.

2   Slide the crankshaft sprocket part way onto the front of the crankshaft by lining up the keyway in the sprocket with the key on the shaft.

1988 and earlier models

Refer to illustrations 13.3, 13.5, 13.6 and 13.8

3   Install the balance shaft chain onto the crankshaft sprocket and the left balance shaft sprocket. The dished or recessed side of the left balance shaft sprocket must face out. Line up the plated links on the chain with the mating marks stamped into the sprockets **(see illustration)**.

4   With the dished or recessed side facing in, slide the right balance shaft sprocket part way onto the lower oil pump gear shaft. Line up the plated link on the chain with the mating mark on the sprocket. Push the balance shaft sprockets all the way onto their respective shafts, lining up the keyways in the sprockets with the keys on the shafts. Simultaneously, push the crankshaft sprocket back until it bottoms on the crankshaft timing chain sprocket. Recheck the position of the mating marks on the chain and sprockets, then install the balance shaft sprocket bolts and tighten them to the specified torque.

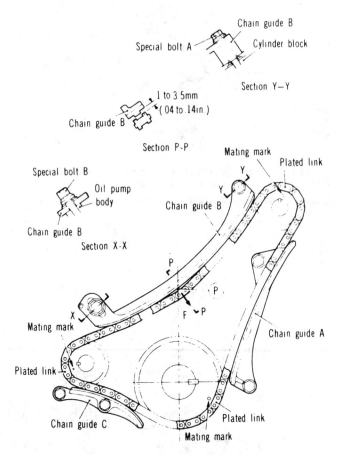

13.3   Balance shaft chain installation and adjustment details (1988 and earlier 2.6L engine)

---

5   Install the chain guides labeled A, B and C **(see illustration)** and tighten the mounting bolts for chain guides A and C securely (leave the mounting bolts for chain guide B finger-tight). Note the difference between the upper and lower chain guide B mounting bolts. Make sure they are installed in the proper location.

6   Adjust the chain slack as follows: rotate the right balance shaft

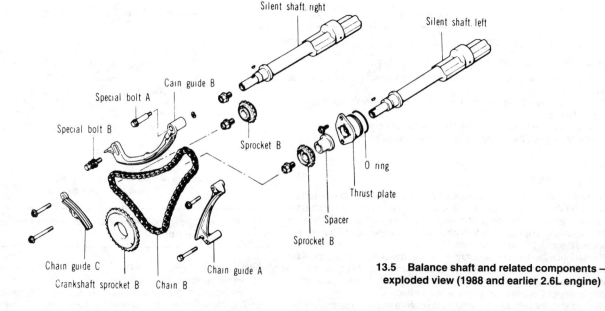

13.5   Balance shaft and related components – exploded view (1988 and earlier 2.6L engine)

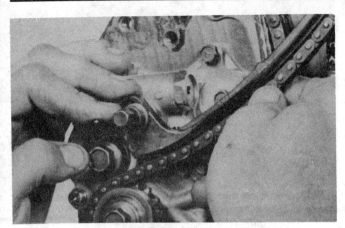

13.6   Adjusting the balance shaft chain slack (1988 and earlier 2.6L engine)

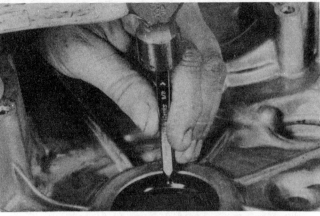

13.8   Drive the old oil seal out of the timing chain cover with a hammer and punch

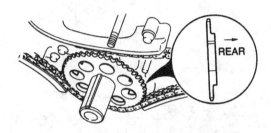

13.12a   Assembly direction of the balance shaft gear on the crankshaft (1989 and later models)

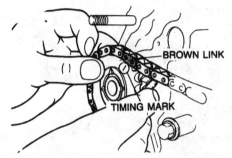

13.12b   Line up the brown link of the balance shaft chain with the mark on the idler gear (1989 and later models)

2A

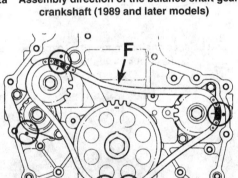

13.12c   Make sure all five marks are in alignment when the balance shaft chain is installed (F indicates the point where excess chain slack is taken up during adjustment) (1989 and later models)

clockwise and the left balance shaft counterclockwise so the chain slack is collected at point P. Pull the chain with your finger tips in the direction of arrow F, then move the lower end of the chain guide B up or down, as required **(see illustration)**, until the clearance between the chain and the guide (chain slack) is as specified. Tighten the chain guide B mounting bolts securely, then recheck the slack to make sure it has not changed. If the chain is not tensioned properly, engine noise and damage will result.

7   Apply a coat of clean moly-base grease to the chain and chain guides.

8   Using a hammer and punch, drive the oil seal out of the timing chain case **(see illustration)**.

9   Lay a new seal in place – make sure the spring faces in – and tap around it with a block of wood and a hammer until it's properly seated.

10   Reinstall the timing chain cover and related components (see Section 9).

11   Apply a thin layer of clean moly-base grease to the seal contact surface of the crankshaft pulley, then slide it onto the crankshaft. Install the bolt and tighten it finger-tight only. **Note:** *The bolt should be tightened to*

the specified torque only after the cylinder head and camshaft have been installed.

1989 and later models

Refer to illustrations 13.12a, 13.12b 13.12c, 13.15a, 13.15b and 13.15c

12   Install the balance shaft sprocket part way onto the crankshaft. The raised side of the gear faces to the rear, towards the engine block **(see illustration)**. Install the sprockets part way onto the idler shaft and the left side balance shaft. Install the balance shaft chain onto the sprocket. Line up the brown link on the chain with the mark on the idler sprocket (which drives the right side balance shaft). Install the chain over the other balance shaft sprocket and make sure all of the marks are in alignment **(see illustrations)**.

13   Push the sprockets all the way onto their respective shafts. Re-check the position of the mating marks, then install the balance shaft sprocket bolts and tighten them to the torque listed in this Chapter's Specifications.

14   Apply a coat of moly-based grease to the chain and chain guides. Install the chain guides labeled A, B and C **(see illustration 12.2b)** and tighten the mounting bolts for chain guides A and B securely (leave the mounting bolts for chain guide C finger-tight). Note the difference between the upper and lower chain guide C mounting bolts. Make sure they are installed in the proper location.

15   Adjust the chain slack as follows: rotate the right (passenger side) balance shaft clockwise and the left (driver's side) balance shaft counterclockwise so the chain slack is collected at point F **(see illustration 13.12)**. Pull the chain with your finger tips in the direction of arrow F, then move the lower end of chain guide C up or down, as required, until the clearance between the chain and the guide (chain slack) **(see illustration)** is as listed in this Chapter's Specifications. Tighten the mounting bolts for chain guide C securely, then re-check the slack to make sure it hasn't changed. If the chain is not tensioned properly, engine noise will result. **Note:** *To adjust the chain without removing the timing chain cover, remove the access cover mounted on the front of the timing chain cover* **(see illustration)**. Loosen bolt "B" **(see illustration)** and using your finger push chain guide "C" down until it bottoms out. Don't use a screwdriver or other implement. Now pull the chain guide up 1/8-inch (3 mm) and tighten bolt "B". Reinstall the access cover.

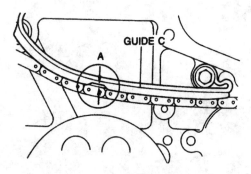

13.15a   Adjust chain guide C until the clearance between the chain and the guide is correct (1989 and later models)

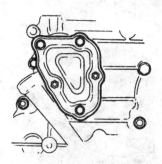

13.15b   Remove this cover from the timing chain cover for access to the balance shaft chain tensioner and the timing chain tensioner (1989 and later models)

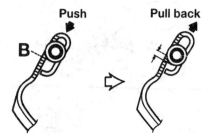

13.15c   Loosen bolt B, push down on the chain guide, then pull it up 1/4-inch and tighten the bolt (1989 and later models)

16   Install a new crankshaft front oil seal in the timing chain cover (see Section 11).

17   Using a new gasket and RTV sealant, install the timing chain cover onto the engine. Tighten the bolts to the torque listed in this Chapter's Specifications. If the gasket protrudes beyond the top or bottom of the case and engine block, trim off the excess with a razor blade.

18   Apply a thin layer of multi-purpose grease to the seal contact surface of the crankshaft pulley, then slide it onto the crankshaft. Install the bolt and tighten it finger-tight only. **Note:** *The bolt should be tightened to the specified torque only after the cylinder head and camshaft have been installed.*

19   The remainder of installation is the reverse of removal. Once the camshaft sprocket has been bolted to the camshaft, remove the pin from the timing chain tensioner, push the chain guide in (towards the driver's side), then install the access cover. Be sure to use a new gasket.

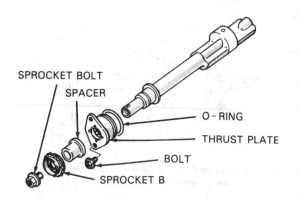

14.5   Left balance shaft components – exploded view (typical 2.6L engine)

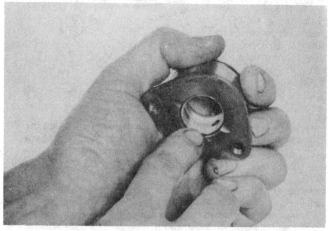

14.7   Checking the bearing in the thrust plate for wear and damage

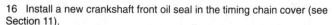

14   Balance shafts – removal, inspection and installation (2.6L engine only)

Refer to illustrations 14.5, 14.7, 14.8 and 14.11

1   The balance shaft chain and sprockets, the timing chain and sprockets and the oil pump should be removed before the balance shafts.

2   Remove the left balance shaft chamber cover plate from the engine block. It is held in place with two bolts. You may have to tap the cover with a soft-faced hammer to break the gasket seal.

3   Remove the two bolts attaching the left balance shaft thrust plate to the engine block, then carefully pull out the thrust plate and the balance shaft as an assembly. Support the rear of the shaft (by reaching through the access hole) to prevent damage to the rear bearing as the shaft is withdrawn from the engine. If the thrust plate proves to be difficult to pull out, screw an appropriate size bolt into each of the threaded holes in the thrust plate flange until they bottom on the engine block. Continue turning them with a wrench, one turn at a time, alternating between the two, until the

thrust plate is backed out of the engine block. Remove the bolts from the thrust plate flange.

4   On 1988 and earlier models, the right balance shaft is removed with the oil pump (see Section 17).

5   To disassemble the left balance shaft, slip off the spacer and the thrust plate/bearing assembly. Do not lose the key in the end of the shaft. Remove the O-ring from the thrust plate – if equipped **(see illustration)**.

6   Clean the components with solvent and dry them thoroughly. Make sure that the oil holes in the shafts and thrust plate are clean and clear.

7   Check both balance shafts and the thrust plate for cracks and other damage. Check the bearings in the engine block and the thrust plate **(see**

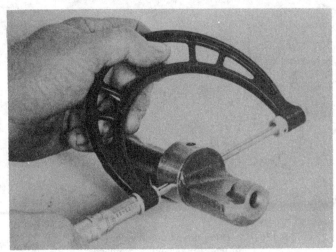

14.8   Measuring the balance shaft bearing journal outside diameter with a micrometer

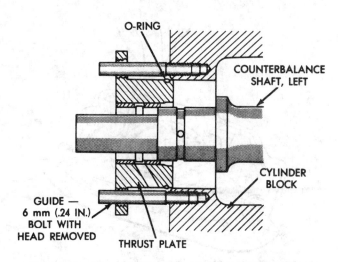

14.11   Install the left balance shaft thrust plate using bolts (with the heads removed) as guides (1988 and earlier 2.6L engine)

2A

illustration) for scratches, scoring and excessive wear. Check the bearing journals on the balance shafts for excessive wear and scoring.

8   Measure the outside diameter of each bearing journal **(see illustration)** and the inside diameter of each bearing. Subtract the journal diameter from the bearing diameter to obtain the bearing oil clearance. Compare the measured clearance to the Specifications. If it is excessive, have an automotive machine shop or dealer service department replace the bearings with new ones. If new bearings do not restore the oil clearance, or if the bearing journals on the shafts are damaged or worn, replace the shafts too. If the bearing in the left balance shaft thrust plate is bad, replace the bearing and thrust plate as an assembly.

9   Apply a thin layer of clean moly-based grease (or engine assembly lube) to the bearing journals on the left balance shaft, then carefully insert it into the engine block. Support the rear of the shaft so the rear bearing is not scratched or gouged as the shaft is inserted into its chamber.

10   On 1988 and earlier models, install a new O-ring on the outside of the thrust plate and lubricate it with clean multi-purpose grease. Also, apply a layer of grease to the thrust plate balance shaft bearing.

11   On 1988 and earlier models, cut the heads off two 6 x 50 mm bolts and install the bolts in the thrust plate mounting bolt holes. Using the bolts as a guide, carefully slide the thrust plate into position in the engine block **(see illustration)**. The guides are necessary to keep the bolt holes in the thrust plate aligned with the holes in the engine block. If the thrust plate is turned to align the holes, the O-ring could be twisted or damaged.

12   On 1988 and earlier models, remove the guide bolts, install the mounting bolts and tighten them securely.

13   Slip the spacer onto the end of the balance shaft (make sure that the key is in place).

14   Turn the shaft by hand and check for smooth operation.

15   Using a new rubber gasket and RTV-type gasket sealant, as well as new O-rings on the bolts, install the left balance shaft chamber cover plate and tighten the bolts securely.

16   On 1988 and earlier models, the right balance shaft is installed with the oil pump (see Section 17).

---

15   Oil pump – removal, inspection and installation (engines with timing belt)

Removal

Refer to illustration 15.4

1   Remove the timing belt covers, timing belt and crankshaft sprocket (see Section 11).

2   Remove the oil pan (see Section 20).

3   Remove the oil pump mounting bolts.

4   Unbolt and remove the oil strainer **(see illustration)**.

5   Insert a screwdriver at the corner of the pump body to break the gasket seal and remove the pump.

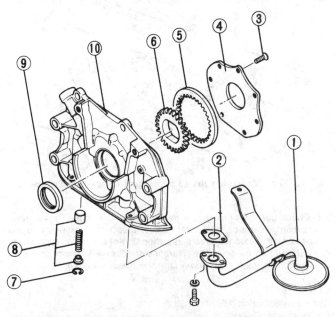

15.4   Oil pump components – exploded view (Mazda engine with timing belt) (gear type pump shown – rotor type similar)

1	Oil strainer	7	Snap-ring
2	Gasket	8	Oil pressure relief valve
3	Screw		plunger assembly
4	Pump cover	9	Crankshaft front oil seal
5	Outer gear	10	Pump body
6	Inner gear		

6   Clean the oil pump body mating surfaces to remove old gasket material.

Inspection

Refer to illustrations 15.12a, 15.12b and 15.12c

7   Remove the retaining screws and cover from the rear of the pump **(see illustration 15.4)**.

8   Remove the gears from the pump body. It may be necessary to turn the body over to remove the gears by allowing them to fall out.

9   Mount the pump body in a vise and remove the oil pressure sending unit, the snap-ring and the relief valve plunger assembly.

10   Wash the oil pump parts in solvent.

11   Inspect the components for wear, cracks and other damage.

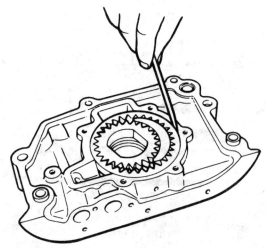

15.12a   Checking the oil pump outer gear-to-body clearance

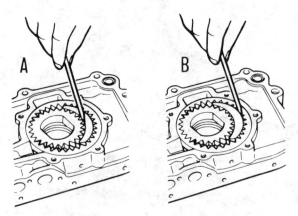

15.12b   Checking the oil pump inner (A) and outer (B) gear-to-crescent clearances

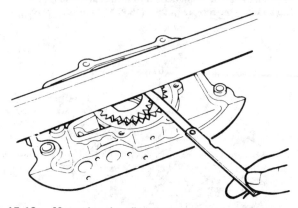

15.12c   Measuring the oil pump gear-to-cover clearance

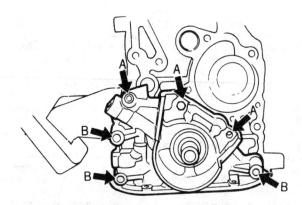

15.14   On 1988 and later models, the oil pump mounting bolts labelled A must be tightened to 14 to 19 ft-lbs – bolts labelled B must be tightened to 27 to 38 ft-lbs (on 1986 and 1987 models, tighten all bolts to 14 to 19 ft-lbs)

12 Check the outer (idler) gear-to-body clearance, inner (drive) gear-to-crescent clearance, the outer gear-to-crescent clearance and the gear-to-cover clearance **(see illustrations)**. Note: *A rotor type pump is used on 1988 models. The clearance checks are very similar to the checks for the gear type pump (see the Specifications).*

Installation
Refer to illustration 15.14

13 Coat the O-ring with petroleum jelly and insert it into the pump. Coat the pump housing with sealant. Apply clean engine oil to the lip of the oil seal.
14 Place the pump and new gasket in position and install the bolts. Tighten the bolts to the specified torque. Note that the bolts are different on 1988 models and require different torque specifications **(see illustration)**.
15 Using a new O-ring, install the strainer. Tighten the bolts to the specified torque.
16 Install the oil pan.
17 Install a new oil filter and reconnect the oil pressure switch harness.
18 Install the crankshaft sprocket, timing belt and covers.

16   Oil pump — removal, inspection and installation (pre-1985 models)

Removal
Refer to illustrations 16.4 and 16.5

1 Remove the oil pan (see Section 20).
2 Remove the timing chain cover (see Section 9).
3 Flatten the locking tab and remove the oil pump sprocket nut.
4 Pull the chain and sprockets off as an assembly **(see illustration)**.

16.4   Once the nut has been removed grasp the sides of the pump sprocket and pull it off the shaft (Mazda engine)

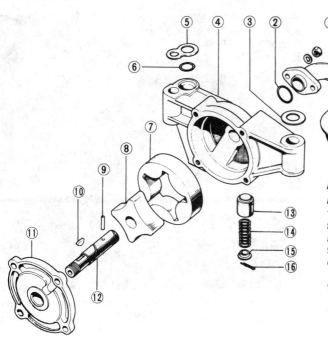

16.5   Oil pump components — exploded view (pre-1985 models)

1	Oil strainer	9	Pin
2	O-ring	10	Key
3	Adjusting shim	11	Cover
4	Body	12	Shaft
5	Adjusting shim	13	Plunger
6	O-ring	14	Spring
7	Outer rotor	15	Spring seat
8	Inner rotor	16	Cotter pin

Inspection

Refer to illustrations 16.9, 16.10, 16.11 and 16.16

7   Inspect the chain and sprockets for wear and damage.

8   Remove the cotter pin and oil pressure relief valve plunger assembly and inspect the parts for wear and damage.

9   Remove the pump cover bolts and measure the outer rotor-to-body clearance **(see illustration)**.

10   Place a straightedge across the pump body opening **(see illustration)** and measure the rotor end play.

11   Measure the clearance between the rotor lobes **(see illustration)**.

12   Compare the results to the Specifications.

13   Remove the inner rotor, the shaft and the outer rotor.

14   Clean all of the parts in solvent. Be sure the small openings are unobstructed. Check the body for wear and score marks.

15   Following the inspection, replace any components that are worn or damaged. If the pump is worn, replace it.

16   Be sure to lubricate all moving parts with engine oil. If the pump is being reused, reassemble it in the reverse order of disassembly. Use new O-rings between the pump and strainer and between the pump and block **(see illustration)**.

2A

5   Remove the nuts and detach the oil strainer **(see illustration)**. Discard the O-ring.

6   Unbolt the oil pump from the engine. Carefully separate the pump and save the adjusting shims, which are located between the pump and block.

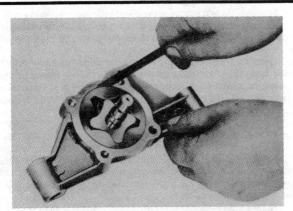

16.9   Checking the outer rotor-to-body clearance

16.10   Checking rotor end play

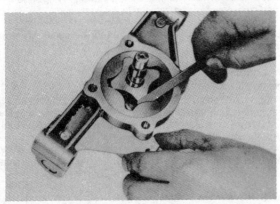

16.11   Checking clearance between rotor lobes

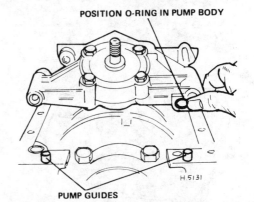

POSITION O-RING IN PUMP BODY

PUMP GUIDES

H.5131

16.16   Position the O-ring in the pump body when installing the oil pump

Installation

Refer to illustration 16.20

17   Mount the pump, using the same shims you took out. Tighten the bolts securely.

18   Install the oil pump drive chain and sprockets, slipping them on together as an assembly. Be sure to align the keys and keyways.

19   Measure the chain slack (deflection) midway between the sprockets before installing the lock tab and nut on the pump sprocket. If the slack is excessive, add adjusting shims (which are 0.006-inch/0.15 mm thick) between the pump and engine **(see illustration 16.5)**. Do not remove all slack.

20   Tighten the sprocket nut to the specified torque and bend over the lock tab **(see illustration)**.

21   Reinstall the remaining parts in the reverse order of removal.

16.20   Bend the lock tab down against the nut with a hammer and punch

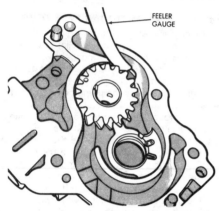

17.11a   Checking the driven gear-to-housing clearance with a feeler gauge

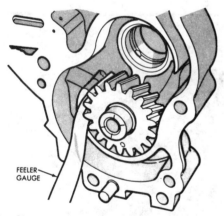

17.11b   Checking the drive gear-to-housing clearance with a feeler gauge

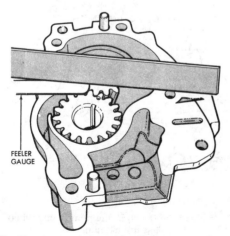

17.11c   Checking gear end play with a feeler gauge and straightedge

17   Oil pump – removal, inspection and installation (2.6L engine)

1988 and earlier models

Removal

1   The oil pump and right balance shaft are removed from the engine as an assembly.

2   Remove the timing chain (see Section 10).

3   Remove the bolt attaching the oil pump to the engine block. Some of the balance shaft chain guide mounting bolts also serve as oil pump mounting bolts; they have already been removed. Leave the Phillips head screw in the front side of the pump in place.

4   Carefully pull straight ahead on the oil pump and remove it, along with the balance shaft, from the engine block. You may have to tap gently on the oil pump body with a soft-face hammer to break the gasket seal. **Caution:** *Prying between the oil pump and engine block could result in damage to the engine.*

5   Remove the bolt from the nose of the balance shaft and pull the shaft out of the oil pump from the rear (do not lose the key in the nose of the shaft). Refer to Section 12 for balance shaft inspection procedures.

6   Remove the plug from the upper side of the pump body and withdraw the relief spring and plunger. You may have to mount the pump body in a vise equipped with soft jaws to loosen the plug. If so, do not apply excessive pressure to the pump body.

7   Remove the Philips head screw from the left side of the pump. Separate the oil pump cover from the body and lift out the two pump gears. Do not lose the key in the lower gear shaft. **Caution:** *Prying between the cover and body may result in damage to the pump body.*

8   Clean the parts with solvent and dry them thoroughly. Use compressed air to blow out all of the oil holes and passages. **Warning:** *Wear eye protection.*

Inspection

Refer to illustrations 17.11a, 17.11b, 17.11c and 17.15

9   Check the entire pump body and cover for cracks and excessive wear. Look closely for a ridge where the gears contact the body and cover.

10   Insert the relief plunger into the pump body and check to see if it slides smoothly. Look for cracks in the relief spring and measure its free length. Inspect the timing chain tensioner plunger sleeve for noticeable wear and the rubber pad for cracks and excessive wear. Measure the tensioner spring free length and compare it to the Specifications.

11   Measure the inside diameter of the bearing surfaces and the outside diameter of each gear shaft. Subtract the two to obtain the gear-to-bearing clearance. Measure the gear-to-housing clearance with a feeler gauge and the gear end play with a feeler gauge and straightedge **(see illustrations)**. Compare the measured clearances to the Specifications.

17.15 Be sure to align the marks on the oil pump gears before installing the cover

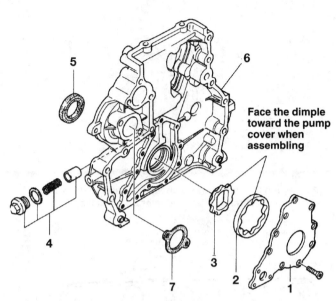

Face the dimple toward the pump cover when assembling

17.27 Exploded view of a typical 1989 and later 2.6L oil pump assembly

1	Cover	5	Oil seal
2	Outer rotor	6	Timing chain cover
3	Inner rotor	7	Gasket
4	Relief valve and spring assembly		

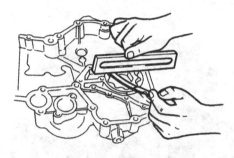

17.28a Using a feeler gauge and straightedge to check the side clearance (1989 and later models)

12   If the oil pump clearances are excessive, or if excessive wear is evident, replace the oil pump as a unit.

Installation

Refer to illustration 17.15

13   The oil pump and right balance shaft are installed as a unit.

14   Coat the oil pump relief plunger with clean moly-based grease and insert the plunger and spring into the oil pump body. Install the cap and tighten it securely.

15   Apply a layer of moly-based grease to the gear teeth, the sides of the gears and the bearing surfaces in the pump body and cover. Lay the gears in place in the body with the mating marks aligned **(see illustration)**. If the mating marks are not properly aligned, the right balance shaft will be out of phase and engine vibration will result.

16   Lay the cover in place using the dowel pins to align it properly. Install the Phillips head screw in the left side of the pump, but do not tighten it completely at this time. Make sure the gears rotate smoothly without binding.

17   Lay a new gasket in place on the cover. It's not necessary to use sealant. The dowel pins will align the gasket properly and hold it in place.

18   Make sure the key is in place in the nose of the shaft, then slip the right balance shaft through the oil pump driven gear as you line up the key in the shaft with the keyway in the gear. Once the shaft and gear are properly mated, clamp the counterweight end of the shaft in a vise equipped with soft jaws, install the bolt in the front end of the shaft and tighten it to the specified torque.

19   Apply a thin layer of clean moly-based grease (or engine assembly lube) to the rear bearing journal of the right balance shaft.

20   Hold the pump upright and fill it with a minimum of 10cc of engine oil. Insert the balance shaft into the engine block and through the rear bearing. Be careful not to scratch or gouge the bearing as the shaft is installed.

21   Make sure the pump is seated against the engine block, then install the mounting bolts and tighten them evenly and securely. Do not forget to tighten the Phillips head screw. The remaining pump mounting bolts will be installed with the chain guides.

22   Temporarily slip the balance shaft drive sprocket onto the lower pump gear shaft and use it to rotate the pump gears/balance shaft. Check for any obvious binding.

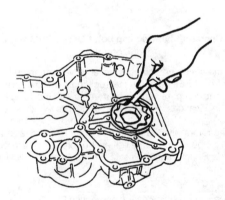

17.28b Using a feeler gauge to check the tooth-tip clearance between the inner and outer rotors (1989 and later 2.6L models)

1989 and later models

Removal

Refer to illustration 17.27

23   Remove rocker arm cover (see Section 4) and unscrew the two bolts attaching the cylinder head to the timing chain cover.

24   Remove the oil pan (see Section 20).

25   Remove oil pickup tube and screen from pump housing.

26   Remove timing chain cover (see Section 9).

27   Remove the screws and disassemble the oil pump **(see illustration)**. You may need to use an impact screwdriver to loosen the pump cover screws without stripping the heads out.

Inspection

Refer to illustrations 17.28a, 17.28b and 17.28c

28   Check the oil pump clearances on both inner and outer rotors to each other and to the pump body **(see illustrations)**. Compare your measurements to the figures listed in this Chapter's Specifications. Replace the pump if any of the measurements are outside of the specified limits.

2A

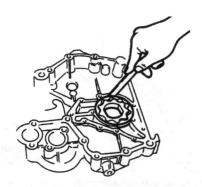

17.28c   **Using a feeler gauge to check the outer rotor-to-pump body clearance (1989 and later 2.6L models)**

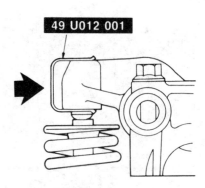

18.6   **Install special holders to prevent the lash adjusters from falling out**

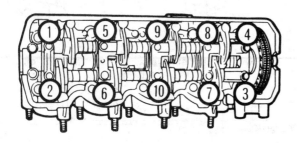

18.7   **Camshaft bearing cap bolt LOOSENING sequence (2.6L engine)**

29 Extract the spring and oil pump relief valve from the pump housing **(see illustration 15.5)**. Measure the free length of the oil pressure relief valve spring and compare your measurement with the value listed in this Chapter's Specifications. Replace the spring if its length is not as specified.

30 Install the rotors with the dimples in alignment and facing the pump cover. Install the pump cover and tighten the screws to the torque listed in this Chapter's Specifications. Install the oil pressure relief valve and spring assembly.

Installation

31 Install the timing chain cover (see Section 9).

32 Install the oil pick-up tube and screen, using a new gasket. Tighten the bolts to the torque listed in this Chapter's Specifications.

33 Install the oil pan (see Section 20).

34 Remainder of installation is the reverse of removal. Add the specified type and quantity of oil and coolant (see Chapter 1), run the engine and check for leaks.

---

18   Rocker arm shafts and camshaft – removal and installation

---

2.6L engine

Refer to illustrations 18.6, 18.7, 18.9, 18.10a and 18.10b

1 Remove the rocker arm cover (see Section 4).

2 Rotate the crankshaft until the number one piston is at top dead center on the compression stroke (see Section 3).

3 Locate the timing mark on the camshaft sprocket and make sure the plated link of the cam chain is opposite the mark.

4 Remove the timing chain tensioner (see Section 8). **Note:** *Place a rag in the timing chain opening to prevent anything from falling into the opening.*

DOWEL PIN

18.9   **Position the camshaft with the dowel pin at the top before installing the rocker arm assembly (2.6L engine)**

5 Remove the camshaft sprocket bolt from the front of the camshaft. To facilitate loosening the camshaft sprocket bolt, you can prevent the crankshaft from turning by holding the large bolt on the end of the crankshaft with a wrench. Remove the distributor drive gear from the front of the camshaft by tapping it with a soft-face hammer. Pull the camshaft sprocket – with the chain in place – off the camshaft, and allow it to rest on the sprocket holder.

6 Install hydraulic lash adjuster holders (Mazda tool no. 49 U 012 001 or equivalent) to prevent the adjusters from falling out when the rocker arm assembly is lifted up **(see illustration)**.

7 Loosen the ten camshaft bearing cap bolts, 1/2-turn each, in sequence, until all pressure from the valve springs has been released **(see illustration)**. Next remove the six inner bolts and lift the rocker arm shaft assembly away from the cylinder head with the four end bolts in place. No further disassembly of these components is necessary unless new parts are required. Carefully lift the camshaft out of the cylinder head and store it someplace where it will not be damaged. See Chapter 2, Part B for inspection procedures.

8 Wipe the camshaft bearing surfaces in the cylinder head clean and apply a coat of clean moly-base grease (or engine assembly lube) to each of them.

9 Make sure the camshaft bearing journals are clean, then carefully lay the camshaft in place in the head. Do not lubricate the cam lobes at this time. Rotate the camshaft until the dowel pin on the front is positioned at 12 o'clock **(see illustration)**.

10 Wipe the camshaft bearing cap bearing surfaces clean and apply a coat of clean moly-based grease (or engine assembly lube) to each of them. Also, apply a very small amount of grease to the end of each valve stem. Lay the rocker arm shaft assembly in place with the number one

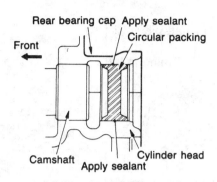

18.10a Apply sealant to the shaded areas of the rear bearing cap (1988 and earlier 2.6L engines)

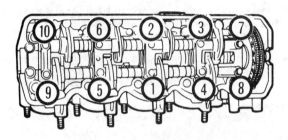

18.10b Camshaft bearing cap bolt TIGHTENING sequence (2.6L engine)

bearing cap toward the timing chain. On 1988 and earlier models apply sealant to the circular packing at the rear bearing cap **(see illustration)**. On 1989 and later models, apply anaerobic-type sealant to the cylinder head contact surfaces of bearing caps 1 and 5. Install the camshaft bearing cap bolts and tighten them to the specified torque in the recommended sequence **(see illustration)**. Note that on some models bolt number 5 requires a different torque.

11 Next, lift up on the camshaft sprocket (with the chain attached) and slip it into place on the end of the camshaft. The dowel pin on the cam should slip into the hole in the sprocket.

12 Install the distributor drive gear (again, line up the dowel pin and hole) and the bolt. Tighten the bolt to the specified torque. To keep the camshaft and crankshaft from turning, hold a large screwdriver against the head and sprocket teeth.

13 Camshaft end play can be checked with a dial indicator set or a feeler gauge (see Chapter 2, Part B).

14 Adjust the jet valves (see Chapter 1).

15 Reinstall the remaining components in the reverse order of removal.

Engines equipped with a timing belt

Refer to illustrations 18.21, 18.28, 18.29 and 18.32

16 Remove the rocker arm cover (see Section 4).

17 Position the number one piston at Top Dead Center (see Section 3).

18 Remove the distributor (see Chapter 5.)

19 Remove the fuel pump (see Chapter 4).

20 Remove the timing belt (see Section 11). Remove the bolt and washer, then detach the sprocket from the end of the camshaft.

21 Unbolt the front housing **(see illustration)**, carefully pry the housing away from the engine and remove it. Remove all traces of old gasket material from the sealing surfaces.

22 Loosen the rocker arm assembly retaining bolts, 1/4-turn at a time, working from the ends toward the center.

23 Once the bolts are loose, remove them and place them in a numbered piece of cardboard for reinstallation in the same positions.

24 Lift the rocker arm assembly off the engine. Remove the camshaft.

25 See Chapter 2, Part B for camshaft and rocker arm inspection procedures.

26 Carefully clean the mating surfaces of the rocker arm assembly and the cylinder head to remove all traces of sealant.

27 Lubricate the camshaft and rocker arm assembly with engine assembly lube.

28 Place the camshaft in position with the dowel pin at the top (12 O'clock position) **(see illustration)**.

29 Apply sealant to the cylinder head-to-rocker arm assembly mating surfaces of the end bearing caps **(see illustration)**.

30 Lower the rocker arm assembly into place and install the bolts finger tight, then tighten them in 1/4-turn increments, working from the center out toward the ends.

31 Install the front housing with a new gasket. Tighten the bolts a little at a time to the specified torque.

32 Install the camshaft sprocket with the dowel pin at the top, making sure the sprocket and front housing marks are aligned **(see illustration)**.

33 Tighten the sprocket bolt to the specified torque. Slip a bar through the cam sprocket to keep it from turning.

34 Install the timing belt as described in Section 11.

35 Check the valve clearances (see Chapter 1).

36 Install the remaining components in the reverse order of removal.

Engines equipped with a timing chain (except 2.6L)

The rocker arm assembly and camshaft are retained by the cylinder head bolts. Whenever the bolts are removed, the cylinder head gasket must be replaced. Follow the procedure outlined in Section 19 *(Cylinder head – removal and installation)*.

2A

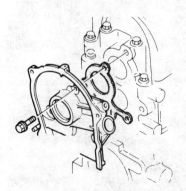

18.21 The front housing is bolted to the cylinder head (Mazda engine with timing belt)

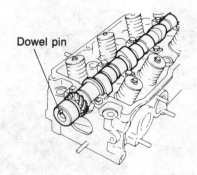

18.28 Install the camshaft with the dowel pin at the top (Mazda engine with timing belt)

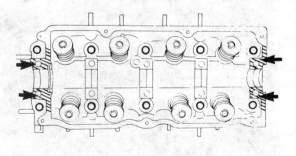

18.29 Apply sealant to the shaded areas of the end bearing caps (arrows) (Mazda engine with timing belt)

19   Cylinder head – removal and installation

Caution: *The engine must be completely cool before beginning this procedure.*

Removal

Refer to illustrations 19.14, 19.15, 19.17a, 19.17b, 19.17c, 19.18 and 19.19

1   Position the number one piston at Top Dead Center (see Section 3).
2   Disconnect the negative cable from the battery.
3   Drain the cooling system and remove the spark plugs (see Chapter 1).
4   Remove the intake manifold (see Section 5).
5   Remove the exhaust manifold (see Section 6).
6   Remove the distributor (see Chapter 5), including the cap and wires.
7   Remove the fuel pump (see Chapter 4).
8   Remove the timing belt, if equipped (see Section 11). **Caution:** *Do not turn the crankshaft while the timing belt is removed.*
9   Remove the rocker arm cover (see Section 4).
10   On 2.6L and all timing belt equipped engines, remove the rocker arm shafts and camshaft as described in Section 18.

Pre-1985 models only

11   Place a rag in the opening of the timing chain cover to prevent anything from falling into it.
12   Secure the timing chain to the camshaft sprocket with a section of wire.
13   Remove the timing chain tensioner (see Section 8).
14   Flatten the lock tab, then remove the first nut, the lock plate and the distributor gear **(see illustration)**.
15   Flatten the lock tab on the front of the camshaft sprocket, then remove the large nut and lock plate **(see illustration)**. **Note:** *Slip a large screwdriver through the camshaft sprocket to prevent it from turning when the nuts are loosened.*
16   Support the sprocket and chain with a wire until the cylinder head is removed.

All models

17   Loosen the cylinder head bolts, 1/4-turn at a time, in the sequence shown **(see illustrations)**. Use the diagram applicable to your vehicle.
18   Be sure to remove the small end bolts **(see illustration)**.
19   On pre-1985 models, lift the rocker shaft assembly straight up with the head bolts still in it **(see illustration)**. This will hold the rocker components in place. Tilt the camshaft slightly and pull it out, leaving the sprocket and chain in place in the front cover.

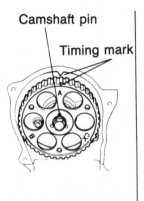
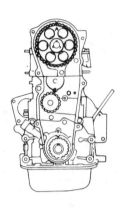

18.32   Install the camshaft sprocket with the pin at the top and the A aligned with the mark on the front housing (Mazda engine with timing belt)

20   Be sure to keep the cam bearing caps (and replaceable bearings – if equipped) in their original positions.
21   Hold a block of wood against the side of the cylinder head and strike it with a hammer to break the gasket seal. Carefully lift the cylinder head straight up (avoid hitting the timing chain guides) and place the head on wooden blocks so the valves don't hit anything.

Installation

Refer to illustrations 19.24a, 19.24b, 19.25, 19.26, 19.27a, 19.27b, 19.27c and 19.27d

22   Remove all traces of old gasket material from the block and head. Don't allow anything to fall into the engine. Clean and inspect all threaded fasteners and be sure the threaded holes in the block are clean and dry.
23   See Chapter 2, Part B for cylinder head, camshaft and rocker arm service information.
24   If you are working on a 2.6L engine, apply sealant to the junction of the timing chain cover and engine block **(see illustration)**. Place a new gasket **(see illustration)** and the cylinder head in position, followed by the camshaft and rocker arm assembly (see Section 18). Be sure to lubricate all moving parts with moly-base grease or assembly lube.
25   On pre-1985 models, make sure the flat surfaces of the rocker arm swivels contact the ends of the valve stems **(see illustration)**.

19.14   Flatten the lock tab, remove the first nut, then pull off the lock plate (arrow)

19.15   Pull off the distributor gear, then flatten the lock tab (arrow) and remove the large sprocket retaining nut

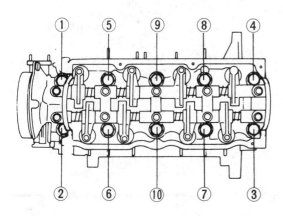

19.17a Cylinder head bolt LOOSENING sequence – Mazda engine with timing belt

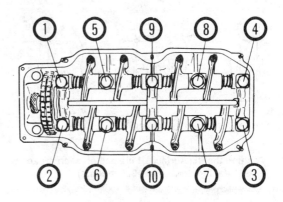

19.17b Cylinder head bolt LOOSENING sequence – Mazda engine with timing chain

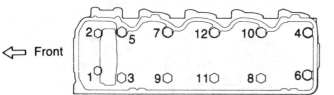

19.17c Cylinder head bolt LOOSENING sequence – 2.6L engine

19.18 Be sure to remove the small bolts as well (arrow)

19.19 Remove the rocker arm shaft assembly (pre-1985 engines) with the head bolts in place to prevent the shaft components from coming apart

19.24b DO NOT use sealant on the new head gasket

26 On pre-1985 models, prior to head bolt tightening, move each rocker arm shaft support on the exhaust side to offset the rocker arm 0.040-inch (1 mm) from the valve center (see illustration).

27 The cylinder head bolts should be tightened in several steps, following the recommended sequence (see illustrations), until the specified torque is reached.

28 Reinstall the timing chain/belt. Be sure to follow the proper installation procedure. Align the timing marks, turning the camshaft, if necessary, to align the cam sprocket.

29 Reinstall the remaining parts in the reverse order of removal. Be sure all fasteners are tightened securely and the locking tabs have been secured, where applicable.

30 Be sure to refill and check all fluid levels. Turn the crankshaft slowly by hand through two complete revolutions. If anything hits, stop immediately and recheck the timing chain/belt installation.

31 Start the engine and set the ignition timing (see Chapter 1). Run the engine until normal operating temperature is reached.

32 Check for leaks and proper operation.

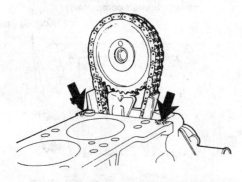

19.24a On 2.6L engines, apply sealant to the junction of the timing chain cover and block (arrows)

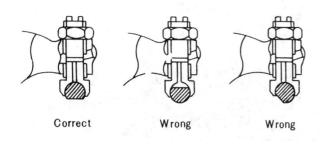

Correct   Wrong   Wrong

19.25   Position the flat surface of the ball on each rocker arm facing down (pre-1985 models)

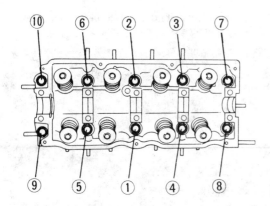

19.27a   Cylinder head bolt TIGHTENING sequence – Mazda engine with timing belt

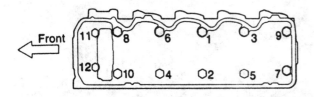

Front

19.27c   Cylinder head bolt TIGHTENING sequence – 1988 and earlier 2.6L engine

33   Shut off the engine and retorque the cylinder head bolts (unless the gasket manufacturer states otherwise).
34   Recheck the valve adjustment.

---

20   Oil pan – removal and installation

Refer to illustrations 20.5, 20.9 and 20.10

1   Disconnect the negative cable from the battery.
2   Raise the vehicle and support it securely on jackstands.
3   Remove the belly pan(s) and dipstick. Drain the engine oil (see Chapter 1).
4   Unbolt and remove the crossmember located below the engine. On 4WD models, detach the front differential from the crossmember (see Chapter 8).
5   Remove the gusset plates (braces) that connect the engine and bellhousing (if equipped). They are located on both sides of the engine at the rear of the oil pan **(see illustration)**.
6   On vehicles so equipped, disconnect the emission line from the oil pan.
7   Remove the bolts and detach the oil pan from the vehicle. If the

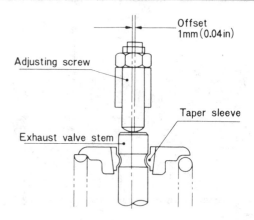

19.26   Move the rocker arm shaft supports on the exhaust side to offset each rocker arm (pre-1985 models)

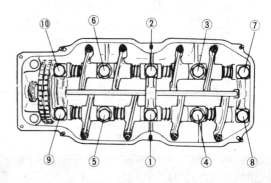

19.27b   Cylinder head bolt TIGHTENING sequence – Mazda engine with timing chain

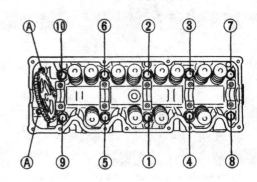

19.27d   Cylinder bolt TIGHTENING sequence – 1989 and later 2.6L engines – (tighten the bolts marked A after the others have been tightened completely)

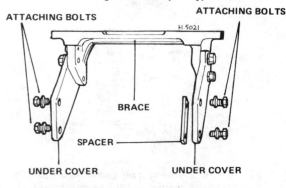

20.5   Typical rear engine gussets (braces)

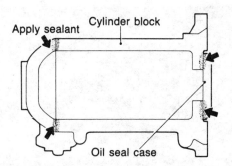

20.9 Apply sealant to the shaded areas (arrows) when installing an oil pan with a gasket

20.10 Apply the sealant to the INSIDE of the bolt holes in a continuous bead all the way around the oil pan flange

pan is stuck, tap it with a soft-face hammer or insert a thin knife blade between the sealing surfaces and work around the perimeter.

8   Thoroughly clean the oil pan and mating surfaces. Remove all traces of old gasket material. Check the oil pan gasket surface for distortion. Straighten or replace as necessary.

9   On engines with an oil pan gasket, apply sealant (Mazda no. 8527 77 739 or equivalent) to the four corners as shown **(see illustration)**. Use a new gasket.

10 On engines with RTV sealant in place of an oil pan gasket, apply a bead of sealant (Mazda no. 8527 77 739 or equivalent) to the oil

pan flange **(see illustration)**, position the pan and install the bolts finger tight.

11 Working in a spiral pattern from the center out, tighten the bolts to the specified torque in three or four steps.

12 Reinstall the remaining parts in the reverse order of removal.

13 Refill the crankcase with the proper quantity and grade of oil and run the engine. Check carefully for leaks.

2A

21 Flywheel/driveplate — removal and installation

Refer to illustrations 21.7a, 21.7b, 21.7c, 21.7d and 21.8

1   Refer to Chapter 7 and remove the transmission. If the vehicle has a manual transmission, the pressure plate and clutch will also have to be removed (see Chapter 8).

2   To keep the crankshaft from turning, insert a large screwdriver into a driveplate hole or pry against the ring gear teeth on the flywheel to prevent it from turning.

3   Remove the mounting bolts. Since it's fairly heavy, support the flywheel as the last bolt is removed. Pull straight back on the flywheel/driveplate to detach it from the crankshaft.

4   On manual transmission equipped vehicles, check the pilot bearing and replace it if necessary (see Chapter 8).

5   Inspect the flywheel/driveplate for cracks and check the ring gear teeth for damage.

6   Apply a light coat of sealant (Mazda no. 8530 77 743 or equivalent) to the bolt threads.

7   On manual transmission equipped models, position the flywheel on the crankshaft. If the flywheel had large washers under some of the flywheel bolts **(see illustration)**, look for a mark on the flywheel **(see illustration)**. The mark must be aligned with the stepped bolt hole in the crankshaft. Install the bolt with the long unthreaded shank **(see illustration)** in the stepped crankshaft hole **(see illustration)**.

21.7a If the flywheel has large washers on some bolts (arrows), . . .

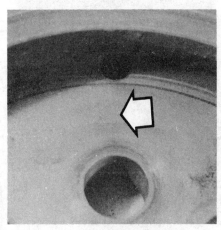

21.7b . . . look for a mark (arrow) adjacent to the bolt hole and . . .

21.7c . . . use the bolt with the long unthreaded shank (arrow) . . .

21.7d . . . in the stepped crankshaft hole (arrow)

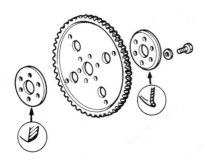

21.8 Driveplate components — exploded view

8   On automatic transmission equipped models, place the adapter, driveplate and backing plate on the crankshaft (**see illustration**).
9   Install and tighten the bolts to the specified torque in a criss-cross pattern.
10   On manual transmission equipped vehicles, install the clutch disc and pressure plate as described in Chapter 8.
11   The remainder of installation is the reverse of removal.

---

22   Crankshaft rear oil seal — replacement

Engines with seal groove in block and rear main cap

1   This procedure applies to engines with the seal flush mounted in the block and main bearing cap.
2   Remove the flywheel/driveplate as described in Section 21.
3   Using an awl, carefully punch two holes in opposite sides of the seal and install self-tapping screws in the holes.
4   Carefully pry the seal out with a claw hammer or two screwdrivers pulling on the screws. **Caution:** *Don't scratch the crankshaft or seal bore.*
5   Clean the seal bore and inspect the crankshaft seal contact surface for nicks and a wear groove.
6   Lubricate the new seal with engine oil or moly-base grease. Position the seal in the bore with the spring side facing in and tap it into place with a soft-face hammer.
7   Reinstall the remaining components in the reverse order of removal.

Engines with seal housing

Refer to illustrations 22.11, 22.14, 22.15 and 22.17

8   This procedure applies to engines with the seal mounted in a removable housing.
9   Remove the flywheel/driveplate (see Section 21).

22.11   Since the seal lip is quite stiff, if won't slide over the end of the crankshaft very easily — if you lubricate the journal and the seal lip with moly-base grease and carefully work the seal over the journal with a smooth, blunt object, you'll get it on without damaging it

10   The seal can be replaced without removing the oil pan or the seal housing. However, this method is not recommended because the lip of the seal is quite stiff and it's possible to cock the seal in the housing or damage it during installation. If you want to take the chance, carefully pry out the old seal with a screwdriver. Clean and inspect the seal cavity.
11   Apply moly-base grease to the crankshaft seal journal and the lip of the new seal and carefully push the seal into place. The lip is stiff so carefully work it onto the seal journal of the crankshaft with a smooth object like the end of an extension (**see illustration**) as you tap the seal into place. Don't rush it or you will damage the seal.
12   The following method is recommended but requires removal of the oil pan (see Section 20) and the seal housing.
13   After the oil pan has been removed, unbolt and remove the seal housing. Thoroughly clean the seal mounting cavity and peel off any old gasket material. On 1988 and earlier 2.6L engines, remove the oil separator.
14   Position the seal housing on wooden blocks and drive the old seal out with a hammer and punch (**see illustration**).
15   Drive the new seal into the housing with a block of wood (**see illustration**). The open (spring) side must face the engine when installed.
16   Lubricate the lip of the new seal with moly-base grease.

22.14   After removing the seal housing from the block, support it on a couple of wood blocks and drive out the old seal with a punch and hammer

22.15   Drive the new seal into the housing with a block of wood — make sure you don't cock the seal

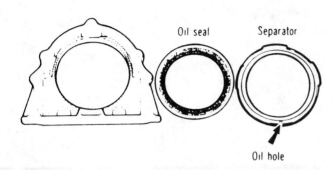

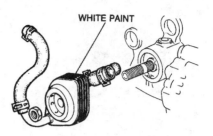

24.3 When installing the oil cooler, make sure the white paint mark faces up

22.17 When installing the engine rear oil seal housing on 1988 and earlier 2.6L models, make sure the separator oil hole is at the bottom

17 Position a new housing gasket on the block. On 1988 and earlier 2.6L engines, place the oil separator into the back of the seal housing with the hole facing down **(see illustration)**.
18 Slowly and carefully push the new seal/housing assembly onto the crankshaft. The seal lip is stiff, so work it onto the crankshaft with a smooth object as you push the housing against the block.
19 Gently tap the seal housing into position. Install and tighten the bolts to the specified torque.
20 The remaining steps are the reverse of removal.

4 Next, the weight of the engine must be taken off the mounts. This can be done from beneath using a jack and wooden block positioned under the oil pan (after removing the belly pan, or from above by removing the air cleaner and using an engine hoist attached to the two engine lifting brackets. The engine should be raised slowly and carefully, while keeping a constant check on clearances around the engine to prevent anything from binding or breaking. Pay particular attention to areas such as the fan, ignition coil wires, vacuum lines leading to the engine and rubber hoses and ducts.
5 Raise the engine just enough to provide adequate room to remove the mounting insulator.
6 Remove the nuts and bolts retaining the insulator, then lift it out, noting how it's installed.
7 Installation is the reverse of removal, but be sure the insulator is installed in the same position it was in before removal.

2A

23 Engine mounts – replacement

Warning: *Don't position any part of your body under the engine when the engine mounts are unbolted!*

1 Engine mounts are non-adjustable and seldom require service. Periodically they should be inspected for hardness and cracks in the rubber and separation of the rubber from the metal backing.
2 To replace the engine mounts with the engine in the vehicle, disconnect the battery and use the following procedure.
3 Loosen the nuts and bolts that retain the front mounting insulator and heat shield (if equipped) to the engine mount bracket and frame. Do this on both sides.

24 Oil cooler (later 2.6L engines) – removal and installation

Refer to illustration 24.3
1 Drain the engine oil and remove the oil filter (see Chapter 1).
2 Drain the engine coolant (see Chapter 1).
3 Disconnect the two coolant hoses at the oil cooler **(see illustration).**
4 Remove the mounting nut and detach the oil cooler.
5 Attach the oil cooler to the engine, using a new gasket, and tighten its mounting nut to the torque listed in this Chapter's Specifications.
6 The remainder of installation is the reverse of removal. Use a new oil cooler gasket and refill the cooling system with the proper mixture of water and coolant (see Chapter 1).

NOTES

Chapter 2   Part B
General engine overhaul procedures

Contents

2B

Specifications

B1600, B1800 and B2000 engines (with timing chain)

General
Cylinder numbers (front-to-rear)	1-2-3-4
Firing order	1-3-4-2
Compression pressure	
Standard	169 PSI
Service limit	118 PSI
Oil pressure (engine at normal operating temperature)	
At idle	4.3 PSI
At 3000 rpm	48 to 64 PSI

Cylinder head
Maximum permissible distortion	0.006 in (0.15 mm)
Maximum refinish	0.010 in (0.25 mm)
Valve seat angle (intake and exhaust)	45°
Valve guide inside diameter	0.3174 to 0.3182 in (8.06 to 8.08 mm)
Valve stem-to-guide clearance	
Intake	0.0007 to 0.0021 in (0.0178 to 0.053 mm)
Exhaust	0.0007 to 0.0023 in (0.0178 to 0.058mm)
Service limit	0.008 in (0.20 mm)
Intake valve	
Stem diameter	
Standard	0.3161 to 0.3167 in (8.029 to 8.044 mm)
Service limit	0.002 in (0.05 mm)
Margin width	
Standard	0.059.1 ± 0.0079 in (1.5 ± 0.2 mm)
Service limit	
B16000	0197 in (0.5 mm)
B1800 and B2000	0.039 in (1.0 mm)
Exhaust valve	
Stem diameter	
Standard	0.3159 to 0.3167 in (8.024 to 8.044 mm)
Service limit	0.002 in (0.05 mm)
Margin width (minimum)	0.039 in (1.0 mm)

Valve spring free length (outer)
  Standard
    B1600 and B1800 .... 1.469 in (373.3 mm)
    B2000 .... 1.598 in (40.6 mm)
  Service limit
    B1600 and B1800 .... 1.425 in (36.2 mm)
    B2000 (except 1984) .... 1.551 in (39.4 mm)
    B2000 (1984 only) .... 1.587 in (40.3 mm)
Valve spring installed height (outer)
  B1600 and B1800 .... 1.339 in (34 mm)
  B2000 .... 1.385 in (34.5 mm)
Valve spring free length (inner)
  Standard .... 1.449 in (36.8 mm)
  Service limit .... 1.406 in (35.7 mm)

Camshaft and related components

Rocker arm bore .... 0.7488 to 0.7501 in (19.02 to 19.053 mm)
Rocker arm shaft diameter
  B1600 .... 0.7469 to 0.7477 in (18.72 to 18.93 mm)
  B1800 .... 0.7477 to 0.7479 in (18.972 to 18.993 mm)
  B2000 .... 0.7483 to 0.7491 in (19.007 to 19.028 mm)
Rocker arm-to-shaft clearance
  Standard .... 0.0011 in to 0.0032 in (0.28 to 0.081 mm)
  Service limit .... 0.004 in (0.1 mm)
Camshaft journal diameter
  Front .... 1.7701 to 1.7695 in (44.96 to 44.945 mm)
  Center .... 1.7691 to 1.7697 in (44.94 to 44.95 mm)
  Rear .... 1.7701 to 1.7695 in (44.96 to 44.945 mm)
  Service limit .... 0.002 in (0.05 mm)
Cam lobe height
  B1800 and B2000
    Standard .... 1.7731 in (45.037 mm)
    Service limit .... 0.008 in (0.020 mm)
  B1600
    Intake .... 1.7605 in (44.715 mm)
    Exhaust .... 1.7592 in (44.682 mm)
Camshaft end play
  Standard .... 0.001 to 0.007 in (0.02 to 0.18 mm)
  Service limit .... 0.008 in (0.20 mm)
Camshaft runout limit .... 0.0012 in (0.03 mm)
Camshaft bearing oil clearance
  Front and rear journals .... 0.0007 to 0.0027 in (0.019 to 0.069 mm)
  Center journal .... 0.0011 to 0.0031 in (0.029 to 0.079 mm)
  Service limit .... 0.0059 in (0.15 mm)

Connecting rods, pistons and bearings

Connecting rod distortion (twist) limit .... 0.002 in per 5 in (0.02 mm per 50 mm)
Connecting rod end play (side clearance)
  Standard .... 0.004 to 0.008 in (0.11 to 0.21 mm)
  Service limit .... 0.014 in (0.356 mm)
Bearing oil clearance
  B1600 .... 0.0011 to 0.003 in (0.027 to 0.077 mm)
  B1800 .... 0.001 to 0.0025 in (0.025 to 0.065 mm)
  B2000 .... 0.0011 to 0.0030 in (0.027 to 0.077 mm)
  Service limit (all) .... 0.0039 in (0.10 mm)
Piston diameter (B1600) — measured 0.67-inch (17 mm) below oil ring groove, 90° to piston pin
  Piston marked A .... 3.0689 to 3.0691 in (77.949 to 77.955 mm)
  Piston unmarked .... 3.0687 ± 0.002 in (77.945 ± 0.004 mm)
  Piston marked C .... 3.0683 to 3.0685 in (77.935 to 77.941 mm)
Piston diameter (B1800) — measured 0.81-inch (20.5 mm)
  below oil ring groove, 90° to piston pin .... 3.1474 to 3.1482 in (79.944 to 79.964 mm)
Piston diameter (B2000) — measured 0.73-inch (18.5 mm)
  below oil ring groove, 90° to piston pin .... 3.4988 to 3.4998 in (88.750 to 88.893 mm)
Piston-to-cylinder clearance
  Standard
    B1600 .... 0.0022 to 0.0028 in (0.057 to 0.072 mm)
    B1800 and B2000 .... 0.0019 to 0.0025 in (0.048 to 0.063 mm)
  Service limit .... 0.006 in (0.15 mm)
Piston ring side clearance
  Top compression ring .... 0.0012 to 0.0028 in (0.035 to 0.070 mm)
  Second compression ring .... 0.0012 to 0.0025 in (0.030 to 0.064 mm)
  Oil control ring .... 0.0012 to 0.0025 in (0.030 to 0.064 mm)
Piston ring end gap
  Compression rings .... 0.008 to 0.016 in (0.2 to 0.4 mm)
  Oil control ring .... 0.012 to 0.035 in (0.3 to 0.9 mm)

B1600, B1800 and B2000 engines (with timing chain) (continued)

Crankshaft and main bearings
Main journal diameter
  Standard
    B1600 . . . . 2.4779 to 2.4875 in (62.94 to 63.18 mm)
    B1800 and B2000 . . . . 2.4780 to 2.4786 in (62.940 to 62.955 mm)
  Service limit . . . . 0.002 in (0.05 mm)
Connecting rod journal diameter
  Standard
    B1600 and B1800 . . . . 2.0842 to 2.0848 in (52.94 to 52.95 mm)
    B2000 . . . . 2.0884 to 2.0890 in (53.045 to 53.060 mm)
  Service limit . . . . 0.002 in (0.05 mm)
Crankshaft end play
  Standard . . . . 0.003 to 0.009 in (0.08 to 0.24 mm)
  Service limit . . . . 0.012 in (0.30 mm)
Crankshaft runout (measured at flywheel face) . . . . 0.0012 in (0.03 mm)
Main bearing oil clearance
  Standard
    B1600 and B1800 . . . . 0.0012 to 0.0024 in (0.031 to 0.061 mm)
    B2000 . . . . 0.0012 to 0.0020 in (0.031 to 0.050 mm)
  Service limit . . . . 0.0031 in (0.08 mm)

Engine block
Bore diameter
  B1600
    Mark A . . . . 3.0714 to 3.0716 in (78.013 to 78.019 mm)
    Mark B . . . . 3.0709 to 3.0711 in (78.000 to 78.006 mm)
    Unmarked . . . . 3.0711 to 3.0714 in (78.006 to 78.013 mm)
  B1800 and B2000 . . . . 3.1497 to 3.1504 in (80.0 to 80.019 mm)
Wear limit . . . . 0.006 in (0.15 mm)
Maximum regrind to correct deck distortion . . . . 0.010 in (0.25 mm)

Torque specifications*
                                                                  Ft-lbs
Main bearing cap bolts . . . . 61 to 65
Connecting rod cap nuts . . . . 30 to 33
Oil pressure switch . . . . 9 to 13

* **Note:** *Refer to Part A for additional torque specifications.*

B2000 and B2200 engines (with timing belt)

General
Compression pressure (at 300 rpm)
  Standard . . . . 173 PSI
  Minimum . . . . 121 PSI
Cylinder numbers (front-to-rear) 1-2-3-4
Firing order 1-3-4-2
Oil pressure . . . . 43 to 57 PSI at 3000 rpm

Valves and related components
Valve face angle . . . . 45°
Valve seat angle . . . . 45°
Valve margin width (minimun)
  Intake . . . . 0.020 in (0.5 mm)
  Exhaust . . . . 0.039 in (1.0 mm)
Valve stem diameter
  Intake . . . . 0.3161 to 0.3167 in (8.030 to 8.045 mm)
  Service limit . . . . 0.3142 in (7.980 mm)
  Exhaust . . . . 0.3159 to 0.3165 in (8.025 to 8.040 mm)
  Service limit . . . . 0.3140 in (7.975 mm)
Stem-to-guide clearance
  Intake . . . . 0.0010 to 0.0024 in (0.025 to 0.060 mm)
  Exhaust . . . . 0.0012 to 0.0026 in (0.030 to 0.065 mm)
  Service limit (intake and exhaust) . . . . 0.0079 in (0.20 mm)
Valve spring out-of-square limit
  Outer . . . . 0.07 in (1.8 mm)
  Inner . . . . 0.06 in (1.5 mm)
Valve spring free length
  Inner . . . . 1.732 in (44.0 mm)
  Service limit . . . . 1.681 in (42.7 mm)
  Outer . . . . 2.047 in (52.0 mm)
  Service limit . . . . 1.984 in (50.4 mm)
Rocker arm and shaft
  Rocker arm bore . . . . 0.6300 to 0.6310 in (16.000 to 16.027 mm)
  Shaft diameter . . . . 0.6286 to 0.6293 in (15.966 to 15.984 mm)
  Rocker arm-to-shaft clearance . . . . 0.0006 to 0.0024 in (0.016 to 0.061 mm)
  Service limit . . . . 0.004 in (0.010 mm)

Crankshaft and connecting rods

Crankshaft end play	0.0031 to 0.0071 in (0.08 to 0.18 mm)
Service limit	0.0118 in (0.030 mm)
Connecting rod end play (side clearance)	0.004 to 0.010 in (0.110 to 0.262 mm)
Service limit	0.012 in (0.30 mm)
Main bearing journal diameter	2.359 to 2.360 in (59.937 to 59.955 mm)
Service limit	0.002 in (0.05 mm)
Grinding limit	0.03 in (0.75 mm)
Main bearing oil clearance	0.0012 to 0.0019 in (0.031 to 0.049 mm)
Service limit	0.0031 in (0.08 mm)
Connecting rod bearing journal diameter	2.005 to 2.006 in (50.940 to 50.955 mm)
Service limit	0.0020 in (0.05 mm)
Grinding limit	0.03 in (0.75 mm)
Connecting rod wrist pin bore diameter	0.8640 to 0.8646 in (21.943 to 21.961 mm)
Connecting rod bearing oil clearance	0.0010 to 0.0026 in (0.027 to 0.067 mm)
Service limit	0.0039 in (0.10 mm)
Crankshaft journal taper/out-of-round limit	0.0020 in (0.05 mm)
Crankshaft runout limit	0.0012 in (0.03 mm)

Engine block

Cylinder bore diameter	3.3859 to 3.3866 in (86.000 to 86.019 mm)
Service limit	0.060 in (0.15 mm)
Deck warpage limit	0.006 in (0.15 mm)

Pistons and rings

Piston diameter	3.3837 to 3.3845 in (85.944 to 85.964 mm)
Piston-to-bore clearance	0.0014 to 0.0030 in (0.036 to 0.075 mm)
Ring groove width	
Compression rings	0.059 to 0.060 in (1.52 to 1.54 mm)
Oil control ring	0.1583 to 0.1591 in (4.02 to 4.04 mm)
Piston ring side clearance (compression rings only)	
Standard	0.0012 to 0.0028 in (0.03 to 0.07 mm)
Service limit	0.006 (0.015 mm)
Piston ring end gap	
Top compression ring	0.008 to 0.014 in (0.2 to 0.3 mm)
Second compression ring	0.006 to 0.012 in (0.15 to 0.3 mm)
Oil control ring	0.012 to 0.035 in (0.3 to 0.9 mm)
Service limit	0.039 in (1.0 mm)
Piston pin diameter	0.8651 to 0.8654 in (21.974 to 21.980 mm)
Pin-to-piston clearance	Loose — 0 to 0.0009 in (0 to 0.024 mm)
Pin-to-rod clearance	Press fit

Camshaft

Runout	0.0012 in (0.03 mm)
End play	0.003 to 0.006 in (0.08 to 0.016 mm)
Service limit	0.008 in (0.20 mm)
Bearing journal diameter	
Front (number 1)	1.257 to 1.258 in (31.940 to 31.965 in
Center (numbers 2, 3, 4)	1.256 to 1.257 in (31.910 to 31.935 mm)
Rear (number 5)	1.257 to 1.258 in (31.940 to 31.965 mm)
Service limit	0.002 in (0.05 mm)
Bearing oil clearance	
Front (number 1)	0.0014 to 0.0033 in (0.035 to 0.085 mm)
Center (numbers 2, 3, 4)	0.0026 to 0.0045 in (0.065 to 0.115 mm)
Rear (number 5)	0.0014 to 0.0033 in (0.035 to 0.085 mm)
Service limit	0.0059 in (0.015 mm)
Lobe lift (intake and exhaust)	
Standard	1.5030 to 1.5050 in (38.176 to 38.226 mm)
Service limit	1.4961 in (38.001 mm)

Torque specifications*

	Ft-lbs
Main bearing cap bolts	61 to 65
Connecting rod nuts	37 to 41
Camshaft cap bolts	13 to 20

Note: *Refer to Part A for additional torque specifications.*

B2600 (2.6L) engine (through 1988)

General

Cylinder numbers (front-to-rear)	1-2-3-4
Firing order	1-3-4-2
Compression pressure	
1972 through 1988	149 psi at 250 rpm
1989 and 1990	185 psi at 280 rpm
1991 and later	182 psi at 270 rpm
Oil pressure (engine warm)	45 to 90 PSI at 3000 rpm (6 PSI at idle)

B2600 (2.6L) engine (continued)

Engine block
Cylinder bore diameter . . . . 3.5874 to 3.5882 in (91.12 to 91.14 mm)
Taper and out-of-round limits . . . . 0.0008 in (0.020 mm)
Block deck distortion limit . . . . 0.0039 in (0.10 mm)

Pistons and rings
Piston diameter* . . . . 3.5874 to 3.5882 in (91.12 to 91.14 mm)
Piston ring side clearance
  Standard
    Top compression ring . . . . 0.0020 to 0.0035 in (0.05 to 0.09 mm)
    Second compression ring . . . . 0.008 to 0.0024 in (0.02 to 0.061 mm)
    Oil control ring . . . . Side rails must rotate freely after assembly
  Service limit
    Top compression ring . . . . 0.006 in (0.15 mm)
    Second compression ring . . . . 0.0039 in (0.099 mm)
Piston ring end gap
  Standard
    Top compression ring . . . . 0.012 to 0.018 in (0.30 to 0.45 mm)
    Second compression ring . . . . 0.010 to 0.016 in (0.25 to 0.40 mm)
    Oil control ring . . . . 0.012 to 0.024 in (0.30 to 0.60 mm)
  Service limit
    Top compression ring . . . . 0.039 in (0.99 mm)
    Second compression ring . . . . 0.039 in (0.99 mm)
    Oil control ring . . . . 0.059 in (1.50 mm)
Measured 90° to pin bore, 1.65-inch up from lower edge of piston

Crankshaft and flywheel
Main journal diameter . . . . 2.3614 to 2.3622 in (59.980 to 60.000 mm)
Taper and out-of-round limits . . . . 0.0012 in (0.030 mm)
Main bearing oil clearance . . . . 0.0008 to 0.0020 in (0.020 to 0.050 mm)
Connecting rod journal diameter . . . . 2.0866 in (53.000 mm)
Connecting rod bearing oil clearance . . . . 0.0008 to 0.0024 in (0.020 to 0.060 mm)
Connecting rod end play (side clearance) . . . . 0.004 to 0.010 in (0.10 to 0.25 mm)
Crankshaft end play . . . . 0.002 to 0.007 in (0.05 to 0.18 mm)

Camshaft
Bearing oil clearance . . . . 0.002 to 0.004 in (0.05 to 0.10 mm)
Lobe height (intake and exhaust)
  Standard . . . . 1.6669 in (42.400 mm)
  Service limit . . . . 1.650 in (41.9 mm)
End play
  Standard . . . . 0.0008 to 0.0070 in (0.02 to 0.18 mm)
  Service limit . . . . 0.008 in (0.20 mm)

Cylinder head and valve train
Head warpage limit . . . . 0.006 in (0.15 mm)
Head resurfacing limit . . . . 0.008 in (0.20 mm)
Valve seat angle . . . . 45°
Valve seat width
  Intake . . . . 0.028 to 0.047 in (0.71 to 1.19 mm)
  Exhaust . . . . 0.039 to 0.079 in (0.99 to 2.01 mm)
Valve stem-to-guide clearance
  Intake
    Standard . . . . 0.0010 to 0.0025 in (0.025 to 0.061 mm)
    Service limit . . . . 0.0079 in (0.20 mm)
  Exhaust
    Standard . . . . 0.0020 to 0.0035 in (0.051 to 0.089 mm)
    Service limit . . . . 0.0079 in (0.20 mm)
Valve spring free length
  Standard . . . . 1.961 in (49.80 mm)
  Service limit . . . . 1.921 in (48.8 mm)
Out-of-square service limit . . . . 3° max
Valve spring installed height . . . . Not available

Torque specifications*
	Ft-lbs
Main bearing cap bolts	54 to 61
Connecting rod bearing cap nuts	33 to 35
Crankshaft rear oil seal housing bolts	7.3 to 8.7
Jet valve assembly	13 to 15
Oil pressure sending unit	11 to 15

Note: Refer to Part A for additional torque specifications.

B2600i (2.6L) engine (1989 and later)

General

Displacement	158.97 cubic inches (2.6 liters)
Bore	3.62 inches
Stroke	3.86 inches
Cylinder compression pressure	
Standard	185 psi
Minimum	142 psi
Oil pressure	
At 1000 rpm	16 to 29 psi
At 3000 rpm	45 to 58 psi

Engine block

Cylinder taper limit	0.0007 inches
Cylinder out-of-round limit	0.0007 inches

Pistons and rings

Piston diameter	
1989	3.6194 to 3.6202 inches
1990 and 1991	3.6195 to 3.6203 inches
1992	3.6194 to 3.6202 inches
Piston ring side clearance	
Top compression ring	
Standard	0.0012 to 0.0028 inches
Service limit	0.006 inch
Second compression ring	
Standard	0.0012 to 0.0028 inches
Service limit	0.006 inch
Piston ring end gap	
Top compression ring	
Standard	0.008 to 0.014 inch
Service limit	Not available
Second compression ring	
Standard	0.010 to 0.016 inch
Service limit	Not available
Oil ring	
Standard	0.008 to 0.028 inch
Service limit	0.039 inch
Piston-to-cylinder wall clearance	
Standard	0.0023 to 0.0029 inch
Service limit	0.006 inch

Crankshaft and connecting rods

Endplay	
Standard	0.0031 to 0.0071 inch
Service limit	0.0118 inch
Crankshaft runout	0.0012 inch
Main bearing journals	
Diameter	
Standard	2.3597 to 2.3604 inches
Minimum	2.358 inches
Out-of-round	0.0020 inch
Main bearing oil clearance	
Standard	0.0010 to 0.0017 inch
Service limit	0.0031 inch
Connecting rod journal	
Diameter	
Standard	2.0055 to 2.0061 inches
Minimum	2.004 inches
Out-of-round	0.0020 inch
Connecting rod bearing oil clearance	
Standard	0.0011 to 0.0026 inch
Service limit	0.0039 inch
Connecting rod endplay (side clearance)	
Standard	0.0044 to 0.0103 inch
Service limit	0.012 inch

Cylinder head and valves

Head warpage limit	0.006 inch
Head warpage at manifold surfaces	0.006 inch
Valve seat angle	45-degrees
Valve face angle	45-degrees
Valve margin width	
Intake	0.039 inch
Exhaust	0.059 inch

Valve stem-to-guide clearance
  Standard
    Intake . . . . 0.0010 to 0.0024 inch
    Exhaust . . . . 0.0012 to 0.0026 inch
  Service limit . . . . 0.008 inch
Valve stem diameter
  Intake . . . . 0.2744 to 0.2750 inch
  Exhaust . . . . 0.2743 to 0.2748 inch
Valve spring
  Free length
    Standard . . . . 1.970 inches
    Minimum . . . . 1.963 inches
  Out-of-square . . . . 0.069 inch
Valve stem installed height
  Standard
    Intake . . . . 1.929 to 1.948 inches
    Exhaust . . . . 1.929 to 1.948 inches
  Service limit
    Intake . . . . 1.949 to 1.988 inches
    Exhaust . . . . 1.949 to 1.988 inches

Torque specifications*

Ft-lbs (unless otherwise indicated)

Main bearing cap bolts . . . . 61 to 65
Connecting rod bearing cap nuts . . . . 48 to 50
Oil jet valves . . . . 104 to 156 in-lbs
Balance shaft thrust plate bolts . . . . 69 to 95 in-lbs
Refer to Part A for additional torque specifications

1   General information

Included in this portion of Chapter 2 are the general overhaul procedures for the cylinder head and internal engine components.

The information ranges from advice concerning preparation for an overhaul and the purchase of replacement parts to detailed, step-by-step procedures covering removal and installation of internal engine components and the inspection of parts.

The following Sections have been written based on the assumption that the engine has been removed from the vehicle. For information concerning in-vehicle engine repair, as well as removal and installation of the external components necessary for the overhaul, see Part A of this Chapter and Section 7 of this Part.

The Specifications included in this Part are only those necessary for the inspection and overhaul procedures which follow. Refer to Part A for additional Specifications.

2   Engine overhaul — general information

Refer to illustration 2.4

It's not always easy to determine when, or if, an engine should be completely overhauled, as a number of factors must be considered.

High mileage is not necessarily an indication that an overhaul is needed, while low mileage doesn't preclude the need for an overhaul. Frequency of servicing is probably the most important consideration. An engine that's had regular and frequent oil and filter changes, as well as other required maintenance, will most likely give many thousands of miles of reliable service. Conversely, a neglected engine may require an overhaul very early in its life.

Excessive oil consumption is an indication that piston rings, valve seals and/or valve guides are in need of attention. Make sure that oil leaks aren't responsible before deciding that the rings and/or guides are bad. Perform a cylinder compression check to determine the extent of the work required (see Section 3).

Check the oil pressure with a gauge installed in place of the oil pressure sending unit **(see illustration)** and compare it to the Specifications. If it's extremely low, the bearings and/or oil pump are probably worn out.

Loss of power, rough running, knocking or metallic engine noises, excessive valve train noise and high fuel consumption rates may also point to the need for an overhaul, especially if they're all present at the same time. If a complete tune-up doesn't remedy the situation, major mechanical work is the only solution.

An engine overhaul involves restoring the internal parts to the specifi-

cations of a new engine. During an overhaul, the piston rings are replaced and the cylinder walls are reconditioned (rebored and/or honed). If a rebore is done by an automotive machine shop, new oversize pistons will also be installed. The main bearings, connecting rod bearings and camshaft bearings are generally replaced with new ones and, if necessary, the crankshaft may be reground to restore the journals. Generally, the valves are serviced as well, since they're usually in less-than-perfect condition at this point. While the engine is being overhauled, other components, such as the distributor, starter and alternator, can be rebuilt as well. The end result should be a like new engine that will give many trouble free miles. **Note:** *Critical cooling system components such as the hoses, drivebelts, thermostat and water pump MUST be replaced with new parts when an engine is overhauled. The radiator should be checked carefully to ensure that it isn't clogged or leaking (see Chapter 3). Also, we don't recommend overhauling the oil pump — always install a new one when an engine is rebuilt.*

Before beginning the engine overhaul, read through the entire procedure to familiarize yourself with the scope and requirements of the job. Overhauling an engine isn't difficult, but it is time consuming. Plan on the vehicle being tied up for a minimum of two weeks, especially if parts must be taken to an automotive machine shop for repair or reconditioning. Check on availability of parts and make sure that any necessary special tools and equipment are obtained in advance. Most work can be done with typical hand tools, although a number of precision measuring tools are required for inspecting parts to determine if they must be replaced. Often an automotive machine shop will handle the inspection of parts and offer advice concerning reconditioning and

2.4   The oil pressure can be checked by removing the oil pressure sending unit and installing a gauge in the hole (located just ahead of the oil filter)

replacement. **Note:** *Always wait until the engine has been completely disassembled and all components, especially the engine block, have been inspected before deciding what service and repair operations must be performed by an automotive machine shop.* Since the block's condition will be the major factor to consider when determining whether to overhaul the original engine or buy a rebuilt one, never purchase parts or have machine work done on other components until the block has been thoroughly inspected. As a general rule, time is the primary cost of an overhaul, so it doesn't pay to install worn or substandard parts.

As a final note, to ensure maximum life and minimum trouble from a rebuilt engine, everything must be assembled with care in a spotlessly clean environment.

3   Cylinder compression check

Refer to illustration 3.6

1   A compression check will tell you what mechanical condition the upper end (pistons, rings, valves, head gaskets) of your engine is in. Specifically, it can tell you if the compression is down due to leakage caused by worn piston rings, defective valves and seats or a blown head gasket. **Note:** *The engine must be at normal operating temperature and the battery must be fully charged for this check. Also, the choke valve must be all the way open to get an accurate compression reading (if the engine's warm, the choke should be open).*

2   Begin by cleaning the area around the spark plugs before you remove them (compressed air should be used, if available, otherwise a small brush or even a bicycle tire pump will work). The idea is to prevent dirt from getting into the cylinders as the compression check is being done.

3   Remove all of the spark plugs from the engine (Chapter 1).

4   Block the throttle wide open.

5   Detach the coil wire from the center of the distributor cap and ground it on the engine block. Use a jumper wire with alligator clips on each end to ensure a good ground.

6   Install the compression gauge in the number one spark plug hole **(see illustration)**.

7   Crank the engine over at least seven compression strokes and watch the gauge. The compression should build up quickly in a healthy engine. Low compression on the first stroke, followed by gradually increasing pressure on successive strokes, indicates worn piston rings. A low compression reading on the first stroke, which doesn't build up during successive strokes, indicates leaking valves or a blown head gasket (a cracked head could also be the cause). Deposits on the undersides of the valve heads can also cause low compression. Record the highest gauge reading obtained.

8   Repeat the procedure for the remaining cylinders and compare the results to the Specifications.

9   Add some engine oil (about three squirts from a plunger-type oil can) to each cylinder, through the spark plug hole, and repeat the test.

10   If the compression increases after the oil is added, the piston rings are definitely worn. If the compression doesn't increase significantly, the leakage is occurring at the valves or head gasket. Leakage past

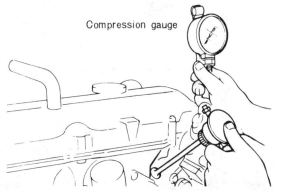

3.6   A compression gauge with a threaded fitting for the spark plug hole is preferred over the type that requires hand pressure to maintain the seal — be sure to open the throttle and choke valves as far as possible during the compression check!

the valves may be caused by burned valve seats and/or faces or warped, cracked or bent valves.

11   If two adjacent cylinders have equally low compression, there's a strong possibility that the head gasket between them is blown. The appearance of coolant in the combustion chambers or the crankcase would verify this condition.

12   If one cylinder is 20 percent lower than the others, and the engine has a slightly rough idle, a worn exhaust lobe on the camshaft could be the cause.

13   If the compression is unusually high, the combustion chambers are probably coated with carbon deposits. If that's the case, the cylinder head should be removed and decarbonized.

14   If compression is way down or varies greatly between cylinders, it would be a good idea to have a leak-down test performed by an automotive repair shop. This test will pinpoint exactly where the leakage is occurring and how severe it is.

4   Engine removal — methods and precautions

If you've decided that an engine must be removed for overhaul or major repair work, several preliminary steps should be taken.

Locating a suitable place to work is extremely important. Adequate work space, along with storage space for the vehicle, will be needed. If a shop or garage isn't available, at the very least a flat, level, clean work surface made of concrete or asphalt is required.

Cleaning the engine compartment and engine before beginning the removal procedure will help keep tools clean and organized.

An engine hoist or A-frame will also be necessary. Make sure the equipment is rated in excess of the combined weight of the engine and accessories. Safety is of primary importance, considering the potential hazards involved in lifting the engine out of the vehicle.

If the engine is being removed by a novice, a helper should be available. Advice and aid from someone more experienced would also be helpful. There are many instances when one person cannot simultaneously perform all of the operations required when lifting the engine out of the vehicle.

Plan the operation ahead of time. Arrange for or obtain all of the tools and equipment you'll need prior to beginning the job. Some of the equipment necessary to perform engine removal and installation safely and with relative ease are (in addition to an engine hoist) a heavy duty floor jack, complete sets of wrenches and sockets as described in the front of this manual, wooden blocks and plenty of rags and cleaning solvent for mopping up spilled oil, coolant and gasoline. If the hoist must be rented, make sure that you arrange for it in advance and perform all of the operations possible without it beforehand. This will save you money and time.

Plan for the vehicle to be out of use for quite a while. A machine shop will be required to perform some of the work which the do-it-yourselfer can't accomplish without special equipment. These shops often have a busy schedule, so it would be a good idea to consult them before removing the engine in order to accurately estimate the amount of time required to rebuild or repair components that may need work.

Always be extremely careful when removing and installing the engine. Serious injury can result from careless actions. Plan ahead, take your time and a job of this nature, although major, can be accomplished successfully.

5   Engine — removal and installation

Refer to illustration 5.24

Warning: *The air conditioning system is under high pressure! Have a dealer service department or service station discharge the system before disconnecting any A/C system hoses or fittings.*

Removal

1   Disconnect the negative cable from the battery.

2   Cover the fenders and cowl and remove the hood (see Chapter 11). Special pads are available to protect the fenders, but an old bedspread or blanket will also work.

3   Remove the air cleaner assembly.

4   Drain the cooling system (see Chapter 1).

5   Label the vacuum lines, emissions system hoses, wiring connec-

tors, ground straps and fuel lines, to ensure correct reinstallation, then detach them. Pieces of masking tape with numbers or letters written on them work well. If there's any possibility of confusion, make a sketch of the engine compartment and clearly label the lines, hoses and wires.

6   Label and detach all coolant hoses from the engine.

7   Remove the cooling fan, shroud and radiator (see Chapter 3).

8   Remove the drivebelts (see Chapter 1).

9   **Warning:** *Gasoline is extremely flammable, so extra precautions must be taken when working on any part of the fuel system. DO NOT smoke or allow open flames or bare light bulbs near the vehicle. Also, don't work in a garage if a natural gas appliance with a pilot light is present.* Disconnect the fuel lines running from the engine to the chassis (see Chapter 4). Plug or cap all open fittings/lines.

10   Disconnect the throttle linkage (and TV linkage/speed control cable, if equipped) from the engine (see Chapter 4).

11   On power steering equipped vehicles, unbolt the power steering pump (see Chapter 10). Leave the lines/hoses attached and make sure the pump is kept in an upright position in the engine compartment (use wire or rope to restrain it out of the way).

12   On A/C equipped vehicles, unbolt the compressor (see Chapter 3) and set it aside. Do not disconnect the hoses.

13   Drain the engine oil (Chapter 1) and remove the filter.

14   Remove the starter motor (see Chapter 5).

15   Remove the alternator (see Chapter 5).

16   Unbolt the exhaust system from the engine (see Chapter 4).

17   If you're working on a vehicle with an automatic transmission, refer to Chapter 7 and remove the torque converter-to-driveplate fasteners.

18   Support the transmission with a jack. Position a block of wood between them to prevent damage to the transmission. Special transmission jacks with safety chains are available — use one if possible.

19   Attach an engine sling or a length of chain to the lifting brackets on the engine.

20   Roll the hoist into position and connect the sling to it. Take up the slack in the sling or chain, but don't lift the engine. **Warning:** *DO NOT place any part of your body under the engine when it's supported only by a hoist or other lifting device.*

21   Remove the gussets (braces) from the rear of the oil pan, then remove the transmission-to-engine block bolts.

22   Remove the engine mount-to-frame bolts.

23   Recheck to be sure nothing is still connecting the engine to the transmission or vehicle. Disconnect anything still remaining.

24   Raise the engine slightly. Carefully work it forward to separate it from the transmission. If you're working on a vehicle with an automatic transmission, be sure the torque converter stays in the transmission (clamp a pair of vise-grips to the housing to keep the converter from sliding out). If you're working on a vehicle with a manual transmission, the input shaft must be completely disengaged from the clutch. Slowly raise the engine out of the engine compartment **(see illustration)**. Check carefully to make sure nothing is hanging up.

25   Remove the flywheel/driveplate and mount the engine on an engine stand.

5.24   Make sure the chain is securely attached to the engine brackets and the hoist before lifting out the engine

Installation

26   Check the engine and transmission mounts. If they're worn or damaged, replace them.

27   If you're working on a manual transmission equipped vehicle, install the clutch and pressure plate (Chapter 7). Now is a good time to install a new clutch.

28   Carefully lower the engine into the engine compartment — make sure the engine mounts line up.

29   If you're working on an automatic transmission equipped vehicle, guide the torque converter into the crankshaft following the procedure outlined in Chapter 7.

30   If you're working on a manual transmission equipped vehicle, apply a dab of high-temperature grease to the input shaft and guide it into the crankshaft pilot bearing until the bellhousing is flush with the engine block.

31   Install the transmission-to-engine bolts and tighten them securely. **Caution:** *DO NOT use the bolts to force the transmission and engine together!*

32   Reinstall the remaining components in the reverse order of removal.

33   Add coolant, oil, power steering and transmission fluid as needed.

34   Run the engine and check for leaks and proper operation of all accessories, then install the hood and test drive the vehicle.

35   Have the A/C system recharged and leak tested.

---

6   Engine rebuilding alternatives

The do-it-yourselfer is faced with a number of options when performing an engine overhaul. The decision to replace the engine block, piston/connecting rod assemblies and crankshaft depends on a number of factors, with the number one consideration being the condition of the block. Other considerations are cost, access to machine shop facilities, parts availability, time required to complete the project and the extent of prior mechanical experience on the part of the do-it-yourselfer.

Some of the rebuilding alternatives include:

Individual parts — If the inspection procedures reveal that the engine block and most engine components are in reusable condition, purchasing individual parts may be the most economical alternative. The block, crankshaft and piston/connecting rod assemblies should all be inspected carefully. Even if the block shows little wear, the cylinder bores should be surface honed.

Short block — A short block consists of an engine block with a crankshaft and piston/connecting rod assemblies already installed. All new bearings are incorporated and all clearances will be correct. The existing cylinder head and external parts can be bolted to the short block with little or no machine shop work necessary.

Long block — A long block consists of a short block plus an oil pump, oil pan, cylinder head, rocker arm cover, camshaft and valve train components, timing sprockets and chain or gears and timing cover. All components are installed with new bearings, seals and gaskets incorporated throughout. The installation of manifolds and external parts is all that's necessary.

Give careful thought to which alternative is best for you and discuss the situation with local automotive machine shops, auto parts dealers and experienced rebuilders before ordering or purchasing replacement parts.

---

7   Engine overhaul — disassembly sequence

Refer to illustrations 7.3a, 7.3b, 7.3c, 7.3d, 5.5a, 5.5b and 5.5c

1   It's much easier to disassemble and work on the engine if it's mounted on a portable engine stand. A stand can often be rented quite cheaply from an equipment rental yard. Before the engine is mounted on a stand, the flywheel/driveplate should be removed from the engine.

2   If a stand isn't available, it's possible to disassemble the engine with it blocked up on the floor. Be extra careful not to tip or drop the engine when working without a stand.

3   If you're going to obtain a rebuilt engine, all external components must come off first, to be transferred to the replacement engine, just as they will if you're doing a complete engine overhaul yourself **(see illustrations)**. These include:

Alternator and brackets*
A/C compressor and brackets*

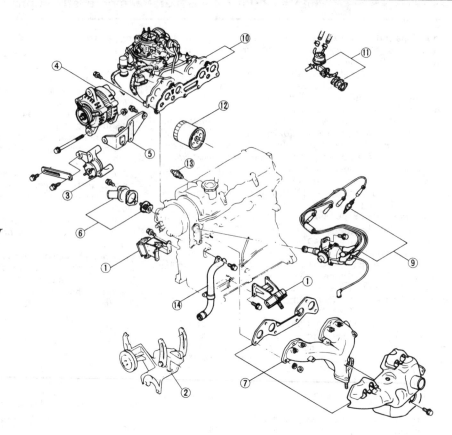

7.3a B2200 engine external components — exploded view

1 Engine mount
2 A/C compressor and power steering pump bracket
3 Cooling fan bracket
4 Alternator
5 Alternator bracket
6 Thermostat and housing
7 Exhaust manifold
8 N/A
9 Distributor
10 Intake manifold
11 Fuel pump
12 Oil filter
13 Oil pressure sending unit
14 Lower radiator hose

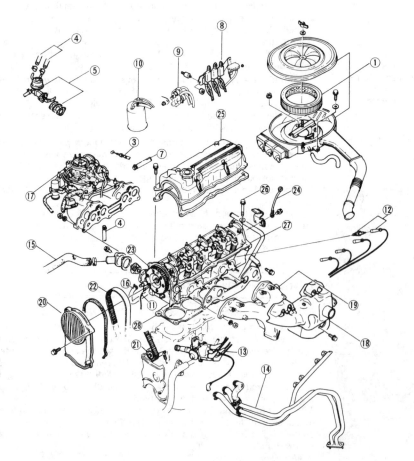

7.3b B2200 engine internal components — exploded view

1 Air cleaner assembly
2 Not used
3 Throttle cable
4 Fuel hose
5 Fuel pump (M/T)
6 Not used
7 Brake vacuum hose
8 3-way solenoid valves and vacuum sensor assembly
9 Duty solenoid valve assembly
10 Canister hose
11 Engine harness connector
12 Spark plugs/wires
13 Distributor
14 Secondary air hose assembly
15 Upper radiator hose
16 Coolant bypass hose
17 Intake manifold
18 Exhaust manifold shroud
19 Exhaust manifold
20 Upper timing belt cover
21 Timing belt tensioner and spring
22 Timing belt
23 Camshaft sprocket
24 Engine ground wire
25 Rocker arm cover
26 Head bolt
27 Cylinder head
28 Head gasket

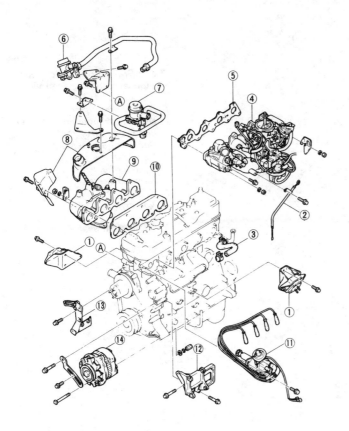

7.3c   Typical 2.6L engine external components — exploded view

1   Engine mount
2   Dipstick and tube
3   Coolant bypass hose
4   Intake manifold
5   Intake manifold gasket
6   No. 2 air control valve
7   No. 1 air control valve
8   Exhaust manifold shroud
9   Exhaust manifold
10 Exhaust manifold gasket
11 Distributor
12 A/C compressor bracket
13 Power steering pump bracket
14 Alternator

2B

7.3d   2.6L engine internal components – exploded view (1988 and earlier model shown)

1   Bracket
2   Exhaust manifold
3   Gasket
4   Coolant bypass pipe
5   Intake manifold
6   Gasket
7   Rocker arm cover
8   Rocker arm shaft assembly
9   Semi-circular seal
10 Distributor drive gear
11 Camshaft
12 Seal
13 Bolt
14 Head bolt
15 Cylinder head
16 Head gasket

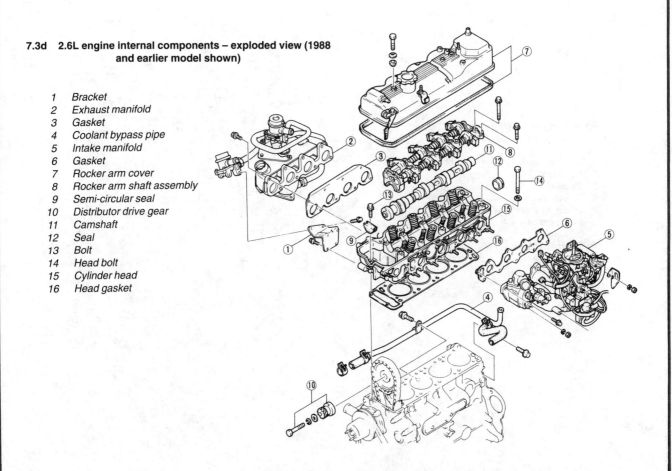

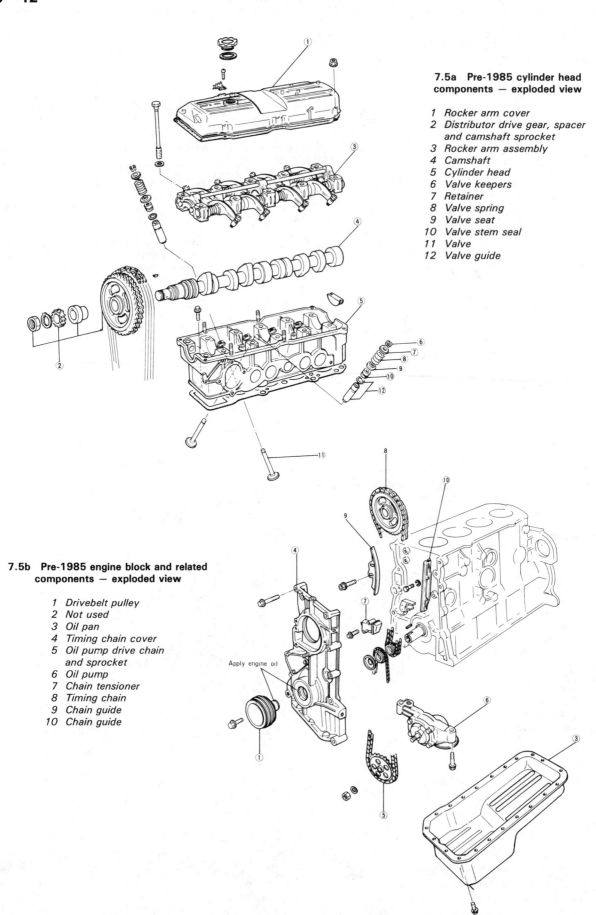

7.5a   Pre-1985 cylinder head components — exploded view

1 Rocker arm cover
2 Distributor drive gear, spacer and camshaft sprocket
3 Rocker arm assembly
4 Camshaft
5 Cylinder head
6 Valve keepers
7 Retainer
8 Valve spring
9 Valve seat
10 Valve stem seal
11 Valve
12 Valve guide

7.5b   Pre-1985 engine block and related components — exploded view

1 Drivebelt pulley
2 Not used
3 Oil pan
4 Timing chain cover
5 Oil pump drive chain and sprocket
6 Oil pump
7 Chain tensioner
8 Timing chain
9 Chain guide
10 Chain guide

Apply engine oil

8.3 A small plastic bag, with an appropriate label, can be used to store the valve train components so they can be kept together and reinstalled in the correct guide

Oil pump
Piston/connecting rod assemblies
Crankshaft and main bearings

6   Before beginning the disassembly and overhaul procedures, make sure the following items are available. Also, refer to *Engine overhaul — reassembly sequence* for a list of tools and materials needed for engine reassembly.

Common hand tools
Small cardboard boxes or plastic bags for storing parts
Gasket scraper
Ridge reamer
Micrometers
Telescoping gauges
Dial indicator set
Valve spring compressor
Cylinder surfacing hone
Piston ring groove cleaning tool
Electric drill motor
Tap and die set
Wire brushes
Oil gallery brushes
Cleaning solvent

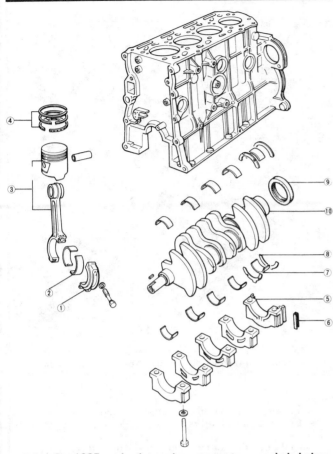

7.5c Pre-1985 engine internal components — exploded view

1 Connecting rod cap	*6 Side seal*
2 Connecting rod bearing	*7 Main bearing*
3 Connecting rod and piston	*8 Thrust bearing*
4 Piston rings	*9 Crankshaft rear oil seal*
5 Main bearing cap	*10 Crankshaft*

Power steering pump and brackets*
Emissions control components
Distributor, spark plug wires and spark plugs*
Thermostat and housing cover
Water pump
Carburetor
Intake/exhaust manifolds
Oil filter*
Engine mounts
Clutch and flywheel/driveplate
Engine rear plate
*Usually done as part of engine removal procedure

Note: *When removing the external components from the engine, pay close attention to details that may be helpful or important during installation. Note the installed position of gaskets, seals, spacers, pins, brackets, washers, bolts and other small items.*

4   If you're obtaining a short block, which consists of the engine block, crankshaft, pistons and connecting rods all assembled, then the cylinder head, oil pan and oil pump will have to be removed as well. See *Engine rebuilding alternatives* for additional information regarding the different possibilities to be considered.

5   If you're planning a complete overhaul, the engine must be disassembled and the internal components **(see illustrations)** removed in the following order:

Rocker arm cover
Intake and exhaust manifolds
Timing cover
Timing chain or belt and sprockets
Rocker arm assembly and camshaft
Cylinder head
Oil pan

8   Cylinder head — disassembly

Refer to illustrations 8.3, 8.4a and 8.4b

Note: *New and rebuilt cylinder heads are commonly available for most engines at dealerships and auto parts stores. Due to the fact that some specialized tools are necessary for the disassembly and inspection procedures, and replacement parts may not be readily available, it may be more practical and economical for the home mechanic to purchase a replacement head rather than taking the time to disassemble, inspect and recondition the original.*

1   Cylinder head disassembly involves removal of the intake and exhaust valves and related components. The camshaft and rocker arm assembly should have been removed previously and the bearing caps (and bearings — if equipped) stored separately in order.
2   The jet valves should be removed from the cylinder head of the 2.6L engine before removal of the intake and exhaust valves. Use a six-point socket and a breaker bar to unscrew them. **Caution:** *Do not tilt the socket — excessive force exerted on the valve spring retainers can easily bend the jet valve stems.* Label each jet valve to ensure installation in its original position. The jet valves can be disassembled by carefully compressing the spring and removing the keepers, the retainer and the spring. Slide the valve out of the body and pull off the seal with a pair of pliers. Discard the old seals. Use new ones during reassembly. Do not allow the parts for one jet valve assembly to become accidentally interchanged with those of another.
3   Before the intake and exhaust valves are removed, arrange to label and store them, along with their related components, so they can be kept separate and reinstalled in the same valve guides they are removed from **(see illustration)**.

8.4a   Measuring the valve spring installed height with a dial caliper

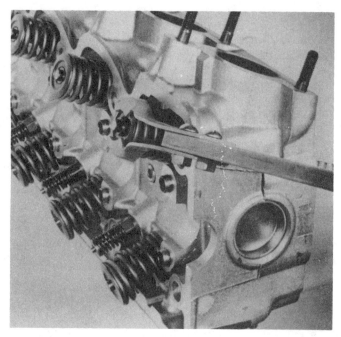

8.4b   Use a valve spring compressor to compress the spring, then remove the keepers from the valve stem

4   Measure the valve spring installed height for each valve and compare it to the Specifications **(see illustration)**. If it is greater than specified the valve seats and faces need attention. Compress the springs on the first valve with a spring compressor and remove the keepers **(see illustration)**. Carefully release the valve spring compressor and remove the retainer, the spring and the spring seat (if used).

5   Pull the valve out of the head, then remove the oil seal from the guide. If the valve binds in the guide (won't pull through), push it back into the head and deburr the area around the keeper groove with a fine file or whetstone.

6   Repeat the procedure for the remaining valves. Remember to keep all the parts for each valve together so they can be reinstalled in the same locations.

7   Once the valves and related components have been removed and stored in an organized manner, the head should be thoroughly cleaned and inspected. If a complete engine overhaul is being done, finish the engine disassembly procedures before beginning the cylinder head cleaning and inspection process.

9   Cylinder head — cleaning and inspection

1   Thorough cleaning of the cylinder head and related valve train components, followed by a detailed inspection, will enable you to decide how much valve service work must be done during the engine overhaul. **Note:** *If the engine was overheated, the cylinder head is probably warped.*

Cleaning

Refer to illustration 9.4

2   Scrape away all traces of old gasket material and sealing compound from the head gasket, intake manifold and exhaust manifold sealing surfaces. **Caution:** *Do not gouge the cylinder head.* Special gasket removal solvents which dissolve the gasket, making removal much easier, are available at auto parts stores.

3   Remove any built up scale around the coolant passages.

4   Run a stiff wire brush through the oil holes, the EGR gas ports and the jet air passages to remove any deposits that may have formed in them **(see illustration)**.

5   Run an appropriate size tap into each of the threaded holes to remove any corrosion and thread sealant that may be present. If compressed air is available, use it to clear the holes of debris produced by this operation. **Warning:** *Wear eye protection when using com-*

pressed air.

6   Clean the exhaust and intake manifold stud threads with an appropriate size die. Clean the rocker arm pivot bolt or stud threads with a wire brush.

7   Clean the cylinder head with solvent and dry it thoroughly. Compressed air will speed the drying process and ensure that all holes and recessed areas are clean. **Note:** *Decarbonizing chemicals may prove helpful for cleaning cylinder heads and valve train components. They are very caustic and should be used with caution. Be sure to follow the instructions on the container.*

8   Without dismantling the rocker arm assembly, clean the rocker arms and shafts with solvent and dry them thoroughly. Compressed air will speed the drying process and can be used to clean out the oil passages.

9   Clean all the valve springs, keepers and retainers with solvent and dry them thoroughly. Clean these assemblies one at a time to avoid mixing up the parts.

10   Scrape off any heavy deposits that may have formed on the valves, then use a motorized wire brush to remove the remaining deposits from

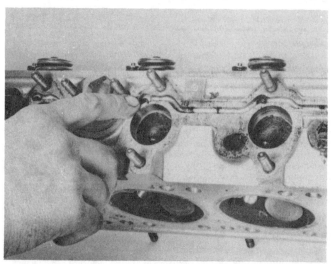

9.4   The Jet air passages, EGR ports and oil holes must be clean and clear

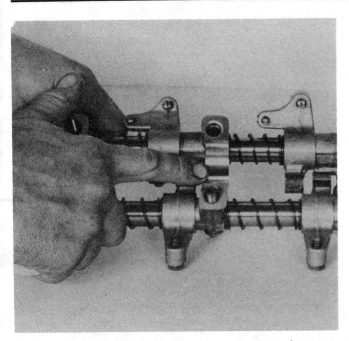

9.11   Inspect the camshaft bearing caps for signs of wear
and damage such as galling and pitting

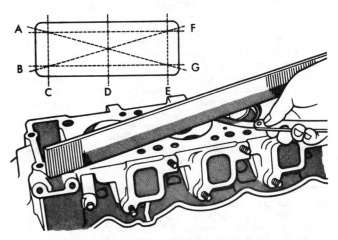

9.12   Check the cylinder head gasket surface for warpage
by trying to slip a feeler gauge under the straightedge
(see the Specifications for the maximum warpage allowed
and use a feeler gauge of that thickness)

the valve heads and stems. Again, do not mix up the valves. If you
are servicing a 2.6L engine cylinder head, also clean the jet valve components with solvent. Do one jet valve assembly at a time so the parts
are not accidentally interchanged. Carefully remove any deposits from
the stems and valve heads with a fine wire brush. **Caution:** *Do not
bend the valve stems of the jet valves while cleaning them.*

Inspection

Cylinder head
Refer to illustrations 9.11, 9.12, 9.14 and 9.15

11 Inspect the head very carefully for cracks, evidence of coolant
leakage and other damage. If cracks are discovered, a new cylinder
head must be obtained. Check the camshaft bearing surfaces in the
head and the bearing caps **(see illustration)**. On engines without
replaceable cam bearings, if there is evidence of excessive cam bearing galling or scoring, the head must be replaced. Failure to do so can
lead to camshaft seizure.

12 Using a precision straightedge and feeler gauges, check the head
gasket mating surface for warpage **(see illustration)**. If the warpage
exceeds the specified amount, the head should be resurfaced at an
automotive machine shop.

13 Examine the valve seats in each of the combustion chambers. If
they are pitted, cracked or burned, take the head to an automotive
machine shop for a valve job. This procedure is beyond the scope of
the home mechanic.

14 Check the valve stem-to-valve guide clearance. Use a dial indicator
to measure the lateral movement of each valve stem with the valve
in the guide and raised off the seat slightly **(see illustration)**. If there
is still some doubt regarding the condition of the valve guides after
this check, the exact clearance and condition of the guides can be
checked by an automotive machine shop.

15 To check the camshaft end play, install the camshaft in the cylinder
head. Mount a dial indicator with the stem resting against the end of
the camshaft **(see illustration)**. Push the camshaft all the way to the
rear and zero the dial indicator. Push the camshaft forward and note
how far it moves. Compare the reading to the Specifications.

Rocker arm assembly (2.6L engine)
*Refer to illustrations 9.16, 9.19a, 9.19b, 9.19c, 9.19d, 9.19e and
9.19f*

16 The rocker arms are mounted on shafts that rest in the camshaft
bearing caps and they are held together by the mounting bolts. The
rocker arms contact the valve on one end and the camshaft on the

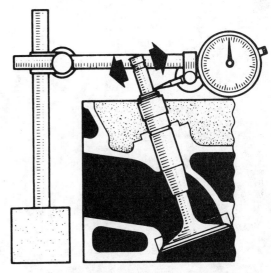

9.14   A dial indicator can be used to determine the valve
stem-to-guide clearance (move the valve
stem as indicated by the arrows)

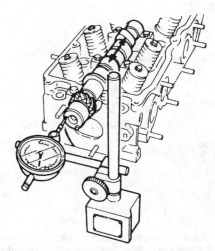

9.15   Measure the camshaft end play with a dial indicator

other end. Check the rocker arm faces that contact the camshaft lobes and the ends of the adjusting screws that contact the valve stems. Look for pitting, excessive wear and roughness **(see illustration)**. Rocker arms should be replaced if worn or damaged — do not reface them.

17 Check the adjusting screw threads for damage. Make sure they can be threaded in and out of the rocker arms.

18 Slide each rocker arm along the shaft, against the locating spring pressure, and check the shaft for excessive wear and evidence of scoring in the areas that normally contact the rocker arms. Measure the shaft diameter and compare it to the Specifications.

19 Any damaged or excessively worn parts must be replaced with new ones. Refer to the accompanying exploded views of the rocker arm assembly components for the correct sequence of disassembly and reassembly **(see illustrations)**.

Camshaft

Refer to illustrations 9.20a, 9.20b, 9.21 and 9.23

20 Inspect the camshaft bearing journals for excessive wear and evidence of galling, scoring or seizure **(see illustration)**. On engines without replaceable cam bearings, if the journals are damaged, the bearing surfaces in the head and bearing caps are probably damaged as well. Both the camshaft and cylinder head will have to be replaced. Pre-1985 models have replaceable cam bearings **(see illustration)** available in several undersizes. This allows the cam to be machined undersize and re-used with the proper bearings.

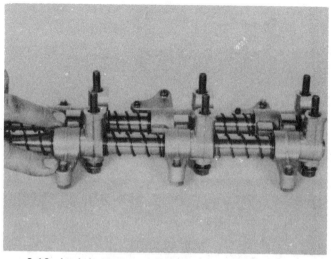

9.16 Look for wear and damage on the rocker arm and adjusting screw surfaces that contact the cam lobe and valve

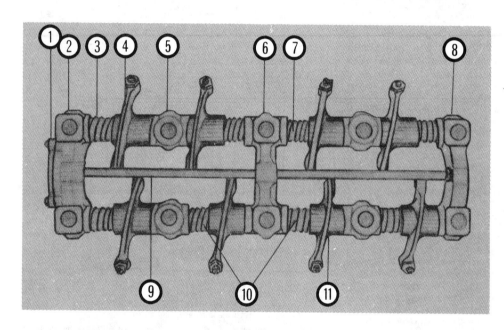

9.19a The oil pipe is installed with the oil ejection holes facing the camshaft and the O-ring in the center bearing cap (pre-1985 models)

1   Thrust plate
2   Front bearing cap
3   Spring
4   Exhaust rocker arm
5   Support
6   Center bearing cap
7   Exhaust rocker shaft
8   Rear bearing cap
9   Oil distribution pipe
10 Intake rocker shaft
11 Intake rocker arm

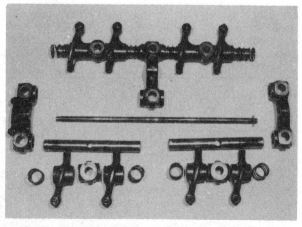

9.19b Partially assembled rocker arm assembly — pre-1985 models (the center bearing cap is installed with the oil hole facing toward the intake side)

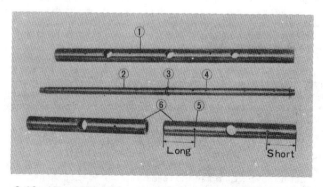

9.19c Pre-1985 rocker shaft components (the ends of the two intake shafts with the longer distance between the oil hole and shaft end must face each other)

1   Exhaust-side shaft
2   Oil distribution pipe
3   O-ring
4   Oil hole
5   Oil hole
6   Intake-side shaft (two-piece)

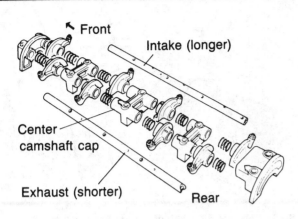

9.19d Rocker arm and shaft components — exploded view (engines with timing belt)

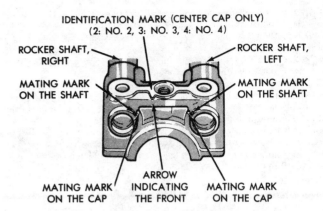

9.19e 2.6L engine camshaft bearing cap marks (1988 and earlier models)

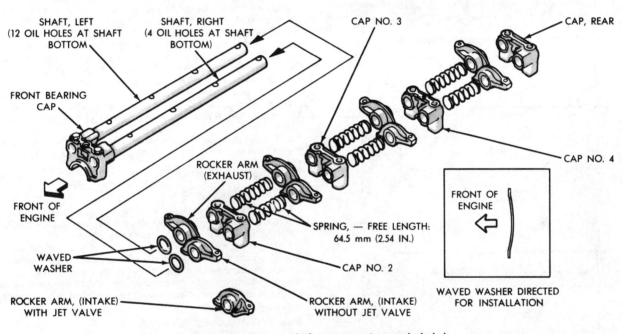

9.19f 2.6L engine rocker arm shaft components – exploded view (1988 and earlier models shown, others similar)

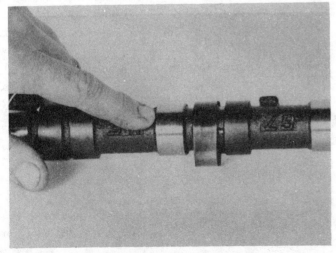

9.20a If the camshaft bearing journals are worn, scored or pitted, a new camshaft is required

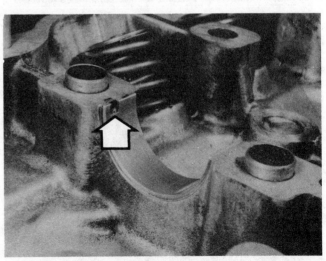

9.20b Pre-1985 models have replaceable cam bearings. The tang (arrow) must line up with the notch in the head

2B

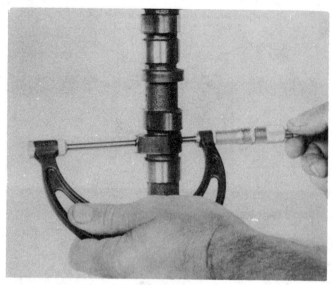

9.21   Measuring camshaft lobe height

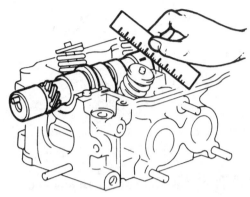

9.23   Compare the width of the crushed Plastigage to the scale on the envelope

21 Check the cam lobes for grooves, flaking, pitting and scoring. Measure the cam lobe height and compare it to the Specifications **(see illustration)**. If the lobe height is less than the minimum specified, and/or the lobes are damaged, get a new camshaft.

22 To measure the camshaft bearing oil clearance, start with clean parts with no oil on them. Temporarily install the camshaft in the head. Place strips of Plastigage lengthwise on the camshaft bearing journals and install the bearing caps. On pre-1985 models, place the head on the engine block, using the old head gasket. Install the bolts and tighten them in the proper sequence (see the appropriate Section in Part A) to the specified torque. **Note:** *Do not turn the camshaft during this procedure.*

23 Remove the caps and compare the Plastigage readings **(see illustration)** to the specifications. Replace any parts which are worn beyond the specified limits.

Valves

Refer to illustration 9.25

24 Carefully inspect each valve face for cracks, pits and burned spots. Check the valve stem and neck for cracks. Rotate the valve and check for any obvious indication that it is bent. Check the end of the stem for pits and excessive wear. The presence of any of these conditions indicates the need for valve service by an automotive machine shop.

25 Measure the width of the valve margin on each valve **(see illustration)** and compare it to the Specifications. Any valve with a margin narrower than specified will have to be replaced with a new one.

Valve components

Refer to illustrations 9.26a and 9.26b

26 Check each valve spring for wear and pitting. Measure the free length and compare it to the Specifications **(see illustration)**. If a spring is shorter than specified, it has sagged and should not be reused. Stand the spring on a flat surface and check it for squareness **(see illustration)**.

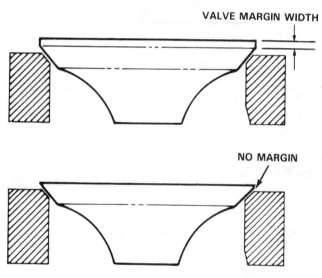

9.25   The margin width on each valve must be as specified (if no margin exists, the valve cannnot be reused)

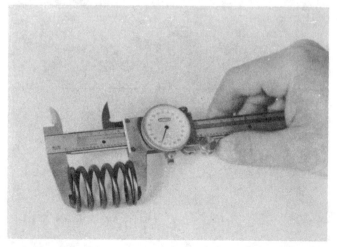

9.26a   Measure the free length of each valve spring with a dial or vernier caliper

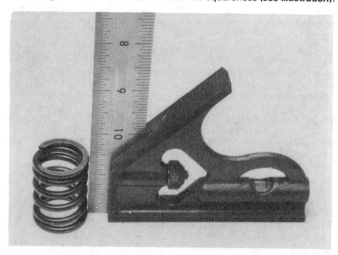

9.26b   Check each valve spring for squareness

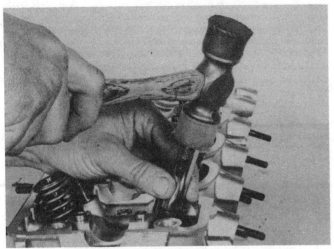

11.4a   Install the new valve guide seals with a hammer and deep socket — don't hammer on the seals once they're seated!

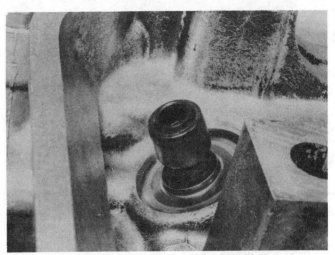

11.4b   Make sure the seals are completely seated on the valve guides

27   Check the spring retainers and keepers for obvious wear and cracks. Any questionable parts should be replaced with new ones. In the event that a retainer or keeper should fail during operation of the engine, extensive damage will occur.

Jet valve assemblies (2.6L engines through 1988)

28   Make sure the valves slide freely in their respective bodies, with no detectable side play. Check each valve head and seat for cracks and pits. Check each spring for wear (on the ends) and cracks. Measure the valve spring free length and the diameter of the stem. Compare the results to the Specifications.

29   If defects are found in any of the components, the entire valve assembly should be replaced with a new one.

30   If the inspection process indicates that the valve components are in generally poor condition and worn beyond the limits specified, which is often the case in an engine being overhauled, reassemble the valves in the cylinder head and refer to Section 10 for valve servicing recommendations.

31   If the inspection turns up no excessively worn parts, and if the valve faces and seats are in good condition, the valve train components can be reinstalled in the cylinder head without major servicing. Refer to the appropriate Section for cylinder head reassembly procedures.

---

10   Valves — servicing

1   Because of the complex nature of the job and the special tools and equipment needed, servicing of the valves, the valve seats and the valve guides, commonly known as a valve job, should be done by a professional.

2   The home mechanic can remove and disassemble the head, do the initial cleaning and inspection, then reassemble and deliver it to a dealer service department or an automotive machine shop for the actual service work. Doing the inspection will enable you to see what condition the head and valvetrain components are in and will ensure that you know what work and new parts are required when dealing with an automotive machine shop.

3   The dealer service department, or automotive machine shop, will remove the valves and springs, recondition or replace the valves and valve seats, recondition the valve guides, check and replace the valve springs, spring retainers and keepers (as necessary), replace the valve seals with new ones, reassemble the valve components and make sure the installed spring height is correct. The cylinder head gasket surface will also be resurfaced if it's warped.

4   After the valve job has been performed by a professional, the head will be in like new condition. When the head is returned, be sure to clean it again before installation on the engine to remove any metal particles and abrasive grit that may still be present from the valve service or head resurfacing operations. Use compressed air, if available, to blow out all the oil holes and passages.

---

11   Cylinder head — reassembly

Refer to illustrations 11.4a, 11.4b, 11.6 and 11.7

1   Regardless of whether or not the head was sent to an automotive repair shop for valve servicing, make sure it's clean before beginning reassembly.

2   If the head was sent out for valve servicing, the valves and related components will already be in place. Begin the reassembly procedure with Step 8.

3   Install the valve spring seats (where applicable) prior to valve seal installation.

4   Install new seals on each of the valve guides with a hammer and deep socket. Gently tap each valve seal into place until it's seated on the guide **(see illustrations)**. *Caution: Don't hammer on the valve seals once they're seated or you may damage them. Don't twist or cock the seals during installation or they won't seal properly on the valve stems.*

5   Apply moly-base grease or engine assembly lube to the first valve and install it in the head. Don't damage the new valve guide oil seal. Set the retainer and keepers in place. Check the installed spring height by lifting up on the retainer until the valve is seated. Measure the distance between the top of the spring seat and the underside of the retainer. Compare your measurement to the specified installed height. Add shims, if necessary to obtain the specified height.

6   Once the correct height is established, remove the keepers and retainer and install the valve springs. **Note:** *The outer spring has a graduated pitch. Install it with the narrow pitch end against the cylinder head* **(see illustration)**.

11.6   Make sure each outer valve spring (right) is installed with the narrow pitch end (arrow) against the cylinder head

11.7   Apply a small dab of grease to each keeper as shown here before installation — it will hold them in place on the valve stem as the spring is released

7   Compress the springs and retainer with a valve spring compressor and slip the keepers into place. Release the compressor and make sure the keepers are seated properly in the valve stem groove. If necessary, grease can be used to hold the keepers in place as the compressor is released **(see illustration)**.
8   Double-check the installed valve spring height for each valve and compare it to the specified installed height **(see illustration 8.4a)**. If it was correct prior to reassembly, it should still be within the specified limits. If it isn't, you must install more shims until it's correct. **Caution:** *Don't, under any circumstances shim the springs to the point where the installed height is less than specified!*
9   If you're working on a 2.6L engine, install new seals on each of the jet valve bodies. Gently tap them into place with a hammer and deep socket. Lubricate and install the valves and make sure the stems slide smoothly in the valve bodies. Install the springs, the retainers and the keepers. When compressing the springs, be careful not to damage the valve stems or the new seals.
10   Install a new O-ring on each jet valve body and apply a thin coat of clean engine oil or grease to each O-ring, the jet valve threads and the seating surfaces.
11   Carefully thread the jet valve assemblies into the cylinder head and tighten them to the specified torque. **Caution:** *Do not tilt the socket — the valve stems bend very easily.*
12   On 2.6L engines and engines with a timing belt, install the camshaft and rocker arm shaft assembly (see Part A, Section 18). **Note:** *Lubricate all moving parts with moly-base grease or engine assembly*

lube. On pre-1985 models, install the camshaft and rocker arm assembly when the head is installed on the engine block.
13   The valves should be adjusted cold (Chapter 1) after installing the head, and again after the engine has been run.
14   Store the head in a clean plastic bag until you're ready to install it.

12   Pistons/connecting rods — removal

Refer to illustrations 12.1, 12.3, 12.4 and 12.6
Note: *Prior to removing the piston/connecting rod assemblies, remove the cylinder head, the oil pan and the oil pump strainer by referring to the appropriate Sections in Chapter 2, Part A.*

1   Use your fingernail to feel if a ridge has formed at the upper limit of ring travel (about 1/4-inch down from the top of each cylinder). If carbon deposits or cylinder wear have produced ridges, they must be completely removed with a special tool **(see illustration)**. Follow the manufacturer's instructions provided with the tool. Failure to remove the ridges before attempting to remove the piston/connecting rod assemblies may result in piston breakage.
2   After the cylinder ridges have been removed, turn the engine upside-down so the crankshaft is facing up.
3   Before the connecting rods are removed, check the end play with feeler gauges. Slide them between the first connecting rod and the crankshaft throw until the play is removed **(see illustration)**. The end play is equal to the thickness of the feeler gauge(s). If the end play exceeds the service limit, new connecting rods will be required. If new rods (or a new crankshaft) are installed, the end play may fall under the specified minimum (if it does, the rods will have to be machined to restore it — consult an automotive machine shop for advice if necessary). Repeat the procedure for the remaining connecting rods.
4   Check the connecting rods and caps for identification marks. If they aren't plainly marked, use a small center punch to make the appropriate number of indentations on each rod and cap (1, 2, 3, etc., depending on the cylinder they're associated with) **(see illustration)**.
5   Loosen each of the connecting rod cap nuts 1/2-turn at a time until they can be removed by hand. Remove the number one connecting rod cap and bearing insert. Don't drop the bearing insert out of the cap.
6   Slip a short length of plastic or rubber hose over each connecting rod cap bolt to protect the crankshaft journal and cylinder wall as the piston is removed **(see illustration)**.
7   Remove the bearing insert and push the connecting rod/piston assembly out through the top of the engine. Use a wooden hammer handle to push on the upper bearing surface in the connecting rod. If resistance is felt, double-check to make sure that all of the ridge was removed from the cylinder.
8   Repeat the procedure for the remaining cylinders.
9   After removal, reassemble the connecting rod caps and bearing

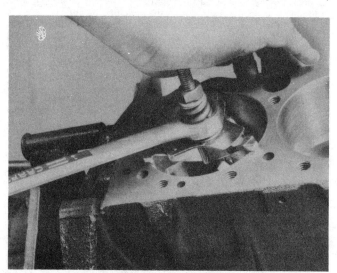

12.1   A ridge reamer is required to remove the ridge from the top of each cylinder — do this before removing the pistons!

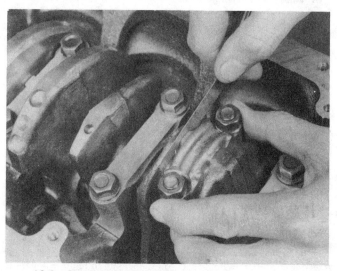

12.3   Check the connecting rod side clearance with a feeler gauge as shown

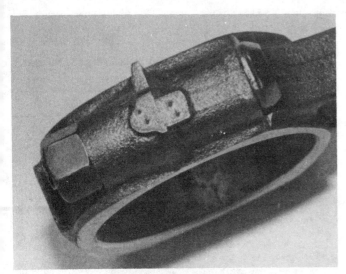

12.4 The connecting rods and caps should be marked to indicate which cylinder they're installed in — if they aren't, mark them with a center punch to avoid confusion during reassembly

12.6 To prevent damage to the crankshaft journals and cylinder walls, slip sections of hose over the rod bolts before removing the pistons

inserts in their respective connecting rods and install the cap nuts finger tight. Leaving the old bearing inserts in place until reassembly will help prevent the connecting rod bearing surfaces from being accidentally nicked or gouged.

10 Don't separate the pistons from the connecting rods (see Section 17 for additional information).

13 Crankshaft — removal

Refer to illustrations 13.1. 13.4 and 13.5

Note: *The crankshaft can be removed only after the engine has been removed from the vehicle. It's assumed that the flywheel or driveplate, vibration damper, timing chain or belt, oil pan, oil pump, front cover and piston/connecting rod assemblies have already been removed. If your engine is equipped with a seal housing, it must be unbolted and separated from the block before proceeding with crankshaft removal.*

1   Before the crankshaft is removed, check the end play. Mount a dial indicator with the stem in line with the crankshaft and just touching one of the crank throws **(see illustration)**.

2   Push the crankshaft all the way to the rear and zero the dial indicator. Next, pry the crankshaft to the front as far as possible and check the reading on the dial indicator. The distance that it moves is the end play. If it's greater than specified, check the crankshaft thrust surfaces for wear. If no wear is evident, new main bearings or thrust bearings should correct the end play.

3   If a dial indicator isn't available, feeler gauges can be used. Gently pry or push the crankshaft all the way to the front of the engine. Slip feeler gauges between the crankshaft and the front face of the thrust main bearing to determine the clearance. The thrust bearing on pre-1985 engines is the rear main, while on 1986 and later engines it's the number three (center) main.

4   Check the main bearing caps to see if they're marked to indicate their locations. They should be numbered consecutively from the front of the engine to the rear. If they aren't, mark them with number stamping dies or a center punch. Main bearing caps generally have a cast-in arrow, which points to the front of the engine **(see illustration)**. Loosen the main bearing cap bolts 1/4-turn at a time each, until they can be removed by hand. Note if any stud bolts are used and make sure they're returned to their original locations when the crankshaft is reinstalled.

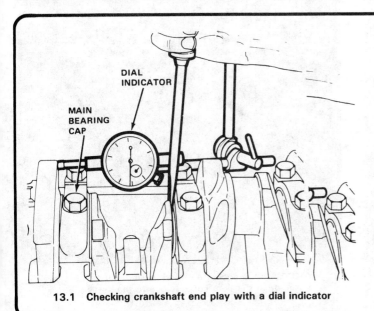

13.1 Checking crankshaft end play with a dial indicator

13.4 The main bearing caps have arrows facing toward the front of the engine

13.5   Using the special tool to remove the rear main bearing cap (pre-1985 engines)

5   Gently tap the caps with a soft-face hammer, then separate them from the engine block. If necessary, use the bolts as levers to remove the caps. **Note:** *On pre-1985 engines, a special puller may be needed to remove the rear bearing cap* (**see illustration**). Try not to drop the bearing inserts if they come out with the caps.

6   Carefully lift the crankshaft out of the engine. It may be a good idea to have an assistant available, since the crankshaft is quite heavy. With the bearing inserts in place in the engine block and main bearing caps, return the caps to their respective locations on the engine block and tighten the bolts finger tight. Store the crankshaft thrust bearings with the appropriate main bearing shells.

14   Engine block — cleaning

Refer to illustrations 14.1, 14.8 and 14.10

Caution: *The core plugs (also known as freeze or soft plugs) may be difficult or impossible to retrieve if they're driven into the block coolant passages.*

1   Drill a small hole in the center of each core plug and pull them out with an auto body type dent puller (**see illustration**).

2   Using a gasket scraper, remove all traces of gasket material from the engine block. Be very careful not to nick or gouge the gasket sealing surfaces.

3   Remove the main bearing caps and separate the bearing inserts

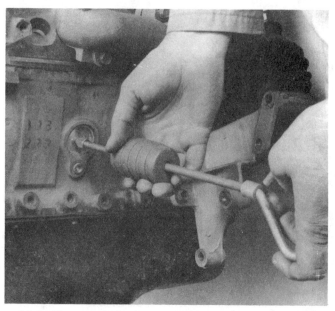

14.1   The core plugs should be removed with a puller — if they're driven into the block they may be impossible to retrieve

from the caps and the engine block. Tag the bearings, indicating which cylinder they were removed from and whether they were in the cap or the block, then set them aside.

4   Remove all of the threaded oil gallery plugs from the block. The plugs are usually very tight — they may have to be drilled out and the holes retapped. Use new plugs when the engine is reassembled.

5   If the engine is extremely dirty it should be taken to an automotive machine shop to be steam cleaned or hot tanked.

6   After the block is returned, clean all oil holes and oil galleries one more time. Brushes specifically designed for this purpose are available at most auto parts stores. Flush the passages with warm water until the water runs clear, dry the block thoroughly and wipe all machined surfaces with a light, rust preventive oil. If you have access to compressed air, use it to speed the drying process and to blow out all the

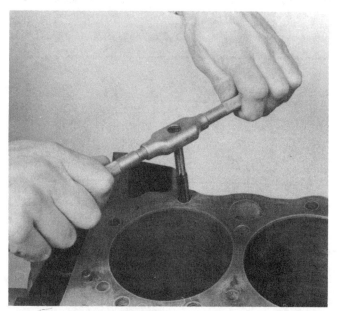

14.8   All bolt holes in the block — particularly the main bearing cap and head bolt holes — should be cleaned and restored with a tap (be sure to remove debris from the holes after this is done)

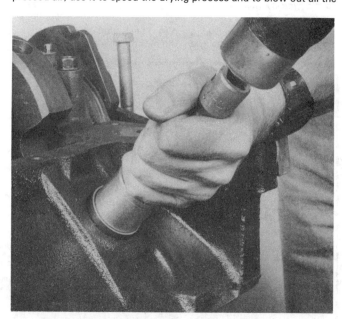

14.10   A large socket on an extension can be used to drive the new core plugs into the bores

oil holes and galleries. **Warning:** *Wear eye protection when using compressed air!*

7   If the block isn't extremely dirty or sludged up, you can do an adequate cleaning job with hot soapy water and a stiff brush. Take plenty of time and do a thorough job. Regardless of the cleaning method used, be sure to clean all oil holes and galleries very thoroughly, dry the block completely and coat all machined surfaces with light oil.

8   The threaded holes in the block must be clean to ensure accurate torque readings during reassembly. Run the proper size tap into each of the holes to remove rust, corrosion, thread sealant or sludge and restore damaged threads **(see illustration)**. If possible, use compressed air to clear the holes of debris produced by this operation. Now is a good time to clean the threads on the head bolts and the main bearing cap bolts as well.

9   Reinstall the main bearing caps and tighten the bolts finger tight.

10   After coating the sealing surfaces of the new core plugs with Permatex no. 2 sealant, install them in the engine block **(see illustration)**. Make sure they're driven in straight and seated properly or leakage could result. Special tools are available for this purpose, but a large socket, with an outside diameter that will just slip into the core plug, a 1/2-inch drive extension and a hammer will work just as well.

11   Apply non-hardening sealant (such as Permatex no. 2 or Teflon pipe sealant) to the new oil gallery plugs and thread them into the holes in the block. Make sure they're tightened securely.

12   If the engine isn't going to be reassembled right away, cover it with a large plastic trash bag to keep it clean.

---

15   Engine block — inspection

Refer to illustrations 15.4a, 15.4b, 15.4c and 15.13

1   Before the block is inspected, it should be cleaned as described in Section 14.

2   Visually check the block for cracks, rust and corrosion. Look for stripped threads in the threaded holes. It's also a good idea to have the block checked for hidden cracks by an automotive machine shop that has the special equipment to do this type of work. If defects are found, have the block repaired, if possible, or replaced.

3   Check the cylinder bores for scuffing and scoring.

4   Measure the diameter of each cylinder at the top (just under the ridge area), center and bottom of the cylinder bore, parallel to the crankshaft axis **(see illustrations)**.

5   Next, measure each cylinder's diameter at the same three locations *across* the crankshaft axis. Compare the results to the Specifications.

6   If the required precision measuring tools aren't available, the piston-to-cylinder clearances can be obtained, though not quite as accurately, using feeler gauge stock. Feeler gauge stock comes in 12-inch lengths and various thicknesses and is generally available at auto parts stores.

7   To check the clearance, select a feeler gauge and slip it into the cylinder along with the matching piston. The piston must be positioned exactly as it normally would be. The feeler gauge must be between the piston and cylinder on one of the thrust faces (90° to the piston pin bore).

8   The piston should slip through the cylinder (with the feeler gauge in place) with moderate pressure.

9   If it falls through or slides through easily, the clearance is excessive and a new piston will be required. If the piston binds at the lower end of the cylinder and is loose toward the top, the cylinder is tapered. If tight spots are encountered as the piston/feeler gauge is rotated in the cylinder, the cylinder is out-of-round.

10   Repeat the procedure for the remaining pistons and cylinders.

11   If the cylinder walls are badly scuffed or scored, or if they're out-of-round or tapered beyond the limits given in the Specifications, have the engine block rebored and honed at an automotive machine shop. If a rebore is done, oversize pistons and rings will be required.

12   If the cylinders are in reasonably good condition and not worn to the outside of the limits, and if the piston-to-cylinder clearances can be maintained properly, then they don't have to be rebored. Honing is all that's necessary (Section 16).

2B

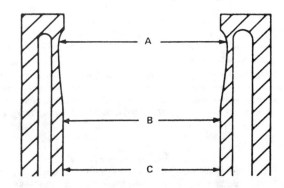

15.4a   Measure the diameter of each cylinder just under the wear ridge (A), at the center (B) and at the bottom (C)

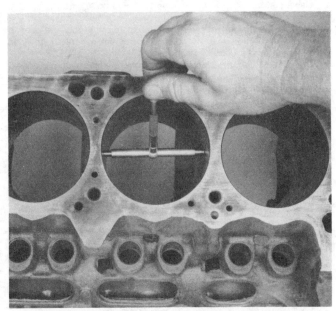

15.4b   The ability to "feel" when the telescoping gauge is at the correct point will be developed over time, so work slowly and repeat the check until you're satisfied that the bore measurement is accurate

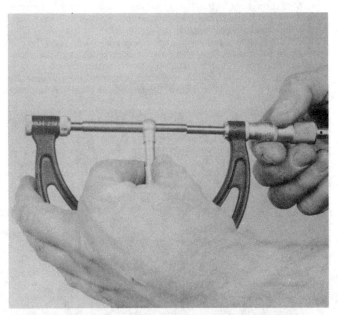

15.4c   The gauge is then measured with a micrometer to determine the bore size

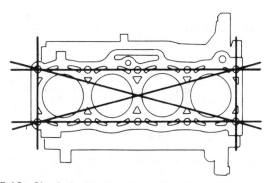

15.13   Check the block deck for distortion with a precision straightedge and feeler gauges

13 Using a precision straightedge and feeler gauge, check the clock deck (the surface that mates with the cylinder head) for distortion **(see illustration)**. If it's distorted beyond the specified limit, it can be resurfaced by an automotive machine shop. The amount that can be taken off is determined by the amount taken off the head, if resurfacing was done. The total that can be removed (head plus block) cannot exceed 0.008-inch. If it does, new components (block and/or head) will be needed. If the block is replaced, new pistons may also be required — check with a dealer service department.

16   Cylinder honing

Refer to illustrations 16.3a and 16.3b

1   Prior to engine reassembly, the cylinder bores must be honed so the new piston rings will seat correctly and provide the best possible combustion chamber seal. **Note:** *If you don't have the tools or don't want to tackle the honing operation, most automotive machine shops will do it for a reasonable fee.*
2   Before honing the cylinders, install the main bearing caps and tighten the bolts to the specified torque.
3   Two types of cylinder hones are commonly available — the flex hone or ''bottle brush'' type and the more traditional surfacing hone with spring-loaded stones. Both will do the job, but for the less experienced mechanic the ''bottle brush'' hone will probably be easier to use. You'll also need some kerosene or honing oil, rags and an electric drill motor. Proceed as follows:

  a) Mount the hone in the drill motor, compress the stones and slip it into the first cylinder **(see illustration)**. Be sure to wear safety goggles or a face shield!
  b) Lubricate the cylinder with plenty of honing oil, turn on the drill and move the hone up-and-down in the cylinder at a pace that will produce a fine crosshatch pattern on the cylinder walls. Ideally, the crosshatch lines should intersect at approximately a 60° angle **(see illustration)**. Be sure to use plenty of lubricant

and don't take off any more material than is absolutely necessary to produce the desired finish. **Note:** *Piston ring manufacturers may specify a smaller crosshatch angle than the traditional 60° — read and follow any instructions included with the new rings.*

  c) Don't withdraw the hone from the cylinder while it's running. Instead, shut off the drill and continue moving the hone up-and-down in the cylinder until it comes to a complete stop, then compress the stones and withdraw the hone. If you're using a ''bottle brush'' type hone, stop the drill motor, then turn the chuck in the normal direction of rotation while withdrawing the hone from the cylinder.
  d) Wipe the oil out of the cylinder and repeat the procedure for the remaining cylinders.

4   After the honing job is complete, chamfer the top edges of the cylinder bores with a small file so the rings won't catch when the pistons are installed. **Be very careful not to nick the cylinder walls with the end of the file.**
5   The entire engine block must be washed again very thoroughly with warm, soapy water to remove all traces of the abrasive grit produced during the honing operation. **Note:** *The bores can be considered clean when a lint-free white cloth — dampened with clean engine oil — used to wipe them out doesn't pick up any more honing residue, which will show up as gray areas on the cloth.* Be sure to run a brush through all oil holes and galleries and flush them with running water.
6   After rinsing, dry the block and apply a coat of light rust preventive oil to all machined surfaces. Wrap the block in a plastic trash bag to keep it clean and set it aside until reassembly.

17   Pistons/connecting rods — inspection

Refer to illustrations 17.4a, 17.4b, 17.5, 17.10 and 17.11

1   Before the inspection process can be carried out, the piston/connecting rod assemblies must be cleaned and the original piston rings removed from the pistons. **Note:** *Always use new piston rings when the engine is reassembled.*
2   Using a piston ring installation tool, carefully remove the rings from the pistons. Be careful not to nick or gouge the pistons in the process.
3   Scrape all traces of carbon from the top of the piston. A hand-held wire brush or a piece of fine emery cloth can be used once the majority of the deposits have been scraped away. Do not, under any circumstances, use a wire brush mounted in a drill motor to remove deposits from the pistons. The piston material is soft and may be eroded away by the wire brush.
4   Use a piston ring groove cleaning tool to remove carbon deposits from the ring grooves. If a tool isn't available, a piece broken off the old ring will do the job. Be very careful to remove only the carbon deposits — don't remove any metal and do not nick or scratch the sides of the ring grooves **(see illustrations)**.
5   Once the deposits have been removed, clean the piston/rod assemblies with solvent and dry them with compressed air (if available). Make sure the oil return holes in the back sides of the ring grooves

16.3a   A ''bottle brush'' hone will produce better results if you have never done cylinder honing before

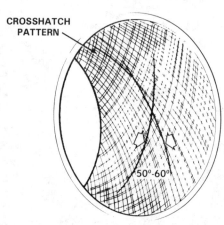

16.3b   The cylinder hone should leave a smooth, crosshatch pattern with the lines intersecting at approximately a 60-degree angle

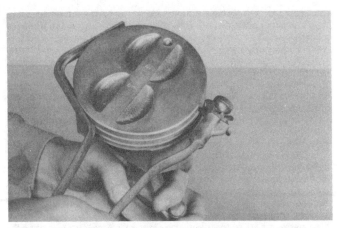

17.4a The piston ring grooves can be cleaned with a special tool, as shown here, . . .

17.4b . . . or a section of a broken ring

and the oil hole in the lower end of each rod are clear **(see illustration)**.

6   If the pistons and cylinder walls aren't damaged or worn excessively, and if the engine block is not rebored, new pistons won't be necessary. Normal piston wear appears as even vertical wear on the piston thrust surfaces and slight looseness of the top ring in its groove. New piston rings, however, should always be used when an engine is rebuilt.

7   Carefully inspect each piston for cracks around the skirt, at the pin bosses and at the ring lands.

8   Look for scoring and scuffing on the thrust faces of the skirt, holes in the piston crown and burned areas at the edge of the crown. If the skirt is scored or scuffed, the engine may have been suffering from overheating and/or abnormal combustion, which caused excessively high operating temperatures. The cooling and lubrication systems should be checked thoroughly. A hole in the piston crown is an indication that abnormal combustion (preignition) was occurring. Burned areas at the edge of the piston crown are usually evidence of spark knock (detonation). If any of the above problems exist, the causes must be corrected or the damage will occur again. The causes may include intake air leaks, incorrect fuel/air mixture, incorrect ignition timing and EGR system malfunctions.

9   Corrosion of the piston, in the form of small pits, indicates that coolant is leaking into the combustion chamber and/or the crankcase. Again, the cause must be corrected or the problem may persist in the rebuilt engine.

10 Measure the piston ring side clearance by laying a new piston ring in each ring groove and slipping a feeler gauge in beside it **(see illustration)**. Check the clearance at three or four locations around each groove. Be sure to use the correct ring for each groove — they are different. If the side clearance is greater than specified, new pistons will have to be used.

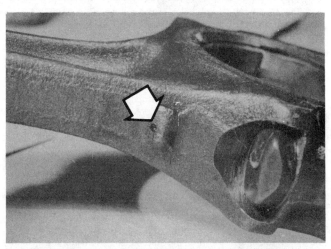

17.5 Make sure the oil hole in the lower end of each connecting rod is clear — if the rods are separated from the pistons, make sure the oil hole is on the correct side when they're reassembled!

11 Check the piston-to-bore clearance by measuring the bore (see Section 15) and the piston diameter. Make sure the pistons and bores are correctly matched. Measure the piston across the skirt, at a 90° angle to the piston pin (refer to the Specifications for the specific location) **(see illustration)**. Subtract the piston diameter from the bore diameter to obtain the clearance. If it's greater than specified, the block will have to be rebored and new pistons and rings installed.

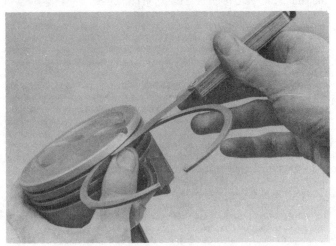

17.10 Check the ring side clearance with a feeler gauge at several points around the groove

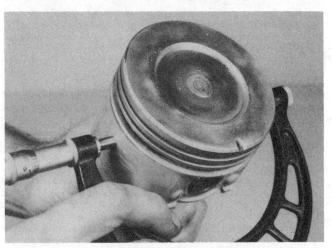

17.11 Measure the piston diameter at the specified point, at right angles to the piston pin

18.4   Check the oil holes in the crankshaft journals to make sure they're clean and smooth — sharp edges here will damage the new bearings!

18.6   Measure the diameter of each crankshaft journal at several points to detect taper and out-of-round conditions

12   Check the piston-to-rod clearance by twisting the piston and rod in opposite directions. Any noticeable play indicates excessive wear, which must be corrected. The piston/connecting rod assemblies should be taken to an automotive machine shop to have the pistons and rods resized and new pins installed.

13   If the pistons must be removed from the connecting rods for any reason, they should be taken to an automotive machine shop. While they are there have the connecting rods checked for bend and twist, since automotive machine shops have special equipment for this purpose. **Note:** *Unless new pistons and/or connecting rods must be installed, do not disassemble the pistons and connecting rods.*

14   Check the connecting rods for cracks and other damage. Temporarily remove the rod caps, lift out the old bearing inserts, wipe the rod and cap bearing surfaces clean and inspect them for nicks, gouges and scratches. After checking the rods, replace the old bearings, slip the caps into place and tighten the nuts finger tight. **Note:** *If the engine is being rebuilt because of a connecting rod knock, be sure to install new rods.*

18   Crankshaft — inspection

Refer to illustrations 18.4 and 18.6

1   Clean the crankshaft with solvent and dry it with compressed air (if available). Be sure to clean the oil holes with a stiff brush and flush them with solvent.

2   Check the main and connecting rod bearing journals for uneven wear, scoring, pits and cracks.

3   Rub a penny accross each journal several times. If a journal picks up copper from the penny, it's too rough and must be reground.

4   Remove all burrs from the crankshaft oil holes with a stone, file or scraper **(see illustration)**.

5   Check the rest of the crankshaft for cracks and other damage. It should be magnafluxed to reveal hidden cracks — an automotive machine shop will handle the procedure.

6   Using a micrometer, measure the diameter of the main and connecting rod journals and compare the results to the Specifications **(see illustration)**. By measuring the diameter at a number of points around each journal's circumference, you'll be able to determine whether or not the journal is out-of-round. Take the measurement at each end of the journal, near the crank throws, to determine if the journal is tapered.

7   If the crankshaft journals are damaged, tapered, out-of-round or worn beyond the limits given in the Specifications, have the crankshaft reground by an automotive machine shop. Be sure to use the correct size bearing inserts if the crankshaft is reconditioned.

8   Check the oil seal journals at each end of the crankshaft for wear and damage. If the seal has worn a groove in the journal, or if it's nicked or scratched, the new seal may leak when the engine is reassembled. In some cases, an automotive machine shop may be able to repair the journal by pressing on a thin sleeve. If repair isn't feasible, a new or

different crankshaft should be installed.

9   Refer to Section 19 and examine the main and rod bearing inserts.

19   Main and connecting rod bearings — inspection

Refer to illustration 19.1

1   Even though the main and connecting rod bearings should be replaced with new ones during the engine overhaul, the old bearings should be retained for close examination, as they may reveal valuable information about the condition of the engine **(see illustration)**.

2   Bearing failure occurs because of lack of lubrication, the presence of dirt or other foreign particles, overloading the engine and corrosion. Regardless of the cause of bearing failure, it must be corrected before the engine is reassembled to prevent it from happening again.

3   When examining the bearings, remove them from the engine block, the main bearing caps, the connecting rods and the rod caps and lay them out on a clean surface in the same general position as their location in the engine. This will enable you to match any bearing problems with the corresponding crankshaft journal.

4   Dirt and other foreign particles get into the engine in a variety of ways. It may be left in the engine during assembly, or it may pass through filters or the PCV system. It may get into the oil, and from there into the bearings. Metal chips from machining operations and normal engine wear are often present. Abrasives are sometimes left in engine components after reconditioning, especially when parts are not thoroughly cleaned using the proper cleaning methods. Whatever the source, these foreign objects often end up embedded in the soft bearing material and are easily recognized. Large particles will not embed in the bearing and will score or gouge the bearing and journal. The best prevention for this cause of bearing failure is to clean all parts thoroughly and keep everything spotlessly clean during engine assembly. Frequent and regular engine oil and filter changes are also recommended.

5   Lack of lubrication (or lubrication breakdown) has a number of interrelated causes. Excessive heat (which thins the oil), overloading (which squeezes the oil from the bearing face) and oil leakage or throw off (from excessive bearing clearances, worn oil pump or high engine speeds) all contribute to lubrication breakdown. Blocked oil passages, which usually are the result of misaligned oil holes in a bearing shell, will also oil starve a bearing and destroy it. When lack of lubrication is the cause of bearing failure, the bearing material is wiped or extruded from the steel backing of the bearing. Temperatures may increase to the point where the steel backing turns blue from overheating.

6   Driving habits can have a definite effect on bearing life. Full throttle, low speed operation (lugging the engine) puts very high loads on bearings, which tends to squeeze out the oil film. These loads cause the bearings to flex, which produces fine cracks in the bearing face (fatigue failure). Eventually the bearing material will loosen in pieces and tear away from the steel backing. Short trip driving leads to corrosion of

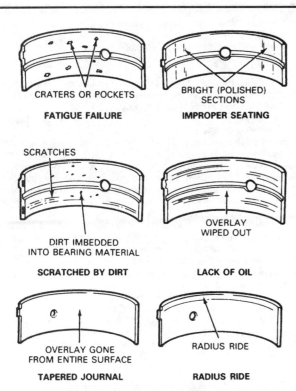

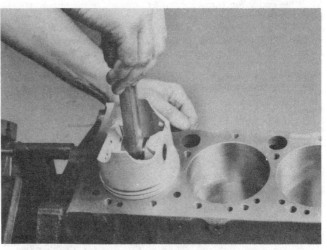

21.3   When checking piston ring end gap, the ring must be square in the cylinder bore (this is done by pushing the ring down with the top of a piston as shown)

19.1   Typical bearing failures

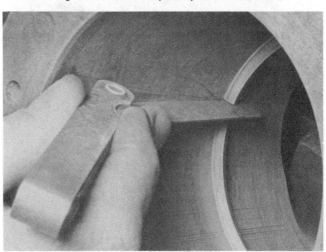

21.4   With the ring square in the cylinder, measure the end gap with a feeler gauge

bearings because insufficient engine heat is produced to drive off the condensed water and corrosive gases. These products collect in the engine oil, forming acid and sludge. As the oil is carried to the engine bearings, the acid attacks and corrodes the bearing material.
7   Incorrect bearing installation during engine assembly will lead to bearing failure as well. Tight fitting bearings leave insufficient bearing oil clearance and will result in oil starvation. Dirt or foreign particles trapped behind a bearing insert result in high spots on the bearing which lead to failure.

20   Engine overhaul — reassembly sequence

1   Before beginning engine reassembly, make sure you have all the necessary new parts, gaskets and seals as well as the following items on hand:
   Common hand tools
   A 1/2-inch drive torque wrench
   Piston ring installation tool
   Piston ring compressor
   Short lengths of rubber or plastic hose
      to fit over connecting rod bolts
   Plastigage
   Feeler gauges
   A fine-tooth file
   New engine oil
   Engine assembly lube or moly-base grease
   Gasket sealant
   Thread locking compound
2   In order to save time and avoid problems, engine reassembly must be done in the following general order:
   Piston rings
   Crankshaft and main bearings
   Piston/connecting rod assemblies
   Crankshaft rear oil seal
   Cylinder head
   Camshaft
   Rocker arm assembly
   Timing chain or belt and sprockets
   Oil pump
   Timing chain cover

   Oil pan
   Intake and exhaust manifolds
   Rocker arm cover
   Engine rear plate
   Flywheel/driveplate

21   Piston rings — installation

Refer to illustrations 21.3, 21.4, 21.5, 21.9a, 21.9b, 21.11 and 21.12

1   Before installing the new piston rings, the ring end gaps must be checked. It's assumed that the piston ring side clearance has been checked and verified correct (Section 17).
2   Lay out the piston/connecting rod assemblies and the new ring sets so the ring sets will be matched with the same piston and cylinder during the end gap measurement and engine assembly.
3   Insert the top (number one) ring into the first cylinder and square it up with the cylinder walls by pushing it in with the top of the piston (**see illustration**). The ring should be near the bottom of the cylinder, at the lower limit of ring travel.
4   To measure the end gap, slip feeler gauges between the ends of the ring until a gauge equal to the gap width is found (**see illustration**). The feeler gauge should slide between the ring ends with a slight amount of drag. Compare the measurement to the Specifications. If the gap is larger or smaller than specified, double-check to make sure you have the correct rings before proceeding.

5   If the gap is too small, it must be enlarged or the ring ends may come in contact with each other during engine operation, which can cause serious damage to the engine. The end gap can be increased by filing the ring ends very carefully with a fine file. Mount the file in a vise equipped with soft jaws, slip the ring over the file with the ends contacting the file face and slowly move the ring to remove material

21.5   If the end gap is too small, clamp a file in a vise and file the ring ends (from the outside in only) to enlarge the gap slightly

from the ends. When performing this operation, file only from the outside in (**see illustration**).
6   Excess end gap isn't critical unless it's greater than 0.040-inch. Again, double-check to make sure you have the correct rings for your engine.
7   Repeat the procedure for each ring that will be installed in the first cylinder and for each ring in the remaining cylinders. Remember to keep rings, pistons and cylinders matched up.
8   Once the ring end gaps have been checked/corrected, the rings can be installed on the pistons.
9   The oil control ring (lowest one on the piston) is usually installed first. It's composed of three separate components. Slip the spacer/expander into the groove (**see illustration**). If an anti-rotation tang is used, make sure it's inserted into the drilled hole in the ring groove. Next, install the lower side rail. Don't use a piston ring installation tool on the oil ring side rails, as they may be damaged. Instead, place one end of the side rail into the groove between the spacer/expander and the ring land, hold it firmly in place and slide a finger around the piston while pushing the rail into the groove (**see illustration**). Next, install the upper side rail in the same manner.
10   After the three oil ring components have been installed, check to make sure that both the upper and lower side rails can be turned smoothly in the ring groove.
11   The number two (middle) ring is installed next. It's usually stamped with a mark which must face up, toward the top of the piston. **Note:** *Always follow the instructions printed on the ring package or box — different manufacturers may require different approaches. Do not mix up the top and middle rings, as they have different cross sections* (**see illustration**).

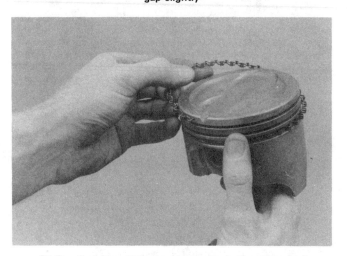

21.9a   Installing the spacer/expander in the oil control ring groove

21.9b   DO NOT use a piston ring installation tool when installing the oil ring side rails

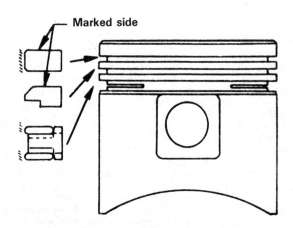

21.11   The piston rings have different shapes, so make sure they aren't mixed up — the marked side must face up!

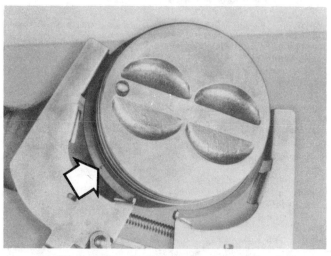

21.12   Installing the compression rings with a ring expander — the mark (arrow) must face up

12 Use a piston ring installation tool and make sure the identification mark is facing the top of the piston, then slip the ring into the middle groove on the piston (**see illustration**). Don't expand the ring any more than necessary to slide it over the piston.

13 Install the number one (top) ring in the same manner. Make sure the mark is facing up. Be careful not to confuse the number one and number two rings.

14 Repeat the procedure for the remaining pistons and rings.

---

22 Crankshaft — installation and main bearing oil clearance check

Refer to illustrations 22.5, 22.6a, 22.6b, 22.11, 22.15, 22.22 and 22.31

1 Crankshaft installation is the first step in engine reassembly. It's assumed at this point that the engine block and crankshaft have been cleaned, inspected and repaired or reconditioned.

2 Position the engine with the bottom facing up.

3 Remove the main bearing cap bolts and lift out the caps. Lay them out in the proper order to ensure correct installation.

4 If they're still in place, remove the original bearing inserts from the block and the main bearing caps. Wipe the bearing surfaces of the block and caps with a clean, lint-free cloth. They must be kept spotlessly clean.

Main bearing oil clearance check

5 Clean the back sides of the new main bearing inserts and lay one in each main bearing saddle in the block. If one of the bearing inserts from each set has a large groove in it, make sure the grooved insert is installed in the block. Lay the other bearing from each set in the corresponding main bearing cap. Make sure the tab on the bearing insert fits into the recess in the block or cap. **Caution:** *The oil holes in the block must line up with the oil holes in the bearing insert* (**see illustration**). *Do not hammer the bearing into place and don't nick or gouge the bearing faces. No lubrication should be used at this time.*

6 On 1986 and newer engines, the flanged thrust bearing must be installed in the number three (center) cap and saddle. On pre-1985 engines, the thrust bearings must be installed in the rear cap and saddle (**see illustrations**).

7 Clean the faces of the bearings in the block and the crankshaft main bearing journals with a clean, lint-free cloth.

8 Check or clean the oil holes in the crankshaft, as any dirt here can go only one way — straight through the new bearings.

9 Once you're certain the crankshaft is clean, carefully lay it in position in the main bearings.

10 Before the crankshaft can be permanently installed, the main bearing oil clearance must be checked.

11 Cut several pieces of the appropriate size Plastigage (they must be slightly shorter than the width of the main bearings) and place one piece on each crankshaft main bearing journal, parallel with the journal axis (**see illustration**).

12 Clean the faces of the bearings in the caps and install the caps in their respective positions (don't mix them up) with the arrows pointing toward the front of the engine. Don't disturb the Plastigage.

13 Starting with the center main and working out toward the ends, tighten the main bearing cap bolts, in three steps, to the specified

2B

22.5   The bearing inserts with the oil groove (arrow) must be installed in the block

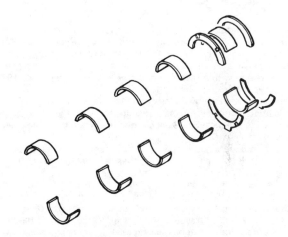

22.6a   On pre-1985 models, install the thrust bearings without tangs in the block and the ones with tangs in the caps

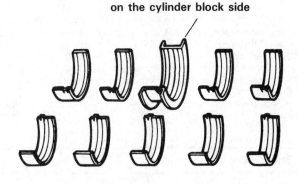

Center main bearing on the cylinder block side

22.6b   1986 and later model main bearings

22.11   Lay the Plastigage strips (arrow) on the main bearing journals, parallel to the crankshaft centerline

22.15 Compare the width of the crushed Plastigage to the scale on the envelope to determine the main bearing oil clearance (always take the measurement at the widest point of the Plastigage); be sure to use the correct scale — standard and metric scales are included

22.22 Slip the new seal over the crankshaft before you install the rear bearing cap (pre-1985 models)

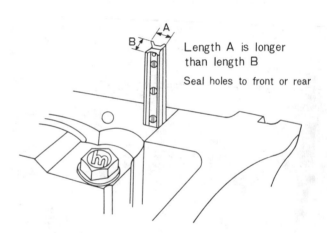

Length A is longer than length B

Seal holes to front or rear

22.31 On pre-1985 models, install the side seals in the rear main bearing cap after coating them with a small amount of RTV sealant

torque. Don't rotate the crankshaft at any time during this operation.

14 Remove the bolts and carefully lift off the main bearing caps. Keep them in order. Don't disturb the Plastigage or rotate the crankshaft. If any of the main bearing caps are difficult to remove, tap them gently from side-to-side with a soft-face hammer to loosen them. Pre-1985 engines may require a puller for the rear cap (see Section 13).

15 Compare the width of the crushed Plastigage on each journal to the scale printed on the Plastigage envelope to obtain the main bearing oil clearance (**see illustration**). Check the Specifications to make sure it's correct.

16 If the clearance is not as specified, the bearing inserts may be the wrong size (which means different ones will be required). Before deciding that different inserts are needed, make sure that no dirt or oil was between the bearing inserts and the caps or block when the clearance was measured. If the Plastigage was wider at one end than the other, the journal may be tapered (refer to Section 18).

17 Carefully scrape all traces of the Plastigage material off the main bearing journals and/or the bearing faces. Use your fingernail or the edge of a credit card — don't nick or scratch the bearing faces.

Final crankshaft installation

18 Carefully lift the crankshaft out of the engine.

19 Clean the bearing faces in the block, then apply a thin, uniform layer of moly-base grease or engine assembly lube to each of the bearing surfaces. Be sure to coat the thrust faces as well as the journal face of the thrust bearing.

20 Make sure the crankshaft journals are clean, then lay the crankshaft back in place in the block.

21 Clean the faces of the bearings in the caps, then apply lubricant to them.

22 Install the caps in their respective positions with the arrows pointing toward the front of the engine. **Note:** *On pre-1985 engines, apply moly-base grease to the lip of the new rear main seal and slide it onto the rear of the crankshaft, then install the rear bearing cap* (**see illustration**).

23 Install the bolts.

24 Tighten all except the thrust bearing cap bolts to the specified torque (work from the center out and approach the final torque in three steps).

25 Tighten the thrust bearing cap bolts to 10-to-12 ft-lbs.

26 Tap the ends of the crankshaft forward and backward with a lead or brass hammer to line up the main bearing and crankshaft thrust surfaces.

27 Retighten all main bearing cap bolts to the specified torque, start-

ing with the center main and working out toward the ends.

28 On manual transmission equipped models, install a new pilot bearing in the end of the crankshaft (see Chapter 8).

29 Rotate the crankshaft a number of times by hand to check for any obvious binding.

30 The final step is to check the crankshaft end play with a feeler gauge or a dial indicator as described in Section 13. The end play should be correct if the crankshaft thrust faces aren't worn or damaged and new thrust bearings have been installed.

31 If you're working on a pre-1985 engine, install new side seals in the rear bearing cap after coating them with a thin layer of RTV sealant (**see illustration**).

32 Refer to Section 23 and install a new rear main seal, then bolt the housing to the block.

23   Rear main oil seal installation

Pre-1985 engines

Refer to Section 22 — rear main oil seal installation on these models is done as part of the crankshaft installation procedure.

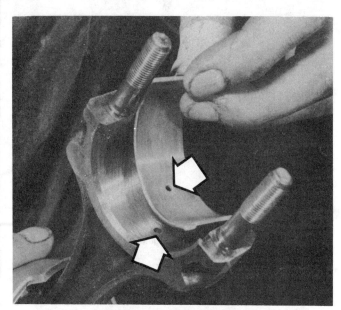

24.3 The tab on each bearing insert must fit into the recess in the rod or cap and the oil holes must line up (arrows)

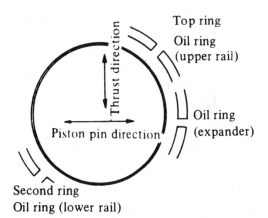

24.5 Stagger the piston ring end gaps as shown here before installing the piston/connecting rod assemblies in the engine

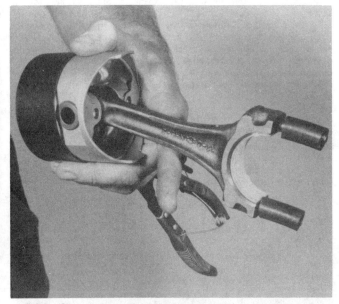

24.7 Slip sections of rubber hose over the rod bolts, then compress the rings with a ring compressor — leave the bottom of the piston sticking out so it will slip into the cylinder

Engines with seal housing that bolts to block

1   The crankshaft must be installed first and the main bearing caps bolted in place, then the new seal should be installed in the housing and the housing bolted to the block.
2   Before installing the crankshaft, check the seal contact surface very carefully for scratches and nicks that could damage the new seal lip and cause oil leaks. If the crankshaft is damaged, the only alternative is a new or different crankshaft.
3   The old seal can be removed from the housing with a hammer and punch by driving it out from the back side. Be sure to note how far it's recessed into the housing bore before removing it; the new seal will have to be recessed an equal amount. Be very careful not to scratch or otherwise damage the bore in the housing or oil leaks could develop.
4   Make sure the housing is clean, then apply a thin coat of engine oil to the outer edge of the new seal. The seal must be pressed squarely

into the housing bore, so hammering it into place is not recommended. If you don't have access to a press, sandwich the housing and seal between two smooth pieces of wood and press the seal into place with the jaws of a large vise. The pieces of wood must be thick enough to distribute the force evenly around the entire circumference of the seal. Work slowly and make sure the seal enters the bore squarely.
5   The seal lips must be lubricated with moly-base grease or engine assembly lube before the seal/housing is slipped over the crankshaft and bolted to the block. Use a new gasket — and RTV sealant — and make sure the dowel pins are in place before installing the housing. If you're working on a 2.6L engine, make sure the oil separator is in place in the housing **(see illustration 22.17 in Part A)**.
6   Tighten the bolts a little at a time until they're all snug.

24 Pistons/connecting rods — installation and rod bearing oil clearance check

Refer to illustrations 24.3, 24.5, 24.7, 24.9a, 24.9b, 24.11, 24.13 and 24.17
1   Before installing the piston/connecting rod assemblies, the cylinder walls must be perfectly clean, the top edge of each cylinder must be chamfered, and the crankshaft must be in place.
2   Remove the cap from the end of the number one connecting rod (refer to the marks made during removal). Remove the original bearing inserts and wipe the bearing surfaces of the connecting rod and cap with a clean, lint-free cloth. They must be kept spotlessly clean.

Connecting rod bearing oil clearance check
3   Clean the back side of the new upper bearing insert, then lay it in place in the connecting rod. Make sure the tab on the bearing fits into the recess in the rod **(see illustration)**. Don't hammer the bearing insert into place and be very careful not to nick or gouge the bearing face. Don't lubricate the bearing at this time.
4   Clean the back side of the other bearing insert and install it in the rod cap. Again, make sure the tab on the bearing fits into the recess in the cap, and don't apply any lubricant. It's critically important that the mating surfaces of the bearing and connecting rod are perfectly clean and oil free when they're assembled.
5   Position the piston ring gaps at staggered intervals around the piston **(see illustration)**.
6   Slip a section of plastic or rubber hose over each connecting rod cap bolt.
7   Lubricate the piston and rings with clean engine oil and attach a piston ring compressor to the piston. Leave the skirt protruding about 1/4-inch to guide the piston into the cylinder. The rings must be compressed until they're flush with the piston **(see illustration)**.
8   Rotate the crankshaft until the number one connecting rod journal is at BDC (bottom dead center) and apply a coat of engine oil to the cylinder walls.

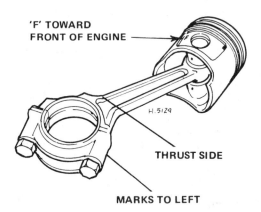

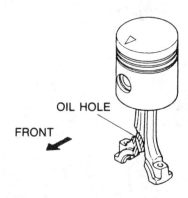

24.9a   The F mark on the side of the piston (pre-1985 model shown) . . .

24.9b   . . . or the arrow (2.6L engine) must face the front of the engine

9   With the F mark on the side of the piston or the arrow on top of the piston (**see illustrations**) facing the front of the engine, gently insert the piston/connecting rod assembly into the number one cylinder bore and rest the bottom edge of the ring compressor on the engine block.

10   Tap the top edge of the ring compressor to make sure it's contacting the block around its entire circumference.

11   Gently tap on the top of the piston with the end of a wooden hammer handle (**see illustration**) while guiding the end of the connecting rod into place on the crankshaft journal. The piston rings may try to pop out of the ring compressor just before entering the cylinder bore, so keep some downward pressure on the ring compressor. Work slowly, and if any resistance is felt as the piston enters the cylinder, stop immediately. Find out what's hanging up and fix it before proceeding. Do not, for any reason, force the piston into the cylinder — you might break a ring and/or the piston.

12   Once the piston/connecting rod assembly is installed, the connecting rod bearing oil clearance must be checked before the rod cap is permanently bolted in place.

13   Cut a piece of the appropriate size Plastigage slightly shorter than the width of the connecting rod bearing and lay it in place on the number one connecting rod journal, parallel with the journal axis (**see illustration**).

14   Clean the connecting rod cap bearing face, remove the protective hoses from the connecting rod bolts and install the rod cap. Make sure the mating mark on the cap is on the same side as the mark on the connecting rod.

15   Install the nuts and tighten them to the specified torque, working

up to it in three steps. **Note:** *Use a thin-wall socket to avoid erroneous torque readings that can result if the socket is wedged between the rod cap and nut. If the socket tends to wedge itself between the nut and the cap, lift up on it slightly until it no longer contacts the cap.* Do not rotate the crankshaft at any time during this operation.

16   Remove the nuts and detach the rod cap, being very careful not to disturb the Plastigage.

17   Compare the width of the crushed Plastigage to the scale printed on the Plastigage envelope to obtain the oil clearance (**see illustration**). Compare it to the Specifications to make sure the clearance is correct.

18   If the clearance is not as specified, the bearing inserts may be the wrong size (which means different ones will be required). Before deciding that different inserts are needed, make sure that no dirt or oil was between the bearing inserts and the connecting rod or cap when the clearance was measured. Also, recheck the journal diameter. If the Plastigage was wider at one end than the other, the journal may be tapered (refer to Section 18).

Final connecting rod installation

19   Carefully scrape all traces of the Plastigage material off the rod journal and/or bearing face. Be very careful not to scratch the bearing — use your fingernail or the edge of a credit card.

20   Make sure the bearing faces are perfectly clean, then apply a uniform layer of clean moly-base grease or engine assembly lube to both of them. You'll have to push the piston into the cylinder to expose the face of the bearing insert in the connecting rod — be sure to slip the protective hoses over the rod bolts first.

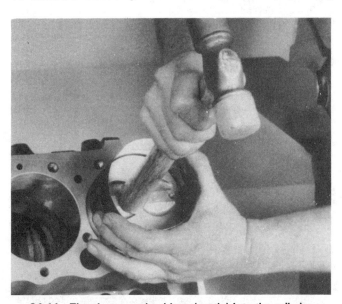

24.11   The piston can be driven (gently) into the cylinder bore with the end of a wooden hammer handle

24.13   Lay the Plastigage strips on each rod bearing journal, parallel to the crankshaft centerline

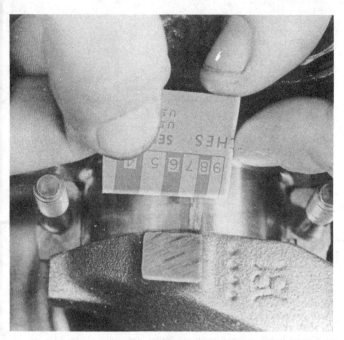

24.17 Measuring the width of the crushed Plastigage to determine the rod bearing oil clearance (be sure to use the correct scale — standard and metric scales are included)

21 Slide the connecting rod back into place on the journal, remove the protective hoses from the rod cap bolts, install the rod cap and tighten the nuts to the specified torque. Again, work up to the torque in three steps.

22 Repeat the entire procedure for the remaining pistons/connecting rods.

23 The important points to remember are . . .
  a) Keep the back sides of the bearing inserts and the insides of the connecting rods and caps perfectly clean when assembling them.
  b) Make sure you have the correct piston/rod assembly for each cylinder.
  c) The arrow or F mark on the piston must face the front of the engine.
  d) Lubricate the cylinder walls with clean oil.
  e) Lubricate the bearing faces when installing the rod caps after the oil clearance has been checked.

24 After all the piston/connecting rod assemblies have been properly installed, rotate the crankshaft a number of times by hand to check for any obvious binding.

25 As a final step, the connecting rod end play must be checked. Refer to Section 12 for this procedure.

26 Compare the measured end play to the Specifications to make sure it's correct. If it was correct before disassembly and the original crankshaft and rods were reinstalled, it should still be right. If new rods or a new crankshaft were installed, the end play may be inadequate. If so, the rods will have to be removed and taken to an automotive machine shop for resizing.

25   Initial start-up and break-in after overhaul

Warning: *Have a fire extinguisher handy when starting the engine for the first time.*

1 Once the engine has been installed in the vehicle, double-check the engine oil and coolant levels.

2 With the spark plugs out of the engine and the ignition system disabled (see Section 3), crank the engine until oil pressure registers on the gauge or the light goes out.

3 Install the spark plugs, hook up the plug wires and restore the ignition system functions (Section 3).

4 Start the engine. It may take a few moments for fuel to reach the carburetor, but the engine should start without a great deal of effort. **Note:** *If backfiring occurs through the carburetor, recheck the valve timing and ignition timing.*

5 After the engine starts, it should be allowed to warm up to normal operating temperature. While the engine is warming up, make a thorough check for fuel, oil and coolant leaks.

6 Shut the engine off and recheck the engine oil and coolant levels.

7 Drive the vehicle to an area with minimum traffic, accelerate at full throttle from 30 to 50 mph, then allow the vehicle to slow to 30 mph with the throttle closed. Repeat the procedure 10 or 12 times. This will load the piston rings and cause them to seat properly against the cylinder walls. Check again for oil and coolant leaks.

8 Drive the vehicle gently for the first 500 miles (no sustained high speeds) and keep a constant check on the oil level. It is not unusual for an engine to use oil during the break-in period.

9 At approximately 500 to 600 miles, change the oil and filter and retorque the cylinder head bolts (if the gasket manufacturer recommends it).

10 For the next few hundred miles, drive the vehicle normally. Do not pamper it or abuse it.

11 After 2000 miles, change the oil and filter again and consider the engine broken in.

2B

Chapter 3 Cooling,
heating and air conditioning systems

Contents

Specifications

General

Radiator cap pressure rating	11 to 15 PSI
Thermostat rating	
B1600 through B2000	180° F
B2200 and B2600	188° F

Torque specifications

Ft-lbs

Thermostat housing cover nuts/bolts	
B2200	14 to 22
All others	
6mm nuts/bolts	5 to 7
8mm nuts/bolts	12 to 17
Water pump bolts	
B2200	14 to 19
B2600	104 to 122 in-lb
All others	
6mm bolts	5 to 7
8mm bolts	12 to 17

---

1 General information

Refer to illustration 1.2

The components of the cooling system are the radiator, upper and lower radiator hoses, water pump, thermostat, radiator cap with pressure relief valve and heater hoses.

The principle of the system is that coolant in the bottom of the radiator circulates up through the lower radiator hose to the water pump, where the pump impeller pushes it around the block and heads through the various cast-in passages to cool the cylinder bores, combustion surfaces and valve seats (see illustration). When sufficient heat has been absorbed by the coolant, and the engine has reached operating temperature, the coolant moves from the cylinder head past the now open thermostat into the top radiator hose and into the radiator header tank. The coolant then travels down the radiator tubes where it is rapidly cooled by the natural flow of air as the vehicle moves down the road. A multi-blade fan, mounted on the water pump pulley, assists this cooling action. The coolant now reaches the bottom of the radiator and the cycle is repeated.

When the engine is cold the thermostat remains closed until the coolant reaches a pre-determined temperature (see the Specifications). This assists rapid warm-up.

The system is pressurized by a spring-loaded radiator filler cap, which prevents premature boiling by increasing the boiling point of the coolant.

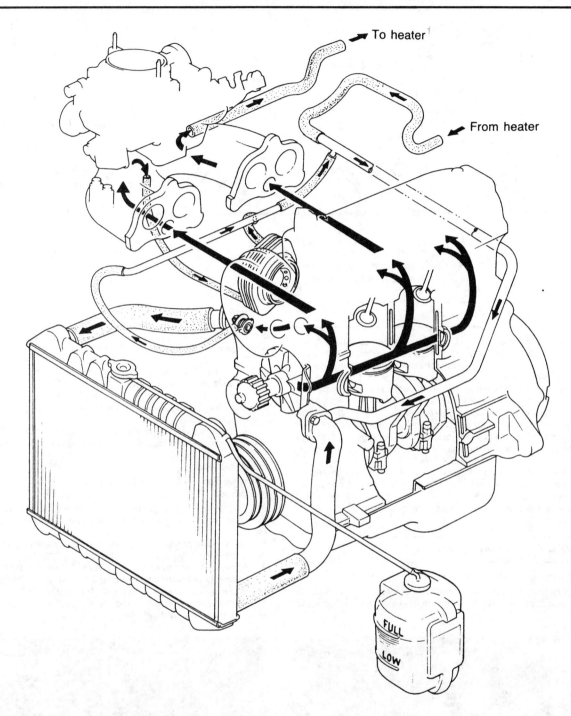

To heater

From heater

FULL

LOW

1.2 Coolant flow diagram — typical

3

If the coolant temperature goes above this increased boiling point, the extra pressure in the system forces the radiator cap internal spring-loaded valve off its seat and exposes the overflow hose, down which displaced coolant escapes into the coolant recovery reservoir.

The coolant recovery system consists of a plastic reservoir into which the overflow coolant from the radiator flows when the engine is hot. When the engine cools, coolant is drawn back into the radiator from the reservoir and maintains the system at full capacity.

Aside from cooling the engine during operation, the cooling system also provides the heat for the vehicles interior heater and heats the intake manifold. On vehicles equipped with an automatic transmission, the transmission fluid is cooled by a cooler attached to the base of the radiator.

On vehicles equipped with an air conditioning system, a condenser is placed ahead of the radiator.

Most radiator cooling fans incorporate either a fluid coupling or a fluid/temperature controlled coupling. The latter device comprises an oil-operated clutch and is a coiled bi-metallic thermostat which functions to permit the fan to slip when the engine is below normal operating temperature and does not require the supplementary air flow provided by the fan at normal running speed. At higher engine operating temperature, the fan is locked and rotates at the speed of the water pump pulley. The fan coupling is a sealed unit and requires no periodic maintenance. **Warning:** *The radiator cap should not be removed while the engine is hot. The proper way to remove the cap is to wrap a thick cloth around it, rotate the cap slowly counterclockwise to the detent and allow any residual pressure to escape. Do not press the cap down until all hissing has stopped, then push down and twist off.*

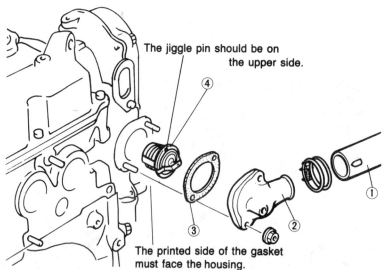

The jiggle pin should be on the upper side.

3.9a   Exploded view of thermostat components — (early model shown — others similar)

1 *Upper radiator hose*
2 *Thermostat housing cover*
3 *Gasket*
4 *Thermostat*

The printed side of the gasket must face the housing.

2   Antifreeze — general information

1   It is recommended that the cooling system be filled with a water/ethylene glycol based antifreeze solution which will give protection down to at least –20 °F. This provides protection against corrosion and increases the coolant boiling point. When handling antifreeze, take care that it is not spilled on the vehicle paint, since it will cause damage if not removed immediately.

2   The cooling system should be drained, flushed and refilled at least every alternate Fall. The use of antifreeze solutions for periods of longer than two years is likely to cause damage and encourage the formation of rust and scale due to the corrosion inhibitors gradually losing their efficiency.

3   The exact mixture of antifreeze to water which you should use depends upon the relative weather conditions. The mixture should contain at least 50 percent antifreeze, but under no circumstances should the mixture contain more than 70 percent antifreeze.

3   Thermostat — check and replacement

Refer to illustrations 3.9a, 3.9b and 3.9c
Note: *Don't drive the vehicle without a thermostat! The computer (when equipped) will stay in open loop and emissions and fuel economy will suffer.*

Check

1   Before condemning the thermostat, check the coolant level, drivebelt tension and temperature gauge (or light) operation.
2   If the engine takes a long time to warm up, the thermostat is probably stuck open. Replace the thermostat.
3   If the engine runs too hot, check the temperature of the upper radiator hose. If the hose isn't hot, the thermostat is probably stuck shut. Replace the thermostat.
4   If the upper radiator hose is hot, it means the coolant is circulating and the thermostat is open. Refer to the troubleshooting section for the cause of overheating.
5   If an engine has been overheated, you may find damage such as leaking head gaskets, scuffed pistons and warped or cracked heads.

Replacement

Warning: *The engine must be completely cool before beginning this procedure!*

6   Disconnect the negative battery cable from the battery.
7   Drain about two quarts of coolant from the cooling system (Chapter 1).
8   Loosen the hose clamp and detach the upper radiator hose from the thermostat housing cover fitting.
9   Remove the nuts/bolts, then detach the thermostat housing cover and gasket **(see illustrations)**. **Note:** *If the cover is difficult to remove, tap it gently with a soft-face hammer or a block of wood. Don't try to pry the cover loose or damage to the gasket sealing surfaces may result and leaks could develop.*

3.9b   On pre-1985 models, the thermostat housing is located at the front of the engine on the intake manifold side

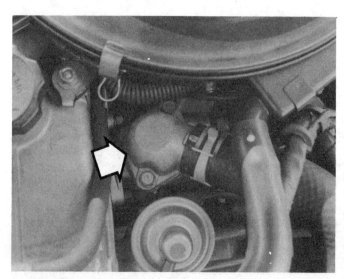

3.9c   On 2.6L engines, the thermostat housing (arrow) is located between the distributor and air cleaner

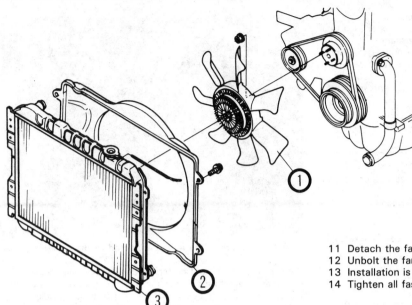

4.10 Fan mounting details (typical)

1 Fan/clutch assembly
2 Fan shroud
3 Radiator

11 Detach the fan and clutch assembly.
12 Unbolt the fan from the clutch (if necessary).
13 Installation is the reverse of removal.
14 Tighten all fasteners securely.

5   Radiator — removal and installation

Refer to illustration 5.9

1   With the engine cold, disconnect the negative battery cable.
2   Remove the undercover (belly pan).
3   Open the drain valve on the underside of the radiator and drain the coolant into a container (see Chapter 1).
4   Remove both the upper and lower radiator hoses.
5   Disconnect the reservoir hose from the radiator filler neck.
6   Remove the screws that attach the shroud to the radiator and slide the shroud toward the engine.
7   If equipped with an automatic transmission, disconnect the cooler hoses from the radiator. Place a drip pan to catch the fluid.
8   Remove the bolts that attach the radiator to the body.
9   Lift out the radiator **(see illustration)**. The shroud may be lifted out now, if desired.
10 With the radiator removed, it can be inspected for leaks or damage. If it requires repair, have a radiator shop or dealer service department perform the work as special techniques are required.
11 Bugs and dirt can be cleaned from the radiator with compressed air and a soft brush. Don't bend the cooling fins as this is done.

10 Note how it's installed (which end is facing up), then lift out the thermostat.
11 Remove all traces of old gasket material and sealant from the housing and cover with a gasket scraper, then clean the gasket mating surfaces with lacquer thinner or acetone.
12 Apply a thin layer of RTV sealant to the gasket mating surfaces of the housing and cover, then install the new thermostat in the housing. Make sure the correct end faces up — the spring is normally directed into the housing.
13 Position a new gasket on the housing and make sure the bolt holes line up.
14 Carefully position the cover on the housing and install the nuts/bolts. Tighten them a little at a time to the specified torque — don't overtighten them or the cover may be distorted.
15 Reattach the radiator hose to the cover fitting and tighten the hose clamp. Now may be a good time to check and replace all of the cooling system hoses and clamps (see Chapter 1).
16 Refer to Chapter 1 and refill the system, then run the engine and check carefully for leaks.

4   Engine cooling fan and clutch — check and replacement

Refer to illustration 4.10
Check

1   Most engines covered in this manual are equipped with thermostatically controlled fan clutches.
2   Begin the clutch check with a lukewarm engine (start it when cold and let it run for two minutes only).
3   Remove the key from the ignition switch for safety purposes.
4   Turn the fan blades and note the resistance. There should be moderate resistance, depending on temperature.
5   Drive the vehicle until the engine is warmed up. Shut it off and remove the key.
6   Turn the fan blades and again note the resistance. There should be a noticeable increase in resistance.
7   If the fan clutch fails this check or is locked up solid, replacement is indicated. If excessive fluid is leaking from the hub or lateral play over 1/4-inch is noted, replace the fan clutch.
8   If any fan blades are bent, don't straighten them! The metal will be weakened and blades could fly off during engine operation. Replace the fan with a new one.

Replacement

9   Remove the fan shroud.
10 Remove the fasteners holding the fan assembly to the water pump hub **(see illustration)**.

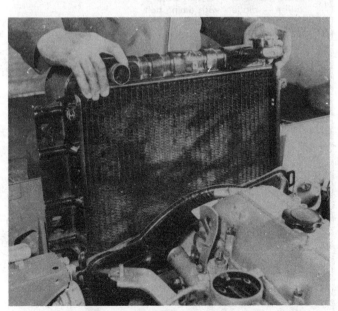

5.9 Let the fan shroud hang on the front of the engine while you lift the radiator out

12 Installation is the reverse of the removal procedure.
13 After installation, fill the cooling system with the proper mixture of antifreeze and water. Refer to Chapter 1 if necessary.
14 Start the engine and check for leaks. Allow the engine to reach normal operating temperature, indicated by the upper radiator hose becoming hot. Recheck the coolant level and add more if required.
15 On automatic transmission equipped models, check and add fluid as needed.

6   Coolant reservoir — removal and installation

Refer to illustration 6.1
1   Disconnect the coolant overflow hose at the reservoir cap **(see illustration)**.
2   Lift the reservoir straight up from its mounting bracket.
3   Pour the contents of the reservoir into a clean container.
4   Installation is the reverse of removal.
5   Refill the container with the proper mixture of antifreeze and water. Refer to Chapter 1 if necessary.

7   Water pump — check

1   Water pump failure can cause overheating of and serious damage to the engine. There are three ways to check the operation of the water pump while it's installed on the engine. If any one of the three following quick checks indicates water pump failure, it should be replaced immediately.
2   Start the engine and warm it up to normal operating temperature. Squeeze the upper radiator hose. If the water pump is working properly,

6.1   Disconnect the hose connected to the radiator (arrow)

a pressure surge should be felt as the hose is released.
3   A seal protects the water pump impeller shaft bearing from contamination by engine coolant. If the seal fails, weep holes in the top and bottom of the water pump snout will leak coolant under the vehicle. If the weep hole is leaking, shaft bearing failure will follow. Replace the water pump immediately.
4   Besides contamination by coolant after a seal failure, the water pump impeller shaft bearing can also be prematurely worn out by an improperly tensioned drivebelt. When the bearing wears out, it emits a high pitched squealing sound. If noise is coming from the water pump during engine operation, the shaft bearing has failed. Replace the water

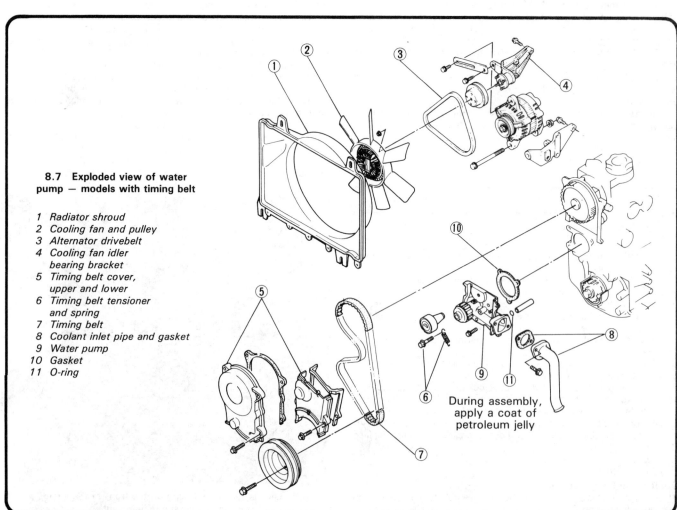

8.7   Exploded view of water pump — models with timing belt

1   *Radiator shroud*
2   *Cooling fan and pulley*
3   *Alternator drivebelt*
4   *Cooling fan idler bearing bracket*
5   *Timing belt cover, upper and lower*
6   *Timing belt tensioner and spring*
7   *Timing belt*
8   *Coolant inlet pipe and gasket*
9   *Water pump*
10 *Gasket*
11 *O-ring*

During assembly, apply a coat of petroleum jelly

pump immediately.

5   To identify excessive bearing wear before the bearing actually fails, grasp the water pump pulley and try to force it up-and-down or from side-to-side. If the pulley can be moved either horizontally or vertically, the bearing is nearing the end of its service life. Replace the water pump.

8 Water pump — removal and installation

1   Disconnect the negative cable from the battery.
2   Drain the cooling system (see Chapter 1).
3   Remove the radiator and shroud for clearance, if necessary (see Section 5).
4   Remove the cooling fan assembly (see Section 4).
5   Remove the drivebelts and any pulleys which are in the way.
6   Disconnect the coolant hoses from the water pump.

Engines with timing belt only

Refer to illustration 8.7

7   Remove the cooling fan idler bearing bracket **(see illustration)**.
8   Remove the timing belt and idler pulley (see Chapter 2, Part A).
9   Remove the coolant inlet pipe.

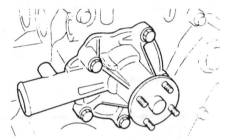

8.10 2.6L water pump — pre-1985 models similar

All models

Refer to illustration 8.10

10   Unbolt and detach the water pump **(see illustration)**.
11   Thoroughly clean away all traces of old gasket and O-ring material.
12   Install the pump with a new gasket, RTV sealer, and an O-ring, where applicable. On 2.6L models, slip the heater hose onto the rear of the pump during installation. Be sure the bolt holes line up with the gasket.
13   Tighten the bolts to the specified torque. The remainder of installation is the reverse of removal.
14   Refill the cooling system, run the engine and check for leaks.

9 Coolant temperature sending unit — check and replacement

Warning: *The engine must be completely cool before removing the sending unit. Antifreeze/coolant is toxic, keep it away from children and pets.*

Refer to illustration 9.10

Check

1   If the coolant temperature gauge is inoperative, check the fuses first (see Chapter 12).
2   If the temperature gauge shows excessive temperature after running a while, see the *Troubleshooting* Section in the front of the manual.
3   If the temperature gauge indicates Hot shortly after the engine is started cold, disconnect the wire at the coolant temperature sensor. If the gauge reading drops, replace the sending unit. If the reading remains high, the wire to the gauge may be shorted to ground or the gauge is faulty.
4   If the coolant temperature gauge fails to show any indication after the engine has been warmed up, (approximately 10 minutes) and the fuses checked out OK, shut off the engine. Disconnect the wire at the sending unit and using a jumper wire, connect it to a clean ground on the engine. Turn on the ignition without starting the engine. If the gauge now indicates Hot, replace the sending unit.
5   If the gauge still does not work, the circuit may be open or the gauge may be faulty, see Chapter 12 for additional information.

Replacement

6   Disconnect the negative cable from the battery.
7   With the engine completely cool, remove the cap from the radiator to release any pressure and then replace the cap. This reduces coolant loss during sending unit replacement.
8   Disconnect the wiring connector from the sending unit.
9   Prepare the new sending unit for installation by applying a light coating of sealer to the threads.
10   Unscrew the sending unit from the engine **(see illustration)** and quickly install the new one to prevent excessive coolant loss.
11   Tighten the sending unit securely and connect the wiring plug.
12   Refill the cooling system and run the engine. Check for leaks and proper gauge operation.

9.10 The coolant temperature sending unit is located adjacent to the thermostat housing on all models (B1600 shown)

10 Blower unit — removal and installation

Refer to illustrations 10.2 and 10.3

Early models

1   Remove the heater assembly as described in Section 11.
2   Separate the two halves of the heater assembly (5 screws). Loosen the fan retaining nut **(see illustration)**, then lightly tap the nut to loosen the fan so that it can be removed from the motor shaft.

FAN

RETAINING NUT

10.2 The fan is located on the firewall side of the heater assembly

3

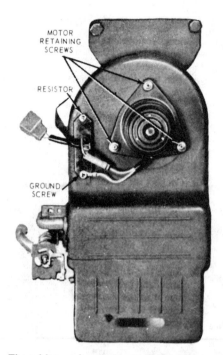

10.3   The wiring and motor mounting screws are located on the side facing the passenger compartment

3   Remove the three motor-to-case retaining screws **(see illustration)**, disconnect the in-line connector to the resistor and the ground screw.
4   Rotate the motor slightly to remove it from the case.
5   Installation is the reverse of removal.

Later models

6   This procedure applies to models where the blower unit is mounted below the glove compartment adjacent to the right kick panel.
7   Disconnect the negative cable from the battery.
8   Remove the right kick panel.
9   Working under the right side of the dash, disconnect the blower motor wires adjacent to the motor.
10   Remove the blower retaining screws and detach the blower unit from the vehicle.
11   nstallation is the reverse of removal.

11   Heater components — removal, installation and adjustment

Refer to illustrations 11.2 and 11.7

Heater assembly

1   Disconnect the negative cable from the battery and drain the cooling system (refer to Chapter 1)
2   Remove the water valve shield (if equipped) at the left-hand side of the heater assembly, and loosen the hose clamps. Remove the hoses **(see illustration)**.
3   Disengage the control cable housing from the heater at the heat/defrost door, water valve and the outside/recirculation door. Disconnect each cable wire at its crank arm.

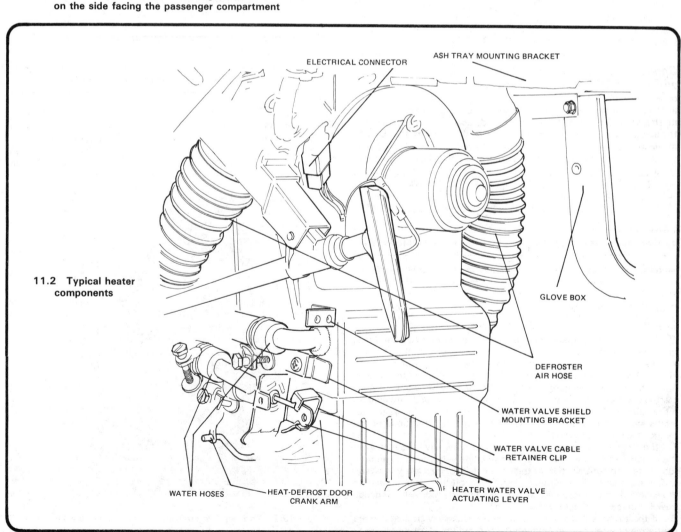

11.2   Typical heater components

ELECTRICAL CONNECTOR

ASH TRAY MOUNTING BRACKET

GLOVE BOX

DEFROSTER
AIR HOSE

WATER VALVE SHIELD
MOUNTING BRACKET

WATER VALVE CABLE
RETAINER CLIP

HEATER WATER VALVE
ACTUATING LEVER

HEAT-DEFROST DOOR
CRANK ARM

WATER HOSES

4 Disconnect the fan motor wires.
5 Remove the glovebox and working in the engine compartment, remove the heater assembly retaining bolt and two retaining nuts. Later models also have a bolt inside the passenger compartment.
6 Disconnect the two defrost ducts from the heater and remove the heater assembly from the vehicle.

Heater core

7 To remove the heater core, remove the screws and separate the two halves of the heater (**see illustration**).
8 Loosen the hose clamps and slide the heater core from the case.
9 Install the replacement core into the case, connecting the core tube to the water valve tube with the short hose and clamps.
10 Assemble the two halves of the heater and fit the retaining screws, then install the heater core to the heater assembly.
11 Position the heater assembly to the firewall, ensuring that the heater duct aligns with the air intake duct and the mounting studs enter the hoses in the firewall.
12 From the engine side of the firewall, install the nuts on the mounting studs. With an assistant lifting the heater up from inside, install the mounting bolt.
13 Connect the defrost ducts. Connect the heat/defrost door control cable wire to the door crank arm and adjust, as described below.
14 Connect the water valve control cable wire to the crank arm on the water valve actuating lever, and locate the housing in the mounting clip. Adjust as described below.
15 Insert the outside/recirculation door control cable wire into the door crank arm hole and tighten the set screw. Adjust as described below.
16 Install the glovebox and secure with the attaching screws.
17 Reconnect the fan motor.
18 Reconnect the heater core hoses and tighten the clamps.
19 Install the water valve shield, fill the cooling system and connect the battery negative cable. Run the engine and bleed the cooling system, if necessary, referring to Chapter 1.

Control cable adjustment

20 Locate the adjustment point by following the cable from the dash control assembly to its other end. Loosen the adjusting clip or screw and move the dash control lever so that the cable is withdrawn into its sheath. Move the under-dash lever toward the cable and tighten the screw or clip. Check the dash mounted control to be sure it can move through its full range of travel. Readjust as necessary.

---

12 Air conditioner and heater control assembly — removal and installation

Early models

1 Disconnect the negative cable from the battery and remove the ashtray and mounting bracket (3 screws).
2 Pull off the heater control knobs, then carefully pry out the control panel and remove the two illumination bulbs.
3 From beneath the instrument panel, remove the two control assembly retaining nuts.
4 Remove the nut retaining the forward end of the control assembly to the bracket on the upper section of the dashpanel.
5 Push the assembly forward and lower it from under the instrument panel. At each of the three cable connections, remove the retaining clip and disconnect the wire from the control lever.
6 When installing, connect the heat/defrost door cable wire to the upper control assembly lever, and the outside/recirculation door cable and the water valve cable wires to the center and lower levers respectively. Secure the housings in the clips.
7 Raise the control assembly up from beneath the instrument panel into the opening, ensuring that the mounting bracket stud on the upper section of the dash panel enters the stud hole in the forward end of the control assembly. Install the mounting nut.
8 Install the nuts (2) which secure the control assembly to the instrument panel and fit the two illumination bulbs.
9 Slide the control panel slots over the center levers and snap the panel into the control assembly.
10 Fit the three control knobs, install the ashtray mounting bracket and ashtray, and reconnect the battery negative cable.

11.7 Remove the retaining screws to separate the case for access to the heater core (early model shown)

3

Later models

Refer to illustration 12.12

11 Disconnect the negative battery cable.
12 Remove the instrument cluster rim (**see illustration**).
13 Remove the glove compartment liner.
14 Pull the control knobs off.
15 Remove the retaining nuts and screws and lift the face plate off.
16 Label and then disconnect the wiring and cables from the control assembly. See Section 11 for the adjustment procedure.
17 Remove the screws retaining the control assembly and carefully pull the unit from the dash.
18 Installation is the reverse of removal.

---

13 Air conditioning system — check and maintenance

Warning: *The air conditioning system is pressurized at the factory and requires special equipment for service and repair. Any work should be left to a dealer service department or a refrigeration shop. Do not, under any circumstances, disconnect the air conditioning hoses while the system is under pressure.*

1 The following maintenance steps should be performed on a regular basis to ensure that the air conditioner continues to operate at peak efficiency.
  a) Check the tension of the drivebelt and adjust if necessary. (Chapter 1).
  b) Inspect the condition of the hoses. Check for cracks, hardening and deterioration. **Warning:** *Do not replace A/C hoses until the system has been discharged by a dealer or air conditioning specialist.*
  c) Inspect the fins of the condenser for leaves, bugs and any other foreign material. A soft brush and compressed air can be used to remove them.
  d) Maintain the correct refrigerant charge.
2 The A/C compressor should be run for about 10 minutes at least once a month. This is particularly important during the winter months because long-term non-use can cause hardening of the internal seals.
3 Because of the complexity of the air conditioning system and the special equipment required to effectively work on it, accurate troubleshooting and repair of the system should be left to a professional mechanic. One probable cause for poor cooling that can be determined

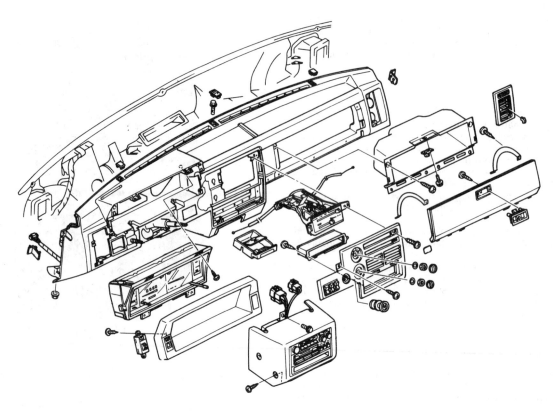

12.12   Exploded view of late model dash components

by the home mechanic is low refrigerant charge. Should the system lose its cooling ability, the following procedure will help you pinpoint the cause.

4   Warm the engine to normal operating temperature.

5   The hood and doors should be open.

6   Set the control mode selector lever to the Norm position.

7   Set the temperature selector lever to the Cold position.

8   Set the blower control selector knob to the Hi position.

9   With the compressor engaged, feel the evaporator inlet pipe between the expansion valve and the evaporator. Compare that to the surface of the accumulator housing.

10 If both surfaces feel about the same temperature and if both feel a little cooler than the ambient temperature, the freon level is probably okay. The problem is elsewhere.

11 If the inlet pipe has frost accumulation or feels cooler than the accumulator surface, the freon charge is low. Add freon as follows.

12 Buy an automotive air conditioner recharge kit and hook it up to the accumulator in accordance with the kit manufacturer's instructions. Add freon until both the accumulator surface and the evaporator inlet pipe feel about the same temperature. Allow stabilization time between each addition.

13 Add one additional can of refrigerant.

14   Air conditioner accumulator — removal and installation

Refer to illustration 14.4

Warning: *The air conditioning system is under high pressure. Do not loosen any hose fittings or remove any components until after the system has been discharged by a dealer service department or automotive air conditioning shop. After the system has been discharged, residual pressure may still remain — be sure to wear eye protection when loosening line fittings!*

1   Have the system discharged.

2   Disconnect the negative cable from the battery.

3   Disconnect the wire from the switch near the top of the accumulator.

4   Detach the refrigerant lines from the accumulator **(see illustration)**

and then cap the open fittings.

5   Unbolt the accumulator from the engine compartment, removing the grille, if necessary (see Chapter 11).

6   Installation is the reverse of removal. Be sure to use new O-rings on the line fittings.

7   Have the system evacuated and recharged by an air conditioning shop or service station.

15   Air conditioner compressor — removal and installation

Refer to illustration 15.6

Warning: *The air conditioning system is under high pressure. Do not loosen any hose fittings or remove any components until after the system has been discharged by a dealer service department, automotive*

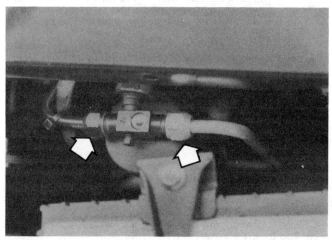

14.4   Detach the refrigerant lines (arrows) from the accumulator

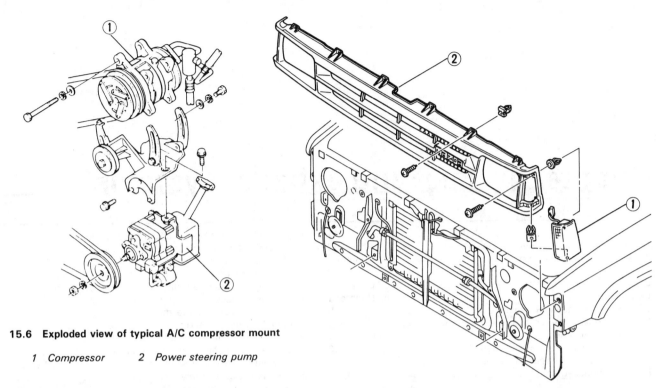

15.6 Exploded view of typical A/C compressor mount

1 Compressor   2 Power steering pump

16.4 Remove the vertical tie bar support (arrow)

air conditioning shop or service station. After the system has been discharged, residual pressure may still remain — be sure to wear eye protection when loosening line fittings!

1 Have the system discharged.
2 Disconnect the negative battery cable from the battery.
3 Remove the drivebelt (Chapter 1).
4 Detach the wire harness from the compressor.
5 Unbolt the refrigerant hose manifold from the compressor and cap all the fittings.
6 Unbolt the compressor and remove it from the vehicle **(see illustration)**.
7 Installation is the reverse of removal. Refer to Chapter 1 and adjust the drivebelt.
8 Have the system evacuated and recharged by an air conditioning shop or service station.

16 Air conditioner condenser — removal and installation

Refer to illustration 16.4
Warning: *The air conditioning system is under high pressure. Do not loosen any hose fittings or remove any components until after the*

system has been discharged by a dealer service department, automotive air conditioning shop or service station. After the system has been discharged, residual pressure may still remain — be sure to wear eye protection when loosening line fittings!

1 Have the system discharged.
2 Disconnect the negative battery cable from the battery.
3 Remove the grille as described in Chapter 11.
4 Remove the radiator tie bar support **(see illustration)**.
5 Disconnect the refrigerant lines from the condenser. Use a back-up wrench to prevent twisting the tubing.
6 Carefully lift the condenser out of the vehicle. Don't lose the rubber mounting pads. Store it upright so the oil won't run out.
7 Cap all open fittings to keep dirt and moisture out.
8 Installation is the reverse of removal. If you're replacing the condenser, drain the oil out of it into a measuring cup and record the amount. The amount drained, plus one ounce, must be replaced during recharging. Use 525 viscosity refrigerant oil.
9 Have the system evacuated, recharged and leak tested by an air conditioning shop or service station.

3

Chapter 4   Fuel and exhaust systems

Contents

Specifications

General

Carbureted

Fuel pressure (mechanical type)	3.7 to 4.7 PSI
Fuel pressure (electrical type)	2.8 to 3.6 PSI
Fuel pump flow rate (electrical type)	52.5 cu in/min at 800 rpm
Fuel pump flow rate (mechanical type)	70.2 cu in/min at 800 rpm

Fuel injected

Fuel pressure	28 to 37 PSI
Fuel pressure drop	21 PSI
Idle speed	See Chapter 1

1   Fuel system – general information

The fuel system is a conventional design. Simply put, fuel is pumped from the fuel tank, through the fuel lines and fuel filter into the carburetor, where it is mixed with air for combustion. The fuel system, as well as the exhaust system, is interrelated with and works in conjunction with various emissions control systems covered in Chapter 6. Thus, some elements that relate directly to the fuel system and carburetor functions are covered in that chapter.

All carburetors are down-draft, two-barrel types. Specific information on the carburetor can be found in Section 9.

Two types of fuel pumps are used. A conventional diaphragm-type, mechanical pump, is attached to the right front side of the cylinder head on earlier models. The operating arm of the pump extends into the cylinder head where it is actuated by an eccentric mounted on the front of the camshaft. This eccentric, when rotating, moves the operating arm back and forth, providing the pump action.

An electric pump is used on some models. It is mounted in the fuel tank or on the frame rail under the truck.

The fuel tank is located under the rear bed of the truck. Besides the fuel feed line leading to the fuel filter and pump, the tank also has an emission vent hose leading to the charcoal canister, an air ventilation line that connects back into the fuel filler hose and a fuel return hose to route excess fuel back to the tank.

2   Fuel tank – removal and installation

Refer to illustration 2.3

Refer to Section 10 for procedures pertaining to the fuel tank on fuel injected models.

Note: *Don't begin this procedure until the gauge indicates that the tank is empty or nearly empty. If the tank must be removed siphon or drain any remaining fuel from the tank prior to removal (see step 3 below).*

Warning: *Gasoline is extremely flammable, so extra precautions must be taken when working on any part of the fuel system. Make sure the engine is cool. Don't smoke or allow open flames or bare light bulbs near the work area. Also, do not work in a garage if a natural gas-type appliance with a pilot light is present. Any repairs to the fuel tank or filler neck should be carried out by a professional who has experience in this critical and potentially dangerous work. While performing any work on the fuel tank, be sure to have a CO2 fire extinguisher on hand and wear safety glasses.*

1   Disconnect the negative battery cable from the battery.
2   Remove the fuel filler cap to relieve pressure in the fuel tank.

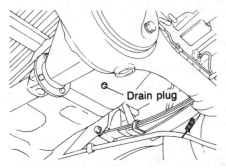

2.3   Most models will have a drain plug in the fuel tank (be careful when draining gasoline because fuel vapors are very flammable – store the gasoline in an appropriate storage container while the fuel tank is being repaired)

3   Remove the drain plug from the bottom of the fuel tank and drain the fuel into an approved gasoline container **(see illustration)**.
4   From the top of the fuel tank, disconnect the fuel filler hose, fuel outlet hose, air ventilation hose, breather hose, fuel return hose and the wiring connector leading to the fuel tank gauge unit. Immediately plug all openings to prevent the entry of dirt.
5   If equipped, remove the fuel tank protector shield mounted in front of the tank.
6   Support the tank with a floor jack and a piece of wood to spread the load. Remove the fuel tank mounting bolts and carefully lower the tank from the truck. Check for any hoses or wiring which may still be connected as the tank is lowered.
7   It is recommended that the tank be cleaned out immediately after removal, especially if it is to be worked on or stored. See Section 3.
8   Before installing the tank make sure that all traces of dirt and corrosion are cleaned from it. If the tank is rusted internally however, it should be replaced with a new one.
9   Installation is the reverse of the removal procedure.

3   Fuel tank – cleaning and repair

1   Repairs to the fuel tank or filler neck should be performed by a professional with the proper training to carry out this critical and potentially dangerous work. Even after cleaning and flushing, explosive fumes can remain and could explode during repair of the tank.
2   If the fuel tank is removed from the vehicle, it should not be placed in an area where sparks or open flames could ignite the fumes

coming out of the tank. Be especially careful inside garages where a natural gas appliance is located because the pilot light could cause an explosion.

4   Fuel tank gauge unit – removal and installation

Warning: *Gasoline is extremely flammable, so extra precautions must be taken when working on any part of the fuel system. Make sure the engine is cool. Don't smoke or allow open flames or bare light bulbs near the work area. Also, do not work in a garage if a natural gas-type appliance with a pilot light is present. While performing any work on the fuel tank be sure to have a CO2 fire extinguisher on hand and wear safety glasses.*
1   Disconnect the negative battery cable.
2   Disconnect the wires leading to the fuel tank gauge unit.
3   Remove the fuel tank as described in Section 2.
4   Remove the gauge unit lock plate by using a hammer and brass punch to turn it clockwise. **Warning:** *Don't use a screwdriver or punch made from any material other than brass. They could cause sparks which could cause an explosion!*
5   Lift the gauge unit from the tank, and cover the tank opening to prevent the entry of dirt.
6   Installation is the reverse of the removal procedure.

5   Fuel lines – repair and replacement

Refer to illustrations 5.1a and 5.1b
Warning: *The fuel tank pressure must be relieved before disconnecting fuel lines and fittings by removing the fuel filler cap. Gasoline is extremely flammable, so extra precautions must be taken when working on any part of the fuel system. Don't smoke or allow open flames or bare light bulbs near the work area. Also, don't work in a garage where a natural gas appliance such as a water heater or clothes dryer is present. Finally, prior to any operation in which a fuel line line will be disconnected, remove the negative cable from the battery to eliminate the possibility of sparks occurring while fuel vapor is present.*

1   If a section of metal fuel line must be replaced, only brazed seamless steel should be used, as copper or aluminum tubing doesn't have enough durability to withstand normal engine vibrations **(see illustrations)**.

4

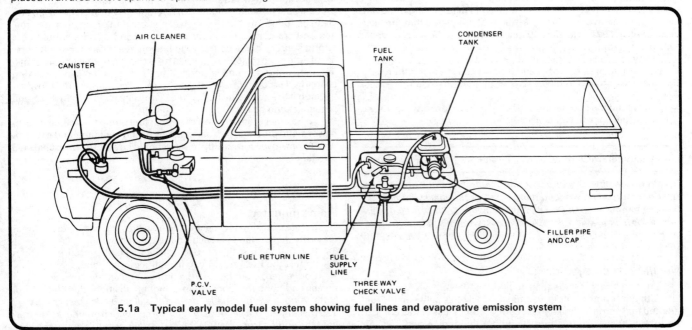

5.1a   Typical early model fuel system showing fuel lines and evaporative emission system

AIR CLEANER

CANISTER

CONDENSER TANK

FUEL TANK

P.C.V. VALVE

FUEL RETURN LINE

FUEL SUPPLY LINE

THREE WAY CHECK VALVE

FILLER PIPE AND CAP

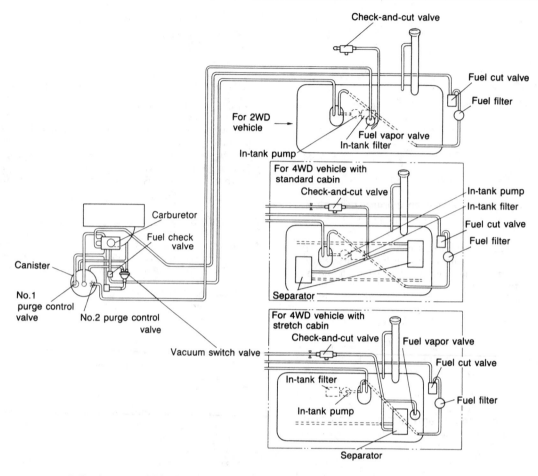

5.1b   Later model fuel system showing fuel lines and evaporative emission system

2   If only one section of a metal fuel line is damaged, it can be cut out and replaced with a piece of rubber hose. The rubber hose should be cut four inches (100 mm) longer than the section it's replacing, so there is about two inches of overlap between the rubber and metal tubing at either end of the section. Hose clamps should be used to secure both ends of the repaired section.

3   If a section of metal line longer than six inches is being removed, use a combination of metal tubing and rubber hose so that the hose lengths will not be longer than 10-inches. **Warning:** *Never use rubber hose within four inches of any part of the exhaust system!*

4   Always replace O-rings and hose clamps.

5   Do not kink or twist hoses and tubes when installing them.

6   To avoid damage to hoses, do not tighten hose clamps excessively.

7   Always run the engine and check for leaks before driving the vehicle after fuel lines have been serviced.

---

6   Fuel pump (carbureted models) – check

Warning: *Gasoline is extremely flammable, so extra precautions must be taken when working on any part of the fuel system. Make sure the engine is cool. Don't smoke or allow open flames or bare light bulbs near the work area. Also, do not work in a garage if a natural gas-type appliance with a pilot light is present. Wear safety glasses.*

Mechanical pump

1   Check that there is adequate fuel in the fuel tank.

2   With the engine running, examine all fuel lines between the fuel tank and fuel pump for leaks, loose connections, kinks or flattening in the rubber hoses. Do this quickly, before the engine gets hot. Air leaks upstream of the fuel pump can seriously affect the pump's output.

3   Check the pump diaphragm flange for leaks.

4   Remove the fuel filler cap to relieve fuel tank pressure. Disconnect the fuel line at the carburetor. Disconnect the ignition coil wire from the coil and ground it on the engine block (use a jumper wire to prevent sparks) so the engine can be cranked without it firing. Place a clean container such as a coffee can at the end of the detached fuel line and crank the engine for several seconds. There should be a strong spurt of gasoline from the line on every second revolution.

5   If little or no gasoline emerges from the line during engine cranking, then either the line is clogged or the fuel pump is not working properly. Disconnect the fuel line from the pump and blow air through it to be sure the line is clear. If the line is clear then the pump is suspect and needs to be replaced with a new one.

6   A more accurate method of testing fuel pump flow capacity is to perform the previous test using a measuring container and a watch. At 800 rpm in one minute, the pump should be able to pump 0.909 US quarts.

Electric pump

Frame mounted

7   Before checking the electric the fuse first and with a test voltmeter verify that voltage is reaching the electric pump.

8   Remove the fuel filler cap to relieve fuel tank pressure and then disconnect the fuel outlet hose from the pump fitting.

9   Connect a rubber hose to the fitting, long enough to reach into a measuring container located in a higher position than the pump. **Note:** *A hose with a smaller diameter will give false test results.*

10   Disconnect the secondary ignition coil wire from the coil to prevent the engine from starting. Use a jumper wire to ground the wire

to the engine block.

11 Turn the ignition switch to the Start position and operate the pump for a total of one minute, in 15-second intervals.

12 A normally operating pump will deliver 0.8 US quart into the container in one minute.

13 If little or no fuel emerged from the hose, either the fuel filter or line is clogged or the pump is defective. Remove the fuel filter and blow air through both fuel lines to be sure they are not clogged. Also, replace the fuel filter if not already done. If this does not improve the test results, the pump should be replaced with a new one.

In fuel tank

14 Before checking the electric fuel pump, always check the fuse first and with a test light or voltmeter verify that voltage is reaching the electric fuel pump.

15 With the engine running, check all metal lines and rubber hoses between the fuel tank (inside of which is the electric pump) and the carburetor to make sure that there are no leaks, kinked, flattened, or bent lines. Turn off the engine.

16 Relieve the fuel tank pressure by removing the fuel filler cap.

17 Detach the cable from the negative terminal of the battery.

18 Disconnect the fuel inlet hose at the carburetor.

19 Install a fuel pressure gauge in-line between the fuel inlet hose and the carburetor.

20 Reattach the cable to the battery negative terminal.

21 Start the engine and check the fuel line for fuel leakage.

22 Note the indicated fuel pressure reading. It should be within the specified range.

23 Detach the cable from the negative terminal of the battery.

24 Remove the pressure gauge from the fuel line.

25 Reconnect the fuel inlet hose.

26 Attach the cable to the negative terminal of the battery.

---

7   Fuel pump (carbureted models) – removal and installation

Warning: *Gasoline is extremely flammable, so extra precautions must be taken when working on any part of the fuel system. Make sure the engine is cool. Don't smoke or allow open flames or bare light bulbs near the work area. Also, do not work in a garage if a natural gas-type appliance with a pilot light is present. Remove the cable from the negative terminal of the battery to eliminate the possibility of sparks occurring while fuel vapor is present.*

Mechanical pump

Refer to illustrations 7.2 and 7.3

1 Relieve fuel tank pressure by removing the fuel filter cap.

2 Locate the fuel pump on the front side of the cylinder head **(see**

7.2   On some vehicles, a mechanical fuel pump is located on the cylinder head – when replacing the fuel pump, always use new gaskets

illustration). Place rags underneath the pump to catch any spilled fuel.

3 Disconnect the fuel lines from the pump. Immediately plug them to prevent the leakage of fuel and the entry of dirt **(see illustration)**.

4 Remove the two bolts or nuts that attach the fuel pump to the cylinder head.

5 Detach the pump from the cylinder head.

6 Installation is the reverse of removal.

7 Always use new gaskets when replacing the fuel pump.

Electric pump

Frame mounted

Refer to illustration 7.11

8 Relieve fuel tank pressure by removing the fuel filler cap.

9 Disconnect the negative cable at the battery.

10 If necessary for clearance, raise the truck and support it on jackstands.

11 Locate the fuel pump on the frame rail, under the right side of the vehicle **(see illustration)**. Remove the fuel pump protector shield.

12 Place rags or a metal container under the pump to catch any fuel. Then disconnect the fuel lines from the pump and immediately plug them.

13 Disconnect the wiring connector leading to the pump.

14 Remove the bolts that attach the pump to its bracket and lift the pump off.

15 Installation is the reverse of the removal procedure.

4

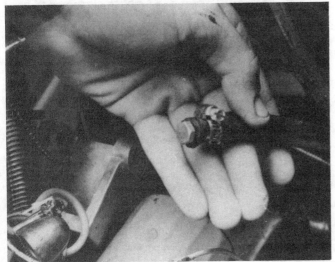

7.3   To plug rubber fuel hoses effectively, insert a bolt into the opening and secure it with a small hose clamp

7.11   Early model electric fuel pumps have a shield that must be removed for access to the pump

In fuel tank

Refer to illustration 7.21

16   Relieve the fuel tank pressure by removing the fuel filler cap.
17   Disconnect the cable from the negative terminal of the battery.
18   Raise the vehicle and place it securely on jackstands.
19   Remove the fuel tank (see Section 5).
20   Remove the fuel tank gauge unit lock plate by using a hammer and brass punch to turn it clockwise. **Warning:** *Sparks caused by the use of a screwdriver or a punch made of any material other than brass could cause an explosion.*
21   Lift the fuel tank gauge unit assembly from the tank **(see illustration).**
22   Separate the fuel pump from the gauge unit.
23   Installation is the reverse of removal.

---

8   Air cleaner housing – removal and installation

Carbureted models

Refer to illustrations 8.3, 8.6a and 8.6b

1   Disconnect the cable from the battery negative terminal.
2   Detach the PCV hose from the elbow fitting on the air cleaner housing.
3   Label the vacuum hoses and fittings, then detach hoses from the air cleaner housing cover **(see illustration).**
4   Remove the center wing nut and/or side clips and detach the cover and filter.
5   Depress the tang that secures the fresh air duct to the air cleaner housing and detach the duct from the housing by pulling it forward.
6   On later models, remove the housing nuts/bolts **(see illustrations).** Raise the air cleaner and detach the pre-heat tube.
7   If you're planning to replace the housing, you'll have to remove both the vacuum motor and the temperature sensor and install them on the new housing. Refer to Chapter 6 for this procedure.
8   Installation is the reverse of removal.

Fuel injected models

Refer to illustration 8.9

9   Loosen the hose clamp screws and detach the inlet and outlet hoses from the housing **(see illustration).**
10   Remove bolts and lift off the housing cover and remove the filter element.
11   Remove the bracket bolts and lift the air cleaner housing out of the engine compartment.
12   Installation is the reverse of removal. the air cleaner-to-bracket mounting bolts and lift the air cleaner housing.

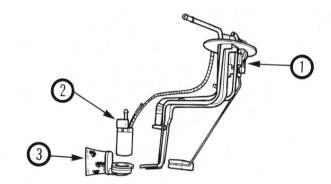

7.21   An exploded view of a typical "in fuel tank" electric fuel pump

| 1 | Fuel tank gauge unit | 3 | Fuel strainer |
| 2 | Electric fuel pump | | |

8.3   Late model vehicles have numerous hoses which must be detached from the air cleaner housing, including the three large hoses shown here. Using tape, label all hoses before disconnecting them. Also visible in this photo are the top cover securing clips and center wing nut.

8.6a   On late models six bolts/nuts secure the air cleaner housing – five are shown here (arrows) with the sixth bolt on the other side of the housing

8.6b   When removing the two nuts (arrows), place a rag in the throat of the carburetor to prevent the nuts or tools from accidentally falling into the carburetor

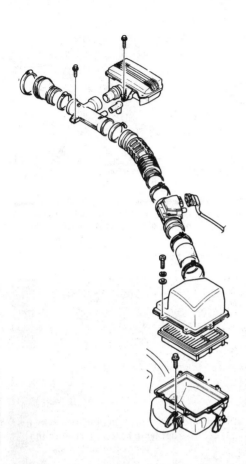

8.9   Fuel injection model air cleaner assembly – exploded view

9   Carburetor – removal and installation

Warning: *Gasoline is extremely flammable so extra precautions must be taken when working on any part of the fuel system. DO NOT smoke or allow open flames or bare light bulbs in or near the work area. Also, don't work in a garage if a natural gas appliance such as a water heater or clothes dryer is present.*

Removal

1   Remove the air cleaner assembly from the carburetor.
2   Disconnect the throttle cable from the throttle lever (some early models will have a choke cable to detach).
3   Label all vacuum hoses and fittings before removing them to simplify installation. Disconnect all vacuum hoses and the fuel line from the carburetor.
4   Label the wires and terminals, then unplug all wire harness connectors.
5   Remove the four mounting nuts and detach the carburetor from the intake manifold. Remove the carburetor mounting gasket.

Installation

6   Clean the gasket mating surfaces of the intake manifold and the carburetor to remove all traces of the old gasket. Be careful not to drop old gasket material into the intake manifold. Place a new gasket on the intake manifold. Position the carburetor on the gasket and install the mounting nuts. Tighten them evenly and securely.
7   The remaining installation steps are the reverse of removal.
8   Check and adjust if necessary the curb idle speed.

10   Fuel injection system – description, checking and component replacement

General information

Later model engines are equipped with an Electronic Fuel Injection (EFI) system. The EFI system is composed of three basic subsystems: a fuel system, an air intake system and an electronic control system **(see illustration 10.20)**.

Fuel delivery system

An electric pump located inside the tank supplies fuel under constant pressure to the fuel distribution pipe, which distributes it to all four injectors. From the distribution pipe, fuel is injected into the intake ports, just above the intake valves, by the four fuel injectors. The amount of fuel supplied by the injectors is precisely controlled by an electronic control module called the EGI control unit. A pressure regulator controls system pressure in relation to intake manifold vacuum. The fuel filter, mounted between the distribution pipe and fuel pump, protects the components of the system.

Air Intake system

The air intake system consists of an air filter housing, an air flow meter and a throttle body. An auxiliary air valve and air bypass solenoid valve control the idle speed under different operating conditions. The air flow meter is an information gathering device for the EGI control unit. A potentiometer measures intake air flow and a temperature sensor measures intake air temperature. This information helps the EGI determine the amount (duration) of fuel to be injected by the injectors. The throttle plate inside the throttle body is controlled by the driver. As the throttle plate opens, the amount of air that can pass through the system increases, so the potentiometer opens further and the EGI signals the injectors to increase the amount of fuel delivered to the intake ports.

Electronic control system

The electronic control system controls the EFI and other systems through an electronic control module, which employs a microcomputer called the EGI control unit. The EGI receives signals from a number of information sensors which monitor such variables as intake air volume, intake air temperature, coolant temperature, engine rpm, acceleration/deceleration and exhaust oxygen content. These signals help the EGI determine the injection duration necessary for the optimum fuel/air ratio. Some of the sensors and the corresponding EGI-controlled solenoids are not contained within EFI components, but are scattered throughout the engine compartment.

General diagnosis

Warning: *Gasoline is extremely flammable, so extra precautions must be taken when working on any part of the fuel system. DO NOT smoke or allow open flames or bare light bulbs near the work area. Also, don't work in a garage if a natural gas appliance (such as a water heater or clothes dryer) is present.*

The EFI system is not usually the direct cause of engine problems. Trouble is usually caused by a bad contact in the wiring connectors or contaminated fuel, which could clog the injectors. Always make sure that all connections are secure by tapping or wiggling the connectors to see if the signal changes. Make sure that the connector terminals are not bent and that the connectors are pushed completely together and locked.

Before troubleshooting the EFI system, always check the condition of the ignition system. Make sure the battery, all fuses, fusible links and ground connections, the ignition coil, the coil high tension wire, the distributor, the plug wires and the spark plugs are all in good condition, properly connected and functioning correctly. Also check the ignition timing and the idle speed.

Check the general engine condition, such as compression pressure and valve clearances. Refer to Chapter 1 for the compression check and valve adjustment procedures.

Check the fuel delivery system for fuel leaks. Make sure the fuel pump is operating properly and the filter is not clogged.

4

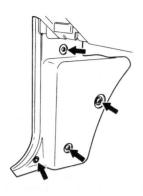

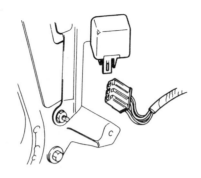

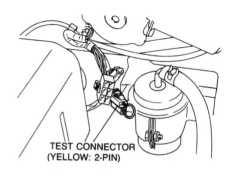

10.1   The circuit opening relay is accessible after removing the driver's side kick panel

10.2   Unplug the circuit opening relay to deactivate the fuel pump

10.3   The fuel pump can be reactivated by bridging the test connector terminals with a jumper wire

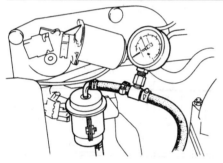

10.5   Connect a fuel pressure gauge between the filter and distribution pipe to check the system pressure

10.9   Fuel regulator details

10.10a   Check the fuel pump by first applying battery power to the connector terminals

Check the air intake system for vacuum leaks. Removal of components such as the engine oil dipstick, oil filler cap, PCV hose, etc. can cause the engine to run poorly. Check for a restricted air filter element.

Although this system requires a special tester for complete diagnosis, some checks of the individual components may be performed using regular shop test equipment.

Fuel pressure relief procedure

Refer to illustrations 10.1 and 10.2

Warning: *Gasoline is extremely flammable, so extra precautions must be taken when working on any part of the fuel system. DO NOT smoke or allow open flames or bare light bulbs near the work area. Also, don't work in a garage if a natural gas appliance (such as a water heater or clothes dryer) is present.*

1   Locate the circuit opening relay located behind the driver's side kick panel **(see illustration)**.
2   Start the engine and unplug the connector from the circuit opening relay **(see illustration)**. The engine will die within a few seconds. Even though the fuel pressure should now be safely relieved, it's always a good idea to disconnect the negative battery cable from the battery and place a shop rag over any fuel fitting before loosening it.

Fuel system priming procedure

Refer to illustration 10.3

3   After it has been depressurized, the fuel system should be primed before putting it back into service to avoid the necessity of excessive cranking to start the engine. Connect the starting relay and bridge the yellow fuel pump test connector terminals (located in the engine compartment next to the fuel filter) with a jumper wire **(see illustration)**. Turn the ignition switch on for 10 seconds, then shut it off and check for fuel leaks. Turn the ignition switch off and remove the jumper wire.

Fuel pressure check

Refer illustration 10.5

4   Relieve the fuel system pressure (see Steps 1 and 2 above). Reconnect the circuit opening relay connector.
5   Disconnect the hose from the fuel filter to the distribution pipe and install a fuel pressure gauge with a T-fitting **(see illustration)**.
6   Start the engine and let it idle. The pressure should be as noted in the Specifications at the beginning of this Chapter.
7   If there is no pressure (even though the pump is running), the in-line fuel filter is probably clogged. Replace it and check the pressure again. If there is still zero pressure, the fuel feed line may be clogged. If the fuel feed line is clear, check the fuel pump in-tank filter.
8   If the fuel pressure is low, the in-line fuel filter may be partially clogged. Replace it and check the pressure again. If it's still low, check for a loose fuel line fitting or a punctured fuel line. Also check the pressure regulator, fuel distribution pipe and injectors for leaks. If nothing is leaking, block the fuel return line (the hose connected to

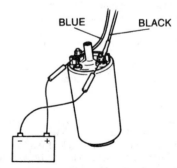

BLUE   BLACK

10.10b   Apply power directly to the fuel pump terminals to see if it runs

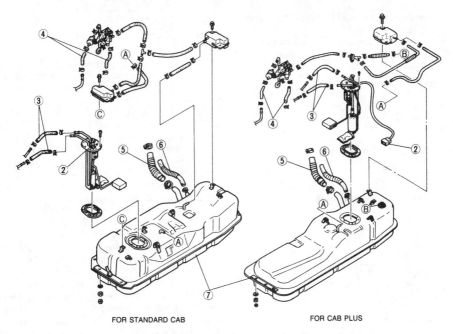

10.12   Fuel tank system details

1   Fuel filler cap
2   Pump electrical connector
3   Fuel hoses
4   Evaporative hoses
5   Filler hose
6   Breather hose
7   Fuel tank

FOR STANDARD CAB

FOR CAB PLUS

the fuel pressure regulator) and bridge the fuel pump test connector terminals on the firewall with a jumper wire **(see illustration 10.3)**. Note the indicated pressure. If the pressure is now above the upper limit, the fuel pressure regulator is faulty. If the pressure is still low, replace the fuel pump.

Fuel pressure drop check

Refer to illustration 10.9

9   Depressurize the fuel system (steps 1 and 2) and install a fuel pressure gauge (step 5). Plug the fuel return line from the pressure regulator side of the return line. Bridge the fuel pump test connector **(see illustration 10.3)** and turn the ignition switch on for 10 seconds. Turn the switch off and remove the jumper wire. After 5 minutes note the fuel pressure, this is the fuel pressure drop. If it is not as specified, depressurize the system, disconnect the hoses and replace the regulator **(see illustration)**.

Fuel delivery components – check, removal and installation

Warning: *Gasoline is extremely flammable, so extra precautions must be taken when working on any part of the fuel system. DO NOT smoke or allow open flames or bare light bulbs near the work area. Also, don't work in a garage if a natural gas appliance (such as a water heater or clothes dryer) is present.*

Fuel pump

Refer to illustrations 10.10a, 10.10b, 10.12, 10.16 and 10.18

10   For fuel pump/pressure diagnosis, refer to Steps 4 through 9. If the fuel pump does not run (make a clicking sound) when the ignition is on, check the circuit opening relay (see Steps 30 thru 33). If the relay is okay, remove the pump and tank gauge unit as described below.

Warning: *For the following test, the pump must be completely removed from the vehicle and away from any source of explosive fuel fumes. Make the electrical connections to the fuel pump connector/terminals before the connections at the battery.* Apply battery power to the connector **(see illustration)**. If the pump does not run, apply battery power directly to the pump terminals **(see illustration)**. If the pump still does not run, replace the pump.

11   To replace the fuel pump, relieve the fuel system pressure, then disconnect the cable from the negative battery terminal.

Fuel tank

Warning: *DO NOT perform the following operation if the fuel tank is full. Using a siphon pump (don't suck on the hose to start a siphon action) drain the fuel into an approved gasoline container.*

12   After depressurizing the system, remove the bolts and lower the fuel tank, referring to Section 2 **(see illustration)**.

13   Unplug the harness connector. Mark the fuel main and return hoses with pieces of tape. Loosen the hose clamps and disconnect the hoses **(see illustration 10.12)**.

14   Remove the pump bracket screws and lift the fuel pump and bracket out of the fuel tank.

15   Disconnect the electrical leads from the pump terminals.

16   Loosen the pump clamp screw, slide the hose clamps toward the center of the hose, then swing the bottom of the pump out of the bracket. Pull the pump assembly and hose from the bracket **(see illustration)**.

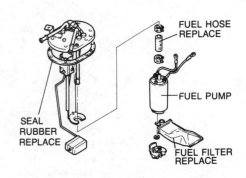

FUEL HOSE
REPLACE

FUEL PUMP

SEAL
RUBBER
REPLACE

FUEL FILTER
REPLACE

10.16   Fuel pump and related components – exploded view

4

17   Remove the rubber cushion and in-tank filter from the lower end of the fuel pump by prying the retaining clip off.

18   Installation is the reverse of removal. Be sure to use a new gasket between the fuel tank and the pump bracket (see illustration).

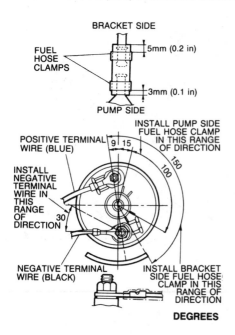

10.18   Fuel pump installation details

Fuel injectors

Refer to illustrations 10.20, 10.22, 10.23, 10.24a, 10.24b, 10.26 and 10.27

19   To check injector operation, place the tip of a screwdriver or stethoscope against each injector body and listen for a clicking noise while the engine is running. If no sound is heard, check the injector resistance (Step 24).

20   Depressurize the fuel system (steps 1 and 2), disconnect the fuel and vacuum hoses, unplug the injector electrical connectors, remove the bolts and remove the distribution pipe and injector assembly (see illustration).

21   To check for injector fuel leakage, connect the hose from the fuel filter to the inlet fitting on the distribution pipe. Using a piece of extra fuel hose and a coupler, connect the return hose to the fuel pressure regulator.

22   Wire the injectors to the distribution pipe so they won't pop off when fuel pressure builds up (see illustration).

23   Place rags under the injectors. Turn the ignition to the On position and energize the fuel pump by jumping the fuel pump test connector terminals (see illustration 10.3). Look for drops or seeping fuel at the injectors. Replace any injectors that leak. **Note:** *A very slight amount of leakage after five minutes is acceptable.*

24   To check injector resistance, unplug the harness and check the resistance at the connector terminals with an ohmmeter (see illustration). It should be 6-to-8 ohms and if it isn't, check for faults in the harness and the injectors themselves. Remove the injector (step 26) and connect an ohmmeter across the injector terminals. The reading should be 12-to-16 ohms (see illustration). If it isn't, replace the injector.

25   To replace a fuel injector, disconnect the extra hose that was connected to perform the leak test. Wrap a rag around the hose when removing it to control the fuel spray, as the pressure relief procedure can't be followed with the distribution pipe removed.

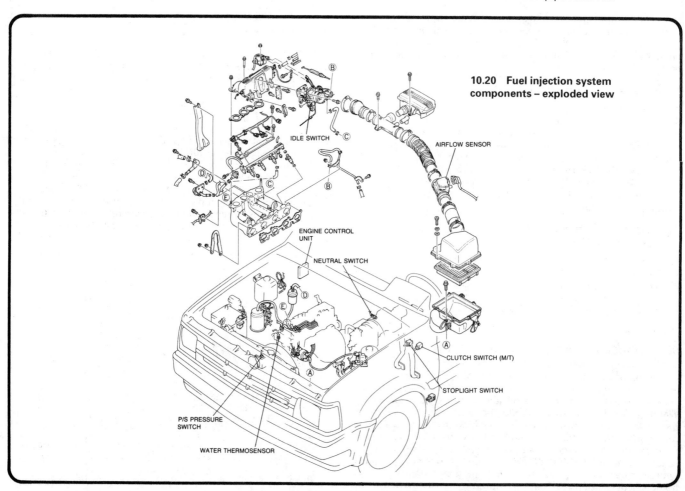

10.20   Fuel injection system components – exploded view

26   Pull the injector out of the distribution pipe using a twisting motion. Inspect the rubber insulator, grommet and O-ring **(see illustration)**. It's a good idea to routinely replace them to eliminate the possibility of fuel leaks.

27   Install the new O-ring, grommet and insulator. Apply a light coat of engine oil to the O-ring and insulator to ease installation and reduce the possibility of tearing them **(see illustration)**.

28   Insert the injector into the fuel distribution pipe. Be sure to push it in straight, otherwise the O-ring may be damaged. The electrical connector must face up.

29   Install the fuel distribution pipe and injectors and tighten the bolts securely. Connect the fuel feed, return and vacuum sensing hoses. Pressurize the fuel system (step 3) and check for leaks.

Circuit opening relay

Refer to illustrations 10.31a, 10.31b and 10.32

30   The circuit opening relay, located under the driver's side kick panel, supplies power to the fuel pump when the starter is operated **(see illustrations 10.1 and 10.2)**. It continues to feed the pump until the key is turned off, at which time the relay resets itself (no power is directed to the pump when the ignition key is turned to the On position – the engine must be turned over first).

31   Check the resistance between the terminals of the relay as shown in the accompanying illustrations. If the resistance values are not within the specified limits, replace the relay.

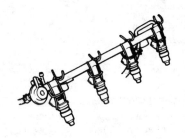

10.22   Wire the injectors to the distribution pipe to prevent them from popping out during the injector leakage check

10.23   The injectors shouldn't leak when moved 60-degrees

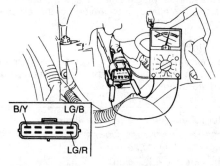

10.24a   Check the injector harness resistance with an ohmmeter at the indicated terminals

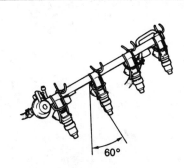

10.24 b   Checking the injector solenoid resistance with an ohmmeter

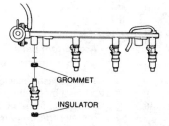

10.26   Injector removal details

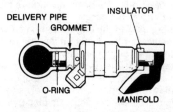

10.27   Fuel injector mounting details (it's a good idea to replace all of the rubber insulators, grommets and O-rings whenever any of the injectors are removed)

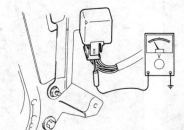

Condition	Terminal	Fp	Fc	B	STA	E1
Ignition switch: ON		0V	12V	12V	0V	0V
Ignition switch: START		12V	0V	12V	12V	0V
At idle		12V	0V	12V	0V	0V

10.31a   Check the circuit opening relay terminal voltages and compare your readings with the chart

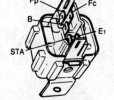

Between terminals	Resistance (Ω)
STA-E1	21—43
B-Fc	109—226
B-Fp	∞

10.31b   Check the circuit opening relay terminal resistance between the indicated terminals – if the values aren't correct, replace the relay

4

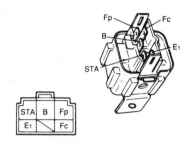

12V	Grounded	Correct result
STA	E₁	B-Fp: Continuity
B	Fc	Fp: Battery voltage

10.32   With battery power applied to the specified terminals, the readings must be as shown

32   Apply battery power to the circuit opening relay terminals and check the operation of the relay **(see illustration)**. Replace the relay with a new one if the results are not as specified in the accompanying chart.
33   To replace the relay, unplug the electrical connector and remove the mounting screw. Installation is the reverse of the removal procedure.

EGI control unit

34   Due to the specialized test equipment and expertise required to check the control unit, diagnosis and replacement should be left to a dealer service department or a repair shop.

11   Accelerator cable – removal and installation

Refer to illustrations 11.2a, 11.2b and 11.7

1   Remove the air cleaner housing.
2   Disconnect the accelerator cable from the carburetor. Early model vehicles have a mechanical linkage set-up and must be unbolted from the carburetor **(see illustrations)**.
3   Working under the dash, disengage the accelerator cable from the upper end of the accelerator pedal.
4   Moving back to the engine compartment, remove the bolts that attach the accelerator cable guide tube to the firewall and then pull the cable out through the opening.
5   Installation is the reverse of the removal procedure.
6   Make sure that the throttle valve opens fully when the accelerator pedal is fully depressed and returns to idle when released.
7   Adjust accelerator pedal free play by turning the adjusting nuts **(see illustration)**.
8   Make sure that the throttle cable does not contact any components in close proximity to it.

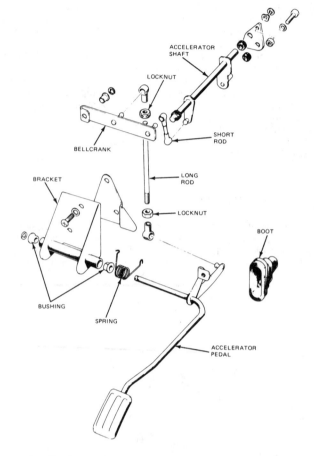

11.2a   Typical early model mechanical operated throttle linkage – to adjust the linkage free play, loosen the locknuts on the long rod and turn the rod just until the free play is taken up

12   Accelerator pedal – removal and installation

1   Disengage the accelerator cable from the upper end of the accelerator pedal by pushing it toward the end of the cable. Then disengage the cable from the pedal.
2   Remove the bolts that retain the accelerator pedal mounting bracket and lift out the pedal.
3   Installation is the reverse of the removal procedure.

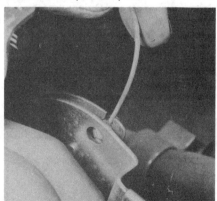

11.2b   Removing a typical accelerator cable

11.7   To adjust the cable operated throttle linkage, simply turn the adjusting nuts (arrows) until the free play is taken up

14.4   On early models the front exhaust pipe is attached to the transmission

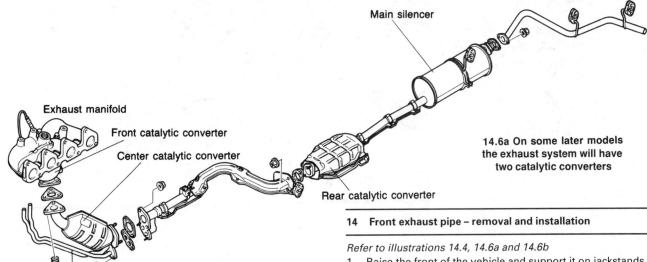

Main silencer

Exhaust manifold

Front catalytic converter

Center catalytic converter

**14.6a On some later models
the exhaust system will have
two catalytic converters**

Rear catalytic converter

Air injection pipe

4   On early models with mechanical linkage, disengage the long rod, remove the clip at the end of the pedal and slide the accelerator pedal out of the bracket **(see illustration 11.2a)**.

13 Exhaust system – general information

The exhaust system consists of the muffler, catalytic converter and exhaust pipes, and includes four main pieces; the front exhaust pipe which attaches to the exhaust manifold, the catalytic converter, the center tube and the muffler/tailpipe assembly.

The catalytic converter is attached to both the front exhaust pipe and the center tube by mounting bolts. The muffler is attached to the center tube by a clamp and is welded to the tailpipe.

The interior of the catlytic converter is a honeycomb-like design that is coated with platinum and rhodium. When these elements interact with the hydrocarbon (HC), carbon monoxide (CO) and oxides of nitrogen (NOx) in the exhaust, it causes reactions to occur that convert the CO to CO_2 (carbon dioxide), the HC to CO and H_2O (water), and reduces the NOx.

Since lead and phosphorus additives in gasoline can poison the converter's catalytic elements, thus rendering it ineffective in altering the gases' toxic elements, only unleaded fuel should be used in the vehicle.

Periodic maintenance of the converter is not required.

In order to accurately test the functioning of the converter, a CO tester is needed. For this reason, we recommend you take the vehicle to a Mazda dealer or other qualified shop to have the converter tested.

If, through physical damage, the use of leaded fuels or because its active elements have been depleted, the catalytic converter is rendered ineffective, it must be replaced as a unit.

Caution: *It should be noted that since the internal chemical conversions occur between the 600-degrees and 1200-degrees F, the converter operates at a very high temperature. Before performing any work on or near the converter be sure it has cooled sufficiently to avoid serious burns.*

When replacing any exhaust system parts, be sure you allow enough clearance from all points on the body to avoid overheating the floor pan and possibly damaging the interior carpet and insulation.

The entire exhaust system is attached to the body with mounting brackets and rubber hangers. If any one of the parts is improperly installed, excessive noise and vibration will be transmitted to the body.

Regular inspection of the exhaust system should be made to keep it at maximum efficiency. Look for any damage or mispositioned parts, open seams, holes, loose connections, excessive corrosion or other defects which could allow exhaust fumes to seep into the vehicle.

14 Front exhaust pipe – removal and installation

Refer to illustrations 14.4, 14.6a and 14.6b

1   Raise the front of the vehicle and support it on jackstands.

2   Remove the lower catalytic converter shield and protector (if equipped).

3   Using a piece of thick wire, secure the catalytic converter to the underside of the vehicle.

4   Remove any insulating shields mounted to the front exhaust pipe. Then disconnect the bracket that attaches the pipe to the body or transmission **(see illustration)**.

5   Loosen , but do not remove the two bolts attaching the front exhaust pipe to the catalytic converter. If the bolts are corroded and cannot be easily broken loose, penetrating oil and tapping with a hammer may help.

6   Remove the bolts that attach the front exhaust pipe to the exhaust manifold **(see illustration)**. Again, penetrating oil and tapping may be necessary. Later models will have two catalytic converters **(see illustration)**.

7   Now, while supporting the front exhaust pipe, remove the two bolts holding the pipe to the converter, and lift out the pipe.

8   Installation is the reverse of the removal procedure. **Note:** *Be sure to use new gaskets between the front exhaust pipe and the exhaust manifold, and the front exhaust pipe and the catalytic converter. Also, before installing the bolts that attach these parts, apply an anti-seize compound to the threads.*

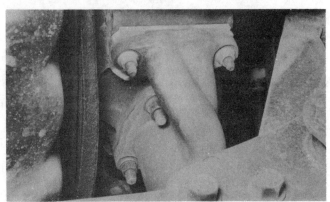

**14.6b The front exhaust pipe-to-manifold nuts on a
late–model vehicle**

15 Muffler/tailpipe assembly – removal and installation

Refer illustrations 15.3a and 15.3b

1   The muffler is welded to the tailpipe, and both pieces are designed to be replaced as a unit. However, if either piece needs replacing, but the other is in good condition, a muffler shop will be able to cut off the muffler or tailpipe and weld on a new one without having to replace both pieces. The cost of this procedure, though, may offset the savings realized as a result of not replacing the entire assembly.

4

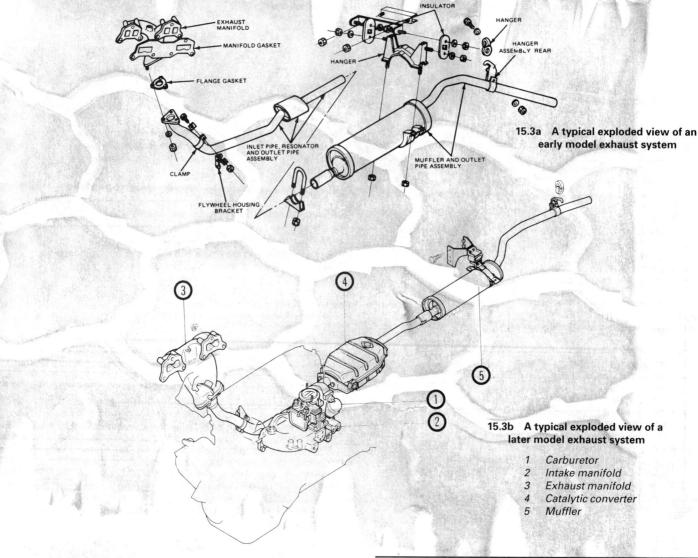

15.3a **A typical exploded view of an early model exhaust system**

15.3b **A typical exploded view of a later model exhaust system**

1   *Carburetor*
2   *Intake manifold*
3   *Exhaust manifold*
4   *Catalytic converter*
5   *Muffler*

2   Raise the rear of the truck and support it on jackstands.
3   Remove the U-bolt clamp that secures the muffler to the center pipe **(see illustrations)**.
4   Lightly tap all around the connection with a hammer to break up the internal sealant.
5   With a soft-faced hammer, tap on the front end of the muffler while pushing it backwards until the muffler is disengaged from the center pipe.
6   Remove the bolts attaching the tailpipe mounting bracket to the frame and lift the assembly out.
7   Installation is the reverse of the removal procedure. **Note:** *To ensure that no exhaust leaks occur at the muffler-to-center tube connection, an exhaust sealant should be used during installation. Follow the directions supplied with the sealant. Always use new exhaust gaskets.*

16   Catalytic converter – removal and installation

Refer to illustration 16.2

1   Raise the front of the vehicle and support it on jackstands.
2   Remove the lower catalytic converter shield and protector **(see illustration)**.
3   Using a piece of strong wire, secure the center pipe to the driveshaft or body.
4   While supporting the catalytic converter, break loose, but do not yet remove the four converter mounting bolts that attach the converter to the front exhaust pipe and center pipe. If the bolts are corroded

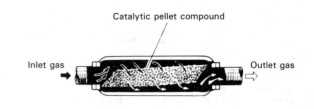

16.2 **A typical catalytic converter used on later model vehicles to 1984**

and cannot be easily broken loose, penetrating oil and tapping with a hammer may help.
5   While supporting the catalytic converter, remove all four mounting fasteners, and detach the converter from the vehicle.
6   Installation is the reverse of the removal procedure. **Note:** *Be sure to use new gaskets during installation and apply anti-seize compound to the mounting bolts.*

Chapter 5 Engine electrical systems

Contents

Specifications

General

Spark plug/coil wire resistance	not to exceed 16,000 ohms per meter (3.28 ft)

Ignition coil

Primary resistance	
Pre-1979	1.3 to 1.7 ohms
1979 thru 1985	0.9 ohms ± 10% at 68-degrees F
1986 and 1987	1.15 ± 0.12 ohms
1988	1.0 to 1.3 ohms
1989	
B2200	1.0 to 1.3 ohms
B2600	
Test 1	0.77 to 0.95 ohms
Test 2	0.9 to 1.1 ohms
1990 and later	
With carb	1.0 to 1.3 ohms
With EFI	0.81 to 0.99 ohms
Secondary resistance	
1986 and 1987	
Hanshin	10.2 ohms
Mitsubishi	8.35 ohms
1988	
B2200	6 to 30 K-ohms
B2600	10 to 20 K-ohms
1989 and later	6 to 30 K-ohms
Insulation resistance (1986 and later)	More than 10 M-ohms
External resistor resistance (1988 B2600 only)	1.0 to 1.5 ohms

1 General information and precautions

The engine electrical systems include all ignition, charging and starting components. Because of their engine-related functions, these components are considered separately from chassis electrical devices like the lights, instruments, etc.

Be very careful when working on the engine electrical components. They are easily damaged if checked, connected or handled improperly. The alternator is driven by an engine drivebelt which could cause serious injury if your hands, hair or clothes become entangled in it with the engine running. Both the starter and alternator are connected directly to the battery and could arc or even cause a fire if mishandled, overloaded or shorted out.

Never leave the ignition switch on for long periods of time with the engine off. Don't disconnect the battery cables while the engine is running. Correct polarity must be maintained when connecting battery cables from another source, such as another vehicle, during jump starting. Always disconnect the negative cable first and hook it up last or the battery may be shorted by the tool being used to loosen the cable clamps.

Additional safety related information on the engine electrical systems can be found in *Safety first* near the front of this manual. It should be referred to before beginning any operation included in this Chapter.

2 Battery — removal and installation

Refer to illustration 2.2

1   Disconnect both cables from the battery terminals. **Caution:** *Always disconnect the negative cable first and hook it up last or the battery may be shorted by the tool being used to loosen the cable clamps.*
2   At the battery, remove the bolt and the hold down clamp **(see illustration)**.
3   Lift out the battery. Special straps that attach to the battery posts are available — lifting and moving the battery is much easier if you use one.
4   Installation is the reverse of removal.

3 Battery — emergency jump starting

Refer to the *Booster battery (jump) starting* procedure at the front of this manual.

4 Battery cables — check and replacement

1   Periodically inspect the entire length of each battery cable for damage, cracked or burned insulation and corrosion. Poor battery cable connections can cause starting problems and decreased engine performance.
2   Check the cable-to-terminal connections at the ends of the cables for cracks, loose wire strands and corrosion. The presence of white, fluffy deposits under the insulation at the cable terminal connection is a sign that the cable is corroded and should be replaced. Check the terminals for distortion, missing mounting bolts and corrosion.
3   When replacing the cables, **always disconnect the negative cable first and hook it up last** or the battery may be shorted by the tool used to loosen the cable clamps. Even if only the positive cable is being replaced, be sure to disconnect the negative cable from the battery first.
4   Disconnect and remove the cable. Make sure the replacement cable is the same length and diameter.
5   Clean the threads of the relay or ground connection with a wire brush to remove rust and corrosion. Apply a light coat of petroleum jelly to the threads to prevent future corrosion.

**2.2   The battery is secured by a clamp across the top —
to remove, unscrew the nut on the threaded rod**

6   Attach the cable to the relay or ground connection and tighten the mounting nut/bolt securely.
7   Before connecting the new cable to the battery, make sure that it reaches the battery post without having to be stretched.
8   Connect the positive cable first, followed by the negative cable.

5 Ignition system — general information

Refer to illustration 5.1

Earlier Mazda pickups are equipped with conventional ignition systems consisting of a battery, an ignition switch, a ballast resistor, an ignition coil, a distributor (with either single or dual contact points) and the spark plugs and wires **(see illustration)**.

In 1979, some models were equipped with "breakerless" ignition systems which substituted an ignition amplifier and module for mechanical breaker points. By 1986, all vehicles employed this type of ignition system.

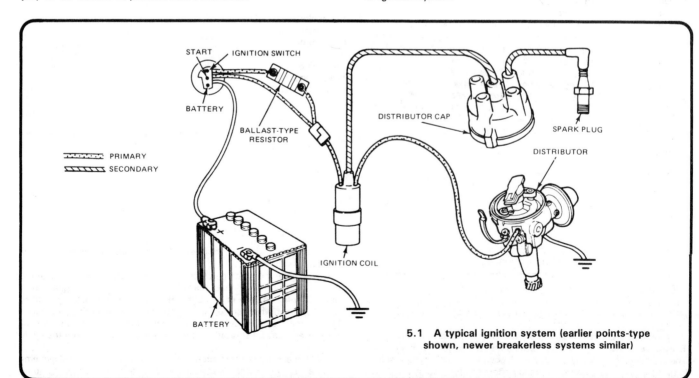

**5.1   A typical ignition system (earlier points-type
shown, newer breakerless systems similar)**

6.2 To use a calibrated ignition tester, disconnect a spark plug wire, attach the wire to the tester, clip the tester to a convenient ground and operate the starter — if there's enough power to fire the plug, sparks will be visible between the electrode tip and the tester body

6 Ignition system — check

Refer to illustration 6.2

Warning: *Because of the very high secondary (spark plug) voltage generated by the ignition system, extreme care should be taken when this check is done.*

Calibrated ignition tester method

1   If the engine turns over but won't start, disconnect the spark plug lead from any spark plug and attach it to a calibrated ignition tester (available at most auto parts stores).
2   Connect the clip on the tester to a bolt or metal bracket on the engine **(see illustration)**, crank the engine and watch the end of the tester to see if bright blue, well-defined sparks occur.
3   If sparks occur, sufficient voltage is reaching the plug to fire it (repeat the check at the remaining plug wires to verify that the distributor cap and rotor are OK). However, the plugs themselves may be fouled, so remove and check them as described in Chapter 1 or install new ones.
4   If no sparks or intermittent sparks occur, remove the distributor cap and check the cap and rotor as described in Chapter 1. If moisture is present, use WD-40 (or something similar) to dry out the cap and rotor, then reinstall the cap and repeat the spark test.
5   If there's still no spark, detach the secondary coil wire from the distributor cap and hook it up to the tester (reattach the plug wire to the spark plug), then repeat the spark check.
6   If no sparks occur, check the primary (small) wire connections at the coil to make sure they're clean and tight. Refer to Section 7 and check the ignition coil. Make any necessary repairs, then repeat the check again.
7   If sparks now occur, the distributor cap, rotor, plug wire(s) or spark plug(s) (or all of them) may be defective.
8   If there's still no spark, the coil-to-cap wire may be bad (check the resistance with an ohmmeter and compare it to the Specifications). If a known good wire doesn't make any difference in the test results, the ignition coil, module or other internal components may be defective.

Alternative method

Note: *If you're unable to obtain a calibrated ignition tester, the following method will allow you to determine if the ignition system has spark, but it won't tell you if there's enough voltage produced to actually initiate combustion in the cylinders.*

9   Remove the wire from one of the spark plugs. Using an insulated tool, hold the wire about 1/4-inch from a good ground and have an assistant crank the engine.
10   If bright blue, well-defined sparks occur, sufficient voltage is reaching the plug to fire it. However, the plug(s) may be fouled, so remove and check them as described in Chapter 1 or install new ones.
11   If there's no spark, check the remaining wires in the same manner.

A few sparks followed by no spark is the same condition as no spark at all.
12   If no sparks occur, remove the distributor cap and check the cap and rotor as described in Chapter 1. If moisture is present, use WD-40 (or something similar) to dry out the cap and rotor, then reinstall the cap and repeat the spark test.
13   If there's still no spark, disconnect the secondary coil wire from the distributor cap, hold it about 1/4-inch from a good engine ground and crank the engine again.
14   If no sparks occur, check the primary (small) wire connections at the coil to make sure they're clean and tight. Refer to Section 7 and check the ignition coil. Make any necessary repairs, then repeat the check again.
15   If sparks now occur, the distributor cap, rotor, plug wire(s) or spark plug(s) (or all of them) may be defective.
16   If there's still no spark, the coil-to-cap wire may be bad (check the resistance with an ohmmeter and compare it to the Specifications). If a known good wire doesn't make any difference in the test results, the ignition coil, module or other internal components may be defective.

7 Ignition coil — check and replacement

Refer to illustrations 7.4, 7.5, 7.6 and 7.8

Check

Coil

1   Inspect the ignition coil for chips, cracks or other damage. If any physical deterioration is visible, replace the coil.
2   Start the engine and allow it to run for a few minutes to heat up the coil to its normal operating temperature.
3   Stop the engine and detach the cable from the negative terminal of the battery.
4   Using an ohmmeter, measure the primary coil resistance by touching one lead of the meter to the positive primary terminal and the other to the negative primary terminal **(see illustration)**. Compare your reading to the specified primary coil resistance. If the indicated measurement does not correspond to the specified primary resistance, replace the coil.
5   Using an ohmmeter, measure the secondary coil resistance by touching one lead of the meter to the positive primary terminal and the other to the high tension terminal **(see illustration)**. Compare your

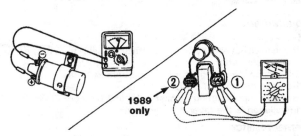

7.4 To check the primary resistance of the coil, touch one lead of an ohmmeter to the primary positive terminal and the other to the primary negative terminal and compare your measurement to the specified primary resistance

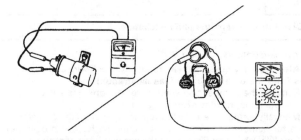

7.5 To check the secondary resistance of the coil, touch one lead of an ohmmeter to the primary positive terminal and the other to the high tension terminal and compare your measurement to the specified secondary resistance

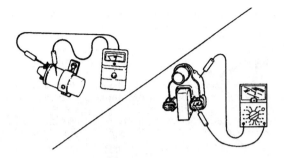
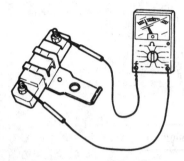

7.6 To check the insulation resistance of the coil, touch one lead of an ohmmeter to the primary negative terminal and the other to the coil case and compare your measurement to the specified insulation resistance

7.8 To check the resistance of the external resistor, touch the leads of an ohmmeter to the terminals of the resistor and compare your measurement to the specified resistance

reading to the specified secondary coil resistance. If the indicated measurement does not correspond to the specified secondary resistance, replace the coil. **Note:** *This test cannot be performed on earlier coils — prior to 1986, no secondary resistance values were provided by the manufacturer.*

6   Using an ohmmeter, measure the insulation resistance of the coil housing by touching one lead of the meter to a primary terminal and the other to the case **(see illustration)**. Compare your reading to the specified insulation resistance of the coil. If the indicated measurement does not correspond to the specified insulation resistance, replace the coil. **Note:** *This test cannot be performed on earlier coils — prior to 1986, no insulation resistance values were provided by the manufacturer.*

External resistor (1988 B2600 models only)

Note: *The external resistor is located to the left of the coil, above and forward of the alternator.*

7   Detach the cable from the negative terminal of the battery.

8   Using an ohmmeter, measure the resistance of the external resistor by touching the leads of the meter to the two resistor terminals **(see illustration)**. Compare your reading to the specified resistance. If the indicated measurement does not correspond to the specified resistance, replace the resistor.

Replacement

Coil

9   If you have not already done so, detach the cable from the negative terminal of the battery.

10   Disconnect the distributor lead and primary wires.

11   Remove the boot (if equipped).

12   Remove the mounting bracket bolts and the coil.

13   Installation is the reverse of removal.

External resistor

14   If you have not already done so, detach the cable from the negative terminal of the battery.

15   Disconnect the wires from the resistor.

16   Remove the mounting bracket bolt and the resistor.

17   Installation is the reverse of removal.

---

8   Distributor — removal and installation

Refer to illustrations 8.1 and 8.10

1   After carefully marking them, remove the coil wire and spark plug wires from the distributor cap **(see illustration)**.

2   Remove the number one spark plug (the one nearest you when you are standing in front of the engine).

3   Manually rotate the engine to top-dead-center on the compression stroke for number one piston (see Chapter 2A for this procedure).

4   Carefully label then disconnect the vacuum hose from the vacuum advance diaphragm.

5   Disconnect the electrical wires to the distributor.

6   Use a small brush and paint, or a scribe to mark the rotor position in relation to the body of the distributor. Make another mark between

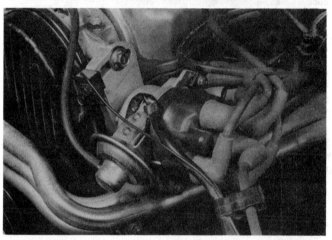

8.1 All spark plug wires, electrical connections and the vacuum advance hose should be carefully marked and numbered with pieces of tape before removing from the distributor body

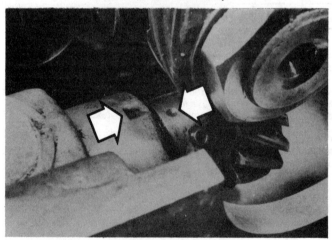

8.10 When installing the distributor, make sure that the drilled mark on the driven gear is aligned with the dimple on the distributor base (arrows)

the distributor body and the mating surface on the engine cylinder head.

7   Remove the distributor hold down nut.

8   Remove the distributor. **Caution:** *Do not rotate the engine with the distributor out.*

9   Before starting installation of the distributor, make certain the number one piston is at top-dead-center on the compression stroke.

10   Align the drilled mark on the driven gear with the dimple on the distributor housing **(see illustration)**. Insert the distributor into the engine with the adjusting clamp centered over the hold-down hole. Make sure that the gear does not turn as the distributor is inserted.

11 Install the hold-down nut. The marks previously made on the distributor housing and on the rotor and cylinder head should be aligned before the bolt is tightened.
12 Install the distributor cap.
13 Connect the wiring for the distributor.
14 Install the spark plug wires.
15 Install the vacuum hoses as previously marked.
16 Time the engine as described in Chapter 1, *Ignition timing — adjustment*.

9 Charging system — general information and precautions

The charging system includes the alternator, either an internal or an external voltage regulator, a charge indicator, the battery, a fusible link and the wiring between all the components. The charging system supplies electrical power for the ignition system, the lights, the radio, etc. The alternator is driven by a drivebelt at the front of the engine.

The purpose of the voltage regulator is to limit the alternator's voltage to a preset value. This prevents power surges, circuit overloads, etc., during peak voltage output.

The fusible link is a short length of insulated wire integral with the engine compartment wiring harness. The link is four wire gauges smaller in diameter than the circuit it protects. Production fusible links and their identification flags are identified by the flag color. See Chapter 12 for additional information regarding fusible links.

The charging system doesn't ordinarily require periodic maintenance. However, the drivebelt, battery and wires and connections should be inspected at the intervals outlined in Chapter 1.

Be very careful when making electrical circuit connections to a vehicle equipped with an alternator and note the following:
a) When reconnecting wires to the alternator from the battery, be sure to note the polarity.
b) Before using arc welding equipment to repair any part of the vehicle, disconnect the wires from the alternator and the battery terminals.
c) Never start the engine with a battery charger connected.
d) Always disconnect both battery leads before using a battery charger.

10 Charging system — on-vehicle check

1 If a malfunction occurs in the charging circuit, don't automatically assume that the alternator is causing the problem. First check the following items:
a) The battery cables where they connect to the battery. Make sure the connections are clean and tight (see Chapter 1).
b) Check the external alternator wiring harness and the connectors at the alternator and voltage regulator. They must be in good condition, clean and tight.
c) Check the drivebelt condition and tension (see Chapter 1).
d) Make sure the alternator mounting and adjustment bolts are tight.
e) Check the fusible link located between the starter relay (refer to Section 19) and the alternator. If it's burned, determine the cause, repair the circuit and replace the link (see Chapter 12).
f) Run the engine and check the alternator for abnormal noise.
2 Using a voltmeter, check the battery voltage with the engine off. It should be approximately 12-volts.
3 Start the engine and check the battery voltage again. It should now be approximately 14-to-15 volts.
4 If the voltage reading is less or more than the specified charging voltage above, replace the voltage regulator (see Section 12).

11 Alternator — removal and installation

Refer to illustration 11.4
1 Detach the cable from the negative terminal of the battery.
2 Unplug the electrical connectors from the alternator and the voltage regulator.
3 Loosen the alternator adjustment and pivot bolts and detach the drivebelt (see Chapter 1).

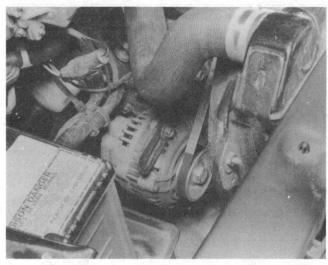

11.4   This view shows the alternator adjustment bolt, which is within the slotted portion of the bracket. The pivot bolt runs through a flange at the bottom of the alternator

4 Remove the adjustment and pivot bolts and separate the alternator from the engine (see illustration).
5 Installation is the reverse of removal.
6 After the alternator is installed, adjust the drivebelt tension (see Chapter 1).

12 Voltage regulator — removal and installation

Refer to illustration 12.2
External
1 Detach the cable from the negative terminal of the battery.
2 Locate the voltage regulator (see illustration) at the front of the engine compartment, next to the coil.
3 Unplug the electrical connector from the regulator.
4 Remove the regulator mounting bolts and remove the regulator from the vehicle.
5 Installation is the reverse of removal.

Internal (IC regulator)
6 Remove the alternator and either exchange it for a rebuilt unit or have the IC regulator replaced.

12.2   A typical external voltage regulator assembly

13 Starting system — general information

The function of the starting system is to crank the engine. The starting system is composed of a starter motor, solenoid and battery. When the ignition switch is turned to Start, electrical energy is supplied by the battery to the solenoid, which completes the circuit to the starter motor, cranking the engine over by turning the ring gear on the flywheel.

A neutral start switch is incorporated into the starting system so that the starter motor can only be operated when the clutch pedal is depressed (manual transmission) or the shift lever is in Park or Neutral (automatic transmission).

Never operate the starter motor for more than 30 seconds at a time without pausing to allow it to cool for at least two minutes. Excessive cranking can cause overheating, which can seriously damage the starter.

14 Starter motor — in-vehicle check

Note: *Before diagnosing starter problems, make sure that the battery is fully charged.*

1   If the starter motor does not turn at all when the switch is operated, make sure that the shift lever is in Park (automatic transmission) or that the clutch pedal is depressed (manual transmission).

2   Make sure that the battery is charged and that all cables, both at the battery and starter solenoid terminals, are secure.

3   If the starter motor spins but the engine is not cranking, then the overrunning clutch in the starter motor is slipping and the starter motor must be replaced.

4   If, when the switch is actuated, the starter motor does not operate at all but the solenoid clicks, then the problem lies with either the battery, the main solenoid contacts or the starter motor itself.

5   If the solenoid plunger cannot be heard when the switch is actuated, the solenoid itself is defective or the solenoid circuit is open.

6   To check the solenoid, connect a jumper lead between the battery positive terminal and the terminal on the solenoid. If the starter motor now operates, the solenoid is OK and the problem is in the ignition switch, neutral start switch or in the wiring.

7   If the starter motor still does not operate, remove the starter/solenoid assembly and have it repaired or replace it.

8   If the starter motor cranks the engine at an abnormally slow speed, first make sure that the battery is charged and that all terminal connections are tight. If the engine is partially seized, or has the wrong viscosity oil in it, it will crank slowly.

9   Run the engine until normal operating temperature is reached, then disconnect the coil wire from the distributor cap and ground it on the engine.

10 Connect a voltmeter positive lead to the ''S'' (Starter motor) terminal of the solenoid and connect the negative lead to ground.

11 Turn the ignition switch to Start and take a voltmeter reading as soon as a steady figure is indicated. Do not allow the starter motor to turn for more than 30 seconds at a time. A reading of 9 volts or more, with the starter motor turning at normal cranking speed, is normal. If the reading is 9 volts or more but the cranking speed is slow, the motor is faulty. Have it repaired or replace it. If the reading is less than 9 volts and the cranking speed is slow, the solenoid contacts are probably burned, or the interlock switch or the starter wiring is faulty. **Note:** *If the magnetic switch is hot, it may not function, even though the voltage is adequate. Also the cranking speed is greatly affected by engine oil viscosity.*

15 Starter motor — removal and installation

1   Disconnect the cable from the negative terminal of the battery.

2   Remove the carburetor air cleaner and air intake tube for access.

3   Disconnect the battery cable from the starter solenoid 'B' terminal and the ignition switch wire from the '50' or 'S' terminal.

4   Raise the front of the vehicle and place it securely on jackstands.

5   Working from below, remove the starter attaching nuts, washers and bolts.

6   Remove the starter from below.

7   Installation is the reverse of the removal procedure.

Chapter 6   Emissions control systems

Contents

1   General information

Refer to illustrations 1.5a, 1.5b, 1.7a and 1.7b

As smog standards have become more stringent, the emissions control systems developed to meet these requirements have not only become increasingly more diverse and complex, but are now designed as integral parts of the operation of the engine. Where once the anti-pollution devices used were installed as peripheral ''add-on'' components, the present systems work closely with such other systems as the fuel, ignition and exhaust systems. All vital engine operations are controlled by the emissions control system.

Because of this close integration of systems, disconnecting or not maintaining the emissions control systems, besides being illegal, can adversely affect engine performance and life, as well as fuel economy.

This is not to say that the emissions systems are particularly difficult for the home mechanic to maintain and service. You can perform general operational checks, and do most (if not all) of the regular maintenance easily and quickly at home with common tune-up and hand tools. **Note:** *The most frequent cause of emissions problems is simply a loose or broken vacuum hose or wire, so always check hoses, wires and connectors before performing major repairs.*

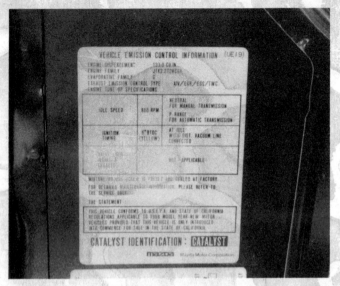

1.5a   A typical Vehicle Emissions Control Information (VECI) label

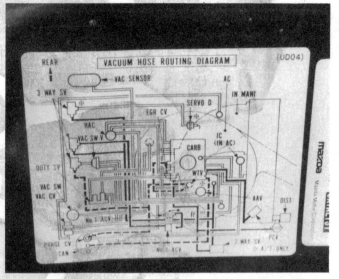

1.5b   A typical vacuum hose routing schematic

While the end result from the various emissions systems is to reduce the output of pollutants into the air (namely hydrocarbons (HC), carbon monoxide (CO), and oxides of nitrogen (NOx), the various systems function independently toward this goal. This is the way in which this Chapter is divided.

Note: *Always refer to the Vehicle Emission Control Information (VECI) label* (**see illustration**) *for specific information regarding emissions components on your vehicle. Similarly, always use the vacuum hose routing diagram* (**see illustration**) *as the final word regarding hose routing for your particular vehicle.*

Malfunction indicator light (Federal vehicles only)

Some model years are equipped with a malfunction indicator light which comes on at 60,000 miles and 80,000 miles to indicate maintenance of the emission control system is required. When the light comes on, the emission system must be inspected and its components adjusted, repaired or replaced as necessary.

To reset the malfunction indicator light, locate the connector under the dash (**see illustration**) and switch the connectors as shown (**see illustration**). Reverse the connection again at 80,000 miles.

2   Positive Crankcase Ventilation (PCV) system

Refer to illustrations 2.2, 2.7, 2.8a and 2.8b

Description

1   The Positive Crankcase Ventilation (PCV) system reduces hydrocarbon emissions by circulating fresh air through the crankcase. This air combines with blow-by gases, or gases blown past the piston rings during compression, and the combination is then sucked into the intake manifold to be reburned.

2   The system consists of one air pipe running from the air cleaner to the rocker arm cover, a one-way PCV valve located in the intake manifold and a second air pipe running from the crankcase to the PCV valve (**see illustration**).

3   During partial throttle operation of the engine, the vacuum created in the intake manifold is great enough to suck the gases from the crankcase, through the PCV valve and into the manifold. The PCV valve allows the gases to enter the manifold but will not allow them to pass in the other direction.

4   The ventilating air is drawn into the rocker arm cover from the air

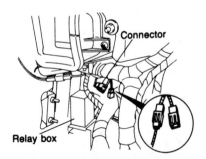

1.7a   The Malfunction Indicator Light (MIL) is located under the dash near the relay box

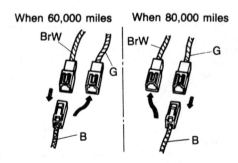

1.7b   When the MIL flashes the first time at 60,000 miles, switch the connectors as shown; when it flashes the second time at 80,000 miles, reverse the connectors again as shown

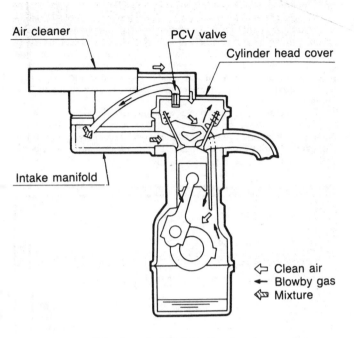

2.7 To check the PCV valve on an older vehicle, detach the ventilation hose from the valve and, with the engine idling, plug the end of the valve with your finger — if the clicking sound of the valve is audible or if the engine speed drops below idle speed, the valve is okay

2.2 A typical Positive Crankcase Ventilation (PCV) system

⇦ Clean air
← Blowby gas
⇦ Mixture

cleaner and then into the crankcase.

5   Under full throttle operation, the vacuum in the intake manifold is not great enough to suck the gases in. Under this condition, the blow-by gases flow backwards into the rocker arm cover, through the air tube and into the air cleaner, where they are carried into the intake manifold in the normal air intake flow.

Check

6   Warm up the engine to normal operating temperature and run it at idle.

7   On older vehicles:

a) Disconnect the ventilation hose from the PCV valve (on the intake manifold next to the carburetor).

b) With the engine idling, plug the inlet of the valve with your finger **(see illustration)**. If the clicking sound of the valve is audible or if the engine speed becomes slightly lower than the idling speed, the valve is okay.

8   On newer vehicles:

a) Detach the PCV valve and the ventilation hose from the cylinder head cover **(see illustration)**.

b) Plug the PCV valve opening with your finger **(see illustration)** and verify that the engine speed drops. If it does, the PCV valve is working properly. If it doesn't, replace the PCV valve.

---

3   Air injection system

Description

Refer to illustrations 3.2a and 3.2b

1   The air injection system (AIS) supplies secondary air into the exhaust system to burn CO and HC in the exhaust gas and to control the 02 signal for the emission control unit.

2.8a   Removing the PCV valve and hose from the cylinder head

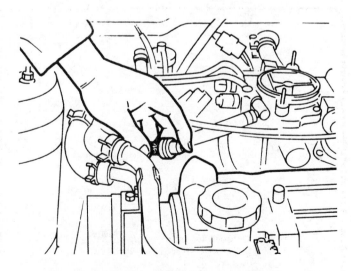

2.8b   To check the PCV valve on a newer vehicle, with the engine idling, plug the valve opening with your finger and verify that the engine speed drops

2   Earlier systems **(see illustration)** employ an air pump which pumps air into the exhaust via an air bypass valve controlled by intake manifold vacuum. In later systems, a passive system was introduced and the pump was eliminated. In 1988, the system was placed under computer control **(see illustration)**.

Check

3   If a fault is suspected in this system, the home mechanic can perform a number of inspection and repair procedures.
4   The first check should be of all rubber vacuum and air delivery hoses in the system. Inspect carefully for cracks, splitting or any damage to these hoses and insure that all are securely connected at each end.
5   All hoses, if defective, can easily be replaced, but always use

replacement hose of the same type and size.
6   If equipped with an air pump, check the tension of the drivebelt which turns the pump. Additional information on belt replacement and tensioning can be found in Chapter 1.
7   If the air pump has failed internally it may make a squealing or other abnormal noise. The air pump cannot be easily repaired, thus a new or factory-rebuilt pump should be used to replace the defective pump.
8   The remaining components can be visually inspected for obvious damage or deterioration.
9   The overall operation of the air injection system can only be checked by a dealer service department equipped with the proper diagnostic tools. You can help the technician by carefully noting engine operation at various engine speeds (idle/high speed, etc.) and engine temperature.

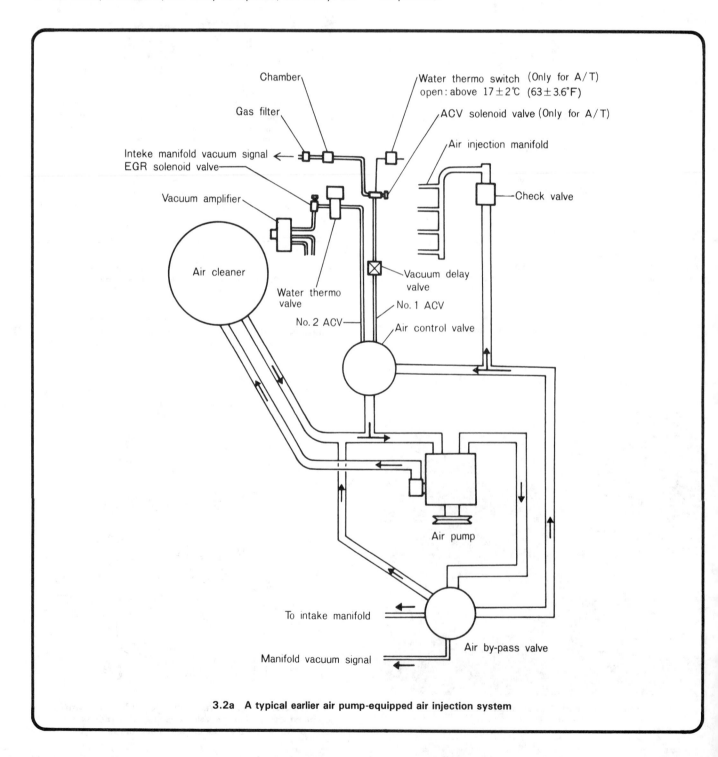

3.2a A typical earlier air pump-equipped air injection system

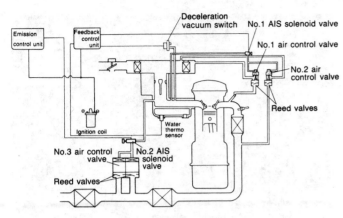

3.2b The electronically controlled air injection system used on 1988 and later models

Replacement

Air pump

10 Disconnect the inlet and outlet hoses from the air pump.
11 Remove the strap bolt and disengage the air pump drive belt.
12 Remove the air pump mounting bolt and nut and remove the pump.
13 Installation is the reverse of removal. Be sure to adjust the belt tension (see Chapter 1).

Check valve

14 Disconnect the air hose from the check valve.
15 Unscrew and remove the check valve from the air injection manifold.
16 Install the check valve.
17 Connect the check valve inlet hose.

Air injection manifold

18 Remove the check valve (see above).
19 Loosen the nuts attaching the air injection manifold to the air injection nozzles, then remove the manifold.
20 Installation is the reverse of removal.

Air injection nozzle

21 Remove the air injection manifold (see above).
22 Remove the hot air duct from the exhaust manifold.
23 Loosen and remove the air injection nozzle from the exhaust manifold. **Note:** *If necessary, remove the exhaust manifold and lightly tap out the air injection nozzle with a plastic hammer.*
24 Installation is the reverse of removal.

Air control valve

25 Disconnect the vacuum sensing tubes from the air control valve.
26 Disconnect the air hoses from the air control valve.
27 Remove the air control valve attaching bolts and remove the air control valve.
28 Installation is the reverse of removal.

Reed valve

29 Disconnect the air hose from the reed valve.
30 Loosen and remove the reed valve from the air pipe.
31 Installation is the reverse of removal.

Air pipe

32 Remove the reed valve.
33 Loosen the nut attaching the air pipe to the bolt connector, then remove the air pipe.
34 Installation is the reverse of removal.

4   Evaporative Emission Control (EEC) system

Description

Refer to illustrations 4.2a, 4.2b and 4.4

1   The Evaporative Emission Control (EEC) system stores the fuel vapor generated in the fuel tank and carburetor when the engine is stopped. When the engine is started, the stored fuel vapors are drawn into the intake manifold and burned.
2   Older, non-electronic systems **(see illustration)** are relatively simple:

a) Vapors from the fuel tank are routed into a condenser tank where they condense back to liquid form and drain into the fuel tank.

6

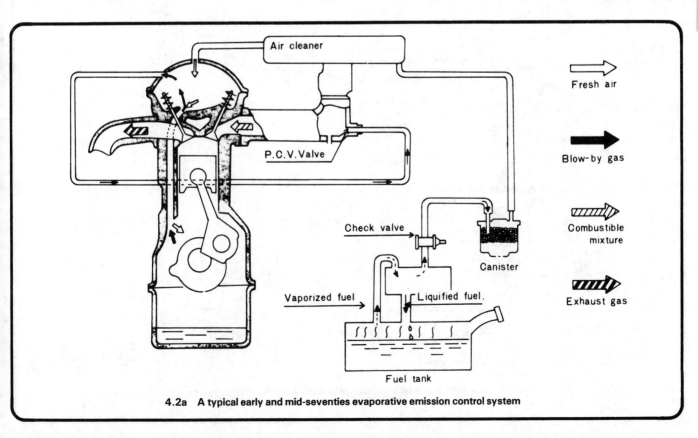

4.2a A typical early and mid-seventies evaporative emission control system

b) When the engine is operating, those fuel vapors which have not condensed are routed through a carbon canister and into the air cleaner to be drawn into the engine.

c) The carbon canister, located in the engine compartment **(see illustration)**, absorbs and stores fuel vapors until they can be burned.

d) A one-way check valve, located in the line between the condenser tank and the canister, allows fuel vapors to flow to the canister when heat causes the pressure of the vapors in the fuel tank to rise.

3   Later versions of the non-electronic system eliminated the condenser tank. Refer to the Vehicle Emission Control Information (VECI) label to determine whether your system is equipped with a condenser tank.

4   The latest version of the EEC system **(see illustration)**, while generally similar in operation to the systems described above, is more complex because it uses system control devices which are operated by the emission control unit:

a) The water thermo valve opens the vacuum passage to the No. 1 and No. 3 purge control valves.

b) The No. 2 purge control valve is a two-way check valve and the No. 1 purge control valve opens the fuel vapor passage between the canister and the intake manifold when the purge solenoid is on. Both valves are in the canister.

c) The No. 3 purge control valve opens the fuel vapor passage between the canister and the intake manifold when the purge solenoid is on on.

d) Port vacuum is applied to the No. 1 purge control valve while the engine is running and to the No. 3 purge control valve during running or heavy-load driving.

e) The check-and-cut valve vents vapors to the atmosphere if the evaporative hoses become clogged. It also prevents fuel leakage if the vehicle overturns.

4.2b   The charcoal cannister is located next to the battery and can be identified by the many vacuum hoses attached to it

Check

System (all vehicles through 1987 models)

5   Inspect the filler cap, fuel tank, fuel lines, condenser tank (if equipped), check valve and canister for leaks. Make sure that there are no loose connections and that all components are in good condi-

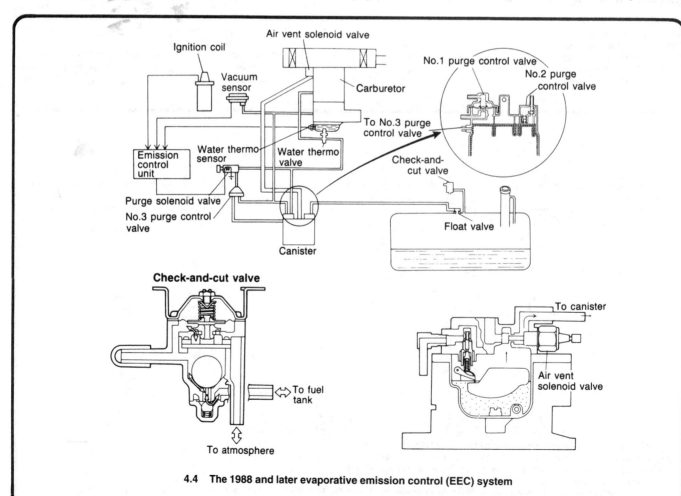

4.4   The 1988 and later evaporative emission control (EEC) system

tion. Inspect all hoses and tubes for deterioration, cracks and holes. Consult the VECI label to determine the hose and fuel line routing on your vehicle and the location of all components.

System (1988 and later models)

Refer to illustrations 4.8, 4.12 and 4.17

6   Inspect the system as described in Step 5 above.

7   Warm up the engine and run it at idle.

8   Disconnect vacuum hose (A) from the No. 1 purge control valve **(see illustration)** and connect a vacuum gauge to the disconnected hose.

9   Increase the engine speed to 2500 rpm and verify that the gauge indicates more than 5.9 in Hg vacuum.

10 It it doesn't, check the water thermo valve (see below).

11 Reconnect hose (A) to the No. 1 purge control valve.

12 Disconnect vacuum hose (B) from the canister and connect a vacuum gauge to the disconnected hose **(see illustration)**.

13 Verify that there is vacuum when the engine speed exceeds 1400 rpm.

14 If no vacuum is evident, check the purge solenoid valve and the No. 3 purge control valve. If they both check out, have the 1V terminal of the emission control unit checked (do not attempt to check it at home without the proper testing equipment or you could damage the control unit).

15 Reconnect hose (B) to the canister.

16 Disconnect the evaporation hose from the evaporation pipe.

17 Connect a vacuum pump to the evaporation pipe **(see illustration)**.

18 Operate the vacuum pump and verify that no vacuum is held.

19 If it is, test the check-and-cut valve and evaporation pipe for clogging.

Canister

20 Inspect the canister for any leakage of the active carbon. Tap the canister. No abnormal sound should be audible.

Check valve (early systems)

Refer to illustration 4.22

21 Remove the check valve **(see illustration 4.45)**, which is located in the tube between the intake manifold and canister.

22 Using a short section of vacuum hose of appropriate diameter, install a pressure/vacuum pump tester or a pressure gauge to one end of the check valve and plug the other end with your finger **(see illustration)**.

23 Pump, or blow, at least 0.57 psi of air into the check valve. Then apply a vacuum. The valve should vent when either the pressure or vacuum is applied. If it doesn't vent both ways, replace it.

Purge control valve (1980 California vehicles and all 1981 thru 1984 vehicles)

Refer to illustration 4.24

24 Disconnect the vacuum sensing tube (A) from the purge control valve port (E) **(see illustration)**.

25 Disconnect the evaporative hose (B) from the purge control valve port (D) and plug the hose.

26 Start the engine and run it at idle.

27 Connect a suitable hose (C) to port (D).

28 Try to blow through the valve by blowing into hose (C). Air should not pass through the valve.

29 Remove the plug from evaporative hose (B) and connect hose (B) to valve port (E).

30 Again, blow through the valve by blowing into hose (C). This time, air should pass through the valve.

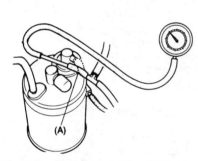

4.8 Disconnect vacuum hose (A) from the No. 1 purge control valve and connect a vacuum gauge to the disconnected hose

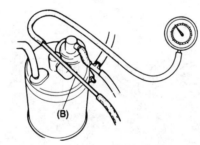

4.12 Disconnect vacuum hose (B) from the canister and connect a vacuum gauge to the disconnected hose

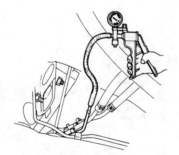

4.17 Disconnect the evaporation hose from the evaporation pipe and connect a vacuum pump to the evaporation pipe

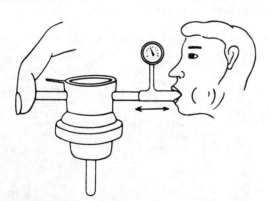

4.22 To test the check valve in earlier EEC systems, connect an air pressure gauge (shown) or a pressure/vacuum pump tester, place your finger over the other pipe, and blow, or pump, air into the valve, then apply a vacuum — the valve should vent when either the pressure or vacuum is applied

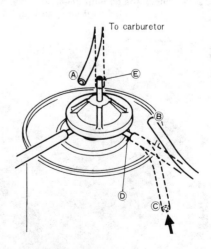

To carburetor

4.24 Checking the purge control valve

6

Evaporative shutter valve (1981 thru 1984 vehicles)

Refer to illustration 4.35

31 Start the engine and warm to operating temperature.
32 Run the engine at normal idle speed.
33 Remove the air cleaner element (see Chapter 1).
34 Make sure that the evaporative shutter valve opens fully.
35 Disconnect the vacuum sensing tube from the vacuum diaphragm **(see illustration)**. Make sure that the evaporative shutter valve closes fully.

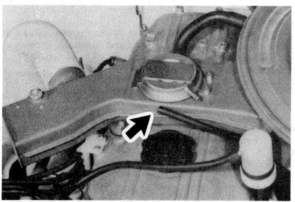

4.35 To check the evaporative shutter valve, start the engine, run it at idle, remove the air cleaner element, make sure the shutter valve opens fully, disconnect the sensing tube (arrow) from the vacuum diaphragm and make sure that the evaporative shutter valve closes fully

Air vent solenoid valve (1986 and later vehicles)

Refer to illustration 4.37

36 Remove the air cleaner (see Chapter 4).
37 Touch the air vent solenoid valve on the carburetor **(see illustration)**.
38 Turn the ignition switch on and off. If there is a clicking noise, the air vent solenoid valve is working properly.

Replacement

Condenser tank (early systems)

Refer to illustration 4.40

39 Raise the vehicle and support it with stands.
40 Locate the tank **(see illustration)**.
41 Disconnect the hoses from the condenser tank.
42 Remove the tank mounting bolts and remove the tank.
43 Installation is the reverse of removal.

Check valve (early systems)

Refer to illustration 4.45

44 Raise the vehicle and support it securely with jackstands.
45 Locate the check valve **(see illustration)**.
46 Disconnect the hoses from the check valve.
47 Remove the bolts securing the check valve and remove the check valve.
48 Installation is the reverse of removal.

Canister

49 Detach the hoses from the canister.
50 Remove the screw holding the canister to the bracket and slip the canister out of the bracket.
51 Installation is the reverse of removal.

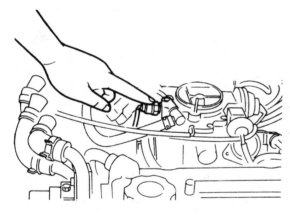

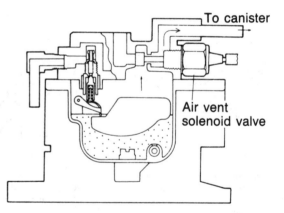

4.37 To check the air vent solenoid valve, remove the air cleaner, touch the valve and turn the ignition switch on and off — if you can hear and feel the solenoid valve clicking on and off, it's okay

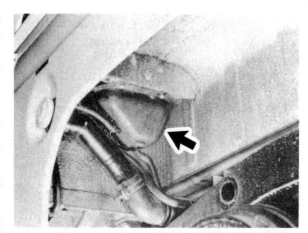

4.40 The condenser tank (arrow) is located in the right rear wheel well

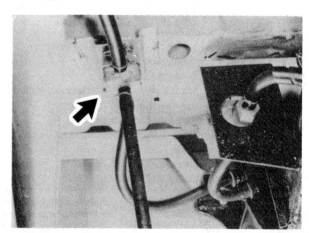

4.45 The check valve (arrow) used in earlier systems is installed in the hose between the intake manifold and the canister

5 Air intake temperature control system

Refer to illustration 5.2

General description

1   The air temperature control system improves engine efficiency and reduces hydrocarbon emissions during the initial warm-up period of the engine by maintaining a controlled air temperature into the carburetor. Temperature control of the incoming air allows leaner carb and choke calibrations and helps prevent carburetor icing in cold weather.

2   The system **(see illustration)** uses an air control valve located in the snorkel of the air cleaner housing to control the ratio of cold and warm air into the carburetor. This valve is controlled by a vacuum motor which is, in turn, modulated by a temperature sensor in the air cleaner. This sensor closes when the intake air temperature is cold, thus allowing intake manifold vacuum to reach the vacuum motor. When the air is hot, the sensor opens, thus closing off the manifold vacuum.

3   It is during the first few miles of driving (depending on outside temperature) that this system has its greatest effect on engine performance and emissions output. When the engine is cold, the air control valve blocks off the air cleaner inlet snorkel, allowing only warm air from the exhaust manifold to enter the carb. Gradually, as the engine warms up, the valve opens the snorkel passage, increasing the amount of cold air allowed in. Once the engine reaches normal operating temperature, the valve completely opens, allowing only cold, fresh air to enter.

4   Because of this cold-engine-only function, it is important to periodically check this system to prevent poor engine performance when cold, or overheating of the fuel mixture once the engine has reached operating temperatures. If the air cleaner valve sticks in the 'no heat' position, the engine will run poorly, stall and waste gas until it has warmed up on its own. A valve sticking in the 'heat' position causes the engine to run as if it is out of tune due to the constant flow of hot air to the carburetor.

5   With the engine off, note the position of the air control valve inside the air cleaner snorkel. If the vehicle is equipped with an air duct on the end of the snorkel, it will have to be removed prior to this check. If visual access to the valve is difficult, use a mirror. The valve should be down, meaning that all air would flow through the snorkel and none through the exhaust manifold hot-air duct at the underside of the air cleaner housing. Move the control valve. It should be easy to move, but some resistance (from the bimetal spring) should be felt.

6   Now have an assistant start the engine and continue to watch the valve inside the snorkel. With the engine cold and at idle, the valve should close off all air from the snorkel, allowing heated air from the exhaust manifold to enter the air cleaner intake. As the engine warms to operating temperature the valve should move, allowing outside air through the snorkel to be included in the mixture. Eventually, the valve should move down to the point where most of the incoming air is through the snorkel and not the exhaust manifold duct.

7   If the valve did not close off snorkel air when the cold engine was first started, disconnect the vacuum hose at the snorkel vacuum motor and place your thumb over the hose end, checking for vacuum. If there is vacuum going to the motor, check that the valve and link are not frozen or binding in the air cleaner snorkel. Replace the vacuum motor if the hose routing is correct and the valve moves freely.

8   If there was no vacuum going to the motor in the above test, check the hoses to make sure they are not cracked, crimped or disconnected. If the hoses are clear and in good condition, replace the temperature sensor inside the air cleaner housing.

Replacement

9   Remove the air cleaner assembly.
10   Remove the vacuum motor mounting nuts.
11   Remove the motor.
12   Installation is the reverse of removal.

6 Carburetor control systems

Description

Altitude compensation system (1986 and later vehicles)

1   This system assures an optimum air-fuel ratio at high altitude

6

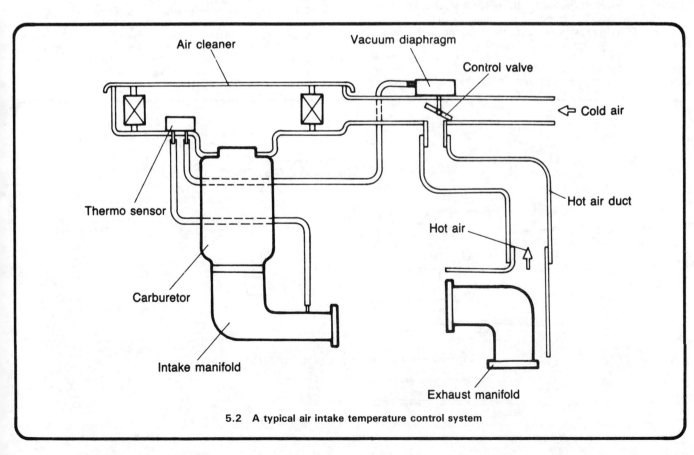

5.2 A typical air intake temperature control system

areas and operates at more than 1640 feet above sea level by increasing the amount of air available to the carburetor to prevent overrich air/fuel ratio at high altitudes. The system consists of the high altitude compensator and the carburetor. The high altitude compensator provides additional air bleeds for the primary main and secondary main fuel circuits and supplies additional air into the intake manifold.

Deceleration control system (all vehicles)

2   The deceleration control system reduces HC and CO during deceleration.

3   The 1988 version of this system consists of a slow fuel cut system and a deceleration spark advance system:

    a) The slow cut fuel system reduces the fuel flow to decrease HC emissions, to improve fuel economy during deceleration and to cut the fuel flow when the ignition switch is off to prevent run-on.

    b) This system advances the ignition timing by controlling the vacuum working on the distributor vacuum diaphragm to reduce HC emissions during deceleration.

Enrichment system (1988 and later vehicles)

4   This system controls the amount of additional fuel fed to the primary system of the carburetor when the engine is cold, during acceleration, when heavy loads are imposed on the engine and during high speed driving.

Hot idle compensation system (1986 and later vehicles)

5   The hot idle system supplies secondary air into the intake manifold to stabilize idle speed when air intake temperature is more than 153-degrees F.

Idle compensation system (1984 vehicles)/Idle-up system (1986 and later vehicles)

6   This system, which is installed on vehicles equipped with an automatic transmission or air conditioning system, raises the idle on those vehicles when either of these systems puts a load on the engine. The system supplies secondary air into the intake manifold to stabilize idle speed when air intake temperature is more than 153-degrees F.

Positive Temperature Coefficient (PTC) heater system (1986 and later vehicles)

7   The PTC heater system warms up the carburetor body to prevent icing. The system consists of the PTC heater, PTC heater relay and water temperature switch. It operates when radiator coolant temperature is less than 41-degrees F (less than 63-degrees F on 1988 models) and engine coolant temperature is less than 153-degrees F.

Vacuum control valve (VCV) systems (1988 and later vehicles)

8   The VCV system prevents fuel from overflowing into the carburetor from the float chamber. While the engine is being driven at full throttle, the float chamber temperature becomes high and may cause fuel in the chamber to bubble and force its way out through the air vent tube and into the carburetor air stream. The VCV system controls float chamber pressure to prevent this bubbling. The vacuum control valve opens the passage from the float chamber to the intake manifold in accordance with the secondary venturi vacuum.

Vacuum switch (1986 vehicles)

9   The vacuum switch improves driveability while driving at high altitudes.

---

7   Exhaust Gas Recirculation (EGR) system

Refer to illustrations 7.2, 7.3 and 7.9

Description

1   The purpose of the exhaust gas recirculation (EGR) system is to introduce small amounts of exhaust gas into the intake manifold to reduce combustion temperatures and the creation of nitrous oxides (NOx). Earlier EGR systems **(see illustration)** are controlled by intake manifold vacuum: When the valve is open, a tiny amount of exhaust gas is allowed into the intake manifold; when the valve is closed, no gas is allowed in.

3   On 1986 thru 1988 models **(see illustration)**, the EGR system is also controlled by engine speed (which is monitored and interpreted by the control unit).

    a) The EGR control valve controls the amount of exhaust gas flowing into the intake manifold.

    b) The duty solenoid valve consists of a vacuum valve and a vent valve. The vacuum valve opens the vacuum passage to the EGR control valve, and the vent valve vents the vacuum from the vacuum valve to control vacuum according to signals from the emission control unit.

    c) The emission control unit senses the amount of EGR gas recirculated by the EGR position sensor on the EGR valve and controls the opening duration of the vacuum and vent valves. The amount of exhaust gas recirculated is determined by the ignition coil signal, water thermo sensor, water temperature sensor, vacuum sensor and atmospheric pressure sensor.

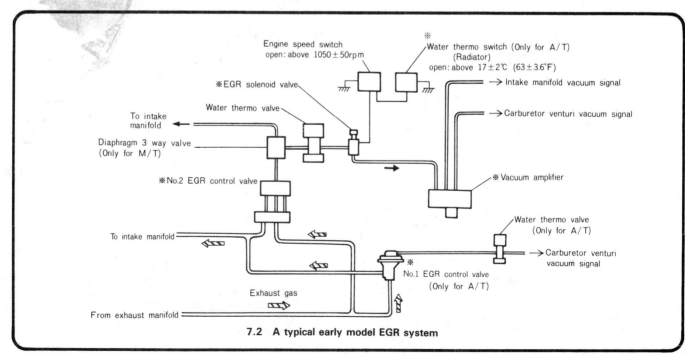

7.2   A typical early model EGR system

Check

4   Due to a number of factors, checking the EGR system on these vehicles by the home mechanic should be limited to simple visual and functional checks as follow.

5   Most problems with this system can be traced to defective vacuum hoses. Carefully inspect all EGR system hoses for splitting or damage and check that they are securely installed at each end.

6   Disconnect each hose (one at a time to prevent confusion) and blow air through the hose to insure there is no blockage.

7   The EGR valve itself will sometimes stick in either the open or closed postion due to hardened deposits.

8   Locate the EGR valve. You will notice that the bottom of the valve has openings, allowing you to see (and feel with your fingers) the diaphragm inside.

9   With the engine cold to prevent burns, use your finger to attempt to move the diaphragm up and down. If it won't move or moves with great difficulty, chances are the valve is defective and should be replaced with a new one **(see illustration)**.

8   Catalytic converter

Description

1   Pre-1984 vehicles are equipped with a single converter located under the vehicle floor pan. Newer vehicles are also equipped with another converter located immediately below the exhaust manifold.

2   The rear converter on all vehicles is a conventional oxidation catalyst. It reduces hydrocarbons (HC) and carbon monoxide (CO).

3   The front converter on newer vehicles is known as a three-way catalyst. It reduces HC, CO and NOx.

Check

4   Because of the special tools required to check catalytic converters, the checking procedure is beyond the scope of the home mechanic. Take the vehicle to a dealer to have it checked by a professional.

5   Whenever the vehicle is raised for any reason, always be sure to inspect the physical condition of the converter(s):

   a) Note any dings or dents in the protective heat shield that might impair the performance of the converter(s).

   b) Make sure that there is adequate clearance between the converter(s) and the vehicle.

   c) Make sure that the flange bolts at either end of the converters are tight. Check the fittings on the air injection pipes attached to the three-way catalyst (if equipped). Make sure they are tight.

Replacement

6   See Chapter 4.

9   Engine control system

Description

1   The engine control system, (called the feedback or "closed loop" system on carbureted models) maintains the air-fuel mixture at an ideal ratio of 14.7:1, reduces CO, HC and NOx emissions and minimizes fuel consumption.

2   There are several versions of this system. They include various combinations of the following components: the ignition coil, the ignition switch, the idle switch, the clutch switch, the neutral switch, the vacuum switch, the vacuum sensor, the oxygen sensor, the intake air temperature sensor, the water thermo sensor, the water temperature switch, the throttle sensor, the deceleration vacuum switch, the A/C switch, the air/fuel (A/F) solenoid valve, fuel injection system and the computer control unit.

Carbureted models

3   The B2200 control unit detects engine speed, intake manifold vacuum, coolant temperature, oxygen concentration in the exhaust gas, position of the valve in the EGR control system, etc. It uses this information to control the fuel control system and the EGR control system.

4   The B2600 has two control units for the fuel and emission control system and responds similarly.

5   The engine control system and control unit(s) regulate the amount of fuel metered through the air/fuel (A/F), or jet mixture, solenoid valve which determines the amount of fuel added to the primary main circuit and air added to the primary slow circuit.

Fuel injected models

6   On these models, the engine control unit computer (called the EGI) gathers information from relays and sensors located in the engine compartment involved with engine and meters the fuel to the injectors to keep the makeup of the exhaust within certain limits. It can do this more precisely because the design of the fuel injection system allows for better fuel management. The emissions system components on fuel injected models are very similar to those on carbureted models except that many are operated by the EGI. More information on the fuel injection system can be found in Chapter 4.

Check

7   Because of the specialized diagnostic equipment required to check the engine control system, the control unit(s) and the components of the system, testing procedures are beyond the scope of the average home mechanic. This system must be checked and repaired by a professional mechanic.

6

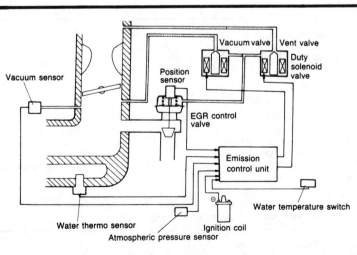

7.3   The computer controlled EGR system as used on 1988 and later models

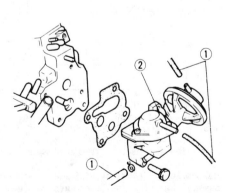

7.9   An exploded view of the EGR control valve on the B2600 — note the cut out portion on the bottom which allows access to the diaphragm

Chapter 7 Part A   Manual transmission

Contents

Specifications

Torque specifications   **Ft-lbs**
Clutch bellhousing-to-engine bolt
   1600/1800/2000/2200 engine . . . . 51 to 65
   2600 engine . . . . 27 to 38

---

1   General information

All vehicles covered in this manual are equipped with either a 4- or 5-speed manual transmission or an automatic transmission. All information on the manual transmission is included in this Part of Chapter 7. Information on the automatic transmission can be found in Part B. Information on the transfer case used on 4WD models can be found in Part C.

Due to the complexity, unavailability of replacement parts and the special tools necessary, internal repair procedures for the manual transmission is not recommended for the home mechanic. The information contained within this manual will be limited to general information, seal replacement and removal and installation procedures.

Depending on the expense involved in having a faulty transmission overhauled, it may be an advantage to consider replacing the unit with either a new or rebuilt one. Your local dealer or transmission shop should be able to supply you with information concerning cost, availability and exchange policy.

Regardless of how you decide to remedy a transmission problem, you can still save considerable expense by removing and installing the unit yourself.

2   Shift lever — removal and installation

Refer to illustration 2.3

1   Remove the console (if equipped) and shift boot screws.
2   Place the shift lever in Neutral.
3   Remove the shift lever cover-to-transmission bolts/screws **(see illustration)**.

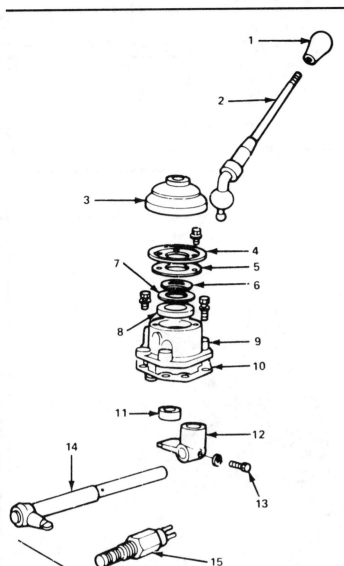

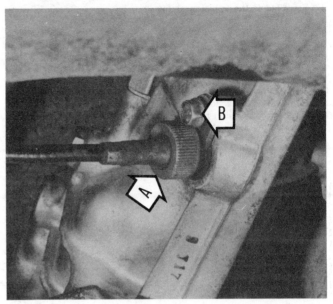

3.9 Unscrew the speedometer cable collar (A) and then remove the gear retaining bolt (B)

2.3 Typical shift lever components — exploded view

1 Knob	9 Shift lever retainer
2 Shift lever	10 Gasket
3 Boot	11 Ball seat
4 Cover	12 Control lever end
5 Gasket	13 Bolt
6 Spring	14 Transmission control lever
7 Shim	15 Backup lamp switch
8 Bushing	

4   Grasp the shift lever securely and pull it straight up and out of the transmission, taking care not to drop the cover, gasket, spring, shims and other components which will come out with the lever **(see illustration 2.3)**.

5   Installation is the reverse of removal.

3   Oil seal replacement

Refer to illustration 3.9

1   Oil leaks frequently occur due to wear of the extension housing oil seal and bushing, and/or the speedometer drive gear oil seal and/or O-ring. Replacement of these seals is relatively easy, since the repairs can usually be performed without removing the transmission from the vehicle.

Extension housing

2   The extension housing oil seal is located at the extreme rear of the transmission, where the driveshaft is attached. If leakage at the seal is suspected, raise the rear of the vehicle and support it securely on jackstands. Be sure to block the front wheels to keep the vehicle from rolling. If the seal is leaking, transmission lubricant will be built up on the front of the driveshaft and may be dripping from the dust shield at the rear of the transmission.

3   Refer to Chapter 8 and remove the driveshaft.

4   Using a screwdriver or pry bar, carefully pry the oil seal and bushing out of the rear of the transmission. Do not damage the splines on the transmission output shaft.

5   Using a large section of pipe or a very large deep socket as a drift, install the new oil seal. Drive it into the bore squarely and make sure that it is completely seated. Install a new bushing using the same method.

6   Reinstall the dust shield by carefully tapping it into place. Lubricate the splines of the transmission output shaft and the outside of the driveshaft sleeve yoke with lightweight grease, then install the driveshaft. Be careful not to damage the lip of the new seal.

Speedometer gear

7   The speedometer cable and driven gear housing is located on the side of the extension housing. Look for transmission oil around the cable housing to determine if the seal and O-ring are leaking.

8   Unscrew the cable housing with pliers.

9   Using a wrench, remove the speedometer driven gear housing **(see illustration)**.

10 Remove the driven gear from the housing.

11 Using a hook, remove the seal.

12 Using a small socket of the appropriate diameter or other similar tool as a drift, install the new seal.

13 Install a new O-ring to the driven gear housing and reinstall the driven gear housing and cable assembly to the extension housing.

4   Manual transmission — removal and installation

Refer to illustrations 4.5a and 4.5b
Removal

1   Disconnect the negative cable at the battery. Place the cable out of the way so it cannot accidentally come in contact with the negative terminal of the battery, as this would once again allow power into the electrical system of the vehicle.

7A

2   From inside the vehicle, remove the shift lever (Section 2).
3   On 4WD models, remove the shift lever assembly.
4   Raise the vehicle and support it securely on jackstands.
5   Disconnect the speedometer cable and electrical connections from the transmission and, if equipped, the transfer case **(see illustrations)**.
6   Drain the transmission and, if equipped, the transfer case.
7   Remove the starter motor.
8   Unbolt the clutch release cylinder and fasten it out of the way.
9   Remove the driveshaft (Chapter 8). Use a plastic bag to cover the end of the transmission to prevent fluid loss and contamination.
10 Remove the exhaust system components as necessary for clear-

ance (Chapter 4).
11 Support the engine. This can be done from above by using an engine hoist, or by placing a jack (with a block of wood as an insulator) under the engine oil pan. The engine should remain supported at all times while the transmission is out of the vehicle.
12 Support the transmission with a jack — preferably a special jack made for this purpose. Safety chains will help steady the transmission on the jack.
13 Remove the rear transmission support-to-crossmember nuts and bolts.
14 Remove the nuts from the crossmember bolts. Raise the transmis-

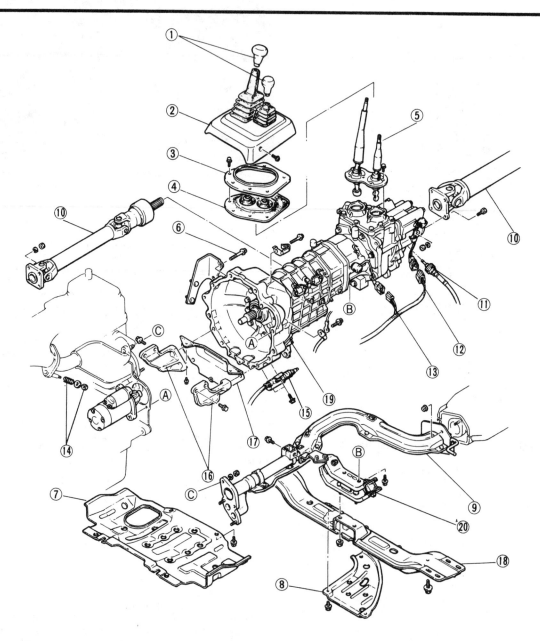

4.5a   Typical transmission/transfer case installation details (4WD models)

1 Shift leaver knobs	8 Transfer case cover	15 Clutch release cylinder
2 Shift console	9 Exhaust pipe	16 Gusset plates
3 Insulator plate	10 Driveshafts	17 Undercover
4 Shift boot	11 Speedometer cable	18 Crossmember
5 Shift lever assembly	12 Transfer case indicator switch	19 Transmission/clutch
6 Bracket bolt	13 Backup switch connector	housing assembly
7 Rear undercover	14 Exhaust pipe bolts	20 Transmission mount bracket

sion slightly and remove the crossmember.

15 Remove the bolts securing the transmission/clutch housing to the engine.

16 Make a final check that all wires and hoses have been disconnected from the transmission and transfer case (4WD models) and then move the transmission and jack toward the rear of the vehicle until the transmission and clutch housing assembly are clear of the engine. Keep the transmission level as this is done.

17 Once it is clear, lower the transmission/clutch housing assembly and remove it from under the vehicle. **Caution:** *Do not depress the clutch pedal while the transmission is removed from the vehicle.*

18 The clutch components can now be inspected (Chapter 8). In most cases, new clutch components should be installed as a matter of course if the transmission is removed.

Installation

19 If removed, install the clutch components (Chapter 8).

20 With the transmission secured to the jack as on removal, raise the transmission into position behind the engine and then carefully slide it forward, engaging the clutch housing with the engine dowel pins. Do not use excessive force to install the transmission — if the dowel pins do not slide into place, readjust the angle of the transmission so it is level.

21 Install the transmission/clutch housing-to-engine bolts. Tighten the bolts to the specified torque.

22 Install the crossmember and transmission support. Tighten all nuts and bolts securely.

23 Remove the jacks supporting the transmission and the engine.

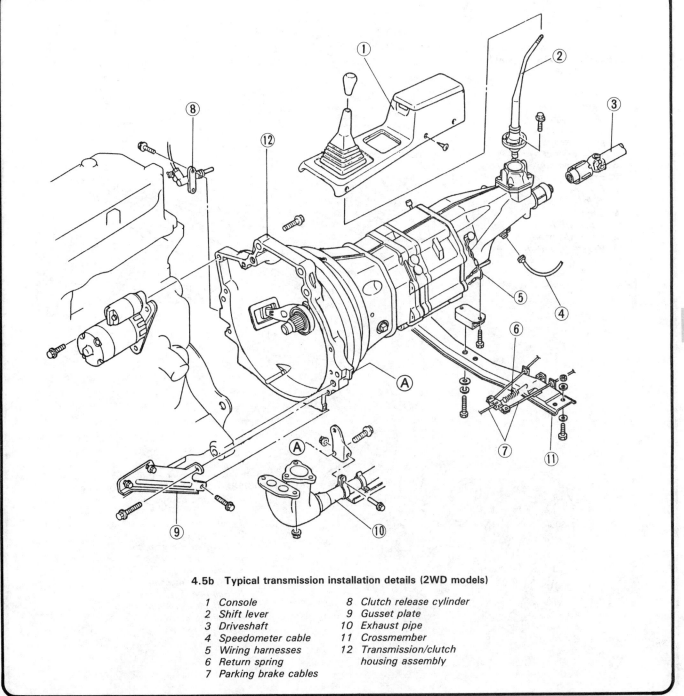

4.5b Typical transmission installation details (2WD models)

1 Console	8 Clutch release cylinder
2 Shift lever	9 Gusset plate
3 Driveshaft	10 Exhaust pipe
4 Speedometer cable	11 Crossmember
5 Wiring harnesses	12 Transmission/clutch
6 Return spring	housing assembly
7 Parking brake cables	

24 Install the various items removed previously, referring to Chapter 8 for the installation of the driveshaft and Chapter 4 for information regarding the exhaust system components.

25 Make a final check that all wires, hoses and the speedometer cable have been connected and that the transmission and transfer case (4WD models) have been filled with lubricant to the proper level (Chapter 1). Lower the vehicle.

26 From inside the vehicle connect the shift lever (see Section 2).

27 On 4WD models, install the transfer case shift lever assembly.

28 Connect the negative battery cable. Road test the vehicle for proper operation and check for leakage.

5   Manual transmission overhaul — general information

Refer to illustrations 5.4a, 5.4b, 5.4c, 5.4d, 5.4e, 5.4f, 5.4g, 5.4h, 5.4i and 5.4j

Overhauling a manual transmission is a difficult job for a do-it-yourselfer. It involves the disassembly and reassembly of many small parts. Numerous clearances must be precisely measured and, if necessary, changed with select fit spacers and snap-rings. As a result, if transmission problems arise, it can be removed and installed by a competent

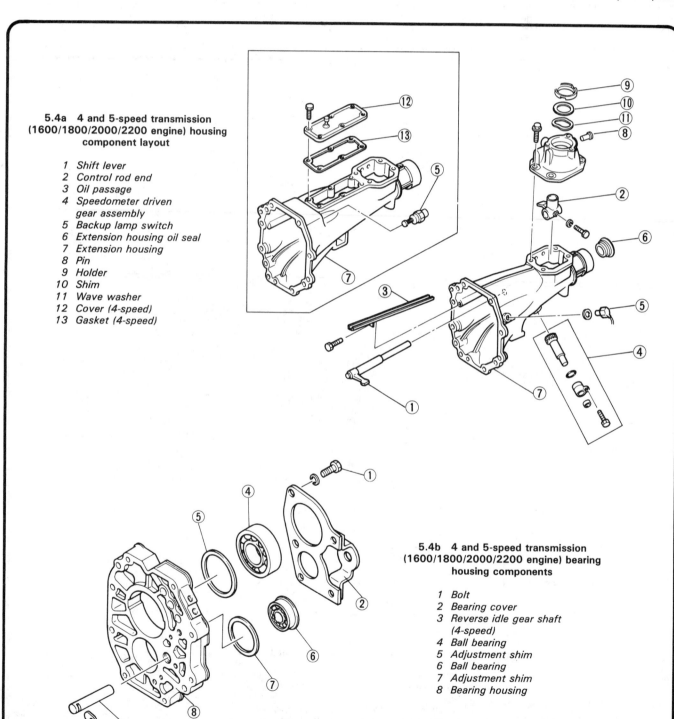

5.4a   4 and 5-speed transmission (1600/1800/2000/2200 engine) housing component layout

1   Shift lever
2   Control rod end
3   Oil passage
4   Speedometer driven gear assembly
5   Backup lamp switch
6   Extension housing oil seal
7   Extension housing
8   Pin
9   Holder
10   Shim
11   Wave washer
12   Cover (4-speed)
13   Gasket (4-speed)

5.4b   4 and 5-speed transmission (1600/1800/2000/2200 engine) bearing housing components

1   Bolt
2   Bearing cover
3   Reverse idle gear shaft (4-speed)
4   Ball bearing
5   Adjustment shim
6   Ball bearing
7   Adjustment shim
8   Bearing housing

do-it-yourselfer, but overhaul should be left to a transmission repair shop. Rebuilt transmissions may be available — check with your dealer parts department and auto parts stores. At any rate, the time and money involved in an overhaul is almost sure to exceed the cost of a rebuilt unit.

Nevertheless, it's not impossible for an inexperienced mechanic to rebuild a transmission if the special tools are available and the job is done in a deliberate step-by-step manner so nothing is overlooked.

The tools necessary for an overhaul include internal and external snap-ring pliers, a bearing puller, a slide hammer, a set of pin punches, a dial indicator and possibly a hydraulic press. In addition, a large, sturdy workbench and a vise or transmission stand will be required.

During disassembly of the transmission, make careful notes of how each piece comes off, where it fits in relation to other pieces and what holds it in place. Exploded views are included **(see illustrations)** to show where the parts go — but actually noting how they are installed when you remove the parts will make it much easier to get the transmission back together.

Before taking the transmission apart for repair, it will help if you have some idea what area of the transmission is malfunctioning. Certain problems can be closely tied to specific areas in the transmission, which can make component examination and replacement easier. Refer to the *Troubleshooting* section at the front of this manual for information regarding possible sources of trouble.

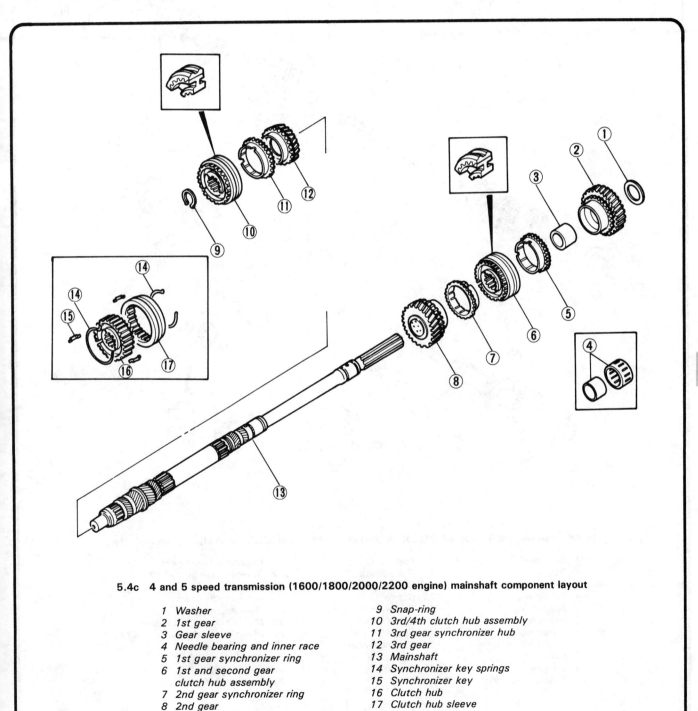

5.4c   4 and 5 speed transmission (1600/1800/2000/2200 engine) mainshaft component layout

1 Washer	9 Snap-ring
2 1st gear	10 3rd/4th clutch hub assembly
3 Gear sleeve	11 3rd gear synchronizer hub
4 Needle bearing and inner race	12 3rd gear
5 1st gear synchronizer ring	13 Mainshaft
6 1st and second gear	14 Synchronizer key springs
clutch hub assembly	15 Synchronizer key
7 2nd gear synchronizer ring	16 Clutch hub
8 2nd gear	17 Clutch hub sleeve

7A

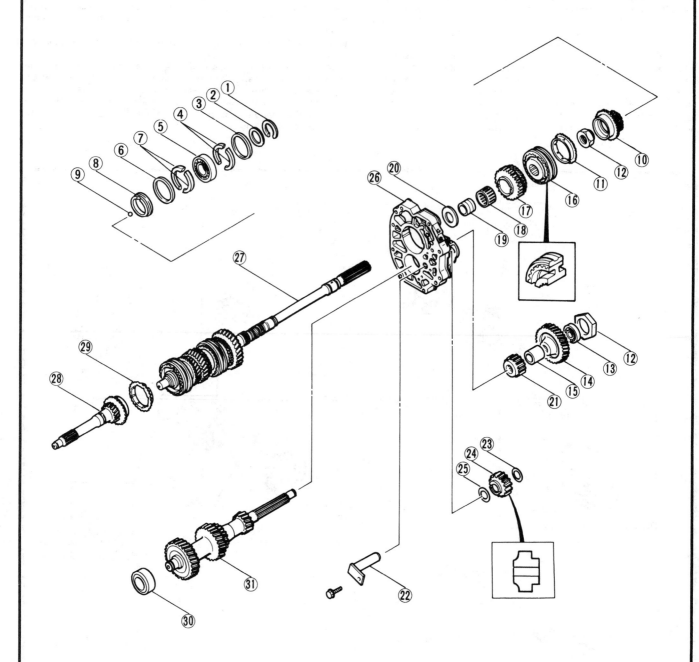

5.4d   5-speed (1600/1800/2000/2200 engine) main and countershaft assembly — exploded view

1	Snap ring	12	Locknut	21	Counter reverse gear
2	Washer	13	Ball bearing	22	Reverse gear idler shaft
3	Retaining ring	14	Countergear	23	Washer
4	C-washers	15	Spacer	24	Reverse idle gear
5	Ball bearing	16	5th/reverse clutch	25	Washer
6	Retaining ring		hub assembly	26	Bearing housing assembly
7	C-washers	17	Reverse gear	27	Mainshaft and gear assembly
8	Thrust lock washer	18	Needle bearing	28	Main drive gear
9	Ball	19	Inner race	29	Synchronizer ring
10	5th gear	20	Washer	30	Ball bearing
11	Synchronizer ring			31	Countershaft gear

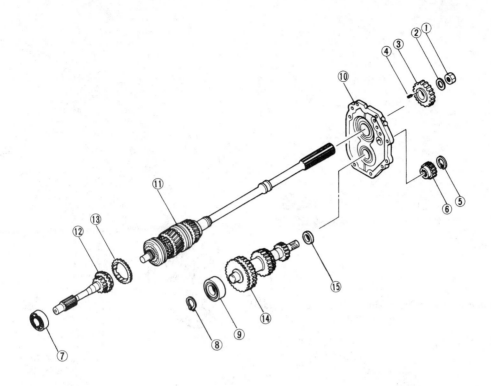

5.4e   4-speed transmission (1600/1800/2000/2200 engine) main and countershaft assembly — exploded view

1 Locknut	6 Counter reverse gear	11 Mainshaft and gear assembly
2 Plain washer	7 Bearing housing assembly	12 Main drive gear
3 Reverse gear	8 Snapring	13 Synchronizer ring
4 Woodruff key	9 Ball bearing	14 Countershaft gear
5 Snapring	10 Bearing housing assembly	15 Spacer

7A

5.4f   4 and 5-speed transmission
(1600/1800/2000/2200 engine) shift
fork and rod assembly — exploded view

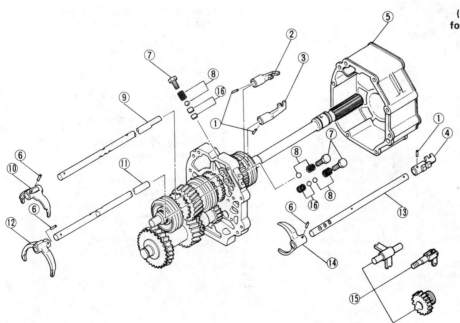

1   Spring pins (5-speed)
2   Shift rod end (1st/2nd)
    (5-speed)
3   Shift rod end (3rd/4th)
    (5-speed)
4   Shift rod end (5th/reverse)
    (5-speed)
5   Intermediate housing
    (5-speed)
6   Spring pins
7   Cap plugs
8   Springs and balls
9   Shift rod (1st/2nd)
10 Shift fork (1st/2nd)
11 Shift rod (3rd/4th)
12 Shift fork (3rd/4th)
13 Shift rod (5th/reverse)
    (5-speed)
14 Shift fork (5th/reverse)
    (5-speed)
15 Shift rod, lever and reverse
    idler gear (4-speed)
16 Springs, balls and
    interlock pins

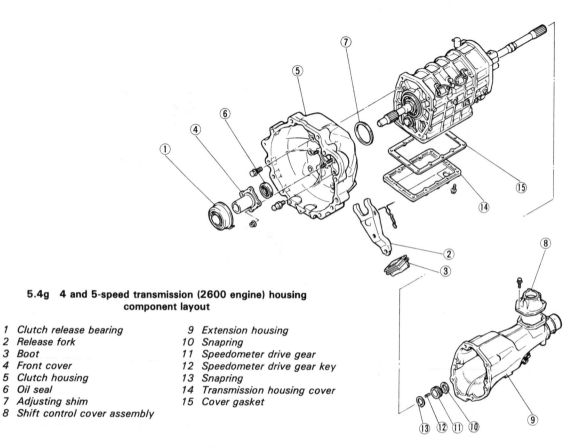

5.4g   4 and 5-speed transmission (2600 engine) housing component layout

1 Clutch release bearing	9 Extension housing
2 Release fork	10 Snapring
3 Boot	11 Speedometer drive gear
4 Front cover	12 Speedometer drive gear key
5 Clutch housing	13 Snapring
6 Oil seal	14 Transmission housing cover
7 Adjusting shim	15 Cover gasket
8 Shift control cover assembly	

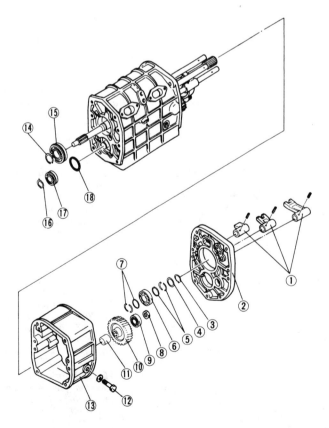

5.4h   4 and 5-speed transmission (2600 engine) bearing housing component layout

1 Shift rod ends
2 Bearing housing
3 Snapring
4 Washer
5 C-washers and retaining ring
6 Mainshaft bearing
7 C-washers and retaining ring
8 Locknut
9 Countershaft rear bearing
10 Counter 5th gear
11 Spacer
12 Idle gearshaft hold bolt
13 Center housing
14 Snapring
15 Main drive gear bearing
16 Snapring
17 Countershaft front bearing
18 Adjusting shim

**5.4i 4 and 5-speed transmission (2600 engine)
mainshaft component layout**

1 Counter reverse gear
2 Mainshaft bearing, adjusting
   shim and thrust washer
3 1st gear
4 Needle bearing and inner race
5 Synchronizer ring (1st)
6 Countershaft center bearing
7 Countershaft
8 Main drive gear
9 Synchronizer ring (4th)
10 Needle bearing
11 Mainshaft
12 Shift forks
13 Transmission case
14 Snapring
15 Clutch hub assembly
   (3rd/4th)
16 Synchronizer ring (3rd)
17 Needle bearing
18 3rd gear
19 Clutch hub assembly
   (3rd/4th)
20 Synchronizer ring (2nd)
21 2nd gear and needle bearing
22 Inner race

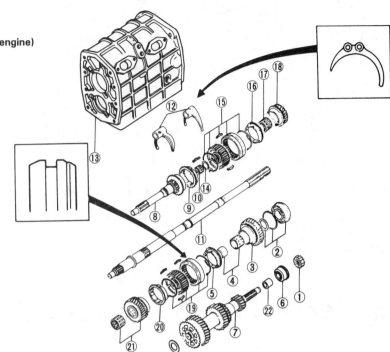

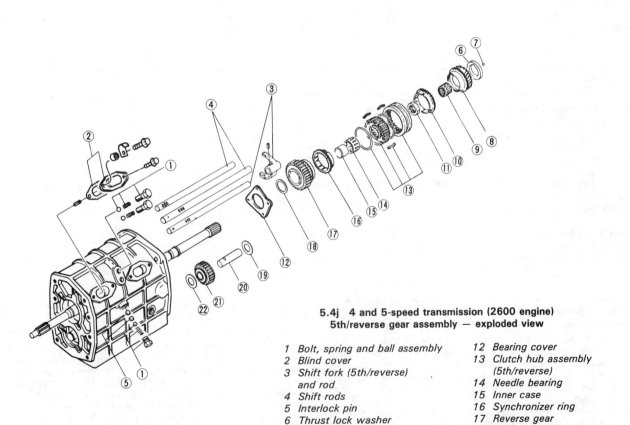

**5.4j 4 and 5-speed transmission (2600 engine)
5th/reverse gear assembly — exploded view**

1 Bolt, spring and ball assembly	12 Bearing cover
2 Blind cover	13 Clutch hub assembly
3 Shift fork (5th/reverse)	(5th/reverse)
and rod	14 Needle bearing
4 Shift rods	15 Inner case
5 Interlock pin	16 Synchronizer ring
6 Thrust lock washer	17 Reverse gear
7 Countershaft	18 Thrust washer
8 5th gear	19 Thrust washer
9 Needle bearing	20 Reverse idle gear shaft
10 Synchronizer ring	21 Reverse idle gear
11 Locknut	22 Thrust washer

Chapter 7 Part B Automatic transmission

Contents

Specifications

Four-speed automatic transmission shift linkage

Adjustment lever-to-locknut A clearance	0.039 in (1.0 mm)
Guide pin-to-guide plate clearance	
Front side	0.039 in (1.0 mm)
Rear side	0.020 in (0.5 mm)

Torque converter end-to-housing end clearance (Dimension A in illustration 6.20)

2600 engine	1.53 in (38.8 mm)
2200 engine	2.13 in (54.2 mm)

Torque specifications

	Ft-lbs
Transmission-to-engine bolt	27 to 38
Torque converter-to-flywheel bolt	25 to 36

1 General information

All vehicles covered in this manual are equipped with either a 4 or 5-speed manual transmission or a 3 or 4-speed automatic transmission. All information on the automatic transmission is included in this Part of Chapter 7. Information for the manual transmission can be found in Part A. Information on the transfer case used on 4WD models can be found in Part C.

Specialized techniques and equipment are required when working on automatic transmissions, due to their complexity. Consequently, this Chapter addresses only those procedures concerned with routine maintenance, general diagnosis and removal and installation.

If the transmission requires major repair work, it should be left to a dealer service department or an automotive transmission repair shop. You can, however, remove and install the transmission yourself and save the expense, even if the repair work is done by a transmission specialist.

2 Diagnosis — general

Note: *Automatic transmission malfunctions may be caused by five general conditions: poor engine performance, improper adjustments, hydraulic malfunctions, or mechanical malfunctions. Diagnosis of these problems should always begin with a check of the easily repaired items: fluid level and condition (Chapter 1), and shift linkage adjustment. Next, perform a road test to determine if the problem has been corrected or if more diagnosis is necessary. If the problem persists after the preliminary tests and corrections are completed, additional diagnosis should be done by a dealer service department or transmission repair shop. Refer to the Troubleshooting Section at the front of this manual for information on symptoms of transmission problems.*

Preliminary checks

1   Drive the vehicle to warm the transmission to normal operating temperature.

2   Check the fluid level as described in Chapter 1:
   a) If the fluid level is unusually low, add enough fluid to bring the level within the designated area of the dipstick, then check for external leaks (see below).
   b) If the fluid level is abnormally high, drain off the excess, then check the drained fluid for contamination by coolant. The presence of engine coolant in the automatic transmission fluid indicates that a failure has occurred in the internal radiator walls that separate the coolant from the transmission fluid (see Chapter 3).
   c) If the fluid is foaming, drain it and refill the transmission, then check for coolant in the fluid or a high fluid level.

3   Check the engine idle speed. **Note:** *If the engine is malfunctioning, do not proceed with the preliminary checks until it has been repaired and runs normally.*

4   Inspect the shift control linkage (Section 3). Make sure that it's properly adjusted and that the linkage operates smoothly.

Fluid leak diagnosis

5   Most fluid leaks are easy to locate visually. Repair usually consists of replacing a seal or gasket. If a leak is difficult to find, the following procedure may help.

6   Identify the fluid. Make sure it's transmission fluid and not engine oil or brake fluid (automatic transmission fluid is a deep red color).

7   Try to pinpoint the source of the leak. Drive the vehicle several miles, then park it over a large sheet of cardboard. After a minute or two, you should be able to locate the leak by determining the source of the fluid dripping onto the cardboard.

8   Make a careful visual inspection of the suspected component and the area immediately around it. Pay particular attention to gasket mating surfaces. A mirror is often helpful for finding leaks in areas that are hard to see.

9   If the leak still cannot be found, clean the suspected area thoroughly with a degreaser or solvent, then dry it.

10   Drive the vehicle for several miles at normal operating temperature and varying speeds. After driving the vehicle, visually inspect the suspected component again.

11   Once the leak has been located, the cause must be determined before it can be properly repaired. If a gasket is replaced but the sealing flange is bent, the new gasket will not stop the leak. The bent flange must be straightened.

12   Before attempting to repair a leak, check to make sure that the following conditions are corrected or they may cause another leak. **Note:** *Some of the following conditions cannot be fixed without highly specialized tools and expertise. Such problems must be referred to a transmission repair shop or a dealer service department.*

Gasket leaks

13   Check the pan periodically. Make sure the bolts are tight, no bolts are missing, the gasket is in good condition and the pan is flat (dents in the pan may indicate damage to the valve body inside).

14   If the pan gasket is leaking, the fluid level or the fluid pressure may be too high, the vent may be plugged, the pan bolts may be too tight, the pan sealing flange may be warped, the sealing surface of the transmission housing may be damaged, the gasket may be damaged or the transmission casting may be cracked or porous. If sealant instead of gasket material has been used to form a seal between the pan and the transmission housing, it may be the wrong sealant.

Seal leaks

15   If a transmission seal is leaking, the fluid level or pressure may be too high, the vent may be plugged, the seal bore may be damaged, the seal itself may be damaged or improperly installed, the surface of the shaft protruding through the seal may be damaged or a loose bearing may be causing excessive shaft movement.

16   Make sure the dipstick tube seal is in good condition and the tube is properly seated. Periodically check the area around the speedometer gear or sensor for leakage. If transmission fluid is evident, check the O-ring for damage.

Case leaks

17   If the case itself appears to be leaking, the casting is porous and will have to be repaired or replaced.

18   Make sure the oil cooler hose fittings are tight and in good condition.

Fluid comes out vent pipe or fill tube

19   If this condition occurs, the transmission is overfilled, there is coolant in the fluid, the case is porous, the dipstick is incorrect, the vent is plugged or the drain back holes are plugged.

---

3   Shift linkage — adjustment

Refer to illustrations 3.5, 3.7, 3.12 and 3.15

1   Place the shift lever in each detent and make sure that the transmission shifts into the corresponding gear as the indicator is moved.

2   If adjustment is required, proceed as follows.

Three-speed transmission

3   Raise the vehicle and support it securely on jackstands.

Early models

4   Working from under the vehicle, place the shift position indicator in Neutral, then disconnect the T-joint from the lower end of the shift operating arm.

5   Loosen the T-joint locknuts and adjust the T-joint so that it freely enters the lever operating arm **(see illustration)**.

6   Tighten the locknuts to secure the adjustment. Connect the T-joint to the shift operating arm.

Later models

7   Working from under the vehicle, loosen the locknuts B and C and lockbolt A **(see illustration)**.

8   Have an assistant position the shift lever in the Park position detent and hold it so it cannot move. Push the transmission control rod to

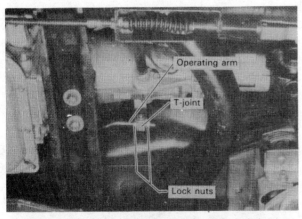

3.5   On earlier three-speed models, the automatic transmission linkage adjustment is done at the T-joint on the operating arm

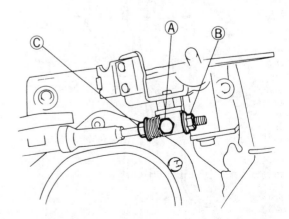

3.7   Later model three-speed transmission shift linkage adjustment points — locknuts B and C, lockbolt A

7B

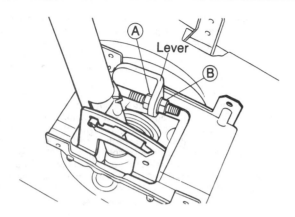

3.12   Four-speed transmission adjustment locknut locations

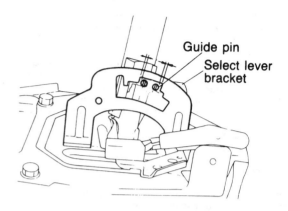

3.15   Shift linkage guide pin details — see specifications for proper clearances

the Park position and tighten the lockbolt A securely.
9   Tighten locknut C finger tight until it just touches the spacer and then tighten locknut B securely.
10   Check the shift lever operation and position indicator alignment.

Four-speed transmission

11   Remove the console.
12   Place the selector lever in the Park position and loosen locknuts A and B **(see illustration)**.
13   Working under the vehicle, move the transmission shift lever to the Park position.
14   With the bolt at 90° to the lever, adjust the distance between the adjustment lever and locknut A to the specified clearance (see specifications).
15   With the shift lever in Park, measure the clearance between the guide plate and the guide pin **(see illustration)**.
16   Move the selector to the Neutral and Drive ranges and make sure that the clearances are as specified. Readjust the A and B locknuts as necessary to obtain the specified clearances.
17   Check the shift lever operation and position indicator alignment.

4   Kick-down switch — check, adjustment and replacement

Refer to illustrations 4.2 and 4.4
1   The kick-down switch is attached to the throttle pedal bracket, under the instrument panel.

Check

2   Unplug the switch wires and connect an ohmmeter or self-powered test light to the switch terminals **(see illustration)**.
3   With the throttle pedal fully depressed, there should be continuity across the switch.

Adjustment

4   Depress the throttle pedal fully, loosen the locknut, then rotate the switch until the threaded case just contacts the stopper on the pedal **(see illustration)**. If there is no continuity after the switch has been adjusted, replace it with a new one.

Replacement

5   Remove the locknut, unplug the connector and lift the switch from the vehicle.
6   Installation is the reverse of removal. Adjust the switch before fully tightening the locknut.

5   Neutral safety switch — check, adjustment and replacement

Refer to illustrations 5.4a, 5.4b, 5.4c, 5.7 and 5.8
1   The neutral safety switch, located on the right-hand side of the transmission, prevents the engine from starting with the transmission in gear.

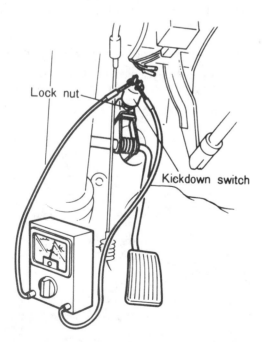

4.2   Check the kick-down switch for continuity with the throttle depressed

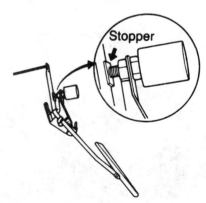

4.4   Adjust the kick-down switch so that it just comes into contact with the stopper when the throttle pedal is fully depressed

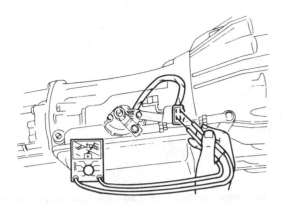

5.4a   Unplug the neutral safety switch electrical connector
and check for continuity with an ohmmeter

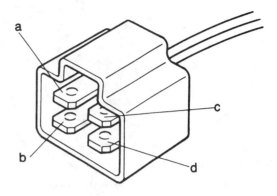

5.4b   Neutral safety switch connector terminals

Check

2   Make sure the engine will start only with the selector lever in Park
and Neutral. With the key in the On position, make sure the backup
lights function when the lever is in Reverse only.
3   If a malfunction is noted, raise the vehicle and support it on
jackstands.
4   Disconnect the switch wire harness, attach the leads of an ohmmeter to the terminals and check for continuity (see illustrations).
5   Adjust the switch (see below) and then check that continuity is
indicated between the switch terminals. If the switch does not operate
properly after adjustment, replace it with a new one.
6   Disconnect the ohmmeter and reconnect the wire harness.

Adjustment

7   Loosen the retaining bolts and remove the screw from the switch
body (see illustration).
8   Rotate the switch and insert a 5/64-inch (2.0 mm) diameter pin
into the alignment hole and through the internal rotor (see illustration).
9   Tighten the mounting bolts, then remove the pin and install the
screw in the hole.
10   Recheck the switch operation as described above.

Replacement

11   Disconnect the negative battery cable.
12   Shift the transmission into Neutral.
13   Remove the retaining nut that secures the shift lever to the lever
shaft and separate the lever from the shaft.
14   Unplug the electrical connector, remove the two retaining bolts
and lift the switch off.

Connection guide

Position	Connector terminal			
	a	b	c	d
P			O—	—O
R	O—	—O		
N			O—	—O
D, 1, 2				

O—O   indicates continuity

5.4c   Continuity should exist between the neutral safety
switch terminals connected by the line when the switch is
in the indicated position

15   Installation is the reverse of removal. Do not tighten the retaining
bolts fully until the switch has been adjusted.
16   Connect the battery negative cable.
17   Start the engine in both Park and Neutral to verify that the switch
is properly adjusted.

6   Automatic transmission — removal and installation

Refer to illustrations 6.8a, 6.8b and 6.20
1   Disconnect the cable from the negative battery terminal.
2   Remove the upper mounting nut on the starter.
3   If equipped, remove the undercover.
4   Disconnect the shift linkage.

7B

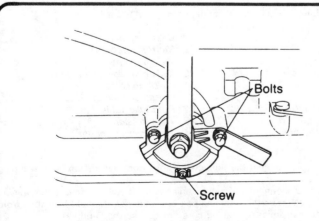

5.7   Neutral safety switch retaining bolt and adjustment
hole screw locations

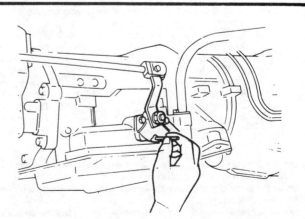

5.8   Insert the alignment pin into the neutral safety
switch hole

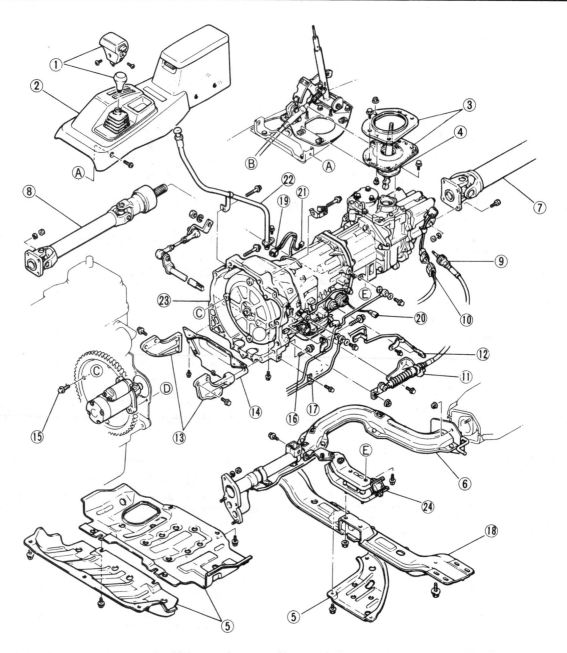

6.8a   Typical automatic transmission installation details (4WD model with transfer case)

1 Shift knob	10 4WD indicator	18 Crossmember
2 Console	switch connector	19 Neutral safety
3 Transfer case shift plate	11 Shift cable and bracket	switch connector
4 Transfer case shift lever	12 Vacuum diaphragm hose	20 Kickdown solenoid connector
5 Under cover	13 Gusset plate	21 4WD indicator
6 Exhaust pipe	14 Driveplate cover	switch connector
7 Rear driveshaft	15 Torque converter bolt	22 Fluid filler tube
8 Front driveshaft	16 Transmission-to-engine bolt	23 Transmission
9 Speedometer cable	17 Fluid cooler line and bracket	24 Transmission mount

5   On 4WD models, disconnect the transfer case shift linkage.

6   Raise the vehicle and support it securely on jackstands.

7   Drain the fluid from the transmission and, if equipped, transfer case (4WD models) (Chapter 1).

8   Disconnect the wiring and vacuum connections at the transmission and, if equipped, transfer case **(see illustrations)**.

9   Remove the starter motor (see Chapter 5).

10   Remove the driveshaft(s) (Chapter 8).

11   Disconnect the speedometer drive cable.

12   Disconnect the fluid cooler lines from the transmission and plug them.

13   Disconnect any exhaust pipes which will interfere with removal.

14   Remove the retaining bolt and then pull the fluid filler tube from the transmission, taking care not to lose the O-ring(s).

15   Remove the driveplate cover.

16   Support the automatic transmission with a jack, then remove the rear support crossmember and mount. Through the open lower half of the torque converter housing, remove the four bolts which join the

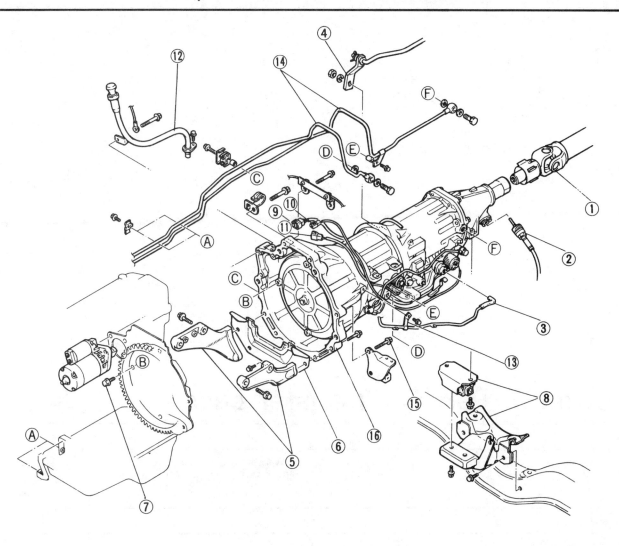

6.8b Typical automatic transmission installation details (2WD model)

1 Driveshaft	7 Torque converter bolt	12 Fluid filler tube
2 Speedometer cable	8 Transmission mount	13 Vacuum pipe bracket
3 Vacuum hose	9 Neutral safety	14 Oil cooler pipe
4 Shift lever	switch connector	15 Transmission mount bolt
5 Gusset plate	10 Kick-down solenoid connector	16 Transmission
6 Driveplate cover	11 Overdrive cancel connector	

driveplate and converter together. Remove them one at a time by rotating the driveplate. To do this, turn the crankshaft with a wrench attached to the pulley securing bolt.

17 Place a jack under the engine oil pan (use a block of wood to protect it), and remove the bolts which attach the torque converter housing to the engine.

18 Lower both jacks progressively until the transmission will clear the lower edge of the firewall. Catch the fluid which may run from the torque converter during this operation.

19 The torque converter can now be pulled forward to remove it from the housing. The driveplate can be unbolted from the crankshaft flange if it has to be replaced because of a worn starter ring gear (see Chapter 2).

20 The installation procedure is basically the reverse of removal. Measure the distance between the end of the torque converter and the end of the bellhousing to make sure it is as specified before raising the transmission into place **(see illustration)**. Tighten all bolts and nuts securely, using a torque wrench where necessary. Be sure to refill the transmission and, if equipped, transfer case with the required fluids (see Chapter 1). Adjust the shift linkage and neutral safety switch as described in this Chapter before road testing the vehicle.

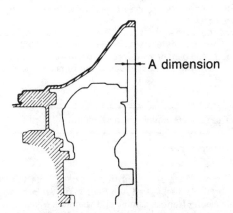

6.20 The distance from the end of the torque converter to the end of the housing (dimension A) must be as specified in the Specifications at the front of this Chapter for the torque converter to be properly installed

Chapter 7 Part C Transfer case

Contents

Specifications

Torque specifications

	Ft-lbs
Transfer case-to-transmission bolt	27 to 35

---

1 General information

Four-wheel drive models are equipped with a transfer case mounted on the rear of the transmission. Drive is passed from the engine through the transmission and the transfer case to the front and rear wheels by the driveshafts.

Because of the special tools and techniques required, disassembly and overhaul of the transfer case should be left to a dealer or properly equipped shop. You can, however, remove and install the transfer case yourself and save the expense, even if the repair work is done by a specialist.

2 Transfer case — removal and installation

Refer to illustration 2.4

Removal

1   Remove the transmission and transfer case from the vehicle as a unit, referring to Section 4, Part A or Section 6, Part B of this Chapter.
2   Carefully clean off the assembly and stand the transfer case/transmission in a vertical position, with the transfer case pointed up.
3   Remove the transfer case-to-transmission mounting bolts.
4   Pull the transfer case straight up and remove it from the transmission, taking care not to damage the control rod or drop the input sleeve **(see illustration)**.

Installation

5   Carefully clean the contact surfaces of the transmission and transfer case, making sure that all traces of sealer are removed. Apply a coat of sealer to the transmission contact surface. Apply sealant to the threads of the retaining bolts.
6   Place the input sleeve in position on the transmission.
7   Carefully lower the transfer case onto the transmission and connect the control lever.
8   Install the retaining bolts. Tighten the bolts to the specified torque.

2.4 After removing the bolts, lift the transfer case off the transmission — be careful not to drop the input sleeve (arrow)

Chapter 8 Clutch and driveline

Contents

Specifications

Clutch

Clutch hydraulic system fluid type	See Chapter 1
Clutch disc minimum thickness	0.039 in (1.0 mm)
Clutch release lever free play (adjustable models only)	0.14 to 0.18 in (3.5 to 4.5 mm)

Driveline

Driveshaft runout limit	0.016 in (0.4 mm)
Driveaxle length (4WD models)	
Right side	24.49 in (622 mm)
Left side	21.81 in (554 mm)
U-joint snap-ring thickness	0.0571 in (1.45 mm)
	0.0583 in (1.48 mm)
	0.0594 in (1.51 mm)
	0.0606 in (1.54 mm)
	0.0618 in (1.57 mm)
	0.0630 in (1.60 mm)
	0.0642 in (1.63 mm)

Rear axle

Rear axle shaft end play

1984 and earlier	
First installed	0.026 to 0.033 in (0.65 to 0.85 mm)
Second installed	0.002 to 0.006 in (0.05 to 0.15 mm)
1986 and later	
First installed	0.026 to 0.037 in (0.65 to 0.95 mm)
Second installed	0.002 to 0.010 in (0.05 to 0.25 mm)

8

Torque specifications

Ft-lbs

Clutch

Pressure plate-to-flywheel bolts

B1600, B1800, B2000 and B2200 . . . .   13 to 20

B2600

    Through 1988 . . . .   16 to 24

    1989 and later . . . .   18 to 26

Transmission-to-engine bolts

    1984 and earlier . . . .   51 to 65

    1986 and later . . . .   27 to 38

Driveline

U-joint flange-to-differential companion flange

    1984 and earlier . . . .   40 to 47

    1986 and 1987 . . . .   36 to 43

    1988 and later . . . .   20 to 22

Center U-joint yoke-to-intermediate shaft nut . . . .   116 to 130

Center bearing support-to-frame bolts . . . .   27 to 39

Rear axle

Rear axle bearing retainer/brake backing plate-to-axle housing nuts

    1984 and earlier . . . .   33 to 36

    1986 and later 2WD . . . .   65 to 80

    4WD . . . .   72 to 87

Rear axle housing-to-leaf spring U-bolt nuts

    1987 and earlier . . . .   47 to 57

    1988 and later . . . .   62 to 101

Differential-to-axle housing bolts . . . .   17 to 20

Front axle (4WD)

Front crossmember-to-frame bolts   57

Center crossmember-to-frame bolts . . . .   69 to 85

Center crossmember-to-differential bolts   57

Differential-to-axle housing bolts . . . .   17 to 20

Freewheel hub cover-to-hub body bolts . . . .   22 to 25

Wheels

Wheel lug nuts

    1981 and earlier . . . .   58 to 65

    1982 thru 1984

        Standard wheels . . . .   72 to 80

        Styled wheels . . . .   87 to 94

    1986 and later . . . .   87 to 108

---

1   General information

The information in this Chapter deals with the components from the rear of the engine to the rear wheels and to the front wheels on 4WD models, except for the transmission and transfer case (4WD models), which are dealt with in the previous Chapter. For the purposes of this Chapter, these components are grouped into four categories; clutch, driveshaft, front axle and rear axle. Separate Sections within this Chapter offer general descriptions and checking procedures for each of these groups.

Since nearly all the procedures covered in this Chapter involve working under the vehicle, make sure it's securely supported on sturdy jackstands or on a hoist where the vehicle can be easily raised and lowered.

2   Clutch — description and check

Refer to illustration 2.1

1   All models equipped with a manual transmission feature a single dry plate, diaphragm spring-type clutch (**see illustration**). The actuation is through a hydraulic system.

2   When the clutch pedal is depressed, hydraulic fluid (under pressure from the clutch master cylinder) flows into the release cylinder. Because the release cylinder is connected to the clutch fork, the fork moves the release bearing into contact with the pressure plate release fingers, disengaging the clutch disc.

3   Early models have an adjustable release cylinder pushrod to adjust the free-play in the clutch release lever. On later models, no such adjustment is possible.

4   Terminology can be a problem regarding the clutch components because common names have in some cases changed from that used by the manufacturer. For example, the driven plate is also called the clutch plate or disc, the clutch release bearing is sometimes called a throwout bearing, the release cylinder is sometimes called the operating or slave cylinder.

5   Due to the slow wearing qualities of the clutch, it is not easy to decide when to go to the trouble of removing the transmission in order to check the wear on the friction lining. The only positive indication that something should be done is when it starts to slip or when squealing noises during engagement indicate that the friction lining has worn down to the rivets. In such instances it can only be hoped that the friction surfaces on the flywheel and pressure plate have not been badly worn or scored.

6   A clutch will wear according to the way in which it is used. Much intentional slipping of the clutch while driving — rather than the correct selection of gears — will accelerate wear. It is best to assume, however, that the disc will need replacement at about 40,000 miles (64,000 km).

7   Because of the clutch's location between the engine and transmission, it cannot be worked on without removing either the engine or transmission. If repairs which would require removal of the engine are not needed, the quickest way to gain access to the clutch is by removing the transmission as described in Chapter 7.

8   Other than to replace components with obvious damage, some preliminary checks should be performed to diagnose a clutch system failure.

   a) The first check should be of the fluid level in the clutch master cylinder. If the fluid level is low, add fluid as necessary and re-test.

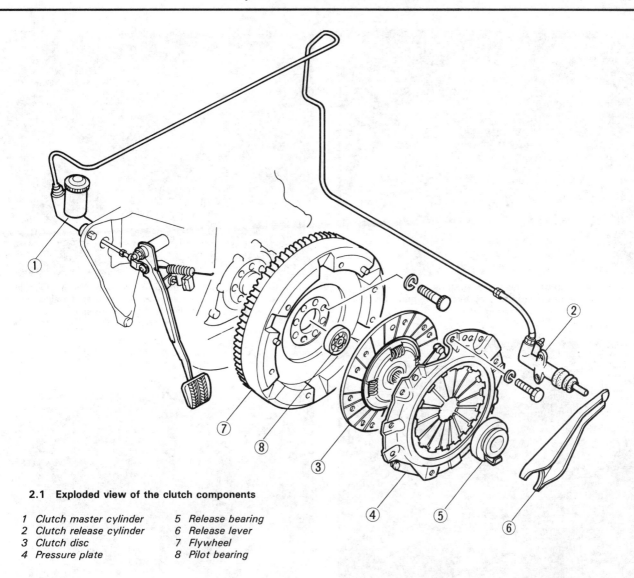

2.1 Exploded view of the clutch components

1 Clutch master cylinder	*5 Release bearing*
2 Clutch release cylinder	*6 Release lever*
3 Clutch disc	*7 Flywheel*
4 Pressure plate	*8 Pilot bearing*

If the master cylinder runs dry, or if any of the hydraulic components are serviced, bleed the hydraulic system as described in Section 8.

b) To check "clutch spin down time", run the engine at normal idle speed with the transmission in Neutral (clutch pedal up — engaged). Disengage the clutch (pedal down), wait nine seconds and shift the transmission into Reverse. No grinding noise should be heard. A grinding noise would indicate component failure in the pressure plate assembly or the clutch disc.

c) To check for complete clutch release, run the engine (with the brake on to prevent movement) and hold the clutch pedal approximately 1/2-inch from the floor mat. Shift the transmission between 1st gear and Reverse several times. If the shift is not smooth, component failure is indicated. Measure the release cylinder pushrod travel. With the clutch pedal completely depressed the release cylinder pushrod should extend substantially. If the pushrod will not extend very far or not at all, check the fluid level in the clutch master cylinder.

d) Visually inspect the clutch pedal bushing at the top of the clutch pedal to make sure there is no sticking or excessive wear.

e) Under the vehicle, check that the release lever is solidly mounted on the ball stud.

Note: *Because access to the clutch components is an involved process, any time either the engine or transmission is removed, the clutch disc, pressure plate assembly and release bearing should be carefully inspected and, if necessary, replaced with new parts. Since the clutch disc is normally the item of highest wear, it should be replaced as a matter of course if there is any question about its condition.*

3 Clutch components — removal, inspection and installation

Refer to illustrations 3.4, 3.5, 3.8, 3.10, 3.12a, 3.12b and 3.14
Warning: *Dust produced by clutch wear and deposited on clutch components contains asbestos, which is hazardous to your health. DO NOT blow it out with compressed air and DO NOT inhale it. DO NOT use gasoline or petroleum-based solvents to remove the dust. Brake system cleaner should be used to flush the dust into a drain pan. After the clutch components are wiped clean with a rag, dispose of the contaminated rags and cleaner in a covered container.*

8

Removal

1   Access to the clutch components is normally accomplished by removing the transmission, leaving the engine in the vehicle. If, of course, the engine is being removed for major overhaul, then the opportunity should always be taken to check the clutch for wear and replace worn components as necessary. The following procedures assume that the engine will stay in place.

2   Remove the release cylinder (see Section 7).

3   Referring to Chapter 7 Part A, remove the transmission from the vehicle. Support the engine while the transmission is out. Preferably, an engine hoist should be used to support it from above. However, if a jack is used underneath the engine, make sure a piece of wood is used between the jack and oil pan to spread the load. **Caution:** *The pickup for the oil pump is very close to the bottom of the oil pan. If the pan is bent or distorted in any way, engine oil starvation could occur.*

3.4   A metal rod or clutch alignment tool can be used to prevent the disc from dropping out as the pressure plate is removed

3.5   Be sure to mark the pressure plate and flywheel in order to insure proper alignment during installation (this won't be necessary if a new pressure plate is to be installed)

3.8   Check the flywheel for cracks, hot spots and other obvious defects (slight imperfections can be removed by a machine shop)

3.10   Once the clutch disc is removed, the rivet depth can be measured and compared to the Specifications

3.12a   Examine the pressure plate friction surface for score marks, cracks and evidence of overheating

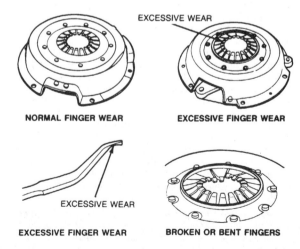

EXCESSIVE WEAR

NORMAL FINGER WEAR

EXCESSIVE FINGER WEAR

EXCESSIVE WEAR

EXCESSIVE FINGER WEAR

BROKEN OR BENT FINGERS

3.12b   Replace the pressure plate if the diaphragm spring fingers exhibit these signs of wear

3.14 Hold the clutch in place with a clutch alignment tool then install the pressure plate

4   To support the clutch disc during removal, install a clutch alignment tool through the clutch disc hub **(see illustration)**.
5   Carefully inspect the flywheel and pressure plate for indexing marks. The marks are usually an X, an O or a white letter. If they cannot be found, apply marks yourself so the pressure plate and the flywheel will be in the same alignment during installation **(see illustration)**.
6   Turning each bolt only 1/2-turn at a time, slowly loosen the pressure plate-to-flywheel bolts. Work in a diagonal pattern and loosen each bolt a little at a time until all spring pressure is relieved. Then hold the pressure plate securely and completely remove the bolts, followed by the pressure plate and clutch disc.

Inspection

7   Ordinarily, when a problem occurs in the clutch, it can be attributed to wear of the clutch disc assembly. However, all components should be inspected at this time.
8   Inspect the flywheel for cracks, heat checking, grooves or other signs of obvious defects **(see illustration)**. If the imperfections are slight, a machine shop can machine the surface flat and smooth, which is highly recommended regardless of the surface appearance. Refer to Chapter 2 for the flywheel removal and installation procedure.
9   Inspect the pilot bearing (Section 5).
10 Inspect the lining on the clutch disc. There should be at least 1mm of lining above the rivet heads. Check for loose rivets, warpage, cracks, distorted springs or damper bushings and other obvious damage **(see illustration)**. As mentioned above, ordinarily the clutch disc is replaced

as a matter of course, so if in doubt about the condition, replace it with a new one.
11 Ordinarily, the release bearing is also replaced along with the clutch disc (see Section 4).
12 Check the machined surfaces of the pressure plate **(see illustrations)**. If the surface is grooved or otherwise damaged, replace the pressure plate. Also check for obvious damage, distortion, cracking, etc. Light glazing can be removed with medium grit emery cloth. If a new pressure plate is indicated, new or factory-rebuilt units are available.

Installation

13 Before installation, carefully wipe the flywheel and pressure plate machined surfaces clean with a rubbing-alcohol dampened rag. It's important that no oil or grease is on these surfaces or the lining of the clutch disc. Handle these parts only with clean hands.
14 Position the clutch disc and pressure plate with the clutch held in place with an alignment tool **(see illustration)**. Make sure it's installed properly (most replacement clutch discs will be marked ''flywheel side'' or something similar — if not marked, install the clutch with the damper springs or bushings toward the transmission).
15 Tighten the pressure plate-to-flywheel bolts only finger tight, working around the pressure plate.
16 Center the clutch disc by ensuring the alignment tool is through the splined hub and into the pilot bearing in the crankshaft. Wiggle the tool up, down, or side-to-side as needed, to bottom the tool in the pilot bearing. Tighten the pressure plate-to-flywheel bolts a little at a time, working in a criss-cross pattern to prevent distorting the cover. After all of the bolts are snug, tighten them to the specified torque. Remove the alignment tool.
17 Using high temperature grease, lubricate the inner groove of the release bearing (refer to Section 4). Also place grease on the fork fingers.
18 Install the clutch release bearing as described in Section 4.
19 Install the transmission, release cylinder and all components removed previously, tightening all fasteners to the proper torque specifications.

---

4   Clutch release bearing — removal and installation

Refer to illustrations 4.4a, 4.4b, 4.5 and 4.8

Removal

1   Disconnect the negative cable from the battery.
2   Remove the transmission (Chapter 7).
3   Remove the clutch release fork from the ball stud by pulling it straight off.
4   Slide the release bearing off the transmission input shaft bearing retainer, then unclip the bearing from the release fork **(see illustrations)**. **Note:** *Later models do not use a spring clip to retain the bearing.*

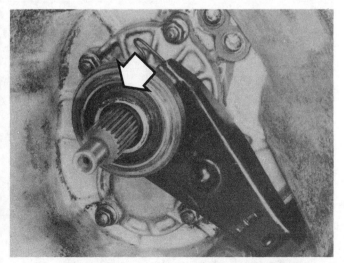

4.4a   Slide the release bearing off the transmission input shaft bearing retainer (with the release lever still attached)

4.4b   The release bearing is held to the clutch release lever by a spring clip (early styles)

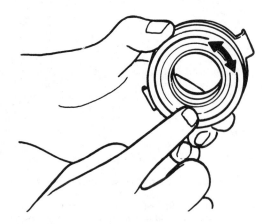

4.5   Check the release bearing to make sure it rotates smoothly

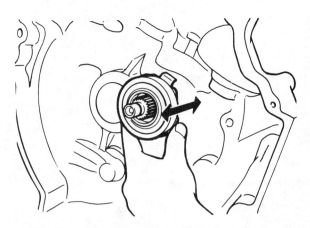

4.8   The release bearing should slide back and forth smoothly on the transmission input shaft bearing retainer

5   Hold the bearing and turn the inner portion **(see illustration)**. If the bearing doesn't turn smoothly or if it's noisy, replace it with a new one. Wipe the bearing with a clean rag and inspect it for damage, wear and cracks. Don't immerse the bearing in solvent — it's sealed for life and to do so would ruin it.

Installation

6   Lubricate the clutch fork ends where they contact the bearing lightly with molybdenum disulphide grease. Apply a thin coat of the same grease to the inner diameter of the bearing and also to the transmission input shaft bearing retainer.

7   Install the release bearing on the clutch fork so that both of the fork ends fit into the bearing tabs. Make sure the spring clip seats in the bearing hub groove (early models).

8   Lubricate the clutch release fork ball socket with molybdenum disulphide grease and push the fork onto the ball stud until it's firmly seated. Check to see that the bearing slides back and forth smoothly on the input shaft bearing retainer **(see illustration)**.

9   The remainder of the installation is the reverse of the removal procedure, tightening all bolts to the specified torque.

---

5   Pilot bearing — inspection, removal and installation

Refer to illustrations 5.5, 5.9, 5.10 and 5.11

1   The clutch pilot bearing is a needle roller type bearing which is pressed into the rear of the crankshaft. Its primary purpose is to support the front of the transmission input shaft. The pilot bearing should be inspected whenever the clutch components are removed from the engine. Due to its inaccessibility, if you are in doubt as to its condition, replace it with a new one. **Note:** *If the engine has been removed from the vehicle, disregard the following steps which do not apply.*

2   Remove the transmission (refer to Chapter 7 Part A)

3   Remove the clutch components (Section 3).

4   Using a clean rag, wipe the bearing clean and inspect for any excessive wear, scoring or obvious damage. A flashlight will be helpful to direct light into the recess.

5   Check to make sure the pilot bearing turns smoothly and quietly **(see illustration)**. If the transmission input shaft contact surface is worn or damaged, replace the bearing with a new one.

6   Removal can be accomplished with a special puller but an alternative method also works very well.

7   Find a solid steel bar which is slightly smaller in diameter than the bearing. Alternatives to a solid bar would be a wood dowel or a socket with a bolt fixed in place to make it solid.

8   Check the bar for fit — it should just slip into the bearing with very little clearance.

9   Pack the bearing and the area behind it (in the crankshaft recess) with heavy grease **(see illustration)**. Pack it tightly to eliminate as much air as possible.

10   Insert the bar into the bearing bore and lightly hammer on the bar, which will force the grease to the backside of the bearing and push

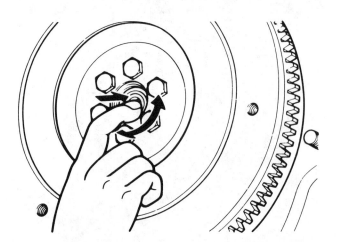

5.5   Turn the pilot bearing by hand while pressing in on it — if it is rough or noisy, a new one should be installed

5.9   Fill the cavity behind the pilot bearing with grease . . .

5.10 . . . then force the bearing out hydraulically with a steel rod slightly smaller than the bore in the bearing — when the hammer strikes the rod, the grease will transmit force to the backside of the bearing and push it out

5.11 Using a hammer and socket, carefully drive the new bearing into place

it out **(see illustration)**. Remove the bearing and clean all grease from the crankshaft recess.

11 To install the new bearing, lubricate the outside surface with oil then drive it into the recess with a hammer and a socket with an outside diameter that matches the bearing outer race **(see illustration)**.

12 Pack the bearing with lithium base grease (NLGI No.2). Wipe off all excess grease so the clutch lining will not become contaminated.

13 Install the clutch components, transmission and all other components removed to gain access to the pilot bearing.

---

6 Clutch master cylinder — removal, overhaul and installation

---

Refer to illustrations 6.1, 6.3, 6.4 and 6.6

Caution: *Do not allow brake fluid to contact any painted surfaces of the vehicle, as damage to the finish may result.*

Removal

1 Disconnect the hydraulic line from the master cylinder and drain the fluid into a suitable container **(see illustration)**.

2 Remove the master cylinder flange mounting nuts from under the dash and withdraw the unit from the engine compartment.

Overhaul

3 Remove the hold-down bolt and pull off the reservoir tank **(see illustration)**. Later models do not have a hold down bolt, so simply pry the reservoir off the cylinder using a screwdriver.

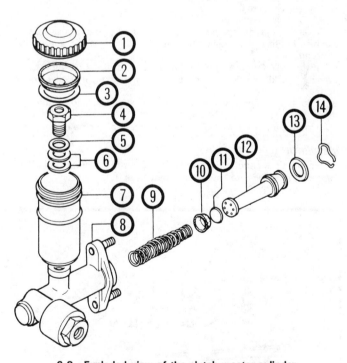

6.3 Exploded view of the clutch master cylinder

1 Cap	9 Spring
2 Fluid baffle	10 Primary piston cup
3 Seal	11 Spacer
4 Hold-down bolt	12 Piston and secondary cup
5 Washer	assembly
6 Cone spring	13 Piston stop washer
7 Reservoir	14 Piston stop ring (snap-ring)
8 Cylinder body	

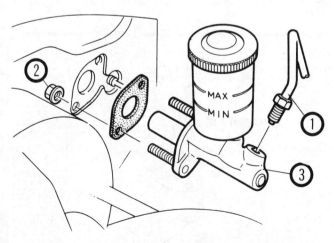

6.1 Clutch master cylinder mounting details

1 Hydraulic line
2 Mounting nut
3 Master cylinder body

8

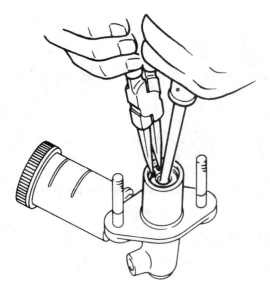

6.4   Using a Phillips screwdriver, push down on the piston and remove the snap-ring with a pair of snap-ring pliers (early models use a different kind of retaining ring which can be pried out with a small screwdriver)

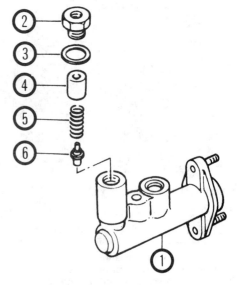

6.6   Exploded view of the one-way fluid valve

1	*Cylinder body*	*4*	*Piston one-way valve*
2	*Outlet fitting*	*5*	*Return spring*
3	*Washer*	*6*	*Pin*

4   Push the piston down and remove the snap-ring with a pair of snap-ring pliers or a small screwdriver **(see illustration)**.
5   Pull out the piston assembly and spring.
6   Some models have a one-way fluid valve incorporated under the outlet fitting. Unscrew the fitting and remove the piston one-way valve, spring and pin **(see illustration)**. Replace these parts with new ones supplied in the rebuild kit.
7   Examine the inner surface of the cylinder bore. If it is scored or exhibits bright wear areas, the entire master cylinder should be replaced.
8   If the cylinder bore is in good condtition, obtain a clutch master cylinder rebuild kit, which will contain all of the necessary replacement parts.
9   Prior to installing any parts, first dip them in brake fluid to lubricate them.
10   Installation of the parts in the cylinder is the reverse of removal.

Installation

11   Position the clutch master cylinder against the firewall, inserting the pedal pushrod into the piston. Install the nuts, tightening them

securely.
12   Bleed the clutch hydraulic system following the procedure in Section 8, then check the pedal height and free play as described in Chapter 1.

---

7   Cluch release cylinder — removal, overhaul and installation

---

Refer to illustrations 7.2a, 7.2b and 7.5

Removal

1   The clutch release cylinder is located on the side of the transmission bellhousing.
2   Using a flare-nut wrench, disconnect the clutch line from the hose at the support bracket, then remove the U-clip that retains the hose to the bracket **(see illustrations)**.
3   Unscrew the hose from the release cylinder.
4   Remove the two bolts and pull off the release cylinder. Early models have a return spring which must be unhooked from the release lever.

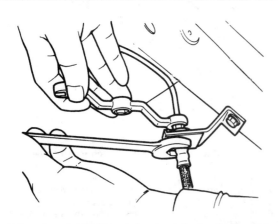

7.2a   Completely loosen the clutch hydraulic line fitting from the clutch release cylinder hose . . .

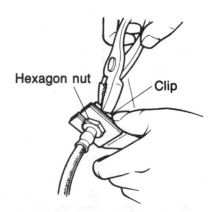

7.2b   . . . then pull the clip of thee hose end and remove the hose from the bracket

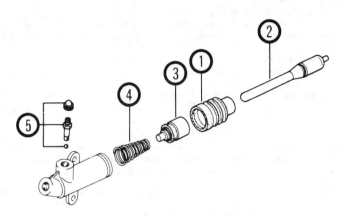

7.5 Exploded view of the release cylinder

1 Boot
2 Pushrod
3 Piston and cup assembly
4 Return spring
5 Bleeder screw, ball and cap

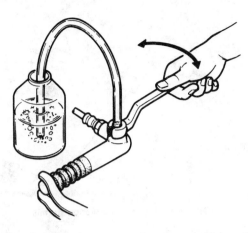

8.3 Open the bleeder screw on the release cylinder when the pedal is held to the floor. Bubbles in the system will pass through the hose and into the fluid. Repeat this procedure until all air is expelled.

Overhaul

5 Pull off the dust boot and pushrod and then tap the cylinder gently on a block of wood to extract the piston and spring **(see illustration)**.
6 Unscrew and remove the bleeder screw.
7 Examine the surfaces of the piston and cylinder bore for scoring or bright wear areas. If any are found, discard the cylinder and purchase a new one.
8 If the components are in good condition, wash them in clean brake fluid. Remove the seal and discard it, noting carefully which way the seal lips face.
9 Obtain a repair kit which will contain all the necessary new items.
10 Install the new seal using your fingers only to manipulate it into position. Be sure the lips face in the proper direction.
11 Dip the piston assembly in clean brake fluid before installing it and the spring into the cylinder.
12 Reinstall the bleeder.
13 Complete the reassembly by installing the pushrod and the dust cover. Be sure the dust cover is secure on the cylinder housing.

Installation

14 Installation is the reverse of the removal procedure. After the cylinder has been installed, bleed the clutch hydraulic system as described in Section 8, then check the release lever free play (Section 9).

8 Clutch hydraulic system — bleeding

Refer to illustration 8.3

Caution: *Do not allow the brake fluid to contact any painted surface of the vehicle, as damage to the finish will result.*

1 Bleeding will be required whenever the hydraulic system has been dismantled and reassembled and air has entered the system.
2 First fill the fluid reservoir with clean brake fluid which has been stored in an airtight container. Never use fluid which has drained from the system or has bled out previously, as it may contain grit.
3 Attach a rubber or plastic bleed tube to the bleeder screw on the release cylinder and immerse the open end of the tube in a glass jar containing an inch or two of fluid **(see illustration)**.
4 Open the bleeder screw about half a turn and have an assistant quickly depress the clutch pedal completely. Tighten the screw and then have clutch pedal slowly released with the foot completely removed. Repeat this sequence of operations until air bubbles are no longer ejected from the open end of the tube beneath the fluid in the jar.
5 After two or three strokes of the pedal, make sure the fluid level in the reservoir has not fallen too low. Keep it full of fresh fluid, otherwise air will be drawn into the system.
6 Tighten the bleeder screw on a pedal down stroke (do not over-

tighten it), remove the bleed tube and jar, top-up the reservoir and install the cap.
7 If an assistant is not available, alternative 'one-man' bleeding operations can be carried out using a bleed tube equipped with a one-way valve or a pressure bleed kit, both of which should be used in accordance with the manufacturer's instructions.

9 Clutch release lever — free play adjustment

Refer to illustration 9.3

1 Raise the vehicle and support it securely on jackstands.
2 Unhook the release lever return spring at the lever.
3 Peel back the rubber boot far enough to expose the locknut then turn the adjusting nut to obtain the specified clearance between the end of the adjusting screw and the release fork **(see illustration)**.
4 After completion of the adjustment, tighten the locknut securely, pull the rubber boot over the nut and install the return spring.

8

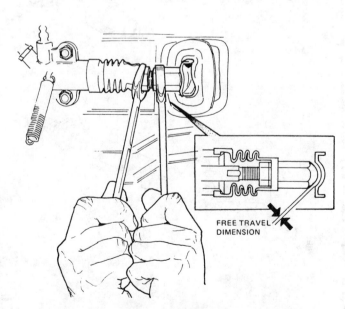

9.3 Loosen the locknut while holding the adjusting nut from turning, then turn the adjusting nut to obtain the specified clearance between the release lever and the pushrod end

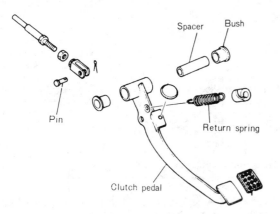

10.1   Clutch pedal installation details

10   Clutch pedal assembly — removal and installation

Refer to illustration 10.1

1   Remove the pedal return spring **(see illustration)**.
2   Disconnect the master cylinder pushrod from the pedal by removing

the spring clip and pulling out the pushrod pin.
3   Remove the pedal shaft nut and washer. Later models utilize an assist lever and spring. Remove the spring clip from the lower end of the lever.
4   Remove the clutch pedal with the bushings and spacer.
5   Clean the parts in solvent and replace any that are damaged or excessively worn.
6   Installation is the reverse of the removal procedure. During installation, apply multi-purpose grease to the pedal boss, return spring, pedal shaft and pushrod pin.

11   Driveshafts, differentials and axles — general information

Refer to illustrations 11.1a and 11.1b

Three different driveshaft assemblies are used on the vehicles covered in this manual **(see illustrations)**. Some use a one-piece driveshaft which incorporates two universal joints, one at either end of the shaft.

Others use a two-piece driveshaft which incorporates a center bearing at the rear of the front shaft. This driveshaft uses three universal joints; one at the transmission end, one behind the center bearing and one at the differential flange.

The 4WD vehicles use two driveshafts; the primary shaft runs between the transfer case and the front differential and the rear driveshaft

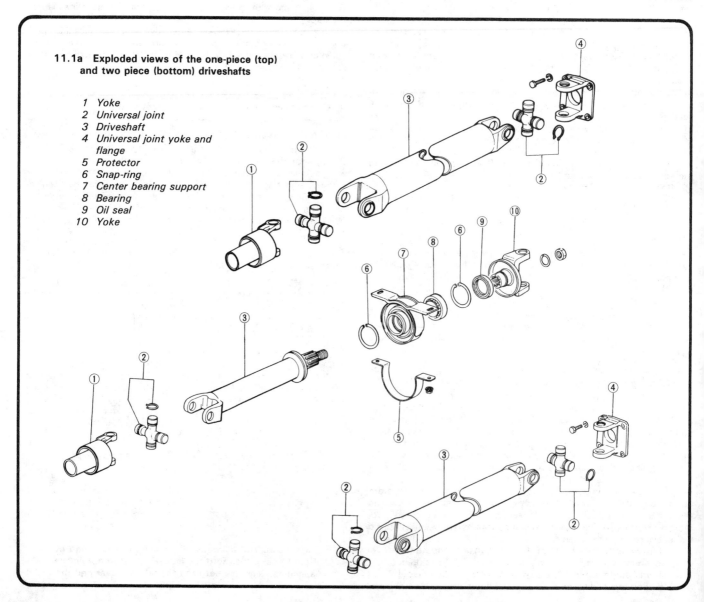

11.1a   Exploded views of the one-piece (top) and two piece (bottom) driveshafts

1   Yoke
2   Universal joint
3   Driveshaft
4   Universal joint yoke and flange
5   Protector
6   Snap-ring
7   Center bearing support
8   Bearing
9   Oil seal
10   Yoke

runs between the transfer case and the rear differential.

All universal joints are of the solid type and can be replaced separate from the driveshaft.

The driveshafts are finely balanced during production and whenever they are removed or disassembled, they must be reassembled and reinstalled in the exact manner and positions they were originally in, to avoid excessive vibration.

The rear axle is of the semi-floating type, having a 'banjo' design axle housing, which is held in proper alignment with the body by the rear suspension.

Mounted in the center of the rear axle is the differential, which transfers the turning force of the driveshaft to the rear axleshafts, on which the rear wheels are mounted.

The axleshafts are splined at their inner ends to fit into the splines in the differential gears; outer support for the shaft is provided by the rear wheel bearing.

The front axle on 4WD vehicles consists of a frame mounted differential assembly and two driveaxles. The driveaxles incorporate two constant velocity (CV) joints each, enabling them to transmit power at various suspension angles independent from each other.

Because of the complexity and critical nature of the differential adjustments, as well as the special equipment needed to perform the operations, we recommend any disassembly of the differential be done by a dealer service department or other repair shop.

---

12   Driveline inspection

1   Raise the rear of the vehicle and support it securely on jackstands.
2   Slide under the vehicle and visually inspect the condition of the driveshaft. Look for any dents or cracks in the tubing. If any are found, the driveshaft must be replaced.
3   Check for any oil leakage at the front and rear of the driveshaft. Leakage where the driveshaft enters the transmission indicates a defective rear transmission seal. Leakage where the driveshaft enters the differential indicates a defective pinion seal. For these repair operations refer to Chapters 7 and 8 respectively.
4   While still under the vehicle, have an assistant turn the rear wheel so the driveshaft will rotate. As it does, make sure that the universal joints are operating properly without binding, noise or looseness. On long bed models, listen for any noise from the center bearing, indicating it is worn or damaged. Also check the rubber portion of the center bearing for cracking or separation, which will necessitate replacement.
5   The universal joint can also be checked with the driveshaft motionless, by gripping your hands on either side of the joint and attempting to twist the joint. Any movement at all in the joint is a sign of considerable wear. Lifting up on the shaft will also indicate movement in the universal joints.
6   Finally, check the driveshaft mounting bolts at the ends to make sure they are tight.
7   On 4WD models, the above driveshaft checks should be repeated on all driveshafts. In addition, check for grease leakage around the sleeve yoke, indicating failure of the yoke seal.
8   Check for leakage at each connection of the driveshafts to the transfer case and front differential. Leakage indicates worn oil seals.
9   At the same time, check for looseness in the joints of the front driveaxles. Also check for grease or oil leakage from around the driveaxles by inspecting the rubber boots and both ends of each axle. Oil leakage at the differential junction indicates a defective side oil seal. Leakage at the wheel side indicates a defective front hub seal, while leakage at the boots means a damaged rubber boot. For servicing of these components, see the appropriate Sections.

---

13   Driveshafts — removal and installation

Refer to illustration 13.2

Front driveshaft (4WD)

1   Raise the front of the vehicle and place it on jackstands.
2   Mark the relationship of the front driveshaft flange to the front differential companion flange so they can be realigned upon installation **(see illustration)**.

8

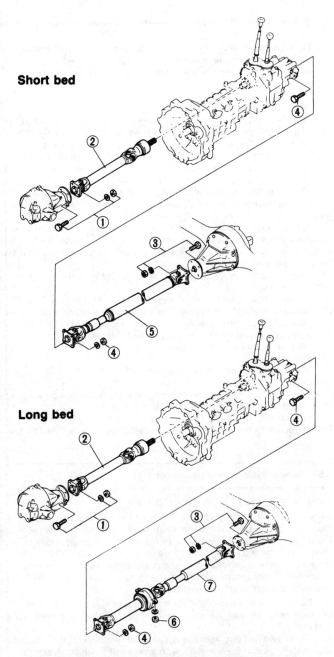

Short bed

Long bed

11.1b Exploded views of the 4WD driveshaft assemblies

1 *Bolts and nuts*   5 *Rear driveshaft (one-piece)*
2 *Front driveshaft*   6 *Nuts*
3 *Bolts and nuts*   7 *Rear driveshaft (two-piece)*
4 *Bolts and nuts*

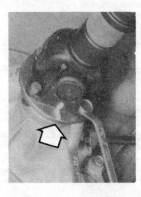

13.2 Mark the driveshaft flange to the differential companion flange (arrow)

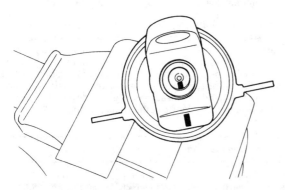

14.4   Mark the intermediate shaft yoke to the shaft to ensure correct installation

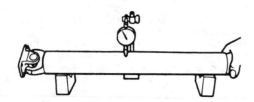

14.8   Check the driveshafts for excessive runout, which can quickly destroy a center bearing

3   Remove the four bolts from the front flange.
4   Push the shaft slightly to the rear to disconnect the front flange, lower the driveshaft then pull it forward to remove it from the transfer case.

Rear driveshaft

5   Raise the rear of the truck and support it on jackstands.
6   Remove the two bolts holding the center support bearing to the frame (3-joint type).
7   Mark the edges of the driveshaft rear flange and the differential companion flange so they can be realigned upon installation.
8   Remove the four nuts and bolts.
9   Push the shaft forward slightly to disconnect the rear flange.
10   Pull the yoke from the transmission while supporting the driveshaft with your hand (2WD models).
11   Mark the driveshaft flange and the flange on the transfer case so they can be realigned upon installation (4WD).
12   Remove the four nuts and bolts from each flange (4WD).
13   Push the shaft slightly to the rear to disconnect the front flange and gently lower the driveshaft (4WD).
14   While the driveshafts are removed, insert a plug in the transmission to prevent lubricant leakage (2WD models).
15   Installation is the reverse of the removal procedures. During installation, make sure all flange marks line up. When connecting the center bearing support to the frame, first finger-tighten the two mounting bolts, then make sure that the bearing bracket is at right angles to the driveshaft. Tighten all nuts and bolts to the specified torque

---

14   Center bearing — replacement

Refer to illustrations 14.4, 14.6 and 14.8

1   Remove the driveshaft (see Section 13). Mark the relationship of the center U-joint yokes to each other and to the intermediate shaft.
2   Disassemble the center universal joint.
3   Remove the center joint nut. To keep the shaft from turning, place the yoke in a vise. Don't tighten the vise excessively, as the yoke may become distorted.
4   Mark the intermediate shaft yoke in relation to the threaded portion of the shaft **(see illustration)**.

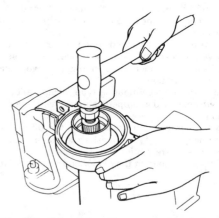

14.6   Partially thread the old nut onto the shaft and knock the shaft out of the bearing with a brass hammer — don't let the intermediate shaft fall when the two separate

5   Pull the yoke off of the shaft.
6   Support the center bearing in a vise with the mounting ears of the bearing resting on the tops of the vise jaws and the intermediate shaft hanging down. Thread the nut back onto the shaft two turns and tap on it lightly with a soft-face hammer **(see illustration)**. If the bearing and shaft don't separate easily, squirt some penetrating oil onto the shaft splines and allow it to soak in for awhile, then try again.
7   Once the bearing is freed, remove the nut and bearing from the shaft. The nut should be discarded and a new one used upon reassembly.
8   Using a dial indicator and V-block arrangement, inspect the two sections of the driveshaft for excessive runout **(see illustration)**. If the readings are greater than the specified maximum, replace the shaft with a new one.
9   Inspect the yokes and flanges for damage and wear, replacing parts where necessary.
10   For universal joint inspection procedures, see Section 15.
11   Begin reassembly by coating the splines of the intermediate shaft with multi-purpose grease and placing the bearing on the shaft. It may be necessary to gently tap the bearing onto the shaft. If this is so, use a hammer and a brass punch, applying force to the inner race of the bearing only.
12   Place the yoke on the shaft, align the match marks and install a new nut.
13   Place the yoke in a vise, clamping the jaws lightly so as not to damage it. Tighten the nut to the specified torque.
14   Attach the rear shaft to the center U-joint yoke by aligning the match marks on the yokes and reassembling the U-joints (Section 15).

---

15   Universal joints — replacement

Refer to illustrations 15.1, 15.2, 15.3 and 15.6

Note: *Selective fit snap-rings are used to retain the universal joint spiders in the yokes. In order to maintain the driveshaft balance, you must use replacement snap-rings of the same size as originally used. Selective snap-rings are listed in the Specifications. On 1986 and later long bed models, selective snap-rings are available for the center U-joint only. If loose joints are found at either end of the shaft, that portion of the shaft must be replaced.*

1   Remove the driveshaft and mark the relationship of all components so that they can all be installed in their original positions **(see illustration)**.
2   Clean away all dirt from the ends of the bearings on the yokes so the snap-rings can be removed with a screwdriver **(see illustration)**. If they are very tight, tap the end of the bearing with a punch and hammer to relieve the pressure.
3   Once the snap-rings are removed tap the universal joints at the yoke with a soft-face hammer; the bearings will come out of the housing and can be removed easily **(see illustration)**.
4   Once the bearings are removed from each opposite journal yoke

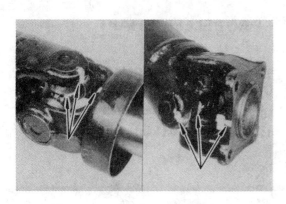

15.1   Place match marks on the driveshaft and yokes to ensure correct reassembly

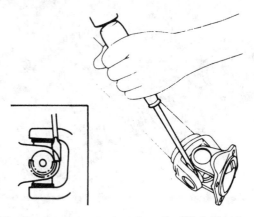

15.2   Remove the snap-rings from the U-joint bearings by tapping them off with a screwdriver and hammer

15.3   With the snap-rings removed, the bearings can be removed by tapping the yoke with a hammer

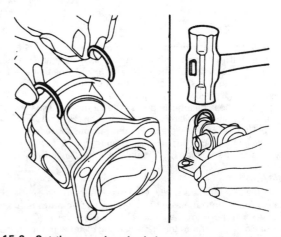

15.6   Set the snap-rings in their grooves and tap them into place with a hammer

the journal can be disengaged.

5   In cases of extreme wear or neglect, it is possible that the bearing housings in the driveshaft, sleeve or flange will be worn so much that the bearings are a loose fit in them. In such a case, it will also be necessary to replace the worn component as well.

6   Installation is the reverse of the removal procedure. **Note:** *Be sure to grease the inner surface of the bearings prior to installing them. Some replacement U-joints are equipped with grease fittings — fill the joint with grease after assembly is completed. Also be sure to install the snap-rings in their proper positions as noted at the beginning of this Section* (**see illustration**). *When assembled, the U-joint should have no play in it and should be reasonably stiff, but should still be able to be flexed easily by hand. If it is loose, install the next thickness snap-ring listed in the Specifications.*

---

16   Rear axleshafts, bearings and oil seals — removal and installation

---

Refer to illustrations 16.1a, 16.1b, 16.8 and 16.11

1   The axleshafts can be removed without disturbing the differential assembly. They must be removed in order to replace the bearings and oil seals and when removing the differential carrier from the rear axle housing (**see illustrations**). **Note:** *Read the entire Section before starting work.*

2   Raise the rear of the vehicle and support it securely on jackstands. Block the front wheels to keep the vehicle from rolling.

3   Remove the rear wheels and release the parking brake, then remove the brake drums (see Chapter 9 for details).

4   Remove the drain plug and drain the differential oil into a suitable container. When the draining is complete, finger-tighten the drain plug in place.

5   Disconnect the brake line from the wheel cylinder (see Chapter 9 for details).

6   Disconnect the parking brake cable from the packing brake lever and the brake backing plate (see Chapter 9).

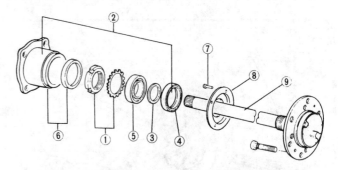

16.1a   Rear axleshaft, bearings and oil seal installation details — 1984 and earlier models

1 Lock nut and washer	6 Bearing housing
2 Bearing housing assembly	7 Rivet
3 Spacer	8 Baffle plate
4 Oil seal	9 Axle shaft
5 Bearing	

8

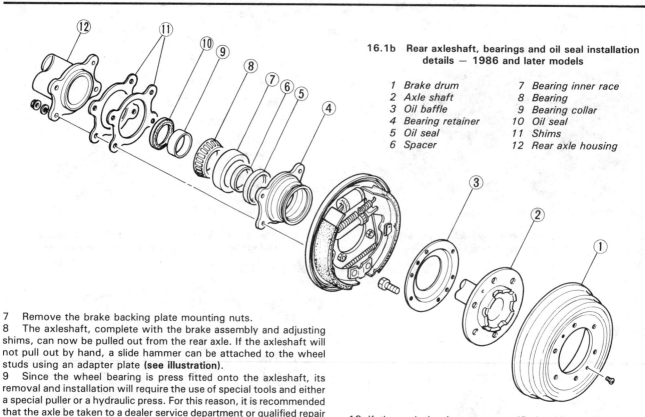

16.1b   Rear axleshaft, bearings and oil seal installation details — 1986 and later models

1	*Brake drum*	*7*	*Bearing inner race*
2	*Axle shaft*	*8*	*Bearing*
3	*Oil baffle*	*9*	*Bearing collar*
4	*Bearing retainer*	*10*	*Oil seal*
5	*Oil seal*	*11*	*Shims*
6	*Spacer*	*12*	*Rear axle housing*

7   Remove the brake backing plate mounting nuts.

8   The axleshaft, complete with the brake assembly and adjusting shims, can now be pulled out from the rear axle. If the axleshaft will not pull out by hand, a slide hammer can be attached to the wheel studs using an adapter plate **(see illustration)**.

9   Since the wheel bearing is press fitted onto the axleshaft, its removal and installation will require the use of special tools and either a special puller or a hydraulic press. For this reason, it is recommended that the axle be taken to a dealer service department or qualified repair shop whenever the bearings, oil seal or axle itself need replacing.

Installation

10   Install the axleshaft assembly, with the shims in place on the bearing retainer studs, into the axle housing. Install two nuts, tightening them securely to perform the axleshaft end play check.

11   Mount a dial indicator to the brake backing plate, with the indicator plunger resting on the face of the axle flange **(see illustration)**. Push the axle in as far as possible and set the dial to zero. Now pull out on the axle flange and read the end play measurement. Compare the reading with the standard bearing play listed in the Specifications section at the beginning of this Chapter (**Note:** *The end play will vary depending on whether one or both of the axles are installed — make sure you use the correct specification. If both of the axles have been removed, set the end play for the first axle alone before installing and adjusting the other axle).*

12   If the dial indicator shows the end play to be within specification, install the remaining two bearing retainer nuts and tighten all four nuts to the specified torque.

13   If the end play is not as specified, add or subtract shims, as necessary, to obtain the desired play. The shims are available in four thicknesses (see the Specifications section).

14   The remaining installation procedures are the reverse of those of removal.

15   Following installation, tighten the drain plug and fill the differential with the proper grade and amount of lubricant as specified in Chapter 1.

16   Bleed the brakes following the procedure described in Chapter 9.

---

17   Rear axle assembly — removal and installation

1   Loosen the rear wheel lug nuts, raise the vehicle and support it securely on jackstands placed underneath the frame. Remove the wheels.

2   Support the rear axle assembly with a floor jack placed underneath the differential.

3   Remove the shock absorber lower mounting nuts and compress

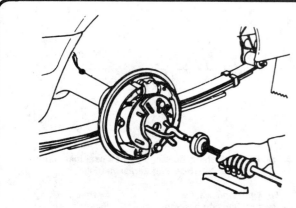

16.8   A rear axle adapter plate and slide hammer may be needed to remove the rear axleshaft assembly

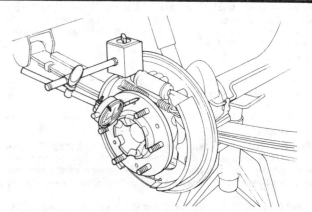

16.11   Check the axleshaft end play with a dial indicator

the shocks to get them out of the way (Chapter 10).
4   Disconnect the driveshaft from the differential companion flange
and hang it with a piece of wire from the underbody (Section 13).
5   Remove the brake drums and disconnect the parking brake cables
from the parking brake levers.
6   Unclip the cables from the backing plates and pull them through
(Chapter 9). Unbolt the load sensing proportioning valve control rod
from the axle housing.
7   Disconnect the rear flexible brake hose from the brake line above
the rear axle housing. Plug the ends of the line and hose or wrap plastic
bags tightly around them to prevent excessive fluid loss and
contamination.
8   Remove the U-bolt nuts from under the leaf spring seats (Chapter
10).
9   Raise the rear axle assembly off of the leaf spring and carefully
maneuver it out from between the leaf spring and the frame (2WD
models). It would be a good idea to have an assistant on hand, as the
assembly is very heavy. On 4WD models, lower the assembly from the
vehicle.
10   Installation is the reverse of the removal procedure. Be sure to
tighten the U-bolt nuts and the driveshaft companion flange bolts to
the specified torque.

18   Front axle assembly — removal and installation

Refer to illustration 18.6

1   Loosen the wheel lug nuts, raise the front of the vehicle and support it securely on jackstands. Remove the wheels.
2   Remove the four bolts that secure the engine undercover and
remove the cover.
3   Drain the front differential gear oil then reinstall the drain plug finger
tight (see Chapter 1).
4   Remove the front driveaxles (see Section 21).
5   Place match marks on the front driveshaft to front differential companion flange, then remove the driveshaft (see Section 13).
6   Support the front axle assembly with two floor jacks — one under
the differential and one under the extension tube. Remove the center
and front crossmember-to-frame mounting bolts **(see illustration)**.
7   Slowly lower the assembly from the vehicle.
8   Installation is the reverse of the removal procedure. Be sure to
tighten the companion flange and crossmember bolts to the specified
torque.

19   Differential — removal and installation

1   Raise the vehicle and support it securely on jackstands. Block the
wheels to keep the vehicle from rolling.
2   Remove the drain plug and drain the differential oil into a suitable
container, then reinstall the drain plug finger-tight.

Rear differential

3   Remove the rear axleshafts (see Section 16).
4   Disconnect the driveshaft flange from the companion flange (see
Section 13). Hang the driveshaft out of the way with a piece of wire.
5   Remove the bolts from the differential carrier assembly and pull
out the differential assembly. The mounting bolts should be loosened
in steps, following a criss-cross pattern. If the differential is stuck to
the axle housing, loosely install two of the bolts, then strike the differential with a hammer and block of wood to dislodge it.
6   The overhaul of the differential unit is not within the scope of the
home mechanic, due to the specialized gauges and tools which are
required. Where the unit requires servicing or repair, due to wear or
excessive noise, it is most economical to exchange it for a factory
reconditioned assembly.
7   Before reinstalling the differential, scrape all traces of old gasket
from the mating surfaces of the axle housing. Position a new gasket
on the housing (use a silicone-type gasket sealant). Later models use
silicone sealant only.
8   Installation is the reverse of the removal procedure. Be sure to
tighten the bolts to the specified torque.
9   Following installation, fill the differential with the proper grade and
quantity of lubricant (see Chapter 1).

Front differential

10   Remove the front axle assembly from the vehicle following the procedure outlined in Section 18.
11   Perform steps 5 through 9 above.

20   Freewheel hub assembly (4WD) — removal,
overhaul and installation

*Refer to illustrations 20.3, 20.4, 20.6, 20.7, 20.11, 20.14, 20.15,
20.17, 20.22 and 20.23*
Note: *When disassembling the freewheel hub, pay very close attention to the way the parts fit together. If confusion is a possibility, make
a sketch as they are disassembled and lay them out in order of removal.*

Removal

1   Set the hub control handle to the Free position.
2   Remove the six bolts and slide the freewheel hub out of the front
hub.

Overhaul

3   To check the operation of the freewheel hub, temporarily install
two bolts through the hub to hold it together, then confirm that the
control handle turns easily and the inner hub rotates smoothly when
the hub is set in the Free position **(see illustration)**. The inner hub should
not turn when the control handle is placed in the Lock position.

8

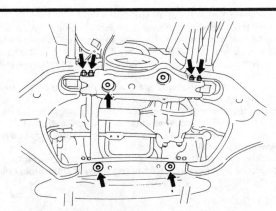

**18.6   Remove the indicated crossmember bolts (arrows) —
the front axle assembly must be supported before
this is done**

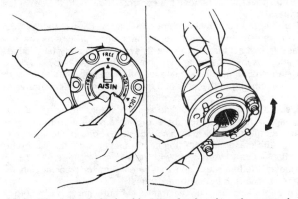

**20.3   The inner hub should rotate freely when the control
knob is in the Free position**

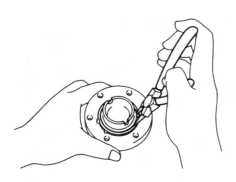

20.4   Remove the snap-ring that retains the control handle to the cover

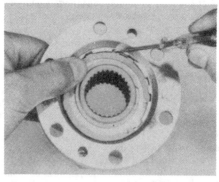

20.6   Removing the snap-ring retaining the inner hub and hub ring to the hub body

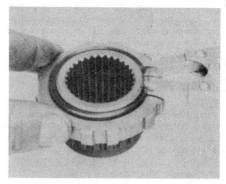

20.7   Removing the snap-ring retaining the hub ring to the inner hub

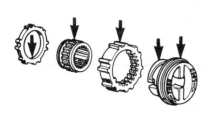

20.11   Lubricate the indicated areas with multi-purpose grease

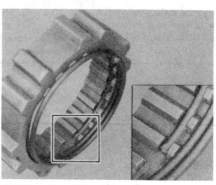

20.14   Proper alignment of the tension spring in the clutch

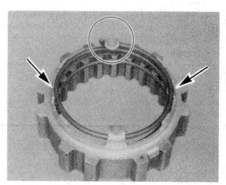

20.15   Spring end abuts one of the large tabs and the top ring rests on the small tabs of the follower pawl

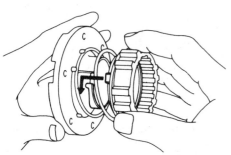

20.17   Install the clutch hub to the clutch cover

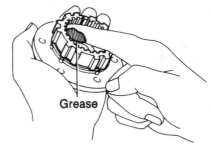

20.22   Lubricate the inner hub splines with multi-purpose grease

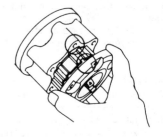

20.23   Align the clutch follower tabs with the hub body and install the clutch assembly

4   Using snap-ring pliers, remove the snap-ring from the underside of the hub cover, then remove the control handle from the cover (**see illustration**).

5   Remove the steel ball and spring from the control handle.

6   Using a screwdriver, remove the snap-ring that retains the inner hub and freewheel hub ring to the freewheel hub body (**see illustration**), then remove the inner hub and ring from the body.

7   Using snap-ring pliers, remove the snap-ring that retains the freewheel hub ring to the inner hub (**see illustration**), then remove the ring and spacer from the inner hub.

8   Inspect the cover, handle and seal for wear or damage. If wear or damage is found, replace the appropriate parts with new ones.

9   Inspect the hub body, clutch spring, clutch body and follower pawl for wear and make sure that the clutch moves smoothly in the hub body. Replace any worn parts with new ones.

10   Inspect the inner hub and free wheel ring for wear or damage. Replace any worn parts with new ones.

11   To begin assembly of the freewheel hub, apply multi-purpose grease to the contact surfaces of all parts (**see illustration**).

12   Attach a new seal and the spring and ball to the control handle.

13   Insert the handle into the cover and install the snap-ring.

14   Install the tension spring in the clutch, with the spring end aligned

with the initial groove (**see illustration**).

15   Place the follower pawl over the tension spring, with one of the large tabs positioned against the bent spring end. The top coil of the spring should rest on the small tabs of the pawl (**see illustration**).

16   Place the spring between the hub cover and clutch, with the large end of the spring toward the cover.

17   Compress the spring and install the clutch with the pawl tab fitted into the handle cam (**see illustration**).

18   Install the spacer and freewheel hub ring in the inner hub, then install the snap-ring with snap-ring pliers (**see illustration 20.7**).

19   Insert the inner hub and freeweel hub ring into the hub body. Using a screwdriver, install the snap-ring.

20   Set the control handle and clutch to the Free position.

21   Insert the cover in the hub body and verify that the inner hub turns freely.

Installation

22   Apply grease to the inner hub splines (**see illustration**).

23   Install the freewheel hub cover onto the body, aligning the follower tabs with the non-toothed lands of the body (**see illustration**). Tighten the six bolts to the specified torque.

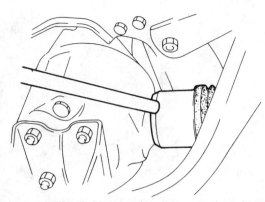

21.10   Use a long drift and a hammer to "pop" the driveaxle out of the differential

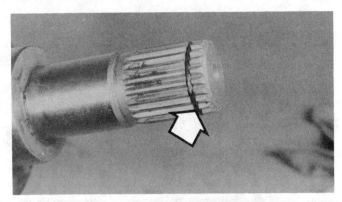

21.12   Always replace the spring clip on the inner stub shaft

---

21   Front driveaxle (4WD) — removal and installation

Refer to illustration 21.10 and 21.12

Removal

1   Loosen the wheel lug nuts, raise the front of the vehicle and support it securely on jackstands. Remove the wheel.
2   Remove the freewheel hub (see Section 20).
3   Unbolt the caliper from the steering knuckle and suspend it with a piece of wire — DON'T let it hang by the brake hose.
4   Using a pair of snap-ring pliers, remove the snap-ring and spacer from the end of the driveaxle.
5   Disconnect the tie-rod end from the steering knuckle arm (Chapter 10).
6   Remove the shock absorber lower mounting bolt and compress the shock absorber as much as possible to get it out of the way.
7   Remove the stabilizer bar-to-lower arm bolt (see Chapter 10).
8   Place a floor jack under the suspension lower arm and raise it slightly, then remove the steering knuckle following the procedure outlined in Chapter 10. Support the outer end of the driveaxle with a piece of wire — allowing it to hang free may damage the inner constant velocity joint.
9   Remove the engine undercover.
10 Using a long drift or pry bar, knock the inner CV joint out of the differential **(see illustration)**, then remove the driveaxle from the vehicle.
11 Inspect the CV joint boots for cracks, holes and tears. Refer to the next Section if the boots need replacing.

Installation

12 If the right side driveaxle is being installed, pry off the old spring clip from the end of the driveaxle stub shaft and install a new one **(see illustration)**. When installing the left driveaxle, this clip is located on the end of the output shaft, and is replaced in the same manner.
13 Lubricate the differential seal (or output shaft seal) with multi-purpose grease or gear oil. Slide the inner end of the driveaxle into the differential side gear (or on the left side, onto the output shaft) until a "click" is felt, indicating that the spring clip has seated in its groove in the side gear (or inner joint, on the left side). Try to pull the driveaxle out — if it won't come out, the clip is properly seated.
14 Once again, hang the outboard end of the driveaxle from a piece of wire as was done in Step 8, then position the steering knuckle over the driveaxle stub shaft and between the balljoint studs.
15 The remainder of the installation procedure is the reverse of the removal sequence. Be sure to tighten all fasteners to the specified torque values where indicated.

---

22   Driveaxle boot replacement and (CV) joint overhaul (4WD)

Refer to illustrations 22.3a, 22.3b, 22.4, 22.5, 22.6, 22.8, 22.9, 22.13, 22.14, 22.15, 22.17, 22.19, 22.20, 22.21a, 22.21b and 22.27

Note: *If the CV joints exhibit signs of wear indicating need for an overhaul (usually due to torn boots), explore all options before begin-*

ning the job. Complete rebuilt driveaxles are available on an exchange basis, which eliminates much time and work. Whichever route you choose to take, check on the cost and availability of parts before disassembling your vehicle.

Inner CV joint and boot

Disassembly
1   Remove the driveaxle from the vehicle (Section 21).
2   Mount the driveaxle in a vise. The jaws of the vise should be lined with wood or rags to prevent damage to the axleshaft.
3   Pry the boot clamps loose with a small screwdriver **(see illustrations)**.

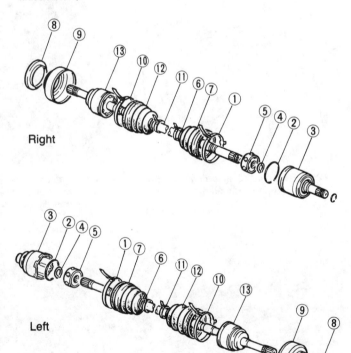

22.3a   Driveaxle assemblies — exploded view

1 Boot clamp	8 Dust cover
2 Ball retainer	9 Boot protector
3 Outer race	10 Boot clamp
4 Snap-ring	11 Boot clamp
5 Inner race and cage (bearing) assembly	12 Boot
6 Boot clamp	13 Outer CV joint and driveaxle assembly
7 Boot	

8

22.3b   The boot clamps can be pried
open with a small screwdriver

22.4   Pry the wire ring from the outer
race with a small screwdriver

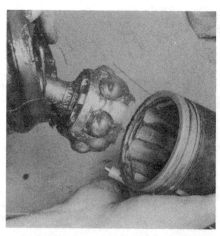

22.5   With the retainer removed, the
outer race can be pulled off the inner
race and cage

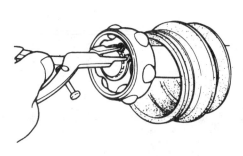

22.6   Remove the snap-ring from the
end of the shaft

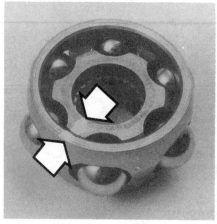

22.8   Make index marks on the inner
race and cage so they'll both be facing
the same direction when reassembled

22.9   Pry the balls from the cage with a
screwdriver (be careful not to nick or
scratch anything)

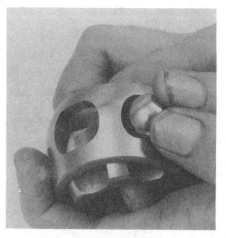

22.13   Press the balls into the cage
through the windows

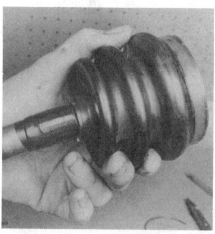

22.14   Wrap the splined area of the
axle with tape to prevent damage to the
boot when installing it

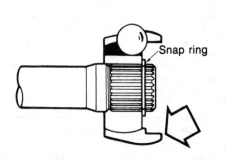

Snap ring

22.15   The larger diameter side of the
inner race and cage (arrow) must face
the end of the shaft

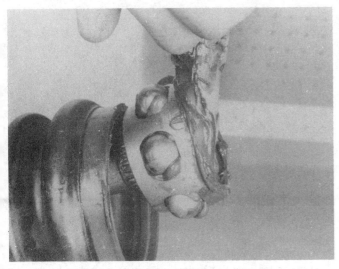

22.17 Pack grease into the bearing until it's completely full

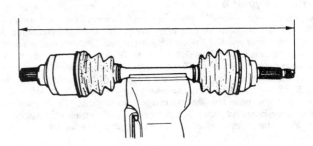

22.19 The driveaxle must be set to the proper length (as stated in the Specifications section) before the inner boot clamp is tightened – it is measured from end-to-end

4   Slide the boot back on the axleshaft and pry the wire ring ball retainer from the outer race (see illustration).
5   Pull the outer race off the inner bearing assembly (see illustration).
6   Remove the snap-ring from the end of the axleshaft with a pair of snap-ring pliers (see illustration).
7   Slide the inner bearing assembly off the axleshaft.
8   Mark the inner race and cage to ensure that they are reassembled with the correct sides facing out (see illustration).
9   Using a screwdriver, pry the balls from the cage (see illustration). Be careful not to scratch the inner race, the balls or the cage.
10 Rotate the inner race 90-degrees, align the inner race lands with the cage windows and rotate the race out of the cage.

Inspection

11 Clean the components with solvent to remove all traces of grease. Inspect the cage and races for pitting, score marks, cracks and other signs of wear and damage. Shiny, polished spots are normal and will not adversely affect CV joint performance.

Reassembly

12 Insert the inner race into the cage. Verify that the matchmarks are on the same side. However, it's not necessary for them to be in direct alignment with each other.
13 Press the balls into the cage windows with your thumbs (see illustration).
14 Wrap the axleshaft splines with tape to avoid damaging the boot. Slide the small boot clamp and boot onto the axleshaft, then remove the tape (see illustration).
15 Install the inner race and cage assembly on the axleshaft with the larger diameter side or ''bulge'' of the cage facing the axleshaft end (see illustration).
16 Install the snap-ring, making sure it seats in it's groove completely.
17 Fill the outer race and boot with the specified type and quantity of CV joint grease (normally included with the new boot kit). Pack the inner race and cage assembly with grease, by hand, until grease is worked completely into the assembly (see illustration).
18 Slide the outer race down onto the inner race and install the wire ring retainer.
19 Wipe any excess grease from the axle boot groove on the outer race. Seat the small diameter of the boot in the recessed area on the axleshaft. Push the other end of the boot onto the outer race and move the race in-or-out to adjust the axle to the proper length (see illustration).
20 With the axle set to the proper length, equalize the pressure in the boot by inserting a dull screwdriver between the boot and the outer race (see illustration). Don't damage the boot with the tool.
21 Install the boot clamps (see illustrations).

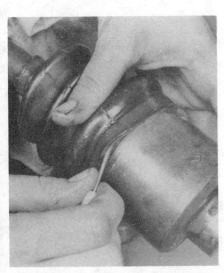

22.20 Equalize the pressure inside the boot by inserting a small screwdriver between the boot and the outer race

22.21a To install a new clamp, bend the tang downward and . . .

22.21b . . . tap the tabs down to hold it in place

8

22 Install a new circlip on the stub axle **(see illustration 21.12).**
23 Install the driveaxle as described in Section 21.

Outer CV joint and boot

24 Remove the inner CV joint and boot following Steps 1 through 7.
25 Remove the boot clamps from the outer joint boot (see Step 3)
26 Thoroughly wash the outer CV joint in clean solvent and blow dry with compressed air, if available. **Note:** *Because the outer joint cannot be disassembled, it is difficult to wash away all the old grease and to rid the bearing of solvent once it's clean. But it is imperative that the job be done thoroughly, so take your time and do it right.*
27 Bend the outer CV joint housing at an angle to the driveaxle to expose the bearings, inner race and cage **(see illustration).** Inspect the bearing surfaces for signs of wear. If the bearings are damaged or worn, replace the driveaxle.
28 Slide the new outer boot onto the driveaxle. It's a good idea to wrap vinyl tape around the spline fo the shaft to prevent damage to the boot. When the boot is in position, add the specified amount of grease (included in the boot replacement kit) to the outer joint and the boot (pack the joint with as much grease as it will hold and put the rest into the boot). Slide the boot on the rest of the way and install the new clamps **(see illustrations 22.21a and 22.21b).**
29 Install the inner CV joint and boot as outlined in this Section.
30 Install the driveaxle as described in Section 21.

22.27   After the joint has been cleaned thoroughly, rotate it through its full range of motion and inspect the bearing surfaces for wear or damage — if any of the balls, the race or cage look damaged, replace the driveaxle and outer joint assembly

Chapter 9 Brakes

Contents

Specifications

General

Brake fluid type .... See Chapter 1
Master cylinder piston-to-pushrod clearance .... 0.004 to 0.020 in (0.1 to 0.5 mm)

Disc brakes

Minimum brake pad thickness .... See Chapter 1
Disc standard thickness
    All 1981 and earlier models, B2000 to 1984 .... 0.4724 in (12 mm)
    1984 and earlier B2200, 1986 and later 2WD .... 0.7874 in (20 mm)
    4WD .... 0.87 in (22 mm)
Disc minimum thickness*
    All 1981 and earlier models, B2000 to 1984 .... 0.4331 in (11 mm)
    1984 and earlier B2200 .... 0.7480 in (19 mm)
    1986 and later 2WD .... 0.71 in (18 mm)
    4WD .... 0.79 in (20 mm)
Lateral runout
    1984 and earlier (all) .... 0.0039 in (0.10 mm)
    1986 and 1987 .... 0.002 in (0.04 mm)
    1988 and later .... 0.006 in (0.15 mm)

Refer to marks stamped on the disc (they supercede information printed here)

Drum brakes

Minimum brake shoe lining thickness .... See Chapter 1
Brake drums (all)
Standard drum diameter .... 10.2364 in (260 mm)
Maximum drum diameter*
    1984 and earlier .... 10.2758 in (261 mm)
    1986 and 1987 .... 10.31 in (262 mm)
    1988 and later .... 10.30 in 261.5 mm)

Refer to marks stamped on the drum (they supercede information printed here)

Torque specifications

	Ft-lbs
Brake caliper mounting bolts	23 to 30
Caliper bracket-to-steering knuckle bolts	36 to 55
Caliper inlet fitting bolt (1986 and later)	16 to 19
Disc-to-hub bolts	33 to 42
Wheel cylinder mounting bolts	
Leading/trailing arrangement	9 to 12
Duo-servo arrangement	15 to 18
Brake backing plate-to-axle housing	
1984 and earlier	33 to 36
1986 and later 2WD	65 to 80
4WD	72 to 87

9

Torque specifications (continued)

	Ft-lbs
Master cylinder mounting nuts	7 to 12
Brake pedal pivot shaft nut	14 to 25
Power brake booster mounting nuts	12 to 17
Wheel lug nuts	
1981 and earlier	58 to 65
1982 thru 1984	
Standard wheels	72 to 80
Styled wheels	87 to 94
1986 and later	87 to 108

1   General information

The vehicles covered by this manual are equipped with hydraulically operated front and rear brake systems (see illustrations). The front brakes on early models are drum type, while 1977 and later models employ front disc brakes. The rear brakes on all models are drum type.

Some early models use a single master cylinder, but the majority are equipped with a dual master cylinder which allows the operation of half of the system if the other half fails. This system also incorporates a proportioning bypass valve which limits pressure to the rear brakes under heavy braking to prevent rear wheel lock-up.

1990 models are equipped with a rear-wheel Anti-Lock Brake System (ABS) on the rear wheels. This system monitors the rear wheel speed, and when it senses a drop in wheel speed, modulates the hydraulic pressure to the rear brakes, inhibiting their tendency to lock up. The system consists of a control unit located under the driver's seat, the hydraulic unit which contains solenoids to pulse the brake line pressure, the speed sensor mounted in the axle housing, a system electrical check connector, a pressure differential switch located near the master cylinder and a system fuse (see illustration).

Each time the vehicle is started, the amber ABS warning light on the dashboard illuminates for a brief time and then goes out, indicating that the system is operating properly. If the dashboard light comes on and stays on while the vehicle is in operation, the ABS system requires attention. About the only check the home mechanic can make at this point is to inspect the ABS fuse to determine if it is burned out. Due to the complicated nature of this system, further diagnosis of the ABS system should be left to a dealer.

On four wheel drive models, the proportioning bypass valve is substituted with a load-sensing G valve (LSGV).

Most models are equipped with a power brake booster which utilizes engine vacuum to assist in application of the brakes.

Early model drum brakes must be adjusted at specified intervals, but late model (rear only) drum brakes are adjusted automatically. The front disc brakes adjust for pad wear automatically, as well.

The parking brake operates the rear brakes only, through cable actuation.

Precautions

There are some notes and cautions involving the brake system on this vehicle:

a) Use only DOT 3 brake fluid in this system

b) The brake pads and linings contain asbestos fibers which are hazardous to your health if inhaled. Whenever you work on the brake system components, carefully clean all parts with brake cleaner. Do not allow the fine asbestos dust to become airborne.

c) Safety should be paramount whenever any servicing of the brake components is performed. Do not use parts or fasteners which are not in perfect condition, and be sure that all clearances and torque specifications are adhered to. If you are at all unsure about a certain procedure, seek professional advice. Upon completion of any brake system work, test the brakes carefully in a controlled area before putting the vehicle into normal service. If a problem is suspected in the brake system, do not drive the vehicle until the fault is corrected.

d) Tires, load and front end alignment are factors which also affect braking performance.

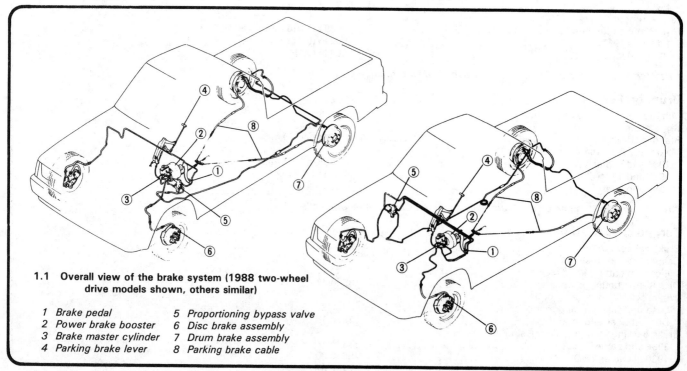

1.1   Overall view of the brake system (1988 two-wheel drive models shown, others similar)

1 Brake pedal	*5 Proportioning bypass valve*
2 Power brake booster	*6 Disc brake assembly*
3 Brake master cylinder	*7 Drum brake assembly*
4 Parking brake lever	*8 Parking brake cable*

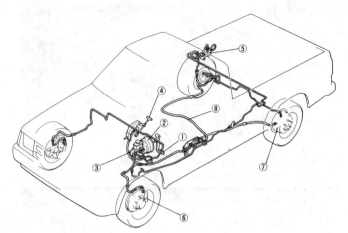

1.2 Overall view of the brake system (4WD models)

1 Brake pedal
2 Power brake booster
3 Brake master cylinder
4 Parking brake lever
5 Load-sensing G valve (LSGV)
6 Disc brake assembly
7 Drum brake assembly
8 Parking brake cable

2 Front brake pads — replacement

Warning: *Disc brake pads must be replaced on both front wheels at the same time — never replace the pads on only one wheel. Also, the dust created by the brake system contains asbestos, which is harmful to your health. Never blow it out with with compressed air and don't inhale any of it. An approved filtering mask should be worn when working on the brakes. Do not, under any circumstances, use petroleum-based solvents to clean brake parts. Use brake cleaner or denatured alcohol only!*

Note: *When servicing the disc brakes, use only high quality, nationally recognized name brand pads.*

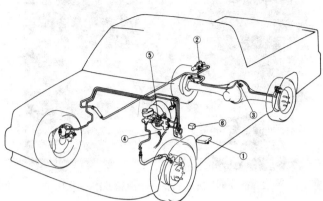

1.3 Overall view of the 1990 model, showing the ABS system

1 Control unit
2 Hydraulic unit
3 Speed sensor
4 System check connector
5 Pressure differential switch
6 ABS fuse

1   Remove the master cylinder reservoir cap and siphon out approximately half of the fluid into a container. Be careful not to spill fluid onto any of the painted surfaces — it will damage the paint.
2   Loosen the wheel lug nuts, raise the vehicle and support it securely on jackstands. Remove the wheels. Work on one brake assembly at a time, using the assembled brake for reference if necessary.
3   Using a large C-clamp, bottom the piston back into the caliper bore. The frame end of the C-clamp should be positioned on the backside of the caliper body and the screw should bear on the outer brake pad.

1977 thru 1981 models (all), 1982 thru 1984 B2000
Refer to illustrations 2.4a, 2.4b and 2.5
4   Remove the four locking clips **(see illustrations)**.

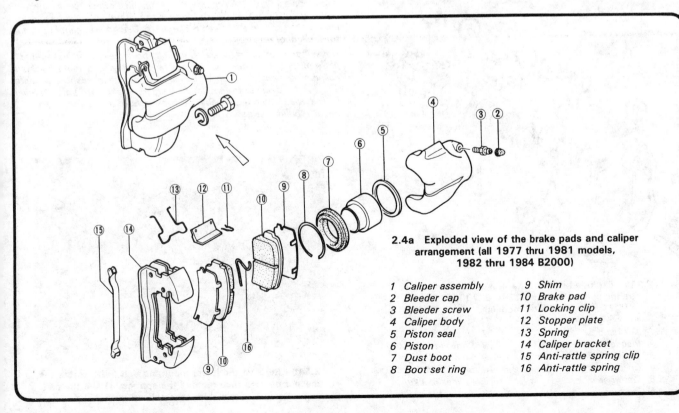

2.4a Exploded view of the brake pads and caliper arrangement (all 1977 thru 1981 models, 1982 thru 1984 B2000)

1 Caliper assembly
2 Bleeder cap
3 Bleeder screw
4 Caliper body
5 Piston seal
6 Piston
7 Dust boot
8 Boot set ring
9 Shim
10 Brake pad
11 Locking clip
12 Stopper plate
13 Spring
14 Caliper bracket
15 Anti-rattle spring clip
16 Anti-rattle spring

9

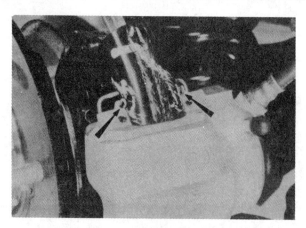

2.4b Pull out the locking clips (arrows)

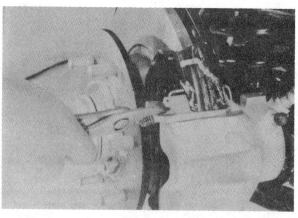

2.5 Remove the stopper plates with a pair of pliers

5 Pull out the stopper plates **(see illustration)** and lift the caliper and anti-rattle springs from the caliper bracket. Support the caliper by a piece of wire — don't allow it to hang by the brake hose.
6 Remove the brake pads and anti-squeal shims from the caliper bracket.
7 Apply a thin coat of disc brake grease to the brake pad backing plates.
8 Install the pads and shims into the caliper bracket.
9 Install the anti-rattle springs then slide the caliper over the pads. Coat the stopper plates with a thin film of disc brake grease and drive them into place. Install the locking clips.
10 Repeat the procedure on the other wheel then proceed to Step 15.

1982 thru 1984 B2200, all 1986 and later models
Refer to illustrations 2.11a and 2.11b

11 Remove the caliper lower mounting bolt and rotate the caliper upward to allow removal of the pads **(see illustrations)**. Remove the anti-

rattle springs and pull the brake pads and shims from the caliper bracket.
12 Coat the pad backing plate with disc brake grease and install the pads and shims into the caliper bracket.
13 Install the anti-rattle springs then swing the caliper down over the pads. Install the lower mounting bolt, tightening it to the specified torque.
14 Repeat the procedure on the other wheel.

All models
15 Firmly depress the brake pedal a few times to bring the pads into contact with the disc. Check the fluid level in the master cylinder, topping it up if necessary.
16 Road test the vehicle carefully before placing it into normal use.

---

3 Disc brake caliper — removal, overhaul and installation

Warning: *Dust created by the brake system contains asbestos, which is harmful to your health. Never blow it out with compressed air and don't inhale any of it. An approved filtering mask should be worn when working on the brakes. Do not, under any circumstances, use petroleum-based solvents to clean brake parts. Use brake cleaner or denatured alcohol only!*

Note: *If an overhaul is indicated (usually because of fluid leakage) explore all options before beginning the job. New and factory rebuilt calipers are available on an exchange basis, which makes this job quite easy. If it's decided to rebuild the calipers, make sure that a rebuild kit is available before proceeding. Always rebuild the calipers in pairs — never rebuild just one of them.*

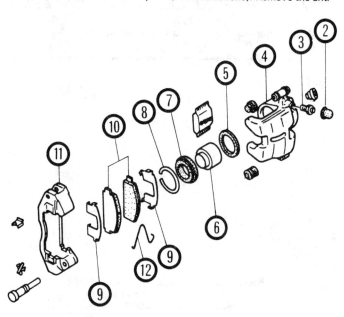

2.11a Exploded view of the brake pads and caliper arrangement (1982 thru 1984 B2200, all 1986 and later models)

1	Not used	7 Dust boot
2	Bleeder cap	8 Boot set ring
3	Bleeder screw	9 Shim
4	Caliper body	10 Brake pads
5	Piston seal	11 Caliper bracket
6	Piston	12 Anti-rattle spring

2.11b Remove the lower mounting bolt (left), rotate the caliper upward then remove the springs (1) and the pad and shim assemblies (2)

3.7a   Using a screwdriver, remove the boot set ring

3.7b   Remove the boot from the cylinder

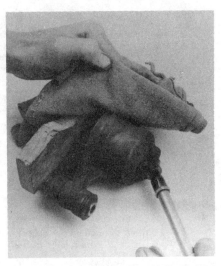

3.8   Apply compressed air to the brake fluid hose connection on the caliper body. Position a wood block between the piston and caliper to prevent damage

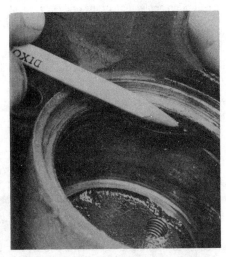

3.9   Because metal tools may cause damage, a wooden or plastic tool should be used to dig the piston seal out of its groove (a sharp pencil works well)

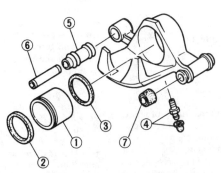

3.10a   Exploded view of the later model caliper

1   Piston
2   Dust boot
3   Piston seal
4   Bleeder screw and cap
5   Boot
6   Pin
7   Bushing

3.10b   On each side of the caliper, push the sliding bushing up through the boot and pull it free, then remove the dust boots

Removal

1   Remove the cap from the brake fluid reservoir, siphon off two-thirds of the fluid into a container and discard it.

2   Loosen the wheel lug nuts, raise the front of the vehicle and support it securely on jackstands. Remove the front wheels.

3   On 1984 and earlier models, disconnect the brake hose from the brake line at the frame bracket. Use a flare nut wrench on the line fitting to avoid rounding-off the peaks of the nut. After the fitting is completely loosened, pull the hose retaining clip out with a pair of pliers. The hose can now be unscrewed from the cliper. Plug the line to prevent excessive fluid loss and contamination.

4   On 1986 and later models, remove the brake hose inlet fitting bolt and detach the hose. Have a rag handy to catch spilled fluid and wrap a plastic bag tightly around the end of the hose to prevent fluid loss and contamination.

5   Remove the caliper, referring to Section 2 — it's part of the brake pad removal procedure.

Overhaul

Refer to illustrations 3.7a, 3.7b, 3.8, 3.9, 3.10a, 3.10b, 3.14 and 3.17

6   Clean the exterior of the caliper with brake cleaner or denatured alcohol. **Never use gasoline, kerosene or petroleum-based cleaning solvents.** Place the caliper on a clean workbench.

7   Remove the set ring and the rubber boot (**see illustrations**).

8   Position a wooden block or several shop rags in the caliper as a cushion, then use compressed air to remove the piston from the caliper (**see illustration**). Use only enough air pressure to ease the piston out of the bore. If the piston is blown out, even with the cushion in place, it may be damaged. **Warning:** *Never place your fingers in front of the piston in an attempt to catch or protect it when applying compressed air, as serious injury could occur.*

9   Using a wood or plastic tool, remove the piston seal from the groove in the caliper bore (**see illustration**). Metal tools may cause bore damage.

10   Remove the caliper bleeder screw, then remove the sliding bushings and dust boots from the caliper ears (1986 and later models only). Discard all rubber parts (**see illustrations**).

11   Clean the remaining parts with brake system cleaner or denatured alcohol then blow them dry with compressed air.

12   Carefully examine the piston for nicks and burrs and loss of plating. If surface defects are present, the parts must be replaced.

13   Check the caliper bore in a similar way. Light polishing with crocus cloth is permissible to remove light corrosion and stains. Discard the mounting bolts if they're corroded or damaged.

9

3.14   Position the seal in the caliper bore groove, making sure it isn't twisted

14   When assembling, lubricate the piston bore and seal with clean brake fluid. Position the seal in the caliper bore groove **(see illustration)**.
15   Lubricate the piston with clean brake fluid, insert the piston squarely in the caliper bore, then apply force to bottom the piston in the bore.
16   Install the new rubber boot and set ring.
17   Lubricate the sliding bushings and boots with the silicone grease supplied in the rebuild kit **(see illustration)**. Push the dust boots into the caliper ears, then install the sliding bushings (1986 and later models only).

Installation

18   Inspect the mounting bolts or stopper plates for excessive corrosion.
19   Place the caliper in position over the disc and mounting bracket, install the bolts and tighten them to the specified torque. On 1984 and earlier models, install the stopper plates and locking clips.
20   Install the brake hose and inlet fitting bolt, using new copper washers, then tighten the bolt to the specified torque (1986 and later models). On 1984 and earlier models, install the brake hose to the caliper and attach it to the frame bracket. Install the clip, then tighten the fitting securely. Be sure to bleed the brakes (Section 11).
21   Install the wheels and lower the vehicle.
22   After the job has been completed, firmly depress the brake pedal a few times to bring the pads into contact with the disc.

---

4   Brake disc — inspection, removal and installation

Refer to illustrations 4.4a, 4.4b, 4.5 and 4.8

Inspection

1   Loosen the wheel lug nuts, raise the vehicle and support it securely

4.4a   Check disc runout with a dial indicator positioned approximately 1/2-inch from the edge of the disc — if the reading exceeds the maximum allowable runout, the disc will have to be resurfaced or replaced

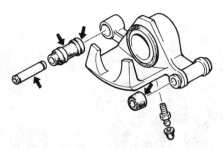

3.17   Apply silicone grease (included in the rebuild kit) to the areas indicated

on jackstands. Remove the wheel.
2   Remove the brake caliper as outlined in Section 3. It's not necessary to disconnect the brake hose. After removing the caliper bolts, suspend the caliper out of the way with a piece of wire. Don't let the caliper hang by the hose and don't stretch or twist the hose.
3   Visually check the disc surface for score marks and other damage. Light scratches and shallow grooves are normal after use and may not always be detrimental to brake operation, but deep score marks — over 0.015-inch (0.38 mm) — require disc removal and refinishing by an automotive machine shop. Be sure to check both sides of the disc. If pulsating has been noticed during application of the brakes, suspect excessive disc runout.
4   To check disc runout, place a dial indicator at a point about 1/2-inch from the outer edge of the disc **(see illustration)**. Set the indicator to zero and turn the disc. The indicator reading should not exceed the specified allowable runout limit. If it does, the disc should be refinished by an automotive machine shop. **Note:** *Professionals recommend resurfacing of brake discs regardless of the dial indicator reading (to produce a smooth, flat surface, that will eliminate brake pedal pulsations and other undesirable symptoms related to questionable discs). At the very least, if you elect not to have the discs resurfaced, deglaze the brake pad surface with medium-grit emery cloth (use a swirling motion to ensure a non-directional finish)* **(see illustration)**.
5   The disc must not be machined to a thickness less than the specified minimum refinish thickness. The minimum wear thickness is cast into the inside of the disc. The disc thickness can be checked with a micrometer **(see illustration)**.

Removal

6   Remove the caliper bracket-to-steering knuckle bolts and lift the bracket off.
7   Remove the hub/disc assembly, referring to Chapter 1, *Front wheel bearing check, repack and adjustment*.
8   Unbolt the disc from the hub **(see illustration)**.

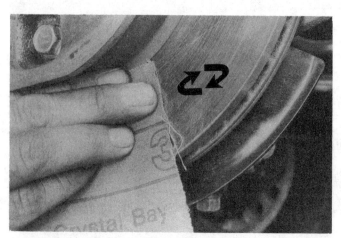

4.4b   Using a swirling motion, remove the glaze from the disc with sandpaper or emery cloth

**4.5   Use a micrometer to measure the thickness
of the disc**

Installation

9   Install the disc to the hub, tightening the bolts to the specified
torque in a criss-cross pattern.
10 Install the disc and hub assembly and adjust the wheel bearing
(Chapter 1).
11 Install the caliper/bracket, tightening the mounting bolts to the
specified torque. Position the pads in the bracket and install the caliper
(refer to Section 3 for the caliper installation procedure, if necessary).
Tighten the caliper bolts to the specified torque (1986 and later models).
12 Install the wheel, then lower the vehicle to the ground. Depress
the brake pedal a few times to bring the brake pads into contact with
the disc. Bleeding of the system will not be necessary unless the brake
hose was disconnected from the caliper. Check the operation of the
brakes carefully before placing the vehicle into normal service.

---

5   Front brake shoes — replacement

Refer to illustrations 5.2 and 5.4

Warning: *Drum brake shoes must be replaced on both front wheels
at the same time — never replace the shoes on only one wheel. Also,
the dust created by the brake system contains asbestos, which is harm-*

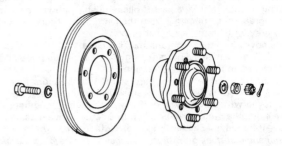

**4.8   Remove the bolts from the backside of the disc/hub
assembly, then separate the two components. It may be
necessary to tap the disc off the hub with a hammer
and a block of wood**

*ful to your health. Never blow it out with compressed air and don't
inhale any of it. An approved filtering mask should be worn when working on the brakes. Do not, under any circumstances, use petroleum-
based solvents to clean brake parts. Use brake cleaner or denatured
alcohol only!* **Caution:** *Whenever the brake shoes are replaced, the
retractor and hold-down springs should also be replaced. Due to the
continous heating/cooling cycle that the springs are subjected to, they
lose their tension over a period of time and may allow the shoes to
drag on the drum and wear at a much faster rate than normal. When
replacing the front brake shoes, use only high quality nationally
recognized brand-name parts.*

1   Loosen the wheel lug nuts, raise the vehicle and support it securely
on jackstands. Remove the wheel.
2   Remove the brake drum attaching screws and pull the drum off
the hub. If it is stuck, install two bolts of the correct size and thread
pitch into the threaded holes in the drum. Tighten the bolts a little at
a time until the drum is free **(see illustration)**.
3   Before removing anything, clean the brake assembly with brake
cleaner or denatured alcohol — DO NOT use compressed air to blow
the dust from the brake assembly!
4   Remove the brake shoe retracting springs **(see illustration)**.

**5.2   If the brake drum refuses to slide off the hub, screw
two bolts of the proper size and thread pitch into the
threaded holes and tighten them evenly, a little at a time.
The drum will be pushed off by the bolts**

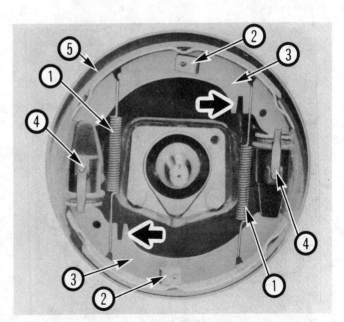

9

**5.4   Assembled view of the front drum brake assembly
(hub removed for clarity). The notches in the shoes
(arrows) must be on the same side as the adjusters**

1 Retracting spring	*4 Wheel cylinder*
2 Hold-down spring and pin	*5 Backing plate*
3 Brake shoe	

5　Remove the hold-down springs and pins. This is accomplished by grasping the spring with a pair of pliers, pushing down and rotating it 90 degrees, disengaging it from the pin. Place a finger behind the pin to prevent it from being pushed out.

6　Remove the shoes from the backing plate.

7　Check the wheel cylinders for signs of leaking fluid, replacing or rebuilding them if necessary (Section 8).

8　Check the brake drum for hard spots, cracks, score marks and grooves. Hard spots will appear as small discolored areas. If they can't be removed with emery cloth or if any of the other conditions listed above exist, the drum must be taken to an automotive machine shop to have it turned (machined on a lathe). **Note:** *Professional mechanics recommend resurfacing the drums whenever a brake job is performed. Resurfacing will eliminate the possibility of out-of-round drums.*

9　Unscrew the brake adjusters from the wheel cylinders, clean them and apply a little high temperature grease to the adjuster screw threads and star wheels. Install the adjusters into the wheel cylinders, turning them in completely.

10　Lubricate the brake shoe contact areas on the backing plate. Position the new shoes on the backing plate, making sure that the slots in the brake shoes are on the same side as the adjuster screw star wheel and the ends of the brake shoes mesh with the slots in the wheel cylinders **(see illustration 5.4).**

11　Install the hold-down pins and springs.

12　Install the retractor springs.

13　Slide the brake drum over the hub and install the retaining screws.

14　Install the wheel and lug nuts. Adjust the brake as described in Section 7. Tighten the lug nuts to the specified torque.

15　Repeat the operation on the other wheel.

16　Road test the vehicle carefully before placing it into normal use.

6　Rear brake shoes — replacement

Warning: *Drum brake shoes must be replaced on both rear wheels at the same time — never replace the shoes on only one wheel. Also, the dust created by the brake system contains asbestos, which is harmful to your health. Never blow it out with compressed air and don't*

inhale any of it. An approved filtering mask should be worn when working on the brakes. Do not, under any circumstances, use petroleum-based solvents to clean brake parts. Use brake cleaner or denatured alcohol only! **Caution:** *Whenever the brake shoes are replaced, the retractor and hold-down springs should also be replaced. Due to the continous heating/cooling cycle that the springs are subjected to, they lose their tension over a period of time and may allow the shoes to drag on the drum and wear at a much faster rate than normal. When replacing the brake shoes, use only high quality nationally recognized brand-name parts.*

1　Loosen the wheel lug nuts, raise the vehicle and support it securely on jackstands. Remove the wheel.

2　Remove the brake drum attaching screws and pull the drum off the axle flange. If it is stuck, install two bolts of the correct size and thread pitch into the threaded holes in the drum. Tighten the bolts a little at a time until the drum is free **(see illustration 5.2).**

3　Before removing anything, clean the brake assembly with brake cleaner or denatured alcohol — DO NOT use compressed air to blow the dust from the brake assembly!

Early style (two wheel cylinders)

Refer to illustrations 6.4 and 6.7

4　Remove the brake shoe retracting springs **(see illustration).**

5　Remove the hold-down springs and pins. This is accomplished by grasping the spring with a pair of pliers, pushing down and rotating it 90 degrees, disengaging it from the pin. Place a finger behind the pin to prevent it from being pushed out.

6　Remove the shoes and parking brake strut from the backing plate.

7　Disconnect the parking brake cable from the parking brake lever **(see illustration).**

8　Remove the pin retaining clip and pin, separating the parking brake lever from the brake shoe.

9　Check the wheel cylinders for signs of leaking fluid, replacing or rebuilding them if necessary (Section 8).

10　Check the brake drum for hard spots, cracks, score marks and grooves. Hard spots will appear as small discolored areas. If they can't be removed with emery cloth or if any of the other conditions listed above exist, the drum must be taken to an automotive machine shop to have it turned (machined on a lathe). **Note:** *Professional mechanics recommend resurfacing the drums whenever a brake job is performed. Resurfacing will eliminate the possibility of out-of-round drums.*

11　Unscrew the brake adjusters from the wheel cylinders, clean them and apply a little high temperature grease to the adjuster screw threads and star wheels. Install the adjuster screws into the wheel cylinders, turning them in completely.

12　Lubricate the brake shoe contact areas on the backing plate with high temperature grease. Connect the parking brake lever to the trailing brake shoe. Attach the parking brake cable to the hook on the lever. Position the new shoes on the backing plate, making sure that the slots in the brake shoes are on the same side as the adjuster screw star wheel and the ends of the brake shoes mesh with the slots in the wheel cylinders **(see illustration 6.4).**

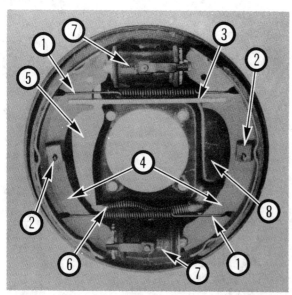

6.4　Assembled view of the rear drum brake assembly (early style)

1　Retracting spring	*5　Parking brake lever*
2　Hold-down spring and pin	*6　Parking brake cable*
3　Parking brake strut	*7　Wheel cylinder*
4　Brake shoe	*8　Backing plate*

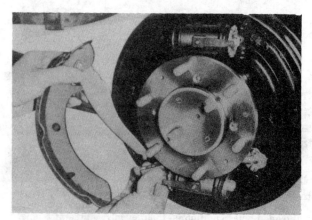

6.7　Unhook the parking brake lever from the cable end

13 Spread the tops of the shoes slightly and install the parking brake strut. Make sure the slots in the strut engage with the slots on the brake shoes.
14 Install the hold-down pins and springs.
15 Install the retractor springs.
16 Slide the brake drum over the axle flange and install the retaining screws.
17 Install the wheel and lug nuts. Adjust the brake as described in Section 7. Tighten the lug nuts to the specified torque.
18 Repeat the operation on the other wheel.
19 Road test the vehicle carefully before placing it into normal service.

Later style (leading/trailing type) (except 4WD models)
Refer to illustration 6.20

20 Remove the brake shoe return springs (see illustration).
21 Remove the front hold-down spring and pin. This is accomplished by grasping the spring with a pair of pliers, pushing down and rotating it 90 degrees, disengaging it from the pin. Place a finger behind the pin to prevent it from being pushed out.
22 Remove the leading brake shoe and parking brake pushrod.
23 Remove the trailing shoe hold down-spring and pin.
24 Remove the trailing brake shoe from the backing plate and discon-

nect the parking brake cable from the parking brake lever.
25 Perform Steps 7 through 11 of this Section.
26 Lubricate the brake shoe contact areas on the backing plate with high temperature grease. Install the parking brake lever to the new trailing shoe.
27 Connect the parking brake cable to the parking brake lever and position the trailing shoe against the backing plate. Install the hold-down pin and spring.
28 Install the adjuster pawl lever and spring to the new leading shoe. Lubricate the adjuster screw on the parking brake pushrod and install the non-threaded end of the pushrod to its slot on the trailing shoe.
29 Place the leading shoe against the backing plate, making sure that the slot in the parking brake pushrod slips into the slot on the shoe. Install the hold-down pin and spring.
30 Install the return springs.
31 Wiggle the brake shoe assembly to center it on the backing plate. Make sure the tops of the shoes are seated in the slots of the wheel cylinder pushrods and the bottoms of the shoes are resting under the tabs of the anchor plate.
32 Install the brake drum and wheel. Adjust the shoes as described in Section 7. Don't forget to tighten the lug nuts to the specified torque. Repeat the operation on the other wheel, then road test the vehicle carefully before placing it into normal service.

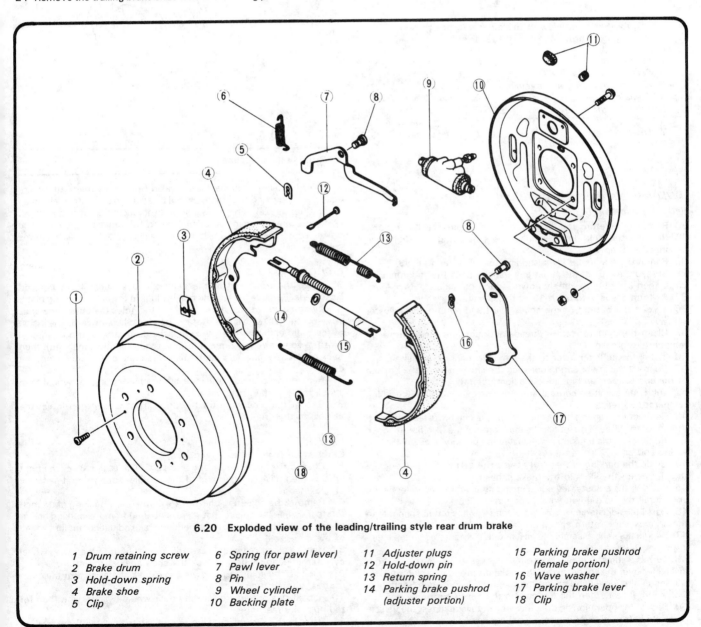

6.20 Exploded view of the leading/trailing style rear drum brake

1 Drum retaining screw	6 Spring (for pawl lever)	11 Adjuster plugs	15 Parking brake pushrod
2 Brake drum	7 Pawl lever	12 Hold-down pin	(female portion)
3 Hold-down spring	8 Pin	13 Return spring	16 Wave washer
4 Brake shoe	9 Wheel cylinder	14 Parking brake pushrod	17 Parking brake lever
5 Clip	10 Backing plate	(adjuster portion)	18 Clip

9

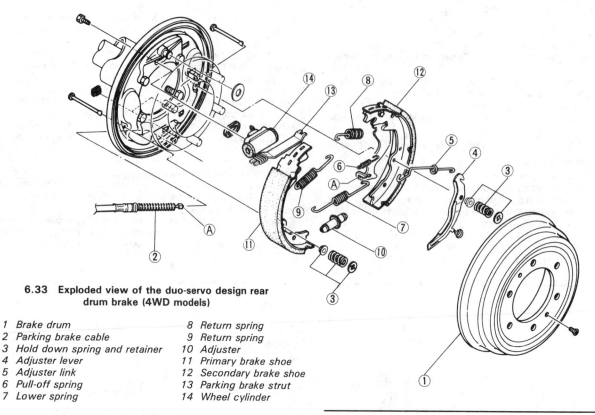

6.33 Exploded view of the duo-servo design rear drum brake (4WD models)

1 *Brake drum*
2 *Parking brake cable*
3 *Hold down spring and retainer*
4 *Adjuster lever*
5 *Adjuster link*
6 *Pull-off spring*
7 *Lower spring*

8 *Return spring*
9 *Return spring*
10 *Adjuster*
11 *Primary brake shoe*
12 *Secondary brake shoe*
13 *Parking brake strut*
14 *Wheel cylinder*

4WD models (duo-servo design)

Refer to illustration 6.33

33 Remove the return springs from the anchor pin **(see illustration)**.
34 Remove the hold-down springs and pins using the technique described in Step 21.
35 Remove the adjuster lever and link **(see illustration 6.33)**.
36 Spread the tops of the shoes apart and remove the parking brake strut, then slide the assembly down around the axle.
37 Perform Steps 7 through 10 of this Section.
38 Spread the bottom of the shoes apart and remove the adjuster screw.
39 Clean the adjuster screw threads and lubricate them with high temperature grease.
40 Install the adjuster lever to the new secondary brake shoe.
41 Connect the lower spring between the shoes, spread the bottom of the shoes apart and install the adjuster screw.
42 Lubricate the shoe contact areas on the backing plate with high temperature grease.
43 Connect the parking brake cable to the parking brake lever. Spread the top of the shoes and maneuver them around the axle flange, positioning them on the backing plate. Install the primary shoe hold-down spring and pin.
44 Guide the parking brake strut behind the axle flange and engage the slots with the slots in the brake shoes.
45 Position the adjuster lever and spring against the secondary shoe and install the hold-down spring and pin.
46 Install the adjuster lever link and secondary shoe return spring, then the primary shoe return spring.
47 Wiggle the shoe assembly to ensure that it is centered on the backing plate.
48 Turn the adjuster screw in or out as necessary, so the brake drum just slides over the shoes. Install the brake drum and retaining screws.
49 Install the wheel and adjust the shoes as described in Section 7. Don't forget to tighten the lug nuts to the specified torque.
50 Repeat the operation on the other wheel, then road test the vehicle carefully before placing it into normal service.

7 Drum brake adjustment

1 In order to maintain maximum braking efficiency the front (where equipped) and rear drum brakes should be adjusted at the intervals given in the Routine Maintenance Section at the beginning of this manual. Perform the adjustment procedure when the brakes are cold, since brakes which are adjusted to hot drums will tend to bind as the drums cool down.

Front brakes

2 Raise the front end of the vehicle and support it securely on jackstands. Remove the adjusting hole plugs in the brake backing plate.
3 Insert a screwdriver through one of the holes to contact the star-wheel of the wheel cylinder. Rotate the star-wheel towards the inside of the drum until the brake shoe hits the drum (try to turn the tire — when it won't turn any more, the shoe is sufficiently expanded), then back off six to eight notches to give clearance of the shoe from the drum.
4 Repeat this procedure for the other adjuster on that wheel then install the adjusting hole covers.
5 Repeat the procedure for the other front wheel then lower the vehicle to the ground.

Rear brakes

Early style (two wheel cylinders)
6 Check to see that the parking brake is fully released. Block the front wheels then raise the rear end of the vehicle, supporting it securely on jackstands.
7 Remove the adjusting hole covers in the brake backing plate then rotate the wheel to ensure that there is no drag from the parking brake. If there is any drag, back off the parking brake adjusting nut just ahead of the equalizer.
8 Using a screwdriver or brake adjusting tool, turn the lower wheel cylinder adjusting wheel to lock the shoe against the drum.
9 Back off the adjusting screw six to eight notches so that the drum rotates without drag.
10 Repeat this procedure for the upper wheel cylinder and then for the opposite rear wheel.
11 After both rear brakes have been adjusted, install the adjusting

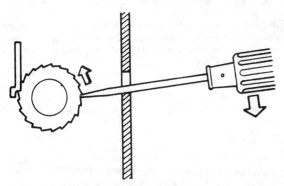

7.15a   Insert a screwdriver through the hole in the backing plate and turn the adjuster star wheel in the direction shown until the brake shoes drag on the drum . . .

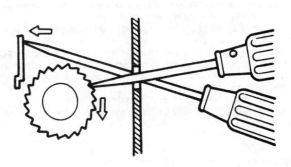

7.15b   . . . then, using another screwdriver, push the pawl lever off the adjuster wheel and back it off 8 to 10 clicks

hole covers, If the parking brake adjusting nut was loosened, refer to Section 13 for the parking brake adjustment procedure.

12 Lower the vehicle to the ground and test drive the car to check for proper brake operation.

Later styles (all)

Refer to illustrations 7.15a and 7.15b

Note: *These rear brakes are self adjusting and require a manual adjustment only after replacement of the brake shoes.*

13 Check to see that the parking brake is fully released. Block the front wheels then raise the rear end of the vehicle, supporting it securely on jackstands.

14 Remove the adjusting hole covers in the brake backing plate then rotate the wheel to ensure that there is no drag from the parking brake. If there is any drag, back off the parking brake adjusting nut just ahead of the equalizer.

15 Using a screwdriver inserted through the correct hole (the slotted hole on two-wheel drive models and the rearmost hole on 4x4 models), turn the adjuster star-wheel until the drum is locked in place **(see illustration)**. Now, back off the star-wheel 8 to 10 notches so that the drum rotates freely. To accomplish this it will be necessary to disengage the pawl lever from the star wheel by inserting a thin screwdriver or punch through the other hole in the backing plate, pushing the pawl off the wheel **(see illustration)**.

16 Adjust the parking brake if necessary, referring to Section 13.

17 Lower the vehicle and road test it for proper braking operation before placing it into normal service.

8   Wheel cylinder — removal, overhaul and installation

Refer to illustrations 8.7a and 8.7b

Note: *If an overhaul is indicated (usually because of fluid leakage or sticky operation) explore all options before beginning the job. New wheel cylinders are available, which make this job quite easy. If it's decided to rebuild the wheel cylinder, make sure that a rebuild kit is available before proceeding. Never overhaul only one wheel cylinder — always rebuild both of them at the same time.*

Removal

1   Raise the vehicle and support it securely on jackstands. Block the wheels to keep the vehicle from rolling.

2   Remove the brake shoe assembly (Section 5 or 6).

3   Remove all dirt and foreign material from around the wheel cylinder.

4   Disconnect the brake line using a flare nut wrench. Don't pull the brake line away from the wheel cylinder.

5   Remove the wheel cylinder mounting bolts.

6   Detach the wheel cylinder from the brake backing plate and place it on a clean workbench. Immediately plug the brake line to prevent fluid loss and contamination.

Overhaul

7   Remove the bleeder screw, piston cups, pistons, boots and spring assembly from the wheel cylinder body **(see illustrations)**.

9

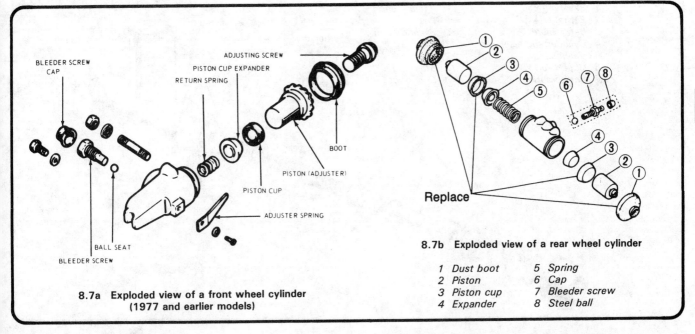

8.7a   Exploded view of a front wheel cylinder (1977 and earlier models)

8.7b   Exploded view of a rear wheel cylinder

1 Dust boot	5 Spring
2 Piston	6 Cap
3 Piston cup	7 Bleeder screw
4 Expander	8 Steel ball

8   Clean the wheel cylinder with brake fluid, denatured alcohol or brake system cleaner. **Warning:** *Do not, under any circumstances, use petroleum based solvents to clean brake parts!*
9   Use compressed air to remove excess fluid from the wheel cylinder and to blow out the passages.
10 Check the cylinder bore for corrosion and score marks. Crocus cloth can be used to remove light corrosion and stains, but the cylinder must be replaced with a new one if the defects cannot be removed easily, or if the bore is scored.
11 Lubricate the new seals with brake fluid.
12 Assemble the brake cylinder components. Make sure the seal lips face in.

Installation

13 Place the wheel cylinder in position and install the bolts.
14 Connect the brake line and install the brake shoe assembly.
15 Bleed the brakes (Section 11).

---

9   Master cylinder — removal, overhaul and installation

Refer to illustrations 9.10, 9.11a, 9.11b and 9.14

Note: *This procedure describes a dual master cylinder overhaul, although it also applies to the older, single piston models. Simply ignore the steps which do not apply, and refer to the appropriate exploded view illustration. Before deciding to overhaul the master cylinder, check on the availability and cost of a new or factory rebuilt unit and also the availability of a rebuild kit.*

Removal

1   The master cylinder is located in the engine compartment, mounted to the power brake booster.
2   Remove as much fluid as you can from the reservoir with a syringe.
3   Place rags under the fluid fittings and prepare caps or plastic bags to cover the ends of the lines once they are disconnected. **Caution:** *Brake fluid will damage paint. Cover all body parts and be careful not to spill fluid during this procedure.*
4   Loosen the tube nuts at the ends of the brake lines where they enter the master cylinder. To prevent rounding off the flats on these

nuts, the use of a flare nut wrench, which wraps around the nut, is preferred.
5   Pull the brake lines slightly away from the master cylinder and plug the ends to prevent contamination. On vehicles with a remotely mounted fluid reservoir, disconnect the feed hoses at the master cylinder and plug them.
6   Disconnect the electrical connector at the master cylinder (if equipped), then remove the nuts attaching the master cylinder to the power booster or firewall. Pull the master cylinder off the studs and out of the engine compartment. Again, be careful not to spill the fluid as this is done.

Overhaul

7   Before attempting the overhaul of the master cylinder, obtain the proper rebuild kit, which will contain the necessary replacement parts and also any instructions which may be specific to your model.
8   Inspect the reservoir or inlet grommet(s) for indications of leakage near the base of the reservoir (except fixed reservoir style). Remove the reservoir.
9   Place the cylinder in a vise and use a punch or Phillips screwdriver to fully depress the pistons until they bottom against the other end of the master cylinder. Hold the pistons in this position and remove the stop bolt on the side of the master cylinder. Remove the two outlet plugs and the copper gaskets.

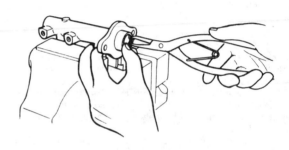

9.10   Push the pistons into the bore and remove the snap-ring

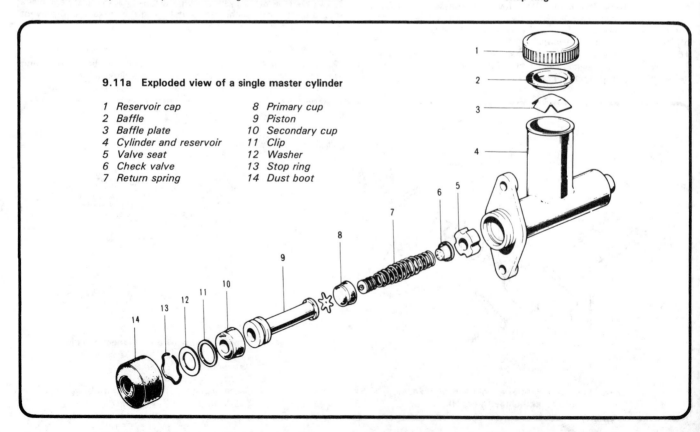

9.11a   Exploded view of a single master cylinder

1 Reservoir cap	8 Primary cup
2 Baffle	9 Piston
3 Baffle plate	10 Secondary cup
4 Cylinder and reservoir	11 Clip
5 Valve seat	12 Washer
6 Check valve	13 Stop ring
7 Return spring	14 Dust boot

10 Depress the pistons once again, then carefully remove the snapring at the end of the master cylinder **(see illustration)**.

11 The internal components can now be removed from the cylinder bore **(see illustrations)**. Make a note of the proper order of the components so they can be returned to their original locations. **Note:** *The two springs are of different tension, so pay particular attention to their order.*

12 Carefully inspect the bore of the master cylinder. Any deep scoring or other damage will mean a new master cylinder is required.

13 Replace all parts included in the rebuild kit, following any instructions in the kit. Clean all reused parts with clean brake fluid or denatured alcohol. Do not use any petroleum-based cleaners. During assembly, lubricate all parts liberally with clean brake fluid. Be sure to tighten all fittings and connections to the specified torque.

14 Install a guide pin (such as the blunt end of a drill bit) into the stop bolt hole **(see illustration)**. Push the assembled components into the bore, bottoming them against the end of the master cylinder. Remove the guide pin and install the stop bolt.

15 Install the new snap-ring, making sure it is seated properly in the groove.

16 Before installing the new master cylinder it should be bench bled. Because it will be necessary to apply pressure to the master cylinder piston and, at the same time, control flow from the brake line outlets, it is recommended that the master cylinder be mounted in a vise, with the jaws of the vise clamping on the mounting flange.

17 Insert threaded plugs into the brake line outlet holes and snug them down so that there will be no air leakage past them, but not so tight that they cannot be easily loosened.

18 Fill the reservoir with brake fluid of the recommended type (see Chapter 1).

19 Remove one plug and push the piston assembly into the master cylinder bore to expell the air from the master cylinder. A large Phillips screwdriver can be used to push on the piston assembly.

20 To prevent air from being drawn back into the master cylinder the plug must be replaced and snugged down before releasing the pressure on the piston assembly.

21 Repeat the procedure until only brake fluid is expelled from the brake line outlet hole. When only brake fluid is expelled, repeat the procedure with the other outlet hole and plug. Be sure to keep the master cylinder reservoir filled with brake fluid to prevent the introduction of air into the system.

22 Since high pressure is not involved in the bench bleeding procedure, an alternative to the removal and replacement of the plugs with each stroke of the piston assembly is available. Before pushing in on the piston assembly, remove the plug as described in Step 19. Before releasing the piston, however, instead of replacing the plug, simply put your finger tightly over the hole to keep air from being drawn back into the master cylinder. Wait several seconds for brake fluid to be drawn from the reservoir into the piston bore, then depress the piston again, removing your finger as brake fluid is expelled. Be sure to put your finger back over the hole each time before releasing the piston, and when the bleeding procedure is complete for that outlet, replace the plug and snug it before going on to the other port.

Installation

23 Install the master cylinder over the studs on the power brake booster and tighten the attaching nuts only finger tight at this time.

24 Thread the brake line fittings into the master cylinder. Since the master cylinder is still a bit loose, it can be moved slightly in order for the fittings to thread in easily. Do not strip the threads as the fittings are tightened.

25 Fully tighten the mounting nuts and the brake fittings.

26 Fill the master cylinder reservoir with fluid, then bleed the master cylinder (only if the cylinder has not been bench bled) and the brake system as described in Section 11. To bleed the cylinder on the vehicle, have an assistant pump the brake pedal several times and then hold the pedal to the floor. Loosen the fitting nut to allow air and fluid to escape. Repeat this procedure on both fittings until the fluid is clear of air bubbles. Test the operation of the brake system carefully before placing the vehicle in normal service.

---

10 Brake lines and hoses — inspection and replacement

---

1 About every six months the flexible hoses which connect the steel brake lines with the front and rear brakes should be inspected for cracks, chafing of the outer cover, leaks, blisters, and other damage (see Chapter 1).

2 Replacement steel and flexible brake lines are commonly available from dealer parts departments and auto parts stores. Do not, under any circumstances, use anything other than genuine steel lines or approved flexible brake hoses as replacement items.

3 When installing the brake line, leave at least 0.75 in (19 mm) clearance between the line and any moving or vibrating parts.

4 When disconnecting a hose and line, first remove the spring clip. Then, using a normal wrench to hold the hose and a flare-nut wrench to hold the tube, make the disconnection. Use the wrenches in the

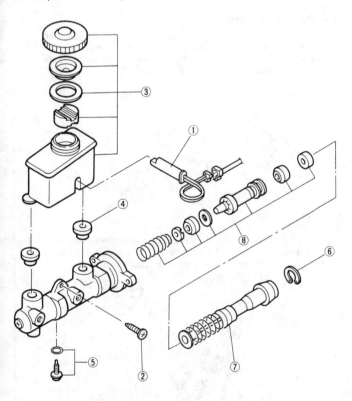

9.11b Exploded view of a dual master cylinder

1 *Fluid level sensor*	5 *Stop bolt*
2 *Screw*	6 *Snap-ring*
3 *Reservoir assembly*	7 *Primary piston assembly*
4 *Grommets*	8 *Secondary piston assembly*

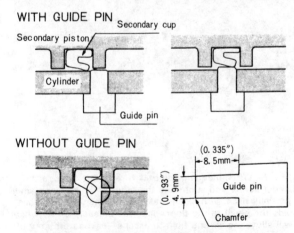

9.14 When installing the secondary piston assembly, install a guide pin into the stop bolt hole to keep the piston cup from catching on the edge of the hole

9

same manner when making a connection, then install a new clip. **Note:** *Make sure the tube passes through the center of its grommet.*

5   When disconnecting two hoses, use normal wrenches on the hose fittings. When connecting two hoses, make sure they are not bent, twisted or strained.

6   Steel brake lines are usually retained along their span with clips. Always remove these clips completely before removing a fixed brake line. Always reinstall these clips, or new ones if the old ones are damaged, when replacing a brake line, as they provide support and keep the lines from vibrating, which can eventually break them.

7   Remember to bleed the hydraulic system after replacing a hose or line.

11   Brake system — bleeding

Refer to illustration 11.7

1   If the brake system has air in it, operation of the brake pedal will be spongy and imprecise. Air can enter the brake system whenever any part of the system is dismantled or if the fluid level in the master cylinder reservoir runs low. Air can also leak into the system through a leak too slight to allow fluid to leak out. In this case, it indicates that a general overhaul of the brake system is required.

2   To bleed the brakes, you will need an assistant to pump the brake pedal, a supply of new brake fluid, an empty glass jar, a plastic or vinyl tube which will fit over the bleeder nipple, and a wrench for the bleeder screw.

3   There are five locations at which the brake system is bled; the master cylinder, the front brake calipers (or wheel cylinders) and the rear brake wheel cylinders. On later models, the rear brakes are bled at the left rear wheel cylinder only (there is no bleeder screw on the right side).

4   Check the fluid level at the master cylinder reservoir. Add fluid, if necessary, to bring the level up to the Full or Max mark. Use only the recommended brake fluid and do not mix different types. Never use fluid from a container that has been standing uncapped. You will have to check the fluid level in the master cylinder reservoir often during the bleed procedure. If the level drops too far, air will enter the system through the master cylinder.

5   Raise the vehicle and set it securely on jackstands.

6   Remove the bleeder screw cap from the wheel cylinder or caliper assembly that is being bled. If more than one wheel must be bled, start with the one farthest from the master cylinder.

7   Attach one end of the clear plastic or vinyl tube to the bleeder screw nipple and place the other end in the glass or plastic jar submerged in a small amount of clean brake fluid **(see illustration)**.

8   Loosen the bleeder screw slightly, then tighten it to the point where it is snug yet easily loosened.

9   Have the asistant pump the brake pedal several times and hold it in the fully depressed position.

10   With pressure on the brake pedal, open the bleeder screw approximately one-half turn. As the brake fluid is flowing through the pedal, hold it in the fully depressed position, and loosen the bleeder screw momentarily. Do not allow the brake pedal to be released with the bleeder screw in the open position.

11   Repeat the procedure until no air bubbles are visible in the brake fluid flowing through the tube. Be sure to check the brake fluid level in the master cylinder reservoir while performing the bleeding operation.

12   Fully tighten the bleeder screw, remove the plastic or vinyl tube and install the bleeder screw cap.

13   Follow the same procedure to bleed the other wheel cylinder or caliper assemblies.

14   To bleed the master cylinder, have the assistant pump and hold the brake pedal. Momentarily loosen the brake line fittings, one at a time, where they attach to the master cylinder. Any air in the master cylinder will escape when the fittings are loosened. Brake fluid will damage painted surfaces, so use paper towels or rags to cover and protect the areas around the master cylinder.

15   Check the brake fluid level in the master cylinder to make sure it is adequate, then test drive the vehicle and check for proper brake operation.

12   Power brake booster — check, removal and installation

Refer to illustrations 12.2, 12.3, 12.7 and 12.14

Operating check

1   Depress the brake pedal several times with the engine off and make sure that there is no change in the pedal reserve distance.

2   Depress the pedal and start the engine. If the pedal goes down slightly, operation is normal **(see illustration)**.

Air tightness check

3   Start the engine and turn it off after one or two minutes. Depress the brake pedal several times slowly. If the pedal goes down farther the first time but gradually rises after the second or third depression, the booster is air tight **(see illustration)**.

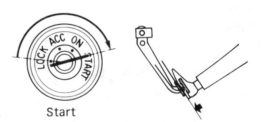

12.2   Push down on the brake pedal then start the engine — the brake pedal should go down slightly, indicating normal booster operation

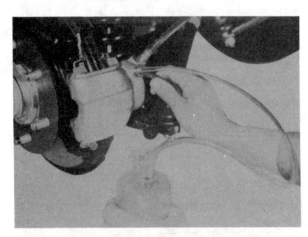

11.7   When bleeding the brakes, attach a hose to the bleeder screw and submerge the other end into a container partially filled with clean brake fluid. When the assistant holds the pedal to the floor, open the bleeder screw, which will allow the air and fluid to escape — when the flow of bubbles ceases, close the valve. Continue this process until no more air bubbles can be seen in the tube or container, then move on to the next wheel

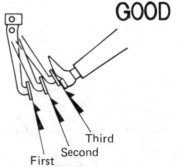

12.3   With the engine turned off, the pedal should build up with each pump if the booster is functioning properly

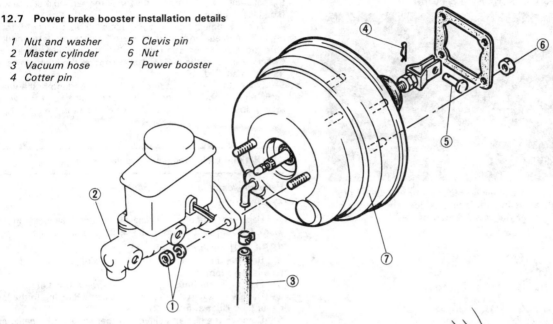

12.7   Power brake booster installation details

1   *Nut and washer*
2   *Master cylinder*
3   *Vacuum hose*
4   *Cotter pin*
5   *Clevis pin*
6   *Nut*
7   *Power booster*

4   Depress the brake pedal while the engine is running, then stop the engine with the pedal depressed. If there is no change in the pedal reserve travel after holding the pedal for 30 seconds, the booster is air tight.

Removal

5   Power brake booster units should not be disassembled. They require special tools not normally found in most automotive repair stations or shops. They are fairly complex and because of their critical relationship to brake performance it is best to replace a defective booster unit with a new or rebuilt one.
6   To remove the booster, first remove the brake master cylinder as described in Section 9.
7   Locate the pushrod clevis connecting the booster to the brake pedal **(see illustration)**. This is accessible from the interior in front of the driver's seat.
8   Remove the clevis pin retaining clip with pliers and pull out the pin.
9   Holding the clevis with pliers, disconnect the clevis locknut with a wrench. The clevis is now loose.
10 Disconnect the hose leading from the engine to the booster. Be careful not to damage the hose when removing it from the booster fitting.
11 Remove the four nuts and washers holding the brake booster to the firewall. You may need a light to see these, as they are up under the dash area.
12 Slide the booster straight out from the firewall until the studs clear the holes and pull the booster, brackets and gaskets from the engine compartment area.

Installation

13 Installation procedures are basically the reverse of those for removal. Tighten the clevis locknut and booster mounting nuts to the specified torque figures.
14 If the power booster unit is being replaced, the clearance between the master cylinder piston and the pushrod in the booster must be measured. Using a depth micrometer or vernier calipers, measure the distance from the seat (recessed area) in the master cylinder to the master cylinder mounting flange. Next, measure the distance from the end of the booster pushrod to the mounting face of the booster where the master cylinder mounting flange seats. Subtract the two measurements to get the clearance. If the clearance is more or less than specified, turn the adjusting screw on the end of the power booster pushrod until the clearance is within the specified limit **(see illustration).**

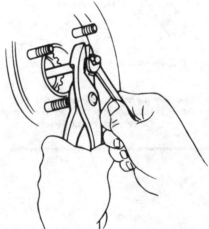

12.14   To adjust the length of the booster pushrod, hold the serrated portion of the rod with a pair of pliers and turn the adjusting screw in or out, as necessary, to achieve the desired setting

15 A second method to measure the pushrod-to-piston clearance is to install the master cylinder on the power booster with a small piece of modeling clay placed on the end of the pushrod. Remove the master cylinder and measure the resulting impression left in the clay. Again adjust as needed to meet the specification. This method may require several trial-and-error fits to reach the proper clearance.
16 After the final installation of the master cylinder and brake hoses and lines, the brake pedal height and free play must be adjusted and the system must be bled. See the appropriate Sections of this Chapter for the procedures.

---

13   Parking brake cable — adjustment

Refer to illustrations 13.3a and 13.3b

1   If the parking brake doesn't keep the vehicle from rolling when the handle is applied 5 to 10 clicks on 1984 and earlier models, or 11 to 13 clicks on later models, adjust the cable.
2   Drive the vehicle in reverse and apply the brakes a few times to

9

activate the automatic adjusters. Raise the vehicle and support it securely on jackstands. Check to see that the brake shoes are not dragging on the drums as the wheels are turned. If they do drag, back off the adjuster wheels as described in Section 7.

13.3a   On 1984 and earlier models, the parking brake cable adjusting nut is located just ahead of the equalizer (arrow)

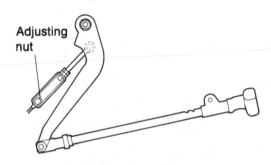

13.3b   The parking brake cable adjusting nut on 1986 and later models is located near the top of the parking brake lever, above the handle

3   Locate the cable adjusting nut for your particular model. On 1984 and earlier models, the adjusting nut is located at the cable equalizer (where the front and rear cables meet). On 1986 and later models, the adjusting nut is located at the top of the parking brake handle linkage (see illustrations).

4   Turn the adjusting nut to provide a handle travel of 5 to 10 clicks on 1984 and earlier models or 11 to 13 clicks on later models. Make sure the rear brakes don't drag when the parking brake is released. Check to see that the parking brake light on the dash glows when the handle is applied.

5   Lower the vehicle and verify that the parking brake will hold the vehicle on a moderate incline. If it still won't keep the vehicle from rolling, inspect the rear brakes as described in Chapter 1.

14   Parking brake cable(s) — replacement

Refer to illustrations 14.2 and 14.8

Front cable

1   Raise the front of the vehicle and support it securely on jackstands. Block the rear wheels and release the parking brake.

1984 and earlier models

2   Remove the clip and pin at the fork joint just ahead of the equalizer (see illustration).

3   Pry the cable housing out of the frame bracket.

4   Remove the clip that secures the cable housing to the lower dash panel (see illustration 14.2).

5   Remove the clip and clevis pin that secures the cable end to the lever, then remove the cable through the lower dash panel.

6   Installation is the reverse of the removal procedure. After the job is completed, adjust the cable following the procedure descibed in Section 13.

1986 and later models

7   Remove the cable adjuster nut (see illustration 13.3b).

8   From under the vehicle, disconnect the two rear cables from the equalizer by turning them 90º, aligning the cables with the slots in the equalizer and passing them through (see illustration).

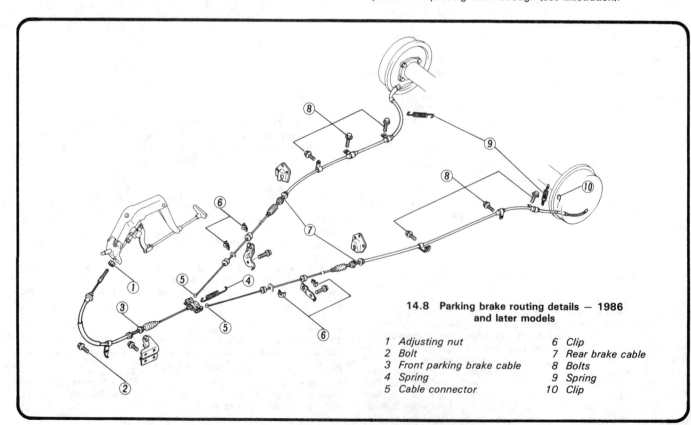

14.8   Parking brake routing details — 1986 and later models

1 *Adjusting nut*	6	*Clip*
2 *Bolt*	7	*Rear brake cable*
3 *Front parking brake cable*	8	*Bolts*
4 *Spring*	9	*Spring*
5 *Cable connector*	10	*Clip*

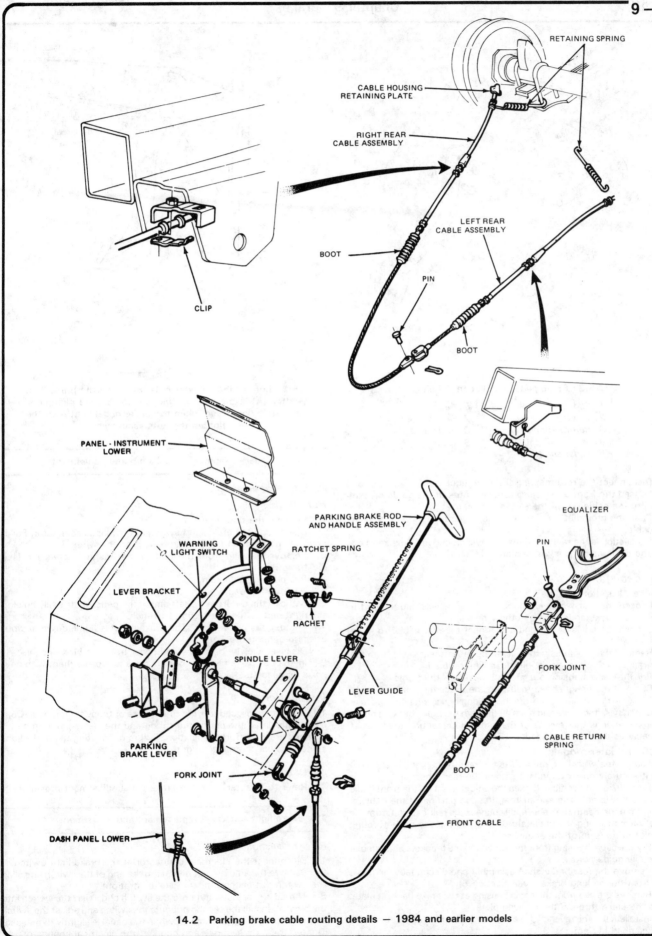

RETAINING SPRING

CABLE HOUSING
RETAINING PLATE

RIGHT REAR
CABLE ASSEMBLY

LEFT REAR
CABLE ASSEMBLY

BOOT

PIN

BOOT

CLIP

PANEL - INSTRUMENT
LOWER

EQUALIZER

PARKING BRAKE ROD
AND HANDLE ASSEMBLY

WARNING
LIGHT SWITCH

RATCHET SPRING

PIN

LEVER BRACKET

RACHET

SPINDLE LEVER

LEVER GUIDE

FORK JOINT

PARKING
BRAKE LEVER

CABLE RETURN
SPRING

FORK JOINT

BOOT

DASH PANEL LOWER

FRONT CABLE

9

14.2 Parking brake cable routing details — 1984 and earlier models

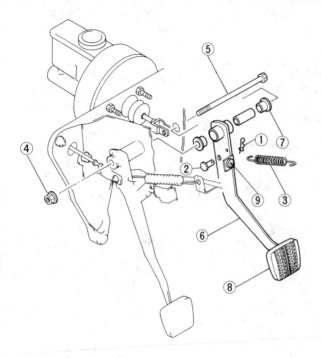

15.3   Brake pedal installation details

1 Clip	6 Pedal
2 Clevis pin	7 Bushing
3 Return spring	8 Pedal pad
4 Nut	9 Stop
5 Pedal shaft	

9   Disconnect the return spring from the equalizer.
10   Loosen the front brake cable retaining nuts at the guide bracket then pry the cable out of the slot in the bracket.
11   Push the grommet through the hole in the floorpan and remove the cable.
12   Installation is the reverse of the removal procedure. Be sure to adjust the cable as outlined in Section 13.

Rear cable(s)

1984 and earlier models
13   Loosen the rear wheel lug nuts, raise the vehicle and support it securely on jackstands. Remove the wheel(s).
14   Loosen the adjuster nut and disconnect the rear cable from the equalizer.
15   Remove the clip and pin then separate the left rear cable from the right rear cable at the clevis joint **(see illustration 14.2)**.
16   Pry the cable housing out of the bracket on the frame.
17   Remove the brake shoes following the procedure in Section 6.
18   Disconnect the cable end from the parking brake lever on the brake shoe, then pass the cable and housing through the brake backing plate.
19   Installation is the reverse of the removal procedure, then adjust the cable as described in Section 13.

1986 and later models
20   Loosen the wheel lug nuts, raise the rear of the vehicle and support it securely on jackstands. Remove the rear wheel(s).
21   From inside the vehicle, loosen the adjuster nut on the front cable until the nut is near the end of the threaded portion of the cable.
22   From underneath the vehicle, disconnect the rear cable(s) from the equalizer by turning the cable(s) 90º and passing the cable through the slot in the side of the equalizer.
23   Pry the cable housing from the various frame brackets and remove the cable guide bolts.
24   Remove the rear brake shoe assembly and disconnect the cable end from the parking brake lever (Section 6).
25   Remove the clip from the cable housing at the brake backing plate. Pass the cable through the backing plate.
26   Installation is the reverse of the removal procedure. Adjust the cable as described in Section 13.

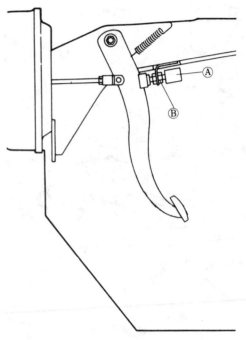

16.2   Loosen the adjuster nuts (B), move the brake light switch (A) in the desired direction so that the plunger is completely depressed when the brake pedal is at rest, then tighten the nuts securely

15   Brake pedal — removal, installation and adjustment

Refer to illustration 15.3
Removal

1   Remove the floor mat.
2   Disconnect the brake light switch at the plastic connector. Pull it apart at the junction rather than pulling on the wires.
3   Remove the clip from the end of the pushrod clevis pin **(see illustration)**.
4   Pull out the clevis pin.
5   Remove the pedal return spring.
6   Remove the nut from the left end of the pedal shaft while holding the right end of the shaft with a wrench.
7   Remove the pedal shaft. The brake pedal will pull down and out of the mounting bracket.
8   Disassemble the bushings and collar from the brake pedal.
9   Inspect all parts for wear or damage and replace them with new parts as needed.

Installation

10   Installation procedures are the reverse of those for removal. Coat all the bushings, the collar, the spring and the clevis pin with multipurpose grease before installation. Before connecting the brake light switch, adjust the pedal height.

Adjustment

11   Refer to Chapter 1 for the brake pedal adjustment procedure.

16   Brake light switch — replacement and adjustment

Refer to illustration 16.2

1   Disconnect the electrical connector at the brake light switch.
2   Remove the adjuster nut nearest to the end of the switch and slide the switch out of the bracket **(see illustration)**.
3   Thread one adjuster nut onto the switch and insert the switch into the bracket. Install the second nut onto the switch and adjust the switch so that the brake lights come on when the pedal is slightly depressed. Tighten the nuts securely and connect the electrical connector.

Chapter 10 Suspension and steering systems

Contents

Specifications

Torque specifications

Front suspension

	Ft-lbs
Upper balljoint-to-steering knuckle	
1984 and earlier	51 to 65
1986 and later	22 to 38
Upper balljoint-to-upper arm	14 to 20
Lower balljoint-to-steering knuckle	
1984 and earlier	51 to 65
1986 and later	87 to 116
Lower balljoint-to-lower arm	60 to 70
Upper arm pivot shaft-to-frame	
2WD	54 to 68
4WD	69 to 83
Lower arm pivot shaft-to-frame (1984 and earlier)	54 to 69
Lower arm pivot bolt(s)	
2WD and 4WD front bolt	87 to 116
4WD rear bolt	115 to 145
Torque plate-to-lower arm.........................	55 to 69
Tension rod-to-lower arm	69 to 86
Knuckle arm-to-knuckle	59 to 74

Rear suspension

Hanger pin nut	62 to 76
Hanger pin-to-frame bracket	14 to 18
Shackle pin nuts.................................	43 to 58
U-Bolt nuts	46 to 58

10

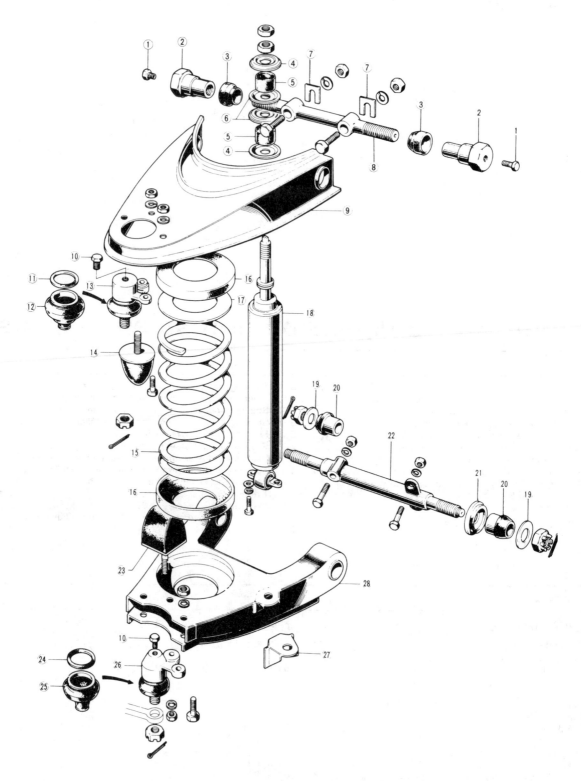

1.1a Exploded view of the front suspension components — coil spring type (1984 and earlier models)

1	Plug	8	Upper arm shaft	15	Coil spring	22	Lower arm shaft
2	Threaded bushing	9	Upper arm	16	Seat	23	Bump stop
3	Dust seal	10	Plug	17	Adjusting plate	24	Set ring
4	Concave washer	11	Set ring	18	Shock absorber	25	Seal
5	Bushing	12	Seal	19	Washer	26	Balljoint
6	Concave washer	13	Balljoint	20	Bushing	27	Bracket
7	Shim	14	Bump stop	21	Stopper	28	Lower arm

Steering

Steering gear-to-frame	33 to 41
Flexible coupling-to-steering gear pinch bolt	22 to 38
Pitman arm-to-steering gear nut	108 to 130
Idler arm-to-frame	
1984 and earlier	33 to 41
1986 and later	46 to 69
Tie-rod ends-to-center link	
1984 and earlier	18 to 25
1986 and later	33 to 43
Tie-rod ends-to-steering knuckle	
1984 and earlier	21 to 28
1986 and later	33 to 43
Center link-to-Pitman arm	
1984 and earlier	21 to 28
1986 and later	33 to 43
Center link-to-idler arm	
1975 and earlier	33 to 47
1976 thru 1984	36 to 58
1986 and later	33 to 43
Steering wheel nut	
1984 and earlier	22 to 29
1986 and later	29 to 36

Wheel lug nuts

1981 and earlier	58 to 65
1982 thru 1984	
Standard wheels	72 to 80
Styled wheels	87 to 94
1986 and later	87 to 108

---

1 General information

Refer to illustrations 1.1a, 1.1b, 1.1c, 1.2a and 1.2b

Warning: *Whenever any of the suspension or steering fasteners are loosened or removed, they must be inspected, and if necessary, replaced with new ones of the same part number or of original equipment quality and design. Torque specifications must be followed for proper reassembly and component retention. Never attempt to heat, straighten or weld any suspension or steering component. Instead, replace any bent or damaged part with a new one. Also, since most of the pro-* cedures involve jacking up the vehicle, be sure to support the vehicle securely on jackstands. If there is any doubt as to where to place them, refer to the Jacking and towing section at the front of this book.

The front suspension on the vehicles covered by this manual is an independent type, made up of upper and lower control arms, coil springs (1984 and earlier models) or torsion bars (1986 and later models), ball-joint mounted steering knuckles and shock absorbers **(see illustrations)**. Some models are equipped with a stabilizer bar to limit body roll during cornering. Four wheel drive models use the same basic arrangement, but with the necessary modifications to accomodate the driveaxles.

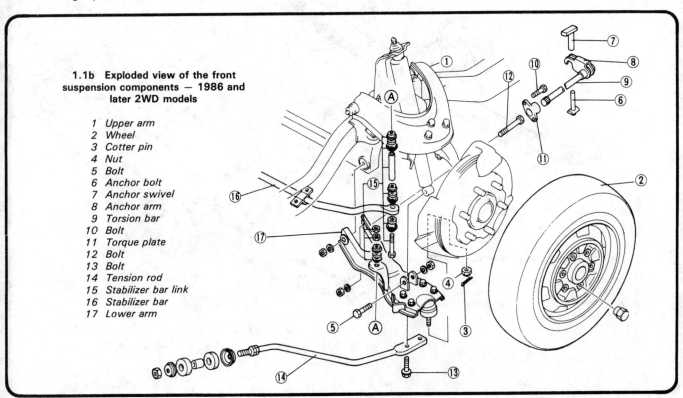

1.1b Exploded view of the front suspension components — 1986 and later 2WD models

1 Upper arm
2 Wheel
3 Cotter pin
4 Nut
5 Bolt
6 Anchor bolt
7 Anchor swivel
8 Anchor arm
9 Torsion bar
10 Bolt
11 Torque plate
12 Bolt
13 Bolt
14 Tension rod
15 Stabilizer bar link
16 Stabilizer bar
17 Lower arm

10

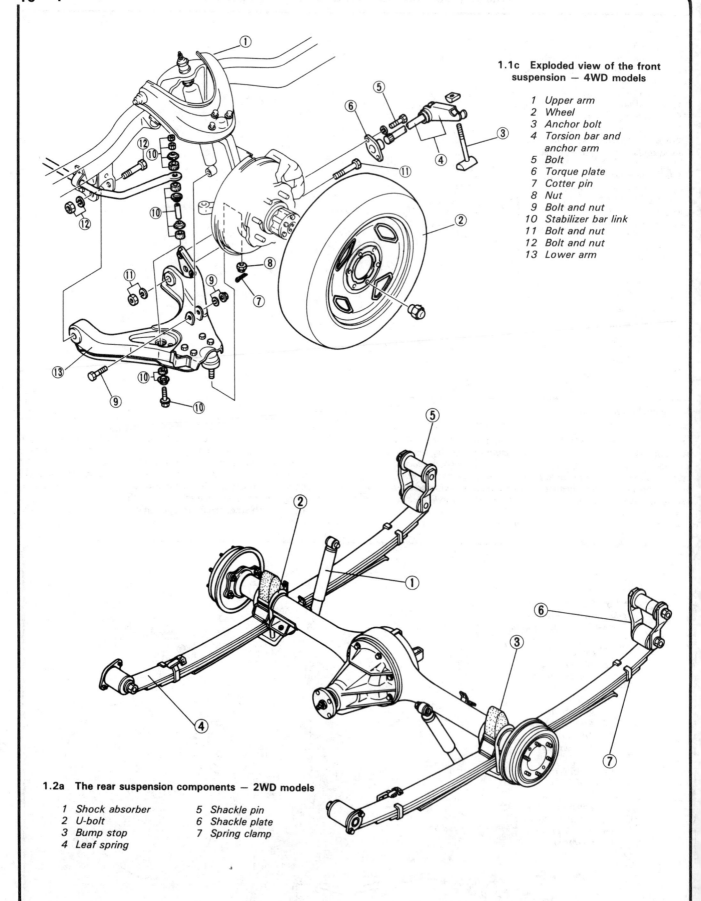

1 Upper arm
2 Wheel
3 Anchor bolt
4 Torsion bar and anchor arm
5 Bolt
6 Torque plate
7 Cotter pin
8 Nut
9 Bolt and nut
10 Stabilizer bar link
11 Bolt and nut
12 Bolt and nut
13 Lower arm

1.2a The rear suspension components — 2WD models

1 Shock absorber
2 U-bolt
3 Bump stop
4 Leaf spring
5 Shackle pin
6 Shackle plate
7 Spring clamp

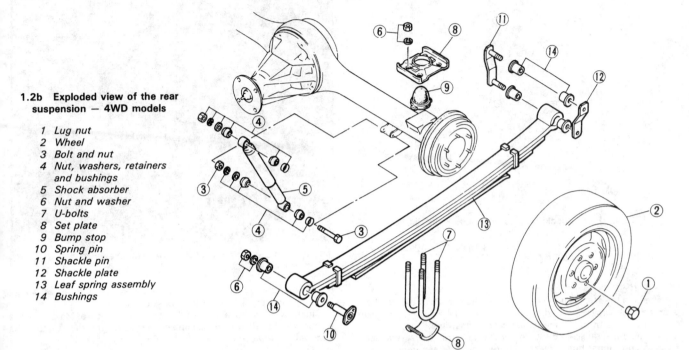

1.2b Exploded view of the rear suspension — 4WD models

1 Lug nut
2 Wheel
3 Bolt and nut
4 Nut, washers, retainers and bushings
5 Shock absorber
6 Nut and washer
7 U-bolts
8 Set plate
9 Bump stop
10 Spring pin
11 Shackle pin
12 Shackle plate
13 Leaf spring assembly
14 Bushings

The rear suspension consists of the rear axle housing, leaf springs and shock absorbers **(see illustrations)**. Information regarding axles and the rear axle housing can be found in Chapter 8.

The steering system is composed of a steering column, steering gear, center link, idler arm and two tie-rod assemblies. Some models feature power assisted steering, which includes a belt-driven pump and associated hoses to provide hydraulic pressure to the steering gear.

2 Front stabilizer bar — removal and installation

Refer to illustrations 2.2a and 2.2b

Removal

1 Raise the vehicle and support it securely on jackstands. Apply the parking brake.

2 Remove the stabilizer bar-to-lower control arm nuts and bolts, noting how the spacers, washers and bushings are positioned **(see illustrations)**.

3 Remove the stabilizer bar bracket bolts and detach the bar from the vehicle.

4 Pull the brackets off the stabilizer bar and inspect the bushings for cracks, hardening and other signs of deterioration. If the bushings are damaged, replace them.

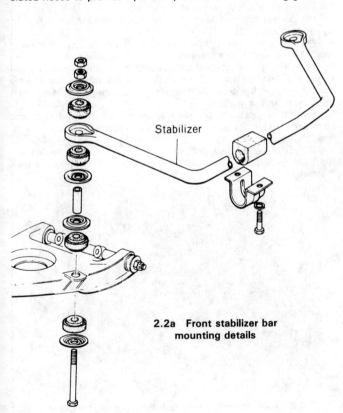

2.2a Front stabilizer bar mounting details

2.2b Stabilizer bar and control arm details

10

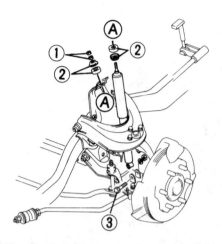

3.3a   Front shock absorber installation details

1   Nuts   *3   Lower mounting bolt*
2   Washers and bushings

Installation

5   Position the stabilizer bar bushings on the bar. Push the brackets over the bushings and raise the bar up to the frame. Install the bracket bolts but don't tighten them completely at this time.
6   Install the stabilizer bar-to-lower control arm bolts, washers, spacers and rubber bushings and tighten the nuts securely.
7   Tighten the bracket bolts.

3   Front shock absorber — removal and installation

Refer to illustrations 3.3a, 3.3b and 3.5

1   Jack up the front of the vehicle and place it securely on jackstands.
2   Remove the front wheels.
3   Remove the nut(s) holding the shock absorber to the frame **(see illustrations)**. Clamp a pair of locking pliers to the flats at the top of the shock rod to prevent it from turning.
4   Remove the washers and the cushions from the shaft of the shock absorber.
5   Disconnect the shock from the lower arm by removing the two bolts (1984 and earlier models) or the single through bolt (1986 and later models) **(see illustration)**.
6   Fully compress the shock absorber.
7   Tilt the shock forward, turn it 90 degrees so the bushing is at right angles to the vehicle and pull it out.

3.5   The lower end of the front shock absorber — late model with a single securing bolt (arrow)

3.3b   The top of the front shock absorber

8   Inspect the shock components for wear, damage or oil leaks. Replace parts as necessary with new ones.
9   Installation is the reverse of the removal procedure. Make sure the washers and bushings are assembled in the proper order. Tighten the bolts and nuts securely.

4   Coil spring — removal and installation

Refer to illustration 4.8

Removal

1   Loosen the wheel lug nuts, raise the vehicle and support it securely on jackstands placed under the frame. Apply the parking brake. Remove the wheel.
2   Remove the shock absorber (Section 3).
3   Disconnect the stabilizer bar from the lower control arm if so equipped (Section 2).
4   Position a jack under the spring pocket of the suspension lower arm. Make sure the jack doesn't cover up the balljoint bolts.
5   Loop a length of safety chain up through the control arm and coil spring and bolt the ends of the chain together. Make sure there's enough slack in the chain so it won't inhibit spring extension when the control arm is lowered.
6   Raise the jack slightly to relieve spring pressure from the balljoint bolts and remove the nuts and bolts. Pull the steering knuckle away from the lower arm.
7   Slowly lower the jack until the coil spring is fully extended.
8   Unbolt the safety chain and maneuver the coil spring out **(see illustration)**.

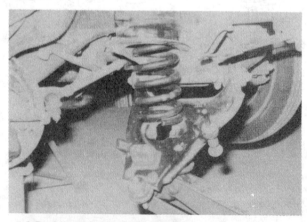

4.8   After the coil spring is fully extended, unbolt the safety chain and guide the spring out

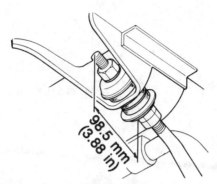

5.6 When installed, the distance from the inner washer to the end of the tension rod should be 98.5 mm

Installation

9 Place the insulators on the top and bottom of the coil spring.
10 Install the top of the spring into the spring pocket and the bottom in the lower control arm. The lower spring coil must be seated in the recessed portion of the spring seat.
11 Place the jack under the lower control arm, install the safety chain and slowly raise the control arm into place. Swing the steering knuckle and balljoint into position, then install the balljoint bolts and nuts. Tighten the nuts to the specified torque and remove the safety chain.
12 Install the shock absorber (Section 3).
13 Attach the stabilizer bar to the lower control arm (Section 2).
14 Install the wheel and lug nuts. Lower the vehicle and tighten the lug nuts to the specified torque.

5 Tension rod — removal and installation

Note: *This procedure applies to 1986 and later models only.*
Refer to illustration 5.6.

1 Raise the vehicle and support it securely on jackstands.
2 Place alignment marks on the threaded portion of the tension rod and the inner nuts. If the position of the inner nut changes, the caster setting will be affected.
3 Remove the outer nut from the tension rod.
4 Remove the bolts holding the tension rod to the lower arm and remove the tension rod.
5 Inspect the tension rod and components for wear or damage. Replace parts as necessary with new ones.
6 Installation is the reverse of the removal procedure. Make sure to first thread the inside nuts onto the tension rod and align the marks made before removal. Tighten the bolts according to the torque figures in the Specifications. Tighten the outside nut until the distance between the end of the rod and the inner washer is as specified **(see illustration)**.

6.2a The rear end of the torsion bar — note that each torsion bar is clearly marked for either the Left (L) or Right (R) side of the vehicle

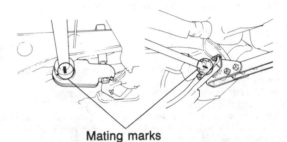

6.2b To simplify the installation and adjustment procedure, mark the relationship of the torsion bar to the anchor arm and the torque plate

6 Torsion bar — removal, installation and adjustment

Refer to illustrations 6.2a, 6.2b, 6.3a, 6.3b, 6.10 and 6.11

Removal

1 Loosen the wheel lug nuts, raise the vehicle and support it securely on jackstands. Remove the wheel.
2 Place alignment marks from the torsion bar to the anchor arm and torque plate **(see illustrations)**.
3 Place alignment marks on the threads of the anchor bolt **(see illustration)**, then remove the anchor bolt (on 4WD models, place the marks on the anchor arm and the bracket).

10

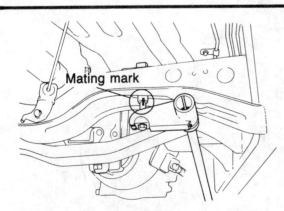

6.3a Mark the position of the anchor bolt to restore the original torsion bar setting during installation

6.3b On 4WD models, place alignment marks from the anchor arm to the bracket

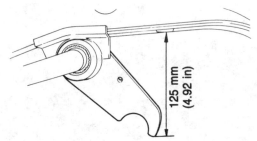

6.10 If a new torsion bar is being installed (or if the original wasn't marked), set the angle of the anchor arm to obtain a distance of 125 mm from the crossmember to the tip of the arm (2WD models)

4   Unbolt the torque plate from the suspension lower arm **(see illustration 1.1b or 1.1c)** and remove the torsion bar assembly from the vehicle.
5   Inspect the torsion bar, anchor arm and torque plate splines for damage and wear. The fit between the bar and the torque plate and anchor arm should be snug, not loose. Inspect the bar for distortion, cracks and nicks, which will cause the bar to fail prematurely.

Installation and adjustment
6   Install the torque plate and tighten the bolts to the specified torque. Apply a coat of multi-purpose grease to the splines of the torsion bar.
7   Slide the anchor arm onto the torsion bar, aligning the match marks.
8   Line up the match marks from the torsion bar to the torque plate and insert the bar into the torque plate. Install the anchor bolt, tightening it until the alignment marks are adjoined.
9   If a new torsion bar has been installed or if alignment marks were not made before disassembly, preset the anchor arm and tighten the bolt a certain amount, as follows:
10   On two-wheel drive vehicles, install the torsion bar into the torque plate then install the anchor arm onto the end of the torsion bar so that there is approximately 125 mm (4.92 in) between the crossmember and the tip of the anchor arm **(see illustration)**. Tighten the anchor bolt until the anchor arm contacts the anchor bolt swivel, then tighten it an additional 45 mm (1.77 in). Install the wheel then lower the vehicle and check the ride height. If the vehicle is not level from side to side, turn the anchor bolt in or out as necessary to even it.
11   On 4WD vehicles, install the torsion bar and anchor arm so that the distance between the anchor arm tip and the frame bracket is

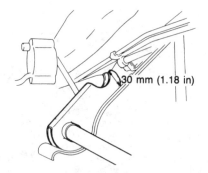

6.11 On 4WD models, set the anchor arm so there is 30 mm clearance between the anchor arm tip and the frame bracket

30 mm (1.18 in) **(see illustration)**. Install the anchor bolt and tighten it. Install the wheel, then lower the vehicle. Tighten or loosen the bolt as necessary to level the vehicle from side-to-side.

---

7   Suspension upper arm — removal and installation

Refer to illustration 7.5
Removal
1   Loosen the wheel lug nuts, raise the front of the vehicle and support it securely on jackstands. Apply the parking brake. Remove the wheel.
2   Support the lower arm with a jack or jackstand. The support point must be as close to the balljoint as possible to give maximum leverage on the lower control arm.
3   Disconnect the upper balljoint from the upper arm by removing the nuts and bolts. Separate the balljoint from the upper arm, but be careful not to let the steering knuckle/brake caliper assembly fall outward, as this may damage the brake hose.
4   If the threaded upper arm shaft bushings are to be replaced, loosen, but do not remove them at this time
5   Remove the upper arm-to-frame nuts and bolts, recording the position of any alignment shims. They must be reinstalled in the same location to maintain wheel alignment **(see illustration)**.
6   Detach the upper arm from the vehicle.
7   Unscrew the bushings if they are to be replaced.

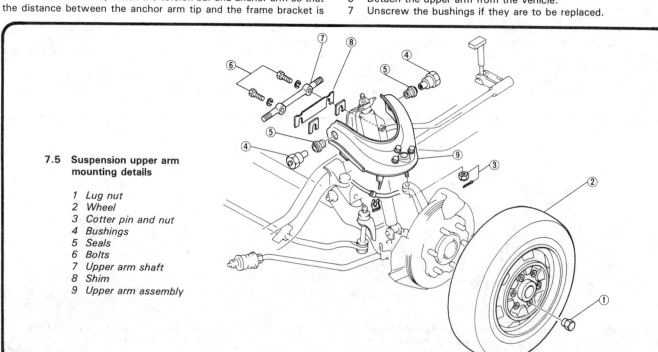

7.5   Suspension upper arm mounting details

1 *Lug nut*
2 *Wheel*
3 *Cotter pin and nut*
4 *Bushings*
5 *Seals*
6 *Bolts*
7 *Upper arm shaft*
8 *Shim*
9 *Upper arm assembly*

Installation

8   Position the arm on the frame and install the bolts and nuts. Install any alignment shims that were removed. Tighten the nuts to the specified torque.

9   Connect the balljoint to the upper arm and tighten the nuts to the specified torque.

10   Install the wheel and lug nuts and lower the vehicle. Tighten the lug nuts to the specified torque.

11   Drive the vehicle to an alignment shop to have the front end alignment checked and, if necessary, adjusted.

8   Suspension lower arm — removal and installation

Removal

1   Loosen the wheel lug nuts, raise the vehicle and support it securely on jackstands. Remove the wheel.

2   On 1984 and earlier models, remove the shock absorber (Section 3). On 1986 and later models, disconnect the shock absorber from the lower arm only.

3   Disconnect the stabilizer bar from the lower arm, if so equipped (Section 2).

4   Remove the coil spring (Section 4) or torsion bar and torque plate (Section 6).

5   Loosen, but do not remove the lower arm pivot bolt(s).

6   Disconnect the balljoint from the lower arm by removing the nuts and bolts (torsion bar models).

7   Unbolt the lower arm from the frame by removing the pivot bolt nut(s) **(see illustration 1.1b or 1.1c)**. On early models, the lower arm has a pivot shaft that is held to the frame by three bolts **(see illustration 1.1a)**.

Installation

8   Position the arm to the frame and install the pivot bolts. The bolts on early styles (with a pivot shaft) may be tightened to the specified torque at this time.

9   On torsion bar models, raise the lower arm to simulate the normal ride angle then tighten the pivot bolt nut(s) to the specified torque. Connect the balljoint to the lower arm and install the bolts and nuts, tightening them to the specified torque. Now allow the arm to hang free and install the torque plate and torsion bar (Section 6).

10   Install the coil spring (1984 and earlier models) and connect the balljoint to the lower arm, tightening the fasteners to the specified torque.

11   Install the shock absorber (Section 3) and connect the stabilizer bar to the lower arm (Section 2).

12   Install the wheel and lug nuts. Lower the vehicle and tighten the lug nuts to the specified torque.

13   With the weight of the vehicle on the wheels, tighten the pivot bolt nuts to the specified torque.

14   Drive the vehicle to an alignment shop to have the front end alignment checked and, if necessary, adjusted.

9   Balljoints — check and replacement

Refer to illustration 9.7

Check

1   Raise the vehicle and support it securely on jackstands.

2   Visually inspect the rubber seal for cuts, tears or leaking grease. If any of these conditions are noticed, the balljoint should be replaced.

3   Place a large pry bar under the balljoint and attempt to push the balljoint upwards. Next, position the pry bar between the steering knuckle and the control arm and apply downward pressure **(see illustrations)**. If any movement is seen or felt during either of these checks, a worn out balljoint is indicated.

4   Have an assistant grasp the tire at the top and bottom and shake the top of the tire in an in-and-out motion. Touch the balljoint stud castellated nut. If any looseness is felt, suspect a worn out balljoint stud or a widened hole in the steering knuckle boss. If the latter problem exists, the steering knuckle should be replaced as well as the balljoint.

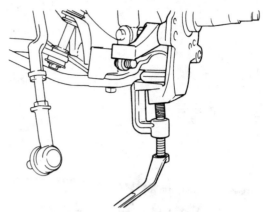

9.7   Break the balljoint loose from the steering knuckle with a separating tool (don't try to hammer the balljoint stud through the knuckle boss)

Replacement

5   With the vehicle still raised and supported, position a floor jack under the lower arm — it must stay there throughout the entire operation. Remove the wheel.

6   Remove the cotter pin and loosen the castle nut a couple of turns, but don't remove it (it will prevent the balljoint and steering knuckle from separating violently).

7   Using a balljoint separating tool, separate the balljoint from the steering knuckle **(see illustration)**. There are several types of balljoint tools available, but the kind that pushes the balljoint stud out of the knuckle boss works the best. The wedge, or ''pickle fork'' type works fairly well, but it tends to damage the balljoint seal. Some two-jaw pullers will do the job, also.

8   Remove the castle nut and disconnect the balljoint from the steering knuckle. If the upper arm balljoint is being worked on, be careful not to let the steering knuckle/hub/brake assembly fall outward, because the brake hose might be damaged. If necessary, wire the assembly to the frame to prevent this from happening.

9   Remove the bolts (and nuts on early models) that retain the balljoint to the suspension arm, then detach the balljoint from the arm. Take note of how the balljoint is positioned on the arm — the new one must be installed the same way.

10   Position the new balljoint on the arm and install the bolts (and nuts), tightening them to the specified torque.

11   Insert the balljoint stud into the steering knuckle boss, install the castle nut and tighten it to the specified torque. Install a new cotter pin. If necessary, tighten the nut an additional amount to line up the slots in the nut with the hole in the balljoint stud (never loosen the nut to align the hole).

12   Install the wheel and lug nuts. Lower the vehicle and tighten the lug nuts to the specified torque.

10   Steering knuckle — removal and installation

Refer to illustration 10.11

Removal

1   Loosen the wheel lug nuts, raise the vehicle and support it securely on jackstands placed under the frame. Apply the parking brake. Remove the wheel.

2   Remove the brake caliper and place it on top of the upper control arm or wire it up out of the way (see Chapter 9 if necessary). Remove the caliper mounting bracket from the steering knuckle.

3   On 4WD models, remove the freewheeling hub assembly and the driveaxle snap-ring and spacer (see the appropriate Sections in Chapter 8).

4   Remove the brake disc and hub assembly (see Chapter 1).

5   Remove the splash shield from the steering knuckle.

6   Separate the tie-rod end from the knuckle arm (see Section 14).

7   If the steering knuckle must be replaced, remove the knuckle arm from the knuckle by removing the two bolts. If it's damaged, replace it with a new one.

10

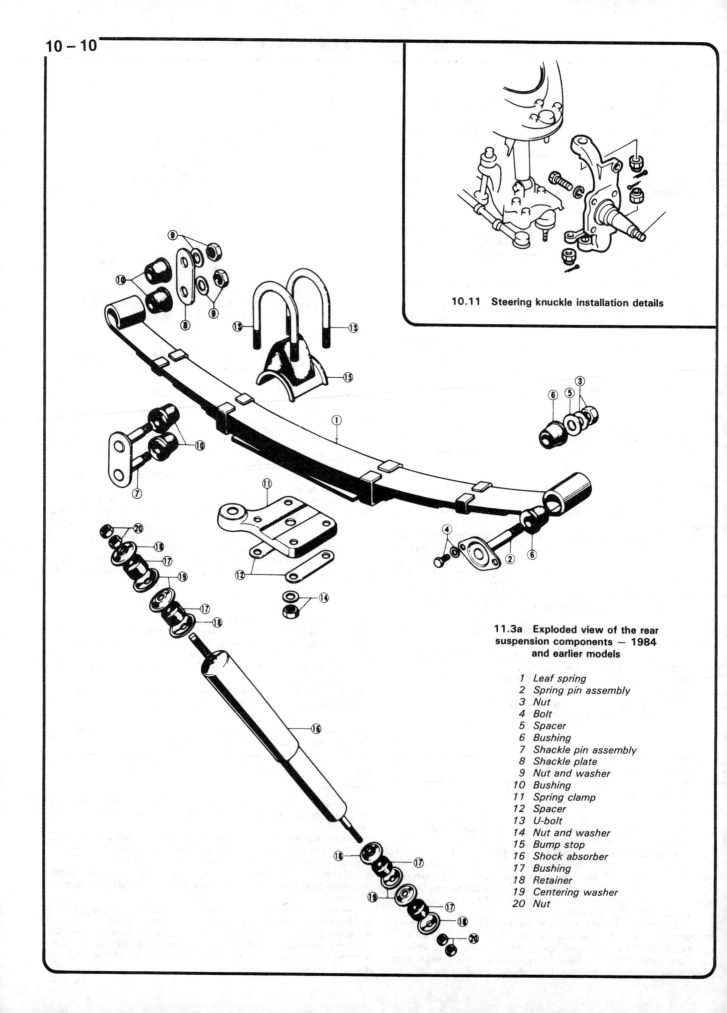

10.11 Steering knuckle installation details

11.3a Exploded view of the rear suspension components — 1984 and earlier models

1   Leaf spring
2   Spring pin assembly
3   Nut
4   Bolt
5   Spacer
6   Bushing
7   Shackle pin assembly
8   Shackle plate
9   Nut and washer
10 Bushing
11 Spring clamp
12 Spacer
13 U-bolt
14 Nut and washer
15 Bump stop
16 Shock absorber
17 Bushing
18 Retainer
19 Centering washer
20 Nut

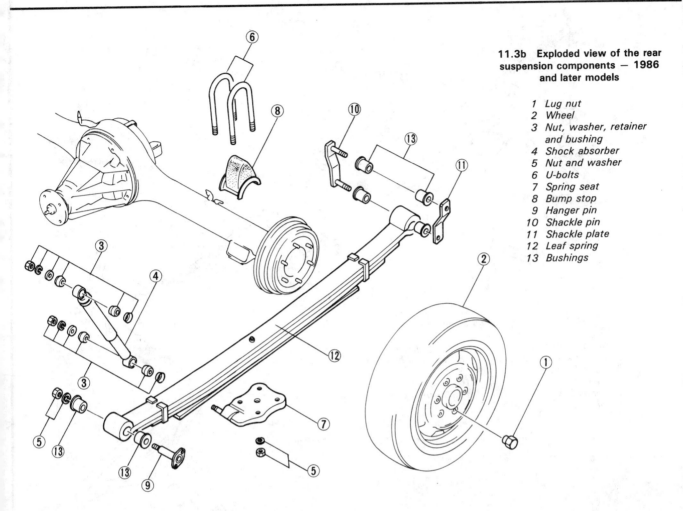

11.3b Exploded view of the rear suspension components — 1986 and later models

1 Lug nut
2 Wheel
3 Nut, washer, retainer and bushing
4 Shock absorber
5 Nut and washer
6 U-bolts
7 Spring seat
8 Bump stop
9 Hanger pin
10 Shackle pin
11 Shackle plate
12 Leaf spring
13 Bushings

8   Position a floor jack under the lower suspension arm and raise it slightly to take the spring pressure off the suspension stop. The jack must remain in this position throughout the entire procedure.

9   Remove the cotter pins from the upper and lower balljoint studs and back off the nuts two turns each.

10   Break the balljoints loose from the steering knuckle (see Section 9).

11   Remove the nuts from the balljoint studs, separate the suspension arms from the steering knuckle and remove the knuckle from the vehicle **(see illustration)**.

Installation

12   Place the knuckle between the upper and lower suspension arms and insert the balljoint studs into the knuckle, beginning with the lower balljoint. Install the nuts and tighten them to the specified torque. Install new cotter pins, tightening the nuts slightly to align the slots in the nuts with the holes in the balljoint studs, if necessary.

13   Install the splash shield.

14   Connect the tie-rod end to the knuckle arm and tighten the nut to the specified torque. Be sure to use a new cotter pin.

15   Install the brake disc and adjust the wheel bearings following the procedure outlined in Chapter 1.

16   On 4WD models, install the driveaxle spacer, snap-ring and the freewheeling hub assembly (Chapter 8).

17   Install the brake caliper mounting bracket and caliper (Chapter 9).

18   Install the wheel and lug nuts. Lower the vehicle to the ground and tighten the nuts to the specified torque.

---

11   Rear shock absorber — removal and installation

Refer to illustrations 11.3a, 11.3b, 11.3c and 11.4

1   If the shock absorber is to be replaced with a new one, it is recommended that both shocks on the rear of the vehicle be replaced at the same time.

2   Raise and support the rear of the vehicle according to the jacking and towing procedures in this manual. Use a jack to raise the differential until the tires clear the ground, then place jackstands under the axle housing. *Do not attempt to remove the shock absorbers with the vehicle raised and the axle unsupported.*

3   Unscrew and remove the lower shock absorber mounting nut to disconnect it at the spring seat **(see illustrations)**.

11.3c The lower end of the rear shock absorber

10

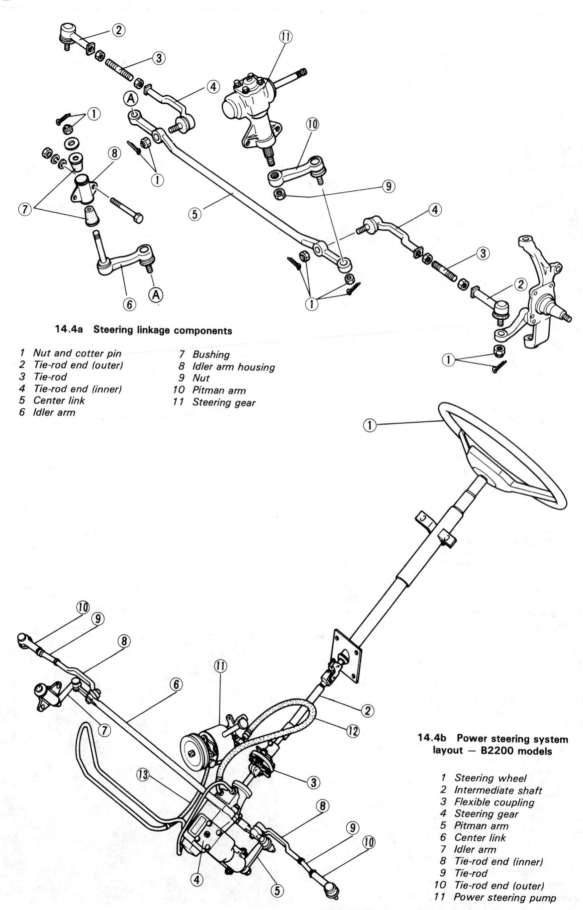

14.4a   Steering linkage components

1 Nut and cotter pin
2 Tie-rod end (outer)
3 Tie-rod
4 Tie-rod end (inner)
5 Center link
6 Idler arm
7 Bushing
8 Idler arm housing
9 Nut
10 Pitman arm
11 Steering gear

**14.4b   Power steering system
layout — B2200 models**

1 Steering wheel
2 Intermediate shaft
3 Flexible coupling
4 Steering gear
5 Pitman arm
6 Center link
7 Idler arm
8 Tie-rod end (inner)
9 Tie-rod
10 Tie-rod end (outer)
11 Power steering pump

11.4 The upper end of the rear shock absorber

4   Unscrew and remove the upper mounting nut at the frame and remove the shock absorber **(see illustration)**.
5   If the unit is defective, it must be replaced with a new one. Replace worn rubber bushings with new ones.
6   Install the shocks in the reverse order of removal, but let the vehicle be free standing before tightening the mounting bolts and nuts.
7   Bounce the rear of the vehicle a couple of times to settle the bushings into place, then tighten the nuts to the specified torque.

12 Rear leaf spring — removal and installation

Refer to illustration 12.10

1   Jack up the vehicle and support the frame securely on jackstands.
2   Remove the rear wheels and tires.
3   Place a jack under the rear differential housing.
4   Lower the axle housing until the leaf spring tension is relieved, and lock the jack in this position.
5   Disconnect the shock absorber from the spring seat.
6   Remove the U-bolt mounting nuts **(see illustration 11.3a or 11.3b)**.
7   Remove the spring seat and U-bolts.
8   Unbolt and remove the shackle pin and hanger pin assemblies.
9   Remove the rubber bushings from the spring ends and frame, then

remove the spring.
10   Installation is the reverse of the removal procedure. Lubricate the shackle pins, hanger pin and bushings with lithium base grease **(see illustration)**. When installing the U-bolt nuts, the hanger pin and shackle pin nuts, tighten them to the specified torque values.

13 Steering wheel — removal and installation

Refer to illustration 13.4

Removal

1   Disconnect the cable from the negative battery terminal.
2   Using a small screwdriver, pry off the horn button or center pad.
3   Mark the steering wheel hub and the column shaft with paint to ensure correct repositioning during reassembly.
4   Unscrew the steering wheel nut and remove the wheel using a steering wheel puller **(see illustration)**. **Note:** *Do not hammer on the wheel or the shaft to separate them.*

Installation

5   Realign the steering wheel and the column shaft using the match marks. Install and tighten the retaining nut to the specified torque, then attach the horn button or center pad.
6   Hook up the negative battery cable to the battery.

14 Steering linkage — removal and installation

Refer to illustrations 14.4a, 14.4b, 14.4c, 14.5 and 14.10

1   All steering linkage removal and installation procedures should be performed with the front end of the vehicle raised and placed securely on jackstands.
2   Before removing any steering linkage components, obtain a ball-joint separator. It may be a screw-type puller or a wedge-type tool, although the wedge-type tool tends to damage the balljoint seals. It is possible to jar a balljoint taper pin free from its eye by striking opposite sides of the eye simultaneously with two large hammers, but the space available to do so is usually very limited.
3   After installing any of the steering linkage components, the front wheel alignment should be checked by a reputable front end alignment and repair shop.

Pitman arm

4   Remove the nut securing the Pitman arm to the steering gear sector shaft **(see illustrations)**.
5   Scribe or paint match marks on the arm and shaft. The Pitman arm has one larger groove that corresponds to one larger spline on the steer-

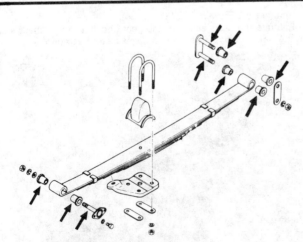

12.10 Apply lithium base grease to the points indicated by arrows

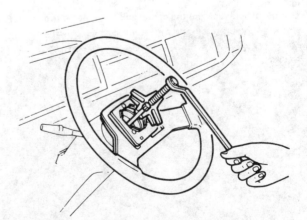

13.4 Remove the steering wheel from the shaft with a puller — DO NOT hammer on the shaft!

10

14.4c   The Pitman arm and its connection to the steering gear box and the center link is shown here

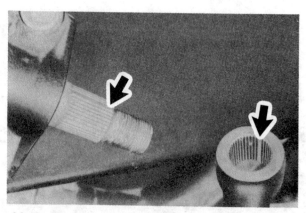

14.10   The tie-rod and its connection to the knuckle arm

ing gear sector shaft, making it possible for the arm to be installed in only one position **(see illustration)**. The match marks will, however, make installation easier.

6   Using a puller, disconnect the Pitman arm from the shaft splines.
7   Remove the cotter pin and castle nut securing the Pitman arm to the center link.
8   Using a puller, disconnect the Pitman arm from the center link.
9   Installation is the reverse of the removal procedure. Be sure to tighten the nuts to the specified torque.

Tie-rod

10   Remove the cotter pins and castle nuts securing the tie-rod to the center link and knuckle arm **(see illustration)**.
11   Separate the tie-rod from the center link and knuckle arm with a puller.
12   If a tie-rod end is to be replaced, loosen the jam nut and mark the relationship of the tie-rod end to the tie-rod with white paint. When installing the new rod end, thread it onto the tie-rod until it reaches the mark, then turn the jam nut until it contacts the rod end. Don't tighten if fully at this time.
13   Turn the tie-rod ends so they are at approximately 90° angles to each other, then tighten the jam nuts to lock the ends in position.
14   The remaining installation steps are the reverse of those for removal. Make sure to tighten the castle nuts to the specified torque.

Center link

15   Remove the cotter pins and castle nuts securing the tie-rod ends to the center link **(see illustration 14.4a)**.
16   Remove the cotter pin and castle nut securing the center link to the Pitman arm.
17   Remove the cotter pin and castle nut securing the center link to the idler arm.
18   Using a puller, separate the center link from the tie-rod ends, Pit-

man arm and idler arm.
19   Installation is the reverse of the removal procedure. Be sure to tighten all nuts to the specified torque.

Knuckle arm

20   Remove the cotter pin and castle nut securing the tie-rod end to the knuckle arm.
21   Using a puller, separate the tie-rod end from the knuckle arm.
22   Unbolt the knuckle arm from the steering knuckle and remove it.
23   Installation is the reverse of the removal procedure. Be sure to tighten all nuts and bolts to the specified torque.

---

15   Steering gear — removal and installation

Refer to illustration 15.4

   Note: *If you find that the steering gear is defective, it is not recommended that you overhaul it. Because of the special tools needed to do the job, it is best to let your dealer service department overhaul it for you (or replace it with a factory rebuilt unit). However, you can remove and install it yourself by following the procedure outlined here.*

   The removal and installation procedures for manual steering and power steering gear housings are identical except that the inlet and outlet lines must be removed from the steering gear housing on power steering-equipped models before the housing can be removed.

   The steering system should be filled and power steering systems should be bled after the gear housing is reinstalled (see Section 18).

1   Raise the front of the vehicle and place it securely on jackstands.
2   Place an alignment mark on the steering coupling and the gear housing worm shaft to assure correct reassembly, then remove the coupling bolt.
3   Remove the Pitman arm (Section 4).
4   Remove the bolts securing the gear housing to the chassis and pull the gear housing from the coupling **(see illustration)**.

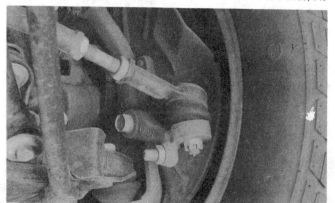

14.5   The Pitman arm has a groove which corresponds with a larger spline on the steering gear sector shaft (arrows)

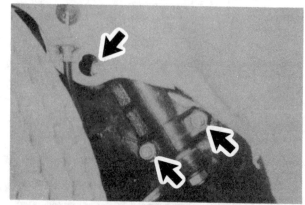

15.4   The steering gear is fastened to the frame by three bolts (1984 and earlier style shown, others similar)

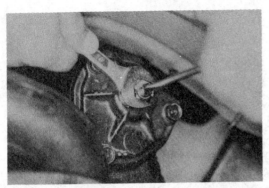

16.6   When tightening the adjusting screw locknut, be sure to hold the screw from turning, otherwise the adjustment will be affected

5   Installation is the reverse of the removal procedure except that the Pitman arm nut should be tightened before the Pitman arm is connected to the center link. Be sure to tighten all nuts and bolts to the specified torque.

16   Steering free play — adjustment

Refer to illustration 16.6
1   Raise the vehicle with a jack so that the front wheels are off the ground and place the vehicle securely on jackstands.
2   Point the wheels straight ahead.
3   Using a wrench, loosen the locknut on the steering gear.
4   Turn the adjusting screw clockwise to decrease wheel free play and counterclockwise to increase it. **Note:** *Turn the adjusting screw in small increments, checking the steering wheel free play between them.*
5   Turn the steering wheel halfway around in both directions, checking that the free play is correct and that the steering is smooth.
6   Hold the adjusting screw so that it will not turn and tighten the locknut **(see illustration)**.
7   Remove the jackstands and lower the vehicle.

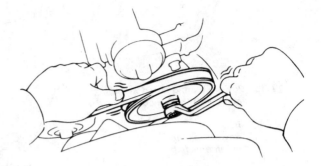

17.1   Push down on the power steering pump drivebelt to prevent the pulley from turning while loosening the nut

17   Power steering pump — removal and installation

Refer to illustrations 17.1, 17.3a and 17.3b.
Note: *If you find that the steering pump is defective, it is not recommended that you overhaul it. Because of the special tools needed to do the job, it is best to let your dealer service department overhaul it for you (or replace it with a factory rebuilt unit). However, you can remove it yourself using the procedure which follows.*

Removal
1   Push on the drivebelt to increase its tension sufficiently to prevent the pulley from turning and loosen the drive pulley nut **(see illustration)**.
2   Loosen the idler pulley nut (B2200 models).
3   Loosen the adjusting bolt and remove the drivebelt **(see illustrations)**.
4   Remove the drive pulley nut and the drive pulley.
5   Disconnect the pressure hose from the pump body. Position a container to catch the pump fluid and plug the hose to prevent contamination.
6   Loosen the return line hose clamp, pull off the hose and plug it to prevent contamination.
7   Remove the pump mounting bolts and lift the pump out of the engine compartment.

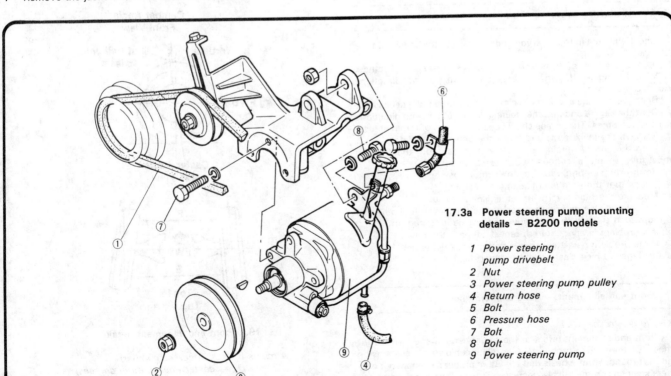

17.3a   Power steering pump mounting details — B2200 models

1   *Power steering pump drivebelt*
2   *Nut*
3   *Power steering pump pulley*
4   *Return hose*
5   *Bolt*
6   *Pressure hose*
7   *Bolt*
8   *Bolt*
9   *Power steering pump*

10

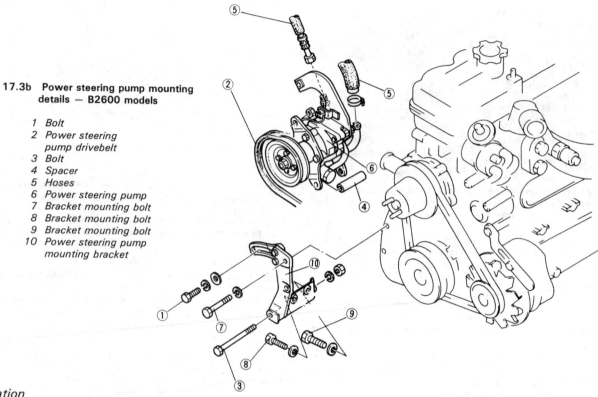

17.3b   Power steering pump mounting details — B2600 models

1   Bolt
2   Power steering
     pump drivebelt
3   Bolt
4   Spacer
5   Hoses
6   Power steering pump
7   Bracket mounting bolt
8   Bracket mounting bolt
9   Bracket mounting bolt
10 Power steering pump
     mounting bracket

Installation

8   Installation is the reverse of the removal procedure. When installing the pressure line, make sure there is sufficient clearance between the line and the exhaust manifold.
9   To adjust the drivebelt tension, see Chapter 1.
10 Fill the power steering fluid reservoir with the specified fluid and bleed the power steering system (see Section 18).
11 Check for fluid leaks.

18   Power steering system — bleeding

1   Check the fluid in the reservoir and add fluid of the specified type if it is low.
2   Jack up the front of the vehicle and place it securely on jackstands.
3   With the engine off, turn the steering wheel fully in both directions two or three times.
4   Recheck the fluid in the reservoir and add more fluid if necessary.
5   Start the engine and turn the steering wheel fully in both directions two or three times. The engine should be running at 1000 rpm or less.
6   Remove the jackstands and lower the vehicle completely.
7   With the engine running at 1000 rpm or less, turn the steering wheel fully in both directions two or three times.
8   Return the steering wheel to the center position.
9   Check that the fluid is not foamy or cloudy.
10 Measure the fluid level with the engine running.
11 Turn the engine and again measure the fluid level. It should rise no more than 0.20 in (5 mm) when the engine is turned off.
12 If a problem is encountered, repeat Steps 7 through 11.
13 If the problem persists, remove the pump (see Section 17), and have it repaired by a dealer service department.

19   Front end alignment — general information

Refer to illustration 19.1

A front end alignment refers to the adjustments made to the front wheels so they are in proper angular relationship to the suspension and the ground. Front wheels that are out of proper alignment not only affect steering control, but also increase tire wear. The front end adjustments normally required are camber, caster and toe-in **(see illustration)**.

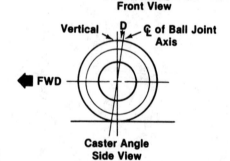

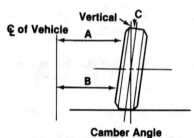

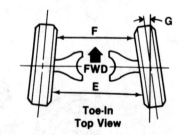

19.1 Front end alignment details

A minus B = C (degrees camber)
         D = caster (measured in degrees)
E minus F = toe-in (measured in inches)
         G = toe-in (expressed in degrees)

Getting the proper front wheel alignment is a very exacting process, one in which complicated and expensive machines are necessary to perform the job properly. Because of this, you should have a technician with the proper equipment perform these tasks. We will, however, use this space to give you a basic idea of what is involved with front end alignment so you can better understand the process and deal intelligently with the shop that does the work.

Toe-in is the turning in of the front wheels. The purpose of a toe specification is to ensure parallel rolling of the front wheels. In a vehicle with zero toe-in, the distance between the front edges of the wheels will be the same as the distance between the rear edges of the wheels. The actual amount of toe-in is normally only a fraction of an inch. Toe-in adjustment is controlled by the tie-rod end position on the inner tie-rod. Incorrect toe-in will cause the tires to wear improperly by making them scrub against the road surface.

Camber is the tilting of the front wheels from the vertical when viewed from the front of the vehicle. When the wheels tilt out at the top, the camber is said to be positive (+). When the wheels tilt in at the top the camber is negative (–). The amount of tilt is measured in degrees from the vertical and this measurement is called the camber angle. This angle affects the amount of tire tread which contacts the road and compensates for changes in the suspension geometry when the vehicle is cornering or travelling over an undulating surface.

Caster is the tilting of the front steering axis from the vertical. A tilt toward the rear is positive caster and a tilt toward the front is negative caster. Caster angle affects the self-centering action of the steering, which governs straight-line stability.

Caster is adjusted by moving shims from one end of the upper control arm mount to the other.

20   Wheels and tires — general information

Wheels can be damaged by an impact with a curb or other solid object. If the wheels are bent, the result is a hazardous condition which must be corrected. To check the wheels, raise the vehicle and set it on jackstands. Visually inspect the wheels for obvious signs of damage such as cracks and deformation.

Tire and wheel balance is very important to the overall handling, braking and ride performance of the vehicle. Whenever a tire is dismounted for repair or replacement, the tire and wheel assembly should be balanced before being installed on the vehicle.

Wheels should be periodically cleaned, especially on the inside, where mud and road salts accumulate and eventually cause rust and, ultimately, possible wheel failure.

Tires are extremely important from a safety standpoint. The tread should be checked periodically to see that the tires have not worn excessively, a condition which can be dangerous, especially in wet weather.

To equalize wear and add life to a set of tires, it is recommended that they be rotated periodically. When rotating, check for signs of abnormal wear and foreign objects in the tread or sidewalls (refer to Chapter 1, Routine Maintenance).

Proper tire inflation is essential for maximum life of the tread and for proper handling and braking.

Tires that are wearing in an abnormal way are an indication that their inflation is incorrect or that the front end components are not adjusted properly. Take the vehicle to a reputable front end alignment and repair shop to correct the situation.

10

Chapter 11 Body

Contents

---

1   General information

The Mazda B series pick-up is available in three basic body styles: the regular bed model, long bed model (which uses the same cab with an extended bed) and the Cab Plus model (which uses the regular bed with an extended cab). Each of these is available in either the two-wheel drive (2WD) or four-wheel drive (4WD) version. In addition, various trim/luxury packages are available with certain models.

The pick-up body consists of a separate cab and bed, both of which are bolted to a pressed steel, box-section frame. The only principle frame difference between pick-up models is the length of the regular bed model and the long bed/Cab Plus models.

Certain body panels which are particularly vulnerable to accident damage can be replaced by unbolting them and installing replacement items. These panels include the fenders, inner fender skirts, grille, front apron, bumpers, hood and rear gate. In addition, whether due to damage or for conversion reasons, the entire rear bed can be easily removed from the frame.

---

2   Maintenance – body and frame

1   The condition of your vehicle's body is very important, because it is on this that the second hand value will mainly depend. It is much more difficult to repair a neglected or damaged body than it is to repair mechanical components. The hidden areas of the body, such as the fender wells, the frame, and the engine compartment, are equally important, although they obviously do not require as frequent attention as the rest of the body.

2   Once a year, or every 12,000 miles, it's a good idea to have the underside of the body and the frame steam cleaned. All traces of dirt and oil will be removed and the underside can then be inspected carefully for rust, damaged brake lines, frayed electrical wiring, damaged cables and other problems. The front suspension components should be greased after completion of this job.

3   At the same time, clean the engine and the engine compartment using either a steam cleaner or a water soluble degreaser.

4   The fender wells should be given particular attention, as undercoating can peel away and stones and dirt thrown up by the tires can cause the paint to chip and flake, allowing rust to set in. If rust is found, clean down to the bare metal and apply an anti-rust paint.

5   The body should be washed as needed. Wet the vehicle thoroughly to soften the dirt, then wash it down with a soft sponge and plenty of clean soapy water. If the surplus dirt is not washed off very carefully, it will in time wear down the paint.

6   Spots of tar or asphalt coating thrown up from the road should be removed with a cloth soaked in solvent.

7   Once every six months, give the body and chrome trim a thorough waxing. If a chrome cleaner is used to remove rust from any of the vehicle's plated parts, remember that the cleaner also removes part of the chrome, so use it sparingly.

---

3   Maintenance – upholstery and carpets

1   Every three months remove the carpets or mats and clean the interior of the vehicle (more frequently if necessary). Vacuum the uphol-

stery and carpets to remove loose dirt and dust.
2   If the upholstery is soiled, apply upholstery cleaner with a damp sponge and wipe it off with a clean, dry cloth.

4   Body repair – minor damage

See photo sequence

Repair of minor scratches

1   If the scratch is superficial and does not penetrate to the metal of the body, repair is very simple. Lightly rub the scratched area with a fine rubbing compound to remove loose paint and built up wax. Rinse the area with clean water.
2   Apply touch-up paint to the scratch, using a small brush. Continue to apply thin layers of paint until the surface of the paint in the scratch is level with the surrounding paint. Allow the new paint at least two weeks to harden, then blend it into the surrounding paint by rubbing with a very fine rubbing compound. Finally, apply a coat of wax to the scratch area.
3   If the scratch has penetrated the paint and exposed the metal of the body, causing the metal to rust, a different repair technique is required. Remove all loose rust from the bottom of the scratch with a pocket knife, then apply rust inhibiting paint to prevent the formation of rust in the future. Using a rubber or nylon applicator, coat the scratched area with glaze-type filler. If required, the filler can be mixed with thinner to provide a very thin paste, which is ideal for filling narrow scratches. Before the glaze filler in the scratch hardens, wrap a piece of smooth cotton cloth around the tip of a finger. Dip the cloth in thinner and then quickly wipe it along the surface of the scratch. This will ensure that the surface of the filler is slightly hollow. The scratch can now be painted over as described earlier in this section.

Repair of dents

4   When repairing dents, the first job is to pull the dent out until the affected area is as close as possible to its original shape. There is no point in trying to restore the original shape completely as the metal in the damaged area will have stretched on impact and cannot be restored to its original contours. It is better to bring the level of the dent up to a point which is about 1/8-inch below the level of the surrounding metal. In cases where the dent is very shallow, it is not worth trying to pull it out at all.
5   If the back side of the dent is accessible, it can be hammered out gently from behind using a soft-face hammer. While doing this, hold a block of wood firmly against the opposite side of the metal to absorb the hammer blows and prevent the metal from being stretched.
6   If the dent is in a section of the body which has double layers, or some other factor makes it inaccessible from behind, a different technique is required. Drill several small holes through the metal inside the damaged area, particularly in the deeper sections. Screw long, self-tapping screws into the holes just enough for them to get a good grip in the metal. Now the dent can be pulled out by pulling on the protruding heads of the screws with locking pliers.
7   The next stage of repair is the removal of paint from the damaged area and from an inch or so of the surrounding metal. This is easily done with a wire brush or sanding disk in a drill motor, although it can be done just as effectively by hand with sandpaper. To complete the preparation for filling, score the surface of the bare metal with a screwdriver or the tang of a file or drill small holes in the affected area. This will provide a good grip for the filler material. To complete the repair, see the Section on filling and painting.

Repair of rust holes or gashes

8   Remove all paint from the affected area and from an inch or so of the surrounding metal using a sanding disk or wire brush mounted in a drill motor. If these are not available, a few sheets of sandpaper will do the job just as effectively.
9   With the paint removed, you will be able to determine the severity of the corrosion and decide whether to replace the whole panel, if possible, or repair the affected area. New body panels are not as expensive as most people think and it is often quicker to install a new panel than to repair large areas of rust.

10   Remove all trim pieces from the affected area except those which will act as a guide to the original shape of the damaged body, such as headlight shells, etc. Using metal snips or a hacksaw blade, remove all loose metal and any other metal that is badly affected by rust. Hammer the edges of the hole inward to create a slight depression for the filler material.
11   Wire brush the affected area to remove the powdery rust from the surface of the metal. If the back of the rusted area is accessible, treat it with rust-inhibiting paint.
12   Before filling is done, block the hole in some way. This can be done with sheet metal riveted or screwed into place, or by stuffing the hole with wire mesh.
13   Once the hole is blocked off, the affected area can be filled and painted. See the following sub-section on filling and painting.

Filling and painting

14   Many types of body fillers are available, but generally speaking, body repair kits which contain filler paste and a tube of resin hardener are best for this type of repair work. A wide, flexible plastic or nylon applicator will be necessary for imparting a smooth and contoured finish to the surface of the filler material. Mix up a small amount of filler on a clean piece of wood or cardboard (use the hardener sparingly). Follow the manufacturer's instructions on the package, otherwise the filler will set incorrectly.
15   Using the applicator, apply the filler paste to the prepared area. Draw the applicator across the surface of the filler to achieve the desired contour and to level the filler surface. As soon as a contour that approximates the original one is achieved, stop working the paste. If you continue, the paste will begin to stick to the applicator. Continue to add thin layers of paste at 20-minute intervals until the level of the filler is just above the surrounding metal.
16   Once the filler has hardened, the excess can be removed with a body file. From then on, progressively finer grades of sandpaper should be used, starting with a 180-grit paper and finishing with 600-grit wet-or-dry paper. Always wrap the sandpaper around a flat rubber or wooden block, otherwise the surface of the filler will not be completely flat. During the sanding of the filler surface, the wet-or-dry paper should be periodically rinsed in water. This will ensure that a very smooth finish is produced in the final stage.
17   At this point, the repair area should be surrounded by a ring of bare metal, which in turn should be encircled by the finely feathered edge of good paint. Rinse the repair area with clean water until all of the dust produced by the sanding operation is gone.
18   Spray the entire area with a light coat of primer. This will reveal any imperfections in the surface of the filler. Repair the imperfections with fresh filler paste or glaze filler and once more smooth the surface with sandpaper. Repeat this spray-and-repair procedure until you are satisfied that the surface of the filler and the feathered edge of the paint are perfect. Rinse the area with clean water and allow it to dry completely.
19   The repair area is now ready for painting. Spray painting must be carried out in a warm, dry, windless and dust free atmosphere. These conditions can be created if you have access to a large indoor work area, but if you are forced to work in the open, you will have to pick the day very carefully. If you are working indoors, dousing the floor in the work area with water will help settle the dust which would otherwise be in the air. If the repair area is confined to one body panel, mask off the surrounding panels. This will help minimize the effects of a slight mismatch in paint color. Trim pieces such as chrome strips, door handles, etc., will also need to be masked off or removed. Use masking tape and several thicknesses of newspaper for the masking operations.
20   Before spraying, shake the paint can thoroughly, then spray a test area until the spray painting technique is mastered. Cover the repair area with a thick coat of primer. The thickness should be built up using several thin layers of primer rather than one thick one. Using 600-grit wet-or-dry sandpaper, rub down the surface of the primer until it is very smooth. While doing this, the work area should be thoroughly rinsed with water and the wet-or-dry sandpaper periodically rinsed as well. Allow the primer to dry before spraying additional coats.
21   Spray on the top coat, again building up the thickness by using several thin layers of paint. Begin spraying in the center of the repair area and then, using a circular motion, work out until the whole repair area and about two inches of the surrounding original paint is covered. Remove all masking material 10 to 15 minutes after spraying on the

11

final coat of paint. Allow the new paint at least two weeks to harden, then use a very fine rubbing compound to blend the edges of the new paint into the existing paint. Finally, apply a coat of wax.

5 Body and frame repair — major damage

1   Major damage must be repaired by an auto body/frame repair shop with the necessary welding and hydraulic straightening equipment.
2   If the damage has been serious, it is vital that the frame be checked for proper alignment or the vehicle's handling characteristics may be adversely affected. Other problems, such as excessive tire wear and wear in the driveline and steering may occur.
3   Due to the fact that many of the major body components (hood, doors, etc.) are separate and replaceable units, any seriously damaged components should be replaced rather than repaired. Sometimes these components can be found in a wrecking yard that specializes in used vehicle components, often at considerable savings over the cost of new parts.

6 Maintenance — hinges and locks

Every 3000 miles or three months, the door and hood hinges should be lubricated with a few drops of oil. The door striker plates should

also be given a thin coat of white lithium-base grease to reduce wear and ensure free movement. Lubricate the door locks with spray-on graphite lubricant, available at auto parts stores.

7 Windshield and fixed glass — replacement

Replacement of the windshield and fixed glass requires the use of special fast-setting adhesive/caulk materials and some specialized tools. It is recommended that these operations should be left to a dealer or a shop specializing in glass work.

8 Grille — removal and installation

Refer to illustration 8.3

1   The grille is secured to the body by screws located along the top edge. Remove the screws and pull the grille free.
2   On earlier models it will be necessary to remove the headlight bezel before removing the grille. On later models, remove the combination lamp assemblies and unplug their electrical connectors.
3   Lift the grille straight up and remove it from the vehicle (**see illustration**).
4   Installation is the reverse of removal

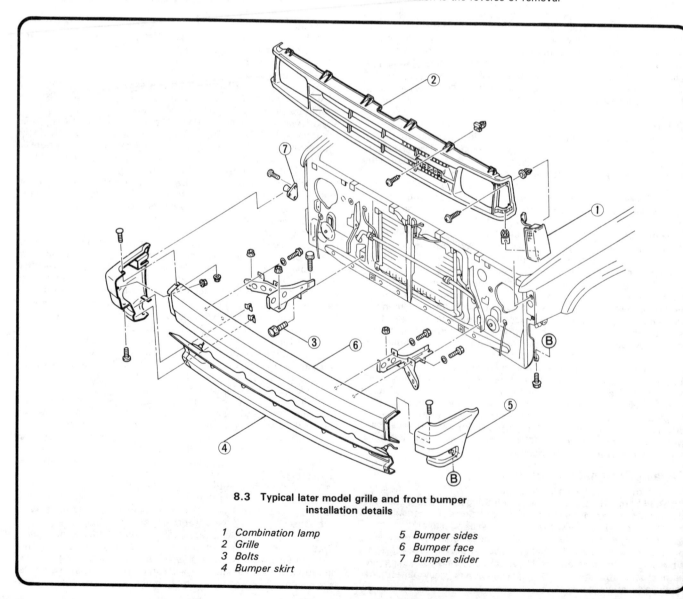

**8.3   Typical later model grille and front bumper
installation details**

1 Combination lamp	5 Bumper sides
2 Grille	6 Bumper face
3 Bolts	7 Bumper slider
4 Bumper skirt	

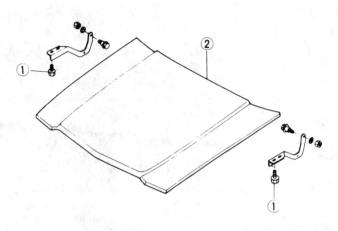

9.3 Typical later model hood details

1 Retaining bolts   2 Hood

9.8 On later models, the hood position can be adjusted after loosening the bolts (arrows)

---

9 Hood — removal, installation and adjustment

Refer to illustrations 9.3, 9.8 and 9.9

Removal and installation

1   Use blankets or pads to cover the cowl area of the body and fenders. This will protect the body and paint as the hood is lifted free.
2   Mark the position of the hood on its hinges by outlining the hinge plate. This will allow reinstallation of the hood to the original position.
3   Have an assistant support the weight of the hood. On earlier models, remove the cotter pin from the hinge stop retaining nut, then remove the pin and stop. Tilt the hood forward, position the torsion bar to one side and remove the hinge-to-body screws. On later models, remove the retaining nuts or bolts and lift out any hinge shims **(see illustration)**.
4   Lift off the hood.
5   Installation is the reverse of removal.

Adjustment

6   Fore-and-aft and side-to-side adjustment of the hood is made by moving the hinge plate slot after loosening the bolts or nuts.
7   Scribe a line around the entire hinge plate so you can judge the amount of movement.
8   Loosen the bolts or nuts and move the hood into correct alignment **(see illustration)**. Move the hood only a little at a time. Tighten the hinge bolts or nuts and carefully lower the hood to check the position.
9   If necessary, the entire hood latch assembly can be adjusted up-and-down as well as side-to-side to properly align with the hood lock in the radiator support. To do this scribe a line around the hood latch mounting screws to provide a reference point. Then loosen them and reposition the latch assembly as necessary. Following adjustment, retighten the mounting bolts **(see illustration)**.
10   Finally, adjust the hood bumpers on the radiator support so that the hood, when closed, is flush with the fender.
11   The hood latch assembly, as well as the hinges, should be periodically lubricated with white lithium base grease to prevent sticking or jamming.

---

10 Door trim panel — removal and installation

Refer to illustrations 10.2 and 10.4

1   Remove the screws that retain the arm rest to the trim panel.
2   Remove the window crank handle. The crank handle is held onto its shaft by a spring clip on later models requiring the use of a small hooked tool to remove it. One can be fabricated out of a piece of coat

9.9 After loosening the attaching bolts (arrows), the hood latch can be moved to adjust hood closing

hanger. With one hand, press the trim panel inward slightly to expose the shaft and clip, and with the other hand insert the tool behind the crank handle until you can hook the spring clip. Then pull the clip toward the handle knob and remove it. On earlier models drive out the retaining pin with a hammer and punch **(see illustration)**. Lift off the crank handle and plastic washer.
3   Remove the door handle escutcheon.

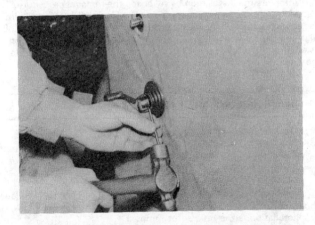

10.2 On earlier models, the window crank can be removed after driving out the retaining pin with a punch and hammer

11

10.4   One of the retaining clips which secure the door trim panel to the door (earlier model shown)

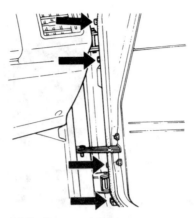

11.2   Door retaining bolt locations (arrows) (later model shown)

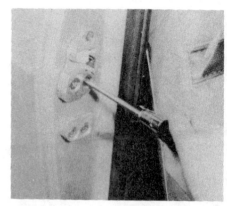

11.4a   On early models, be sure to loosen all the screws before moving the door striker

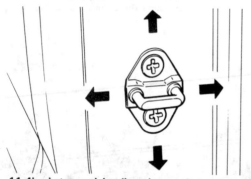

11.4b   Later model strikers have only two screws

4   The trim panel is attached to the door with retaining clips (**see illustration**). To disengage these clips, insert a flat, blunt tool (like a screwdriver wrapped with tape) between the metal door skin and the trim panel. Carefully pry the door panel away from the door, keeping the tool close to the clips to prevent damage to the panel. Start at the bottom and work around the door toward the top. Once the retaining clips are pried free, lift the trim panel upward and away from the door.

5   Before installing the trim panel, check that all the trim retaining clips are in good condition and the sealing screen is correctly applied to the door.

6   Engage the top of the trim panel first and then position the panel correctly on the door. The shaft for the window winder can be used as a rough guide.

7   Press the retaining clips into their respective cups or holes in the door. Pressure can be applied with the palm of your hand or with a clean rubber mallet.

8   Complete the installation by reversing the removal procedure. To install the crank handle on later models, first install the spring clip into its groove on the handle with the closed end facing the handle knob, align the handle with the one on the opposite door and push it onto its shaft until the spring clip clicks into place. On earlier models, place the crank in position and install the retaining pin.

11   Door — removal, installation and adjustment

Refer to illustrations 11.2, 11.4a and 11.4b

1   Either place a jack or stand under the door or have an assistant on hand to support it when the hinge bolts are removed. **Note:** *If a jack or stand is being used, place a rag between it and the door to protect the door's painted surfaces.*

2   Remove the hinge-to-door bolts and carefully lift off the door (**see illustration**).

3   Installation is the reverse of removal.

4   Following installation of the door, check that it is in proper alignment and adjust it if necessary as follows:
   a) Up-and-down and forward-and-backward adjustments are made

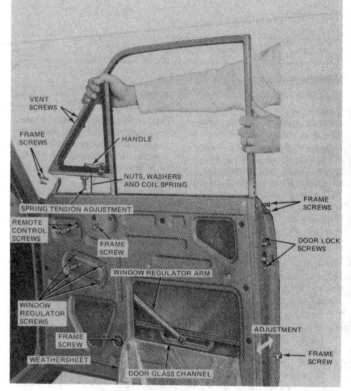

12.2   Early model door window glass frame removal details

by loosening the hinge-to-body bolts and moving the door as necessary. The inner fender protector will have to be removed in order to reach these bolts.
   b) The door lock striker can also be adjusted both up-and-down and sideways to provide a positive engagement with the locking mechanism. This is easily done by loosening the securing bolts and moving the striker as necessary (**see illustrations**).

12   Door window and regulator — removal and installation

Refer to illustrations 12.2, 12.3 and 12.6

1   Remove the door trim panel and plastic sealing screen (Section 10).

Early models

2   Remove the seven screws from the window frame assembly and

12.3 Early model door window glass removal

carefully detach the frame from the door **(see illustration)**.
3   Lower the window glass. Remove the window glass by tilting it to detach the regulator arm from the glass channel and then sliding the glass up and out of the door **(see illustration)**.
4   If necessary, remove the regulator retaining screws and slide the regulator out of the opening in the door.
5   Installation is the reverse of removal.

Later models

6   Remove the bolts that attach the window to the regulator assembly **(see illustration)**.
7   Remove the inner and outer weatherstrips and the glass guide mounting bolt.
8   Pull the glass up, tilt it inward and then guide it up and out of the door.
9   If it is necessary to remove the regulator, remove the retaining screws and slide the regulator out of the large opening in the door.
10 Installation is the reverse of removal.

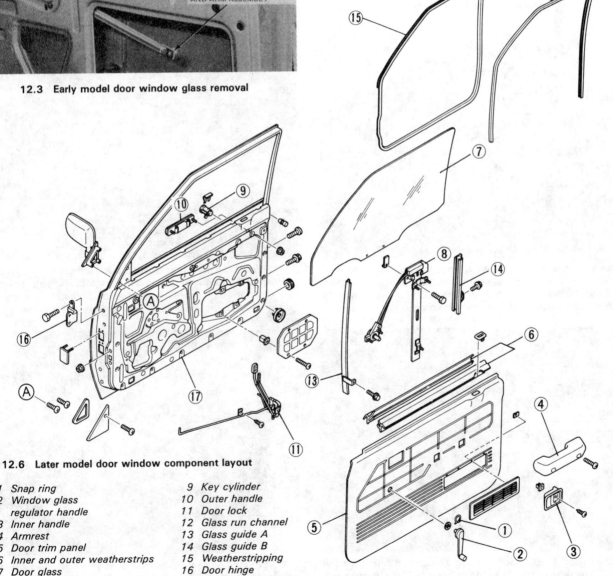

12.6   Later model door window component layout

1 Snap ring	9 Key cylinder
2 Window glass	10 Outer handle
regulator handle	11 Door lock
3 Inner handle	12 Glass run channel
4 Armrest	13 Glass guide A
5 Door trim panel	14 Glass guide B
6 Inner and outer weatherstrips	15 Weatherstripping
7 Door glass	16 Door hinge
8 Regulator assembly	17 Door

11

These photos illustrate a method of repairing simple dents. They are intended to supplement *Body repair - minor damage* in this Chapter and should not be used as the sole instructions for body repair on these vehicles.

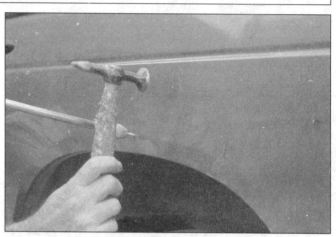

1   If you can't access the backside of the body panel to hammer out the dent, pull it out with a slide-hammer-type dent puller. In the deepest portion of the dent or along the crease line, drill or punch hole(s) at least one inch apart . . .

2   . . . then screw the slide-hammer into the hole and operate it. Tap with a hammer near the edge of the dent to help 'pop' the metal back to its original shape. When you're finished, the dent area should be close to its original contour and about 1/8-inch below the surface of the surrounding metal

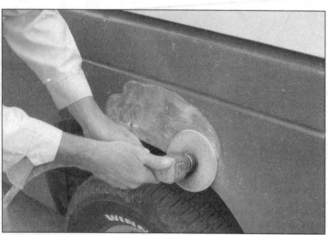

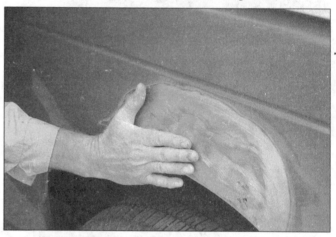

3   Using coarse-grit sandpaper, remove the paint down to the bare metal. Hand sanding works fine, but the disc sander shown here makes the job faster. Use finer (about 320-grit) sandpaper to feather-edge the paint at least one inch around the dent area

4   When the paint is removed, touch will probably be more helpful than sight for telling if the metal is straight. Hammer down the high spots or raise the low spots as necessary. Clean the repair area with wax/silicone remover

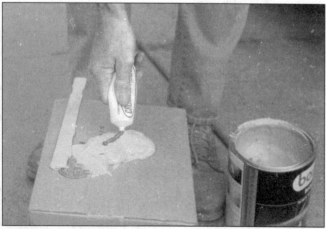

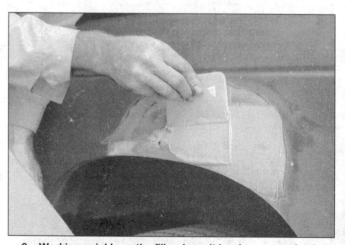

5   Following label instructions, mix up a batch of plastic filler and hardener. The ratio of filler to hardener is critical, and, if you mix it incorrectly, it will either not cure properly or cure too quickly (you won't have time to file and sand it into shape)

6   Working quickly so the filler doesn't harden, use a plastic applicator to press the body filler firmly into the metal, assuring it bonds completely. Work the filler until it matches the original contour and is slightly above the surrounding metal

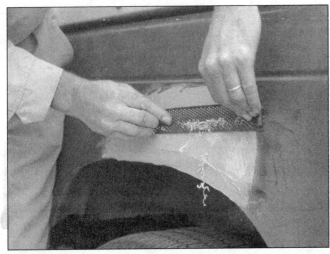

7 Let the filler harden until you can just dent it with your fingernail. Use a body file or Surform tool (shown here) to rough-shape the filler

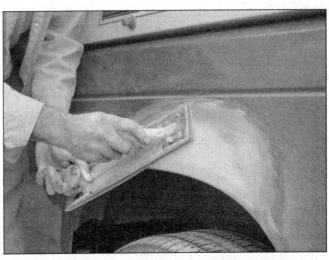

8 Use coarse-grit sandpaper and a sanding board or block to work the filler down until it's smooth and even. Work down to finer grits of sandpaper - always using a board or block - ending up with 360 or 400 grit

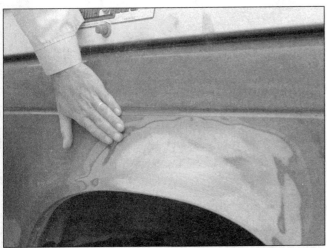

9 You shouldn't be able to feel any ridge at the transition from the filler to the bare metal or from the bare metal to the old paint. As soon as the repair is flat and uniform, remove the dust and mask off the adjacent panels or trim pieces

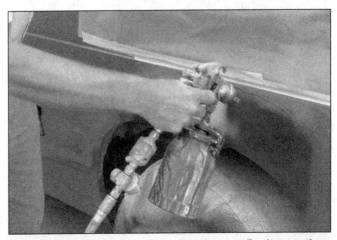

10 Apply several layers of primer to the area. Don't spray the primer on too heavy, so it sags or runs, and make sure each coat is dry before you spray on the next one. A professional-type spray gun is being used here, but aerosol spray primer is available inexpensively from auto parts stores

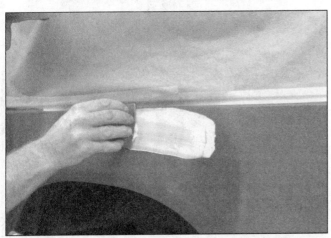

11 The primer will help reveal imperfections or scratches. Fill these with glazing compound. Follow the label instructions and sand it with 360 or 400-grit sandpaper until it's smooth. Repeat the glazing, sanding and respraying until the primer reveals a perfectly smooth surface

12 Finish sand the primer with very fine sandpaper (400 or 600-grit) to remove the primer overspray. Clean the area with water and allow it to dry. Use a tack rag to remove any dust, then apply the finish coat. Don't attempt to rub out or wax the repair area until the paint has dried completely (at least two weeks)

13   Door lock and lock control — removal and installation

Refer to illustrations 13.5 and 13.8

1   Remove the door trim panel as described in Section 10.
2   Remove the plastic sealing screen, taking care not to tear it.
3   Disengage the interior handle rod from the connection at the door lock assembly.
4   Remove the screws that retain the interior handle assembly and lift it out.
5   Remove the retaining clip from the door lock cylinder and remove the cylinder **(see illustration)**.
6   Disengage the door lock rod from the door lock assembly.
7   Remove the three door lock assembly mounting screws, located on the outside rear of the door, and lift out the door lock assembly.
8   If necessary, remove the two nuts retaining the exterior handle and lift it out **(see illustration)**.
9   Installation is the reverse of removal. **Note:** *During installation, apply grease to the sliding surface of all levers and springs.*

14   Bumpers — removal and installation

Refer to illustrations 14.5 and 14.6

1   Disconnect the negative battery cable from the battery.
2   Disconnect any wiring leading to the bumper.
3   On the front bumper, remove the bolts attaching the side bumpers to the fenders.
4   The bumper can be removed either by removing the nuts that attach the bumper to its bracket, or by removing the bolts that attach the bumper brackets to the body.
5   On the front bumper, the side bumpers and molding can be removed, if necessary, by simply removing the bolts that secure them to the bumper **(see illustration)**.
6   On rear bumpers, disconnect any wiring, remove the bolts and lower the bumper **(see illustration)**.
7   Installation is the reverse of removal.

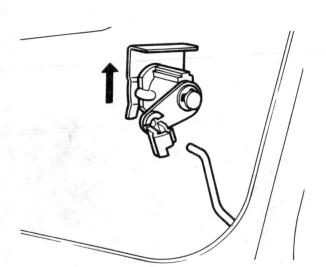

13.5   Push the clip off to detach the door lock cylinder

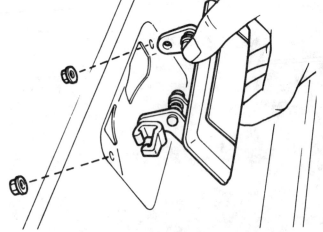

13.8   Exterior door handle details

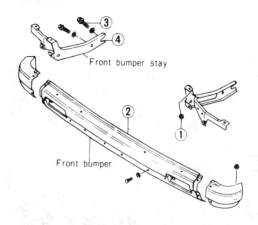

14.5   Front bumper details

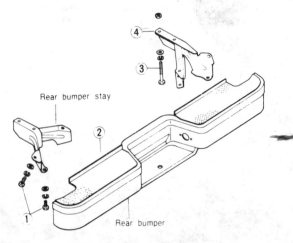

14.6   Rear bumper details

| 1   Left bracket | 3   Bolt |
| 2   Bumper assembly | 4   Right bracket |

| 1   Bolts | 3   Bolt |
| 2   Bumper assembly | 4   Bracket |

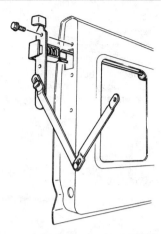

15.5   Later model tailgate latch assembly details

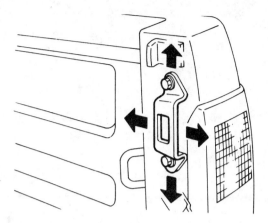

15.8   On later models, the tailgate closing can be adjusted by loosening the bolts and moving the latch striker

15   Tailgate latch — removal and installation

Refer to illustrations 15.5 and 15.8

Early models

1   With the tailgate closed, loosen the chain retaining bracket and move it to one side. Remove the retaining screws and lift the latch off.
2   Installation is the reverse of removal.

Later models

3   Remove the retaining screws from the inside of the cover plate and remove the plate.
4   Remove the nuts or screws retaining the tailgate latch, disconnect the control rods and remove the latch assembly.
5   Remove the two bolts and lift off the latch assembly **(see illustration)**.
6   Remove two screws and lift off the control handle.
7   Installation is the reverse of removal.
8   Adjustment of the tailgate position is made by loosening the tailgate latch striker bolts and moving the striker fore-and aft and/or up and down until the tailgate locks securely **(see illustration)**.

11

Chapter 12   Chassis electrical system

Contents

Specifications

Bulbs

Application	Wattage
Headlight	
1981 and earlier	37.5, 37.5/50, 40/45, 45, 50/40, 50/37.5
1982 and later	65/55, 65/35 (halogen)
Front parking light	8
Turn signal	27
Side marker light	3.8, 8
Tail light	8, 27
Back-up light	27
License plate light	6, or 4 for models with step bumper
Interior light	
1984 and earlier	5
1986 and later	10

---

1   General information

The electrical system is a 12-volt, negative ground type. Power for the lights and all electrical accessories is supplied by a lead/acid-type battery which is charged by the alternator.

This Chapter covers repair and service procedures for the various electrical components not associated with the engine. Information on the battery, alternator, distributor and starter motor can be found in Chapter 5.

It should be noted that when portions of the electrical system are serviced, the negative battery cable should be disconnected from the battery to prevent electrical shorts and/or fires.

2   Electrical troubleshooting — general information

A typical electrical circuit consists of an electrical component, any switches, relays, motors, etc. related to that component and the wiring and connectors that connect the component to both the battery and the chassis. To aid in locating a problem in any electrical circuit, wiring diagrams are included at the end of this Chapter.

Before tackling any troublesome electrical circuit, first study the appropriate diagrams to get a complete understanding of what makes up that individual circuit. Trouble spots, for instance, can often be narrowed down by noting if other components related to that circuit are operating properly or not. If several components or circuits fail at one

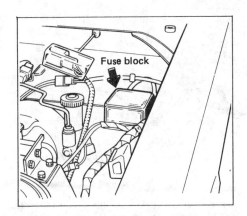

3.2a Fuse block location — 1984 and earlier models

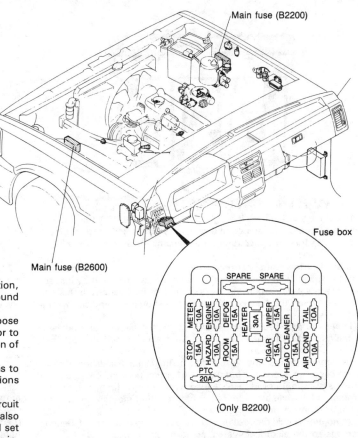

3.2b Fuse block location — 1986 and later models

time, chances are the problem lies in the fuse or ground connection, as several circuits often are routed through the same fuse and ground connections.

Electrical problems often stem from simple causes, such as loose or corroded connections, a blown fuse or melted fusible link. Prior to any electrical troubleshooting, always visually check the condition of the fuse, wires and connections of the problem circuit.

If testing instruments are going to be utilized, use the diagrams to plan ahead of time where you will make the necessary connections in order to accurately pinpoint the trouble spot.

The basic tools needed for electrical troubleshooting include a circuit tester or voltmeter (a 12 volt bulb with a set of test leads can also be used), a continuity tester (which includes a bulb, battery and set of test leads) and a jumper wire, preferably with a circuit breaker incorporated, which can be used to bypass electrical components.

Voltage checks should be performed if a circuit is not functioning properly. Connect one lead of a circuit tester to either the negative battery terminal or a known good ground. Connect the other lead to a connector in the circuit being tested, preferably nearest to the battery or fuse. If the bulb of the tester lights, voltage is reaching that point (which means the part of the circuit between that connector and the battery is problem free). Continue checking along the entire circuit in the same fashion. When you reach a point where no voltage is present, the problem lies between there and the last good test point. Most of the time the problem is due to a loose connection. Keep in mind that some circuits receive voltage only when the ignition key is in the Accessory or Run position.

A method of finding shorts in a circuit is to remove the fuse and connect a test light or voltmeter in its place to the fuse terminals. There should be no load in the circuit. Move the wiring harness from side-to-side while watching the test light. If the bulb lights, there is a short to ground somewhere in that area, probably where insulation has rubbed off a wire. The same test can be performed on other components of the circuit, including the switch.

A ground check should be done to see if a component is grounded properly. Disconnect the battery and connect one lead of a self-powered test light, such as a continuity tester, to a known good ground. Connect the other lead to the wire or ground connection being tested. If the bulb lights, the ground is good. If the bulb does not light, the ground is not good.

A continuity check is performed to see if a circuit, section of circuit or individual component is passing electricity through it properly. Disconnect the battery, and connect one lead of a self-powered test light, such as a continuity tester, to one end of the circuit being tested and the other lead to the other end of the circuit. If the bulb lights, there is continuity, which means the circuit is passing electricity through it properly. Switches can be checked in the same way.

Remember that all electrical circuits are composed basically of electricity running from the battery, through the wires, switches, relays, etc. to the electrical component (light bulb, motor, etc.). From there it is run to the body (ground) where it is passed back to the battery. Any electrical problem is basically an interruption in the flow of electricity to and from the battery.

3 Fuses — general information

Refer to illustrations 3.2a, 3.2b, 3.3 and 3.4

The electrical circuits of the vehicle are protected by a combination of fuses and fusible links.

The fuse box is located underneath the dash on the left side or under the hood in the rear of the engine compartment **(see illustrations)**. Access to the fuses is achieved by simply unsnapping the fuse cover.

Each of the fuses is designed to protect a specific circuit, as identified on the fuse cover or fuse block. Early models use glass-tube fuses, while later models use the miniaturized blade-terminal style. The entire circuit is protected by a main fuse, located along the right-side inner fender panel, behind the battery **(see illustration)**.

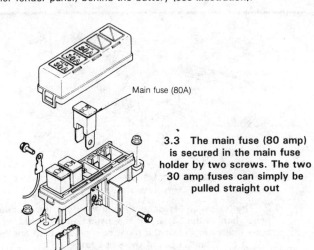

3.3 The main fuse (80 amp) is secured in the main fuse holder by two screws. The two 30 amp fuses can simply be pulled straight out

12

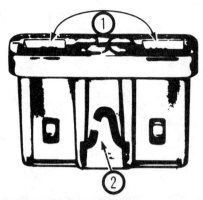

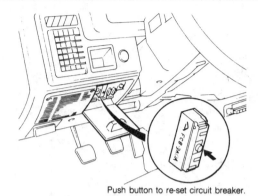

Push button to re-set circuit breaker.

3.4   To check the fuses in the fuse block, probe each terminal (1) with a test lamp — if it lights on one side but not the other, the fuse is blown. This condition can be confirmed by removing the fuse and inspecting the element for a break (2)

5.2   Some models are equipped with circuit breakers, which protect the heater and air conditioner circuits — if it "pops", open the fuse panel cover and press the button in the center of the breaker to reset it

If an electrical component has failed, your first check should be the fuse. A fuse which has "blown" can be readily identified by inspecting the metal element inside the housing (see illustration). If this element is broken the fuse is inoperable and should be replaced with a new one.

Fuses are replaced by simply pulling out the old one and pushing in the new one with the exception of the main fuse, which is secured by screws (see illustration 3.3).

It is important that the correct fuse be installed. The different electrical circuits need varying amounts of protection, indicated by the amperage rating on the fuse. A fuse with too low a rating will blow prematurely, while a fuse with too high a rating may not blow soon enough to avoid serious damage.

At no time should the fuse be bypassed by using metal or foil. Serious damage to the electrical system could result.

If the replacement fuse immediately fails, do not replace it with another until the cause of the problem is isolated and corrected. In most cases this will be a short circuit in the wiring system caused by a broken or deteriorated wire.

If an electrical failure occurs in a circuit or group of circuits, and there are no blown fuses, check for a melted fusible link. If the link is melted, it should be replaced, but only after checking and correcting the electrical fault that caused it.

5   Circuit breakers — general information

Refer to illustration 5.2

Circuit breakers, which are located in the main fuse block on some models, protect accessories such as the heater and air conditioner.

An electrical overload in the system will cause the blower or air compressor to go off and come on or, in some cases, to remain off. If this happens, check the malfunctioning circuit. The circuit breaker can be reset by pushing the button in the center of the breaker (see illustration). Refer to the wiring diagrams at the end of this book for the application of circuit breakers in your vehicle.

4   Fusible links — general information

Refer to illustration 4.2

In addition to fuses, the wiring system incorporates fusible links for additional overload protection. These links are used in circuits which are not ordinarily fused, such as the ignition circuit.

The fusible links are located near the positive battery terminal, and are easily removed by unplugging the connectors at either end (see illustration).

6   Hazard warning and turn signal flashers — check and replacement

Refer to illustrations 6.3a, 6.3b and 6.4

1   If the flashers fail to work properly, first check the bulbs, then make sure that the nuts which hold the light units to the vehicle are tight and free from corrosion. These complete the circuit and any resistance here could affect the operation of the flasher unit.

2   Check the security of all wiring connectors after referring to the proper wiring diagram. Make sure all of the fuses are good.

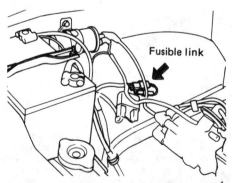

4.2   The fusible link is located along the right inner fender panel, behind the battery. If the insulation is burned or appears bubbly or swollen, it must be replaced with another fusible link of the same rating

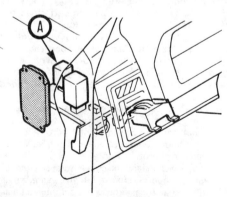

6.3a   The hazard warning/turn signal flasher unit (A) is located under the dash near the left kick panel on 1986 and later models

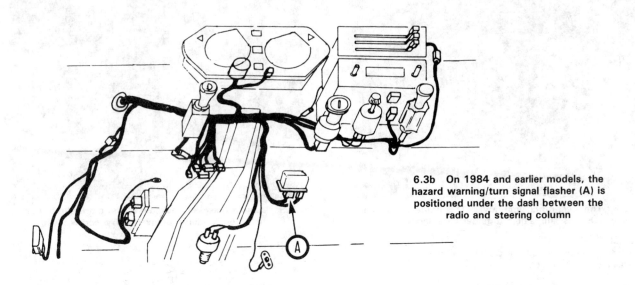

6.3b On 1984 and earlier models, the hazard warning/turn signal flasher (A) is positioned under the dash between the radio and steering column

3   If everything is secure after making the above checks, then the hazard warning/turn signal flasher unit itself must be faulty. Since it cannot be repaired, it must be replaced with a new unit. It is located under the dash, approximately between the left side kick panel and the air conditioning duct on 1986 and later models, or between the steering column and the radio on 1984 and earlier models **(see illustrations)**. To replace it, slide it from its bracket mount, disconnect the electrical connector and install a new unit.

4   Some very early models employ separate turn signal and hazard flasher units. They are mounted on separate sides of the steering column **(see illustration)**.

7 Ignition switch — removal and installation

Refer to illustrations 7.6 and 7.8

1   Disconnect the cable from the negative terminal of the battery.

Dash mounted switch

2   Reach under the dash and unplug the electrical connector from the back of the switch.

3   Hold the switch from behind the dash panel, then unscrew the re-

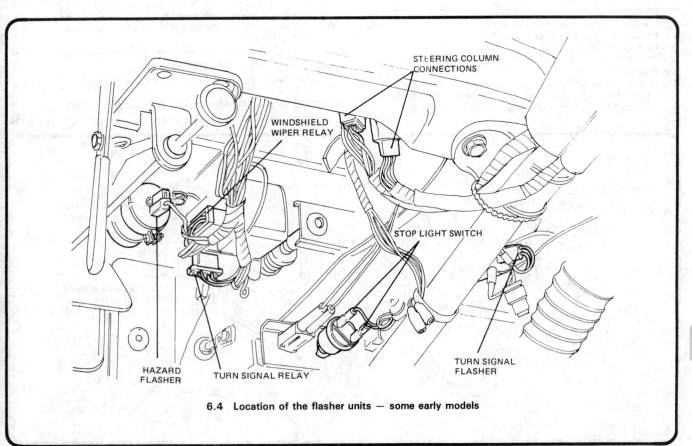

6.4 Location of the flasher units — some early models

7.6   The steering column cover (1) is made up of two halves and is held together with screws

taining nut.
4   Push the switch through the panel to remove it.
5   Installation is the reverse of the removal procedure.

Steering column mounted switch

6   Remove the steering column cover (see illustration).
7   Unplug the ignition switch wiring harness.
8   Remove the two ignition switch/steering lock mounting bolts. On models with shear-head bolts it will be necessary to cut slots in the tops of the bolts with a chisel or hacksaw blade, then unscrew them with a screwdriver (see illustration).
9   Remove the switch assembly from the steering column.
10 Installation is the reverse of the removal procedure.

---

8   Combination switch (light control, wiper and washer switch) — removal and installation

---

1   Disconnect the cable from the negative terminal of the battery.
2   Remove the steering wheel (see Chapter 10).
3   Remove the steering column covers.
4   Slide the stop ring, turn signal cancelling cam and spring off the steering shaft.
5   Unplug the electrical connector from the combination switch.
6   Loosen the clamp screw and pull the switch from the shaft.
7   To install the switch, reverse the removal procedure.

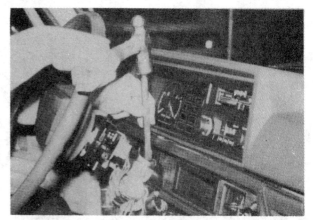

7.8   Using a chisel or hacksaw blade, cut a slot in each shear bolt to allow removal with a screwdriver

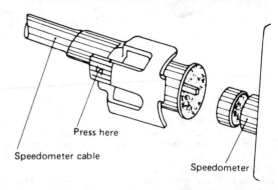

Press here
Speedometer cable
Speedometer

9.8   Some speedometer cables are fastened to the cluster by a threaded collar, others by a spring clip retainer as shown here

---

9   Combination meter (instrument cluster) — removal and installation

---

Refer to illustrations 9.8, 9.9 and 9.13
1   Disconnect the cable from the negative terminal of the battery.

Oblong dial combination meter (early models)

2   Reach up behind the instrument panel and remove the two bolts

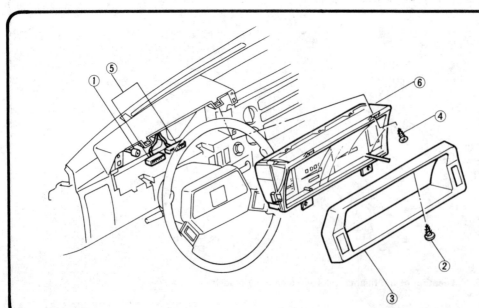

9.9   Combination meter mounting details (typical)

1   *Speedometer cable*
2   *Screw*
3   *Meter hood*
4   *Screw*
5   *Electrical connectors*
6   *Meter assembly*

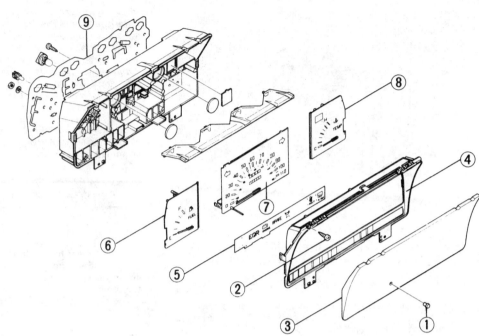

9.13 Exploded view of the combination meter assembly (1988 model shown, others similar)

1 Trip meter knob
2 Screws
3 Front lens
4 Window plate
5 Warning plate
6 Fuel gauge
7 Speedometer
8 Coolant temperature gauge
9 Printed circuit board

and washers and the two nuts and washers.

3   Pull the cluster out as far as possible then unscrew the speedometer cable from the back of the unit.

4   Using pieces of numbered tape, carefully mark the positions of the wires that must be disconnected to remove the unit, then disconnect them.

5   Remove the meter assembly from the dash.

6   Installation is the reverse of the removal procedure.

All others

7   Remove the meter hood, if so equipped.

8   Reach behind the meter from under the dash and disconnect the speedometer cable. Some models have a threaded collar that must be unscrewed, others have a spring clip type device that must be pressed in to free the cable casing (**see illustration**).

9   Remove the four cluster assembly-to-dash panel screws (**see illustration**).

10 Pull the meter assembly out as far as possible and unplug the multi-wire connector(s) from the back of the unit. Some models have additional wires that must be disconnected, so be sure to mark them before removing.

11 Remove the combination meter from the dash panel.

12 If it is necessary to remove the printed circuit board from the rear of the meter assembly, remove all of the bulbs and retainers. Remove the gauge retaining screws and the lens screws and carefully lift the printed circuit from the unit.

13 The combination meter assembly can be dismantled to allow access to the enclosed gauges and indicators by removing the lens and plate retaining screws (**see illustration**).

14 Installation is the reverse of the removal procedure.

10   Headlights — removal and installation

Refer to illustrations 10.2a, 10.2b and 10.4

1   Depending on the vehicle, it may be necessary to remove the headlight trim or grille for access to the bezel screws. Refer to Chapter 11 for the grille or headlight trim piece removal procedure.

2   On vehicles with round headlights, loosen, but do not remove the three screws in the keyhole slots in the light bezel. Do not disturb the adjusting screws. Turn the bezel clockwise, then lift the bezel off the screw heads (**see illustrations**).

10.2a   To remove a round headlight, loosen the bezel retaining screws . . .

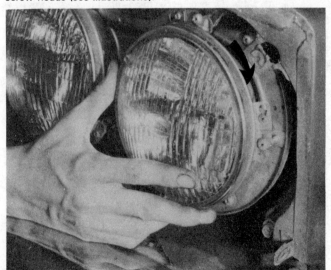

10.2b   . . . rotate the bezel to line up the screw "keyhole" slots and pull it off

12

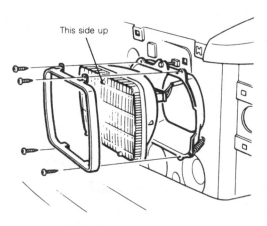

10.4   To remove rectangular headlights, remove the four trim ring screws, then remove the trim ring and headlight

3   Hold the headlight and disconnect the plug from the contacts at the rear.
4   On vehicles with rectangular headlights, remove the screws holding the headlight trim ring, then lift off the trim ring **(see illustration)**.
5   Pull out the headlight and disconnect the plug from the contacts at the rear.
6   Installation is the reverse of removal.

11   Headlights — adjustment

Refer to illustration 11.2

1   It's important that the headlights be aimed correctly. If adjusted incorrectly they could blind an oncoming driver and cause a serious accident or seriously reduce your ability to see the road. The headlights should be checked for proper aim every 12 months and each time a new sealed beam headlight is installed or front end body work is performed.
2   Each headlight has two spring-loaded adjusting screws, one on the top controlling up-and-down movement and one on the side controlling left-and-right movement **(see illustration)**. There are several methods of adjusting the headlights. The simplest method requires an empty wall 25 feet in front of the vehicle and a level floor.
3   Park the vehicle on a level floor 25 feet from the wall.
4   Position masking tape vertically on the wall in reference to the vehicle centerline and the centerlines of both headlights.
5   Position a horizontal tape line in reference to the centerline of all the headlights. **Note:** *It may be easier to position the tape on the wall with the vehicle parked only a few inches away.*
6   Adjustment should be made with the vehicle sitting level, the gas tank half-full and no unusually heavy load in the vehicle.
7   Starting with the Low beam adjustment, position the high intensity zone two inches below the horizontal line and two inches to the right of the headlight vertical line. Adjustment is made by turning the top

11.2   Location of the headlight aim adjusting screws

adjusting screw clockwise to raise the beam and counterclockwise to lower the beam. The adjusting screw on the side should be used in the same manner to move the beam left-or-right.
8   With the High beams on, the high intensity zone should be vertically centered with the exact center just below the horizontal line. **Note:** *It may not be possible to position the headlight aim exactly for both High and Low beams. If a compromise must be made, keep in mind that the Low beams are the most used and have the greatest effect on driver safety.*
9   Any adjustments which are made should be regarded only as interim measures and the alignment should be checked as soon as possible by a dealer service department or other service station with optical alignment equipment.

12   Windshield wiper motor — removal and installation

Refer to illustrations 12.3 and 12.4

Removal

1   Disconnect the cable from the negative terminal of the battery.
2   Mark the wiper arms as to which side of the vehicle they are on, lift up the covers and remove the wiper arm securing nuts. Remove the arms.
3   Remove the cowl grille **(see illustration)**.

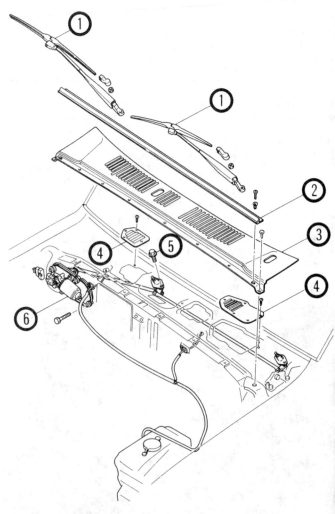

12.3   Wiper motor and related components

1 *Wiper arms and blades*	5 *Bolt*
2 *Weatherstrip*	6 *Wiper motor and link*
3 *Cowl grille*	*assembly*
4 *Seal covers*	

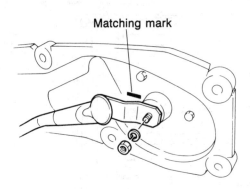

12.4 Mark the position of the motor arm to the motor to ensure correct wiper operation

4 Apply a match mark from the wiper motor arm to the wiper motor **(see illustration)**, then remove the nut and washer, separating the motor arm from the motor shaft.
5 Disconnect the motor electrical connector, remove the mounting bolts and separate the motor from the firewall.

Installation

6 Position the motor on the firewall and install the bolts, tightening them securely. Plug in the electrical connector.

7 Install the wiper motor arm to the motor shaft, aligning the previously applied match mark. Install the lock washer and nut, tightening the nut securely.
8 Install the cowl grille.
9 Install the wiper arms.
10 Connect the negative cable to the battery.
11 Operate the wipers, noting the sweep pattern on the winsdshield. If the wiper arms travel too high or too low, remove and reposition them as necessary.

13 Bulbs — replacement

Refer to illustrations 13.2a, 13.2b and 13.3
1 The lenses of most lights are held on by screws, which makes it a simple procedure to gain access to the bulbs.
2 A few lights have their lenses held in by clips. On these, the lens can either be removed by unsnapping it by hand or, as with the interior overhead light, using a small screwdriver inserted in the rear to pry it off **(see illustrations)**.
3 Four different types of bulbs are used **(see illustration)**. Type A and B are removed by pushing in and turning counterclockwise. Type D simply unclips from its terminals and Type C simply pulls out of its socket.
4 To gain access to the instrument panel illumination light bulbs, the combination meter must be removed as described in Section 9.

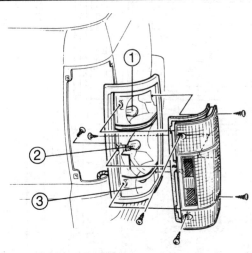

13.2a Rear combination light installation details — 1986 and later

1 *Turn signal light*   3 *Back-up light*
2 *Brake and tail light*

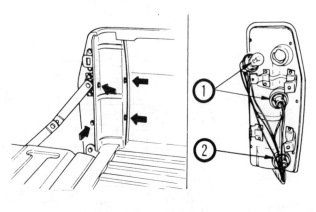

13.2b Rear combination light installation details — 1984 and earlier models. Remove the four screws to separate the light housing from the body, then the rear turn signal/stoplight bulbs (1) or the back-up light bulb (2) can be removed

A   B   C   D

 REMOVE   INSTALL

13.3 The four types of bulbs used on these vehicles

12

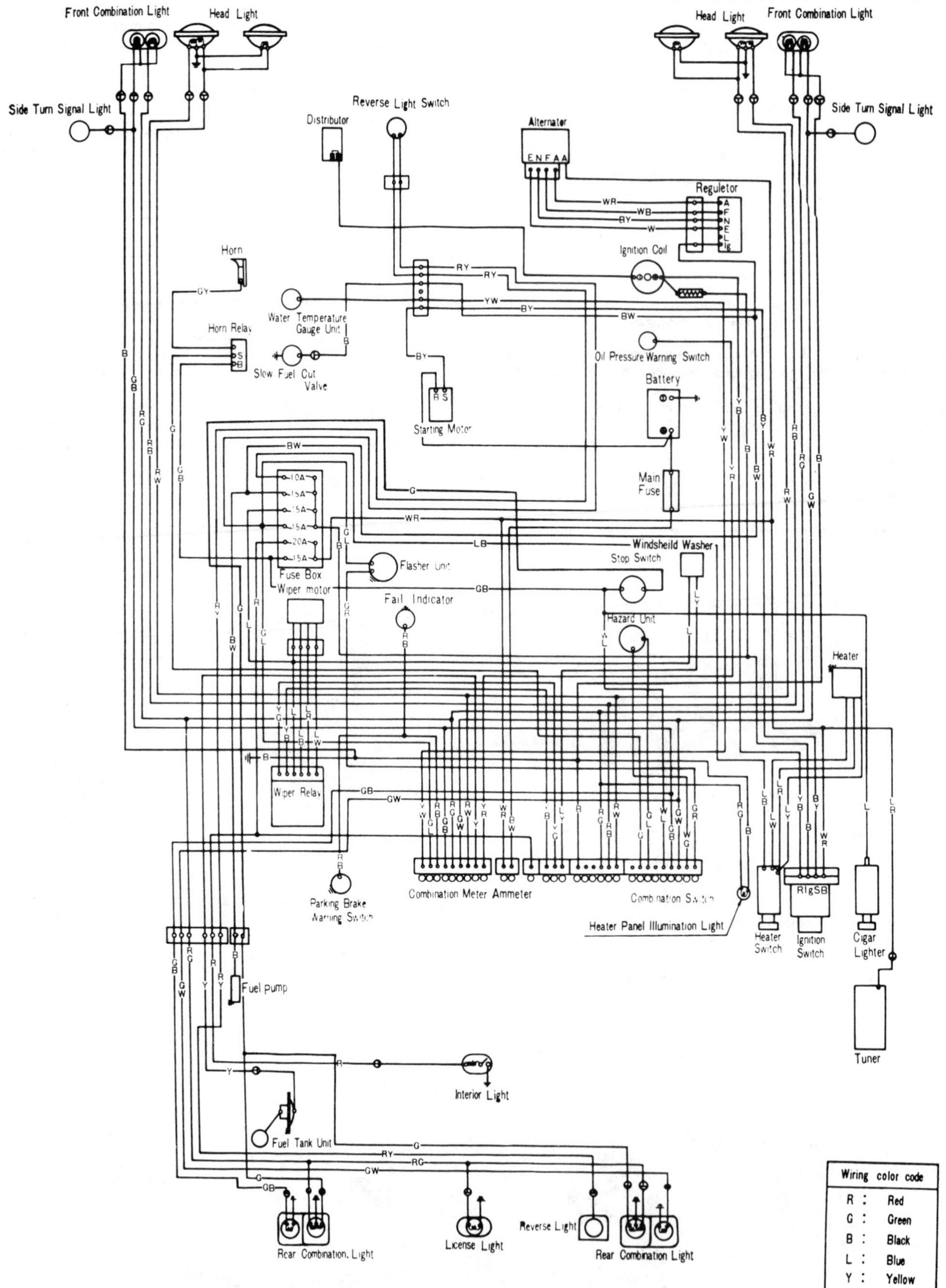

Front Combination Light · Head Light · Head Light · Front Combination Light

Side Turn Signal Light

Reverse Light Switch

Distributor

Alternator

E N F A A

Regulator

A F N E L Ig

WR WB
BY

Ignition Coil

Horn

Horn Relay

Water Temperature Gauge Unit

Slow Fuel Cut Valve

Oil Pressure Warning Switch

Battery

Starting Motor

Main Fuse

Side Turn Signal Light

Fuse Box

10A
15A
15A
15A
20A
15A

Flasher Unit

Wiper motor

Fail Indicator

Windsheild Washer

Stop Switch

Hazard Unit

Heater

Wiper Relay

Parking Brake Warning Switch

Combination Meter   Ammeter

Combination Switch

Heater Panel Illumination Light

Heater Switch

Ignition Switch

Cigar Lighter

Tuner

Fuel pump

Interior Light

Fuel Tank Unit

Rear Combination Light

License Light

Reverse Light

Rear Combination Light

Wiring color code	
R :	Red
G :	Green
B :	Black
L :	Blue
Y :	Yellow
W :	White

Wiring diagram — early model B1600

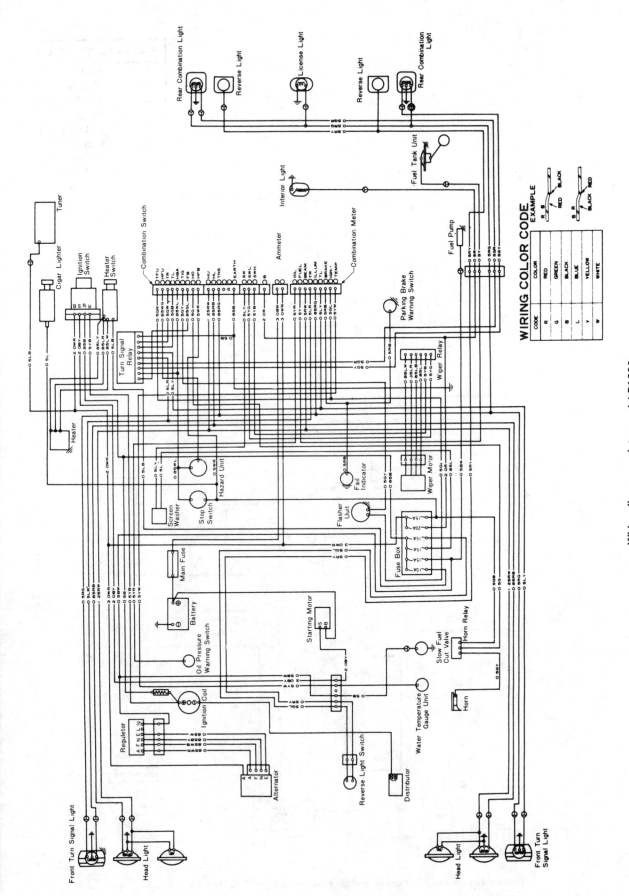

Wiring diagram — later model B1600

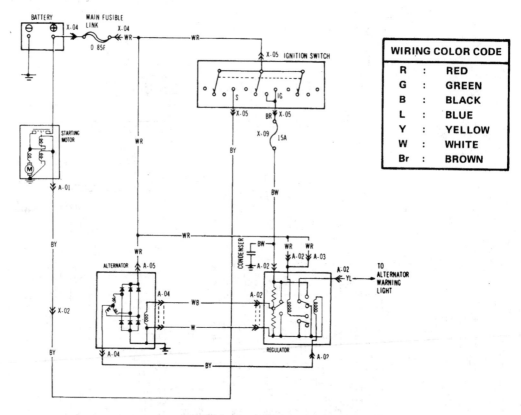

Charging system/starting system — 1979 thru 1981 B2000

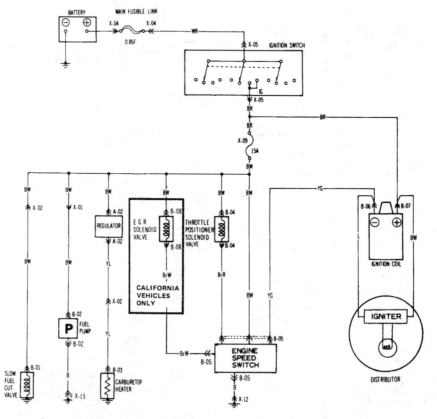

Ignition system/slow fuel cut valve/fuel pump circuit — 1979 thru 1981 B2000

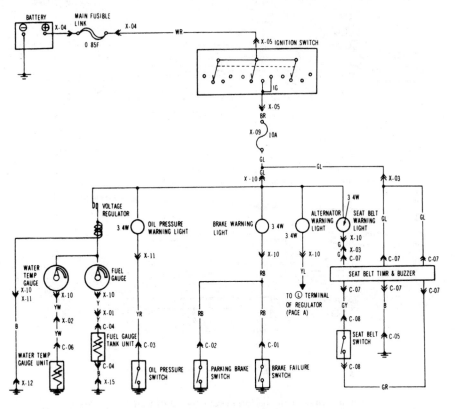

Meter and warning system/seat belt warning system — 1979 thru 1981 B2000

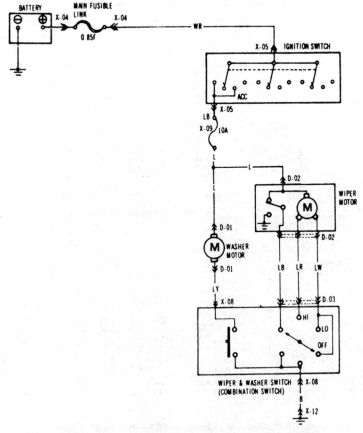

Wiper and washer system — 1979 thru 1981 B2000

12

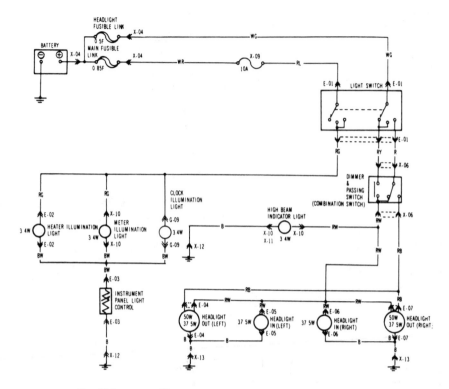

Headlight system/illumination system — 1979 thru 1981 B2000

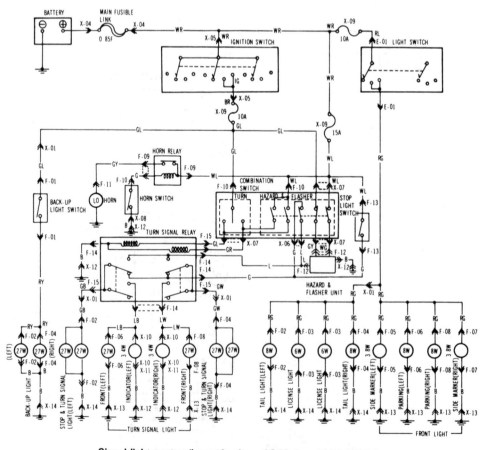

Signal light system/horn circuit — 1979 thru 1981 B2000

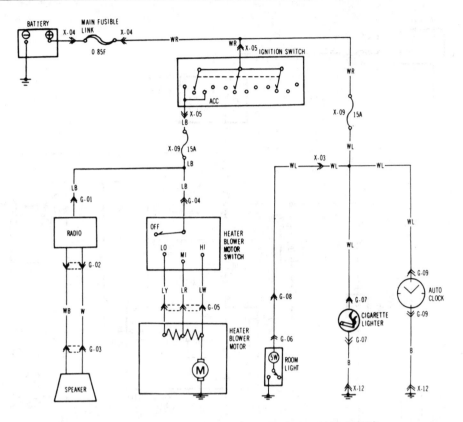

Heater system/room light/lighter/clock — 1979 thru 1981 B2000

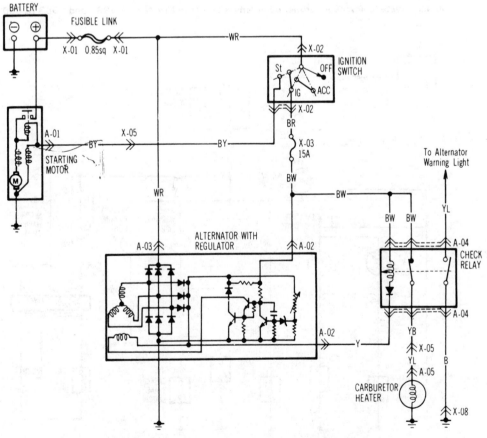

Charging system/starting system — 1982 thru 1984 B2000

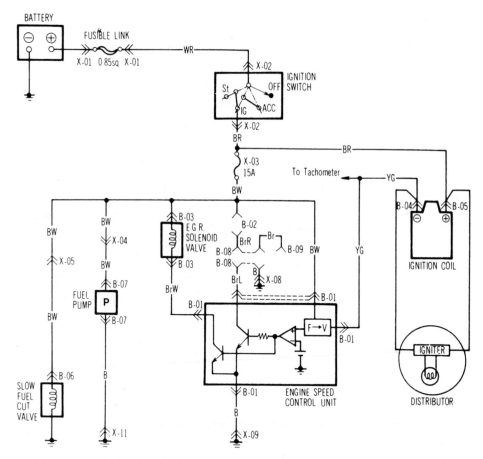

Ignition system/slow fuel cut/fuel pump/emission control system — 1982 and 1983 B2000

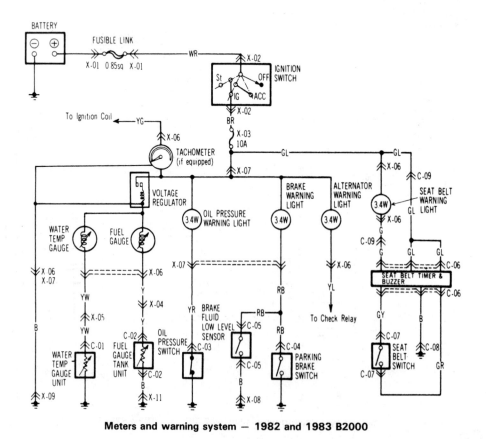

Meters and warning system — 1982 and 1983 B2000

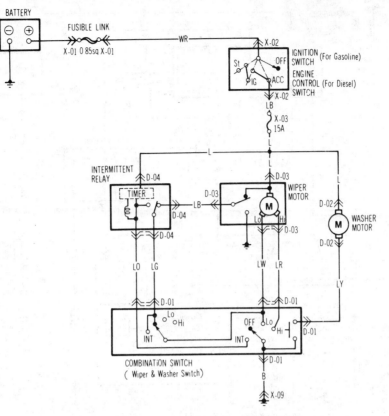

Wiper and washer — 1982 thru 1984 B2000

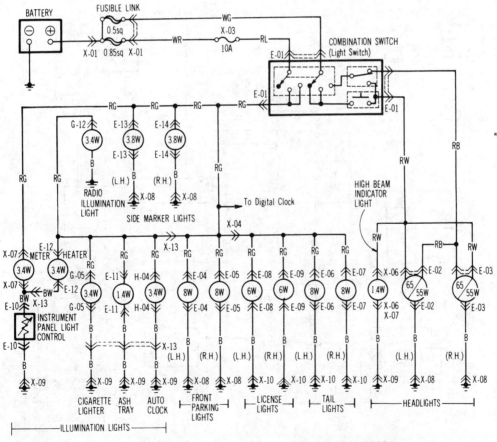

Lighting and illumination system — 1982 thru 1984 B2000

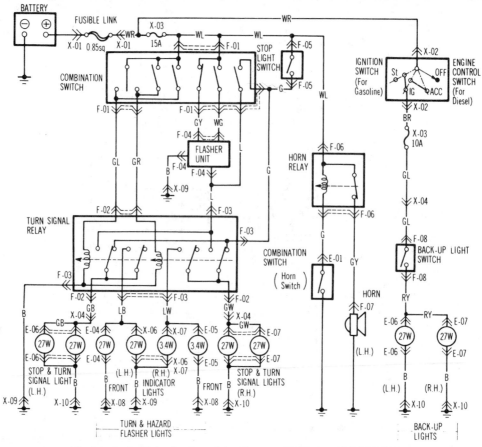

Flashers/brake lights/back-up lights/horn — 1982 thru 1984 B2000

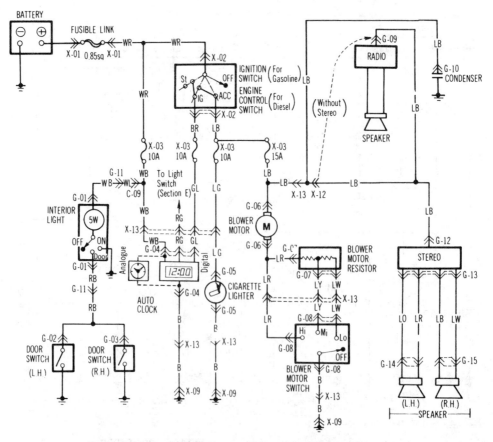

Heater/lighter/radio/clock/interior light — 1982 and 1983 B2000

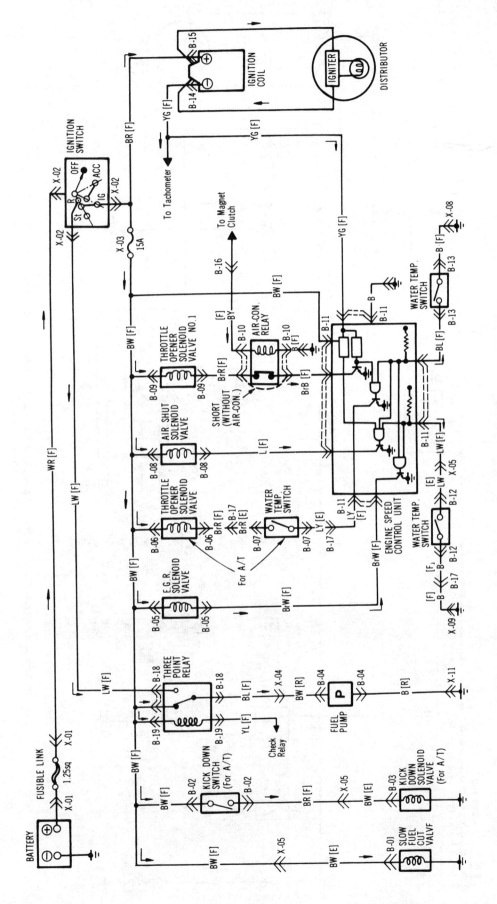

Ignition system/slow fuel cut valve/fuel pump/emission control system/kick-down system for A/T
(1984 B2000 Federal models)

12

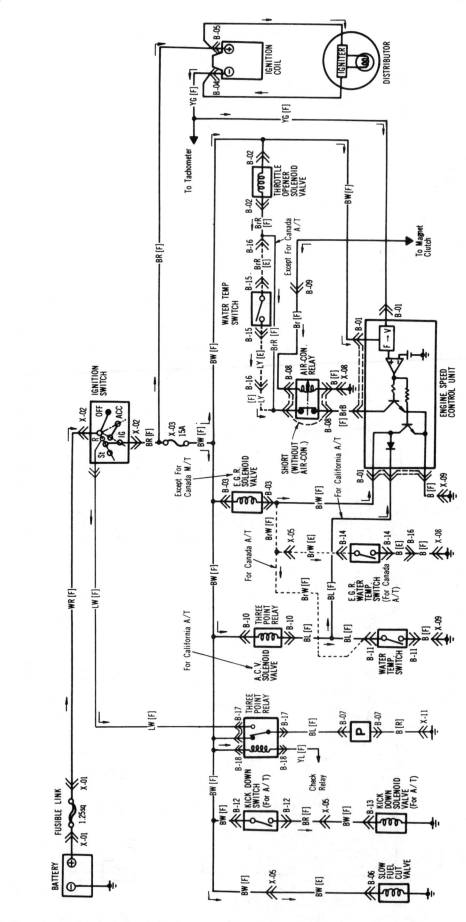

Ignition system/slow fuel cut valve/fuel pump/emission control system/kick-down system for A/T
(1984 B2000 non-Federal models)

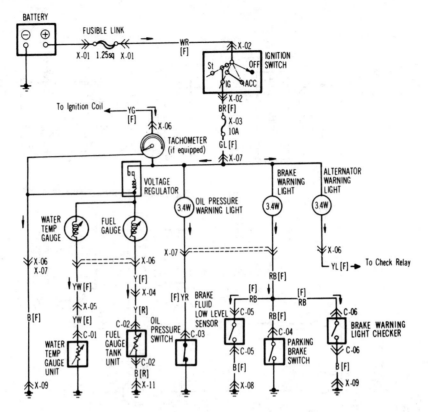

Meters and warning system — 1984 B2000

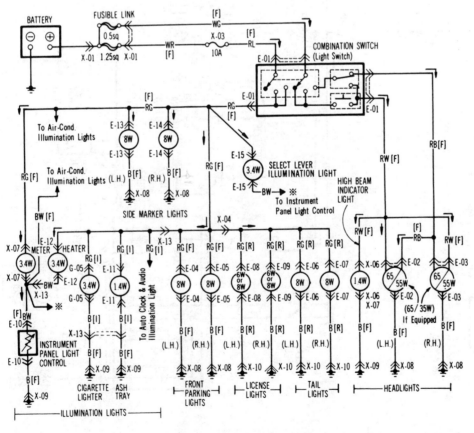

Exterior lights — 1984 B2000

12

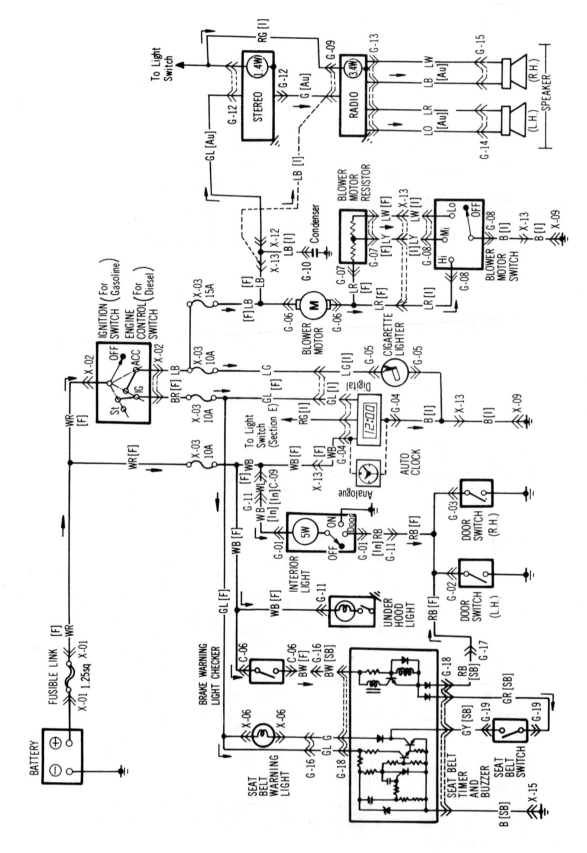

Heater/lighter/radio/clock/interior light/seat belt warning system — 1984 B2000

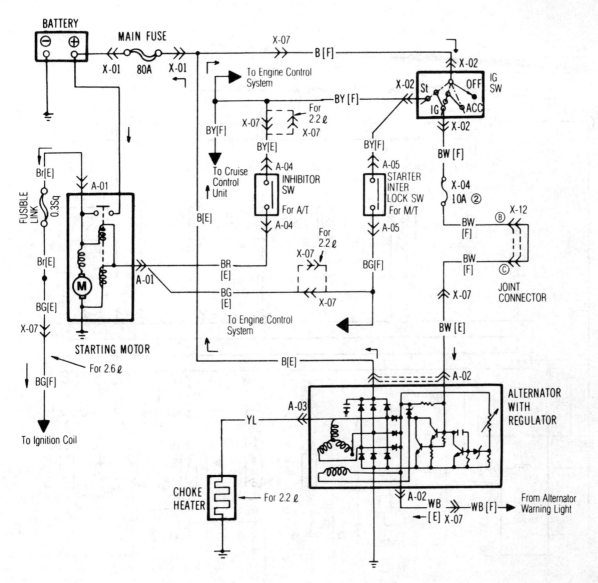

Starting system/charging system — 1984 and later models

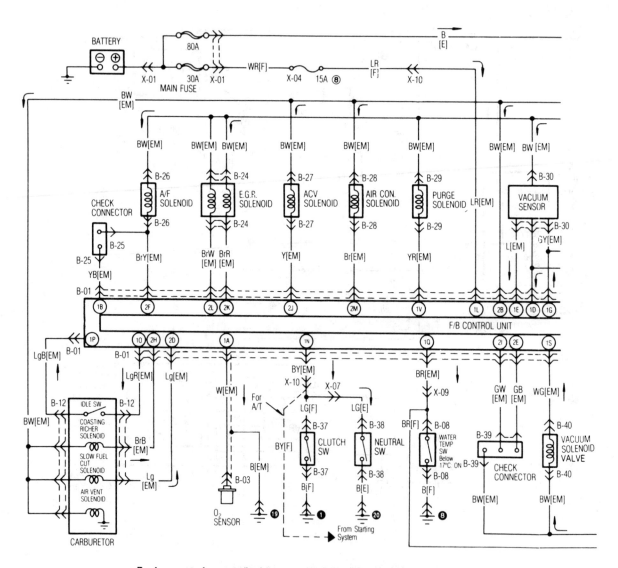

Engine control system/ignition system/fuel pump circuit — B2200 models

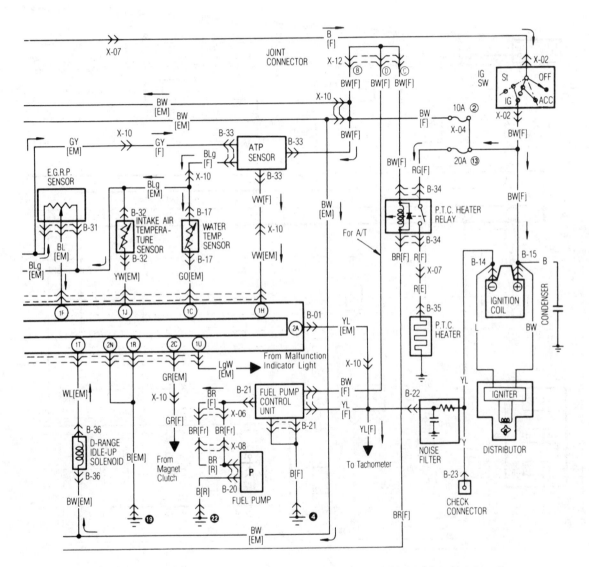

Engine control system/ignition system/fuel pump circuit — B2200 models (continued)

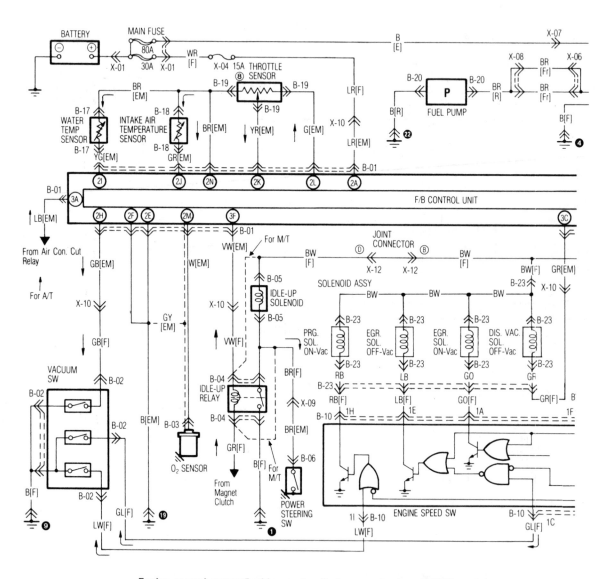

Engine control system/ignition system/fuel pump circuit — B2600 models

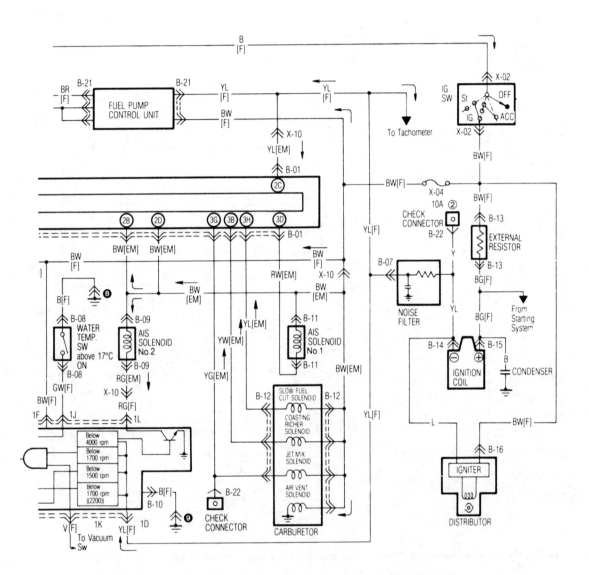

Engine control system/ignition system/fuel pump circuit — B2600 models (continued)

12

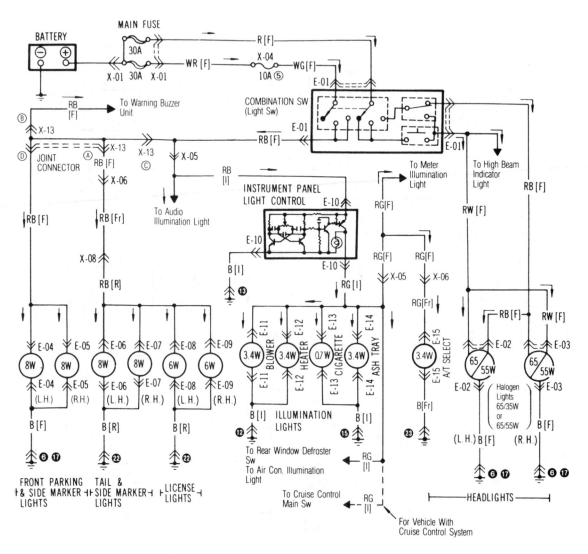

Headlights/tail lights/parking, side marker and license plate lights/illumination lights — 1986 and later models

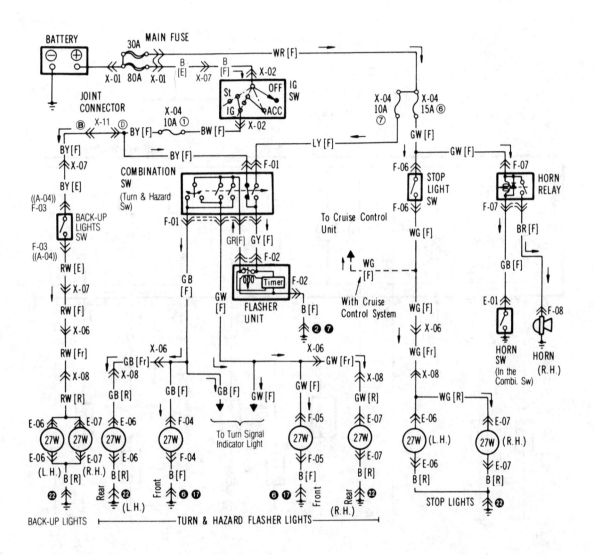

Turn signal and hazard flasher lights/back-up and stop lights/horn — 1986 and later models

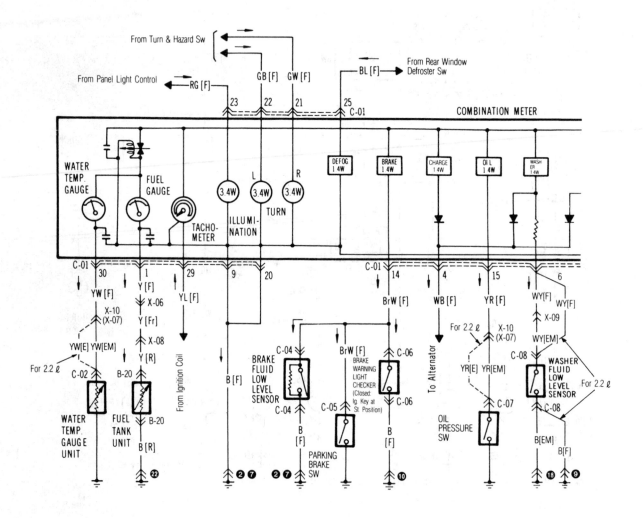

Warning lights/meters – 1988 and later models (1986 and 1987 models similar)

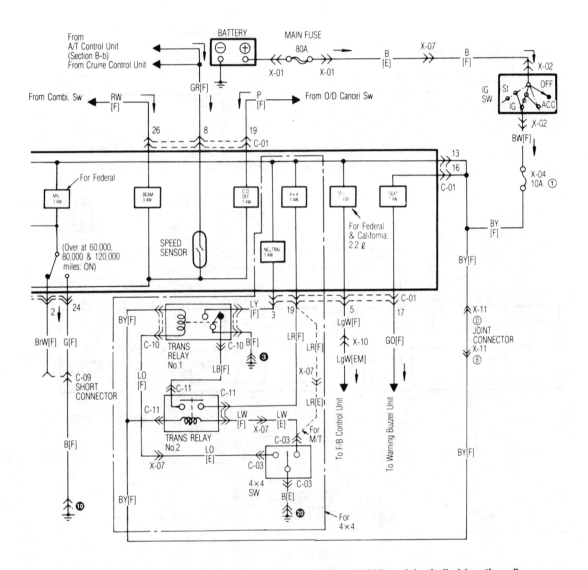

Warning lights/meters – 1988 and later models (1986 and 1987 models similar) (continued)

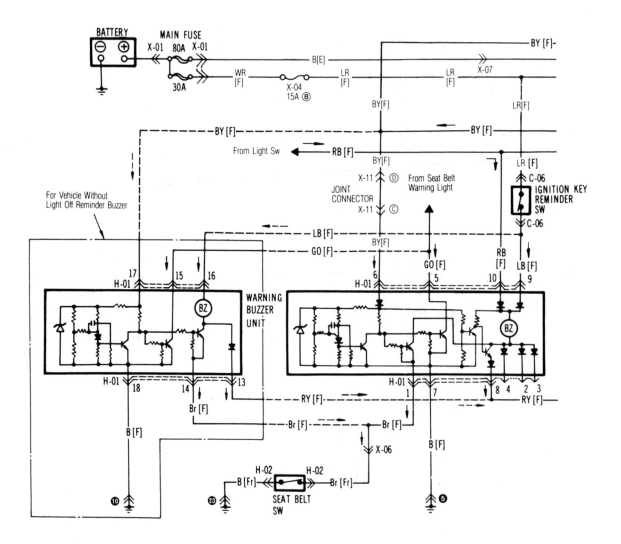

Interior lights/cigarette lighter/ignition key and seat belt warning buzzers — 1986 and later models

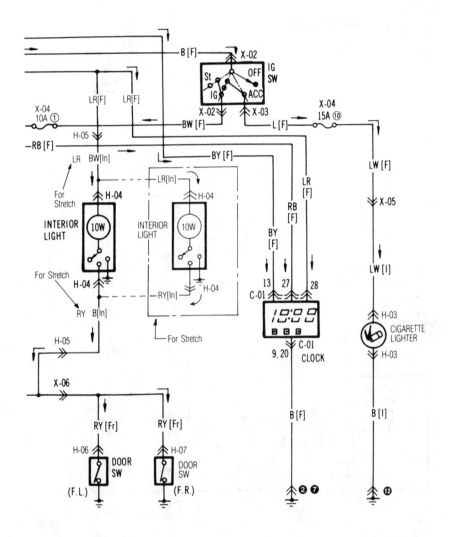

Interior lights/cigarette lighter/ignition key and seat belt warning buzzers — 1986 and later models (continued)

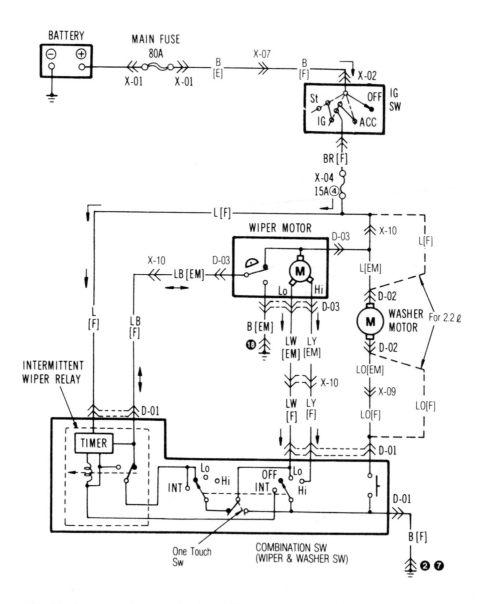

Windshield wiper and washer circuits – 1988 and later models (1986 and 1987 models similar)

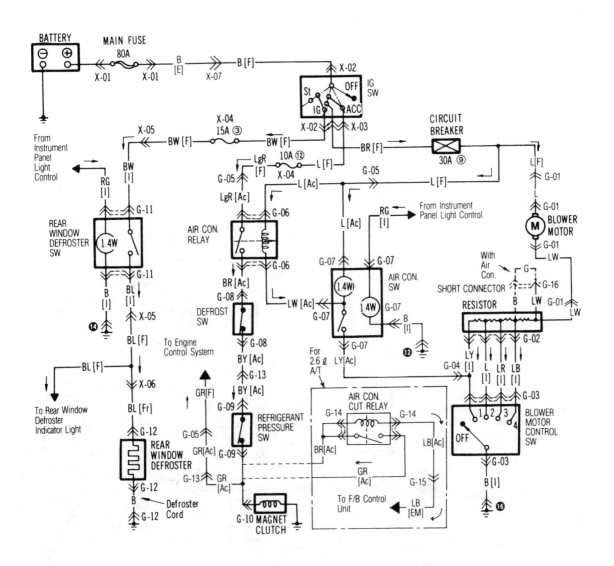

Heater and air conditioner/rear window defroster – 1988 and later models (1986 and 1987 models similar)

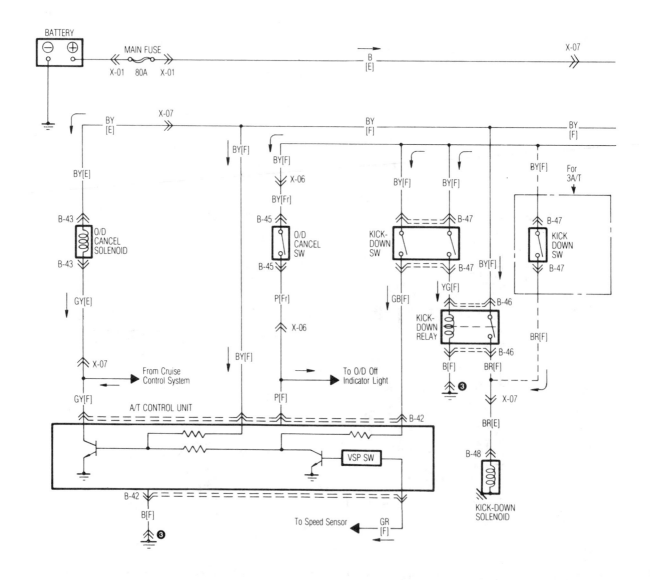

Automatic transmission control system – 1988 and later models

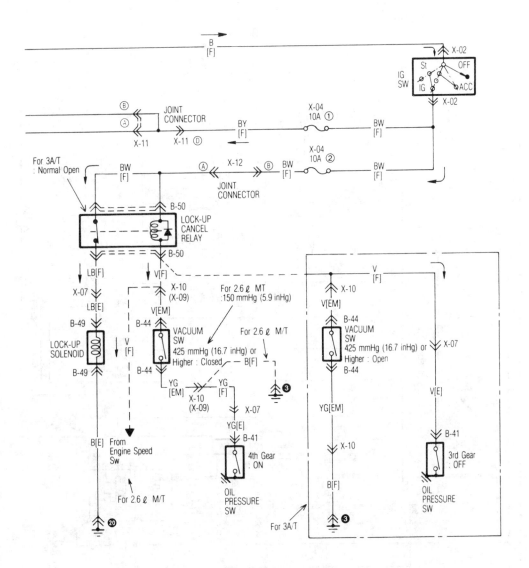

Automatic transmission control system – 1988 and later models (continued)

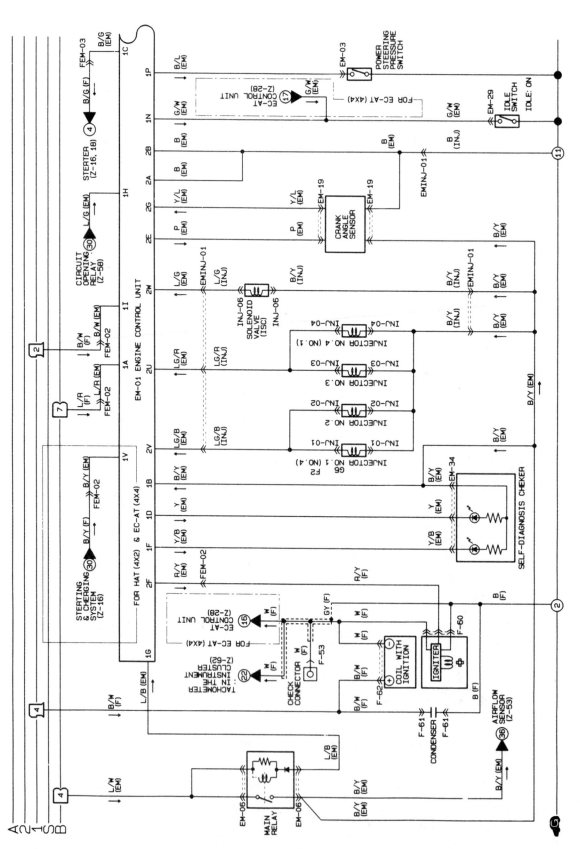

Fuel injection system – 1990 on

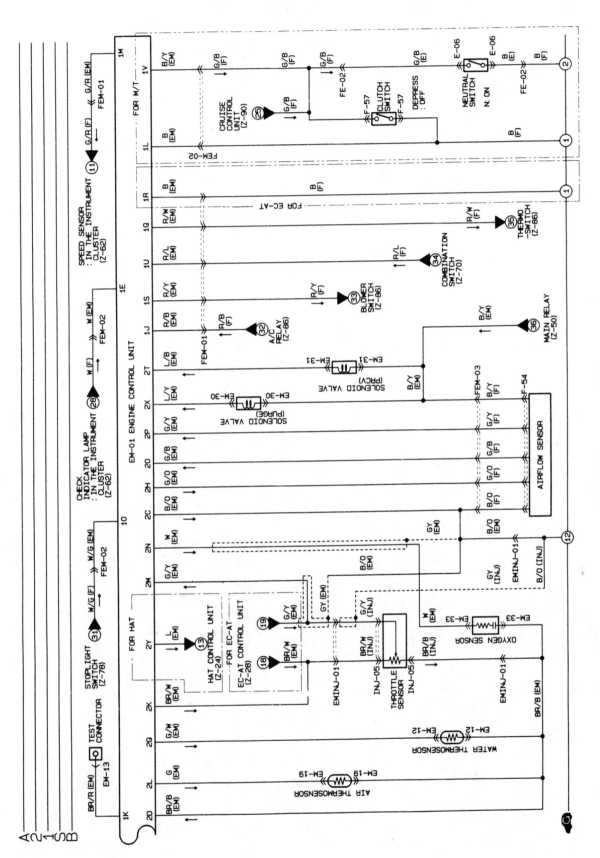

Fuel injection system – 1990 on

NOTES

Index

A

B

NOTES

HAYNES AUTOMOTIVE MANUALS

NOTE: New manuals are added to this list on a periodic basis. If you do not see a listing for your vehicle, consult your local Haynes dealer for the latest product information.

ACURA
1776 **Integra & Legend** '86 thru '90

AMC
    Jeep CJ – *see JEEP (412)*
694 **Mid-size models**, Concord, Hornet, Gremlin & Spirit '70 thru '83
934 **(Renault) Alliance & Encore** all models '83 thru '87

AUDI
615 **4000** all models '80 thru '87
428 **5000** all models '77 thru '83
1117 **5000** all models '84 thru '88

AUSTIN
    Healey Sprite – *see MG Midget Roadster (265)*

BMW
276 **320i** all 4 cyl models '75 thru '83
632 **528i & 530i** all models '75 thru '80
240 **1500 thru 2002** all models except Turbo '59 thru '77
348 **2500, 2800, 3.0 & Bavaria** '69 thru '76

BUICK
    Century (front wheel drive) – *see GENERAL MOTORS A-Cars (829)*
*1627 **Buick, Oldsmobile & Pontiac Full-size (Front wheel drive)** all models '85 thru '93 **Buick** Electra, LeSabre and Park Avenue; **Oldsmobile** Delta 88 Royale, Ninety Eight and Regency; **Pontiac** Bonneville
*1551 **Buick Oldsmobile & Pontiac Full-size (Rear wheel drive)** **Buick** Electra '70 thru '84, Estate '70 thru '90, LeSabre '70 thru '79 **Oldsmobile** Custom Cruiser '70 thru '90, Delta 88 '70 thru '85, Ninety-eight '70 thru '84 **Pontiac** Bonneville '70 thru '81, Catalina '70 thru '81, Grandville '70 thru '75, Parisienne '84 thu '86
627 **Mid-size** all rear-drive **Regal & Century** models with V6, V8 and Turbo '74 thru '87
    Regal – *see GENERAL MOTORS (1671)*
    Skyhawk – *see GENERAL MOTORS J-Cars (766)*
552 **Skylark** all X-car models '80 thru '85

CADILLAC
*751 **Cadillac Rear Wheel Drive** all gasoline models '70 thru '90
    Cimarron – *see GENERAL MOTORS J-Cars (766)*

CAPRI
296 **2000 MK I Coupe** all models '71 thru '75
205 **2600 & 2800 V6 Coupe** '71 thru '75
375 **2800 Mk II V6 Coupe** '75 thru '78
    Mercury Capri – *see FORD Mustang (654)*

CHEVROLET
*1477 **Astro & GMC Safari Mini-vans** all models '85 thru '91
554 **Camaro** V8 all models '70 thru '81
*866 **Camaro** all models '82 thru '91
    Cavalier – *see GENERAL MOTORS J-Cars (766)*
    Celebrity – *see GENERAL MOTORS A-Cars (829)*
625 **Chevelle, Malibu & El Camino** all V6 & V8 models '69 thru '87
449 **Chevette & Pontiac T1000** all models '76 thru '87
550 **Citation** all models '80 thru '85
*1628 **Corsica/Beretta** all models '87 thru '92
274 **Corvette** all V8 models '68 thru '82
*1336 **Corvette** all models '84 thru '91

704 **Full-size Sedans** Caprice, Impala, Biscayne, Bel Air & Wagons, all V6 & V8 models '69 thru '90
    Lumina – *see GENERAL MOTORS (1671)*
    Lumina APV – *see GENERAL MOTORS (2035)*
319 **Luv Pick-up** all 2WD & 4WD models '72 thru '82
626 **Monte Carlo** all V6, V8 & Turbo models '70 thru '88
241 **Nova** all V8 models '69 thru '79
*1642 **Nova and Geo Prizm** all front wheel drive models, '85 thru '90
*420 **Pick-ups '67 thru '87** – Chevrolet & GMC, all full-size models '67 thru '87; Suburban, Blazer & Jimmy '67 thru '91
*1664 **Pick-ups '88 thru '92** – Chevrolet & GMC, all full-size (C and K) models, '88 thru '92
*1727 **Sprint & Geo Metro** '85 thru '91
*831 **S-10 & GMC S-15 Pick-ups** all models '82 thru '92
*345 **Vans** – Chevrolet & GMC, V8 & in-line 6 cyl models '68 thru '92

CHRYSLER
*1337 **Chrysler & Plymouth Mid-size** front wheel drive '82 thru '93
    K-Cars – *see DODGE Aries (723)*
    Laser – *see DODGE Daytona (1140)*

DATSUN
402 **200SX** all models '77 thru '79
647 **200SX** all models '80 thru '83
228 **B-210** all models '73 thru '78
525 **210** all models '78 thru '82
206 **240Z, 260Z & 280Z Coupe** & 2+2 '70 thru '78
563 **280ZX Coupe & 2+2** '79 thru '83
    300ZX – *see NISSAN (1137)*
679 **310** all models '78 thru '82
123 **510 & PL521 Pick-up** '68 thru '73
430 **510** all models '78 thru '81
372 **610** all models '72 thru '76
277 **620 Series Pick-up** all models '73 thru '79
    720 Series Pick-up – *see NISSAN Pick-ups (771)*
376 **810/Maxima** all gasoline models '77 thru '84
124 **1200** all models '70 thru '73
368 **F10** all models '76 thru '79
    Pulsar – *see NISSAN (876)*
    Sentra – *see NISSAN (982)*
    Stanza – *see NISSAN (981)*

DODGE
*723 **Aries & Plymouth Reliant** all models '81 thru '89
*1231 **Caravan & Plymouth Voyager Mini-Vans** all models '84 thru '91
699 **Challenger & Plymouth Saporro** all models '78 thru '83
236 **Colt** all models '71 thru '77
610 **Colt & Plymouth Champ (front wheel drive)** all models '78 thru '87
*556 **D50/Ram 50/Plymouth Arrow Pick-ups & Raider** '79 thru '91
*1668 **Dakota Pick-up** all models '87 thru '90
234 **Dart & Plymouth Valiant** all 6 cyl models '67 thru '76
*1140 **Daytona & Chrysler Laser** all models '84 thru '89
*545 **Omni & Plymouth Horizon** all models '78 thru '90
*912 **Pick-ups** all full-size models '74 thru '91
*1726 **Shadow & Plymouth Sundance** '87 thru '91
*1779 **Spirit & Plymouth Acclaim** '89 thru '92
*349 **Vans** – Dodge & Plymouth V8 & 6 cyl models '71 thru '91

FIAT
094 **124 Sport Coupe & Spider** '68 thru '78

479 **Strada** all models '79 thru '82
273 **X1/9** all models '74 thru '80

FORD
*1476 **Aerostar Mini-vans** all models '86 thru '92
788 **Bronco and Pick-ups** '73 thru '79
*880 **Bronco and Pick-ups** '80 thru '91
268 **Courier Pick-up** all models '72 thru '82
789 **Escort & Mercury Lynx** all models '81 thru '90
*2046 **Escort & Mercury Tracer** all models '91 thru '93
*2021 **Explorer & Mazda Navajo** '91 thru '92
560 **Fairmont & Mercury Zephyr** all in-line & V8 models '78 thru '83
334 **Fiesta** all models '77 thru '80
754 **Ford & Mercury Full-size,** Ford LTD & Mercury Marquis ('75 thru '82); Ford Custom 500, Country Squire, Crown Victoria & Mercury Colony Park ('75 thru '87); Ford LTD Crown Victoria & Mercury Gran Marquis ('83 thru '87)
359 **Granada & Mercury Monarch** all in-line, 6 cyl & V8 models '75 thru '80
773 **Ford & Mercury Mid-size,** Ford Thunderbird & Mercury Cougar ('75 thru '82); Ford LTD & Mercury Marquis ('83 thru '86); Ford Torino, Gran Torino, Elite, Ranchero pick-up, LTD II, Mercury Montego, Comet, XR-7 & Lincoln Versailles ('75 thru '86)
*654 **Mustang & Mercury Capri** all models including Turbo '79 thru '92
357 **Mustang V8** all models '64-1/2 thru '73
231 **Mustang II** all 4 cyl, V6 & V8 models '74 thru '78
649 **Pinto & Mercury Bobcat** all models '75 thru '80
*1670 **Probe** all models '89 thru '92
*1026 **Ranger & Bronco II** all gasoline models '83 thru '92
*1421 **Taurus & Mercury Sable** '86 thru '92
*1418 **Tempo & Mercury Topaz** all gasoline models '84 thru '91
1338 **Thunderbird & Mercury Cougar/XR7** '83 thru '88
*1725 **Thunderbird & Mercury Cougar** '89 and '90
*344 **Vans** all V8 Econoline models '69 thru '91

GENERAL MOTORS
*829 **A-Cars** – Chevrolet Celebrity, Buick Century, Pontiac 6000 & Oldsmobile Cutlass Ciera all models '82 thru '90
*766 **J-Cars** – Chevrolet Cavalier, Pontiac J-2000, Oldsmobile Firenza, Buick Skyhawk & Cadillac Cimarron all models '82 thru '92
*1420 **N-Cars** – Buick Somerset '85 thru '87; Pontiac Grand Am and Oldsmobile Calais '85 thru '91; Buick Skylark '86 thru '91
*1671 **GM: Buick** Regal, **Chevrolet** Lumina, **Oldsmobile** Cutlass Supreme, **Pontiac** Grand Prix, all front wheel drive models '88 thru '90
*2035 **GM: Chevrolet Lumina APV, Oldsmobile Silhouette, Pontiac Trans Sport** '90 thru '92

GEO
    Metro – *see CHEVROLET Sprint (1727)*
    Prizm – *see CHEVROLET Nova (1642)*
    Tracker – *see SUZUKI Samurai (1626)*

GMC
    Safari – *see CHEVROLET ASTRO (1477)*
    Vans & Pick-ups – *see CHEVROLET (420, 831, 345, 1664)*

(continued on next page)

** Listings shown with an asterisk (*) indicate model coverage as of this printing. These titles will be periodically updated to include later model years – consult your Haynes dealer for more information.*

Haynes North America, Inc., 861 Lawrence Drive, Newbury Park, CA 91320 • (805) 498-6703

HAYNES AUTOMOTIVE MANUALS

(continued from previous page)

NOTE: New manuals are added to this list on a periodic basis. If you do not see a listing for your vehicle, consult your local Haynes dealer for the latest product information.

HONDA

351	**Accord CVCC** all models '76 thru '83
*1221	**Accord** all models '84 thru '89
160	**Civic 1200** all models '73 thru '79
633	**Civic 1300 & 1500 CVCC** all models '80 thru '83
297	**Civic 1500 CVCC** all models '75 thru '79
*1227	**Civic** all models '84 thru '91
*601	**Prelude CVCC** all models '79 thru '89

HYUNDAI

*1552 **Excel** all models '86 thru '91

ISUZU

*1641 **Trooper & Pick-up,** all gasoline models '81 thru '91

JAGUAR

*242 **XJ6** all 6 cyl models '68 thru '86
*478 **XJ12 & XJS** all 12 cyl models '72 thru '85

JEEP

*1553 **Cherokee, Comanche & Wagoneer Limited** all models '84 thru '91
412 **CJ** all models '49 thru '86
*1777 **Wrangler** all models '87 thru '92

LADA

*413 **1200, 1300. 1500 & 1600** all models including Riva '74 thru '86

MAZDA

648 **626** Sedan & Coupe (rear wheel drive) all models '79 thru '82
1082 **626 & MX-6 (front wheel drive)** all models '83 thru '91
370 **GLC Hatchback (rear wheel drive)** all models '77 thru '83
757 **GLC (front wheel drive)** all models '81 thru '86
*2047 **MPV** '89 thru '93
Navajo – see FORD Explorer (2021)
*267 **Pick-ups** '72 thru '92
460 **RX-7** all models '79 thru '85
*1419 **RX-7** all models '86 thru '91

MERCEDES-BENZ

*1643 **190 Series** all four-cylinder gasoline models, '84 thru '88
346 **230, 250 & 280** Sedan, Coupe & Roadster all 6 cyl sohc models '68 thru '72
983 **280 123 Series** all gasoline models '77 thru '81
698 **350 & 450** Sedan, Coupe & Roadster all models '71 thru '80
697 **Diesel 123 Series** 200D, 220D, 240D, 240TD, 300D, 300CD, 300TD, 4- & 5-cyl incl. Turbo '76 thru '85

MERCURY

For all PLYMOUTH titles see FORD Listing

MG

111 **MGB** Roadster & GT Coupe all models '62 thru '80
265 **MG Midget & Austin Healey Sprite** Roadster '58 thru '80

MITSUBISHI

*1669 **Cordia, Tredia, Galant, Precis & Mirage** '83 thru '90
*2022 **Pick-ups & Montero** '83 thru '91

MORRIS

074 **(Austin) Marina 1.8** all models '71 thru '80
024 **Minor 1000** sedan & wagon '56 thru '71

NISSAN

1137 **300ZX** all Turbo & non-Turbo models '84 thru '89

*1341 **Maxima** all models '85 thru '91
*771 **Pick-ups/Pathfinder** gas models '80 thru '91
*876 **Pulsar** all models '83 thru '86
*982 **Sentra** all models '82 thru '90
*981 **Stanza** all models '82 thru '90

OLDSMOBILE

Custom Cruiser – see BUICK Full-size (1551)
658 **Cutlass** all standard gasoline V6 & V8 models '74 thru '88
Cutlass Ciera – see GENERAL MOTORS A-Cars (829)
Cutlass Supreme – see GENERAL MOTORS (1671)
Firenza – see GENERAL MOTORS J-Cars (766)
Ninety-eight – see BUICK Full-size (1551)
Omega – see PONTIAC Phoenix & Omega (551)
Silhouette – see GENERAL MOTORS (2035)

PEUGEOT

663 **504** all diesel models '74 thru '83

PLYMOUTH

For all PLYMOUTH titles, see DODGE listing.

PONTIAC

T1000 – see CHEVROLET Chevette (449)
J-2000 – see GENERAL MOTORS J-Cars (766)
6000 – see GENERAL MOTORS A-Cars (829)
1232 **Fiero** all models '84 thru '88
555 **Firebird** all V8 models except Turbo '70 thru '81
*867 **Firebird** all models '82 thru '91
Full-size Rear Wheel Drive – see Buick, Oldsmobile, Pontiac Full-size (1551)
Grand Prix – see GENERAL MOTORS (1671)
551 **Phoenix & Oldsmobile Omega** all X-car models '80 thru '84
Trans Sport – see GENERAL MOTORS (2035)

PORSCHE

*264 **911** all Coupe & Targa models except Turbo & Carrera 4 '65 thru '89
239 **914** all 4 cyl models '69 thru '76
397 **924** all models including Turbo '76 thru '82
*1027 **944** all models including Turbo '83 thru '89

RENAULT

141 **5 Le Car** all models '76 thru '83
079 **8 & 10** all models with 58.4 cu in engines '62 thru '72
097 **12 Saloon & Estate** all models 1289 cc engines '70 thru '80
768 **15 & 17** all models '73 thru '79
081 **16** all models 89.7 cu in & 95.5 cu in engines '65 thru '72
Alliance & Encore – see AMC (934)

SAAB

247 **99** all models including Turbo '69 thru '80
*980 **900** all models including Turbo '79 thru '88

SUBARU

237 **1100, 1300, 1400 & 1600** all models '71 thru '79
*681 **1600 & 1800** 2WD & 4WD all models '80 thru '89

SUZUKI

*1626 **Samurai/Sidekick and Geo Tracker** all models '86 thru '91

TOYOTA

*1023 **Camry** all models '83 thru '91
150 **Carina Sedan** all models '71 thru '74
*2038 **Celica** Front Wheel Drive '86 thru '92
935 **Celica** Rear Wheel Drive '71 thru '85
*1139 **Celica Supra** '79 thru '92
361 **Corolla** all models '75 thru '79
961 **Corolla** all models (rear wheel drive) '80 thru '87
*1025 **Corolla** all models (front wheel drive) '84 thru '91
*636 **Corolla Tercel** all models '80 thru '82
230 **Corona & MK II** all 4 cyl sohc models '69 thru '74
360 **Corona** all models '74 thru '82
*532 **Cressida** all models '78 thru '82
313 **Land Cruiser** all models '68 thru '82
200 **MK II** all 6 cyl models '72 thru '76
*1339 **MR2** all models '85 thru '87
304 **Pick-up** all models '69 thru '78
*656 **Pick-up** all models '79 thru '92

TRIUMPH

112 **GT6 & Vitesse** all models '62 thru '74
113 **Spitfire** all models '62 thru '81
322 **TR7** all models '75 thru '81

VW

159 **Beetle & Karmann Ghia** all models '54 thru '79
238 **Dasher** all gasoline models '74 thru '81
*884 **Rabbit, Jetta, Scirocco, & Pick-up** all gasoline models '74 thru '91 & **Convertible** '80 thru '92
451 **Rabbit, Jetta & Pick-up** all diesel models '77 thru '84
082 **Transporter 1600** all models '68 thru '79
226 **Transporter 1700, 1800 & 2000** all models '72 thru '79
084 **Type 3 1500 & 1600** all models '63 thru '73
1029 **Vanagon** all air-cooled models '80 thru '83

VOLVO

203 **120, 130 Series & 1800 Sports** '61 thru '73
129 **140 Series** all models '66 thru '74
*270 **240 Series** all models '74 thru '90
400 **260 Series** all models '75 thru '82
*1550 **740 & 760 Series** all models '82 thru '88

SPECIAL MANUALS

1479 **Automotive Body Repair & Painting Manual**
1654 **Automotive Electrical Manual**
1480 **Automotive Heating & Air Conditioning Manual**
1762 **Chevrolet Engine Overhaul Manual**
1736 **Diesel Engine Repair Manual**
1667 **Emission Control Manual**
1763 **Ford Engine Overhaul Manual**
482 **Fuel Injection Manual**
1666 **Small Engine Repair Manual**
299 **SU Carburetors** thru '88
393 **Weber Carburetors** thru '79
300 **Zenith/Stromberg CD Carburetors** thru '76

See your dealer for other available titles

---

* *Listings shown with an asterisk (*) indicate model coverage as of this printing. These titles will be periodically updated to include later model years – consult your Haynes dealer for more information.*

Over 100 Haynes motorcycle manuals also available

1-93

Haynes North America, Inc., 861 Lawrence Drive, Newbury Park, CA 91320 • (805) 498-6703